IRS ENROLLED AGENT

STUDY GUIDE

FAST FORWARD ACADEMY

Published by Fast Forward Academy, LLC
https://fastforwardacademy.com
(888) 798-PASS (7277)

ISBN-13: 978-1-938440-89-2

1st Edition

Printed in the United States of America

The information provided in this publication is for educational purposes only, and does not necessarily reflect all laws, rules, or regulations for the tax year covered. This publication is designed to provide accurate and authoritative information concerning the subject matter covered, but it is sold with the understanding that the publisher is not engaged in rendering legal, accounting or other professional services. If legal advice or other expert assistance is required, the services of a competent professional person should be sought.

To the extent any advice relating to a Federal tax issue is contained in this communication, it was not written or intended to be used, and cannot be used, for the purpose of (a) avoiding any tax related penalties that may be imposed on you or any other person under the Internal Revenue Code, or (b) promoting, marketing or recommending to another person any transaction or matter addressed in this communication.

ABOUT US

Fast Forward Academy, LLC provides companies and individuals around the world with the tools to efficiently manage their professional education needs. As the industry-leader in exam review, Fast Forward Academy's modern approach empowers students to make data driven decisions as they learn. Our goal is to make it easier to learn so that it is easier for you to succeed.

Expert Instruction

The foundation of a great course is expert instruction and content. We organize the most important exam topics in a clear and efficient way, allowing you to focus on the essentials you need to know to pass.

Powerful Technology

We have spent millions developing personalized learning technology to improve the way you learn, earning a patent along the way. You simply won't find a learning experience like this anywhere else.

Unparalleled Support

Self-study doesn't mean you're alone. We are your partner in success—in your corner every step of the way. Give us the opportunity and we will exceed your expectations.

Additional study tools including 3,500+ questions, practice exams, video lectures, and more are available for purchase at **fastforwardacademy.com**.

PREFACE

The use of the singular male pronoun throughout this text is not intended to suggest any gender bias. It is used to make the text easier to read. In every instance, the word "he" should be understood to refer equally to "he or she." Likewise, all references to singular taxpayers should be understood to refer to plural taxpayers, such as joint filers or married persons filing separately, except where it is specified or clear from the context that only the singular reference is appropriate.

THE MATERIALS

Thank you for choosing our *IRS Enrolled Agent Exam Study Guide*. This course, along with our online question bank, will provide you with everything you need to pass the IRS Special Enrollment Exam. We designed our course to save you time, utilizing the experience of Enrolled Agents, CPAs, and former IRS employees. It provides only the essential material you need to pass the test and leaves out unnecessary information that would only bog you down. Our course is half the size on purpose!

OUTLINE FORMAT FOR STUDY-EFFICIENCY

The IRS has a "study kit" for the exam that lists 112 separate forms, form instructions, and publications that "provide much of the basic information to assist you in preparing for the examination." There are thousands of pages within these documents, yet not one is designed to help you prepare for the exam. While the information within these publications may appear overwhelming, you do not need to remember it all to pass.

In the field of taxation, there are often exceptions, additional details, or extenuating circumstances that could affect a situation. While this course is comprehensive, it does not include every rule (or variation of a rule) that "could" appear on the exam. This is intentional. Spending time on rules that do not show up on the exam will not help you pass. In this course, we cover the relevant information you must know to pass. If you stray too far from the path, you risk losing focus on the important details needed for success.

The chapters within our study guide contain comprehensive outlines whenever possible. This format helps you better *visualize* and *retain* the important points of each section, resulting in maximum study efficiency and reduced study time.

UNDERSTANDING THE TERMS USED IN THIS BOOK

TIP: Practical information you might want to remember.

EXAMPLE: An example to demonstrate a point or concept.

An important concept you should master. This information is very important in your review.

TCJA: The Tax Cuts and Jobs Act of 2017 is the biggest overhaul of the tax code in decades.

ABOUT THE IRS SPECIAL ENROLLMENT EXAM

The EA Exam, officially known as the Special Enrollment Examination (SEE), is a three-part exam administered by Prometric on behalf of the Internal Revenue Service. You will take each part as a separate, 100-question exam. You will have up to 3 1/2 hours to complete each exam, which equates to just over two minutes per question. We suggest that you not study for all three exams at once. Pass one exam, and then move on to the next one. If you are like most people, you will probably study the Individuals (Part 1) exam first. Part 2 is the most challenging of the three exams, so after you pass Part 1, we suggest you take the representation exam next. There is much less content to study, and passing it can give you a boost of confidence going into the last exam. The IRS does not require you to take the tests in any particular order.

Part 1 – Individuals	Percent of Exam
Section 1: Preliminary Work and Taxpayer Data	16%
Section 2: Income and Assets	20%
Section 3: Deductions and Credits	20%
Section 4: Taxation	18%
Section 5: Advising the Individual Taxpayer	13%
Section 6: Specialized Returns for Individuals	13%
TOTAL	**100%**

Part 2 – Businesses	Percent of Exam
Section 1: Business Entities and Considerations	35%
Section 2: Business Tax Preparation	44%
Section 3: Specialized Returns and Taxpayers	21%
TOTAL	**100%**

Part 3 – Representation, Practices, and Procedures	Percent of Exam
Section 1: Practices and Procedures	31%
Section 2: Representation before the IRS	29%
Section 3: Specific Areas of Representation	24%
Section 4: Filing Process	16%
TOTAL	**100%**

A new examination period commences each year on May 1 and continues through the end of February the following year. No testing occurs during March or April. The period that begins on May 1, 2021, will include questions based on the 2020 tax year, as the law exists on Dec 31, 2020. A passing score on each part of the exam is required before the IRS will admit an enrolled agent to practice. Scaled scores are determined by ranking your exam results against others taking the exam, on a scale ranging between 40 and 130. A score of 105 is the minimum required to pass. Test results are available immediately following the exam. Those who pass are informed, but they do not receive a score. Those who fail receive a score and a diagnostic report indicating the areas of weakness. A candidate may re-take each part up to four times during each testing period. Once a candidate passes the first part, he must pass the other two parts of the exam during a two-year window.

HOW TO REGISTER FOR THE IRS SPECIAL ENROLLMENT EXAM

To schedule an exam, you need a Preparer Tax Identification Number (PTIN). To obtain a PTIN, you must complete a W-12 by mail, fax, or online at www.irs.gov. The online method is quickest and provides you with the instantaneous issuance of the PTIN.

Examinations are administered by computer at Prometric testing centers. Currently, the Special Enrollment Examination is given at nearly 300 Prometric testing centers located across the United States and internationally. Test centers are located in most major metropolitan areas. Once you have your PTIN, you may register for your exam online at www.prometric.com/irs.

QUESTION TYPES

The IRS Special Enrollment Exam contains only multiple-choice questions. Each provides four options from which you choose your answer. Three different multiple-choice formats are used.

Format 1 – Direct question

Which of the following entities are required to file Form 709, U.S. Gift Tax Return?

A. An individual
B. An estate or trust
C. A corporation
D. All of the above

Format 2 – Incomplete sentence

Supplemental wages are compensation paid in addition to an employee's regular wages. They **do not** include payments for the following:

A. Accumulated sick leave
B. Nondeductible moving expenses
C. Vacation pay
D. Travel reimbursements paid at the Federal Government per diem rate

Format 3 – All of the following except

There are five tests that must be met for you to claim an exemption for a dependent. Which of the following is **not** a requirement?

A. Citizen or Resident Test
B. Member of Household or Relationship Test
C. Disability Test
D. Joint Return Test

INDIVIDUALS

SEE EXAM PART 1

LESSON 1

Taxpayers and Dependents

CITIZENS AND DEPENDENTS

U.S. CITIZENS

Federal income tax rules apply to <u>all</u> *U.S. citizens*, regardless of where they live. The term U.S. citizen includes:

- An individual born in the United States
- An individual whose parent is a U.S. citizen
- A former alien who has been naturalized as a U.S. citizen
- An individual born in Puerto Rico, Guam, or the U.S. Virgin Islands (these are "U.S. possessions")

TIP: For tax purposes, the term "U.S. national" refers to individuals who were born in the U.S. possessions of American Samoa or the Northern Mariana Islands who are <u>not</u> U.S. citizens. There are also special rules that apply, which we will not cover.

These U.S possessions have their own governments and their own tax systems. Special rules exist for taxpayers that reside in U.S. possessions, but this is beyond the scope of this course. This course will focus more generally on citizens who do <u>not</u> reside in U.S. possessions and accordingly are required to **report <u>all</u> income from worldwide sources on their U.S. income tax return**.

TESTS FOR CLAIMING DEPENDENTS

Determining when a taxpayer is able to claim another person as a *dependent* is an important consideration in filing a tax return. A dependent is a person that relies on the taxpayer to provide the majority of their support. For this reason, a taxpayer is able to report dependents on their tax return and claim certain benefits.

In prior years, taxpayers were able to exempt a small amount of income from tax for themselves and qualifying dependents. Beginning in 2018, and continuing through 2025, taxpayers can **no longer deduct exemptions**.

To claim a person as a dependent, the taxpayer must meet <u>all</u> three of the following tests:

- **Dependent Taxpayer Test** – The taxpayer cannot qualify as a dependent of another person.
- **Joint Return Test** – A taxpayer cannot claim a married person who files a joint return as a dependent unless the married person files the return only as a claim for refund.
- **Citizenship or Resident Test** – A dependent must be a U.S. citizen, U.S. resident alien, U.S. national, or a resident of Canada or Mexico, for some part of the year.

In general, a taxpayer cannot claim a person as a dependent unless they provide more than half of the total annual support <u>and</u> that person is a *qualifying child* or *qualifying relative*.

QUALIFYING CHILD

There are additional tests for a child to be a qualifying child, these four tests <u>must</u> be met:

- **Relationship Test** – The child must be a son, daughter, stepchild, foster child, brother, sister, half-brother, half-sister, step-brother, step-sister, or a descendant of any of them.
- **Age Test** – To meet this test, a child must be younger than the taxpayer (<u>or</u> spouse if filing jointly) and meet one of the following conditions:
  1. Younger than age 19 at the end of the year
  2. Younger than age 24 at the end of the year and a full-time student

3. Any age if permanently and totally disabled (does not need to be younger than the taxpayer)

- **Residency Test** – Child must live with the taxpayer more than half of the year. A child who is born or dies during the year qualifies if the home was the child's home the entire time the child was alive. A child is considered to live with a taxpayer when at the hospital following birth, or temporary absences due to special circumstances such as illness, education, business, vacation, or military service. If born alive but living for a moment (not stillborn) official documentation must prove live birth.
- **Support Test** – The child cannot provide more than half of their own support.

TIP: If a child can be a qualifying child of more than one person, the taxpayer claiming certain benefits must be the person entitled to claim the child as a qualifying child. In most cases, because of the residency test, a child of divorced or separated parents is the qualifying child of the **custodial parent**. A noncustodial parent may claim the child for purposes of the child tax credits and credit for other dependents if the custodial parent agrees in writing (Form 8332).

> **EXAMPLE:** Your unmarried son lived with you all year and was 18 years old at the end of the year. He didn't provide more than half of his own support and doesn't meet the tests to be a qualifying child of anyone else. As a result, he is your qualifying child and, because he is single, your qualifying person for you to claim head of household filing status.

QUALIFYING RELATIVE

A qualifying relative can be any age. There are four tests that must be met:

- **Not a Qualifying Child Test** – The person cannot be a qualifying child of any taxpayer.
- **Support Test** – A taxpayer generally must provide more than **half of a person's total support** during the year. A person's own funds are not support unless they are actually spent for support.

> **EXAMPLE:** Your mother received $2,400 in social security benefits and $300 in interest. She paid $2,000 for lodging and $400 for recreation. She put $300 in a savings account. Even though your mother received a total of $2,700 ($2,400 + $300), she spent only $2,400 ($2,000 + $400) for her own support. If you spent more than $2,400 for her support and no other support was received, you have provided more than half of her support.

TIP: Under a written *multiple support agreement* if two or more persons together provide more than half of the support they can agree that one will claim the dependent. The person claiming the dependent must provide more than 10% of the total support for the qualifying individual, and no other person can pay over half of the total support. Each eligible person who pays over 10% of support must provide the taxpayer with a signed statement agreeing not to claim the qualifying individual as a dependent. The taxpayer will file *Form 2120, Multiple Support Declaration* with their tax return attesting to the agreement.

- **Gross Income Test** – The person's gross income for 2020 must be **less than $4,300**.

> **EXAMPLE:** Your unmarried son lived with you all year and was 25 years old at the end of the year. His gross income was $5,000 but he didn't provide more than half of his own support and doesn't meet the tests to be a qualifying child of anyone else. Because he doesn't meet the age test, your son isn't your qualifying child. Because he doesn't meet the gross income test, he isn't your qualifying relative. Also, as a result, he isn't a qualifying person for head of household purposes.

- **Member of Household <u>or</u> Relationship Test** – To meet this test, a person must meet one of the following conditions:
    1. Live with the taxpayer all year as a **member of the household**, <u>or</u>
    2. Must be **related** to the taxpayer in one of the following ways:
        A. A child, step-child, foster child, or a descendant of any of them (for example, a grandchild). Treat a legally adopted child the same as a child.
        B. A brother, sister, half-brother, half-sister, step-brother, or step-sister.
        C. A father, mother, grandparent, or other direct ancestors, but <u>not</u> foster parent.
        D. A step-father or step-mother.
        E. A son or daughter of the taxpayer's brother or sister (e.g. nephew or niece).
        F. A brother or sister of the taxpayer's father or mother (e.g. uncle or aunt).
        G. A son or daughter-in-law, father or mother-in-law, brother or sister-in-law.

TIP: A qualifying relative must be related in one of these ways, <u>or</u> live with the taxpayer all year as a member of the household. If the relationship does not violate local law, any person meeting the tests above can be a "qualifying relative," even if not a blood relative. A *qualifying relative* by virtue of **family lineage need not live with the taxpayer.**

FILING STATUS

CHOOSING THE RIGHT FILING STATUS

Taxpayers that are required to file a tax return must specify a filing status. Filing status is important because many benefits, deductions, credits, and applicable tax rates vary by filing status. In general, filing status depends on the taxpayer's marital status on the last day of the tax year.

> **The IRS considers a person unmarried for the whole year if—on the last day of the tax year—he is unmarried or legally separated from a spouse under a divorce or separate maintenance decree.** If a spouse dies during the year, the IRS considers the surviving spouse married for the whole year and allows married filing jointly as the filing status.
>
> For federal tax purposes, taxpayers of the same sex are considered married if they were lawfully married in a state (or foreign country) whose laws authorize the marriage of two individuals of the same sex, even if the state (or foreign country) in which they now live does not recognize same-sex marriage.

SINGLE (S)

A taxpayer is "single" if, on the last day of the year, he is unmarried or legally separated from a spouse under a final court decree and does not qualify for another status.

HEAD OF HOUSEHOLD (HH)

Filing as *head of household* usually results in lower tax rates than those for single or married filing separately.

- To qualify, a person <u>must</u> be *unmarried* or *considered unmarried* on the last day of the year <u>and</u> pay **more than half the cost** of keeping up a home for the year.
    - For filing as head of household, a person is *considered unmarried* if they file a separate return <u>and</u> a spouse did not live in the home the **last 6 months of the tax year**.
- A **qualifying person** <u>must</u> live with the taxpayer <u>more</u> than **half of the year**, with the exception of a mother or father (i.e., parents need not live with the taxpayer).

- A **qualifying person** generally <u>must</u> be a *qualifying child* or *qualifying relative* for whom the taxpayer can claim as a dependent.

> **EXCEPTION:** The *custodial parent* may claim a child as a qualifying person for head of household filing status even if the other parent claims the same child as a dependent for other benefits.

- A **qualifying relative** <u>must</u> be a member of the taxpayer's family (not merely a member of the household) in order to be a qualifying person for head of household status.

> **EXAMPLE:** Your girlfriend lived with you all year. Even though she may be your qualifying relative if the gross income and support tests are met (and therefore a dependent on your tax return), she isn't your qualifying person for head of household purposes because she isn't related to you in one of the ways listed in the qualifying relative relationship test.

- The taxpayer <u>must</u> **pay more than half** the cost of maintaining the parent's home (or the cost of a facility) if claiming head of household based on a *dependent parent*.

TIP: In most cases, because of the residency test, a child of divorced or separated parents is the qualifying child of the custodial parent. The custodial parent is the parent with whom the child lived for the greater number of nights during the year. The other parent is the noncustodial parent. Therefore, in most cases, because of the residency test, the custodial parent may claim head of household filing status.

The custodial parent can sign a written declaration (Form 8332), that he or she won't claim the child as a dependent for the year, and the noncustodial parent attaches this written declaration to his or her return. The **noncustodial parent** can claim the child as a **dependent** and as a qualifying child for the **child tax credit**. However, this does <u>not</u> allow the noncustodial parent to claim head of household filing status, the credit for child and dependent care expenses, the exclusion for dependent care benefits, the earned income credit, or the health coverage tax credit. In prior years this form also released the dependency exemption, but that benefit is suspended for tax years 2018 through 2025 by the Tax Cuts and Jobs Act.

Paid tax return preparers have **elevated due diligence** requirements in the determination of eligibility to file as head of household. This means that preparers are required to ask questions and obtain all the information needed to determine if a taxpayer is eligible for certain benefits. A tax preparer can use *Form 8867 Paid Preparer's Due Diligence Checklist* to document due diligence. Failure to perform the required due diligence for a return filed in 2021 (generally 2020 tax returns) shall pay a penalty of **$540 for each failure**.

MARRIED FILING JOINTLY (MFJ)

Taxpayers may <u>choose</u> *married filing jointly* as the filing status if they are married and agree to file a joint return. Both are responsible, jointly and individually, for the tax and any interest or penalty due. While different accounting methods are allowable, both must use the same accounting period and are generally required to sign the return. All combined income and allowable expenses must be reported. They may file a joint return even if one spouse has no income or deductions. When a court decree of annulment reverses a marriage, they must amend previous joint returns. If one spouse is a nonresident alien, they must have either an SSN or an ITIN to file a joint return.

MARRIED FILING SEPARATELY (MFS)

Married couples can <u>choose</u> *married filing separately* as a status if they want to be responsible only for their respective taxes or if it results in less tax than filing a joint return. They will generally pay more combined tax on separate returns than when using another filing status. When choosing this filing status, the following special rules apply:

- Cannot take the credit for child and dependent care expenses in most cases, and the limit on income excluded under an employer's dependent care assistance program is $2,500 (instead of $5,000 for joint returns).
- No earned income credit.
- No exclusion or credit for adoption expenses in most cases.
- Cannot take the education credits (Lifetime Learning or American Opportunities) or the deduction for student loan interest.
- No exclusion on interest income from U.S. savings bonds when used for education expenses.
- If the taxpayer lived with a spouse at any time during the tax year, the following conditions apply:
  1. Cannot claim the credit for the elderly or the disabled
  2. Must include in income more (up to 85%) of any Social Security the taxpayer received
- The *child tax credit* and *retirement savings contribution credit* reduce at a level of income equal to one-half of the amount allowable to joint filers.
- The deduction limit for a capital loss is $1,500 (instead of $3,000 for joint returns).
- The standard deduction is half that allowed to joint filers. If one spouse itemizes deductions, the other cannot claim the standard deduction.

TIP: If you are married, you and your spouse can file a joint return or separate returns. You should figure your tax both ways, on a joint return and on separate returns. This way you can make sure you are using the filing status that results in the lowest combined tax.

QUALIFYING WIDOW(ER) (QW)

If one spouse dies during the tax year, the survivor can file jointly (MFJ) if he otherwise qualifies for that status. The year of death is the last year to file jointly with a deceased spouse. In certain cases, *qualifying widow(er)* is the **filing status for two tax years** following the year a spouse died. This filing status entitles them to use joint return tax rates and the highest standard deduction amount (if not itemizing deductions). To file as a qualifying widow(er) the taxpayer must meet <u>all</u> of the following tests:

- Must be entitled to file a joint return with their spouse for the year the spouse died
- Must not remarry before the end of the tax year
- Must have a child or stepchild (not a foster child) for whom he **can claim** as a dependent <u>or</u> **could claim** as a dependent <u>except</u> that, for 2020:
  1. The child had gross income of **$4,300** or more,
  2. The child filed a joint return, or
  3. The taxpayer could be claimed as a dependent on someone else's return.

TIP: The IRS no longer requires a taxpayer to claim a dependent on the tax return to file as Qualifying Widow(er) provided the child would qualify as a dependent if it were not for one of these exceptions.

- A child lived in the person's home all year, except for temporary absences
- The taxpayer and the deceased spouse paid more than half of the cost of maintaining a home

> **EXAMPLE:** Jane files a joint return the year her husband dies (2020). If her son meets the requirements discussed above, she can choose Qualifying Widow(er) as her filing status for 2021 and 2022.

FILING REQUIREMENTS AND FORM 1040

FILING REQUIREMENTS

The *gross income threshold* (based on filing status and age) determines whether or not a taxpayer must file a federal income tax return. *Gross income* is the total of *earned* and *unearned income*.

- **Earned income** includes salaries, wages, tips, professional fees, taxable scholarships, and fellowship grants.
- **Unearned income** includes unemployment compensation, taxable Social Security benefits, taxable pensions, annuity income, canceled debt, unearned income from a trust, taxable interest, dividends, and capital gains.

A taxpayer is <u>not</u> required to file a return if gross income does <u>not</u> exceed the gross income threshold.

INDIVIDUALS

Table 1-1. Filing Requirements for Most Taxpayers – 2020

IF filing status is …	AND at the end of the year, the taxpayer was …	THEN file a return if the gross income was at least …
Single	younger than 65	$12,400
	65 or older	$14,050
Married Filing Jointly	younger than 65 (both spouses)	$24,800
	65 or older (one spouse)	$26,100
	65 or older (both spouses)	$27,400
Married Filing Separately	any age	$5
Head of Household	younger than 65	$18,650
	65 or older	$20,300
Qualifying Widow(er)	younger than 65	$24,800
	65 or older	$26,100

DEPENDENTS

Dependents must file individual returns under the circumstances described in Table 1-2.

Table 1-2. Filing Requirements for Single Dependents – 2020

Single dependents – Were you either age 65 or older or blind?

☐ **No.** You must file a return if any of the following apply:

- Your unearned income was more than $1,100.

- Your earned income was more than $12,400.

- Your gross income was more than the larger of:

   - $1,100, or

   - Your earned income (up to $12,050) plus $350.

☐ **Yes.** You must file a return if any of the following apply:

- Your unearned income was more than $2,750 ($4,400 if 65 or older and blind).

- Your earned income was more than $14,050 ($15,700 if 65 or older and blind).

- Your gross income was more than the larger of:

   - $2,750 ($4,400 if 65 or older and blind), or

   - Your earned income (up to $12,050) plus $2,000 ($3,650 if 65 or older and blind).

EXAMPLE: Henry has two dependents, Mary and Lulu. Neither is over age 65 or blind. Mary has earned income of $5,600 and $500 in dividends. Lulu has earned income of $4,500 and $200 in dividends.

Neither Mary nor Lulu is required to file a return based solely on their earned or unearned income. The third test is the gross income threshold. The 2020 rule states, if gross income is greater than $1,100 or earned income plus $350, the dependent must file.

Mary's gross income of $6,100 ($5,600 + $500) is more than $5,950 (the greater of $1,100 or earned income plus $350). Mary must file a return.

Lulu's gross income of $4,700 ($4,500 + $200) is less than than $4,850 (the greater of $1,100 or earned income plus $350). Lulu does not need to file a return.

ADDITIONAL FILING REQUIREMENTS

A taxpayer is required to file a return if any of the conditions listed below apply, even if income is less than the amount shown in Table 1-1 or Table 1-2:

- Net earnings from self-employment are at least $400.
- Wages are $108.28 or more from a church or qualified church-controlled organization that is exempt from employer Social Security and Medicare taxes.
- The taxpayer (or spouse, if filing jointly) received HSA, Archer MSA, or Medicare Advantage MSA distributions.
- Advance payments of the premium tax credit or the health coverage tax credit were made for the taxpayer, spouse, or a dependent.
- The taxpayer owes special taxes or must recapture certain credits, including any of the following:
   1. Alternative minimum tax.

2. Additional tax on a qualified plan, including an individual retirement arrangement (IRA), or other tax-favored accounts. The taxpayer can file Form 5329 by itself if this is the only reason for filing a return.

3. Household employment taxes. The taxpayer can file Schedule H by itself if this is the only reason for filing a return.

4. Social security and Medicare tax on tips not reported to the employer or on wages received from an employer who did not withhold these taxes.

5. Recapture of first-time homebuyer credit.

6. Write-in taxes, including uncollected social security and Medicare or RRTA tax on tips reported to an employer or on group-term life insurance and additional taxes on health savings accounts.

7. Recapture taxes.

TIP: Even if a taxpayer does not otherwise have to file a return, the taxpayer should file one to get a refund of any federal income tax withheld. A taxpayer also should file if eligible for any of the following credits:

- Earned income credit
- Additional child tax credit
- American opportunity credit
- Credit for federal tax on fuels
- Premium tax credit
- Health coverage tax credit

FORM 1040 AND SCHEDULES

A citizen or resident of the United States who is required to file a tax return will use Form 1040 to report information to the IRS.

FORM 1040

A determination of **total income** must be made in order to calculate a taxpayer's income tax obligation. This is accomplished on the recently redesigned Form 1040. This version of Form 1040 uses a "building block" approach that requires additional numbered schedules (1 through 3) to complete more complex tax returns. A taxpayer with a straightforward tax situation can file Form 1040 without the numbered schedules.

> **Taxpayers no longer use Forms 1040A or 1040EZ** to file tax returns. Taxpayers who used these forms in the past will now file Form 1040.

> **Form 1040-SR** is available as an <u>optional</u> alternative to using Form 1040 for taxpayers who are **age 65 or older**. Form 1040-SR uses the same schedules and instructions as Form 1040 does.

FORM 1040 SCHEDULES

A taxpayer with a straightforward tax situation can file Form 1040 without the numbered schedules. These additional schedules are used as needed to complete more complex tax returns.

The 2020 Form 1040 has three numbered schedules (Schedules 1 through 3) in addition to the following existing schedules:

- **Schedule A, Itemized Deductions** – When itemized deductions exceed the amount of the standard deduction, a taxpayer attaches Schedule A to Form 1040 in order to claim the higher amount.

- **Schedule B, Interest and Ordinary Dividends** – A taxpayer attaches Schedule B to Form 1040 if <u>any</u> of the following conditions apply:

  1. The taxpayer has <u>over</u> **$1,500** of taxable interest or ordinary dividends
  2. Receipt of interest from a seller-financed mortgage and the buyer used the property as a personal residence
  3. The taxpayer has accrued interest from a bond
  4. The taxpayer reports original issue discount (OID) less than the amount shown on Form 1099-OID
  5. The taxpayer reduces interest income on a bond by the amount of amortizable bond premium
  6. The taxpayer claims an exclusion of interest from series EE or I U.S. savings bonds issued after 1989
  7. The taxpayer receives interest or ordinary dividends as a nominee
  8. The taxpayer has a certain interest in a financial account in a foreign country or a foreign trust

- **Schedule D, Capital Gains and Losses** – A taxpayer uses Schedule D to report the sale or exchange of capital assets. Most property held for personal purposes, pleasure, or investment is a capital asset. Many transactions that, in previous years, would have been reported on Schedule D must be reported on *Form 8949*. A taxpayer uses Form 8949 to list all capital gain and loss transactions. The subtotals from this form are carried to Schedule D, where gain or loss is calculated in aggregate. The transactions reportable on this schedule include the following:

  1. Sales, exchanges, or involuntary conversions of capital assets
  2. Capital gain distributions not reported directly on Form 1040
  3. Nonbusiness bad debts

- **Schedule J, Income Averaging for Farmers and Fishermen** – Use Schedule J to elect to figure income tax by averaging, over the previous 3 years (base years), all or part of current year taxable income from farming or fishing. This election does not apply when figuring the alternative minimum tax.

- **Schedule 8812, Additional Child Tax Credit** – A taxpayer uses Schedule 8812 to figure the additional child tax credit (ACTC).

- **Schedule EIC, Earned Income Credit** – A taxpayer uses Schedule EIC to give the IRS information about their qualifying child(ren).

Schedule 1, Additional Income and Adjustments To Income

A taxpayer uses Schedule 1 to report additional income, such as unemployment compensation, prize or award money, gambling winnings, and to claim adjustments to income, such as student loan interest deduction, self-employment tax, educator expenses.

A taxpayer using Schedule 1 may need to attach the following additional schedules:

- **Schedule C, Net Profit or Loss from Business** – A "self-employed" taxpayer files Schedule C with Form 1040 to report income and deductions resulting from their trade or business. To file this schedule, the taxpayer must operate a business as one of the following:

  1. Sole proprietor or disregarded entity (single-member LLC treated as a sole proprietor)
  2. Qualified joint venture
  3. Statutory employee

- **Schedule E, Supplemental Income and Loss** – A taxpayer attaches Schedule E to report income or loss from rental real estate, royalties, partnerships, S corporations, estates, trusts, and residual interests in REMICs.

- **Schedule F, Profit or Loss from Farming** – Farmers use Schedule F to figure net profit or loss from regular farming operations. This includes farm products raised for sale or products bought for resale.

Schedule 2, Additional Taxes

A taxpayer uses Schedule 2 to report amounts if they owe other taxes, such as self-employment tax, household employment taxes, additional tax on IRAs or other qualified retirement plans and tax-favored accounts, Alternative Minimum Tax (AMT), or if they need to make an excess advance premium tax credit repayment.

A taxpayer using Schedule 2 may need to attach the following additional schedules:

- **Schedule SE, Self-Employment Tax** – Withholding tax for social security or Medicare does not apply to net earnings from self-employment. A self-employed taxpayer uses Schedule SE to figure the tax due on net earnings from self-employment. The taxpayer uses *Schedule SE* and calculates self-employment tax, which is essentially social security and Medicare tax for the self-employed. A taxpayer must include their share of certain partnership income and guaranteed payments as income from self-employment. For 2020, the first **$137,700** of net earnings is subject to Social Security tax. **All** net earnings are subject to Medicare tax.
- **Schedule H, Household Employment Taxes** – To report employment taxes withheld for household employees if the taxpayer paid cash wages of **$2,200** or more in 2020 to any one household employee.

Schedule 3, Additional Credits and Payments

A taxpayer uses Schedule 3 to claim any credit that they did not claim on Form 1040, such as the foreign tax credit, education credits, general business credit, or if they have other payments, such as an amount paid with a request for an extension to file or excess social security tax withheld.

A taxpayer using Schedule 3 may need to attach the following additional schedule:

- **Schedule R, Credit for the Elderly or the Disabled** – A U.S. citizen or resident alien with limited income who is age 65 or older at the end of the year can file this schedule to receive a credit.

TIP: If filing a paper return, assemble any schedules and forms behind Form 1040 in order of the "Attachment Sequence No." shown in the upper right corner of the schedule or form.

GENERAL RETURN REQUIREMENTS

TAXPAYER IDENTIFICATION NUMBER

A taxpayer, and spouse (if filing jointly) and all qualifying dependents on the return <u>must</u> have a valid *taxpayer identification number* (TIN) **issued by the due date of the return** (including extensions).

A TIN is a *Social Security number* (SSN), an *individual taxpayer identification number* (ITIN), or an *adoption taxpayer identification number* (ATIN).

Taxpayers are generally required to provide the SSN for <u>all</u> parties on the return, including each **dependent** claimed. An ITIN or ATIN may be used in place of the SSN in certain circumstances.

Certain credits require <u>all</u> parties on the return to have a valid TIN prior to the return due date (including extensions):

- Earned Income Tax Credit, Child Tax Credit, and Additional Child Tax Credit requires a valid **SSN only**
- The Credit for Other Dependents and American Opportunity Tax Credit requires a valid **SSN, ITIN, or ATIN**

The child must have a taxpayer identification number **by the due date of the return** (including extensions), even if that child later gets a TIN, the taxpayer can not use the child to claim these credits on either their original or amended tax return. A taxpayer looking to claim these credits should obtain a TIN prior to filing their tax return.

TIP: The IRS allows as a dependent a child that is **born and dies in the same year** even if the taxpayer does not have an SSN for the child. If a dependent child was born and died in the tax year and the taxpayer does not have an SSN for the child, enter "Died" for the SSN in the Dependents section of Form 1040. The taxpayer <u>must</u> attach a copy of the child's birth certificate, death certificate, or hospital records. The document <u>must</u> show the child was **born alive**. The taxpayer may claim the Earned Income Tax Credit (EITC), the Child Tax Credit (CTC), and the Additional Child Tax Credit (ACTC) using this approach.

INDIVIDUAL TAXPAYER IDENTIFICATION NUMBER

Any individual filing a U.S. tax return is required to state his or her taxpayer identification number on such return. Generally, a taxpayer identification number is the individual's SSN. However, in the case of an individual who is not eligible to be issued an SSN, but who has a tax filing obligation, the IRS issues an ITIN for use in connection with the individual's tax filing requirements. An individual who is eligible to receive an SSN may not obtain an ITIN for purposes of his or her tax filing obligations.

Examples of individuals who are not eligible for SSNs, but potentially need ITINs in order to file U.S. returns include a nonresident alien filing a claim for a reduced withholding rate under a U.S. income tax treaty, a nonresident alien required to file a U.S. tax return, an individual who is a U.S. resident alien under the substantial presence test and who therefore must file a U.S. tax return, a dependent or spouse of the prior two categories of individuals, or a dependent or spouse of a nonresident alien visa holder.

ITINs are issued regardless of immigration status because both resident and nonresident aliens may have a U.S. filing or reporting requirement under the Internal Revenue Code.

Individuals generally must have a filing requirement and file a valid federal income tax return to receive an ITIN. There are four exceptions to this income tax return requirement. The first exception is for information reporting and/or tax withholding requirements of third parties (such as banks) who need an SSN or ITIN from an individual to comply with U.S. Treasury Regulations. The second exception is when tax withholding is required on wages, scholarships, etc. for payments to foreign individuals who otherwise do not have to file a U.S. tax return. The third exception is for mortgage interest reporting and the final exception relates to when a U.S. real property interest is acquired from a foreign person.

ITINs are for federal tax reporting only and are <u>not</u> intended to serve any other purpose. The IRS issues ITINs to help individuals comply with the U.S. tax laws and to provide a means to efficiently process and account for tax returns and payments for those not eligible for Social Security Numbers.

An ITIN does <u>not</u> authorize work in the U.S. or provide eligibility for Social Security benefits. Individuals filing tax returns using an ITIN are <u>not</u> eligible for the earned income credit (EIC). Also, a child who has an ITIN <u>cannot</u> be claimed as a qualifying child for purposes of the EIC.

A taxpayer applies for an ITIN by filing *Form W-7, Application for IRS Individual Taxpayer Identification Number*. Generally, a taxpayer files Form W-7 with the federal income tax return. The taxpayer must also include originals of his or her proof of identity (or copies certified by issuing agency and foreign status documents). Individuals may also apply for an ITIN using the services of an IRS-authorized "Acceptance Agent."

TIP: If an ITIN is applied for on or before the due date of the tax return (including extensions) and the IRS issues an ITIN as a result of the application, the IRS will consider the ITIN as issued on or before the due date of the return. After the Form W-7 is processed, the IRS will assign an ITIN to the return and process the return.

If an individual has an application for an SSN pending, they should not file Form W-7. Rather, they should complete Form W-7 only if and when notified by the Social Security Administration that an SSN cannot be issued. Under such circumstances, proof that the request for an SSN was denied must be included with the Form W-7.

A taxpayer can't electronically file (e-file) a return using an ITIN in the calendar year the ITIN is assigned. Once an ITIN is assigned, the taxpayer can e-file returns in the following years. For example, a taxpayer that receives an ITIN in 2020 may not e-file any tax return using that ITIN (including prior-year returns) until 2021.

> Any ITIN that is <u>not</u> used on a federal tax return for three consecutive tax years, either as the ITIN of an individual who files the return or as the ITIN of a dependent included on a return, will **expire on December 31 of the third consecutive tax year of nonuse.**

An ITIN only needs to be renewed if it will be included on a U.S. federal tax return and it is expiring or has expired.

ACCOUNTING PERIODS AND METHODS

ACCOUNTING PERIOD

The typical period covered by personal income tax returns is the 12-month period from January 1 through December 31, also known as a **calendar year**. A **fiscal year** is another typical accounting period. A regular fiscal year is a 12-month period that **ends on the last day of any month except December**. A taxpayer will choose the type of accounting period (tax year) when they file their first income tax return.

CASH METHOD

Most individual taxpayers use the **cash method**. If this method is used, the taxpayer must report income in the year of **constructive receipt**. Constructive receipt occurs when the income is available for a taxpayer's unrestricted withdrawal. Physical possession is not a requirement. Examples of constructive receipt include the following:

- Garnished wages (considered income received for the year)
- Debt canceled or paid for a taxpayer but not as a gift or loan (gross income to the recipient)
- Income payments paid directly to a third party from property owned by a taxpayer (treated as received by the taxpayer and paid to the third party)
- Income paid in advance (includable in gross income for the year received)
- Checks received and available to the taxpayer without restriction

> **EXCEPTION:** There is one exception. Do not report the interest on Series E and EE U.S. savings bonds until the final maturity date.

> **EXAMPLE:** Jill is a cash basis taxpayer. To earn extra money, she works as a photographer in the month of December. Jill shot a family portrait for the Johnson family on December 15, 2019, and receives a check for her work on that date. The Johnsons dated the check January 2, 2020, and asked Jill not to cash it until that time. Jill does not recognize this income in 2019 because of the restriction on withdrawal. Jill will recognize this income in 2020 since she can cash the check in 2020.

ACCRUAL METHOD

Another method is the **accrual method**. When using the accrual method, report income when earned, whether the taxpayer has received it or not. The IRS considers the taxpayer to have earned income when all the events have occurred that fix the right to receive such income and the amount can be determined with reasonable accuracy.

LESSON 2

Income

WAGES, SALARIES, AND OTHER EARNINGS

WAGES

Wages, salaries, and other forms of employee compensation are included in gross income. Generally, the employer reports annual employee compensation to employees on Form W-2, which the employer must provide to the employee by the end of January each year. The employee should attach copy B of Form W-2 to the federal income tax return if mailing the return to the IRS (not required for e-file).

An employee who receives *Form 1099-NEC, Nonemployee Compensation*, instead of *Form W-2, Wage and Tax Statement*, because their employer did not consider them an employee, uses *Form 8919* to report *Uncollected Social Security and Medicare Tax on Wages*.

CHILDCARE PROVIDERS

When taxpayers provide childcare, regardless of location, the pay received must be included in gross income. Taxpayers who are not employees must include payments for services on Schedule C (Form 1040) and complete Schedule 1. The same rules apply for persons babysitting, even if only periodically and/or just for relatives.

FOREIGN INCOME

U.S. citizens and resident aliens must report income from sources outside the United States (foreign income) on their tax return unless it is exempt by U.S. law. This applies to earned income (such as wages and tips) as well as unearned income (such as interest, dividends, capital gains, pensions, rents, and royalties). U.S. citizens and resident aliens residing outside the United States may be able to exclude all or part of their foreign source earned income. *See foreign earned income exclusion.*

ADVANCE COMMISSIONS

Under the cash method, a taxpayer receiving advance commissions or other amounts for future services must include these amounts as income in the year received.

COST-OF-LIVING ALLOWANCES AND REIMBURSEMENTS

Cost-of-living allowances are generally included in income. However, allowances for a federal civilian or federal court employee stationed in Alaska, Hawaii, or outside the United States are exempt from the rule and are not included as income. Allowances that increase an employee's basic pay as an incentive for taking a less desirable assignment are part of compensation and must be included in income.

BACK PAY

Amounts awarded in a settlement or judgment for back pay should be included in income. These include payments made to a person for damages, unpaid life insurance premiums, and unpaid health insurance premiums. Employers should report on Form W-2.

BONUSES AND AWARDS

Bonuses or awards received from an employer are included in income and should appear on Form W-2. If the award is goods or services, include the fair market value in income.

SEVERANCE PAY

Severance pay and any payment received due to the cancellation of an employment contract must be included in income amounts. This includes any payment received for accrued leave and monies withheld from severance for outplacement services. If a taxpayer accepts a reduced amount of severance pay in order to receive outplacement services (such as training in resume writing and interview techniques), he must include the unreduced amount of the severance pay in income.

SICK PAY

Pay received from an employer while sick or injured is part of salary or wages. In addition, employees must include in income sick pay benefits received from any of the following payors:

- A welfare fund
- A state sickness or disability fund
- An association of employers or employees
- An insurance company, if the employer paid for the plan

However, if the employee paid the premiums on an accident or health insurance policy, the benefits received under the policy are not taxable.

DISABILITY INCOME

Generally, employees must report as income any amount received for personal injury or sickness through an accident or health plan when the employer pays plan premiums. If both the employee and employer pay for the plan, the employee must report only the amount received that is due to the employer's payments. However, certain payments may not be taxable to the employee. For example, a taxpayer need not report as income any reimbursement for medical expenses incurred after the plan was established. A taxpayer may need to include reimbursements for medical expenses deducted on a prior return as income in the current year.

ACCIDENT OR HEALTH PLAN

Generally, the value of accident or health plan coverage provided to a taxpayer by an employer is not included in income. Benefits received from the plan may be taxable.

FRINGE BENEFITS

Fringe benefits received in connection with the performance of services are included in income as compensation unless the employee paid fair market value for the benefits or specifically excluded by law. The IRS treats abstaining from the performance of services (for example, under a covenant not to compete) as the performance of services for purposes of these rules.

GROUP TERM LIFE INSURANCE

Generally, the cost of up to **$50,000** of group term life insurance coverage provided by an employer (or former employer) is not included in income. However, the cost of employer-provided insurance that exceeds the cost of $50,000 of coverage reduced by any amount paid toward the purchase of the insurance must be included in income. If an employer provides more than $50,000 of coverage, the employer must report the amount included in income as part of wages in Box 1 of Form W-2. Employer-paid premiums for whole life or permanent insurance are included in the employee's income.

RESTRICTED PROPERTY

Generally, the fair market value of property received for services is income in the year the taxpayer receives the property. A taxpayer does not include the value of stock or other property in income if there are certain restrictions that affect its value, e.g., a substantial risk of forfeiture. The taxpayer must report the property as income once it substantially vests (is no longer restricted). A taxpayer can choose to include the value of the property in income in the year the transfer occurs if making a proper *83(b) election* within 30 days of the grant date. The election is made by sending a letter to the IRS (see Rev. Proc. 2012-29 for example). The IRS treats restricted stock dividends as compensation and not as dividend income unless the taxpayer has recognized the stock as income. The holding period begins when the taxpayer includes the amount in income. The benefit of the 83(b) election is that future income or gains may receive the more preferential dividend and capital gain tax treatment.

> **EXAMPLE:** Your employer gives you $50,000 in stock for services performed under the condition that you'll have to return the stock unless you complete 5 years of service. The stock is under a substantial risk of forfeiture and isn't substantially vested when you receive it. You don't report income from the stock until you have completed the 5 years of service that satisfy the condition.
>
> You could elect under 83(b) to include $50,000 (the value of the stock) in income within 30 days of the grant date. Essentially, an 83(b) election is utilized when the underlying asset is expected to appreciate or substantial dividends are expected. In the absence of such an election, the value of the property (including any appreciation since the grant date) is taxed at ordinary rates when the restriction period ends. If the stock is worth $150,000 after 5 years the taxpayer would report the entire amount in income, taxed at ordinary rates. As an alternative, the 83(b) election would cause recognition of $50,000 in the first year, and any appreciation is taxed at more favorable capital gains rates when the stock is sold.

STOCK OPTIONS

If an employee receives a ***non-statutory stock option*** (also called ***non-qualified stock option*** or ***NSO)*** that has a readily determinable fair market value at the time it is granted, the option is treated similarly to other property received as compensation. Otherwise, the amount of income to include (and the time to include it) depends on the fair market value of the option when the employee does one of the following:

- Exercises the option (uses it to buy or sell the stock or other property)
- Sells or otherwise disposes of the option

However, if the option is a ***statutory stock option*** (also called ***incentive stock option*** or ***ISO***), the employee will <u>not</u> have any income until they sell or exchange the stock. The tax treatment for ISOs is more favorable than that of NSOs. Capital gain tax rates apply to gain from ISOs if an employee holds the stock more than one year from the date of exercise and more than two years from the option grant date prior to disposing of the stock; otherwise, ordinary income rates apply to the gain at the time of sale.

> **EXAMPLE:** In 2008, MicroMedia grants Doug non-statutory options giving him the right to purchase 1,000 shares of MicroMedia stock for a price of $25 per share. On the grant date, MicroMedia shares traded at $5. Douglas does not recognize income when he receives the options because his exercise price is above the current share price; therefore, there is no readily determinable market value. In 2020, Doug exercises his options when the price of the stock is $95. He receives $70,000 in compensation, which is the difference between what he pays ($25,000) and the value of the stock at exercise ($95,000). MicroMedia should include the compensation on Doug's W-2, and withhold any applicable social security and Medicare tax.

TIP INCOME

<u>All</u> tips received are income and subject to federal income tax. Include in gross income <u>all</u> tips received directly, charged tips paid by an employer, and any tips received under a tip-splitting or tip-pooling arrangement. The IRS also considers non-cash tips such as tickets, passes, or other items of value as taxable income, based on their value. To report tip income correctly, employees must:

- Keep a daily tip record
- Report cash and charge tips to the employer **by the 10th of the following month if $20 or more**

- Report all tips on the income tax return, with the exception of tips reported to the employer after the end of the year that will be reflected on the employee's W-2 in the following year

Tips reported to the employer **on time** are considered income in the **month reported**. Tips that are not reported on time are considered income in the **month actually received**.

TIP: Employees who receive tips of less than $20 in a calendar month aren't required to report tips to their employer but must report these amounts as income on their tax returns and pay taxes, if any.

EXAMPLE: Ben Smith began working at the Blue Ocean Restaurant (his only employer in 2020) on June 30 and received $10,000 in wages during the year. Ben kept a daily tip record showing that his tips for June were $18 and his tips for the rest of the year totaled $7,000. He wasn't required to report his June tips to his employer, but he reported all of the rest of his tips to his employer as required.

Ben's Form W-2 from Blue Ocean Restaurant shows $17,000 ($10,000 wages + $7,000 reported tips) in box 1. He adds the $18 unreported tips to that amount and reports $17,018 as wages on his tax return.

Tip income is subject to social security and Medicare tax. The taxpayer must give the employer a written report of all cash and charge tips if receiving $20 or more in tips during a month. A taxpayer uses *Form 4137* to figure the social security and Medicare tax owed on tips they did not report to their employer, including any allocated tips shown on Form(s) W-2 that they must report as income.

The taxpayer must report the value of non-cash tips to the IRS on the tax return, but not to the employer. The taxpayer does not pay social security, Medicare, Additional Medicare, or railroad retirement taxes on non-cash tips.

A taxpayer may be subject to a 6652(b) penalty equal to 50% of unpaid social security and Medicare taxes due on unreported tips. The penalty amount is in addition to those taxes. The taxpayer can avoid this penalty if there is a reasonable cause for not reporting the tips to the employer. To do so, the taxpayer attaches a statement to the tax return explaining the reason for not reporting the tips.

SPECIAL RULES FOR CERTAIN EMPLOYEES

CLERGY

Members of the clergy must include in income any salary and fees received for masses, marriages, baptisms, funerals, etc. Payments to the religious institution are not taxable. Members of religious organizations who give outside earnings to the organization must include the earnings as income and may take a charitable deduction for the amount paid to the organization.

- **Pension** – Pension or retirement pay for a clergy member usually receives normal treatment.
- **Housing** – The rental value of a home (including utilities) or any designated *housing allowance* is **excludable** from income. The exclusion cannot be more than the reasonable pay for services rendered. Any allowance designated for the cost of utilities is excludable, up to the actual utility cost. The home or allowance must represent compensation for services rendered as an ordained, licensed, or commissioned minister. However, the rental value of the home or the housing allowance must be included as **earnings from self-employment** (on Schedule SE) if self-employment tax is applicable.

EXAMPLE: Rev. Joanna Baker is a full-time minister. The church allows her to use a parsonage that has an annual fair rental value of $24,000. The church pays her an annual salary of $67,000, of which $7,500 is designated for utility costs. Her actual utility costs during the year were $7,000.

For income tax purposes, Rev. Baker excludes $31,000 from gross income ($24,000 fair rental value of parsonage + $7,000 from the allowance for utility costs, up to the actual utility costs). She will report gross income of $60,000 ($59,500 salary + $500 unused utility allowance). Her income for self-employment tax purposes, however, is $91,000 ($67,000 salary including allowance for utility costs + $24,000 fair rental value of parsonage).

TIP: If you have church employee income of **$108.28** or more, you <u>must</u> pay self-employment tax. Church employee income is wages you received as an employee (other than as a minister or member of a religious order) of a church or qualified church-controlled organization that has a certificate in effect electing an exemption from employer social security and Medicare taxes.

MEMBERS OF RELIGIOUS ORDERS

The treatment of renounced earnings turned over to a religious order by a member under a vow of poverty depends on whether or not the member performed the services specifically for the order.

- **Services performed for the order** – If the member performed services as an agent of the order in the exercise of duties required by the order, the amounts turned over to the order should not be included as income. If the member performed services for another agency of the supervising church or an associated institution, and the order mandated said service, the IRS considers the member to have performed the services as an agent of the order. Any wages a member earns as an agent of an order and turns over to the order are not included as income.
- **Services performed outside the order** – If a member of an order is directed to work outside the order, the services rendered are not an exercise of duties required by the order unless they meet both of the following requirements:
  1. The services are the kind of services that are ordinarily the duties of members of the order.
  2. They are part of the duties that the member must exercise for the religious order as its agent.

EXAMPLE: Pat Brown and Chris Green are members of a religious order and have taken vows of poverty. They renounce all claims to their earnings. The earnings belong to the order.

Pat is a licensed attorney. The superiors of the order instructed her to get a job with a law firm. Pat joined a law firm as an employee and, as she requested, the firm made the salary payments directly to the order.

Chris is a secretary. The superiors of the order instructed him to accept a job with the business office of the church that supervises the order. Chris took the job and gave all his earnings to the order.

Pat's services aren't duties required by the order. Her earnings are subject to social security and Medicare tax under FICA and to federal income tax. Chris' services are duties required by the order. He is acting as an agent of the order and not as an employee of a third party. He doesn't include the earnings in gross income, and they aren't subject to income tax withholding or to social security and Medicare tax under FICA or SECA.

FOREIGN EMPLOYER

Compensation for services performed within or outside the United States by an employee or officer (regardless of citizenship or residence) of an **international organization** is <u>not</u> considered to be wages for social security and Medicare tax purposes. A **U.S. citizen** reports income paid for services rendered to an international organization as **self-employment income** on their U.S. federal income tax return and is subject to self-employment tax to the extent such services are performed within the United States.

Compensation for services performed as an employee of a **foreign government**, without regard to citizenship, residence, or where services are performed, is not considered to be wages for social security and Medicare tax purposes. This includes services performed by ambassadors, other diplomatic and consular officers and employees, and nondiplomatic representatives.

MILITARY PAY

A member of the military must generally report payments received as a service member as wages for tax purposes, except for retirement pay, which is taxable as a pension.

INTEREST INCOME

TAXABLE INTEREST

Interest is money paid in exchange for the use of money. Interest is generally earned through deposit accounts, investments, and loans to others.

A taxpayer should receive Form 1099-INT from each payor who paid interest of **$10 or more.** Certain taxpayers may receive Schedule K-1 if they have reportable interest from partnerships, S corporations, estates, and trusts.

> A taxpayer with over **$1,500** of taxable interest or ordinary dividends must attach Schedule B to Form 1040.

Taxable interest includes income from various sources such as the following:

- Bank, savings and loan, or credit union accounts
- Certificates of deposit
- U.S. Treasury bills, notes, and bonds (exempt from all state and local income taxes)
- Loans made to others
- Gifts more than $10 for opening financial accounts ($20 if the account is more than $5,000)
- Interest received on tax refunds
- U.S. Savings Bond interest
    1. Series H and HH – Report semi-annual interest payments in the year received.
    2. Series I, E, and EE – Interest is credited at maturity. Taxpayers who use the cash method of accounting may elect to defer reporting interest until maturity; those using the accrual method must report interest on U.S. savings bonds each year as it accrues. Interest may be tax-free if used for qualified education expenses.

TIP: Interest from Series I or EE bonds may be tax-free if used to pay for qualified education expenses the same year. This exclusion is known as the Education Savings Bond Program and is not available when married filing separately. A taxpayer uses Form 8815 to figure the exclusion and attaches the form to Form 1040.

NOMINEES

Generally, if someone receives interest as a nominee for you, that person will give you a Form 1099-INT showing the interest received on your behalf. If you receive a Form 1099-INT that includes amounts belonging to another person, report the full amount shown as interest on Schedule B. Then, on Schedule B, below a subtotal of all interest income listed, enter "Nominee Distribution" and the amount of interest income that actually belongs to someone else. Subtract that nominee amount from the interest income subtotal. An example of when this occurs is a joint account with one owner indicated as the tax-reporting holder.

A taxpayer who receives interest as a nominee on 2020 Form 1099-INT <u>must</u> file Form 1099-INT for that interest with the IRS with a Form 1096, Annual Summary and Transmittal of U.S. Information Returns, by February 28, 2021 (March 31, 2021 if filing electronically). In addition, the taxpayer must furnish the actual owner of the interest with copy B of Form 1099-INT by January 31, 2021.

In certain circumstances, a shareholder may receive dividends as a nominee on Form 1099-DIV. When this occurs, the same rules apply except the taxpayer must submit Form 1099-DIV.

> **EXAMPLE:** You and your sister have a joint savings account that paid $1,500 interest for 2020. Your sister deposited 30% of the funds in this account, and you and she have agreed to share the yearly interest income in proportion to the amount each of you has invested. Because your SSN was given to the bank, you received a Form 1099-INT for 2020 that includes the interest income earned belonging to your sister. This amount is $450, or 30% of the total interest of $1,500.
>
> You must give your sister a Form 1099-INT by January 31, 2021, showing $450 of interest income she earned for 2020. You also must send a copy of the nominee Form 1099-INT, along with Form 1096, to the Internal Revenue Service Center by February 28, 2021 (March 31, 2021, if you file Form 1099-INT electronically). Show your own name, address, and SSN as that of the "Payer" on the Form 1099-INT. Show your sister's name, address, and SSN in the blocks provided for identification of the "Recipient."
>
> When you prepare your own federal income tax return, report the total amount of interest income, $1,500, on Schedule B (Form 1040), Part I, line 1, and identify the name of the bank that paid this interest. Show the amount belonging to your sister, $450, as a subtraction from a subtotal of all interest on Schedule B (Form 1040) and identify this subtraction as a "Nominee Distribution." (Your sister will report the $450 of interest income on her own tax return, if she has to file a return, and identify you as the payer of that amount.)

ORIGINAL ISSUE DISCOUNT (OID)

Original issue discount (OID) is a form of interest. Taxpayers include a portion of the discount as income as it accrues over the term of the debt instrument, even if they do not receive any payments from the issuer. A debt instrument generally has OID when the debtor issues the instrument for a price that is less than its stated redemption price at maturity. OID is the difference between the stated redemption price at maturity and the issue price. The IRS presumes that all debt instruments that do not pay interest before maturity are issued at a discount. Zero-coupon bonds are one example of these instruments.

The OID accrual rules generally do not apply to short-term obligations (those with a fixed maturity date of one year or less from date of issue). The taxpayer may treat the discount as zero if it is less than one-fourth of 1% (.0025) of the stated redemption price at maturity multiplied by the number of full years from the date of original issue to maturity. This small discount is known as "*de minimis*" OID.

> **EXAMPLE:** You bought a 10-year bond with a stated redemption price at maturity of $1,000, issued at $980 with OID of $20. One-fourth of 1% of $1,000 (stated redemption price) times 10 (the number of full years from the date of original issue to maturity) equals $25. Because the $20 discount is less than $25, the OID is treated as zero. (If you hold the bond at maturity, you will recognize $20 ($1,000 − $980) of capital gain.)
>
> Assume the facts are the same, except that the bond was issued at $950. The OID is $50. Because the $50 discount is more than the $25 (one-fourth of 1%), you must include the OID in income as it accrues over the term of the bond.

EXCEPTIONS TO REPORTING OID

The OID rules do <u>not</u> apply to the following debt instruments:

- Tax-exempt obligations
- U.S. savings bonds
- Short-term debt instruments (with a fixed maturity date one year or less from the date of issue)
- Obligations issued by an individual before March 2, 1984
- Loans between individuals, if <u>all</u> the following are true:
  1. The lender is not in the business of lending money
  2. All outstanding loans between the same individuals total $10,000 or less
  3. Avoiding any federal tax is not one of the principal purposes of the loan

DIVIDENDS AND OTHER CORPORATE DISTRIBUTIONS

CLASSIFICATION OF DIVIDENDS

A taxpayer that receives a distribution from a corporation may have taxable income if the distribution is classified as a dividend. A dividend is a distribution of property paid by the corporation to its stockholders. A dividend is the most common type of distribution from a corporation. A dividend is paid out of the earnings and profits of the corporation.

A dividend is classified either as ordinary or qualified. Whereas ordinary dividends are taxable as ordinary income, qualified dividends that meet certain requirements are taxed at the same low rates that apply to long-term capital gains.

The payer of the dividend is required to correctly identify each type and amount of dividend and report to the taxpayer on Form 1099-DIV for distributions of **at least $10**. A taxpayer that is a partner in a partnership or a beneficiary of an estate or trust, may be required to report a share of any dividends received by the entity, whether or not the dividend is paid out. A share of the entity's dividends is generally reported on a Schedule K-1.

ORDINARY DIVIDENDS

A corporation pays ordinary dividends out of its earnings and profits. This means they are not capital gains. A taxpayer can assume that any dividend received on common or preferred stock is an ordinary dividend unless the paying corporation or mutual fund tells them otherwise. Ordinary dividends are the most common type of distribution from a corporation, and as the name implies, shareholders generally report such payments as **ordinary** income.

QUALIFIED DIVIDENDS

Qualified dividends also are included in the ordinary dividend total, but qualified dividends are eligible for a lower tax rate than other ordinary income. The maximum rate of tax on qualified dividends is:

- **0%** on any amount that otherwise would be taxed below the 15% rate,
- **15%** on any amount that otherwise would be taxed at rates between 15% and 37%, and
- **20%** on any amount that otherwise would be taxed at a 37% rate.

To qualify for the maximum rate, the dividends must be paid by a U.S. corporation or a qualified foreign corporation, <u>and</u> the taxpayer must hold the stock for **more than 60 days** during the 121-day period that begins 60 days before the ex-dividend date.

TIP: In calculating the holding period, include the day the stock was disposed of, but not the day acquired. The ex-dividend date is the first date following the declaration of a dividend on which the buyer of a stock will not receive the next dividend payment. Instead, the seller will get the dividend.

EXAMPLE: You bought 5,000 shares of XYZ Corp. common stock on July 5. XYZ Corp. paid a cash dividend of 10 cents per share. The ex-dividend date was July 12. Your Form 1099-DIV from XYZ Corp. shows $500 in box 1a (ordinary dividends) and in box 1b (qualified dividends). However, you sold the 5,000 shares on August 8 of the same year. You held your shares of XYZ Corp. for only 34 days of the 121-day period (from July 6, through August 8). The 121-day period began on May 13 (60 days before the ex-dividend date) and ended on September 10. You have no qualified dividends from XYZ Corp. because you held the XYZ stock for less than 61 days.

Assume the same facts except that you bought the stock on July 11 (the day before the ex-dividend date) and you sold the stock on September 13. You held the stock for 63 days (from July 12, through September 13). The $500 of qualified dividends shown in box 1b of your Form 1099-DIV are all qualified dividends because you held the stock for 61 days of the 121-day period (from July 12, through September 13).

EXAMPLE: You bought 10,000 shares of ABC Mutual Fund common stock on July 5. ABC Mutual Fund paid a cash dividend of 10 cents per share. The ex-dividend date was July 12 of the same year. The ABC Mutual Fund advises you that the portion of the dividend eligible to be treated as qualified dividends equals 2 cents per share. Your Form 1099-DIV from ABC Mutual Fund shows total ordinary dividends of $1,000 and qualified dividends of $200. However, you sold the 10,000 shares on August 8. You have no qualified dividends from ABC Mutual Fund because you held the ABC Mutual Fund stock for less than 61 days.

DIVIDENDS USED TO BUY MORE STOCK

Some corporations have dividend reinvestment plans that allow for the purchase of more stock in the corporation instead of receiving the dividends in cash. Taxpayers who are members of this type of plan must still report the dividends as income. If the plan allows the purchase of more stock at a price less than its fair market value, the taxpayer must report the fair market value of the additional stock as dividend income on the dividend payment date.

MONEY MARKET FUNDS

A taxpayer reports amounts received from money market funds as dividend income. Money market funds are a type of mutual fund, not to be confused with bank money market accounts that pay interest.

CAPITAL GAIN DISTRIBUTIONS

Capital gain distributions reflect income paid or credited to the taxpayer's account by mutual funds (or other regulated investment companies) and real estate investment trusts (REITs). A taxpayer must report capital gain distributions as long-term capital gains (not dividends) regardless of how long the taxpayer has owned the shares of the mutual fund or REIT. Some mutual funds and REITs keep their long-term capital gains and pay tax on them.

Shareholders receive *Form 2439* reflecting their share of undistributed long-term capital gains. Each must treat their share of gain as a distribution, even if not actually received. Report undistributed capital gains as long-term capital gains on Schedule D. A taxpayer can apply for a refund or credit of any payments made by including the amount in the "Payments" section of their tax return, and checking the appropriate box next to "2439."

NON-DIVIDEND DISTRIBUTIONS

A *non-dividend distribution* (return of capital) is a distribution that is <u>not</u> a payment from the earnings and profits of a corporation. A non-dividend distribution is <u>not</u> a dividend, it is a return of an investment in the stock of the company and reduces the basis of the stock. It is <u>not</u> taxable until the taxpayer **fully recovers their basis**. When stock basis reaches zero, report any additional non-dividend distribution as a capital gain. Whether the taxpayer should report it as a long-term or short-term capital gain depends on their holding period.

DISTRIBUTIONS OF STOCK AND STOCK RIGHTS

Distributions by a corporation of its own stock or stock rights (also known as "stock options") are generally not taxable, and a holder of such options need not report them on a return. Distributions of stock dividends and stock rights are taxable if <u>any</u> of the following apply:

- Shareholders have the choice to receive cash or other property instead of stock or stock rights.
- The distribution gives cash or other property to some shareholders and an increase in the percentage interest in the corporation's assets or earnings and profits to other shareholders.
- The distribution is in convertible preferred stock, resulting in a change of ownership.
- The distribution is preferred stock for some common shareholders and common stock to others.
- The distribution is on preferred stock.

IRAS, QUALIFIED RETIREMENT PLANS, PENSIONS, AND ANNUITIES

A taxpayer must include distributions other than the taxpayer's cost (basis) from certain retirement plans or annuities in gross income. The IRS treats distributions of basis as a tax-free return of principal (<u>not</u> income). A loss may arise if the entire account is withdrawn and a taxpayer receives less than their cost basis.

TIP: The taxpayer should receive a 1099-R reflecting information about the distribution, such as the gross distribution and taxable amount. A taxpayer filing a paper return should attach Form 1099-R, but <u>only</u> if federal income tax was withheld.

QUALIFIED RETIREMENT PLANS

The term *qualified retirement plan* has varied meanings within the tax code and IRS publications. In a broad sense, the term describes plans that qualify for favorable tax benefits such as tax deferral on contributions, investment gains, and earnings. As a result, plans such as IRAs, annuities, 403(b)s, and 457(b)s are at times describes as qualified retirement plans for the application of specific rules and regulations.

There is, however, a common usage of the term that identifies a specific subset of retirement plans. A qualified retirement plan is an employer-sponsored retirement plan that qualifies for special tax treatment under Section 401(a) of the Internal Revenue Code. These plans are sometimes called *ERISA qualified plans* because employer plans must adhere to the minimum standards set forth in the *Employee Retirement Income Security Act of 1974 (ERISA)*. Other terms used to describe these plans include a *qualified employee plan*, or simply *qualified plan*. To avoid confusion, we will <u>not</u> use this terminology to describe other types of plans that share similar tax advantages.

There are two basic kinds of qualified plans—defined contribution plans (e.g., a profit sharing or 401(k) plan) and defined benefit plans (e.g., a pension plan)—and different rules apply to each. Employers establish these plans and generally make contributions to fund the plan for the benefit of employees. Some plans also allow for elective deferrals of salary. This is where an employee can direct the employer to contribute **pre-tax** compensation to the plan rather than receive the amount in cash. Contributions to the plan are generally <u>not</u> included in the employee's taxable income until withdrawn.

INDIVIDUAL RETIREMENT ACCOUNT (IRA)

An *individual retirement account (IRA)* is a trust or custodial account set up in the United States for the exclusive benefit of a taxpayer or his beneficiaries. A taxpayer creates this account with a written document. The document must show that the account meets all of the following requirements:

- The trustee or custodian must be a bank, a federally insured credit union, a savings and loan association, or an entity approved by the IRS to act as trustee or custodian.
- The trustee or custodian generally should not accept contributions of more than the deductible amount for the year. However, rollover contributions and employer contributions to a simplified employee pension (SEP) can be more than this amount.
- Contributions, except for rollover contributions, must be in cash.
- The taxpayer must have a non-forfeitable right to the amount at all times.
- The account holder cannot use money in the account to buy a life insurance policy.
- The account holder cannot use money in the account to buy collectibles other than certain gold or silver coins minted by the Treasury Department. It can also invest in certain platinum coins and certain gold, silver, palladium, and platinum bullion.
- The account holder cannot combine assets with other property, except in a common trust or investment fund.

TRADITIONAL IRA

A *traditional IRA* (sometimes called an ordinary or regular IRA) is an IRA that is not a Roth IRA or a SIMPLE IRA. A traditional IRA can be an individual retirement account or annuity.

Two advantages of a traditional IRA are as follows:

- Traditional IRA contributions may be **tax-deductible**, depending on the circumstances
- Amounts in a traditional IRA, including earnings and gains, are **not taxed until distributed**

Money cannot remain in a *traditional IRA* indefinitely, and eventually, a taxpayer must take a *required minimum distribution (RMD)*. The taxpayer generally must make annual withdrawals from an IRA, SIMPLE IRA, SEP IRA, or retirement plan when reaching age 72 (or age 70.5 if 70.5 prior to January 1, 2020).

TIP: For 401(k), profit-sharing, 403(b), or other defined contribution plans, the taxpayer generally must make annual withdrawals the later of reaching age 72 (or age 70.5 prior to January 1, 2020), or **retires** from the employer sponsoring the plan.

ROTH IRA

A *Roth IRA* is an individual retirement plan that is subject to the rules that apply to a traditional IRA, with the following exceptions:

- Contributions to a Roth IRA are not tax-deductible. Do not report them on the tax return.
- Amounts can remain in the Roth IRA until the taxpayer dies (**no RMD**). Mandatory distributions are not required when attaining age 72 (or age 70.5 prior to January 1, 2020).
- Certain *qualified distributions* may be **tax-free**.

Two advantages of a Roth IRA over a traditional IRA are as follows:

- Amounts can remain in a Roth IRA, RMDs are not required
- Amounts in a Roth IRA, including earnings and gains, are generally **not taxed, even when distributed**

ROTH CONVERSIONS

A taxpayer can withdraw all or part of the assets from a traditional IRA and reinvest them (within 60 days) in a Roth IRA. The amount that the taxpayer withdraws and timely contributes (converts) to the Roth IRA is called a conversion contribution. If properly (and timely) rolled over, the 10% additional tax on early distributions will <u>not</u> apply. The taxpayer must roll over into the Roth IRA the same property received from the traditional IRA. The taxpayer can roll over part of the withdrawal into a Roth IRA and keep the rest of it. The amount kept will generally be taxable (except for the part that is a return of nondeductible contributions) and may be subject to the 10% additional tax on early distributions.

The IRS treats the converted amount as a taxable distribution in the year of the conversion. A taxpayer recognizes the entire amount of the conversion (other than basis) in income. A taxpayer may convert a traditional IRA or Simple IRA into a Roth IRA, regardless of filing status or income.

RECHARACTERIZATION

A recharacterization allows the taxpayer to treat a regular contribution made to a Roth IRA or to a traditional IRA as having been made to the other type of IRA. To recharacterize a regular IRA contribution, the taxpayer instructs the trustee of the financial institution holding the IRA to transfer the amount of the contribution plus earnings to a different type of IRA (either a Roth or traditional) in a trustee-to-trustee transfer or to a different type of IRA with the same trustee. If this is done by the due date for filing the tax return (including extensions), the taxpayer can treat the contribution as made to the second IRA for that year (effectively ignoring the contribution to the first IRA).

> **TCJA:** Effective January 1, 2018, pursuant to the Tax Cuts and Jobs Act, a conversion from a traditional IRA, SEP, or SIMPLE to a Roth IRA <u>cannot</u> be recharacterized. The new law also prohibits recharacterizing amounts rolled over to a Roth IRA from other retirement plans, such as 401(k) or 403(b) plans.

DESIGNATED ROTH ACCOUNTS

Designated Roth accounts are separate accounts under 401(k), 403(b), or 457(b) plans that accept elective deferrals that are referred to as Roth contributions. A taxpayer includes these elective deferrals in income, but qualified distributions from these accounts are not included in income. Designated Roth accounts are <u>not</u> IRAs and should not be confused with Roth IRAs. Contributions, up to their respective limits, can be made to Roth IRAs and designated Roth accounts according to a taxpayer's eligibility to participate. A contribution to one does not impact eligibility to contribute to the other.

BASIS OF QUALIFIED RETIREMENT PLANS AND IRAS

For **qualified retirement plans** and **individual retirement arrangements (IRA)** basis equals the amount of after-tax (non-deductible) contributions remaining within the plan. A taxpayer who made nondeductible contributions has a cost basis equal to the sum of the nondeductible contributions minus any withdrawals or distributions of nondeductible contributions. Contributions that the taxpayer excludes from gross income do <u>not</u> increase basis.

TIP: The custodian of a qualified plan maintains records for nondeductible contributions. For a traditional IRA, the taxpayer files **Form 8606** to report nondeductible contributions. Form 8606 is filed in subsequent years to report any changes to basis (i.e., distributions from a traditional, SEP, or SIMPLE IRA that impact basis).

Distributions from a qualified plan are usually taxable because most recipients do not have a basis in the qualified plan. If the taxpayer has a basis, the pro-rata portion of each withdrawal that represents basis is not taxed. Withdrawals, other than required distributions, can maintain tax-deferred treatment if transferred into another qualified plan or IRA within 60 days. This is commonly referred to as a **rollover**. Any amount withdrawn and not rolled over within this period is subject to tax. A *conversion* is a distribution from a qualified retirement plan or IRA into a Roth IRA. Conversions are taxed as ordinary distributions.

TRADITIONAL IRA NONDEDUCTIBLE CONTRIBUTIONS

Although the deduction for traditional IRA contributions may be reduced or eliminated, contributions can be made up to the general limit or, if it applies, the spousal IRA limit. The difference between the total permitted contributions and the IRA deduction is a *nondeductible contribution*. A nondeductible contribution increases the basis of the IRA and is not taxable when withdrawn.

TIP: To designate contributions as nondeductible, a taxpayer must file *Form 8606*, even if not required to file a tax return for the year. If a taxpayer does not report nondeductible contributions, the IRS treats all contributions to a traditional IRA as deductible contributions—meaning distributions will be taxed!

A traditional IRA consisting only of deductible contributions and earnings does not have a basis. If the IRA has a basis resulting from nondeductible contributions, distributions consist partly of nondeductible contributions (basis) and partly of deductible contributions, earnings, and gains (if any). Until the entire basis has been distributed, each distribution is partly nontaxable and partly taxable. To determine the nontaxable percentage of the distribution, divide the basis at the beginning of the year (plus contributions for the tax year) by the total value of all IRAs at the end of the year (plus distributions in the tax year).

> **EXAMPLE:** Jim makes a $6,000 nondeductible contribution in 2020 to his IRA and properly files Form 8606. His prior-year deductible contributions to the account total $15,000. Jim withdraws $10,000 during 2020. The balance in his IRA at the end of 2020 is $50,000. The nontaxable portion of his withdrawal is 10% ($6,000 ÷ ($50,000 + $10,000)) of the distribution amount or $1,000 ($10,000 × 10%).

QUALIFIED DISTRIBUTIONS

Most retirement plan withdrawals are subject to income tax, including *qualified distributions*. Withdrawals other than qualified distributions may be subject to a 10% additional tax on the distribution. This additional tax applies to the part of the distribution the individual must include in income and is in addition to any regular income tax on that amount. Generally, the amounts an individual withdraws from a retirement plan before reaching age 59.5 (or age 55 and separated from service for a qualified plan) are called "early" or "premature" distributions (Age 59.5 Rule). Individuals must pay an additional 10% early withdrawal tax unless an exception applies. A number of exceptions apply to this Age 59.5 Rule and are discussed in the chapter *Additional Taxes on Tax-Favored Accounts*.

QUALIFIED CHARITABLE DISTRIBUTION

A qualified charitable distribution (QCD) is a nontaxable distribution **made directly by the trustee of an IRA** (other than a SEP or SIMPLE IRA) to an organization eligible to receive tax-deductible contributions. The taxpayer must have been **at least age 70.5** when making the distribution. The taxpayer must keep the same type of acknowledgment of the contribution that he would need to claim a deduction for a charitable contribution. Total QCDs for the year cannot be more than $100,000 ($200,000 if MFJ) reduced by deductible contributions for all taxable years after the taxpayer attains age 70.5. The amount of the QCD is limited to the amount of the distribution that would otherwise be included in income. If the IRA includes nondeductible contributions, the distribution is first considered to be paid out of otherwise taxable income. The *PATH Act of 2015* made this deduction permanent.

TIP: QCDs are available for traditional or Roth IRAs only. Employer-sponsored plans (e.g. 401(k) or 403(b) plans) are not eligible for QCD treatment.

EXAMPLE: On December 23, 2020, Jeff, age 75, directed the trustee of his IRA to make a distribution of $25,000 directly to a qualified 501(c)(3) organization (a charitable organization eligible to receive tax-deductible contributions). The total value of Jeff's IRA is $30,000 and consists of $20,000 of deductible contributions and earnings and $10,000 of nondeductible contributions (basis). Since Jeff is at least age 70.5 and the distribution is made directly by the trustee to a qualified organization, the part of the distribution that would otherwise be includible in Jeff's income ($20,000) is a QCD.

In this case, Jeff has made a QCD of $20,000 (his deductible contributions and earnings). Because Jeff made a distribution of nondeductible contributions from his IRA, he must file Form 8606 with his return. Jeff includes the total distribution ($25,000) on line 4a of Form 1040. He completes Form 8606 to determine the amount to enter on line 4b of Form 1040 and the remaining basis in his IRA. Jeff enters -0- on line 4b. This is Jeff's only IRA and he took no other distributions in 2020. He also enters "QCD" next to line 4b to indicate a qualified charitable distribution.

After the distribution, his basis in his IRA is $5,000. If Jeff itemizes deductions and files Schedule A with Form 1040, the $5,000 portion of the distribution attributable to the nondeductible contributions can be deducted as a charitable contribution, subject to AGI limits. He can't take the charitable contribution deduction for the $20,000 portion of the distribution that wasn't included in his income.

TIP: Taxpayers often use QCD to meet annual RMD requirements. The Secure Act of 2019 increased the mandatory distribution age to 72 but *kept the QCD age at 70.5*. For these taxpayers, QCDs made prior to age 72 do not impact RMD.

DISTRIBUTION OF EMPLOYER SECURITIES IN QUALIFIED PLAN

26 U.S. Code §402 allows a participant in a **qualified plan** the opportunity to pay capital gains tax on the *net unrealized appreciation (NUA)* of employer securities that were purchased in the plan. NUA is the net increase in the securities' value (the amount in excess of basis) while inside the retirement plan.

To receive this benefit, the taxpayer distributes the entire account in a *lump-sum distribution* and **pays ordinary income tax on the basis** of the securities, which includes both participant and employer contributions used to purchase the securities. The taxpayer can rollover any part of the distribution (other than the securities). No tax is currently due on the part rolled over. Report any part not rolled over as ordinary income.

A lump-sum distribution is a distribution **within a single tax year** of a plan participant's **entire balance** from all of the employer's qualified plans of one kind (for example, pension, profit-sharing, or stock bonus plans). Additionally, a lump-sum distribution is a distribution that's paid:

- Because of the plan participant's death,
- After the participant reaches age 59.5,
- Because the participant, if an employee, separates from service, or
- After the participant, if a self-employed individual, becomes totally and permanently disabled.

The taxpayer will generally defer paying tax on the NUA until the securities are sold. At that time, any **gain due to NUA is a long-term capital gain**, regardless of the actual holding period of the securities. The character of the gain on any further appreciation (above the NUA) after the distribution will depend on the actual holding period.

This tax deferral applies to distributions of the employer corporation's stocks, bonds, registered debentures, and debentures with interest coupons attached.

TIP: This tax benefit has the potential to be substantial, and is especially valuable when highly appreciated company stock is held within a 401K plan. Use caution when advising a client on a rollover as the tax benefits are lost if the securities are rolled into an IRA or another qualified plan.

PROHIBITED TRANSACTIONS

Generally, a prohibited transaction is a transaction between a plan and a taxpayer, a beneficiary, or any other disqualified person. Disqualified persons include a fiduciary and members of a taxpayer's family (spouse, ancestor, lineal descendant, and any spouse of a lineal descendant).

Prohibited transactions generally include the following transactions:

- a transfer of plan income or assets to, or use of them by or for the benefit of, a disqualified person;
- any act of a fiduciary by which plan income or assets are used for his or her own interest;
- the receipt of consideration by a fiduciary for his or her own account from any party dealing with the plan in a transaction that involves plan income or assets;
- the sale, exchange, or lease of property between a plan and a disqualified person;
- lending money or extending credit between a plan and a disqualified person; and
- furnishing goods, services, or facilities between a plan and a disqualified person.

Certain transactions are exempt from being treated as prohibited transactions. For example, a prohibited transaction does not take place if a disqualified person receives a benefit to which he or she is entitled as a plan participant or beneficiary. However, the benefit must be figured and paid under the same terms as for all other participants and beneficiaries.

Generally, if there is a prohibited transaction in connection with an IRA account at any time during the year, the account stops being an IRA as of the first day of that year. At that time, the **entire account balance is considered a distribution**, and the taxpayer may need to pay a 10% penalty if under age 59.5.

If someone other than the owner or beneficiary of an IRA engages in a prohibited transaction, that person may be liable for certain taxes. There is a **15%** tax on the amount of the prohibited transaction and a **100%** additional tax if the transaction is not corrected.

DISTRIBUTIONS DUE TO DEATH

The surviving spouse may elect to treat an inherited IRA or qualified retirement plan as their own by rolling the account into their name. Except for certain eligible designated beneficiaries, all other beneficiaries generally must withdraw the entire balance of the retirement account within **10 years** or over a specified period, depending on several factors, including the age of the decedent, age of the beneficiary, and the type of beneficiary (i.e., individual, trust, or estate).

TIP: A portion of funds within retirement plans or annuities has never been taxed or has accumulated free of tax. This amount, if withdrawn by the original account owner, would be subject to income tax. If the account owner dies, this amount becomes *income in respect of a decedent (IRD)* and is taxable to the beneficiary of the account upon withdrawal.

INHERITED IRA - INHERITED AFTER 2019

The Secure Act of 2019 dramatically changes the distribution rules for inherited retirement accounts. The Act provides new required distribution rules for designated beneficiaries upon the death of the IRA owner after December 31, 2019. All distributions must be made by the end of the 10th year after death, except for distributions made to certain eligible designated beneficiaries.

SECURE ACT – Effective January 1, 2020, for account owners who die after December 31, 2019, (with a delayed effective date for certain collectively bargained plans), the Secure Act requires the entire balance of the participant's account be distributed within **ten years**. There is an exception for a surviving spouse, a child who has not reached the age of majority, a disabled or chronically ill person, or a person not more than ten years younger than the employee or IRA account owner. The new 10-year rule applies regardless of whether the participant dies before, on, or after, the required beginning date, which effective January 1, 2020, is age 72.

Most beneficiaries of a traditional IRA from decedents who die <u>after</u> December 31, 2019, must withdraw the entire IRA account balance by the **end of the 10th year after the IRA owner's death**. The 10-year withdrawal rule offers flexibility regarding the timing and amount of distributions, as it does not require annual withdrawals, funds can be withdrawn in any amount, at any time over the course of the 10 years, as long as all funds are withdrawn within 10 years after the year of the account owner's death.

There is an **exception** to the 10-year withdrawal rule for certain *eligible designated beneficiaries*. Eligible designated beneficiaries include:

- a *surviving spouse*
- a *child of the account owner* who has <u>not</u> *reached the age of majority*
    1. does <u>not</u> include minor grandchild of account owner
    2. the age of majority is a matter of state law (most states deem an individual to have reached the age of majority upon turning 18)
    3. a child may be treated as having not reached the age of majority if the child has not completed a "specified course of education" and is under the age of 26
    4. once the child reaches the age of majority, the child is no longer an eligible designated beneficiary and the 10-year withdrawal rule applies
- a *disabled or chronically ill* person
- a person <u>not</u> *more than ten years younger than the IRA account owner*

These eligible designated beneficiaries are subject to the pre-Secure Act withdrawals rules described below for non-spouse designated beneficiaries.

INHERITED IRA - INHERITED BEFORE 2020 (PRE-SECURE ACT OF 2019)

Beneficiaries of a traditional IRA from decedents who die before January 1, 2020, must begin withdrawals from a traditional IRA by December 31 of the year following the IRA owner's death.

For non-spouse designated beneficiaries (not a trust or estate), these required distributions must occur under one of the following methods:

- **Lump-sum** – Distribute the entire account immediately.
- **Life expectancy** – Use the divisor from the *Single Life Table*, minus one each year.
- **Five-year deferral** – The IRS does not allow this method when an IRA owner is beyond the *required beginning date* at the time of death. A beneficiary who is an individual may be required to take the entire account by the end of the fifth year following the year of the owner's death. If this rule applies, no distribution is required for any year before that fifth year.

A taxpayer who inherits an IRA from a spouse can elect to treat the IRA as his or her own. This alternative to treatment as a beneficiary is available <u>only</u> if the surviving spouse is the sole beneficiary.

Beneficiaries of retirement accounts and IRAs calculate RMDs using the Single Life Table (Table I, Appendix B, of Publication 590-B). The table shows a life expectancy based on the beneficiary's age. The account balance is divided by this life expectancy to determine the first RMD. The life expectancy is reduced by one for each subsequent year.

TIP: Generally, the *designated beneficiary* is determined on September 30 of the calendar year following the calendar year of the IRA owner's death. In order to be a designated beneficiary, an individual must be a beneficiary as of the date of death. Any person who was a beneficiary on the date of the owner's death, but isn't a beneficiary on September 30 following the calendar year of the owner's death (because, for example, he or she disclaimed entitlement or received his or her entire benefit), won't be taken into account in determining the designated beneficiary.

TIP: These minimum distribution rules apply to traditional IRAs, SEP IRAs, SIMPLE IRAs, 401(k) plans, 403(b) plans, 457(b) plans, profit-sharing plans, and other defined contribution plans.

ANNUITIES

An annuity in a qualified plan or IRA will receive the same tax treatment afforded to those plans. If the annuity is a *non-qualified annuity* (funded with after-tax dollars), individuals do <u>not</u> receive a tax deduction for the investment; therefore, the initial basis is the total of all contributions to the policy. Factors in addition to cost basis may also determine the tax treatment of withdrawals:

- **Annuitization** – The process of converting an annuity into a series of periodic payments.
  1. Accumulation phase – Prior to annuitization, withdrawals are removed earnings first. The IRS treats any amount in excess of basis as ordinary income.
  2. Distribution phase – After annuitization, allocate the periodic payments to income and basis according to an exclusion ratio. The exclusion ratio refers to the basis portion of each payment that is exempt from tax.

     Under the Simplified Method, figure the tax-free part of each annuity payment by dividing the cost by the total number of anticipated monthly payments. For an annuity that is payable for the lives of the annuitants, this number is based on the annuitants' ages on the annuity starting date and is determined from a table. For any other annuity, this number is the number of monthly annuity payments under the contract.

- **Exchanges** – During the accumulation phase, a policyholder may exchange an annuity under §1035 for a policy with another provider without recognition of taxes.

> **EXAMPLE:** George spends $100,000 for an immediate annuity. The insurance company will pay George $500 each month for the next 20 years. The tax-free portion of each payment is $416.67 ($100,000 ÷ 240).

SOCIAL SECURITY BENEFITS

AMOUNT TO INCLUDE IN INCOME

A taxpayer must include in income a portion of social security benefits received when *provisional income* exceeds a specified base amount.

Determine provisional income as follows:

- **One-half** of Social Security benefits, <u>plus</u>
- All other income, including tax-exempt interest.

A taxpayer cannot exclude income received from interest from qualified U.S. Savings bonds, employer-provided adoption benefits, foreign earned income or foreign housing, or income earned as a resident of American Samoa or Puerto Rico.

CALCULATING THE TAXABLE AMOUNT

The calculation to determine the percentage of benefits to include in income is a multi-step process. How much is taxable, depends on the total amount of benefits and other income. Generally, the higher that total amount, the greater the taxable part of benefits.

Determine Maximum Limits

The percentage of benefits a taxpayer includes in income is limited to 50% when provisional income exceeds the lower base amount and 85% when above the upper base amount. A taxpayer with provisional income below the lower base amount excludes all social security benefits from income.

Threshold to determine maximum percentage of benefits subject to tax		
Filing Status	**50%** **Lower Base**	**85%** **Upper Base**
Single	$25,000	$34,000
Head of Household	$25,000	$34,000
Qualifying Widow(er)	$25,000	$34,000
Married Filing Separately*	$25,000	$34,000
Married Filing Jointly	$32,000	$44,000

*This table does not apply to a taxpayer who is married filing separately and lives with a spouse at <u>any</u> time during the year. This taxpayer must include in income 85% of provisional income or 85% of social security benefits, whichever is lower.

EXAMPLE: A married taxpayer receives $20,000 in social security benefits. The taxpayer has $10,000 in tax-free municipal bond interest and $30,000 in taxable IRA withdrawals during the year.

Step 1: Determine provisional income as follows:

1/2 social security benefits ($20,000 × 50%)	$10,000
plus all other income (including tax-exempt)	$40,000
Provisional Income	**$50,000**

The provisional income of $50,000 exceeds the upper threshold for MFJ status. For this taxpayer, the taxable portion of social security benefits to include in income **can be as high as 85% of benefits, or $17,000** ($20,000 social security benefits × 85%). This amount may be further limited (see Example continued).

TIP: It is unlikely you will need to perform complex calculations for this topic. However, you should understand the level where a taxpayer will <u>not</u> pay any tax on benefits, and the level subjecting 85% of benefits to tax.

The Calculation

Allocate provisional income based on filing status. Multiply the amount of provisional income that is between the lower and upper base amount by 50%, and the amount above the upper base amount by 85%, and then add together. The taxable portion of social security benefits to include in income is the lower of this amount, or that maximum limit discussed earlier.

> **EXAMPLE** (continued): The taxpayer in this example uses the MFJ status and the provisional income of $50,000 exceeds the upper threshold for MFJ status. Apportion the amount of provisional income above $44,000 (upper base amount) to the 85% bracket, and any remaining that is above $32,000 (lower base amount) to the 50% bracket.
>
> Now compare provisional income to the brackets to determine the taxable amount of social security benefits.
>
> **Step 2: Allocate provisional income to each bracket based on MFJ filing status:**
>
> | | | | |
> |---|---|---|---|
> | Above $44,000 ($50,000 provisional income – $44,000) | $6,000 | × 85% | $5,100 |
> | Between $32,000 and $44,000 | $12,000 | × 50% | $6,000 |
> | Below base amount, up to $32,000 | $32,000 | × 0% | $0 |
> | **Benefits subject to tax** | | | **$11,100** |
>
> The amount of **social security benefits to include in income is $11,100, as this is lower than the $17,000 maximum amount** (calculated in Step 1).

ADDITIONAL INCOME

A taxpayer reports income from various sources as "Additional Income" on their tax return by attaching additional required forms and schedules and completing Form 1040 Schedule 1. This schedule generally includes farm, business, and rental income, which we will cover separately.

REFUND OF STATE AND LOCAL INCOME TAXES

Taxpayers who itemize deductions may claim a deduction for a *state and local taxes (SALT)* paid. This deduction, which includes state and local income taxes, is limited to $10,000 ($5,000 MFS).

Sometimes a taxpayer receives a SALT refund for income taxes paid in the prior year, and in that case, the taxpayer may need to report the refund as **additional income** on Schedule 1. The taxpayer can exclude the refund from income if the amount did not benefit the prior income tax return. Essentially, a refund is not considered to the extent of any disallowed deduction resulting from the overall limit on SALT.

> **EXAMPLE:** A single taxpayer itemizes and claims deductions totaling $15,000 on the taxpayer's 2019 federal income tax return. A total of $12,000 in state and local taxes is listed on the return, including state and local income taxes of $7,000. Because of the limit, however, the taxpayer's SALT deduction is only $10,000.
>
> In 2020, the taxpayer receives a $750 refund of state income taxes paid in 2019, meaning the taxpayer's actual 2019 state income tax liability was $6,250 ($7,000 paid minus $750 refund). Accordingly, the taxpayer's 2019 SALT deduction would still have been $10,000, even if it had been figured based on the actual $6,250 state and local income tax liability for 2019. The taxpayer did not receive a tax benefit on the taxpayer's 2019 federal income tax return from the taxpayer's overpayment of state income tax in 2019. Thus, the taxpayer is not required to include the taxpayer's 2020 state income tax refund on the taxpayer's 2020 return.

TIP: None of the refund is taxable if, in the year the taxpayer paid the tax, the taxpayer either (a) didn't itemize deductions, or (b) elected to deduct state and local general sales taxes instead of state and local income taxes.

ALIMONY

Payments to a former spouse that meet the criteria of ***alimony*** under a divorce or separate maintenance agreement, may or may not qualify as income or deduction items. ***Property settlements*** or payments of court-ordered ***child support*** are not alimony and do not qualify as income or deduction items.

The taxation of alimony payments will depend on when the divorce or separation instrument was **executed** or **modified**.

AGREEMENTS EXECUTED AFTER 2018

Under the Tax Cuts and Jobs Act, the payment of alimony and separate maintenance under a divorce or separate maintenance agreement (or modifications to prior agreements that account for the new TCJA provision) **executed after** December 31, 2018, is **no longer deductible** by the payor spouse and **no longer includible** in income by the payee spouse.

The intent of the provision is to follow the rule of the United States Supreme Court's holding in ***Gould v. Gould 245 U.S. 151 (1917)***, in which the Court held that such payments are not income to the recipient. Income used for alimony payments is taxed at the rates applicable to the payor spouse rather than the recipient spouse.

Under the provision, any divorce or separation instrument executed after December 31, 2018, including the modification of a prior instrument that expressly provides that the amendments made by this section apply to such modification, alimony and separate maintenance payments are not deductible by the payor spouse. The provision also repeals Code provisions that specify that alimony and separate maintenance payments are included in income by the payee spouse. Effectively, payments of alimony under this provision will be handled in the same manner as child support, not deductible and not includible in income.

AGREEMENTS EXECUTED IN 2018 OR EARLIER

Under prior rules, alimony is **deductible** by the payor and **includible** in the recipient's income for a divorce or separation instrument **executed on or before** December 31, 2018, even when payments are made after 2018.

If a prior year agreement is **modified after December 31, 2018**, the tax treatment will follow the old rules unless the modification expressly states the repeal of the deduction for alimony payments applies to the modification or if the agreement is changed to expressly provide that alimony received is not included in income, then the tax treatment will follow the new rules. If following the old rules, alimony is deductible by the payor and includible in the recipient's income. If following the new rules, alimony is not deductible by the payor and not includible in the recipient's income.

OTHER GAINS (OR LOSSES)

A taxpayer uses ***Form 4797*** to report the sale or exchange of business property, certain involuntary conversions, the recapture of depreciation on certain business property that falls below 50% business use, and ordinary gains or losses of securities traders using the mark-to-market election.

Some of the gains on Form 4797 are reported on Schedule D as long-term capital gain, while other gains are ordinary and reported as "Other Gains or (Losses)" on Schedule 1.

UNEMPLOYMENT BENEFITS

The IRS considers the amount of unemployment compensation received to be income. Unemployment compensation generally includes any amount received under an unemployment compensation law of the United States or of a state. The taxpayer should receive a Form 1099-G, Certain Government Payments, showing the amount of unemployment compensation paid.

OTHER INCOME

A taxpayer must include certain other sources of income on their tax return. If applicable, a taxpayer combines income from a variety of sources and reports as "Other Income" on Schedule 1.

BARTERING INCOME

Bartering is an exchange of property or services. The taxpayer must report the fair market value of property or services received in bartering as income. The fair market value should be determined at the time of the exchange.

BRIBES AND KICKBACKS

If a taxpayer receives bribe, kickback, side commission, push money, or similar payments, it must be included in income on Schedule 1 as "Other Income" or on Schedule C if from a self-employment activity.

CANCELED DEBT

Generally, if a creditor cancels or forgives a debt, the debtor <u>must</u> report the canceled or forgiven amount as income. If the creditor intends the canceled debt as a gift or bequest, the debtor does not have to report it as income. A debt includes any indebtedness for which the taxpayer is liable or which attaches to property held by the taxpayer. Do <u>not</u> consider canceled debt as income in these cases:

- **Bankruptcy** – Debt canceled in a title 11 bankruptcy case.
- **Insolvency** – Immediately before the cancellation, liabilities exceed assets.
- **Price reduction** – When the seller reduces the taxpayer's debt and the taxpayer is not insolvent or bankrupt. The taxpayer reduces basis in the property by the amount of debt reduction. See §108(e)(5).
- **Certain student loan indebtedness:**
  1. Excluded if the creditor canceled the debt due to the performance of services.
  2. Excluded if due to death or total and permanent disability. **TCJA:** Discharges of loans <u>after</u> December 31, 2017, and <u>before</u> January 1, 2026.
- **Qualified real property business indebtedness** – Debt used to acquire, construct, or substantially improve new business real property; or to refinance business real property acquired before 1993.
- **Qualified principal residence indebtedness** – Debt incurred in acquiring, constructing, or substantially improving a principal residence and secured by the principal residence. It also includes any debt resulting from the refinancing of such debt but only to the extent of the prior debt. Cash taken during refinancing is <u>not</u> qualified principal residence indebtedness. Up to **$2 million** ($1 million married filing separately) may be excluded for debt discharged (or agreed to in writing) before January 1, 2021.

> **CONSOLIDATED APPROPRIATIONS ACT UPDATE:** The Consolidated Appropriations Act, 2021 extended the exclusion to discharges made before January 1, 2026, and reduced the exclusion amount to $750,000 ($375,000 married filing separate return) for discharges of indebtedness after December 31, 2020. Thus, up to $750,000 ($375,000 married filing separate) may be excluded for debt discharged 2021 through 2025.

- **Qualified farm indebtedness** – Debt directly related to the business of farming, and more than 50% of gross receipts for the past three years are from farming.

GAMBLING WINNINGS

A taxpayer must report gambling winnings, such as lotteries and raffles, as income. In addition to cash winnings, the fair market value of bonds, cars, houses, and other non-cash prizes must be included as income.

A taxpayer may take **gambling losses** as an itemized deduction on Schedule A but <u>only</u> **to the extent of gambling winnings**. The taxpayer may <u>not</u> report a net loss from gambling.

HOBBY INCOME

Many people enjoy hobbies that are also a source of income. From painting and pottery to scrapbooking and soapmaking, these activities can be sources of both fun and finances. Taxpayers who make money from a hobby must report that income on their tax return.

If someone has a business, they operate the business to make a profit. In contrast, people engage in a hobby for sport or recreation, not to make a profit.

In determining whether you are carrying on an activity for profit, several factors are taken into account. Among the factors to consider are whether:

- You carry on the activity in a businesslike manner,
- The time and effort you put into the activity indicate you intend to make it profitable,
- You depend on the income for your livelihood,
- Your losses are due to circumstances beyond your control (or are normal in the start-up phase of your type of business),
- You change your methods of operation in an attempt to improve profitability,
- You (or your advisors) have the knowledge needed to carry on the activity as a successful business,
- You were successful in making a profit in similar activities in the past,
- The activity makes a profit in some years, and
- You can expect to make a future profit from the appreciation of the assets used in the activity.

With the exception of certain horse-related activities, the IRS presumes an activity is carried on for profit if it produced a profit in at least three of the last five tax years, including the current year.

Hobby expenses are no longer deductible as miscellaneous itemized deductions. The taxpayer must still report the income they receive on Schedule 1, Form 1040.

ILLEGAL ACTIVITIES

Income from illegal activities, such as money from dealing illegal drugs, must be included in income on Schedule 1 as "Other Income" or on Schedule C if from a self-employment activity.

JURY DUTY PAY

Compensation for jury duty is included in income on Form 1040. If the taxpayer must give the pay to an employer because the employer continues to pay a salary while serving on the jury, the taxpayer may deduct the amount turned over to the employer as an adjustment to income.

RENTAL OF PERSONAL PROPERTY

Other income includes income from the rental of personal property if the taxpayer engages in the rental for profit but is <u>not</u> in the business of renting such property.

COURT AWARDS AND DAMAGES

To determine if settlement amounts received are income, the taxpayer must consider the item that the settlement replaces. Include the following as ordinary income:

- Interest on any award

- Compensation for lost wages or lost profits in most cases
- *Punitive damages* (punishment), it does not matter if related to a physical injury or sickness
- Amounts received in settlement of pension rights (if the taxpayer did not contribute to plan)
- Damages for one of the following:
  1. Patent or copyright infringement
  2. Breach of contract
  3. Interference with business operations
- Back pay and damages for emotional distress under Title VII of the Civil Rights Act of 1964
- Attorney fees and costs where the underlying recovery is included in gross income

> Do not include in income *compensatory damages* (compensation) for personal physical injury, physical sickness, or emotional distress attributable to a physical injury or physical sickness.

PRIZES AND AWARDS

If a taxpayer wins a prize in a lucky number drawing, television or radio quiz program, beauty contest, or other event, it must be included in income. For example, if a taxpayer wins a $50 prize in a photography contest, the taxpayer must report this income. If the taxpayer refuses to accept a prize, its value is not included in income.

RENTAL INCOME AND EXPENSES

RENTAL REAL ESTATE

Several factors determine the amount of rental income to include on a taxpayer's return. The IRS allows certain expenses as a deduction against gross rental income, resulting in either a gain or loss from rental activities.

Most taxpayers report income and expenses from rental real estate on *Schedule E* and transfer the resulting net gain or allowable loss amount to Form 1040 Schedule 1.

Generally, Schedule C is used when a taxpayer provides substantial services in conjunction with the property or the rental is part of a trade or business as a real estate dealer. Examples of substantial services include regular cleaning, changing linen, or maid service. Substantial services don't include the furnishing of heat and light, cleaning of public areas, trash collection, etc.

TIP: Big differences when reporting a real estate rental on Schedule C are that losses are not subject to the passive activity limits, and income is subject to SE tax.

PERSONAL USE PROPERTY

The IRS treats rental real estate property as a *home* if used for personal purposes more than the greater of 14 days or 10% of the total days rented to others.

- If the taxpayer does not use the property as a home, report all the rental income and deduct all the rental expenses. Deductible rental expenses can be more than gross rental income.
- If the taxpayer uses the property as a home, the rental income and deductions depend on how many days the taxpayer rented the unit at a fair rental price.
  1. If rented **fewer than 15 days** during the year, do not treat that period as rental activity. Do not include any of the rent as income and do not deduct any of the rental expenses.
  2. If rented 15 days or more, include all rental income and allocate expenses between rental and personal use. If resulting in a loss, not all expenses may be deductible.
     A. Personal use is used by owners, family members, or anyone for less than fair value.

B. Any day that the taxpayer rents the unit at a fair rental price is a day of rental use even if used for personal purposes that day.

C. Any day that the unit is available but not actually rented is not a day of rental use.

RENTAL INCOME

Generally, a taxpayer must include all amounts received as rent in gross income. Rental income is any payment received for the use or occupation of property. In addition to amounts received as normal rent payments, other amounts may be rental income.

- **Advance rent** – Advance rent is any amount received before the period that it covers. Include advance rent as rental income during the year the taxpayer **receives the income**, regardless of the period covered or the method of accounting used.

  > **EXAMPLE:** You sign a 10-year lease to rent your property. In the first year, you receive $5,000 for the first year's rent and $5,000 as rent for the last year of the lease. You must include $10,000 in your income in the first year.

- **Security deposits** – Do not include a security deposit as income when the taxpayer receives the deposit if the taxpayer is to return the deposit to the tenant at the end of the lease. Include any part of the security deposit the taxpayer keeps because the tenant does not live up to the terms of the lease as income in that year. A taxpayer must treat a security deposit as income (advance rent) when received if the security deposit may be used as a final payment of rent.

- **Expenses paid by tenant** – If a taxpayer's tenant pays any of the taxpayer's expenses, the taxpayer must report the payments as rental income. These payments should be included as income. The taxpayer may deduct certain deductible rental expenses.

- **Property or services** – Include the fair market value of the property or services a tenant provides the taxpayer in place of rent as rental income when received. If the tenant provides the services at an agreed-upon or specified price, that price is generally considered the fair market value.

- **Rents from personal property** – If renting out personal property, such as equipment or vehicles, the method for reporting income and expenses depends upon whether or not the rental activity is a business conducted for profit. In general, if the primary purpose is income or profit and the taxpayer is regularly involved in the rental activity, it is a business. Report income and expenses on Schedule C. If a rental activity is not a business, report rental income as other income on Form 1040 and include any expenses as an adjustment to gross income.

RENTAL EXPENSES

- **Related expenses** – Deductions from rental income include advertising, cleaning and maintenance, utilities, taxes, interest, commissions for the collection of rent, travel, and transportation.

- **Fire and liability insurance** – If the taxpayer pays insurance premiums for more than 12 months in advance, the taxpayer cannot deduct the entire premium payment in the year it was paid.

- **Depreciation** – Depreciate rental property when it is ready and available for rent. Depreciation is a method to recover the cost of income-producing property through yearly tax deductions. The recovery period for **residential** real property is **27.5 years**. The recovery period for **non-residential** real property is **39 years**. Taxpayers may not depreciate the cost of land.

- **Repairs** – A repair keeps property in good operating condition. Repairs do not materially add to the value of the property or substantially prolong its life. Repainting the property inside or out, fixing gutters or floors, fixing leaks, plastering, and replacing broken windows are examples of repairs. If the taxpayer makes repairs as part of an extensive remodeling or restoration of the property, the whole job is considered an improvement. The taxpayer may deduct the cost of repairs to the rental property.

- **Improvements** – An improvement adds to the value of property, prolongs its useful life, or adapts it to new uses. The taxpayer does not immediately deduct the cost of improvements in the current year. Instead, costs are *capitalized* (included in the value of the asset and the taxpayer recovers the cost of improvements by taking depreciation over the useful life of the property). Examples of improvements include putting a recreation room in an unfinished basement, adding a bathroom or bedroom, building a fence, installing new plumbing, wiring, or cabinets, putting on a new roof, and paving a driveway.

TIP: A unit of property that has an economic useful life of 12 months or less, or an acquisition cost of **$200 or less**, is generally <u>not</u> required to be capitalized and is treated instead as **materials and supplies**. All costs to improve eight specified building systems must be treated as capital expenditures. Those systems are HVAC, plumbing, electrical, escalators, elevators, fire protection and alarm, security, and gas distribution.

> Under the final tangibles regulations, a taxpayer may <u>elect</u> to apply a *de minimis safe harbor* of $2,500 to amounts paid to acquire or produce tangible property to the extent such amounts are deducted for financial accounting purposes or in keeping the books and records. The de minimis safe harbor allows the taxpayer to elect to deduct, rather than capitalize, the cost of the property if the expenditure is less than $2,500. A taxpayer that files an applicable financial statement (AFS) may use the de minimis safe harbor rule to deduct up to $5,000.

ADDITIONAL CONSIDERATIONS

- **Local benefit taxes** – Generally, a taxpayer may not deduct charges for local benefits that increase the value of the property. Examples of these charges include charges for putting in streets, sidewalks, or water and sewer systems. These charges are non-depreciable capital expenditures, and the taxpayer must add them to the basis of the property.

- **Vacant rental property** – If holding property for rental purposes, ordinary and necessary expenses may be deducted (including depreciation) for managing, conserving, or maintaining the property while the property is vacant. Income loss due to a vacancy is not deductible.

- **Uncollected rent** – Cash basis taxpayers do not deduct uncollected rent because it was never considered as income. Under the accrual method, taxpayers report income when earned. If the taxpayer is unable to collect the rent, they may be able to deduct it as a bad business debt.

- **Not rented for profit** – If the taxpayer rents a property but does not rent the property to make a profit, the taxpayer may deduct rental expenses, but only up to the amount of the rental income. The taxpayer cannot deduct losses nor carry them forward to the next year if rental expenses are more than the rental income for the year.

- **Property changed to rental use** – If a property converts to rental use at any time after the beginning of the tax year, taxpayers divide yearly expenses such as taxes and insurance between rental and personal use. Only the portion of expenses relative to the rental use is deductible. The IRS does not permit deductions for depreciation or insurance during periods of personal use.

- **Renting part of property** – If the taxpayer rents part of the property, the taxpayer must divide certain expenses between the part of the property used for rental purposes and the part of the property used for personal purposes; it would be as though two separate pieces of property existed. The taxpayer need not divide expenses that belong only to the rental part of the property. The taxpayer may deduct depreciation on the part of the house used for rental purposes as well as on the furniture and equipment used for rental purposes.

LIMITS ON RENTAL LOSSES

The following rules may limit the loss deduction allowed on a rental real estate activity. One must consider these rules in the order shown below:

- **At-risk rules** – Apply these rules first if there is an investment in the taxpayer's rental real estate activity for which the taxpayer is not at risk. This applies only if the real property was placed in service after 1986. Generally, the IRS allows any loss from an activity subject to the at-risk rules only to the extent of the total amount that is at risk in the activity at the end of the tax year. A taxpayer is at risk in an activity to the extent of cash and the adjusted basis of other property contributions and certain amounts borrowed for use in the activity. Losses disallowed because of the at-risk limits are deductions from the same activity in the next tax year.

- **Passive activity limits** – Generally, the IRS considers rental real estate activities as passive activities, and a loss is not deductible unless income from another passive activity exists to offset it. The taxpayer may carry any excess *passive activity loss (PAL)* or credit forward to the next tax year.

An otherwise passive rental loss may offset ordinary income under the following two exceptions:

1. A *real estate professional* may deduct losses against ordinary income when both of the following conditions exist:

   A. More than half of work is involved in real property trades or businesses in which the taxpayer *materially participates*, and

   B. More than **750 hours** of material participation in real property trades or businesses.

2. If rental losses are not more than **$25,000**, and the taxpayer or spouse *actively participates* in the rental activity, the passive activity limits may not apply. Active participation is a less stringent standard than material participation. Active participation includes management decisions such as approving tenants, rental terms, approving expenditures, etc.

> If a taxpayer or spouse actively participated in a passive rental real estate activity, they may be able to **deduct up to $25,000** of loss from the activity from their nonpassive income. This special allowance is an exception to the general rule disallowing losses in excess of income from passive activities. If a taxpayer has modified adjusted gross income (MAGI) of $100,000 or less, the loss is deductible up to the $25,000 special allowance. If MAGI is more than $100,000, the $25,000 special allowance is limited to 50% of the difference between $150,000 and MAGI. There is no allowance if MAGI is more than **$150,000**.

Modified adjusted gross income (MAGI)

Adjusted gross income figured without considering:

- The taxable amount of Social Security or equivalent tier 1 railroad retirement benefits
- The deduction allowed for contributions to IRAs or certain other qualified retirement plans
- The exclusion from income of interest from Series EE and I U.S. savings bonds
- The exclusion of amounts received under an employer's adoption assistance program
- Any passive activity income or loss included on Form 8582
- Any rental real estate loss allowed to real estate professionals
- Any overall loss from a publicly traded partnership
- The deductions allowed for self-employment tax, student loan interest, qualified tuition and fees

EXAMPLE: Pedro and his wife manage the daily activities of his 10-unit apartment building. He collects rent and orders repairs. The loss from this rental activity is $40,000. They also own an oil partnership generating $5,000 in passive income. MAGI is $125,000. They actively participate in the rental activity and can deduct $12,500 (50% of the difference between MAGI and $150,000) against ordinary income on a jointly filed return. The remaining $27,500 is a passive loss. They can use $5,000 of that loss in the current year against other passive income and may carry forward the remaining $22,500 into the following year.

BUSINESS INCOME AND LOSS

BUSINESS INCOME

A self-employed taxpayer (other than a partner) that carries on a trade or business as a sole proprietor or an independent contractor reports business income and expenses on **Schedule C.** The net income or loss from the business is part of gross income on their personal tax return.

TRADE OR BUSINESS

An activity qualifies as a trade or business if the taxpayer's primary purpose for engaging in the activity is for income or profit and they are involved in the activity with continuity and regularity. The facts and circumstances of each case determine if an activity is a trade or business. The regularity of activities and transactions and the production of income are important elements. Taxpayers do not need to actually make a profit to be in a trade or business as long as they have a profit motive. However, taxpayers do need to make ongoing efforts to further the interests of their business. If the taxpayer owns an interest in a pass-through entity, the trade or business determination is made at that entity's level.

Trade or business income or (loss) can include income reported as:

- Business income or (loss), Schedule C
- Capital gain or (loss), Schedule D
- Other gains or (losses), Form 4797
- Rental real estate, royalties, partnerships, S corporations, trusts, etc., Schedule E
- Farm income or (loss), Schedule F
- Unemployment compensation
- Any other income, gain, or losses from a trade or business

Section 162(a) allows a deduction for all the **ordinary and necessary expenses** paid or incurred during the taxable year in carrying on any trade or business. Section 262, however, provides that no deduction is allowed for personal, living, or family expenses.

There is a small problem here—section 162 does _not_ provide a definition of a trade or business. Welcome to tax!

Because there is no statutory or regulatory definition of a section 162 trade or business, courts have established two definitional requirements to determine the existence of a trade or business. One, in relation to **profit motive**, is said to require the taxpayer to enter into and carry on the activity with a good faith intention to make a profit or with the belief that a profit can be made from the activity. The second is in relation to the scope of the activities and is said to require **considerable, regular, and continuous activity**.

TIP: As usual, a determination of whether or not an activity is a trade or business will depend on the facts and circumstances. A hobby will not qualify, however, a gambling activity could qualify. See Commissioner v. Groetzinger, 480 U.S. 23 (1987).

PARTNERSHIP AND S CORPORATION INCOME

Generally, certain flow-through entities such as partnerships or S corporations do not pay tax on income. Instead, the entity files an informational return with the IRS and distributes a Schedule K-1 to each partner or shareholder. The income, gains, losses, deductions, and credits pass through to the owners based on their respective shares. A taxpayer with income or loss from a flow-through entity attaches *Schedule E* to the tax return.

BUSINESS LOSS LIMITATIONS

A taxpayer that has a loss from a trade or business can claim a deduction against ordinary income, within limits, on their individual income tax return.

There are four potential limitations on losses for individual taxpayers. These limitations, in the order in which they apply, are the *basis rules*, the *at-risk limitations*, the *passive activity limitations*, and the *excess business loss limitations*.

A taxpayer may <u>not</u> take a deduction against ordinary income for a loss, if the loss is in *excess of basis*, if the amount is not *at-risk*, or if the loss is the result of a *passive activity*. If a loss is allowed after the basis rules, the at-risk and passive activity loss limitations, the deduction for the loss is then subject to the *excess business loss* limitation (**suspended** for 2018, 2019, and 2020 by the *CARES Act*).

CARES ACT UPDATE: The TCJA introduced the *excess business loss* limitation by creating a provision, section 461(l), for taxable years beginning after 2017 and before 2026. However, the CARES Act **retroactively suspends** the provision by amending section 461(l) to restrict the limitation on excess business losses of noncorporate taxpayers to tax years beginning <u>after</u> 2020 and <u>before</u> 2026. The CARES Act **repealed** the excess business loss limitation for tax years 2018, 2019, and 2020. A taxpayer who filed a return for tax years 2018, 2019, or 2020 subject to the limitation can file an amended return to claim a refund.

BASIS RULES

Generally, a taxpayer may not claim a loss greater than the adjusted basis of his S corporation or partnership interest. The taxpayer may carry forward disallowed losses and deductions due to the basis limit **indefinitely** and deduct them subject to the basis limit for that year.

AT-RISK LIMITS

Generally, any loss from an activity subject to the at-risk rules is allowed <u>only</u> to the extent of the total amount at risk in the activity at the end of the tax year. Losses disallowed because of the at-risk limits are deductions from the **same activity** in the next tax year. A taxpayer is at-risk in any activity for:

- The money and adjusted basis of property he contributes to the activity, and
- Amounts he borrows for use in the activity if:
  1. He is personally liable for repayment, or
  2. He pledges property (other than property used in the activity) as security for the loan.

EXAMPLE: Jim contributes $50,000 to a partnership that limits his liability. He also personally guarantees a recourse loan of $25,000 made to the partnership to purchase equipment. He is "at risk" for $75,000.

PASSIVE ACTIVITIES

> A taxpayer with a loss from a passive activity can offset the loss with income from other passive activities. Generally, a taxpayer is **unable to deduct a loss from a passive activity.** Carry forward any excess *passive activity loss (PAL)* or credit to the next tax year and use to offset only passive income.

The passive activity rules apply to:

- Individuals
- Estates
- Trusts (other than grantor trusts)
- Personal service corporations
- Closely held corporations

TIP: Even though the rules don't apply to grantor trusts, partnerships, and S corporations directly, they do apply to the owners of these entities.

> For a **closely held corporation**, the passive activity loss is the excess of passive activity deductions over the sum of passive activity gross income <u>and</u> **net active income.**

There are two kinds of passive activities:

- Business activities in which the taxpayer does <u>not</u> *materially* participate during the year
- *Rental activities* (even with material participation, <u>unless</u> the taxpayer is a real estate professional)

The IRS will consider participation to be material if the taxpayer can satisfy any of the following tests:

- The taxpayer participated in the activity for **more than 500** hours during the tax year.
- The taxpayer's participation was substantially **all of the participation** in the activity of all individuals for the tax year, including the participation of individuals who did not own any interest in the activity.
- The taxpayer participated in the activity for **more than 100** hours during the tax year, and at least as much as <u>any</u> other individual for the year.

NET OPERATING LOSS (NOL)

A taxpayer with annual business deductions that exceed business income may have a *net operating loss (NOL)*.

Some typical losses that may produce an NOL include losses incurred from the following:

- A trade or business
- A casualty or theft
- Moving expenses (for military)
- Rental property

A loss from operating a business is the most common reason for an NOL. Individuals may use a net operating loss to offset taxable income in other periods. A net operating loss may be **carried forward indefinitely** and used as a deduction in the future period it is carried to. Individuals, Estates, and Trusts follow similar rules. Partnerships and S corporations generally <u>cannot</u> use an NOL, but partners or shareholders can use their separate shares of pass-through loss to figure their individual NOLs.

TCJA: The TCJA introduced new rules for NOLs arising in taxable years beginning after December 31, 2017. The general 2-year NOL carryback rule does not apply and the taxpayer may carry the loss forward indefinitely. Exceptions apply to certain farming losses (2-year carryback) and NOLs of property and casualty insurance companies. There is also a provision that limits the NOL deduction to **80% of taxable income** (determined without regard to the deduction). These rules are **temporarily suspended** by the *CARES Act*.

TIP: NOLs arising in taxable years beginning before 2018 remain subject to **prior law**. Accordingly, such NOLs are not subject to the 80-percent limitation and remain subject to the prior law carryback rules (generally 2-year carryback) and the 20-year carryover limitation.

CARES ACT UPDATE: As authorized by the CARES Act, the IRS issued Revenue Procedure 2020-24 providing guidance on procedures for **carrying back NOLs arising in taxable years 2018, 2019, or 2020** to each of the **five preceding tax years.** As a result of this amendment, taxpayers take into account such NOLs in the earliest taxable year in the carryback period, carrying forward unused amounts to each succeeding taxable year. Also, the NOL deduction is not limited to 80% of taxable income for losses arising in 2018, 2019, or 2020.

If a taxpayer chooses to carry back an NOL, they must first carry the entire NOL back 5 years. Carry back the entire NOL to the 5th tax year before the loss year. Any NOL not used in the 5th preceding year is then carried to the 4th preceding year, and so on. Any NOL not applied in the 5 preceding years can be carried forward to tax years following the year of loss. Any NOL not carried back may be carried forward indefinitely and used as a deduction in the future period it is carried to.

A taxpayer within the scope of this revenue procedure may **elect to waive** the carryback period in the case of a net operating loss arising in a taxable year beginning after December 31, 2017, and before January 1, 2021. Such an election must be made no later than the due date, including extensions, for filing the taxpayer's income tax return for the first taxable year ending after March 27, 2020.

EXAMPLE 1: On a previously filed 2019 tax return, Nick, a single taxpayer has $400,000 dividend income and $800,000 net business losses. Under the **TCJA**, the 2019 business loss was limited to $255,000 and the taxpayer reported 2019 taxable income of $145,000 ($400,000 dividend – $255,000 business loss allowed). The taxpayer had an excess business loss of $545,000 ($800,000 net business losses – $255,000 business loss allowed), which was carried forward as an NOL to the next year (2019 NOL of $545,000 carried forward to 2020). Under the TCJA, the taxpayer may deduct the carried forward NOL in the subsequent tax year, subject to the 80% of taxable income limitation.

Pursuant to the **CARES Act**, the originally filed 2019 tax return can be amended. Since in 2019, business losses are no longer subject to the excess business loss limitation, a taxpayer may utilize the entire loss to reduce taxable income. This would reduce the taxpayer's 2019 taxable income from $145,000 to $0 as $400,000 of the business loss is used to offset the $400,000 dividend income. The remaining $400,000 business loss ($800,000 net business losses – $400,000 business loss utilized) becomes part of the taxpayer's NOL. After amending the 2019 tax return, Nick now has a 2019 NOL of $400,000, which also receives favorable treatment under the CARES Act.

EXAMPLE 2: Using the facts from the previous example, after amending the 2019 tax return pursuant to the CARES Act, Nick had a 2019 NOL of $400,000. This NOL may be carried back five years by amending prior tax returns or filing **Form 1045 Application for Tentative Refund** (quick tax refund from the carryback of an NOL). Below is an illustration of the application of an NOL carried back five years using Nick's 2019 NOL of $400,000:

Tax Year	Taxable Income before Carryback	NOL Carryback	Taxable Income after Carryback	Carryforward NOL
2014	$100,000	($100,000)	$0	$300,000
2015	$50,000	($50,000)	$0	$250,000
2016	$125,000	($125,000)	$0	$125,000
2017	$100,000	($100,000)	$0	$25,000
2018	$200,000	($25,000)	$175,000	$0
	$575,000	($400,000)	$175,000	

A 2019 NOL carried back five years is carried back first to 2014, then to 2015, 2016, 2017, and lastly to 2018. In this example, Nick was able to carry back an NOL of $400,000 to reduce $575,000 of taxable income before NOL carryback to $175,000 of taxable income after NOL carryback. Nick's entire 2019 net business losses of $800,000 ($400,000 utilized on 2019 amended tax return and $400,000 carried back and utilized in the prior 5 tax years) are applied to provide a substantial tax benefit.

TIP: The CARES Act provisions could be of substantial benefit for taxpayers with losses in 2018, 2019, or 2020. Taxpayers with business losses in those tax years are no longer subject to the excess business loss limitation and may utilize the entire loss to reduce taxable income by amending previously filed tax returns to claim previously disallowed losses that were subject to the limitation. Also, taxpayers with an NOL in those tax years have the ability to carry the NOL back five years and the NOL deduction is not limited to 80% of taxable income for NOLs arising in those years.

HOW TO FIGURE NOL

There are rules that limit which deductions from income are allowed for NOL purposes. Calculate the NOL only on the income and expenses directly related to a trade or business. In general, the following items are not allowed when figuring an NOL:

- Capital losses in excess of capital gains of taxpayers other than corporations
- The Section 1202 exclusion of the gain from the sale of qualified small business stock
- Non-business deductions in excess of non-business income
- Net operating loss deduction

A loss resulting from non-business deductions that are not connected to a trade or business or employment cannot contribute to the NOL. Examples of **non-business deductions** include:

- Alimony paid
- Deductions for contributions to an IRA or a self-employed retirement plan
- Health savings account deduction for a taxpayer, spouse, or dependents
- Most itemized deductions (except for casualty and theft losses and state income tax on business profit)

HOW TO REPORT NOL

For an individual taxpayer, carry forward NOL to a tax year after the NOL year, list the NOL deduction as a negative figure on the "Other income" line of Schedule 1 (Form 1040).

The taxpayer must attach a statement that shows all the important facts about the NOL. The statement should include a computation showing the calculation for the NOL deduction.

LESSON 3

Gains and Losses

BASIS OF PROPERTY

COST BASIS

Basis is the amount of a taxpayer's investment in a property for tax purposes. A gain or loss is determined by subtracting the adjusted basis from the proceeds of the sale, exchange, or other disposition of property. A taxpayer uses basis to figure deductions for depreciation, amortization, depletion, and casualty losses. If a taxpayer uses property for business (or investment) purposes and for personal purposes, the taxpayer must properly allocate basis based on the property use. Only the basis allocated to business or investment use of the property is depreciable. The basis of property is usually its cost. The cost is the amount paid in cash, debt obligations, other property, or services. A taxpayer's cost basis also includes (but is not limited to) amounts paid for:

• Commissions

• Sales tax, freight, installation, and testing

• Legal and accounting fees (when they must be capitalized)

• Excise taxes, revenue stamps, recording fees, and real estate taxes (if assuming seller's liability)

The original basis in the property is adjusted (increased or decreased) by certain events:

• Improvements to a property will increase basis

• Deductions for depreciation or casualty losses or claiming certain credits will reduce basis

REAL PROPERTY

Real property, also called real estate, is land and generally anything built on, growing on, or attached to the land. Certain fees and other expenses are part of the cost basis of the property. If a taxpayer buys buildings and the land on which the buildings stand for a lump sum, the taxpayer should allocate cost basis among the land and the buildings. The taxpayer should allocate cost basis according to the respective fair market value (FMV) of the land and buildings at the time of purchase. The basis of each asset is calculated by multiplying the lump sum by a fraction. The numerator is the FMV of that asset, and the denominator is the FMV of the whole property at the time of purchase.

TIP: Since land is not depreciable, a taxpayer must allocate a portion of the purchase price to land prior to calculating the depreciation deduction. Improvements that increase the value of a structure apply only to the structure and do not increase the basis of the land.

If a taxpayer buys property and assumes an existing mortgage on the property, the basis includes the amount paid for the property plus the amount to be paid on the mortgage. The basis is adjusted by certain settlement costs as described below:

> A taxpayer's basis includes the *settlement fees* and *closing costs* paid for buying the property. A fee for buying property is a cost that the taxpayer must pay even if they buy the property with cash. Do <u>not</u> include fees and costs for getting a loan on the property in the basis.

• Taxpayers <u>may</u> add the following settlement fees or closing costs to basis:

1. Abstract fees (abstract of title fees)

2. Charges for installing utility services

3. Legal fees (fees for the title search and preparation of the sales contract and deed)

4. Recording fees

5. Survey fees

6. Transfer taxes

7. Owner's title insurance

8. Any amounts the buyer agrees to pay for the seller, such as back taxes or interest, recording or mortgage fees, cost of improvements or repairs, and sales commissions

- Taxpayers may <u>not</u> add the following settlement fees and closing costs to basis:

1. Casualty insurance premiums

2. Rent for occupancy of the property before closing

3. Charges for utilities or other services related to the property before closing

4. Charges connected with getting a loan, such as points (discount points, loan origination fees), mortgage insurance premiums, loan assumption fees, cost of a credit report, and fees for an appraisal required by a lender

5. Fees for refinancing a mortgage. If a taxpayer pays points to get a loan (including a mortgage, second mortgage, a line of credit, or a home equity loan), the points may not be added to the basis of the related property. Generally, the taxpayer will deduct points over the term of the loan. Special rules may apply to points taxpayers and sellers pay when they receive mortgages to buy their primary homes. If certain requirements are met, a taxpayer may deduct the points in full for the year in which they are paid. The basis of a home must be reduced by any seller-paid points.

6. Amounts placed in escrow for the future payment of taxes and insurance

The term *"points"* is used to describe certain charges paid to obtain a home mortgage. Points are prepaid interest and may be deductible as home mortgage interest. Special rules apply to points paid on a mortgage to buy a main home. If certain requirements are met, a taxpayer may deduct the points in full for the year in which they are paid. Points paid for refinancing generally can only be deducted over the life of the new mortgage. Points do not increase basis.

Points charged for specific services, such as preparation costs for a mortgage note, appraisal fees or notary fees are not interest and cannot be deducted. Points paid by the seller of a home cannot be deducted as interest on the seller's return, but they are a selling expense which will reduce the amount of gain realized. Points paid by the seller may be deducted by the buyer provided the buyer subtracts the amount from the basis, or cost, of the residence. Points you pay on loans secured by your second home can be deducted only over the life of the loan.

ADJUSTED BASIS

Before figuring gain or loss on a sale, exchange, or other disposition of property or figuring allowable depreciation, depletion, or amortization, a taxpayer must usually make certain adjustments (increases and decreases) to the cost of the property. The result is the adjusted basis.

- **Increase** the basis of any property by all items properly added to a capital account. These include, but are not limited to, the following items:

1. **Capital improvements** – The costs of improvements having a useful life of more than one year, which increase the value of the property, lengthen its life or adapt it to a different use. Improvements include the following:

   A. Putting a recreation room in an unfinished basement

   B. Adding another bathroom or bedroom

   C. Building a fence

   D. Installing new plumbing or wiring

    E. Installing a new roof

    F. Paving the driveway

  2. **Assessments for local improvements** – Add property assessments for improvements that increase the value of the property assessed to the basis. Do not deduct these assessments as taxes. Examples include assessments for roads, sidewalks, water connections, and extending utility service to the property.

- **Decrease** the basis of any property by all items that represent a return of capital for the period during which the taxpayer held the property. Examples of items that decrease basis include (but are not limited to) the following items:

  1. **Non-taxable corporate distributions** – Also known as non-dividend distributions. This amount reflects a return of capital and reduces basis.

  2. **Casualty and theft losses** – Decrease the basis of property by any insurance proceeds or other reimbursement and by any deductible loss not covered by insurance. Increase the basis in the property by the amount spent on repairs that restore the property to its pre-casualty condition.

  3. **Depreciation and Section 179 deduction** – The basis of a taxpayer's qualifying business property will be decreased by any Section 179 deductions taken and the depreciation deducted, or could have deducted (including any special depreciation allowance), on the taxpayer's returns under the method of depreciation selected.

  4. **Easements** – Compensation for granting an easement is generally treated the same as proceeds from the sale of an interest in real property. Reduce basis by the amount received.

  5. **Certain Credits** – Basis may be reduced by certain credits received due to the purchase of the property. Examples include the alternative motor vehicle credit and the residential energy efficient property credit.

PROPERTY RECEIVED FOR SERVICES

If a taxpayer receives property for services rendered, its FMV must be included in income. The amount included in income becomes the basis. If the taxpayer performed the services for a price agreed on beforehand, the IRS will accept that price as the FMV of the property if there is no evidence to the contrary. If the property is subject to certain restrictions, the basis in the property is its FMV when it vests substantially. However, this rule does not apply if the taxpayer makes an election to include in income the FMV of the property at the time the transfer of property occurs, less any amount the taxpayer paid for it. Property is substantially vested when it is transferable or when it is not subject to a substantial risk of forfeiture (the taxpayer does not have a good chance of losing it).

DEPRECIATION

There are two basic types of property:

1. **Tangible property** – Is physical in nature and includes land, structures, equipment, natural resources, etc. Tangible property is further divided into the following categories:

  ◦ *Real property* – Real estate including land, houses, buildings, etc.

  ◦ *Personal property* – Any tangible property other than real property.

2. **Intangible property** – Does not have a physical presence and includes computer software, patents, goodwill, stocks, and bonds.

Expenditures that do not have a useful life beyond one year are *expenses.* A taxpayer may generally deduct expenses in the year they incur them. Property acquired with a useful life greater than one year or an *improvement* that increases the value of the property, lengthens the life of the property, or adapts it to a different use is a *capital expenditure*. A capital expenditure is *capitalized* (added to capital), and the cost is systematically *recovered* (written off) each year, in various ways, depending on the type of property. The methods for recovering the cost of an asset over its useful life include the following:

- **Depreciation** – For tangible income producing property, other than natural resources
- **Depletion** – For assets that diminish over time such as oil, gas, and other natural resources
- **Amortization** – For intangible assets, such as patents and goodwill

The taxpayer may recover the cost of tangible income producing property through yearly tax deductions by depreciating the property, that is, by deducting some of the cost each year on the tax return. Three basic factors determine how much depreciation the taxpayer may deduct:

- The basis in the property
- The recovery period for the property
- The depreciation method used

A taxpayer cannot simply deduct mortgages, principal payments, or the cost of furniture, fixtures, or equipment as an expense. The taxpayer may deduct depreciation only on the part of the property used for a business or income-producing activity. A taxpayer cannot depreciate personal-use property. Depreciation reduces the basis for figuring gain or loss on a later sale or exchange.

WHAT PROPERTY CAN BE DEPRECIATED

A taxpayer may depreciate property if it meets all the following requirements:

- The taxpayer owns the property
- The taxpayer uses the property in business or income-producing activity (rental property)
- The property has a determinable useful life
- The taxpayer expects the property to last more than one year

TIP: A taxpayer **cannot depreciate personal-use property**. Deduct depreciation only on the part of the property used for a business or income-producing activity. A farmer can elect to claim 75% business use without records if using the vehicle in farming business most of the normal business day.

Depreciation begins when a taxpayer places the property in service for the production of income and ends when either the taxpayer fully recovers the cost, or the property is retired from service, whichever happens first. Property is placed in service in a rental activity when it is ready and available for a specific use in that activity. Even if unused, it is in service when it is ready and available for its specific use.

REPAIRS AND IMPROVEMENTS

Modifications to property have traditionally been categorized as either *improvements* that must be capitalized or *repairs* that are currently deductible and do not affect basis. Improvement means an addition to or partial replacement of property that is a *betterment* to the property, restores the property, or adapts it to a new or different use.

Generally, the taxpayer may deduct the cost of repairing business property in the same way as any other business expense. However, a taxpayer must capitalize a repair or replacement that increases the value of the property, makes it more useful, or lengthens its life.

A taxpayer treats each improvement as <u>separate</u> depreciable property. Annual deductions for depreciation are determined by class life of the property. MACRS recovery periods apply to property used in rental activities. Using the General Depreciation System (GDS), appliances, carpeting, and furniture used in a rental real estate activity can be depreciated over a 5-year recovery period. Land improvements, such as roads, shrubbery, and fences can be depreciated over a 15-year recovery period.

Additions and improvements, such as a new roof use the same recovery period as that of the property to which the addition or improvement is made, determined as if the property were placed in service at the same time as the addition or improvement (generally, 27.5 years residential real property or 39 years for nonresidential real property).

Common Examples of Improvements to Real Property

Additions	Miscellaneous	Plumbing
Bedroom	Storm windows, doors	Septic system
Bathroom	New roof	Water heater
Deck	Central vacuum	Soft water system
Garage	Wiring upgrades	Filtration system
Porch	Satellite dish	
Patio	Security system	**Interior Improvements**
		Built-in appliances
Lawn & Grounds	**Heating & Air Conditioning**	Kitchen modernization
Landscaping	Heating system	Flooring
Driveway	Central air conditioning	Wall-to-wall carpeting
Walkway	Furnace	
Fence	Duct work	**Insulation**
Retaining wall	Central humidifier	Attic
Sprinkler system	Filtration system	Walls, floor
Swimming pool		Pipes, duct work

Generally, the taxpayer may deduct the cost of repairing business property in the same way as any other business expense. This generally includes the costs of routine repairs and maintenance to the property that result from use of the property and that keep the property in an ordinary efficient operating condition.

TIP: A small taxpayer is <u>not</u> required to capitalize expenditures (even if they would otherwise meet the definition of improvements) if the total amount expended during the year does <u>not</u> exceed the <u>lesser</u> of **$10,000** <u>or</u> **2% of the unadjusted basis** of the building.

A small taxpayer is defined as <u>average</u> annual gross receipts of no more than **$10 million** during the preceding three years. Specifically, **with respect to buildings** that have an unadjusted basis (i.e., original cost) of **$1 million or less**, a taxpayer with no more than $10 million in annual gross receipts may be able to elect to treat expenditures as deductible repairs, regardless of their nature.

TIP: A taxpayer can elect to treat up to $2,500 per invoice of certain expenditures as an expense under the *de minimis safe harbor election*.

TIP: A unit of property with an acquisition cost of **$200 or less** is generally not required to be capitalized and is treated instead as materials and supplies. All costs to improve eight specified building systems must be treated as capital expenditures. Those systems are HVAC, plumbing, electrical, escalators, elevators, fire protection and alarm, security, and gas distribution.

BARGAIN PURCHASES

A bargain purchase is a purchase of an item for less than its FMV. If, as compensation for services, a taxpayer buys goods or other property at less than FMV, the difference between the purchase price and the property's FMV must be included in income. The basis in the property is its FMV (the purchase price plus the amount included in income).

INVOLUNTARY CONVERSIONS

A taxpayer may receive replacement property after an *involuntary conversion*, such as a casualty, theft, or condemnation. The basis of the replacement property is based on the converted property.

- **Similar or related property** – If a taxpayer receives replacement property similar or related in service or use to the converted property, the replacement property's basis is the same as the converted property's basis on the date of the conversion, with the following adjustments:

  1. The basis is decreased by the following:

     A. Any loss recognized on the involuntary conversion

     B. Any money received that the taxpayer does not spend on similar property

  2. The basis is increased by the following:

     A. Any gain recognized on the involuntary conversion

     B. Any cost of acquiring the replacement property

- **Money or property not similar or related** – If a taxpayer receives money or property not similar or related in service or use to the converted property, and they buy replacement property similar or related in service or use to the converted property, the basis of the replacement property will be its cost decreased by the gain not recognized on the conversion.

> **EXAMPLE:** Bill's dog knocks over a glass of milk destroying his business laptop. His basis in the laptop is $2,000. He receives a $2,500 insurance reimbursement and purchases another laptop for $2,200. Bill realizes a gain of $500 ($2,500 insurance reimbursement – $2,000 basis). Bill will recognize the $300 ($2,500 insurance reimbursement – $2,200 new laptop) that he did not spend on the replacement property as a capital gain. His gain not recognized or deferred gain is $200 ($500 realized gain – $300 recognized gain). His adjusted basis in the new laptop is $2,000 ($2,200 cost – $200 gain not recognized).

The TCJA temporarily modifies the itemized deduction for **personal casualty and theft losses**. Under the provision, an individual may claim an itemized deduction for a personal casualty loss only if such loss was attributable to a disaster **declared by the President**. An exception applies to the extent a loss of an individual does not exceed the individual's personal casualty gains.

PROPERTY RECEIVED AS A GIFT

To establish the basis of property received as a gift, a taxpayer must know the adjusted basis to the *donor* (source of gift), its fair market value (FMV) at the time the donor gifted the property, and any gift tax paid on it. The annual exclusion is **$15,000** in 2020 and 2021. The relationship between the FMV and the donor's basis determines the applicable rule. If a taxpayer receives a gift of property and the donor's adjusted basis determines the basis, the IRS considers the taxpayer's holding period to have started on the same day the donor's holding period started. If the fair market value of the property determines the basis, the holding period starts on the day after the date of the gift.

FMV LESS THAN DONOR'S ADJUSTED BASIS

Basis depends on whether a gain or a loss occurs when the property is disposed of. The following *dual basis rules* prevent taxpayers from shifting unrealized losses to other taxpayers:

- The basis for figuring gain is the same as the donor's adjusted basis.
- The basis for figuring loss is its FMV when the taxpayer received the gift.

TIP: If calculating a loss, use the basis that works best for the IRS (i.e., the smallest loss). If you use the donor's adjusted basis for figuring a gain and get a loss, and then use the FMV for figuring a loss and get a gain, you have neither a gain nor loss on the sale.

> **EXAMPLE:** You received an acre of land as a gift. At the time of the gift, the land had an FMV of $8,000. The donor's adjusted basis was $10,000. After you received the land, no events occurred to increase or decrease your basis. If you sell the land for $12,000, you'll have a $2,000 gain because you must use the donor's adjusted basis ($10,000) at the time of the gift as your basis to figure gain. If you sell the land for $7,000, you'll have a $1,000 loss because you must use the FMV ($8,000) at the time of the gift as your basis to figure a loss.
>
> If the sales price is between $8,000 and $10,000, you have neither gain nor loss. For instance, if the sales price was $9,000 and you tried to figure a gain using the donor's adjusted basis ($10,000), you would get a $1,000 loss. If you then tried to figure a loss using the FMV ($8,000), you would get a $1,000 gain.

FMV EQUAL TO OR GREATER THAN DONOR'S ADJUSTED BASIS

Basis is the **same as the donor's adjusted basis** at the time the taxpayer received the gift.

If the donor paid gift tax on the transfer, basis increases by the part of the gift tax that is due to the net increase in the value of the gift. The net increase in the value of the gift is the FMV of the gift minus the donor's adjusted basis. Figure the increase by multiplying the gift tax paid by a fraction.

Basis increase:

$$\text{Gift tax paid} \times \frac{FMV \text{ at time of gift} - Donor's \text{ basis}}{Amount \text{ of gift (after annual exclusion)}}$$

> **EXAMPLE:** In 2020, you received a gift of property from your mother that had an FMV of $50,000. Her adjusted basis was $20,000. She paid a gift tax of $7,100.
>
> | | |
> |---|---:|
> | Fair market value | $50,000 |
> | Minus: Adjusted basis | – 20,000 |
> | Net increase in value | $30,000 |

The amount of the gift for gift tax purposes was $35,000 ($50,000 – $15,000 annual exclusion). Your basis, $26,106, is figured as follows:

Gift tax paid	$7,100
Multiplied by ($30,000 ÷ $35,000)	× 0.86
Gift tax due to net increase in value	$6,106
Adjusted basis of property to your mother	+ 20,000
Your basis in the property	**$26,106**

PROPERTY TRANSFERRED FROM A SPOUSE

The basis and holding period of property transferred to a taxpayer (or in trust for the taxpayer's benefit) by the taxpayer's spouse are the same as the spouse's adjusted basis and holding period. The same rule applies to a transfer by a taxpayer's former spouse that is incident to divorce. The taxpayer does not recognize any gain or loss on property transferred to a spouse or former spouse incident to divorce. This is true even if receiving cash or other consideration.

INHERITED PROPERTY

With the exception of 2010 transfers electing modified carryover basis, a gain on inherited property is always long-term. The basis of an inherited capital asset is generally the FMV of the property on the date of death or an alternate valuation date if elected by the personal representative. The executor can make this election only if it **reduces both the gross estate and estate tax due**. The alternate valuation date is **6 months** from the date of death (or the disposition date if earlier). A *step-up* in basis occurs when the FMV is greater than the *decedent's* (person who died) basis.

EXCEPTION: The step-up rule does not apply to appreciated property you receive from a decedent if you or your spouse originally gave the property to the decedent **within 1 year** before the decedent's death. Your basis in this property is the same as the decedent's adjusted basis in the property immediately before his or her death, rather than its FMV.

The form of ownership can affect the amount of the step-up:

- **Qualified Joint Interest** – A qualified joint interest is any interest in property held by a married couple as *tenants by the entirety* or *tenants with rights of survivorship*. One-half of the value of the property receives a step-up in basis to FMV.

   EXAMPLE: Lou and his wife Julia own 5,000 shares of Cocomart stock in a joint account, with rights of survivorship. Their basis in the stock is $75,000. At the time of Julia's death in November of 2020, the stock had a fair market value of $200,000. Lou's new basis in the Cocomart stock is $137,500, which represents ½ of the original basis plus a step-up of ½ of the fair market value on date of death.

- **Joint tenancy with rights of survivorship (JTWROS)** – Joint tenants with rights of survivorship share an equal interest in the property. As such, they participate equally in income and deductions. If one owner dies, only the portion included in the decedent's estate receives a step-up in basis. The amount is dependent upon the percentage of the total consideration for the property provided by the decedent and whether or not it was a gift. Where the capital contribution was 75%, and the decedent did not gift any portion of the property, 75% of the property receives a step-up in basis.

> **EXAMPLE:** John and Jim owned, as joint tenants with right of survivorship, business property they purchased for $30,000. John furnished two-thirds of the purchase price and Jim furnished one-third. Depreciation deductions allowed before John's death were $12,000. Under local law, each had a half interest in the income from the property. At the date of John's death, the property had an FMV of $60,000, two-thirds of which is includible in John's estate. Jim figures his basis in the property at the date of John's death as follows:
>
> | | | |
> |---|---:|---:|
> | Interest Jim bought with his own funds—$1/3$ of $30,000 cost | $10,000 | |
> | Interest Jim received on John's death—$2/3$ of $60,000 FMV | 40,000 | $50,000 |
> | Minus: ½ of $12,000 depreciation before John's death | | 6,000 |
> | **Jim's basis at the date of John's death** | | **$44,000** |
>
> If Jim hadn't contributed any part of the purchase price, his basis at the date of John's death would be $54,000. This is figured by subtracting from the $60,000 FMV, the $6,000 depreciation allocated to Jim's half interest before the date of death.
>
> If under local law Jim had no interest in the income from the property and he contributed no part of the purchase price, his basis at John's death would be $60,000, the FMV of the property.

- **Community Property** – In community property states (Arizona, California, Idaho, Louisiana, Nevada, New Mexico, Texas, Washington, and Wisconsin), each spouse usually owns half of the community property. When either spouse dies, the total value of all community property, even the part belonging to the surviving spouse, can receive a step-up in basis, provided the decedent's share is part of their gross estate.

PROPERTY CHANGED FROM PERSONAL TO BUSINESS OR RENTAL USE

If a taxpayer holds property for personal use and then changes it to business use or uses it to produce rent, the taxpayer may begin to depreciate the property at the time of the change. To do so, calculate the property's basis for depreciation. An example of changing property held for personal use to business or rental use would be renting a former personal residence. The basis for depreciation is the lesser of the following:

- The FMV of the property on the date of the change
- The adjusted basis on the date of the change

> **EXAMPLE:** Several years ago, you paid $160,000 to have your home built on a lot that cost $25,000. You paid $20,000 for permanent improvements to the house and claimed a $2,000 casualty loss deduction for damage to the house before changing the property to rental use last year. Because land isn't depreciable, you include only the cost of the house when figuring the basis for depreciation.
>
> Your adjusted basis in the house when you changed its use was $178,000 ($160,000 + $20,000 − $2,000). On the same date, your property had an FMV of $180,000, of which $15,000 was for the land and $165,000 was for the house. The basis for figuring depreciation on the house is its FMV on the date of change ($165,000) because it's less than your adjusted basis ($178,000).

If the taxpayer sells the property at a profit, the original basis (with adjustments) is used.

> **EXAMPLE:** Assume the same facts as in the previous example except that you sell the property at a gain after being allowed depreciation deductions of $37,500. Your adjusted basis for figuring gain is $165,500 ($178,000 + $25,000 (land) − $37,500).

If the taxpayer sells the property at a loss, the cost for purposes of determining basis is the FMV on the date of conversion (with adjustments). This rule prevents a taxpayer from shifting nondeductible losses on personal property to deductible losses on business property.

> **EXAMPLE:** Assume the same facts as in the previous example, except that you sell the property at a loss after being allowed depreciation deductions of $37,500. In this case, you would start with the FMV on the date of the change to rental use ($180,000) because it's less than the adjusted basis of $203,000 ($178,000 + $25,000) on that date. Reduce that amount ($180,000) by the depreciation deductions to arrive at a basis for loss of $142,500 ($180,000 − $37,500).

> **EXCEPTION:** If you hold the gift as business property, your basis for figuring any depreciation, depletion, or amortization deduction is the same as the donor's adjusted basis plus or minus any required adjustments to basis while you hold the property.

SECURITIES

The rules explained below apply to most investors. Dealers in securities and day-traders may utilize different methods to account for their transactions.

STOCKS OR BONDS

The basis of purchased stocks or bonds is generally the purchase price and any costs of purchase, such as commissions and recording or transfer fees.

- **Nontaxable stock dividends or stock splits** – In this situation, a shareholder's percentage of ownership does not change. Allocate the total adjusted basis of all shares *pro-rata* to each share. Reduce the basis of existing shares by the amount of basis allocated to the new shares. This rule applies only when the additional stock received is identical to the stock held. For example, if a corporation declares a 2 for 1 split, each shareholder receives 2 shares for each share held. A shareholder with 100 shares and a basis of $10 per share has a total of 200 shares with a basis of $5 per share after the split. The total basis is unchanged at $1,000.
- **Return of capital** – Also known as non-dividend distributions. This amount reflects a return of capital and reduces basis.
- **Subsequent Transactions** – If transactions occur at various times in varying quantities and the taxpayer cannot adequately identify the shares sold, the basis used is the basis of the securities acquired first. This is the *first in, first out (FIFO)* method. If adequate identification is possible, the taxpayer may elect to report the specific shares sold, regardless of their order of purchase.

MUTUAL FUNDS

The rules for other securities also apply to mutual funds with one addition.

- **Subsequent Transactions** – In addition to FIFO or specific identification, a mutual fund may use the *average cost method* to calculate basis. Average cost reflects the average basis of all shares. Accounting for re-invested dividends or capital gains is easier with this method.

OPTIONS

Gain or loss that results from the expiration of an option to buy or sell property or a ***closing transaction*** (sale or trade to close position) is reported as a capital gain or loss in the year these events occur. Upon expiration, if the option to buy or sell is unexercised, the IRS considers the taxpayer to have sold or traded the option on the date that it expired. The tax treatment of transactions is different if the taxpayer ***exercises*** the options. The option is not reported separately; instead, the option's cost (or proceeds) modifies the basis (or amount realized) on the underlying stock. A ***put option*** is the right to sell to the ***writer (seller)***, at any time before a specified future date, a stated number of shares at a specified price. Conversely, a ***call option*** is the right to buy from the writer of the option, at any time before a specified future date, a stated number of shares of stock at a specified price. This adjustment depends on several factors:

- **Put buyer** – Reduces the amount realized on the sale of stock by the cost of the put
- **Call buyer** – Adds the cost of call to the basis of stock purchased
- **Put writer** – Reduces the basis of the stock purchased by the amount received for the put
- **Call writer** – Increases the amount realized on sale of stock by the amount received for call

WASH SALES

A taxpayer may not deduct losses from sales of stock or securities in a ***wash sale***. A wash sale occurs when the taxpayer sells securities at a loss and, within 30 days before or after the sale, the taxpayer obtains the same securities or rights (options) to acquire identical securities. Do not include the date of sale in the calculation of the 30 days. Add the basis of any disallowed loss to the cost of the new securities. This adjustment postpones the loss deduction until the disposition of the new stock or securities. The holding period for the new stock or securities includes the holding period of the stock or securities sold.

> **EXAMPLE:** Moe buys 1,500 shares of Acme stock on December 7, 2020. He sells the shares on December 31, 2020, at a loss of $3,000. Regretting his decision, he buys 1,000 shares of Acme stock on January 29, 2021. This partial wash sale prevents him from claiming the entire loss. He can deduct only $1,000 of the loss due to the 500 shares he did not replace. The remaining loss of $2,000 increases the basis of the replacement stock. On Form 8949, he should report the entire loss with the appropriate box checked; enter "W" in column (f); enter as a positive number in column (g) the amount of the wash sale loss not allowed.

DISPOSITION OR SALE OF PROPERTY

WORTHLESS SECURITIES

Stocks, stock rights, and bonds (other than those held for sale by a securities dealer) that became completely worthless during the tax year are treated as though they were sold on the **last day of the tax year**. Worthless securities also include abandoned securities. To abandon a security, the taxpayer must permanently surrender and relinquish all rights in the security and receive no consideration in exchange for it. Consider all the facts and circumstances to determine whether the taxpayer should characterize the transaction as abandonment or another type of transaction, such as an actual sale or exchange, contribution to capital, dividend, or gift.

NON-BUSINESS BAD DEBT

A taxpayer who is owed money that they cannot collect is said to have a ***bad debt***. The bad debt may be deductible during the year it becomes worthless. There are two kinds of bad debts—business and nonbusiness. A business bad debt, generally, is one that comes from operating a trade or business and is deductible as a business loss. All other bad debts are **nonbusiness bad debts** and are deductible as **short-term capital losses** if the debt meets the following conditions:

- A debt must be **totally worthless**.
- The debt must be genuine. A debt is genuine if it arises from a debtor-creditor relationship based on a valid and enforceable obligation to repay a fixed or determinable sum of money.
- There must be an intention at the time of the transaction to make a loan and **not a gift**. If a taxpayer lends money to an individual with the understanding that the individual does not have to pay it back, it is a gift and not a loan. A taxpayer may not take a bad debt deduction for a gift. There cannot be a bad debt unless there is a true creditor-debtor relationship between the taxpayer and the individual or organization that owes the money.
- There is no genuine debt when minor children borrow from their parents to pay for their basic needs. A taxpayer may not take a bad debt deduction for such a loan.
- To deduct a bad debt, the taxpayer **must have a basis** in it. The amount must have already been included in income or loaned out in cash. For example, a taxpayer cannot claim a bad debt deduction for unpaid court-ordered child support. A cash method taxpayer (most individuals) generally may not deduct unpaid salaries, wages, rents, fees, interest, dividends, and similar items.
- A taxpayer can only take a bad debt deduction in **the year the debt becomes worthless**. A taxpayer does not have to wait until a debt is due to determine whether it is worthless. A debt becomes worthless when there is no longer any chance that the debtor will pay the amount owed. A taxpayer can amend a prior year return to claim a refund based on a bad debt or worthless security **within 7 years after the due date** of the return for the tax year in which the debt or security became worthless.
- It is not necessary to go to court if the taxpayer can show that a judgment from the court would be uncollectible. A taxpayer need only show that they have taken reasonable steps to collect the debt. The bankruptcy of the debtor is generally good evidence of the worthlessness of a debt.
- If a taxpayer guarantees a debt that becomes worthless, they may not take a bad debt deduction for payments on the debt unless it can be shown that either the reason for making the guarantee was to protect the investment or that the taxpayer entered the guarantee transaction with a profit motive. If the taxpayer made the guarantee as a favor to friends without any consideration in return, the IRS will treat the payments as a gift and the taxpayer may not take a bad debt deduction.

SALE OF PROPERTY

Calculate the gain or loss on the sale property by subtracting the adjusted basis from the amount *realized* to get the gain or loss. The amount realized is the selling price minus selling expenses. Selling expenses include commissions, advertising fees, legal fees, and loan charges paid by the seller, such as loan placement fees or points.

A taxpayer may exclude from income a gain up to certain levels on the sale of their *main home* (*see Exclusions*). A taxpayer may not deduct a loss on the sale of their main home. However, a taxpayer may have to report the gain or loss on Schedule D even though it is not taxable (main home exclusion) or not deductible (personal loss).

INVOLUNTARY CONVERSION

A taxpayer has had a disposition when property is destroyed or *condemned* and the taxpayer receives another property or money in payment, such as insurance or a condemnation award. The IRS treats this as a sale, and the taxpayer may be able to exclude all or part of any gain from the destruction or condemnation of the main home, as explained above.

INSTALLMENT SALE

Some sales involve arrangements that provide for part or the entire selling price to be paid in a later year. These sales are *installment sales.* The buyer's obligation to make future payments can be in the form of a deed of trust, note, land contract, mortgage, or other evidence of the buyer's debt. If a sale qualifies as an installment sale, the taxpayer must report the gain under the *installment method* unless the taxpayer elects to report the gain in the current year. If the sale results in a loss, a taxpayer **may not use the installment method**. The following conditions apply to an installment sale:

- Increase the adjusted basis for installment sale purposes by selling expenses (commissions, attorney fees, and any other expenses paid on the sale) and depreciation recapture.

- If a taxpayer sells a property on which a depreciation deduction was claimed or could have been claimed, the taxpayer must report the amount of the deduction (or amount that could have been claimed) as *depreciation recapture* income in the year of sale, whether or not an installment payment was received that year. Report the recapture income in **full** as ordinary income in the year of sale; report only the gain greater than the recapture income on the installment method.

- Each payment on an installment sale usually consists of three parts—interest income, return of adjusted basis in the property, and gain on the sale.

- The method to determine the amount of gain recognized as installment income is as follows:

  1. **Determine gross profit** – Gross profit is the selling price less the adjusted basis for installment sale purposes. If the property is the taxpayer's main home, subtract any gain that the taxpayer can exclude from the gross profit.

  2. **Gross profit percentage** – A certain percentage of each payment (after subtracting interest) is reported as installment sale income. Calculate this *gross profit percentage* by dividing the gross profit from the sale by the contract price.

  3. **Installment sale income recognized** – To arrive at the amount recognized, multiply the payments received each year (**less interest**) by the gross profit percentage.

> **EXAMPLE:** Jim and Jean purchased a vacation home in 1997 for $100,000. They sold the property for $500,000 and received a down payment of $200,000. They took a mortgage from the purchaser for the remaining $300,000. Gross profit is $400,000 ($500,000 selling price – $100,000 basis). Determine the gross profit percentage by dividing the gross profit from the sale by the contract price. Gross Profit Percentage is 80% ($400,000 gross profit divided by $500,000 selling price). Jim and Jean must report 80% of each payment (after subtracting interest) as installment sale income.

TIP: The gross profit percentage is always 100% if the buyer assumes a liability that is greater than the installment sale basis of the property sold. Treat the amount of the liability that exceeds basis as a payment received in the year of sale.

- In each year that a taxpayer receives an installment payment, the taxpayer must include in income both the interest and the part that is the taxpayer's gain on the sale. If an installment sale contract does not provide for adequate stated interest (when compared to the *applicable federal rate*), the taxpayer may reclassify part of the stated principal amount of the contract as interest. The taxpayer should not include in income the part that is the return of the basis in the property. Basis is the amount of the investment in the property for installment sale purposes.

- If the taxpayer sells depreciable property to certain *related persons*, the taxpayer may not report the sale using the installment method. Instead, all payments due are considered received in the year of sale. However, the taxpayer may use the installment method in a related party transaction if they derive no significant tax deferral benefit from the sale. The taxpayer must show, to the satisfaction of the IRS, that avoidance of federal income tax was not a principal purpose of the sale.

- If the taxpayer sells property to a related person and, within **two years**, the related person disposes of the property before the taxpayer receives all payments with respect to the sale, the taxpayer may have a reporting obligation. The taxpayer may have to treat part or all of the amount the related person realizes (or the FMV if the disposed property is not sold or exchanged) from the second disposition as if the taxpayer received it at the time of the second disposition.

- **Disposition of an installment obligation** – A disposition generally includes a sale, exchange, cancellation, bequest, distribution, or transmission of an installment obligation. An installment obligation is the buyer's note, deed of trust, or other evidence that the buyer will make future payments to the taxpayer.

  1. If a taxpayer is using the installment method and the installment obligation is disposed of, generally, the taxpayer will have a gain or loss to report. The gain or loss applies to the sale of the property for which the taxpayer received the installment obligation. If the original installment sale produced ordinary income, the disposition of the obligation will result in ordinary income or loss. If the original sale resulted in a capital gain, the disposition of the obligation will result in a capital gain or loss.

  2. **Rules to figure gain or loss** – Use the following rules to figure gain or loss from the disposition of an installment obligation:

     A. If the taxpayer sells or exchanges the obligation, or accepts less than face value in satisfaction of the obligation, the gain or loss is the difference between the basis of the obligation and the amount realized.

     B. If the obligation is disposed of in any other way, the gain or loss is the difference between the basis in the obligation and FMV at the time of the disposition. This rule applies, for example, when the taxpayer gives the installment obligation to someone else or cancels the buyer's debt.

  3. Calculate the basis of an installment obligation by multiplying the unpaid balance on the obligation by the gross profit percentage. Subtract that amount from the unpaid balance. The result is the basis in the installment obligation.

EXAMPLE: In 2004, Sue sold an airplane on the installment method. She needed cash in 2020 so she sold the note for $110,000 when the balance due her was $140,000. Her gross profit percentage was 60%. Of the $140,000 still owed to Sue, $84,000 is profit owed to her on the obligation, and $56,000 is her basis. She receives $110,000 for the note so she has a profit of $54,000.

LIKE-KIND EXCHANGES OF REAL PROPERTY

If a taxpayer trades *business or investment real property* for other business or investment real property it's a *like-kind exchange (Section 1031 Exchange)*, and the taxpayer does not pay tax on any gain or deduct any loss until the taxpayer sells or disposes of the property received. The taxpayer may realize a partial gain to the extent of cash and the fair market value of any unlike property received. If a taxpayer trades property with a *related party* in a like-kind exchange, if either the taxpayer or the related party disposes of the like property within two years after the trade, both parties must report any gain or loss not recognized on the original trade on the return for the year in which the later disposition occurs.

Nonrecognition of gain under Section 1031 in the case of like-kind exchanges completed after December 31, 2017, applies only to **real property** that is not held primarily for sale. A taxpayer can no longer defer gain on tangible personal property held for use in a trade or business or held for investment.

RELATED PARTY

A taxpayer **may not deduct a loss** on the sale or trade of property, other than a distribution in complete liquidation of a corporation if the transaction is directly or indirectly between the taxpayer and the following related parties:

- Members of taxpayer's family, which includes only brothers and sisters, half-brothers and half-sisters, spouse, ancestors (parents, grandparents, etc.), and lineal descendants (children, grandchildren, etc.)
- A partnership or corporation with more than 50% directly or indirectly owned by the taxpayer
- A tax-exempt charitable or educational organization controlled by taxpayer or family member

If a taxpayer sells property that was purchased from a related party, the taxpayer **recognizes gain only to the extent that it is more than the loss previously disallowed** to the related party. This rule applies only to the original transferee and only if the property was acquired by purchase or exchange.

EXAMPLE: Your brother sells you stock for $7,600. His cost basis is $10,000. Your brother cannot deduct the loss of $2,400. Later, you sell the same stock to an unrelated party for $10,500, realizing a gain of $2,900. Your reportable gain is $500 (the $2,900 gain minus the $2,400 loss not allowed to your brother).

A taxpayer that sells property at a loss cannot **recognize the loss that was not allowed to the related party**.

EXAMPLE: Same details as the prior example, but assume you sold the stock for $6,900 instead of $10,500, your recognized loss is only $700 (your $7,600 basis minus $6,900). You cannot deduct the loss that was not allowed to your brother.

REPORTING GAINS AND LOSSES

INVESTORS

Investors typically buy and sell securities and expect income from dividends, interest, or capital appreciation. They buy and sell these securities and hold them for personal investment; they're **not conducting a trade or business.** Most investors are individuals and hold these securities for a substantial period of time.

Sales of these securities result in capital gains and losses that must be reported on Form 1040, Schedule D, Capital Gains and Losses, and on Form 8949, Sales and Other Dispositions of Capital Assets, as appropriate. Investors are subject to the capital loss limitations described in section 1211(b), in addition to the section 1091 wash sales rules.

Investors may be able to benefit from a deduction for the interest paid for money to buy or carry investment property that produces taxable income on Schedule A, but under section 163(d), the deduction can't exceed the net investment income. Commissions and other costs of acquiring or disposing of securities aren't deductible but must be used to figure gain or loss upon disposition of the securities. **Investment income isn't subject to self-employment tax.**

SECURITIES TRADERS

Special rules apply to a trader in securities, in the business of buying and selling securities for their own account. The law considers this to be a business, even though a trader doesn't maintain an inventory and doesn't have customers (unlike a dealer). To be engaged in business as a trader in securities, a taxpayer must meet <u>all</u> of the following conditions:

- Must seek to profit from daily market movements in the prices of securities and not from dividends, interest, or capital appreciation,
- Activity must be substantial, and
- Must carry on the activity with continuity and regularity.

The following facts and circumstances should be considered in determining if the activity is a **securities trading business**:

- Typical holding periods for securities bought and sold,
- The frequency and dollar amount of trades during the year,
- The extent to which the taxpayer pursues the activity to produce income for a livelihood, and
- The amount of time devoted to the activity.

If the nature of trading activities doesn't qualify as a business, the taxpayer is considered an investor and not a trader. A taxpayer may be a trader in some securities and may hold other securities for investment. The special rules for traders don't apply to those securities held for investment. A trader must keep detailed records to distinguish the securities held for investment from the securities in the trading business. The securities held for investment must be identified as such in the trader's records on the day he acquires them (for example, by holding them in a separate brokerage account).

A trader can elect to report business expenses on **Schedule C**, Profit or Loss From Business (Sole Proprietorship). **The Schedule A limitations on investment interest expense, which apply to investors, do not apply to interest paid or incurred in a trading business.** Commissions and other costs of acquiring or disposing of securities aren't deductible but must be used to figure gain or loss upon disposition of the securities. Gains and losses from selling securities from being a trader are <u>not</u> **subject to self-employment tax.** If a trader doesn't make a mark-to-market election, then they must treat the gains and losses from sales of securities as capital gains and losses and **report the sales on Schedule D**, Capital Gains and Losses and on Form 8949, Sales and Other Dispositions of Capital Assets, as appropriate.

MARK-TO-MARKET ELECTION

Traders can elect to use the mark-to-market rules of Section 475, **reporting a change in the fair value of securities as income (or loss) each year**. A trader utilizing mark-to-market accounting recognizes income (or loss) even though the underlying securities are not sold.

If a trader makes a timely mark-to-market election, then he can treat the gains and losses from sales of securities as **ordinary gains and losses** (except for securities held for investment) that must be reported on Part II of Form 4797, Sales of Business Property. **Neither the limitations on capital losses nor the wash sale rules apply to traders using the mark-to-market method of accounting.**

If a trader doesn't make a valid mark-to-market election, then he must treat the gains and losses from sales of securities as capital gains and losses and report the sales on Form 1040, Schedule D, Capital Gains and Losses and on Form 8949, Sales and Other Dispositions of Capital Assets, as appropriate. When reporting on Schedule D, both the limitations on capital losses and the wash sales rules continue to apply.

In general, a trader must make the mark-to-market election by the due date (not including extensions) of the tax return for the year prior to the year for which the election becomes effective. The election is made by attaching a statement either to the income tax return or to a request for an extension of time to file the return. It's important to note that in general, late Section 475(f) elections are not allowed.

HOLDING PERIOD

In general, the holding period for investment property begins the day <u>after</u> the day the property is acquired (*trade date*) or receipt of title and includes the date of disposition, transfer, or sale. Gain or loss is *short-term* on property held one year or less; otherwise, the holding period is *long-term*.

GAIN RECOGNITION

- **Amount realized** – The amount *realized* from a sale or trade of property is everything received for the property. This includes the money, the fair market value of any property or services, and debt or other liabilities assumed by the buyer.
- **Realized gains** – The difference between adjusted basis and the amount realized in a sale is the realized gain (or loss) on the transaction.
- **Amount recognized** – The amount of income or loss *recognized* is the amount a taxpayer includes in taxable income for the tax year. Certain transactions such as *like-kind exchanges* and *installment sales* may defer recognition of gain.

TIP: Pay careful attention to the language of each exam question. Multiple questions may test your understanding of the difference between realized and recognized gains.

CAPITAL ASSETS

If a taxpayer has a taxable gain or a deductible loss from a transaction, circumstance will dictate whether it is a *capital gain* or loss or an *ordinary gain* or loss.

Generally, a sale or trade of a *capital asset* results in a capital gain or loss. A sale or trade of a non-capital asset results in ordinary gain or loss. In some situations, part of the gain or loss may be a capital gain or loss and part may be an ordinary gain or loss.

> Rather than defining capital assets, the law provides a list of properties that are <u>not</u> capital assets:
>
> - Intangibles such as a patent, invention, model or design (whether or not patented), secret formula or process, copyright, and a composition (literary, musical, or artistic) **created by the efforts of the taxpayer** <u>or</u> having a substituted or **transferred basis** from the taxpayer who created the property (or for whom the property was created).
> - Supplies regularly used or consumed in the ordinary course of a taxpayer's trade or business
> - Accounts or notes receivable acquired in the ordinary course of a trade or business for services rendered or from the sale of property held mainly for sale to customers
> - Inventory or property held mainly for sale to customers or property that will physically become a part of the merchandise that is for sale to customers
> - Depreciable property and real property (real estate) used in the taxpayer's trade or business

TIP: Use the acronym "I SAID" to help remember what is <u>not</u> a capital asset.

TIP: The TCJA amends section 1221(a)(3) for dispositions after 2017 adding to the list a patent, invention, model or design (whether or not patented), and a secret formula or process.

For the most part, everything owned and used for personal purposes, pleasure, or investment is a capital asset. Some examples include the following:

- Stocks or bonds held in a personal account
- House owned and used by the taxpayer and the taxpayer's family
- Household furnishings
- A car used for pleasure or commuting
- Coin or stamp collections
- Gems and jewelry

> In general, a taxpayer reports overall capital gains and losses on Schedule D and includes the amount of net capital gain in gross income on Form 1040. Schedule D is not necessary if the taxpayer is without capital losses, and the only capital gains are distributions from Form 1099-DIV.

INVESTMENT PROPERTY

Investment property is a capital asset. Any gain or loss from its sale or trade is generally a capital gain or loss unless a dealer holds them for sale. Examples include gold, silver, stamps, coins, gems, stocks, bonds, etc. The taxpayer recaptures depreciation on the investment property when he/she sells the property.

PERSONAL USE PROPERTY

Property held for personal use only is a capital asset. If a taxpayer sells personal use property, he/she must report the difference between the sale price and the basis in the asset, if positive, as a capital gain. The IRS does not permit a deduction for a capital loss on the sale of personal use property.

VIRTUAL CURRENCY TRANSACTIONS

A checkbox appears on page 1 of the Form 1040— "At any time during 2020, did you receive, sell, send, exchange, or otherwise acquire any financial interest in any virtual currency?"

Cryptocurrency (e.g., Bitcoin) is a common form of virtual currency. A **transaction** involving virtual currency includes:

- The receipt or transfer of virtual currency for free (without providing any consideration)
- An exchange of virtual currency for goods or services
- A sale of virtual currency
- An exchange of virtual currency for other property, including for another virtual currency

For income tax purposes, virtual currency is **treated as property** and general tax principles applicable to property transactions apply to transactions using virtual currency.

- A taxpayer reports a transaction involving virtual currency that was held as a capital asset (such as an investment) using Form 8949 (and Schedule D) to figure capital gain or loss.
- A taxpayer who received virtual currency as compensation for services or disposed of any virtual currency held for sale to customers in a trade or business reports the income the same as other income of the same type (for example, W-2 wages on Form 1040, or inventory or services from Schedule C on Schedule 1).

CAPITAL GAINS RATES

Capital gains receive more favorable tax treatment than ordinary gains, to which ordinary income tax rates apply. The tax rates that apply to a *net capital gain* are generally lower than the tax rates that apply to other income. These lower rates are the *maximum capital gain rates*.

In general, the holding period for investment property begins the day <u>after</u> the day the property is acquired (*trade date*) or receipt of title and includes the date of disposition, transfer, or sale. Gain or loss is *short-term* on property held one year or less; otherwise, the holding period is *long-term*.

- **Long-term** capital gains (other than gains on collectibles, small business stock, or un-recaptured 1250 gains) receive special tax treatment and are taxed at a **maximum rate of 20%**.
- **Short-term** capital gains are taxed at the same rates as **ordinary income**.

What is the Maximum 2020 Capital Gain Rate?	
IF the net capital gain is from...	**THEN the maximum capital gain rate is...**
Gain on collectibles or qualified small business stock	28%
Un-recaptured Section 1250 gain	25%
All other capital gains	20%

Reduced maximum rates apply to gains from stocks and bonds (except qualified small business stock) as well as real property for certain entities.

Capital Gain Breakpoints for 2020		
Filing Status	**15-percent Breakpoint**	**20-percent Breakpoint**
Married Individuals Filing Joint Returns and Surviving Spouses	$80,000	$496,600
Married Individuals Filing Separate	$40,000	$248,300
Heads of Households	$53,600	$469,050
Unmarried Individuals (other than Surviving Spouses and Heads of Households)	$40,000	$441,450
Estates and Trusts	$2,650	$13,150

In the case of an individual (including an estate or trust) with an adjusted net capital gain, to the extent the gain would <u>not</u> result in *taxable income* exceeding the 15-percent breakpoint, such **capital gain is not taxed.** Any adjusted net capital gain which would result in *taxable income* exceeding the 15-percent breakpoint but <u>not</u> exceeding the 20-percent breakpoint, such **capital gain is taxed at 15-percent.** The remaining adjusted net **capital gain is taxed at 20-percent.**

TIP: Qualified dividends are subject to the same 0%, 15%, or 20% maximum tax rates that apply to net capital gain.

FORM 8949

A taxpayer uses *Form 8949* to list all capital gain and loss transactions and carries the subtotals from this form to Schedule D (Form 1040), where gain or loss will be calculated in aggregate. Short-term gains are listed together in Part I, while long-term gains are listed in Part II.

A taxpayer uses Form 8949 to report:

- The sale or exchange of a capital asset not reported on another form or schedule,
- Gains from involuntary conversions (other than from casualty or theft) of capital assets not held for business or profit, and
- Nonbusiness bad debts.

CALCULATING NET GAINS AND LOSSES

Tax rates differ, depending upon the nature of the gain and the type of property involved. Combine gains and losses in each category to arrive at a net gain or loss.

- **Short-term gains and losses** – Sale or trade of investment property **held one year or less**. Combine the taxpayer's share of short-term capital gain or loss from partnerships, S corporations, fiduciaries, and any short-term capital loss carryover with other short-term capital gains and losses to figure the *net short-term capital gain* (NSTCG) *or loss* (NSTCL).
- **Long-term gains and losses** – Sale or trade of investment property **held more than one year** is a long-term capital gain or loss. Combine the taxpayer's share of long-term capital gain or loss from partnerships, S corporations, and fiduciaries, as well as any long-term capital loss carryover with other long-term capital gains and losses, to figure *net long-term capital gain* (NLTCG) *or loss* (NLTCL).
- **Total net gain or loss** – A taxpayer may calculate total net gain or loss by comparing the net short-term capital gain or loss to the net long-term capital gain or loss. If a taxpayer has a:
  1. **Net gain and a net loss** (NLTCG and NSTCL <u>or</u> NLTCL and NSTCG) – The resulting gain or loss maintains the character of the <u>larger</u> item.

     > **EXAMPLE:** If net short-term losses exceed net long-term gains, the character of the resulting net loss is short-term. If net short-term gains exceed net long-term losses, the resulting net gain is short-term and is taxed at ordinary income tax rates. If net long-term gains exceed net short-term losses, the resulting net gain is long-term and is taxed at the maximum net capital gain tax rates.

  2. **Both short and long-term losses** (NLTCL and NSTCL) – Each loss maintains its character, either long or short-term.
  3. **Both short and long-term gains** (NLTCG and NSTCG) – Each gain maintains its character. The maximum net capital gain tax rates apply to the long-term capital gain, while ordinary income tax rates apply to the short-term capital gain.

CAPITAL LOSS CARRYOVER

If capital losses are more than capital gains, a taxpayer may claim a capital loss deduction. The allowable capital loss deduction, figured on Schedule D, is the <u>lesser</u> of the following:

- **$3,000** ($1,500 if the taxpayer is married and files a separate return), or
- The taxpayer's total net capital loss, as shown on Schedule D

A taxpayer may use a net capital loss to reduce income dollar for dollar, up to the $3,000 limit. If the taxpayer's total net capital loss exceeds the yearly limit on capital loss deductions, carry the unused part over to the next year and treat it as though it had incurred in that next year. If part of the loss is still unused, the taxpayer may carry the unused part over to later years until none of the loss remains.

TIP: A capital loss sustained by a decedent during the final tax year (or carried over to that year from an earlier year) can be deducted (subject to the $3,000 limit) only on the final income tax return filed for the decedent.

Capital loss carryovers do <u>not</u> transfer to an estate or the surviving spouse. A taxpayer filing jointly with the decedent for the year of death should consider recognizing capital gains to take advantage of any capital loss carryforward that will expire if it is not used on the final return.

When calculating the amount of any capital loss carryover to the next year, consider the current year's allowable deduction, whether or not the taxpayer has claimed the allowable deduction. When a taxpayer carries over a loss, it remains long-term or short-term. Any long-term capital losses carried over to the next tax year will reduce that year's long-term capital gains before it reduces that year's short-term capital gains. In calculating the capital loss carryover, a taxpayer should use the short-term capital losses first, even if the taxpayer incurred those losses after a long-term capital loss. If a taxpayer has not reached the limit on the capital loss deduction after using the short-term capital losses, use the long-term capital losses until the taxpayer has reached the limit.

> **EXAMPLE:** Sheila has both long and short-term capital losses in 2020. Her net STCL is $5,000 and a net LTCL is $10,000. She can only deduct $3,000 in the current year and must use her short-term loss first. She carries $2,000 STCL and $10,000 LTCL forward to 2021.

SECTION 1244 SMALL BUSINESS STOCK

A *small business corporation* may qualify for special treatment under *Section 1244*. If so, any **gain on the sale of stock is a capital gain** if the stock is a capital asset. A taxpayer may deduct the loss on the sale, trade, or worthlessness of Section 1244 stock as an **ordinary loss**, rather than as a capital loss. The amount a taxpayer may deduct as an ordinary loss is limited to $50,000 each year. On a joint return, the limit is $100,000, even if only one spouse has this type of loss.

- A corporation shall be treated as a small business corporation if the aggregate amount of money and other property received by the corporation for stock, as a contribution to capital, and as paid-in surplus, does not exceed $1,000,000.
- During the 5-year period ending before the date the loss, the corporation must derive more than 50 percent of its aggregate gross receipts from sources other than royalties, rents, dividends, interests, annuities, and sales or exchanges of stocks or securities.
- Section 1244 relates to **stock issued for money or property** (other than stock and securities). An increase in the basis of outstanding stock as a result of a contribution to capital is <u>not</u> treated as an issuance of stock under Section 1244.
- The taxpayer **must be the original owner of the stock to be allowed ordinary loss treatment.** To claim a deductible loss on stock issued to a partnership, the taxpayer must have been a partner when the stock was issued and have remained so until the time of the loss.

SECTION 1202 EXCLUSION

Certain eligible C corporations with gross assets under $50 million may qualify for special treatment under *Section 1202* as *qualified small business stock (QSB)*. A taxpayer (other than a corporation) selling QSB stock held for <u>more</u> than **five years** can exclude up to 50% of the eligible gain from income.

> For stock acquired after September 27, 2010, the §1202 exclusion is **100% of eligible gains**. The amount of gain eligible for the exclusion is limited to the <u>greater</u> of **$10,000,000 or 10 times the adjusted basis.**

- Certain corporations do not qualify, such as a REIT, REMIC, RIC, DISC, FASIT, cooperative, or corporation electing treatment as a possessions corporation.

- The C corporation must be an active business using at least 80% of assets in the active conduct of a qualified trade or business. The following trades or businesses do <u>not</u> qualify:

  1. Services performed in the fields of health, law, engineering, architecture, accounting, actuarial science, performing arts, consulting, athletics, financial services, or brokerage services

  2. One whose principal asset is the reputation or skill of one or more employees

  3. Any banking, insurance, financing, leasing, investing, or similar business

  4. Any farming business (including the business of raising or harvesting trees)

  5. Oil or gas operations if percentage depletion can be claimed

  6. Any business of operating a hotel, motel, restaurant, or similar business

PASSIVE ACTIVITY CAPITAL GAINS AND LOSSES

A taxpayer reports capital gains or losses from a passive activity on Form 8582. Passive activities occur when there is income from certain businesses where no material participation occurs. A passive loss is not deductible on an individual income tax return, but the loss may be used to offset income from other passive activities.

LESSON 4

Income Exclusions

ITEMS EXCLUDED FROM GROSS INCOME

Certain forms of income are <u>not</u> subject to federal income tax. An ***exclusion*** item is any income that is specifically <u>not</u> taxed. A few of the major exclusions from income are as follows:

- **Municipal bond interest** – Interest from state and local government bonds that serve a public purpose is generally excluded.
- **Gain on sale of main home** – Up to $250,000 ($500,000 for qualifying married filers).
- **Discharge of debt due to bankruptcy or insolvency** – Excluded from income.
- **Discharge of qualified principal residence indebtedness:**
    - Up to $2 million ($1 million married filing separate) for discharges in 2020
    - Up to $750,000 ($375,000 married filing separate) for discharges made 2021 through 2025
- **Discharge of certain student loan indebtedness:**
    - Excluded if the creditor canceled the debt due to the performance of services.
    - Excluded if due to death or total and permanent disability. **TCJA:** Discharges of loans <u>after</u> December 31, 2017, and <u>before</u> January 1, 2026.
- **Price reduction** – When the seller reduces the taxpayer's debt and the taxpayer is not insolvent or bankrupt. The taxpayer reduces basis in the property by the amount of debt reduction. See §108(e)(5).
- **Social Security benefits** – Up to 85% of benefits may be included in gross income; therefore, exclude a minimum of 15% from gross income.
- **Employee achievement awards** – Up to $1,600 for a length of service or safety achievement may be excluded.
- **Fringe benefits** – Certain employer-provided fringe benefits are specifically excluded.
- **Housing allowance for member of clergy** – A reasonable housing allowance may be excluded.
- **Military and government disability pensions** – Must <u>not</u> be based on years of service.
- **Veterans (VA) benefits** – Do not include veterans' benefits paid under any law, regulation, or administrative practice administered by the Department of Veterans Affairs (VA) in income.
- **Gifts and inheritances** – Generally, property received as a gift, bequest, or inheritance.
- **Scholarships and fellowships** – Exempt if used for qualified educational expenses.
- **Distributions from Coverdell ESA or 529 Plan** – When a taxpayer uses distributions to pay for qualified educational expenses of the designated beneficiary.
- **Interest on Series EE and I savings bonds** – When used for qualified higher education expenses.
- **Workers' compensation** – Payments for occupational sickness or injury under the workers' compensation act.
- **Compensation for sickness or injury** – Compensatory damages from a lawsuit, benefits under a health insurance plan where the taxpayer paid the premiums or reimbursements for medical care.
- **Welfare or public assistance** – Exclude unless payment for services or obtained fraudulently.
- **Life insurance proceeds** – Death payouts are generally tax-free to the beneficiary.
- **Accelerated death benefits** – Exclude payments to the terminally or chronically ill.
- **Casualty insurance** – Exclude insurance settlements received to compensate for damaged or stolen property from income. However, include in income any payments for living expenses that are more than the temporary increase in actual living expenses.
- **Qualified disaster relief payments** – Due to terrorist or military action, a federally declared disaster area, or an accident involving a common carrier determined to be catastrophic.
- **Property settlements** – A taxpayer does not recognize any gain on a transfer of property to a spouse due to divorce. However, any gain on later distribution or sale of the property may be taxable.
- **Child support** – Child support payments are excluded.

- **Foster care** – In general, exclude payments received as a provider of foster care.
- **Reimbursements for certain employment-related expenses** – Exclude from the employee's income any ordinary and necessary business expenses related to travel and meals paid by the employee and later reimbursed under an employer's *accountable plan*. Within a reasonable period of time, the employee must provide the employer with records to substantiate the expense and return any excess reimbursement.
- **Foreign earned income exclusion** – Up to $107,600 of foreign earnings per qualifying person in 2020.

MUNICIPAL BOND INTEREST

Generally, interest on a bond used to finance government operations is not taxable if a state, the District of Columbia, a U.S. possession, or any of their political subdivisions issues the bond for a public purpose. Even if interest is not subject to tax, capital gain or loss may apply when sold. Political subdivisions include:

- Port authorities
- Toll road commissions
- Utility services authorities
- Community redevelopment agencies
- Qualified volunteer fire departments (for certain obligations issued after 1980)

PRIVATE ACTIVITY BONDS

Not all Municipal bond interest is exempt from federal income tax. Interest on bonds used for most private activities is not exempt from income tax. A bond is generally considered a *private activity bond* if the amount of the proceeds to finance loans to persons other than government units is more than 5% of the proceeds or $5 million (whichever is less). This is called the "private loan financing test." If the bond is a private activity bond but is exempt it is referred to as a *qualified bond* or *qualified private activity bond*. Private activity bonds are often used to build a sports facility or industrial park, airport, for-profit hospital, etc.

> **EXAMPLE:** Interest on a bond to finance a bridge is exempt from federal income tax. Interest on a bond to build a new sports arena is taxable. Report both on Form 1040, but exclude exempt interest from income.

Interest listed on Form 1099 as private activity bond interest is from qualified private activity bonds. Qualified private activity bond interest is listed separately on Form 1099 because it is a tax preference item for AMT. Interest from nonqualified private activity bonds is simply added into the taxable interest on the Form 1099 and not separately stated. This is likely to appear on the exam (i.e., Which of the following items is a preference or adjustment item for AMT?), with *qualified private activity bond interest* being one of the items on a list.

GAIN ON SALE OF MAIN HOME

A taxpayer who meets certain qualifications may exclude gains on the sale of a principal residence. This is a *Section 121 exclusion*. Otherwise, the taxpayer will report the sale or exchange of the main home on Form 8949, which will flow to Schedule D.

Usually, the home in which the taxpayer lives most of the time is the main home. In addition to a house, a main home may also be a condominium, cooperative apartment, houseboat, or mobile home. If a taxpayer uses only part of the property as main home, these rules apply only to the gain or loss on the sale of that part. A taxpayer may not exclude gain on a home acquired in a like-kind exchange for a period of 5 years.

The taxpayer must own and live in the property as his *main home* for at least **two years during the five-year period** ending on the date of sale.

OWNERSHIP AND USE TESTS

During the five-year period ending on the date of the sale, the taxpayer must meet the following ownership and use tests in order to claim the exclusion:

- **Ownership test** – Owned the home for at least two years.
- **Use test** – Lived in the home as a main home for at least two years. Occupancy does not have to be consecutive so long as periods of residence total 24 months (730 days). Occupancy does not have to begin or end on the dates of purchase or sale of the property.
  1. Taxpayers with occupancy of fewer than two years may claim a reduced exclusion if the move is due to unexpected changes in employment, health, or other unforeseen circumstances.
  2. Certain members of the military, intelligence community, or Peace Corps volunteers may suspend the five-year test by up to 10 additional years if on qualified official extended duty while serving at a duty station that is at least 50 miles from his or her main home, or living in government quarters under government orders. Extended duty is for a period of more than 90 days or for an indefinite time.

EXCEPTION: There is an exception to the use test if a taxpayer becomes physically or mentally unable to care for himself, and he owns and lives in the home as a main home for at least 1 year during the 5-year period before the sale of the home. Under this exception, the taxpayer is considered to live in the home during any time within the 5-year period that he owns the home and lives in a facility (including a nursing home). This exception is for the use test only, as the taxpayer still must meet the 2-out-of-5-year ownership test to claim the exclusion.

Death of spouse rule: If you sell your home after your spouse dies (within 2 years after your spouse dies), and you haven't remarried as of the sale date, you can count any time when your spouse owned the home as time you owned it, and any time when the home was your spouse's residence as time when it was your residence.

MAXIMUM EXCLUSION

- A taxpayer may exclude **up to $250,000** of the gain if all of the following are true:
  1. The taxpayer meets the ownership test.
  2. The taxpayer meets the use test.
  3. The taxpayer did not exclude the gain from the sale of another home during the **two-year period ending on the date of the sale**.
- A taxpayer may exclude **up to $500,000** of the gain if all of the following are true:
  1. The taxpayer is married and files a joint return for the year.
  2. Either the taxpayer or spouse meets the ownership test.
  3. Both the taxpayer and spouse meet the use test.
  4. During the two-year period ending on the date of the sale, neither the taxpayer nor spouse excluded gain from the sale of another home.

PERIODS OF NONQUALIFIED USE

Generally, the gain from the sale or exchange of a main home will not qualify for the exclusion to the extent that the taxpayer allocates gains to periods of nonqualified use. Nonqualified use is any period after December 31, 2008, during which the taxpayer does not use the property as his main home. Allocate the gain resulting from the sale of the property between qualified and nonqualified use periods based on the amount of time the taxpayer held the property for qualified and nonqualified use. Gain from the sale or exchange of a main home allocable to periods of qualified use will continue to qualify for the exclusion for the sale of a main home. Gain from the sale or exchange of property allocable to nonqualified use will not qualify for the exclusion.

- A period of nonqualified use does not include:
  1. Any portion of the five-year period ending on the date of the sale or exchange that is after the last date the taxpayer (or spouse) used the property as a main home.
  2. Any period (not to exceed an aggregate period of 10 years) during which taxpayer or spouse is serving on qualified official extended duty for any of the following:
     A. As a member of the uniformed services
     B. As a member of the Foreign Service of the United States
     C. As an employee of the intelligence community
  3. Any other period of temporary absence (not to exceed an aggregate period of two years) due to change of employment, health conditions, or such other unforeseen circumstances as may be specified by the IRS.
- To figure the portion of the gain that is allocated to the period of nonqualified use, multiply the gain by the following fraction:

Portion of gain allocated to nonqualified use

$$\text{Gain on sale} \times \frac{\textit{Total nonqualified use after 2008}}{\textit{Total period of ownership}}$$

EXAMPLE: Liam purchases a home for $250,000 on January 1, 2006.

- Jan 1, 2006 – Liam lists the home as a vacation rental property to help him generate income.
- Jan 1, 2012 – Liam no longer rents the property and begins to treat the home as his main home.
- Jan 1, 2019 – Liam no longer lives in the property and lists the home as a rental.
- Dec 31, 2020 – Liam sells the property for $450,000.

A period of non-use is measured in days. For simplification of this example, we will assume each year is 365 days.

Period	Use	Non-use	Description
1/1/2006 – 12/31/2008	1,095		Non-use days are days after 12/31/2008.
1/1/2009 – 12/31/2011		1,095	The 3 years rental period after 12/31/2008 is nonqualified use.
1/1/2012 – 12/31/2018	2,555		Liam lives in the house for 7 years as his main home.
1/1/2019 – 12/31/2020	730		Non-use days do not include days after a taxpayer stops using the home as a main home if the days are within the 5-year period ending on the date of the sale.

Determine the portion of gain allocated to nonqualified by dividing the total days of non-use by the total days owning the home. 1,095 ÷ 5,475 = .2

Accordingly, **20%** of the gain is allocated to nonqualified use and does <u>not</u> qualify for the exclusion.

BUSINESS USE OR RENTAL OF HOME

A taxpayer may be able to exclude gain from the sale of a home that he uses for business or to produce rental income. However, a taxpayer <u>must</u> meet the ownership <u>and</u> use tests. If a taxpayer is entitled to take depreciation deductions because the main home was used for business purposes or as a rental property (even if he did not actually claim them), he may <u>not</u> exclude the part of the gain equal to any **depreciation** allowed or allowable as a deduction for periods after May 6, 1997. If the taxpayer can show, by adequate records or other evidence, that the depreciation allowed was less than the amount allowable, the amount a taxpayer may not exclude is the amount allowed.

EXAMPLE: Using the same facts as the prior example we will calculate the amount of gain Liam may exclude. There is one additional fact we need to know, and which is:

- While the property is rented, Liam claims $50,000 in depreciation.

We know from the prior example that Liam's purchased the home for $250,000. He will adjust his basis in the property to $200,000 ($250,000 cost – $50,000 depreciation) to account for the depreciation.

He realizes a gain on the sale of $250,000 ($450,000 sales price – $200,000 adjusted basis) but cannot exclude the entire gain. He cannot exclude the $50,000 portion of his gain that is due to depreciation. The first step is reducing the gain by the amount of depreciation claimed.

$250,000 – $50,000 = $200,000 net gain

Now, if you recall from the prior example, Liam rented the property and a portion of the net gain is attributed to periods of non-use and is <u>not</u> eligible for exclusion.

$200,000 × 20% = $40,000 nonqualified use gain

Liam is able to exclude the remaining $160,000 from his income, but as a result of the rental, he must include $50,000 as an unrecaptured Section 1250 gain (taxed at 25%) and $40,000 as a long-term capital gain (taxed at a maximum 20% rate).

$50,000	Unrecaptured Section 1250 gain (depreciation)
$40,000	Long-term capital gain (nonqualified use)
$160,000	Eligible for Section 121 exclusion
$250,000	Total Realized Gain

DISCHARGE OF QUALIFIED PRINCIPAL RESIDENCE INDEBTEDNESS

A taxpayer may be able to exclude from gross income a *discharge of qualified principal residence indebtedness*. This exclusion applies to discharges made after 2006 and before 2021. If a taxpayer chooses to exclude this income, reduce the basis of the principal residence by the amount excluded from the gross income (not less than zero).

- **Principal residence** – The principal residence is the home where the taxpayer ordinarily lives most of the time. There can only be one principal residence at any one time.

- **Qualified principal residence indebtedness** – Debt that the taxpayer incurs while acquiring, constructing, or substantially improving a principal residence, for which the principal residence serves as security. Also includes any debt resulting from the refinancing of such debt but only to the extent of the prior debt. Cash taken during refinancing is not qualified principal residence indebtedness.

- **Amount eligible for the exclusion** – The maximum amount that the taxpayer may treat as qualified principal residence indebtedness in 2020 is **$2 million** ($1 million married filing separate). The taxpayer may not exclude discharge of qualified principal residence indebtedness from gross income if the discharge was for services performed for the lender or because of any other factor not directly related to a **decline in the value of the residence** or to the **taxpayer's financial condition**.

> **CONSOLIDATED APPROPRIATIONS ACT UPDATE:** The Consolidated Appropriations Act, 2021 extended the exclusion to discharges made before January 1, 2026, and reduced the exclusion amount to $750,000 ($375,000 married filing separate return) for discharges of indebtedness after December 31, 2020. Thus, the maximum amount a taxpayer may treat as qualified principal residence indebtedness is $750,000 ($375,000 married filing separate) for debt discharged 2021 through 2025.

EMPLOYER PROVIDED BENEFITS AND AWARDS

FRINGE BENEFITS

Fringe benefits received in connection with the performance of services are included in income as compensation unless the employee pays fair market value for the benefits or the law specifically excludes them. The IRS treats abstaining from the performance of services (for example, under a covenant not to compete) as the performance of services for purposes of these rules. Certain fringe benefits are specifically excluded:

- **Accident or health plan** – Generally, the value of accident or health plan coverage that an employer provides to a taxpayer is not included as income. Benefits received from the plan may be taxable, as explained later under *Sickness and Injury Benefits*.

- **Long-term care coverage** – Contributions by employers to provide coverage for long-term care services generally are not included as income. However, contributions made through a flexible spending or similar arrangement (such as a cafeteria plan) must be included in income. This amount appears as wages in Box 1 of Form W-2.

- **Archer MSA contributions** – Employer contributions to an Archer MSA generally are not included as income. The total of these contributions appears in Box 12 of Form W-2 with code R. The taxpayer must report this amount on Form 8853, Archer MSAs and Long-Term Care Insurance Contracts. A taxpayer should file Form 8853 with his returns. If a taxpayer does not enjoy employer contributions to his MSA, the taxpayer may make his own contributions.

- **Meals and lodging** – An employee can exclude the value of employer-provided meals or lodging from gross income if provided on the employer's premises for the employer's convenience.

- **Health flexible spending arrangement (health FSA)** – If an employer provides a health FSA that qualifies as an accident or health plan, the amount of salary reduction and reimbursements of medical care expenses for the employee and those of the employee's spouse and dependents are not included in income.

- **Health reimbursement arrangement (HRA)** – If the employer provides an HRA that qualifies as an accident or health plan, coverage and reimbursements of medical care expenses and those of a spouse and dependents generally are not included in income.

- **Health savings accounts (HSA)** – Employer contributions are not included in income. Distributions from the HSA that the taxpayer uses to pay qualified medical expenses are not included in income. Distributions not used for qualified medical expenses are included in income and may be subject to early withdrawal penalties. If a taxpayer does not enjoy employer contributions to his HSA, the taxpayer may make his own contributions.

- **De Minimis (minimal) benefits** – If an employer provides employees with products or services where the cost of it is so small that it would be unreasonable for the employer to account for it, the value is not included in income. Examples of this would include coffee, doughnuts, etc.

- **Holiday gifts** – If an employer gives employees turkeys, hams, or other items of nominal value at Christmas or other holidays, the value of the gift should not be included in income. However, if the employer gives an employee cash, gift certificates, or similar items that may easily be exchanged for cash, the employee should include the value of that gift as extra salary or wages regardless of the amount involved.

- **Dependent care assistance** – Generally, employees may exclude from income up to $5,000 ($2,500 for married employees filing separate returns) received from an employer's dependent care assistance program.

- **Adoption assistance** – For 2020, an employee may exclude up to $14,300 per eligible child ($14,440 for 2021) of expenses incurred by an employer for qualified adoption expenses in connection with the adoption of an eligible child.

- **Educational assistance** – For the tax year, employees may exclude from income up to $5,250 of qualified employer-provided educational assistance (payments of tuition, fees, books, supplies, and equipment for either undergraduate or graduate education). Employees may not exclude expenses for meals, lodging, or transportation. Tools or supplies (other than textbooks) that can be kept after completing the course of instruction do not qualify. The exclusion is generally not available for education related to sports, games or hobbies unless it has a relationship to the business of the employer or is otherwise required to obtain a degree.

- **Moving expense reimbursements** – Qualified moving expense reimbursements are excluded from an employee's gross income. Qualified moving expenses are defined as any amount received (directly or indirectly) from an employer as payment for (or reimbursement of) expenses which would be deductible as moving expenses if directly paid or incurred by the employee. However, any such amount actually deducted by the individual is not eligible for this exclusion.

> The TCJA **repeals the exclusion of qualified moving expense reimbursements** from gross income and wages (except for members of the Armed Forces) for taxable years beginning after December 31, 2017, and before January 1, 2026. All moving expenses paid or reimbursed for taxable years 2018 through 2025, will be taxable to the employee (except for members of the Armed Forces) and subject to tax withholding.

- **Group-term life Insurance** – Generally, the cost of up to $50,000 of group-term life insurance coverage provided by an employer (or former employer) is not included in income. However, the cost of employer-provided insurance that is more than the cost of $50,000 of coverage reduced by any amount the employee pays toward the purchase of the insurance should be included as income. If a group-term life insurance policy includes permanent benefits, such as a paid-up or cash surrender value, an employee should include the cost of the permanent benefits minus the amount paid for them as income in the form of wages. The exclusion is for term life insurance protection (insurance for a fixed period of time), meeting all of the following conditions:

1. The insurance must provide a general death benefit
2. The insurance must be provided to a group of employees
3. The insurance must be under a policy carried by the employer
4. The insurance must provide an amount of insurance to each employee based on a formula that prevents individual selection

- **Retirement planning services** – Qualified retirement planning services that an employer provides to employees are not included in income. Qualified services include retirement planning advice, information about the employer's retirement plan, and information about how the plan may fit into the overall individual retirement income plan. Employees may not exclude the value of any tax preparation, accounting, legal, or brokerage services provided by the employer.

- **Transportation** – Employees may exclude employer-provided qualified transportation fringe benefits from income in 2020, within limits. Qualified transportation fringe benefits include the following:

   1. Transit passes and commuter highway vehicle transportation – In 2020, up to $270 ($270 in 2021) per month for combined commuter highway vehicle transportation and transit passes.

   2. Qualified parking – In 2020, up to $270 ($270 in 2021) per month for qualified parking.

> **TCJA:** For tax years beginning after December 31, 2017, the act suspends the exclusion from gross income and wages for qualified bicycle commuting reimbursements.

- **No additional cost services** – Employees may exclude the value of certain employer-provided services from income when the services do not cause the employer any substantial additional costs. The employer must offer the services to customers in the ordinary course of the line of business in which the employee performs substantial services. Generally, no-additional-cost services are excess capacity services, such as airline, bus, or train tickets; hotel rooms; or telephone services provided free or at a reduced price to employees working in those lines of business.

- **Athletic facilities** – Employees may exclude the value of using employer-owned athletic facilities if substantially all use is by employees, spouses, and dependent children.

- **Employee discounts** – Employees may exclude discounts on either of the following:

   1. Merchandise up to the employer's gross profit percentage

   2. Services up to 20% of the price charged to non-employees

- **Qualified retirement plan contributions** – Employer contributions to a qualified retirement plan for employee accounts are not included in income at the time contributed. Although not immediately taxed, these contributions are not excluded from income when withdrawals occur from the plan.

   1. **Elective deferrals** – An elective deferral (employee contribution), other than a designated Roth contribution, is not included in wages subject to income tax at the time contributed. However, it is included in wages subject to Social Security and Medicare taxes.

EMPLOYEE ACHIEVEMENT AWARDS

Generally, if tangible personal property is received (other than cash, a gift certificate, or an equivalent item) as an award for length of service or safety achievement, its value may be excluded from the taxpayer's income.

> The Tax Cuts and Jobs Act adds a definition of "tangible personal property" that may be considered a deductible employee achievement award. It provides that tangible personal property shall not include cash, cash equivalents, gift cards, gift coupons or gift certificates (other than arrangements conferring only the right to select and receive tangible personal property from a limited array of such items preselected or preapproved by the employer), or vacations, meals, lodging, tickets to theater or sporting events, stocks, bonds, other securities, and other similar items.

The amount the taxpayer may exclude is limited to an employer's cost and **cannot be more than $1,600** ($400 for awards that are not qualified plan awards) for all such awards received during the year. The award must be part of a meaningful presentation, under conditions and circumstances that do not create a significant likelihood of it being disguised pay. This exclusion does not apply to the following awards:

- A length-of-service award for less than 5 years of service or if already received another length-of-service award during the previous 4 years.

- A safety achievement award for managers, administrators, clerical employees, or other professional employees or if more than 10% of eligible employees previously received safety achievement awards during the year.

> **EXAMPLE:** Ben Green received three employee achievement awards during the year: a nonqualified plan award of a watch valued at $250, two qualified plan awards of a stereo valued at $1,000, and a set of golf clubs valued at $500. Assuming that the requirements for qualified plan awards are otherwise satisfied, each award by itself would be excluded from income. However, because the $1,750 total value of the awards is more than $1,600, Ben must include $150 ($1,750 – $1,600) in his income.

MILITARY AND GOVERNMENT DISABILITY PENSIONS

SERVICE-CONNECTED DISABILITY

Taxpayers may exclude from income amounts received as a pension, annuity, or similar allowance for personal injury or sickness resulting from active service in one of the following government services:

- The armed forces of any country
- The National Oceanic and Atmospheric Administration
- The public health service
- The foreign service

CONDITIONS FOR EXCLUSION

Disability payments should <u>not</u> be **included in income** if <u>any</u> of the following conditions apply:

- The taxpayer is entitled to receive a disability payment before September 25, 1975.
- The taxpayer was a member of a listed government service or its reserve component or was under a binding written commitment to become a member on September 24, 1975.
- The taxpayer receives the disability payments for a combat-related injury or sickness that meets one of the following criteria:
  1. Results directly from armed conflict
  2. Takes place while engaged in extra-hazardous service
  3. Occurs under conditions simulating war, including training exercises such as maneuvers
  4. Is caused by an instrumentality of war
- The taxpayer would be entitled to receive disability compensation from the Department of Veterans Affairs (VA) upon the filing of an application. Exclusion under this condition is equal to the amount the taxpayer would be entitled to receive from the VA.

PENSION BASED ON YEARS OF SERVICE

Generally, if a taxpayer receives a disability pension based on years of service, the pension must be included in income. However, if the pension qualifies for exclusion for a service-connected disability as listed above, the part of the pension based on a percentage of disability should not be included as income. The rest of the pension should be included in income.

EDUCATION-RELATED BENEFITS

SCHOLARSHIPS AND FELLOWSHIPS

A candidate **for a degree** may exclude amounts received as a qualified scholarship or fellowship. A qualified scholarship or fellowship is any amount received that is for one of the following:

- Tuition and fees to enroll at or attend an educational institution
- Any fees, books, supplies, and equipment required for courses at the educational institution

Amounts used for **room and board do not qualify** for the exclusion.

A taxpayer must include in income the part of any scholarship or fellowship that represents payment for past, present, or future teaching, research, or other services. This applies even if all candidates for a degree must perform the services to receive the degree.

> **EXCEPTION:** A scholarship prize won in a contest is not a scholarship or fellowship if a taxpayer does not have to use the prize for educational purposes. Include these amounts as income on Form 1040, whether or not the taxpayer uses them for educational purposes.

TIP: Scholarships or fellowships are taxable income if the recipient is not seeking a degree.

EDUCATION SAVINGS BOND PROGRAM

Under the Education Savings Bond Program, a taxpayer may exclude all or part of the interest received on the redemption of qualified U.S. savings bonds during the year if the taxpayer uses that interest to pay for qualified higher educational expenses during the same year. Married taxpayers **must file jointly** to qualify for the exclusion.

- **Qualified U.S. savings bonds** – A qualified U.S. savings bond is a series EE bond issued after 1989 or a series I bond. The bond must be in the taxpayer's name (sole owner) or jointly held with a spouse. The **taxpayer must be at least 24 years old** before the bond's issue date. The issue date of a bond may be earlier than the date the taxpayer purchased the bond because the issue date assigned to a bond is the first day of the month in which it is purchased.
- **Qualified expenses** – Qualified higher educational expenses are tuition and fees required for a taxpayer and dependents (for whom is claimed as a dependent) to attend an eligible educational institution. Qualified expenses include any contribution made to a qualified tuition program or to a Coverdell education savings account.

Qualified expenses do not include expenses for **books, room and board,** or for courses involving **sports, games, or hobbies** that are not part of a degree or certificate-granting program.

- **Eligible educational institutions** – These institutions include most public, private, and nonprofit universities, colleges, and vocational schools that are accredited and are eligible to participate in student aid programs run by the Department of Education.
- **Reduction for certain benefits** – A taxpayer must reduce his qualified higher-educational expenses by all of the following tax-free benefits:
  1. The tax-free part of scholarships and fellowships
  2. Expenses used to figure the tax-free portion of distributions from a Coverdell ESA
  3. Expenses used to figure the tax-free part of distributions from a qualified tuition program

4. Any expense used for the American Opportunity and Lifetime Learning credits
5. Any tax-free payments (other than gifts or inheritances) received for educational expenses:
   A. Veterans' educational assistance benefits
   B. Qualified tuition reductions
   C. Employer-provided educational assistance

- **Amount excludable** – If the total proceeds (interest and principal) from the qualified U.S. savings bonds redeemed during the year are not more than the adjusted qualified higher education expenses for the year, the taxpayer may exclude all of the interest. If the proceeds are more than the expenses, the taxpayer may exclude only part of the interest. To determine the amount to exclude from income, divide the qualified expenses by the total bond proceeds. Multiply this percentage by the amount of bond interest to arrive at the amount excluded from income. The remainder of the interest is included in income.

- **Modified adjusted gross income limit** – The interest exclusion is phased-out at certain levels of modified adjusted gross income (MAGI).

Filing Status	2020	2021
MFJ	$123,550 – $153,550	$124,800 – $154,800
S, HH, or QW	$82,350 – $97,350	$83,200 – $98,200

EXAMPLE: In 2020, Robert cashes in his Series EE bonds to pay for his son's tuition at the University of Central Florida. The amount redeemed includes $2,000 principal and $400 interest. Robert is married, he files jointly with his spouse and has MAGI of $130,000.

Step 1 – Robert's MAGI is in the phase-out range but is below the upper end of the range. Determine the difference between his MAGI and the upper limit of the range. $153,550 – $130,000 MAGI = $23,550

Step 2 – Determine the relationship to the size of the phase-out range. Phase-out range $153,550 – $123,550 = $30,000. $23,550 ÷ $30,000 = .785

Step 3 – Multiply the interest by the applicable percentage to determine the exclusion. $400 interest × .785 = $314 interest exclusion

QUALIFIED EDUCATION EXPENSES

For purposes of the *Coverdell ESA* and *qualified tuition programs (QTP)*, qualified education expenses are the amounts paid for tuition, fees, books, supplies, and equipment required for enrollment or attendance at an eligible educational institution. They also include the reasonable costs of room and board for a designated beneficiary who is at least a half-time student. The **cost of room and board qualifies** only to the extent that it is not more than the greater of the following two amounts:

- The allowance for room and board, as determined by the eligible educational institution, that was included in the cost of attendance (for federal financial aid purposes) for a particular academic period and living arrangement of the student
- The actual amount charged if the student is residing in housing owned or operated by the eligible educational institution

Adjust qualified education expenses to take into account certain credits, such as the *American Opportunity credit* or *Lifetime Learning credit*, and any other tax-free benefits received to pay for expenses. If a designated beneficiary receives distributions from both a QTP and a Coverdell ESA in the same year, and the total of these distributions is more than the beneficiary's adjusted qualified higher education expenses, allocate the expenses between the distributions. For purposes of this allocation, disregard any qualified elementary and secondary education expenses.

> **The cost of room and board is a qualified education expense for ESAs and QTPs,** but is not a qualified expense for the education savings bond program, education credits, scholarships, or fellowships.

COVERDELL EDUCATION SAVINGS ACCOUNT (ESA)

A Coverdell ESA is a trust or custodial account created or organized in the United States only for paying the qualified education expenses of the designated beneficiary of the account. While there is **no tax deduction** for contributions, **earnings are tax-deferred.** Exclude distributions from a Coverdell ESA from income up to the amount of qualified education expenses for the year, adjusted for other benefits received. The expenses may be qualified education expenses or qualified elementary and secondary education expenses.

- The account must be a designated Coverdell ESA when the taxpayer created the account.
- Account documents must be in writing and must satisfy the following requirements:
  1. The trustee or custodian must be a bank or an entity approved by the IRS.
  2. The trustee or custodian may only accept contributions that meet the following conditions:
     A. The contribution is in cash
     B. The contribution is made before the beneficiary (other than a special needs beneficiary) reaches age 18
     C. **Contributions may not be more than $2,000** for the year (not including rollovers)
  3. The taxpayer cannot invest the money in the account in life insurance contracts.
  4. The taxpayer cannot combine the money in the account with other property except in a common trust fund or common investment fund.
     A. The account balance must be distributed within 30 days after the earlier of the following:
        i. The beneficiary reaches age 30 unless a special needs beneficiary
        ii. The beneficiary's death
- If modified adjusted gross income (MAGI) is between $95,000 and $110,000 (between $190,000 and $220,000 if filing a joint return), then the $2,000 contribution limit for each designated beneficiary is gradually reduced. If MAGI is $110,000 or more ($220,000 or more if filing a joint return), the taxpayer cannot contribute to anyone's Coverdell ESA.
- Calculate the reduced contribution amount by multiplying $2,000 by a fraction. The numerator (top number) is the MAGI minus $95,000 ($190,000 if filing a joint return). The denominator (bottom number) is $15,000 ($30,000 if filing a joint return). Subtract the result from $2,000. The taxpayer may contribute this amount for each beneficiary.

QUALIFIED TUITION PROGRAMS (QTP)

A qualified tuition program (also known as a ***529 plan***) is a program set up to allow the taxpayer to either prepay or contribute to an account established for paying a student's qualified education expenses at an eligible educational institution. A state, a state agency, an instrumentality of a state, or an eligible educational institution can establish and maintain a QTP.

- The part of a distribution representing the amount paid or contributed to a QTP is not included in income. This is a return of the investment in the program.
- Earnings accumulate tax free while in the account. The beneficiary generally does not include earnings distributed from a QTP in income if the total distribution is less than or equal to adjusted qualified education expenses. Income is reported to the recipient on Form 1099Q. The beneficiary is the recipient when

distributions are made either directly to the beneficiary or to an eligible educational institution for his benefit. Consequently, taxable distributions constitute income to the beneficiary when paid either directly to the beneficiary or to an eligible educational institution for his benefit. Otherwise, the account owner is the recipient.

- The designated beneficiary is generally the student (or future student) for whom the QTP is intended to provide benefits. The taxpayer **can change the designated beneficiary**.
- Contributions to a QTP on behalf of any beneficiary cannot be more than the amount necessary to provide for the qualified education expenses of the beneficiary.
- There are **no income restrictions** on individual contributors.

TIP: An ESA and a QTP are similar in that neither offers a tax deduction for contributions to the plan, earnings accumulate free of tax until withdrawn, and withdrawals are excluded from income if used for qualified education expenses. A QTP is different from an ESA in the following ways: the beneficiary of a QTP can be any age and can even change, QTP does not have age-based distribution requirements, contributions can be far more than allowed in an ESA, and there are no income restrictions.

The Tax Cuts and Jobs Act consolidates and modifies the education savings rules for distributions made after December 31, 2017. The act modifies Section 529 plans to allow such plans to distribute **not more than $10,000** in expenses for tuition incurred during the taxable year in connection with the enrollment or attendance of the designated beneficiary at a **public, private or religious elementary or secondary school**. The limitation applies on a per-student basis, rather than a per-account basis. Any excess distributions (over $10,000) received would be treated as a taxable distribution.

The Secure Act of 2019 expands the definition of qualified higher education expenses for 529 plans, allowing costs associated with **registered apprenticeships** and up to **$10,000 of principal or interest on qualified student loan repayments** for the beneficiary (and an additional $10,000 for each of the beneficiary's siblings).

For distributions made from qualified tuition programs (QTPs), Section 529 plans can make tax-free distributions of **not more than $10,000 per taxable year, per student,** for:

- Qualified higher education expenses.
- Tuition incurred during the taxable year in connection with the enrollment or attendance of the designated beneficiary at a public, private or religious elementary or secondary school (i.e. kindergarten through grade 12).
- Certain expenses required for a designated beneficiary's participation in certain apprenticeship programs.
- Up to $10,000 paid as principal or interest on a qualified student loan of the designated beneficiary or the designated beneficiary's sibling (reduced by the amount of distributions so treated for all prior taxable years).

TIP: Amounts treated as a qualified higher education expense with respect to the loans of a sibling of the designated beneficiary shall be taken into account with respect to such sibling and not with respect to such designated beneficiary. The $10,000 cap on student loan repayments treated as qualified higher education expenses is a lifetime limit per beneficiary (reduced by the amount of distributions so treated for all prior taxable years).

TIP: A taxpayer can withdraw any amount from their 529 plan, but only qualified distributions are tax-free.

529 ABLE

An *Achieving a Better Life Experience (ABLE)* account (also known as a *529 ABLE* or *529A* account) provides for a tax-favored savings program intended to benefit **disabled** individuals. Similar to a traditional 529 plan, a qualified ABLE program is a program established and maintained by a State or agency or instrumentality thereof.

A designated beneficiary must be an eligible individual. An eligible individual is an individual <u>either</u>:

- For whom a disability certification has been filed with the Secretary for the taxable year, or
- Who is entitled to Social Security Disability Insurance benefits or SSI benefits based on blindness or disability, and such blindness or disability occurred before the individual attained age 26.

A disability certification is made by the eligible individual or the parent or guardian, indicating that the individual has a medically determinable physical or mental impairment, which results in marked and severe functional limitations, and which can be expected to result in death or which has lasted or can be expected to last for a continuous period of not less than 12 months, or is blind. Such blindness or disability must have occurred before the date the individual attained age 26. Such certification must include a copy of the diagnosis of the individual's impairment and be signed by a licensed physician.

Amounts in an ABLE account may be rolled over without income tax liability to another ABLE account for the same beneficiary or another ABLE account for the designated beneficiary's brother, sister, stepbrother or stepsister who is also an eligible individual. Once an ABLE account has been established by a designated beneficiary, no account subsequently established by such beneficiary shall be treated as an ABLE account.

Contributions to an ABLE account must be made in cash and are not deductible for Federal income tax purposes. An ABLE account must provide that it may not receive aggregate contributions during a taxable year in excess of the annual gift tax exclusion (**$15,000** for 2020), except in the case of a rollover contribution from another ABLE account. Amounts in an ABLE account accumulate on a tax-deferred basis.

A contribution to an ABLE account is treated as a completed gift of a present interest to the designated beneficiary of the account. Such contributions qualify for the per-donee annual gift tax exclusion ($15,000 for 2020) and, to the extent of such exclusion, are exempt from the generation-skipping transfer (GST) tax. A distribution from an ABLE account generally is not subject to gift tax or GST tax.

Distributions from an ABLE account are generally includible in the distributee's income to the extent consisting of earnings on the account. Distributions from an ABLE account are excludable from income to the extent that the total distribution does not exceed the qualified disability expenses of the designated beneficiary during the taxable year. If a distribution exceeds the qualified disability expenses of the designated beneficiary, a pro-rata portion of the distribution is excludable from income. The portion of any distribution that is includible in income is subject to an additional 10% tax unless the distribution is made after the death of the beneficiary.

The earnings on distributions from an ABLE account are excluded from income only to the extent total distributions do not exceed the qualified disability expenses of the designated beneficiary. For this purpose, qualified disability expenses are any expenses related to the eligible individual's blindness or disability which are made for the benefit of the designated beneficiary. Such expenses include the following expenses: education, housing, transportation, employment training and support, assistive technology and personal support services, health, prevention and wellness, financial management and administrative services, legal fees, expenses for oversight and monitoring, funeral and burial expenses, and other expenses, which are approved by the Secretary under regulations and consistent with the purposes of section 529A.

> **TCJA:** Effective for taxable years beginning after the date of enactment (December 22, 2017):
>
> - The act allows a designated beneficiary of an ABLE account to claim the saver's credit for contributions made to an ABLE account.
> - Under the act, the limitation is increased with respect to contributions made by the designated beneficiary of the ABLE account. After the overall limitation on contributions (the per-donee annual gift tax exclusion) is reached, an ABLE account's **designated beneficiary may contribute an additional amount**, up to the <u>lesser</u> of, the Federal poverty line for a one-person household ($12,490 in 2020) or the individual's compensation for the taxable year.
> - Effective for distributions after the date of enactment, the act allows for amounts from qualified tuition programs (529 accounts) to be rolled over to a qualified ABLE account without penalty, provided that the ABLE account is owned by the designated beneficiary of that 529 account or a member of such designated beneficiary's family. Such rolled-over amounts count towards the overall limitation on amounts that can be contributed to an ABLE account within a taxable year. Any amount rolled over that is in excess of this limitation shall be includible in the gross income of the distributee.

PAYMENTS FOR SICKNESS, INJURY, OR DEATH

WORKERS' COMPENSATION

An amount received as workers' compensation for an occupational sickness or injury is **fully exempt from tax** if paid under a workers' compensation act or similar statute. The exemption also applies to the victim's survivors. The exemption does not apply to retirement plan benefits received based on age, length of service, or prior contributions to the plan, even if an occupational sickness or injury caused retirement. If a taxpayer returns to work after qualifying for workers' compensation, salary payments received for performing light duties are taxable as wages.

COMPENSATION FOR SICKNESS OR INJURY

Many other amounts taxpayers receive as compensation for sickness or injury are <u>not</u> **taxable**. These include the following amounts:

- Compensatory (not punitive) damages received from a lawsuit for physical injury or physical sickness, whether paid in a lump sum or in periodic payments. Damages for *emotional distress* on account of physical injuries or sickness are excludable by IRC § 104(a)(2). However, costs incurred to treat emotional distress, even those due to physical injury, are taxable if they were previously deducted as a medical expense in a prior year.

   TIP: The term emotional distress includes physical symptoms, such as insomnia, headaches, and stomach disorders, which may result from emotional distress. Emotional distress itself is <u>not</u> considered a physical injury or physical sickness.

- Benefits under an accident or health insurance policy on which either a taxpayer paid the premiums, or the taxpayer's employer paid the premiums and those premiums were included in income.
- Disability benefits received for loss of income or earning capacity because of injuries under a no-fault car insurance policy.
- Compensation for permanent loss (or loss of use) of a part or function of the body, or for permanent disfigurement. This compensation must be based only on the injury and not on the period of absence from work. These benefits are not taxable, even if an employer pays for the accident and health plan that provides these benefits.

- Reimbursement for medical care is generally not taxable. However, it may reduce the medical expense deduction.

LIFE INSURANCE PROCEEDS

Life insurance proceeds paid because of the death of the insured person are not **taxable** unless the taxpayer sold the policy to another for a price (***Viatical Settlement***). This is true even if the taxpayer received proceeds under an accident or health insurance policy or an endowment contract.

- If the taxpayer receives death benefits paid in a **lump sum** or other than at regular intervals, include in income only the benefits that are more than the amount payable at the time of the death.
- If the taxpayer receives payment of life insurance proceeds in installments, exclude part of each installment from income. To determine the excluded part, divide the amount held by the insurance company (generally the total lump sum payable at the death of the insured person) by the number of installments to be paid. Include anything more than this excluded part in income as interest.
    1. If the spouse of the taxpayer died before October 23, 1986, and the taxpayer receives payment in installments of insurance proceeds because of the death, the taxpayer may exclude up to $1,000 per year of the interest included in the installments, even if the taxpayer remarries.
- **Endowment contract proceeds** – An endowment contract is a policy under which the taxpayer receives a specified amount of money on a certain date. If the taxpayer dies before that date, the money goes to the designated beneficiary. Endowment proceeds paid in a lump sum at maturity are taxable only if the proceeds are more than the cost of the policy. To determine the cost, take any amount previously received under the contract (and excluded from income) and subtract that from the total premiums (or other consideration) paid for the contract. Include the part of the lump sum payment that is more than the cost in income.
- **Accelerated death benefits** – Exclude certain amounts paid as accelerated death benefits under a life insurance contract or viatical settlement before the insured's death if the insured is terminally or chronically ill.
    1. **Exclusion for terminal illness** – Accelerated death benefits are fully excludable if the insured is a terminally ill individual, certified by a physician as having an illness or condition reasonably expected to result in death within 24 months from the date of the certification.
    2. **Exclusion for chronic illness** – If the insured is a chronically ill individual, who is not terminally ill, accelerated death benefits paid based on costs incurred for qualified long-term care services are fully excludable. Accelerated death benefits paid on a ***per diem*** or other periodic basis are excludable up to a limit.
    3. **Viatical settlement** – This is the sale or assignment of any part of the death benefit under a life insurance contract to a ***viatical settlement provider*** in the business of buying insurance contracts on the lives of insured individuals who are terminally or chronically ill.

FOREIGN EARNED INCOME EXCLUSION AND FOREIGN HOUSING EXCLUSION

A U.S. citizen or resident alien of the United States who lives abroad must pay taxes on worldwide income. However, a taxpayer may qualify to exclude some or all of their foreign earnings from income. For the tax year 2020, the foreign earned income exclusion cannot be more than the smaller of the following:

- **$107,600** (if MFJ $107,600 for each spouse if both spouses qualify and meet the requirements)
- Foreign earned income for the tax year minus the amount of foreign housing exclusion or housing deduction

The taxpayer may exclude or deduct certain foreign housing amounts, limited to the lesser of the foreign housing costs paid for with employer-provided amounts or the amount of foreign earned income. For purposes of determining the foreign housing exclusion or deduction, a taxpayer cannot consider housing expenses that exceed a certain limit. The limit on housing expenses is generally **30%** of the maximum foreign earned income exclusion, but it may vary depending upon the location in which you incur housing expenses.

TIP: All taxpayers use *Form 2555* to claim the foreign earned income exclusion. Starting with the 2019 tax year, Form 2555-EZ can no longer be used.

- **Married couples** – If both the taxpayer and spouse qualify for the foreign earned income exclusion, figure the amount of the exclusion separately for each using Part VII of separate Forms 2555.

To claim the *foreign earned income exclusion* and the *foreign housing exclusion* or the *foreign housing deduction* (deduction only available if the taxpayer is self-employed), a taxpayer **must meet all three of the following requirements:**

- The *tax home* must be in a foreign country. A tax home is a place where a taxpayer permanently or indefinitely engages to work as an employee or self-employed individual. The tax home is not in a foreign country for any period in which the taxpayer's abode is in the United States. An abode is one's home, habitation, residence, domicile, or place of dwelling.
- The taxpayer **must have foreign earned income.**
- The taxpayer must meet either the *Bona Fide Residence Test* or *Physical Presence Test*.

BONA FIDE RESIDENCE TEST

A taxpayer does not automatically acquire bona fide resident status merely by living in a foreign country for one year. The length of stay and the nature of the job are additional factors that determine whether a taxpayer meets the test. A taxpayer who travels to a foreign country to work on a particular construction job for a specified period-of-time ordinarily is not a bona fide resident of that country even if working there for more than one tax year.

> **EXAMPLE:** You could have your domicile in Cleveland, Ohio, and a bona fide residence in Edinburgh, Scotland, if you intend to return eventually to Cleveland. The fact that you go to Scotland does not automatically make Scotland your bona fide residence. If you go there as a tourist, or on a short business trip, and return to the United States, you haven't established bona fide residence in Scotland. But if you go to Scotland to work for an indefinite or extended period and you set up permanent quarters there for yourself and your family, you probably have established a bona fide residence in a foreign country, even though you intend to return eventually to the United States. You are clearly not a resident of Scotland in the first instance. However, in the second, you are a resident because your stay in Scotland appears to be permanent.

To be a bona fide resident a taxpayer must be:

- A U.S. citizen who is a bona fide resident of a foreign country or countries for an **uninterrupted period that includes an entire tax year**, or
- A U.S. resident alien who is a citizen or national of a country with which the United States has an income tax treaty in effect and who is a bona fide resident of a foreign country or countries for an uninterrupted period that includes an entire tax year.

> **EXAMPLE 1:** You arrived with your family in Lisbon, Portugal, on November 1, 2019. Your assignment is indefinite, and you intend to live there with your family until your company sends you to a new post. You immediately established residence there. You spent April of 2020 at a business conference in the United States. Your family stayed in Lisbon. Immediately following the conference, you returned to Lisbon and continued living there. On January 1, 2021, you completed an uninterrupted period of residence for a full tax year (2020), and you meet the bona fide residence test.

EXAMPLE 2: Assume the same facts, except that you transferred back to the United States on December 13, 2020. You would not meet the bona fide residence test because your bona fide residence in the foreign country, although it lasted more than a year, didn't include a full tax year. You may, however, qualify for the foreign earned income exclusion or the housing exclusion or deduction under the physical presence test.

PHYSICAL PRESENCE TEST

A U.S. citizen or a U.S. resident alien physically present in a foreign country or countries for **at least 330 full days during any period of 12 consecutive months.** The physical presence test is based only on how long the taxpayer is in a foreign country. This test does not depend on the kind of residence established, intentions about returning, or the nature and purpose of the stay abroad.

EXAMPLE 1: You are a construction worker who works on and off in a foreign country over a 20-month period. You might pick up the 330 full days in a 12-month period only during the middle months of the time you work in the foreign country because the first few and last few months of the 20-month period are broken up by long visits to the United States.

EXAMPLE 2: You work in New Zealand for a 20-month period from January 1, 2019, through August 31, 2020, except that you spend 28 days in February 2019 and 28 days in February 2020 on vacation in the United States. You are present in New Zealand for at least 330 full days during each of the following two 12-month periods: January 1, 2019 – December 31, 2019 and September 1, 2019 – August 31, 2020. By overlapping the 12-month periods in this way, you meet the physical presence test for the whole 20-month period.

TIP: There is a difference between the *Physical Presence Test* and the *Substantial Presence Test* used to determine U.S. residency status. Aside from the number of days required, the former measures time in a foreign country while the latter measures time in the United States.

COVID-19 UPDATE: Due to the global health emergency caused by COVID-19, the IRS has provided relief related to the time requirement necessary to meet either the bona fide residence test or physical presence test for purposes of claiming the foreign earned income exclusion. A taxpayer may be treated as meeting these tests if he can establish a reasonable expectation that the tests would be met if it had not been for the COVID-19 emergency. See Revenue Procedure 2020-27.

LESSON 5

Adjustments to Income

HEALTH SAVINGS ACCOUNTS (HSA)

A taxpayer establishes a *health savings account (HSA)* with a qualified trustee to pay or reimburse certain medical expenses. The maximum contribution to an HSA depends on the type of *high deductible health plan (HDHP)* coverage, age, the date the taxpayer became an eligible individual, and the date a taxpayer ceases to be an *eligible individual*. The taxpayer has until April 15, 2021, to make contributions for 2020.

For 2020, taxpayers who have **self-only** HDHP coverage can contribute up to **$3,550**. For **family** HDHP coverage, the maximum contribution is up to **$7,100**. An additional **$1,000 catch-up contribution** is available if age 55 or older.

The benefits of an HSA are as follows:

- The taxpayer receives a tax deduction for contributions that he or someone other than an employer made to the HSA even if not itemizing deductions on Form 1040.
- A taxpayer may exclude employer contributions to an HSA from gross income.
- The contributions remain in the HSA account from year to year until used.
- The interest or other earnings on the assets in the account accumulate tax-free.
- Distributions may be tax-free if used to pay for *qualified medical expenses* (costs that would generally qualify for the medical and dental expenses deduction). However, the **additional tax** on distributions <u>not</u> used for qualified medical expenses is **20%** <u>unless</u> made after the date the taxpayer reaches age 65, is disabled, or deceased.
- An HSA is "portable" so it stays with the taxpayer when changing employers or leaving the workforce.

To qualify for an HSA, an individual must meet all the following requirements:

- Must be covered under a high deductible health plan (HDHP) on the first day of the month:
  - Under the last-month rule, individuals are eligible for the entire year if covered on the first day of the last month of the tax year (December 1 for most taxpayers).
- Must not have other health coverage.
- Must not be enrolled in Medicare.
- Must not be claimed as a dependent on someone else's tax return.

A taxpayer that meets these requirements is an eligible individual even if a spouse has non-HDHP family coverage, provided the spouse's coverage does not cover the taxpayer.

An HDHP has the following features:

- A higher annual deductible than typical health plans.
- A maximum limit on the sum of the annual deductible and out-of-pocket medical expenses that the taxpayer must pay for covered expenses. Out-of-pocket expenses include copayments and other amounts but do <u>not</u> include premiums.

HDHP Maximums and Minimums - 2020		
	Self-only Coverage	Family Coverage
Maximum contribution*	$3,550	$7,100
Minimum deductible	$1,400	$2,800
Maximum out-of-pocket expenses	$6,900	$13,800
*An additional $1,000 catch-up contribution is available if age 55 or older.		

Form 8889 Health Savings Accounts (HSAs) is used to report:

- HSA Contributions and Deduction
- HSA Distributions

MOVING EXPENSES

Prior law permitted an above-the-line deduction for moving expenses paid or incurred during the taxable year in connection with the commencement of work by the taxpayer as an employee or as a self-employed individual at a new principal place of work. Such expenses were deductible only if the move met certain conditions related to distance from the taxpayer's previous residence and the taxpayer's status as a full-time employee in the new location.

> The TCJA **suspends the deduction for moving expenses** (except for members of the Armed Forces) for taxable years 2018 through 2025.

Special rules apply in the case of a member of the Armed Forces of the United States. In the case of any such individual (or their spouse or dependents) who is on active duty, who moves pursuant to a military order and incident to a permanent change of station, the limitations related to distance from the taxpayer's previous residence and status as a full-time employee in the new location do not apply.

> The TCJA also **repeals the exclusion of qualified moving expense reimbursements** from gross income and wages (except for members of the Armed Forces) for taxable years beginning after December 31, 2017, and before January 1, 2026. All moving expenses paid or reimbursed for taxable years 2018 through 2025, will be taxable to the employee (except for members of the Armed Forces) and subject to tax withholding.

> **EXCEPTION:** The TCJA retains the deduction for moving expenses and the rules providing for exclusions of amounts attributable to in-kind moving and storage expenses (and reimbursements or allowances for these expenses) for **members of the Armed Forces** (or their spouse or dependents) on active duty that move pursuant to a military order and incident to a permanent change of station.

DEDUCTIBLE MOVING EXPENSES FOR MEMBERS OF THE ARMED FORCES

Members of the armed forces may deduct the reasonable expenses of the following:

- Moving household goods and personal effects, including the following:
  1. The cost of packing, crating and transporting household goods and personal effects.
  2. Storing and insuring household goods and personal effects within any period of 30 consecutive days after moving the items from the former home (includes in-transit or foreign-move storage).

Deductible costs also include the cost of moving household goods and personal effects from a place other than a former home. The deduction is limited to the amount it would have cost to move them from the former home.

> **EXAMPLE:** Paul Brown has been stationed in North Carolina for the last four years. Because he has been renting a small apartment, he stored some furniture at his parents' home in Georgia. Paul received a permanent change in duty station to Washington, DC. It cost him $900 to move the furniture from his North Carolina apartment to Washington and $3,000 to move the stored furniture from Georgia to Washington. It

> would have cost $1,800 to ship the stored furniture from North Carolina to Washington. He can deduct only $1,800 of the $3,000 he paid. The amount he can deduct for moving his furniture is $2,700 ($900 + $1,800).

- Traveling to a new home, consisting of:

   1. Transportation and lodging for the taxpayer and household members. This includes expenses for the day of arrival. There is no deduction for meals.

   2. If traveling by car, a taxpayer may deduct actual expenses such as gasoline or oil if he keeps an accurate record of each expense. There is no deduction for certain automobile expenses such as general repairs, general maintenance, insurance, or depreciation. An alternative is to use the 2020 standard mileage rate of **17 cents per mile** driven for moving. Taxpayers can deduct parking fees and tolls regardless of the method used.

   Members of a household don't have to travel together or at the same time. However, a taxpayer can only deduct expenses for one trip per person.

> **EXAMPLE:** In February 2020, Josh and Robyn moved from Nebraska, where Robyn was stationed, to her new duty station in Washington, DC. Josh drove the family car to Washington, a trip of 1,000 miles. His expenses were $170 for mileage (1,000 x 17 cents a mile) plus $40 for tolls and $150 for lodging, for a total of $360. One week later, Robyn flew to Washington. Her only expense was her $400 plane ticket. Their deduction is $760 (Josh's $360 + Robyn's $400).

NONDEDUCTIBLE EXPENSES

A taxpayer cannot deduct the following items as moving expenses:

- Meals while traveling
- Any part of the purchase price of a new home
- Car tags
- Driver's license
- Expenses of buying or selling a home (including closing costs, mortgage fees, and points)
- Expenses of entering into or breaking a lease
- Home improvements to help sell a home
- Loss on the sale of a home
- Losses from disposing of memberships in clubs
- Mortgage penalties
- Pre-move house hunting expenses
- Real estate taxes
- Refitting of carpet and draperies
- Return trips to a former residence
- Security deposits (including any given up due to the move)
- Storage charges except those incurred in transit and for foreign moves

ADJUSTMENTS IF SELF-EMPLOYED

DEDUCTIBLE PART OF SELF-EMPLOYMENT TAX

The IRS considers a taxpayer that carries on a trade or business as a sole proprietor or an independent contractor to be self-employed. A partner's distributive share of ordinary income or loss is also self-employment income. A self-employed taxpayer includes Schedule SE with their individual income tax return to pay self-employment tax on net earnings from self-employment.

> A self-employed taxpayer may **deduct 50% of self-employment taxes** reported on Schedule SE as an adjustment to gross income on Form 1040, Schedule 1.

SELF-EMPLOYED HEALTH INSURANCE

A self-employed taxpayer may adjust income on his personal income tax return (using Form 1040, Schedule 1) for the amount of medical, dental, and qualified long-term care insurance premiums (limited) that he pays on behalf of himself, his spouse, his dependents, and his child who was under age 27 at the end of the year, even if the child was not a dependent.

> For the purposes of this adjustment (and no others) a taxpayer is considered self-employed if he receives **wages from an S corporation** in which he is <u>more</u> than a **2% shareholder.**

The adjustment cannot be more than the earned income from the business. The taxpayer must establish the plan under the business. A taxpayer establishes a plan under a business if the policy is in the name of the following:

- A self-employed individual who files Schedule C, or his trade or business
- A partnership or S corporation
- Partners, if the partnership reimburses the partner for premiums paid, and the amount of the reimbursement is included in the partner's income on the K-1 as a guaranteed payment
- More than 2% shareholders, if S corporation reimburses them for the premiums paid, and the amount of the reimbursement is included in the shareholder's wages on Form W-2

A taxpayer cannot deduct payments for medical insurance for any month in which he was eligible to participate in a health plan subsidized by his employer, his spouse's employer, or an employer of his dependent or child under age 27 at the end of the year.

SELF-EMPLOYED RETIREMENT PLAN CONTRIBUTIONS

Retirement plans for self-employed people were formerly referred to as "***Keogh plans***" after the law that first allowed unincorporated businesses to sponsor retirement plans. Since the law no longer distinguishes between corporate and other plan sponsors, the term is seldom used. A Keogh plan is nothing more than a *qualified plan* for the self-employed. By in large, the SEP and SIMPLE options are more popular for self-employed taxpayers due to the lower administrative costs (no Form 5500, discrimination testing, etc.), and similar contribution and benefit limits.

KEOGH PLANS

A *qualified plan* is a retirement plan that offers a tax-favored way to save for retirement. Employers may deduct contributions made to the plan for employees. Earnings on these contributions are generally tax-free until distributed at retirement. Profit-sharing, money purchase, and defined benefit plans are qualified plans. A 401(k) plan is also a qualified plan. The qualified plan rules are more complex than the SEP plan and SIMPLE plan rules.

However, there are advantages to qualified plans, such as increased flexibility in designing plans and increased contribution and deduction limits in some cases. There are two basic kinds of qualified plans—*defined contribution* plans and *defined benefit* plans—and different rules apply to each. An employer can have more than one qualified plan, but contributions to all plans must not total more than the overall limits.

One difference is that with a Keogh the business owner will **use net earnings from self-employment to determine contributions** instead of compensation. A **defined contribution** plan's annual contributions and other additions (excluding earnings) to the account of a participant can't exceed the lesser of the following amounts:

- 100% of the participant's compensation (net earnings from self-employment for the owner's contribution)
- $57,000 for 2020 ($58,000 for 2021)

SEP IRA

A SEP plan allows employers to contribute to traditional IRAs (SEP-IRAs) set up for employees. A business of any size, even self-employed, can establish a SEP.

The SEP rules permit an employer to contribute a limited amount of money each year to each employee's SEP-IRA. A self-employed taxpayer can contribute to a SEP-IRA established on his own behalf. Contributions must be in the form of **money** (cash, check, or money order), not **property**.

> Contributions made by the employer for 2020 to a common-law employee's **SEP-IRA** cannot exceed the lower of **25% of the employee's compensation** or **$57,000**. Compensation generally does not include the employer's contributions to the SEP.

SIMPLE IRA

Generally, an employer with **100 or fewer** employees making at least $5,000 in compensation last year can set up a *Savings Incentive Match Plan for Employees (SIMPLE)*. The employer cannot maintain another qualified plan unless the other plan is for collective bargaining (union) employees. Under a **SIMPLE** plan, **employees** can choose to make salary reduction contributions up to **$13,500** in 2020 (and 2021) rather than receiving these amounts as part of their regular pay. In addition, the **employer** will contribute either up to **3% matching** or **2% non-elective** contributions.

> In order to avoid additional tax, the participant must maintain a SIMPLE IRA for at least two years from the date of initial contribution. If a withdrawal, rollover distribution, or transfer from a SIMPLE IRA does not satisfy the 2-year rule and is otherwise an early distribution, the additional tax imposed because of the early distribution increases from 10% to 25% of the amount distributed.

The two types of SIMPLE plans are the SIMPLE IRA plan and the SIMPLE 401(k) plan. A SIMPLE plan cannot be a Roth IRA. Contribution methods and limits of a SIMPLE IRA and SIMPLE 401(k) are the same. Unlike the IRA version, the SIMPLE 401(k) is a qualified plan and is subject to those rules (under certain conditions, a SIMPLE 401(k) plan is not subject to the nondiscrimination and top-heavy rules).

COMPENSATION

Compensation for plan allocations is the pay a participant receives from the employer for personal services for a year. Compensation includes all of the following payments:

- Wages and salaries
- Fees for professional services

- Other amounts received (cash or noncash) for personal services actually rendered by an employee, including, but not limited to commissions, tips, fringe benefits, and bonuses

COMPENSATION FOR THE SELF-EMPLOYED

Those who are self-employed must make a special computation to determine contributions for their own accounts. The deduction for contributions to the plan and net earnings **depend on each other**. For this reason, a self-employed individual determines the deduction for contributions to his account indirectly by reducing the contribution rate called for in the plan. The formula to determine the contribution percentage is *rate÷(1+rate).*

> When figuring the deduction made to one's own SEP-IRA, compensation is **net earnings from self-employment** (provided that personal services are a material income-producing factor), reduced by the total of:
>
> - The deduction for the deductible part of self-employment tax (7.65%)
> - The deduction for contributions to his own account

EXAMPLE: Peter is a sole proprietor with $100,000 net income on his Schedule C. His deduction for self-employment tax on Form 1040 is $7,650. Peter subtracts the deductible part of self-employment tax, arriving at $92,350. The contribution rate for his SEP plan for employees is 25%. Peter needs to adjust the contribution percentage for his own contribution .25 ÷ 1.25 =.20. His SEP contribution is $18,470 ($92,350 × 20%).

Compensation, after deducting his own contribution, is $73,880 ($92,350 – $18,470).

There is a simple way to quickly verify the accuracy of his contribution/deduction amount:

	$100,000	Schedule C net profit
–	$7,650	Deductible part of self-employment tax
–	$18,470	Deduction for contributions to his own SEP
=	$73,880	Compensation subject to plan's **full** rate
×	25%	Plan's full rate
=	$18,470	Deduction for contributions to his own SEP

Net earnings from self-employment is gross income from a trade or business (provided personal services are a material income-producing factor) <u>minus</u> allowable business deductions. Allowable deductions include contributions for common-law employees and the deduction allowed for the deductible part of self-employment tax. A sole proprietor or partner cannot deduct contributions made to a retirement plan for himself as a business expense, only those made for his common-law employees. Sole proprietors and partners deduct contributions on Form 1040.

Net earnings from self-employment does not include items excluded from gross income (or their related deductions) other than foreign earned income and foreign housing cost amounts.

Net earnings include a partner's distributive share of partnership income or loss (other than separately stated items, such as capital gains and losses). It doesn't include income passed through to shareholders of S corporations. Guaranteed payments to limited partners are net earnings from self-employment if they are paid for services to or for the partnership. Distributions of other income or loss to limited partners aren't net earnings from self-employment.

ALIMONY

Alimony is a payment to (or for) a spouse or former spouse under a divorce or separation instrument. It does not include a voluntary payment made by the taxpayer that is not under a divorce or separation instrument. Payments to a former spouse that meet the criteria of *alimony* under a divorce or separate maintenance agreement, may or may not qualify as income or deduction items.

Not all payments under a divorce or separation instrument are alimony. Alimony does not include the following items:

- Child support
- Noncash property settlements
- Payments that are a spouse's part of community income
- Payments to maintain the payer's property
- Use of the payer's property

> Mortgage payments on a **house owned by the taxpayer** do not qualify as alimony, even if the ex-spouse lives there. If the mortgage payments are for a house **totally owned by the ex-spouse** 100% could be alimony.

A payment to or for a spouse under a divorce or separation instrument is alimony if the spouses do not file a joint return with each other and all the following requirements are met:

- The payment is in cash (checks and money orders)
- The instrument cannot designate the payment as not alimony
- The spouses are not members of the same household at the time the taxpayer makes the payments
- There is no liability to make any payment (cash or property) after the death of the recipient spouse
- The payment is not treated as child support

Cash payments, checks, or money orders to a third party on behalf of a spouse under the terms of a divorce or separation instrument can be alimony if they otherwise qualify. These include payments for a spouse's medical expenses, housing costs (rent, utilities, etc.), premiums for insurance on your life to the extent your spouse owns the policy, taxes, tuition, etc. The payments are treated as received by the spouse and then paid to the third party. In addition, cash payments made to a third party at the written request of a taxpayer's spouse may qualify as alimony if they meet all of the following requirements:

- The payments are in lieu of payments of alimony directly to the spouse
- The written request states that both spouses intend to treat the payments as alimony
- The taxpayer receives the written request from a spouse before filing the return

If a divorce or separation instrument requires a taxpayer to pay mortgage payments for a home jointly owned with a spouse or former spouse, **one-half of the payments are alimony.**

The deductibility of alimony payments will depend on when the divorce or separation instrument was **executed** or **modified**.

AGREEMENTS EXECUTED AFTER 2018

Under the Tax Cuts and Jobs Act, the payment of alimony and separate maintenance under a divorce or separate maintenance agreement (or modifications to prior agreements that account for the new TCJA provision) **executed after December 31, 2018**, is **no longer deductible** by the payor spouse and **no longer includible** in income by the payee spouse.

The intent of the provision is to follow the rule of the United States Supreme Court's holding in *Gould v. Gould 245 U.S. 151 (1917)*, in which the Court held that such payments are <u>not</u> income to the recipient. Income used for alimony payments is taxed at the rates applicable to the payor spouse rather than the recipient spouse.

Under the provision, any divorce or separation instrument executed <u>after</u> December 31, 2018, including the modification of a prior instrument that expressly provides that the amendments made by this section apply to such modification, alimony and separate maintenance payments are not deductible by the payor spouse. The provision also repeals Code provisions that specify that alimony and separate maintenance payments are included in income. Effectively, payments of alimony under this provision will be handled in the same manner as child support, not deductible and not includible in income.

AGREEMENTS EXECUTED IN 2018 OR EARLIER

Under prior rules, alimony is **deductible** by the payor and **includible** in the recipient's income for a divorce or separation instrument **executed <u>on or before</u> December 31, 2018**, even when payments are made <u>after</u> 2018.

If a prior year agreement is **modified <u>after</u> December 31, 2018**, the tax treatment will follow the old rules <u>unless</u> the modification **expressly states** the repeal of the deduction for alimony payments applies to the modification or if the agreement is changed to **expressly provide** that alimony received is not included in income, then the tax treatment will follow the new rules. If the agreement follows the old rules, alimony is deductible by the payor and includible in the recipient's income. If the agreement follows the new rules, alimony is not deductible by the payor and not includible in the recipient's income.

RECAPTURE RULE

The recapture provision prevents a taxpayer from disguising nondeductible property settlements as deductible alimony. If alimony payments decrease or terminate during the first three calendar years, the taxpayer may have to include in the third year part of the alimony payments previously deducted from income as alimony received on Form 1040. The receiving spouse can deduct part of the alimony payments he previously included in income as an adjustment to gross income. A taxpayer is subject to the recapture rule in the third year if one of the following conditions exists:

- Alimony paid in the third year (Y_3) decreases by more than $15,000 from the second year (Y_2)
- The average alimony paid in Y_2 and Y_3 decreases by more than $15,000 from Y_1

Calculate recapture in each of the first two years:	
Recapture amount for second year:	$R_2 = (Y_2 - Y_3) - \$15,000$
Recapture amount for first year:	$R_1 = Y_1 - (Y_2 + Y_3 - R_2) \div 2 - \$15,000$

The calculation for a decrease in alimony does not include the following amounts:

- Payments made under a temporary support order
- Payments required over a period of at least three calendar years that vary because they are a percentage of income from a business or property, or from compensation for employment
- Payments that decrease because of the death of either spouse or the remarriage of the spouse receiving the payments before the end of the third year

TIP: This rule only applies to divorces executed on or before December 31, 2018. The last year to recapture alimony for a 2018 divorce is 2020.

CHILD SUPPORT

A payment that is *specifically designated as child support* or treated as specifically designated as child support under a divorce or separation instrument is <u>not</u> **alimony**.

> Child support payments are <u>not</u> **deductible** by the payer and are <u>not</u> **taxable** to the recipient.

The IRS will treat a payment as child support to the extent that the payment declines under either of the following conditions:

- On the happening of a contingency relating to a child, such as becoming employed, dying, leaving the household, leaving school, married, or reaching a specified age or income level
- At a time that can be clearly associated with the contingency

> **EXAMPLE:** Mike and Judy are divorced in May of 2018. Mike is ordered to pay child support for their 16-year old son of $300 per month, as well as alimony of $1,000 per month. The alimony will reduce to zero when their son reaches age 18. The alimony is treated as child support because it reduces based on an age-related event pertaining to the child.

INDIVIDUAL RETIREMENT ARRANGEMENTS (IRA)

IRA CONTRIBUTION DEADLINE

A taxpayer can make contributions to traditional IRAs and Roth IRAs at any time during the year or by the due date for filing the return for that year, not including extensions. For most taxpayers, this is April 15.

> **EXAMPLE:** Jim makes a contribution to his IRA on February 3, 2021. Jim can apply his contribution to 2020 <u>or</u> 2021. He can apply the contribution to the 2020 tax year since it is made before the due date of his 2020 tax return. He can apply the contribution to 2021, the actual year of deposit.

A taxpayer can withdraw contributions before the due date of the return, including extensions. To do so, the taxpayer must not take a deduction for the contribution and must include in income any interest or gain earned on the contribution. If there was a loss, the net income earned on the contribution may be a negative amount.

> **EXAMPLE:** On May 2, 2020, when her IRA is worth $4,800, Cathy makes a $1,600 regular contribution to her IRA. Cathy requests that $400 of the May 2 contribution be returned to her. On February 2, 2021, when the IRA is worth $7,600, the IRA trustee distributes to Cathy the $400 plus net income attributable to the contribution. No other contributions have been made to the IRA for 2020 and no distributions have been made.
>
> The adjusted opening balance is $6,400 ($4,800 + $1,600) and the adjusted closing balance is $7,600. The net income due to the May 2, 2020, contribution is $75 ($400 × ($7,600 − $6,400) ÷ $6,400). Therefore, the total to be distributed on February 2, 2021, is $475.

COMPENSATION FOR IRA PURPOSES

Taxpayers can set up and contribute to *traditional IRAs* or *Roth IRAs* <u>only</u> if the taxpayer or spouse received *taxable compensation* during the year.

Individuals can have a traditional IRA even if covered by another retirement plan. Contributions may not be deductible if the taxpayer (or spouse) is covered by an employer retirement plan. If both a taxpayer and a spouse have compensation each can set up an IRA; however, they cannot participate in the same IRA. If filing a joint return, only one spouse needs to have compensation.

- **Compensation** – Generally, compensation is the amount earned from working. Compensation includes wages, salaries, tips, professional fees, bonuses, and other amounts individuals receive for providing personal services. *For IRA purposes*, compensation includes amounts considered taxable alimony and nontaxable combat pay. For the *self-employed* (a sole proprietor or a partner), compensation is the *net earnings* (do not consider a net loss) from a trade or business (provided the personal services are a material income-producing factor) reduced by the total of the following:
    1. The deduction for contributions made on the **taxpayer's own behalf** to retirement plans
    2. The **deductible portion of self-employment taxes**
- Compensation does not include any of the following:
    1. Earnings and profits from property, such as rental, interest, and dividend income
    2. Pension or annuity income
    3. Deferred compensation received (compensation payments postponed from a past year)
    4. Income from a partnership if the taxpayer does not provide services that are a material income-producing factor
    5. Amounts excluded from income (other than combat pay), such as foreign earned income

TIP: For IRA purposes, compensation includes any **taxable** alimony and separate maintenance payments received under a decree of divorce or separate maintenance.

IRA CONTRIBUTION LIMIT

For 2020, the **total contributions** a taxpayer can make to all their *traditional IRAs* and *Roth IRAs* cannot exceed the smaller of the following:

- **$6,000 ($7,000 if age 50 or older**, due to a $1,000 catch-up contribution)
- 100% of taxable compensation for the year

TIP: For 2021 the IRA contribution limit is unchanged.

The total contributions a taxpayer can make each year to all their traditional IRAs and Roth IRAs can not exceed the general IRA contribution limit.

Roth IRA contributions might be further limited if the taxpayer's income exceeds a certain level (discussed later under Roth IRA Contribution Limit). *Traditional IRA contributions* are not limited based on the taxpayer's income level.

For 2020 and later, there is **no age limit** on making *regular contributions* to traditional IRAs or Roth IRAs. *Catch-up contributions* for traditional and Roth IRAs, are if age 50 or older.

TIP: In years prior to 2019, contributions to traditional IRAs were not allowed unless the taxpayer was younger than age 70.5 at the end of the tax year. This requirement was **eliminated** with the passage of the *Secure Act of 2019*.

A taxpayer can contribute to a traditional IRA or Roth IRA even if they participate in another retirement plan through their employer or business. The IRA contribution limit is not limited if an employer retirement plan covers either the taxpayer or spouse at any time during the year. Employer retirement plans do <u>not</u> affect the amount a taxpayer can contribute to a traditional IRA or Roth IRA.

TIP: The IRA contribution limit does not apply to rollover contributions.

SPOUSAL IRA CONTRIBUTION LIMIT

If a taxpayer files a joint return, the taxpayer may be able to contribute to a *traditional IRA* or *Roth IRA* even if the taxpayer did not have taxable compensation as long as the taxpayer's spouse did. Each spouse can make a contribution up to the current limit; however, the total of the combined contributions (taxpayer's and spouse's) can <u>not</u> be more than the taxable compensation reported on their joint return.

TIP: A taxpayer can contribute to a *Roth IRA* for their spouse provided their modified AGI is less than the Roth IRA contribution limit.

For 2020, if filing a joint return with a spouse, the **total spousal IRA contributions (*traditional* <u>and</u> *Roth*)** for the spouse with the lowest compensation cannot exceed the <u>smaller</u> of the following:

- $6,000 ($7,000 if age 50 or older)
- Total taxable compensation of both spouses for the year, reduced by the other spouse's IRA contributions (traditional and Roth) for the year

For 2020, the total combined contributions that a taxpayer can make for the year to <u>both</u> IRAs (taxpayer's and spouse's) can be as much as $12,000 ($13,000 if one is age 50 or older and $14,000 if both are age 50 or older).

Spousal Roth IRA contributions might be further limited if the taxpayer's income exceeds a certain level (discussed below under Roth IRA Contribution Limit). *Spousal traditional IRA contributions* are <u>not</u> limited based on the taxpayer's income level.

> **EXAMPLE 1:** Kristin, a full-time student with no taxable compensation, marries Carl during the year. Neither of them was age 50 by the end of 2020. For the year, Carl has taxable compensation of $30,000. He plans to contribute (and deduct) $6,000 to a traditional IRA. If he and Kristin file a joint return, each can contribute $6,000 to a traditional IRA. This is because Kristin, who has no compensation, can add Carl's compensation, reduced by the amount of his IRA contribution ($30,000 – $6,000 = $24,000), to her own compensation ($0) to figure her maximum contribution to a traditional IRA. In her case, $6,000 is her contribution limit, because $6,000 is less than $24,000 (her compensation for purposes of figuring her contribution limit).

> **EXAMPLE 2:** Tom and Darcy are married and both are 53. They both work and each has a traditional IRA. Tom earned $3,800 and Darcy earned $48,000 in 2020. Because of the spousal IRA limit rule, even though Tom earned less than $7,000, they can contribute up to $7,000 to his IRA for 2020 if they file a joint return. They can contribute up to $7,000 to Darcy's IRA. If they file separate returns, the amount that can be contributed to Tom's IRA is limited by his earned income, $3,800.

ROTH IRA CONTRIBUTION LIMIT

A **Roth IRA contribution is <u>never</u> deductible** and is **<u>not</u> an adjustment to income**. The following Roth IRA contribution requirements are illustrated to help you absorb its differences and similarities to the traditional IRA rules and limits.

If a taxpayer contributes to both Roth IRAs and traditional IRAs, the general limit for Roth IRAs is the same as the limit would be if contributions were made only to Roth IRAs or only to traditional IRAs. The total contributions a taxpayer can make each year to all their traditional IRAs and Roth IRAs can not exceed the general IRA contribution limit.

In addition to the general contribution limit that applies to both Roth IRAs and traditional IRAs, a *Roth IRA* contribution may also be limited based on the taxpayer's filing status and income.

If a taxpayer's modified adjusted gross income (MAGI) is above a certain amount, the Roth IRA contribution limit is gradually reduced.

Effect of MAGI on Roth IRA Contributions – 2020		
IF your filing status is	**AND your modified AGI is**	**THEN you can make**
married filing jointly or qualifying widow(er)	$196,000 or less	a full contribution
	between $196,000 – $206,000	a partial contribution
	$206,000 or more	no contribution
married filing separately and live with spouse	$0	a full contribution
	between $0 – $10,000	a partial contribution
	$10,000 or more	no contribution
all others	$124,000 or less	a full contribution
	between $124,000 – $139,000	a partial contribution
	$139,000 or more	no contribution

EXCESS CONTRIBUTIONS

Contributions above the allowed limits are *excess contributions*. For purposes of determining excess contributions, any contribution that is withdrawn on or before the due date (including extensions) for filing the tax return for the year is **treated as an amount not contributed**. This treatment only applies if any earnings on the contributions are also withdrawn. The earnings are considered earned and received in the year the excess contribution was made.

TRADITIONAL IRA DEDUCTION LIMIT

Although a taxpayer can contribute to a traditional IRA even if they participate in another retirement plan through their employer or business, however, a taxpayer may not be able to **deduct** all of their *traditional IRA* contributions if the taxpayer or taxpayer's spouse participates in another retirement plan at work.

Traditional IRA contributions may be tax-deductible. The deduction may be limited if the taxpayer or taxpayer's spouse is covered by a retirement plan at work and the taxpayer's modified adjusted gross income (MAGI) exceeds certain levels.

Generally, the **deduction** is the lesser of the following:

- The actual contributions to a traditional IRA for the year

- The general limit on contributions (or the spousal IRA contribution limit, if it applies)

The **deduction may be limited** if an employer retirement plan covers either spouse at any time during the year for which contributions are made. **The deduction limitation does <u>not</u> affect the amount that the taxpayer can contribute.**

Effect of MAGI on Deduction if Taxpayer Is Covered by a Retirement Plan at Work – 2020		
IF your filing status is	**AND your modified AGI is**	**THEN you can take**
single or head of household	$65,000 or less	a full deduction
	between $65,000 – $75,000	a partial deduction
	$75,000 or more	no deduction
married filing jointly or qualifying widow(er)	$104,000 or less	a full deduction
	between $104,000 – $124,000	a partial deduction
	$124,000 or more	no deduction
married filing separately	less than $10,000	a partial deduction
	$10,000 or more	no deduction

Effect of MAGI on Deduction if Taxpayer Is <u>NOT</u> Covered by Retirement Plan at Work – 2020		
IF your filing status is	**AND your modified AGI is**	**THEN you can take**
single, head of household, or qualifying widow(er)	any amount	a full deduction
married filing jointly or **separately** and spouse <u>is not</u> covered by a plan at work	any amount	a full deduction
married filing jointly and spouse <u>is</u> covered by a plan at work	$196,000 or less	a full deduction
	between $196,000 – $206,000	a partial deduction
	$206,000 or more	no deduction
married filing separately with a spouse who <u>is</u> covered by a plan at work	less than $10,000	a partial deduction
	$10,000 or more	no deduction

The deduction amount is decreased (phased out) when income rises above a certain amount, and it is eliminated altogether when it reaches a higher amount. These amounts vary depending on filing status.

TIP: If you file separately and did <u>not</u> live with your spouse **at any time** during the year, your IRA deduction is determined under the "Single" filing status.

To determine if the deduction is subject to phase-out, compare modified adjusted gross income (MAGI) to the base amounts.

- When MAGI is **less than the lower base amount**, taxpayers receive a **full deduction**.
- If MAGI is **more than the upper base amount**, the contribution is **not deductible**.

- If MAGI is **between the base amounts**, the taxpayer will receive a **partial deduction** determined by subtracting MAGI from the upper base amount and multiplying it by a percentage based on filing status:

    1. **Married Filing Jointly/Qualifying Widow(er) and you are covered by an employer plan** – The total IRA deduction is 27.5% (32.5% if 50 or older) of the difference between MAGI and the upper base amount.

    2. **All others** – The total IRA deduction is 55% (65% if 50 or older) of the difference between MAGI and the upper base amount.

> **EXAMPLE:** Tony is 29 years old and single. In 2020, he was covered by a retirement plan at work. His salary is $67,000. His modified AGI is $80,000. Tony makes a $6,000 IRA contribution for 2020. Because he was covered by a retirement plan and his modified AGI is above $75,000, he can't deduct his $6,000 IRA contribution. He must designate this contribution as a nondeductible contribution by reporting it on Form 8606.
>
> If Tony was not covered by a retirement plan at work, he would not be limited by his modified AGI and could take a full deduction for his IRA contribution.

TRADITIONAL IRA NONDEDUCTIBLE CONTRIBUTIONS

Although the deduction for traditional IRA contributions may be reduced or eliminated, contributions can be made up to the general IRA contribution limit or, if it applies, the spousal IRA contribution limit. The difference between the total permitted traditional IRA contributions and the traditional IRA deduction is a ***nondeductible contribution***. A nondeductible contribution increases the basis of the traditional IRA and is not taxable when withdrawn. For a traditional IRA, the taxpayer files *Form 8606* to report nondeductible contributions.

> **EXAMPLE:** Matt is covered by a retirement plan at work. He contributes $6,000 to his traditional IRA for the tax year, which he can't deduct because his income exceeds the limit for a taxpayer covered by a retirement plan at work. He must designate this contribution as a nondeductible contribution by reporting it on Form 8606.

TIP: To designate contributions as nondeductible, a taxpayer must file *Form 8606*, even if not required to file a tax return for the year. If a taxpayer does not report nondeductible contributions, the IRS treats all contributions to a traditional IRA as deductible contributions—meaning distributions will be taxed!

EDUCATION RELATED ADJUSTMENTS

EDUCATOR EXPENSES

An *eligible educator* may deduct up to $250 (for 2020 and 2021) of *qualified expenses* as an adjustment to gross income, rather than as a miscellaneous itemized deduction. If filing jointly and both are eligible educators, the maximum deduction is $500. Neither spouse can deduct more than $250 of qualified expenses. This deduction was made permanent by the *PATH Act of 2015* and is set to increase with inflation in increments of $50.

- **Eligible educator** – An eligible educator is a kindergarten through grade 12 teacher, instructor, counselor, principal, or aide who worked in a school for at least 900 hours during a school year.
- **Qualified expenses** – Qualified expenses include ordinary and necessary expenses paid in connection with books, supplies, equipment (including computer equipment, software, and services), and other materials used in the classroom. Qualified expenses do not include costs for homeschooling or nonathletic supplies for courses in health or physical education.

> **Consolidated Appropriations Act, 2021 UPDATE:** Expenses paid or incurred after March 12, 2020, that fit the category of personal protective equipment (PPE), including disinfectant and other supplies used for the prevention of the spread of COVID-19, are treated as qualified expenses for the educator expense deduction.

STUDENT LOAN INTEREST DEDUCTION

Individuals may deduct up to **$2,500** of the interest paid on a ***qualified student loan*** used for higher education. The loan cannot be from a related person or a qualified employer plan and must be for qualified educational expenses that are as follows:

- For the taxpayer, a spouse, or a dependent at the time of the loan, who is **enrolled at least half-time** in a program leading to a degree, certificate, or other recognized educational credential
- Paid or incurred within a reasonable period of time before or after obtaining the loan
- For education provided during an academic period for an eligible student

Generally, the deduction is available when all of the following apply:

- The taxpayer paid interest on a qualified student loan
- Filing status is not married filing separately
- Modified adjusted gross income (MAGI) is less than $85,000 ($170,000 MFJ) for 2020
- The taxpayer and spouse, if filing jointly, cannot be claimed as a dependent on another return

> For 2020, the $2,500 maximum deduction begins to phase out for taxpayers with MAGI in excess of $70,000 ($140,000 MFJ) and is completely phased out for taxpayers with MAGI of $85,000 or more ($170,000 or more MFJ).

To figure the phaseout, multiply the interest deduction (before the phaseout, but not more than $2,500) by a fraction. The numerator (top part) is MAGI minus $70,000 ($140,000 in the case of a joint return). The denominator (bottom part) is $15,000 ($30,000 in the case of a joint return). Subtract the result from the deduction (before the phaseout) to determine the deductible amount.

> **EXAMPLE 1:** During 2020, you paid $800 interest on a qualified student loan. Your 2020 MAGI is $155,000 and you are filing a joint return. You must reduce your deduction by $400, figured as follows.
>
> $$\$800 \times \frac{\$155{,}000 - \$140{,}000}{\$30{,}000} = \$400$$

> **EXAMPLE 2:** The facts are the same as in Example 1, except that you paid $2,750 interest. Your maximum deduction for 2020 is $2,500. You must reduce your maximum deduction by $1,250, figured as follows.
>
> $$\$2{,}500 \times \frac{\$155{,}000 - \$140{,}000}{\$30{,}000} = \$1{,}250$$

TUITION AND FEES DEDUCTION

A taxpayer may deduct up to **$4,000** for qualified tuition and related education expenses paid during the tax year. The educational institution should provide the taxpayer with *Form 1098-T, Tuition Statement*. This form reports either payments received or amounts billed. The taxpayer reports qualified expenses for the tuition and fees deduction using *Form 8917*. The taxpayer must reduce the qualified education expenses by the amount of any tax-free educational assistance and refunds received.

> The **$4,000** deduction may be reduced or eliminated at higher income levels. The maximum deduction is reduced to **$2,000** if MAGI is more than $65,000 ($130,000 MFJ). No deduction is allowed if MAGI is larger than $80,000 ($160,000 MFJ).

- Generally, a taxpayer can claim the deduction if all three of the following requirements are met:
    1. Taxpayer paid qualified education expenses required to attend an eligible educational institution
    2. Taxpayer paid the education expenses for an eligible student
    3. The eligible student is the taxpayer, a spouse, or qualifying dependent on the taxpayer's income tax return
- A taxpayer cannot claim the tuition and fees deduction if any of the following apply:
    1. Filing status is **married filing separately**
    2. The person qualifies as a dependent of another taxpayer, regardless if actually claimed
    3. MAGI is more than $80,000 ($160,000 MFJ)
    4. The taxpayer is a nonresident alien for any part of the year and did not elect treatment as a resident alien for tax purposes
    5. The taxpayer or anyone else claims an American Opportunity or Lifetime Learning credit for the student for whom the taxpayer paid the qualified education expenses

TIP: A taxpayer may be able to take an education credit instead of a deduction, but not both. An individual can choose the one providing the lower tax.

TIP: Congress allowed this deduction (and several others) to expire after 2017. The *Taxpayer Certainty and Disaster Tax Relief Act of 2019*, enacted on December 20, 2019, extends this benefit to tax years 2018, 2019, and 2020. Since this act applies retroactively to 2018 additional deductions could be available for previously filed tax returns. The *Consolidated Appropriations Act, 2021* repeals the deduction for qualified tuition and fees and increases the phaseout limits for the lifetime learning credit, effective for taxable years beginning after December 31, 2020, as a transition from the tuition and fees deduction to an increased income limitation on lifetime learning credit.

LESSON 6

Deductions from Adjusted Gross Income

STANDARD AND ITEMIZED DEDUCTIONS

STANDARD DEDUCTION

The standard deduction reduces the amount of income subject to tax. Taxpayers generally benefit from the standard deduction if it is more than the allowable *itemized deductions*.

The following taxpayers are <u>not</u> eligible for the standard deduction:

- Married filing a separate return (MFS) <u>and</u> the other spouse itemizes deductions.
- The tax return is for a **short tax year** because of a change in the annual accounting period.
- *Nonresident* or *dual-status alien* during the year. A dual-status alien is both a nonresident and resident alien during the year.

EXCEPTION: A nonresident alien who is married to a U.S. citizen or resident alien at the end of the year can choose tax treatment as a U.S. resident and as such may claim the standard deduction. Students and business apprentices from India may be eligible to claim the standard deduction under Article 21 of the U.S.A.-India Income Tax Treaty.

STANDARD DEDUCTION AMOUNT

A taxpayer's filing status determines the amount of the standard deduction:

Filing Status	2020	2021
S or MFS	$12,400	$12,550
HH	$18,650	$18,800
MFJ or QW	$24,800	$25,100

The standard deduction is higher for taxpayers who are **65 or older** at the end of the year **and/or blind** (vision not better than 20/200). This extra deduction applies to both the taxpayer <u>and</u> to a spouse if married. Increase the standard deduction by the following for **each occurrence** of the conditions above.

Filing Status	2020	2021
MFJ, MFS or QW	$1,300	$1,350
S or HH	$1,650	$1,700

EXAMPLE: A blind taxpayer and spouse who is not blind, both age 66, may add $3,900 ($1,300 × 3) to the 2020 basic standard deduction of $24,800 for a total deduction of $28,700. A taxpayer who qualifies as both blind and elderly is entitled to two additional standard deductions, for a total additional amount of $2,600 or $3,300 (if filing S or HH) for 2020.

INCREASED STANDARD DEDUCTION FOR NET QUALIFIED DISASTER LOSS IF NOT ITEMIZING

If a taxpayer has a net qualified disaster loss and is not itemizing their deductions, they can claim an increased standard deduction for the net qualified disaster loss using Schedule A (see details under Casualty and Theft Losses).

INCREASED STANDARD DEDUCTION FOR QUALIFIED CASH CHARITABLE CONTRIBUTIONS IF NOT ITEMIZING

CARES ACT UPDATE: Individual taxpayers can claim an "above-the-line" deduction of up to **$300 per return** for *qualified cash donations* made to charity during 2020. The special $300 deduction is designed especially for people who take the standard deduction, rather than itemizing their deductions. Previously, charitable contributions could <u>only</u> be deducted if taxpayers itemized their deductions. Contributions of non-cash property do <u>not</u> qualify for this relief. *Cash contributions* <u>include</u> those paid by cash, check, electronic funds transfer, credit card, debit card, or payroll deduction. They don't include securities, household items, or other property.

TIP: The *Consolidated Appropriations Act, 2021* increased this special deduction up to $600 for married filing jointly but only for 2021. For 2020, the charitable deduction was up to $300 per "tax unit"—meaning those married filing jointly can only get up to a $300 deduction. For 2021, married filing jointly can each take up to a $300 deduction, for a total deduction of up to $600.

STANDARD DEDUCTION FOR DEPENDENTS

The standard deduction for a dependent cannot exceed the regular standard deduction, based on filing status. The basic standard deduction for an individual who is a dependent on another person's tax return is generally limited to the greater of:

- $1,100 in 2020 (unchanged in 2021) <u>or</u>
- The individual's earned income for the year, <u>plus</u> $350

EXAMPLE 1: Michael is 16 years old and single. His parents can claim him as a dependent on their 2020 tax return. He has interest income of $780 and wages of $150. He has no itemized deductions.

Michael's standard deduction is $1,100 because it is greater than $500 ($150 earned income + $350).

EXAMPLE 2: Joe, a 22-year-old college student, can be claimed as a dependent on his parents' 2020 tax return. Joe is married and files a separate return. His wife doesn't itemize deductions on her separate return. Joe has $1,500 in interest income and wages of $3,800. He has no itemized deductions.

Joe's standard deduction is $4,150 ($3,800 earned income + $350) because it is greater than $1,100.

ITEMIZED DEDUCTIONS

A taxpayer with deductions that surpass the standard deduction amount, or one who does not qualify for the standard deduction, may wish to itemize on *Schedule A* (Form 1040) if it provides a greater benefit.

Common deductions include:

- Medical and dental expenses
- Certain taxes
- Interest expense
- Non-business casualty and theft losses attributable to a federally declared disaster
- Charitable contributions
- Certain miscellaneous expenses (other itemized deductions not subject to the 2% limit)

NONDEDUCTIBLE EXPENSES

A deduction is <u>not</u> available for the following expenses:

- Adoption expenses (may claim credit)
- Broker's commissions that paid in connection with IRA
- Burial or funeral expenses, including the cost of a cemetery lot
- Campaign expenses
- Capital expenses
- Check-writing fees
- Club dues and health spa expenses
- Commuting expenses
- Fees and licenses, such as car licenses, marriage licenses, and dog tags
- Fines and penalties, such as parking tickets
- Hobby losses
- Home repairs, insurance, and rent
- Home security system
- Illegal bribes and kickbacks
- Investment-related seminars
- Life insurance premiums
- Lobbying expenses
- Losses from the sale of taxpayer's home, furniture, personal car, etc.
- Lost or misplaced cash or property
- Lunches with co-workers or meals while working late
- Medical expenses as business expenses
- Personal disability insurance premiums
- Personal legal expenses
- Personal, living, or family expenses
- Political contributions
- Professional accreditation fees
- Professional reputation, expenses to improve
- Relief fund contributions
- Residential telephone line
- Stockholders' meeting, expenses of attending
- Tax-exempt income, expenses of earning or collecting
- The value of wages never received or lost vacation time
- Travel expenses for another individual
- Voluntary unemployment benefit fund contributions
- Wristwatches

MISCELLANEOUS DEDUCTIONS SUBJECT TO THE 2% LIMIT

The TCJA **suspends** <u>all</u> miscellaneous itemized deductions subject to the 2% floor for tax years 2018 through 2025.

Three categories of deductions were subject to the 2% limit and are **no longer deductible:**

- **Unreimbursed employee expenses** (examples include the home office deduction, unreimbursed travel and meals, qualified expenses for eligible educators not taken as an adjustment to gross income, and union dues)
- **Tax preparation fees**
- **Other expenses**
  - Appraisal fees for a casualty loss or charitable contribution
  - Excess deductions (including administrative expenses) allowed a beneficiary on termination of an estate or trust
  - Fees to collect interest and dividends
  - Hobby expenses, but generally not more than hobby income
  - Indirect miscellaneous deductions of pass-through entities
  - Investment fees and expenses
  - Legal fees related to producing or collecting taxable income or getting tax advice
  - Loss on deposits in an insolvent or bankrupt financial institution
  - Loss on traditional IRAs or Roth IRAs, when all amounts have been distributed
  - Repayments of income
  - Repayments of Social Security benefits
  - Safe-deposit box rental
  - Service charges on dividend reinvestment plans
  - Tax advice fees
  - Trustee's fees for IRA, if separately billed and paid

OTHER ITEMIZED DEDUCTIONS NOT SUBJECT TO THE 2% LIMIT

The following are other itemized deductions that remain deductible:

- Amortizable premium on taxable bonds
- Casualty and theft losses from income-producing property
- Federal estate tax on income in respect of a decedent
- Gambling losses (including otherwise deductible expenses incurred in connection with the activity before **2025,** such as travel to and from a casino) up to the amount of **gambling winnings**
- Impairment-related work expenses of persons with disabilities
- Loss from other activities from an electing large partnership (Form 1065-B, Schedule K-1 Box 2 losses)
- Losses from Ponzi-type investment schemes
- Repayments of more than $3,000 under a claim of right
- Unrecovered investment in an annuity

PHASE-OUT OF ITEMIZED DEDUCTIONS

TCJA: Congress repealed the overall limitation on itemized deductions for tax years 2018 through 2025.

MEDICAL AND DENTAL EXPENSES

Medical expenses are the costs of diagnosis, cure, mitigation, treatment, or prevention of disease, and the costs for treatments affecting any part or function of the body. They include the costs of equipment, supplies, and diagnostic devices needed for these purposes. Medical expenses also include dental care and the cost of insurance.

- Medical expenses <u>must</u> be primarily to alleviate or prevent a physical or mental defect or illness. Do <u>not</u> include expenses for procedures that are purely cosmetic or those that are merely beneficial to general health, such as vitamins or a vacation.

- Include only the expenses **paid this tax year**, even if services were provided in a prior year. Payment made in advance for medical treatment is <u>not</u> deductible until the medical treatment is actually rendered.

- A taxpayer can generally deduct medical expenses paid for himself, and someone who was a spouse or dependent, or would have been a dependent (see below) when the services were provided <u>or</u> when the taxpayer paid for them.

- Medical expenses include expenses paid for a dependent <u>or</u> for an individual that **would have been a dependent** <u>except</u> that, for 2020:

  1. He or she had gross income of **$4,300** or more,
  2. He or she filed a joint return, or
  3. Taxpayer, or taxpayer's spouse if filing jointly, could be claimed as a dependent on someone else's return.

  TIP: The IRS no longer requires a taxpayer to claim a dependent on the tax return to deduct medical expenses provided the individual would qualify as a dependent if it were not for one of these exceptions.

  EXAMPLE 1: Mary received medical treatment before she married Bill. Bill paid for the treatment after they married. Bill can include these expenses in figuring his medical expense deduction even if Bill and Mary file separate returns.

  If Mary had paid the expenses, Bill couldn't include Mary's expenses in his separate return. Mary would include the amounts she paid during the year in her separate return. If they filed a joint return, the medical expenses both paid during the year would be used to figure their medical expense deduction.

  EXAMPLE 2: This year, John paid medical expenses for his wife Louise, who died last year. John married Belle this year and they file a joint return. Because John was married to Louise when she received the medical services, he can include those expenses in figuring his medical expense deduction for this year.

Only the amount of medical and dental expenses **that exceed 7.5% of AGI** are deductible in 2020.

TIP: Employees who contribute through payroll deductions towards their medical insurance premiums—or any other benefits—can't claim a deduction on their personal tax returns for amounts not included in wages, as doing so would provide a double benefit.

DEDUCTIBLE MEDICAL EXPENSES

- **Medical insurance premiums** (including Medicare parts B and D) for policies that cover:
  1. Hospitalization, surgical services, x-rays
  2. Prescription drugs and insulin
  3. Dental care
  4. Replacement of lost or damaged contact lenses
  5. Long-term care (limited)

TIP: An employee may not deduct the cost of insurance premium payments made with pre-tax income that is not included in his wages on Form W-2 (Box 1). Certain self-employed taxpayers or S corporation shareholders with a qualifying plan established under the business may benefit more by deducting the cost of insurance as an adjustment to gross income.

- **Meals and lodging:**
  1. Include the cost of meals and lodging **at a hospital** or similar institution if a principal reason for being there is to get medical care.
  2. The cost of such lodging not provided in a hospital or similar institution while away from home if <u>all</u> of the following requirements are met:
     A. The lodging is primarily for and essential to medical care.
     B. A doctor in a licensed hospital or in a medical care facility related to, or the equivalent of, a licensed hospital provided the services.
     C. The lodging is not lavish or extravagant under the circumstances.
     D. There is no significant element of personal pleasure, recreation, or vacation in the travel away from home.
     E. The deduction for lodging cannot be more than $50 for each night for each person. Also, include lodging for a person traveling with the person receiving medical care. For example, if a parent is traveling with a sick child, up to $100 per night can be included as a medical expense for lodging. Meals are <u>not</u> included.
- **Nursing home** – Costs of medical care in a nursing home, home for the aged, or similar institution.
- **Transportation** – Amounts paid for transportation primarily for, and essential to, medical care:
  1. Bus, taxi, train, or plane fares, or ambulance service
  2. Transportation expenses of a parent who must go with a child who needs medical care
  3. Transportation expenses of a nurse or other person who can give injections, medications, or other treatment required by a patient who is traveling to get medical care and is unable to travel alone
  4. Transportation expenses for regular visits to see a mentally ill dependent if the medical provider recommended these visits as a part of treatment
- **Car expenses** – Out-of-pocket expenses, such as the cost of gas and oil, when using a car for medical reasons. Individuals <u>cannot</u> include depreciation, insurance, general repair, or maintenance expenses. If preferred, the taxpayer may use the 2020 standard mileage rate of **17 cents per mile** driven for medical instead of actual expenses incurred.
- **Capital expenses** – Amounts paid for special equipment installed in a home, or for improvements, if their main purpose is medical care for the taxpayer, spouse, or dependent. The cost of permanent improvements that increase the value of the property may be partly included as a medical expense. The cost of the improvement is <u>reduced</u> by the **increase in the value** of the property. The difference is a medical expense. If the value of the property isn't increased by the improvement, the entire cost is included as a medical expense.

  Certain improvements don't usually increase the value of the home and the cost can be included in full as medical expenses. These improvements include, but aren't limited to, the following items.

  1. Constructing entrance or exit ramps.
  2. Widening doorways at entrances or exits.
  3. Widening or otherwise modifying hallways and interior doorways.
  4. Installing railings, support bars, or other modifications to bathrooms.
  5. Lowering or modifying kitchen cabinets and equipment.
  6. Moving or modifying electrical outlets and fixtures.

7. Installing porch lifts and other forms of lifts (but elevators generally add value to the house).

8. Modifying fire alarms, smoke detectors, and other warning systems.

9. Modifying stairways.

10. Adding handrails or grab bars anywhere (whether or not in bathrooms).

11. Modifying hardware on doors.

12. Modifying areas in front of entrance and exit doorways.

13. Grading the ground to provide access to the residence.

TAX EXPENSE

DEDUCTIBLE TAXES

For taxable years beginning in 2018, the itemized deduction for taxes is limited. The TCJA allows a taxpayer to claim an itemized deduction on Schedule A of **up to $10,000** ($5,000 married filing a separate return) for the **aggregate** of property taxes and state and local income (or sales) taxes paid or accrued in the taxable year.

A taxpayer receives a deduction for taxes he is legally liable to pay:

- State and local income taxes, if applicable, or general sales taxes, but not both.
- Foreign income taxes paid. Generally, one may take either a deduction or a credit for income taxes imposed by a foreign country or a U.S. possession.
- Real estate taxes on real property levied for the general public welfare. Deduct only the taxes that are based on the *assessed value* of the real property and charged uniformly against all property under the jurisdiction of the taxing authority.
  1. If property was bought or sold during the year, divide the current real estate taxes between buyer and seller according to the number of days owned, pro-rata. The seller pays the taxes up to, but not including, the date of sale.
  2. If mortgage payments include taxes placed in escrow, no tax is deductible until paid by the mortgage servicing company.
- Personal property taxes that meet the following criteria:
  1. Based only on the value of personal property.
  2. Charged on a yearly basis, even if they are collected more or less than once a year.

NONDEDUCTIBLE TAXES

TCJA: For taxable years beginning in 2018, the tax act modifies the deduction for taxes not paid or accrued in a **trade or business**. An individual's state, local, and foreign property taxes and state and local sales taxes are allowed as a deduction only when paid or accrued in carrying on a trade or business or relating to expenses for the production of income. Thus, deductions for property taxes and sales taxes are only deductible in computing income on an individual's Schedule C, Schedule E, or Schedule F.

Also, under the new act, an individual is not allowed a deduction for state and local income taxes. An exception allows a taxpayer to claim an itemized deduction on Schedule A of up to **$10,000** ($5,000 married filing a separate return) for the aggregate of property taxes and state and local income (or sales) taxes paid or accrued in the taxable year. Foreign real property taxes are nondeductible.

- Real estate items individuals generally <u>cannot</u> deduct include the following:
    1. Special assessments for local benefits that increase the property value, such as sidewalks or sewer
    2. Itemized fixed charge assessments for services. Service charges used to maintain or improve services (such as trash collection or police and fire protection) are deductible as real estate taxes if the following conditions exist:
        A. Fees or charges are imposed at a like rate against all property in the taxing jurisdiction
        B. The funds collected are not earmarked; and are part of general revenue funds
        C. Funds used to maintain or improve services are not limited to or determined by the amount of these fees or charges collected
    3. Transfer taxes (or stamp taxes)
    4. Rent increases due to higher real estate taxes
    5. Homeowners' association charges
- Foreign real property taxes
- Employment taxes, including Social Security and Medicare
- Estate, inheritance, legacy, or succession taxes
- Federal income taxes
- Fines and penalties
- Gift taxes
- License fees, and per capita taxes

INTEREST EXPENSE

HOME MORTGAGE INTEREST

A taxpayer may deduct interest paid on **home acquisition debt** to buy, build, or improve a **qualified home** (main home or second home).

TIP: Do not confuse a home equity loan with home equity debt. Interest on a home equity loan may be deductible as home acquisition debt if used to buy, build, or improve the qualified home that secures the loan.

For taxable years beginning **after 2017** and beginning before 2026, a taxpayer may treat no more than **$750,000** ($375,000 married filing separately) as acquisition indebtedness. In the case of acquisition indebtedness incurred <u>on or before</u> December 15, 2017, this limitation is $1,000,000 ($500,000 married filing separately). For taxable years beginning <u>after</u> 2025, a taxpayer may treat up to $1,000,000 ($500,000 married filing separately) of indebtedness as acquisition indebtedness, regardless of when the indebtedness was incurred.

TIP: Special rules apply in the case of indebtedness from **refinancing** <u>existing</u> acquisition indebtedness. Specifically, the $1,000,000 ($500,000 married filing separately) limitation continues to apply to refinanced prior qualified residence indebtedness to the extent the amount of the new indebtedness resulting from the refinancing does not exceed the amount of the prior indebtedness refinanced. Thus, the maximum dollar amount that may be treated as principal residence acquisition indebtedness will not decrease by reason of a refinancing.

Interest on *home equity debt* (mortgage taken other than to buy, build, or improve a home) is **no longer deductible.**

Mortgage interest on home acquisition debt to buy, build, or improve a qualified home is deductible if <u>all</u> the following conditions exist:

- File Form 1040 and itemize deductions on Schedule A
- The taxpayer is legally liable for the loan
- There is a true debtor-creditor relationship between the taxpayer and the lender
- The taxpayer has an ownership interest in the qualified home that secures the mortgage

TIP: Taxpayers who sell their home can deduct the home mortgage interest paid up to, but not including the date of sale. If the taxpayer paid $600 or more of mortgage interest (including certain points and mortgage insurance premiums) during the year on any mortgage, the mortgage holder will send a Form 1098 or similar statement to the taxpayer.

POINTS

The term "points" describes certain charges paid, or treated as paid, by a borrower to obtain a home mortgage. In general, taxpayers amortize points (deduct ratably over the life of the mortgage). A taxpayer may fully *deduct* points in the year paid if the following conditions exist:

- The taxpayer must use the loan proceeds to buy, build or improve a **main home** (points on a second home or to refinance an existing loan are *amortized* over the life of the loan)
- Paying points is an established business practice in the area where the loan was made
- The points paid were not more than the points generally charged in that area
- The taxpayer uses the cash method of accounting
- The points are not in place of amounts that ordinarily are stated separately on the settlement statement, such as appraisal fees, inspection fees, title fees, attorney fees, and property taxes
- The points are not financed into the mortgage amount
- The points were computed as a percentage of the principal amount of the mortgage
- The amount clearly appears on the settlement statement as points charged for the mortgage

EXAMPLE: Lamont purchased a new home to use as his primary residence. He pays $5,000 in points to improve the rate on his 15-year loan. On Schedule A, he deducts the points as interest in the year paid. If this were an investment property, he would amortize the points over a period of 15 years.

Points on *home equity debt* (mortgages taken other than to buy, build, or improve a home) are **no longer deductible.**

MORTGAGE INSURANCE PREMIUMS

Treat the amount paid during the year for *qualified mortgage insurance* as home mortgage interest. The insurance must be purchased in connection with acquisition indebtedness of the taxpayer's qualified residence. This deduction decreases by 10% for each $1,000 ($500 MFS) of AGI above **$100,000** ($50,000 MFS).

TIP: Congress allowed this deduction (and several others) to expire after 2017. The *Taxpayer Certainty and Disaster Tax Relief Act of 2019*, enacted on December 20, 2019, extends this benefit to tax years 2018, 2019, and 2020.

Since this act applies retroactively to 2018 additional deductions could be available for previously filed tax returns. The *Consolidated Appropriations Act, 2021* further extends this deduction through 2021.

INVESTMENT INTEREST

Interest on loans to buy property held for investment is *investment interest*.

> The deduction for investment interest is limited to the taxpayer's *net investment income.* If the taxpayer does not use the deduction, he may carry it forward into the next year. Interest incurred to produce tax-exempt income is not deductible.

An individual, estate, or trust must use *Form 4952* to claim a deduction for investment interest expenses. Form 4952 is not necessary if a taxpayer meets both the following conditions:

- Income from interest and ordinary dividends (minus any qualified dividends) exceeds the amount of investment interest expenses
- The taxpayer does not have any other deductible investment expenses or carryover of disallowed prior-year investment interest expense

CHARITABLE CONTRIBUTIONS

Deductions for contributions to a *qualified organization* are generally limited to 60% of adjusted gross income, but in some cases, 50%, 30%, or 20% limits may apply. Qualified organizations include:

- Churches, association of churches, temples, synagogues, mosques, and other religious organizations
- Most nonprofit charitable organizations such as the Red Cross and the United Way
- Most nonprofit educational organizations (Boy and Girl Scouts of America, colleges, and museums)
- Nonprofit hospitals and medical research organizations
- Utility company emergency energy programs, if the utility company is an agent for a charitable organization that assists individuals with emergency energy needs
- Nonprofit volunteer fire companies
- Public parks and recreation facilities
- Civil defense organizations

NONDEDUCTIBLE CONTRIBUTIONS

- Contributions of the value of taxpayer-provided time or services
- Contributions of less than the entire interest in property:
  1. Right to use property – A contribution of the right to use property is a contribution of less than the taxpayer's entire interest in that property (a contribution of a partial interest) and isn't deductible.

     Example: You own a 10-story building and donate rent-free use of the top floor to a charitable organization. Because you still own the building, you have contributed a partial interest in the property and can't take a deduction for the contribution.

- Contributions to **specific individuals**, including the following:
  1. Contributions to fraternal societies for paying medical or burial expenses of deceased members
  2. Contributions to individuals who are needy or worthy
  3. Payments to a member of the clergy that the member may spend as he wishes

4. Expenses paid for another person who provided services to a qualified organization

5. Payments to a hospital for a specific patient's care or for services for a specific patient

- Contributions to nonqualified organizations:

1. Groups that are run for a profit

2. Certain state bar associations

3. Chambers of commerce and other business leagues or organizations

4. Civic leagues and associations

5. Country clubs and other social clubs

6. Foreign organizations except certain Canadian, Israeli, or Mexican charitable organizations

7. Homeowners' associations

8. Labor unions

9. Political organizations and candidates

CONTRIBUTIONS OF PROPERTY

The deductible amount for **capital gain property** is generally the fair market value of the property at the time of the contribution.

The deduction for ordinary income property is limited to the gifts fair market value <u>minus</u> the **amount that would be ordinary income or a short-term capital gain** if the taxpayer sold the property for its fair market value. Ordinary income property includes short-term gain property, inventory, works of art created by the taxpayer, property subject to depreciation recapture, etc.

EXAMPLE: You donate stock you held for 5 months to your church. The fair market value of the stock on the day you donate it is $1,000, but you paid only $800 (your basis). Because the $200 of appreciation would be a short-term capital gain if you sold the stock, your deduction is limited to $800 (fair market value minus the appreciation).

EXCEPTION: Do <u>not</u> reduce the charitable contribution if reporting the ordinary or capital gain income in the same year as the contribution.

The deduction for contributed property that has decreased in value (i.e., fair market value is less than cost basis) is limited to the value of the property. A taxpayer can't claim a deduction for the original cost. Common examples of property that decrease in value include clothing, furniture, appliances, and cars.

Donated clothing or household items must be in good used condition or better in order to qualify for a deduction. A good measure of value might be the price that buyers of these used items actually pay in consignment or thrift shops. However, a taxpayer may take a deduction for items in poor condition if the deduction is more than $500 and the taxpayer includes a qualified appraisal with the return.

A taxpayer claiming a deduction for non-cash gifts of <u>more</u> than **$500** must file Form 8283. The IRS requires an **appraisal** for any single item or group of related items with a value exceeding **$5,000**.

A taxpayer looking to deduct more than $500 resulting from a donation of a qualified vehicle must attach a copy of the contemporaneous written acknowledgment. In general, a contemporaneous acknowledgment must be issued within 30 days of the contribution or later sale. The organization receiving the property may use Form

1098-C copy B as the acknowledgment. The deduction is limited to the smaller of the vehicle's FMV on the date of the contribution or the gross proceeds received from a later sale of the vehicle. An acceptable measure of the FMV of a donated vehicle is an amount not in excess of the price listed in a used vehicle pricing guide for a private party sale of a similar vehicle.

LIMITS ON CHARITABLE DEDUCTIONS

CARES ACT UPDATE: The CARES Act temporarily suspends limits on certain **cash contributions** made in 2020. Individuals may deduct qualified contributions of cash up to **100% of adjusted gross income**. Contributions of non-cash property do <u>not</u> qualify for this relief. This relief also applies to qualified cash contributions made in 2021, as the relief was extended by the *Consolidated Appropriations Act, 2021*.

The limit that applies to a contribution depends on the type of property donated and the category of the qualified organization that receives the property. The charitable contribution deduction generally is limited to a percentage of adjusted gross income.

The charitable contribution deduction is generally **limited to 100% of adjusted gross income** for **cash contributions**. This 100% limit does <u>not</u> apply to non-cash charitable contributions. Gifts of **appreciated property** or gifts **to certain organizations** are subject to additional limits of 50%, 30%, or 20%, depending on the circumstances. The limits apply to all charitable contributions made during the year and any carryover from a prior year.

A taxpayer can carry over any contributions he can't deduct in the current year because they exceed the AGI limits. The taxpayer may be able to deduct the excess in each of the next **5 years** until it is used up, but not beyond that time. A carryover of a *qualified conservation contribution* can be carried forward for **15 years**.

- **50% limit organizations** – The following is a partial list of the types of organizations that are 50% limit organizations:
  1. Churches and conventions or associations of churches.
  2. Educational organizations with a regular faculty and curriculum that normally have a regularly enrolled student body attending classes on-site.
  3. Hospitals and certain medical research organizations associated with these hospitals.
  4. Publicly-supported charities.

A 2020 **cash** contribution to a 50% limit organization is limited to **100% of AGI.**

A **non-cash** contribution to a 50% limit organization is limited to **50% of AGI.**

EXCEPTION: A **special 30% limit** applies to **gifts of capital gain property** to 50% limit organizations. The special 30% limit does <u>not</u> apply when using cost in place of FMV as the amount of the gift. Instead, only the 50% limit applies.

- **30% limit** – A 30% limit applies to the following gifts:
  1. Gifts to <u>all</u> qualified organizations <u>other than</u> 50% limit organizations. This includes gifts to veterans' organizations, fraternal societies, nonprofit cemeteries, and certain private non-operating foundations.

2. Cash contributions **for the use of** any organization. A 30% limit applies to cash contributions that are "for the use of" the qualified organizations instead of "to" the qualified organization. A contribution is "for the use of" a qualified organization when it is held in a legally enforceable trust for the qualified organization or in a similar legal arrangement.

- **20% limit** – A 20% limit applies to all non-cash **gifts of capital gain property** to organizations other than 50% limit organizations, or for the use of any qualified organization.

TIP: The **special 30% limit** for **capital gain property** is separate from the other 30% limit. Therefore, the deduction of a contribution subject to one 30% limit does not reduce the amount taxpayers can deduct for contributions subject to the other 30% limit. However, the total cannot be more than 50% of adjusted gross income.

EXAMPLE: Your adjusted gross income is $50,000. During the year, you gave capital gain property with a fair market value of $15,000 to a 50% limit organization. You do not choose to reduce the property's fair market value by its appreciation in value. You also gave $10,000 cash to a qualified organization that is not a 50% limit organization. The $15,000 gift of property is subject to the special 30% limit. The $10,000 cash gift is subject to the other 30% limit. Both gifts are fully deductible because neither is more than the 30% limit that applies ($15,000 in each case) and together they are not more than the 50% limit ($25,000).

Limit if Benefit Received

If a taxpayer receives a benefit because of a contribution to a qualified organization, reduce the charitable deduction by the FMV of the benefit received.

EXAMPLE 1: You pay $65 for a ticket to a dinner dance at a church. Your entire $65 payment goes to the church. The ticket to the dinner-dance has a fair market value of $25. When you buy your ticket, you know its value is less than your payment. To figure the amount of your charitable contribution, subtract the value of the benefit you receive ($25) from your total payment ($65). You can deduct $40 as a charitable contribution to the church.

EXAMPLE 2: At a fundraising auction conducted by a charity, you pay $600 for a week's stay at a beach house. The amount you pay is no more than the fair rental value. You haven't made a deductible charitable contribution.

A charitable deduction is not allowed for any payment to a higher education institution in exchange for the right to purchase tickets or seating at an athletic event.

RECORDS FOR CASH CONTRIBUTIONS

Cash contributions include those paid by cash, check, electronic funds transfer, credit card, debit card, or payroll deduction. To claim a cash contribution, taxpayers must have one of the following:

- Bank records (canceled check or statement)
- A receipt (or other written communication) from the qualified organization showing the name of the organization, the date of the contribution, and the amount of the contribution
- Payroll deduction records

To deduct a cash contribution of **$250 or more**, the taxpayer <u>must</u> receive an acknowledgment of the contribution from the qualified organization or have certain payroll deduction records.

OUT-OF-POCKET EXPENSES IN GIVING SERVICES

The value of taxpayer-provided services given to a qualified organization is not deductible; however, costs (automobile or travel expenses, etc.) associated with providing the services may be. The 2020 standard mileage rate is **14 cents per mile** driven in service of charitable organizations.

A taxpayer cannot deduct personal expenses for sightseeing, fishing parties, theater tickets, nightclubs, or expenses for family members. To receive a deduction, the expenses must be as follows:

- Unreimbursed
- Directly connected with the services
- Expenses incurred only because of the services provided
- Not personal, living, or family expenses

CONVENTIONS

If a taxpayer is a chosen representative attending a convention of a qualified charitable organization, he may deduct actual unreimbursed expenses for travel and transportation, including a reasonable amount for meals and lodging, while away from home overnight in connection with the convention. Expenses are <u>not</u> deductible if attending as a member of the organization rather than as a chosen representative.

INCREASED STANDARD DEDUCTION

CARES ACT UPDATE: Individual taxpayers can claim an "above-the-line" deduction of up to **$300 per return** for *qualified cash donations* made to charity during 2020. The special $300 deduction is designed especially for people who take the standard deduction, rather than itemizing their deductions. Previously, charitable contributions could <u>only</u> be deducted if taxpayers itemized their deductions. Contributions of non-cash property do <u>not</u> qualify for this relief. *Cash contributions* <u>include</u> those paid by cash, check, electronic funds transfer, credit card, debit card, or payroll deduction. They don't include securities, household items, or other property.

TIP: The *Consolidated Appropriations Act, 2021* increased this special deduction up to $600 for married filing jointly but only for 2021. For 2020, the charitable deduction was up to $300 per "tax unit"—meaning those married filing jointly can only get up to a $300 deduction. For 2021, married filing jointly can each take up to a $300 deduction, for a total deduction of up to $600.

If the taxpayer is taking the standard deduction, the special deduction for cash charitable contributions is an adjustment to income. If the taxpayer is not taking the standard deduction, the taxpayer may claim cash and non-cash charitable contributions as an itemized deduction, subject to the normal limits.

INCREASED PENALTY FOR OVERSTATED DEDUCTION

The *Consolidated Appropriations Act, 2021* also increased the penalty for overstatement of this special deduction. Any portion of an underpayment that is attributable to an overstatement of the special deduction shall be **50%** instead of 20%.

NON-BUSINESS CASUALTY AND THEFT LOSSES

CASUALTY AND THEFT LOSSES ATTRIBUTABLE TO A FEDERALLY DECLARED DISASTER

For tax years 2018 through 2025, the personal casualty and theft losses of an individual are deductible <u>only</u> to the extent they are attributable to a **federally declared disaster**.

EXCEPTION: An exception applies to the extent the personal casualty loss of an individual does <u>not</u> exceed the individual's personal casualty gains. In this case, you will reduce your personal casualty gains by any casualty losses not attributable to a federally declared disaster. Any excess gain is used to reduce losses from a federally declared disaster.

EXAMPLE: Martin and Grace experienced multiple personal casualties. Grace's diamond necklace was stolen, resulting in a $15,500 casualty loss. Martin and Grace also lost their camper as a result of a lightning strike. They have replacement-value insurance on the camper, so they have a $13,000 gain. Finally, they lost their car in a flood determined to be a federally declared disaster, resulting in a casualty loss of $25,000. Because Martin and Grace experienced a $13,000 personal casualty gain as a result of the replacement-value insurance, they can offset that gain with a portion of their personal casualty loss attributable to the stolen necklace and can claim the full federally declared disaster casualty loss of $25,000 subject to the 10% of AGI and $100 limitations. Note: The remaining personal casualty loss from the stolen necklace is not deductible, since the loss was not from a federally declared disaster. Also, since the flood was classified as a federally declared disaster (but not a qualified disaster), the loss is deductible subject to the $100 and 10% of AGI limitations. If the flood had been a "qualified disaster loss (major disaster)" the loss would have only been subject to the $500 limitation.

A *casualty* is the damage, destruction, or loss of property resulting from an identifiable event that is sudden, unexpected, or unusual (e.g., terrorist attacks, earthquakes, fires, floods, hurricanes, and tornadoes). A taxpayer may have multiple losses from a single casualty. A taxpayer must use a **separate Form 4684** for <u>each</u> casualty or theft event involving personal use property.

An individual may claim an itemized deduction for a personal casualty loss <u>only</u> if such loss was attributable to a disaster declared by the President under section 401 of the *Robert T. Stafford Disaster Relief and Emergency Assistance Act*.

TIP: Victims of fraudulent investment schemes can claim a theft loss deduction if certain conditions apply.

GAIN OR LOSS

The taxpayer must determine if the result of a nonbusiness casualty or theft is a gain or a loss.

FIGURING A LOSS

- The loss is the smaller of the adjusted basis in the property before the casualty or theft, or the decrease in FMV of the property because of the casualty or theft, minus any insurance or other reimbursements.

There are two types of disaster declarations provided for in the Stafford Act: *emergency declarations* and *major disaster declarations*.

- For **emergency declarations**, there are two limits on the deductible amount for casualty or theft loss on personal-use property:
  1. Reduce each casualty or theft loss by $100 (**$100 rule**)
  2. The total of all casualty and theft losses is further reduced by 10% of AGI (**10% rule**)

- A **major disaster declaration** receives more favorable treatment as a *qualified disaster loss.* Net casualty losses from qualified disasters do not need to exceed 10% of adjusted gross income to qualify for the deduction but the $100 limit per casualty is increased to **$500** per casualty. A qualified disaster loss may be claimed in addition to the standard deduction if not itemizing.

TIP: A **qualified disaster loss** is now expanded to include an individual's casualty and theft of personal-use property that is attributable to a **major disaster** that was declared before February 26, 2021. However, this change does not include those losses attributable to a major disaster that has been declared only by reason of **COVID-19**. Examples of major disasters include Hurricane Harvey, Irma, and Maria, or the California wildfires in 2017 and January 2018.

EXAMPLE: In June, a tornado destroyed your lakeside cottage, which cost $144,800 (including $14,500 for the land) several years ago. (Your land wasn't damaged.) **The tornado was classified as a federally declared disaster by the President, but it is not a qualified disaster loss.** This was your only casualty or theft loss for the year. The FMV of the property immediately before the tornado was $180,000 ($145,000 for the cottage and $35,000 for the land). The FMV immediately after the tornado was $35,000 (value of the land). You collected $130,000 from the insurance company. Your adjusted gross income for the year the tornado occurred is $80,000. Your deduction for the casualty loss is $6,700, figured in the following manner.

1.	Adjusted basis of the entire property (cost in this example)	$144,800
2.	FMV of entire property before tornado	$180,000
3.	FMV of entire property after tornado	35,000
4.	Decrease in FMV of entire property (line 2 – line 3)	$145,000
5.	Loss (smaller of line 1 or line 4)	$144,800
6.	Subtract insurance proceeds received	– 130,000
7.	Loss after reimbursement	$14,800
8.	Subtract $100	– 100
9.	Loss after $100 rule	$14,700
10.	Subtract 10% of $80,000 AGI	– 8,000
11.	**Casualty loss deduction**	$6,700

If the result is a loss and the taxpayer is:

- **Itemizing deductions** – Use Schedule A to report the casualty and theft loss(es) from a federally declared disaster and attach a **separate Form 4684** for each **casualty or theft event** involving personal use property. In 2020, the taxpayer reports casualty and theft loss(es) from a federally declared disaster (other than net qualified disaster losses) on line 15 of Schedule A. The taxpayer reports any net qualified disaster loss on line 16 as "Other itemized deductions."

- **Not itemizing deductions** – If a taxpayer has a **net qualified disaster loss** on Form 4684 and is not itemizing deductions, they can claim an **increased standard deduction** for the net qualified disaster loss. The taxpayer still files Form 4684 (for each casualty or theft event) along with Schedule A showing the net qualified disaster loss on line 16 "Other itemized deductions." Also, enter on the dotted line next to line 16, your standard deduction amount and the description "Standard Deduction Claimed With Qualified Disaster Loss.

TIP: It is important to recognize when a loss is a *qualified disaster loss (major disaster)*, as that is the only type that may be claimed as an increase to the standard deduction. A qualified disaster loss must exceed $500 before it is deductible, but it is not subject to the 10% reporting threshold like other federal disaster losses. Other federal disaster losses can only be claimed as an itemized deduction.

Election to deduct loss in the preceding year

A taxpayer may deduct the loss from a federally declared disaster on his return for the tax year of the disaster or elect to deduct the loss in the preceding tax year on an amended return for the tax year immediately **preceding the tax year of the disaster**. If an individual chooses an amended return, treat the loss as having occurred in the preceding tax year. Claiming the loss on the previous year's return may result in a lower tax for that year, often producing or increasing a refund or overpayment.

TIP: To make this election for a loss in disaster year **2020**, complete Part I of Section D on the 2019 Form 4684, Casualties and Thefts, and attaching it to taxpayer's return or **amended return for 2019** that claims the disaster loss deduction on or before the date that is six months after the regular due date for filing the original return (without extensions) for the disaster year. For a calendar year taxpayer, a taxpayer can make the election to deduct a disaster loss sustained in 2020 on their amended 2019 return on or before October 15, 2021.

FIGURING A GAIN

A taxpayer may have a reportable **gain** if he receives an insurance payment or other reimbursement that is more than his adjusted basis in the destroyed, damaged, or stolen property.

- Gain is figured as follows—
  1. The amount received, minus
  2. The adjusted basis in the property at the time of the casualty or theft.

The amount received includes any money plus the value of any property received minus any expenses in obtaining the reimbursement. It also includes any reimbursement used to pay off a mortgage or other lien on the damaged, destroyed, or stolen property.

> Even if the decrease in FMV of the property is smaller than its adjusted basis, **use the adjusted basis to figure the gain.**

> **EXAMPLE:** A hurricane destroyed your personal residence and the insurance company awarded you $145,000. You received $140,000 in cash. The remaining $5,000 was paid directly to the holder of a mortgage on the property. The amount you received includes the $5,000 reimbursement paid on the mortgage.

If the result is gain, the taxpayer may elect to account for it is as a capital gain on Schedule D, or postpone reporting the gain (must acquire related replacement property within two tax years).

SECTION 199A QUALIFIED BUSINESS INCOME DEDUCTION

With the passage of the *Tax Cuts and Jobs Act of 2017 (TCJA)* business taxpayers received a multitude of benefits, including the permanent reduction of the corporate tax rate from a maximum of 35% down to 21%.

That's a sweet deal—if you happen to own a corporation!

A mere 5% of all businesses in the United States are taxed as corporations. While many corporations are classified as small (85% have less than 20 employees) the corporate form is often the entity of choice for big business.

So, you might wonder, is there anything in the "Cut Cut Cut Act" for the other 95%? Plumbers, doctors, contractors, dentists, lawyers, consultants, financial advisors... tax preparers? If the goal of the TCJA is to create jobs surely you cannot ignore the single biggest contributor—small business.

What about the rest of us?

From a tax perspective, the most common forms of small business are sole proprietorships, partnerships, and S corporations. I have a sneaky suspicion that most business returns you encounter will fall into one of these classifications.

TIP: A *limited liability company (LLC)* is a business structure allowed by state statute. Depending on elections made by the LLC, and the number of members, the IRS will treat an LLC as either a corporation ("C" or "S"), partnership, or as part of the LLC's owner's tax return (a "disregarded entity").

SECTION 199A OVERVIEW

Lurking deep within the pages of the TCJA, there is something for the rest of us.

A temporary deduction—called the *Section 199A deduction* or *QBI deduction*—is available for taxable years beginning after December 31, 2017, and before January 1, 2026.

TIP: Take note that the Section 199A deduction will expire unless extended. Pay close attention to this date as the planning implications are significant for business owners.

Section 199A provides that a taxpayer **other than a corporation** generally may deduct:

- **20 percent** of *qualified business income (QBI)*, plus
- **20 percent** of aggregate qualified real estate investment trust (REIT) dividends and qualified publicly traded partnership (PTP) income.

The deduction is subject to an **overall limitation** as it cannot exceed **20% of taxable income**, calculated before the QBI deduction, minus net capital gain.

NOTE: In an effort to avoid distracting you from the most important aspects of 199A that apply broadly, this course does not cover the many additional rules and regulations unique to specified agricultural and horticultural cooperatives and their patrons.

While this deduction is far more complex than the flat 21% corporate rate, you should familiarize yourself with it because many small businesses qualify. There are exceptions of course, and a number of new terms to learn, so we will start with a general overview before we dig deep.

S corporations and partnerships (other than a PTP) are generally not taxpayers and cannot take the deduction themselves. Instead, these *relevant passthrough entities (RPE)* must report the necessary information to owners on Schedule K-1 so they may figure the deduction. Section 199A does not require a taxpayer's material participation in the business to qualify for the deduction.

TIP: Section 199A amounts are **presumed to be $0** if the RPE omits the information on Schedule K-1. If this information is missing, the taxpayer should request a correction to the K-1.

Taxpayers eligible to claim the deduction generally include individuals and certain trusts and estates with QBI. An individual taxpayer claims the deduction on Form 1040 while a trust or estate with QBI uses Form 1041. For the remainder of the discussion, we will focus on individual taxpayers.

The deduction is subject to multiple limitations such as the type of trade or business, the taxpayer's taxable income, the amount of W-2 wages paid with respect to the qualified trade or business, and the unadjusted basis immediately after acquisition (UBIA) of qualified property held by the trade or business.

The business type limitation may eliminate the 199A deduction for certain large service businesses classified as a *Specified Service Trade or Business (SSTB)*. Many businesses fall into this category, which we will cover later. It is easy to assume that a taxpayer with an SSTB does not qualify, but that is a huge mistake!

The **50% W-2 wage limitation** is also a potential deduction killer because a sole proprietor or partnership with no employees does not have W-2 wages.

> The **SSTB limitation** and the **W-2 wage limitation** that reduce or eliminate the deduction **do not apply** if taxable income is below **$163,300** for single filers (**$326,600** if filing jointly) in 2020. A partial deduction is available below $213,300 ($426,600).

TIP: It's easy to spot a missing deduction. Is there an amount entered for the QBI deduction on the 2020 Form 1040 (line 13)? If a taxpayer has a business that isn't a corporation and has taxable income (line 15) below the threshold amount, it's time to dig deeper. It is good practice to review returns starting in 2018 for a missed QBI deduction.

QUALIFIED TRADE OR BUSINESS

The QBI component of section 199A is dependent on whether the individual has QBI from a *qualified trade or business*. The term "trade or business" generally includes any activity carried on for the production of income from selling goods or performing services.

So, what makes a business "qualified" for this deduction?

Section 199A(d) defines a qualified trade or business as any trade or business other than a **specified service trade or business** or the **trade or business of performing services as an employee**.

> **EXCEPTION:** The code provides an exception for any SSTB if taxable income is less than a threshold amount plus $50,000 ($100,000 in the case of a joint return). For 2020 the threshold is **$163,300** for single filers (**$326,600** if filing jointly). Simply put, if taxable income does not exceed this limit treat an SSTB just like any other qualified trade or business.

The IRS released final regulations further defining a "trade or business" in section 1.199A-1(b)(14) as a **trade or business under Section 162** other than the trade or business of performing services as an employee.

There is a small problem here—section 162 does not define a trade or business. Welcome to tax!

Because there is no statutory or regulatory definition of a section 162 trade or business, courts have established elements to determine the existence of a trade or business. The courts have developed two definitional requirements. One, in relation to **profit motive**, is said to require the taxpayer to enter into and carry on the activity with a good faith intention to make a profit or with the belief that a profit can be made from the activity. The second is in relation to the scope of the activities and is said to require **considerable, regular, and continuous**

activity. If the taxpayer owns an interest in a pass-through entity, the trade or business determination is made at that entity's level.

TIP: The trade or business requirement is a critical component to establish QBI. As usual, a determination of whether or not an activity is a trade or business will depend on the facts and circumstances. A hobby will not qualify, however, a gambling activity could qualify. See Commissioner v. Groetzinger, 480 U.S. 23 (1987).

REAL ESTATE TRADE OR BUSINESS

The ownership of rental real estate is common, but is it a business?

Whether an interest in rental real estate rises to the level of a trade or business for purposes of section 199A is the subject of uncertainty for some taxpayers. To help mitigate this uncertainty, ***Revenue Procedure 2019-38*** provides a safe harbor under which ***rental real estate enterprise*** will be treated as a trade or business for purposes of the QBI deduction. Rental real estate that does <u>not</u> meet the requirements of the safe harbor may still be treated as a trade or business for purposes of the QBI deduction if it otherwise meets the definition of a trade or business in the section 199A regulations.

This safe harbor is available for taxpayers who seek to claim the section 199A deduction with respect to a "rental real estate enterprise." Solely for purposes of this safe harbor, a rental real estate enterprise is defined as an interest in real property held to generate rental or lease income. It may consist of an interest in a single property or interests in multiple properties.

The taxpayer or a relevant passthrough entity (RPE) relying on this revenue procedure <u>must</u> **hold each interest directly** <u>or</u> through an entity **disregarded** as an entity separate from its owner, such as a limited liability company with a single member.

Safe Harbor Requirements

The following requirements <u>must</u> be met by taxpayers or RPEs to qualify for this safe harbor:

- **Separate books and records** are maintained to reflect income and expenses for **each** rental real estate enterprise.
- For rental real estate enterprises that have been in existence for less than four years, **250 or more hours of rental services** are performed per year. For other rental real estate enterprises, 250 or more hours of rental services are performed in at least three of the past five years.
- The taxpayer maintains **contemporaneous records**, including time reports, logs, or similar documents, regarding the following: hours of all services performed; description of all services performed; dates on which such services were performed; and who performed the services.
- The taxpayer or RPE **attaches a statement to a timely filed original return** (or an amended return for the 2018 taxable year only) filed for the tax year(s) the safe harbor is relied upon.

Certain Rental Real Estate Arrangements Excluded

The following types of property may <u>not</u> be included in a rental real estate enterprise and are therefore <u>not</u> eligible for the safe harbor:

- Real estate used by the taxpayer (including an owner or beneficiary of an RPE) as a residence more than the greater of 14 days or 10 percent of the number of days rented at fair value.
- Real estate rented or leased under a triple net lease. For purposes of this revenue procedure, a triple net lease includes a lease agreement that requires the tenant or lessee to pay taxes, fees, and insurance, and to pay for maintenance activities for a property in addition to rent and utilities.
- Real estate rented to a trade or business conducted by a taxpayer or an RPE which is commonly controlled.

- The entire rental real estate interest if any portion of the interest is treated as an SSTB under § 1.199A-5(c)(2) (which provides special rules where property or services are provided to an SSTB).

PERFORMING SERVICES AS AN EMPLOYEE

The trade or business of performing services as an employee is <u>not</u> a trade or business for purposes of section 199A. Therefore, no items of income, gain, deduction, and loss from the trade or business of performing services as an employee constitute QBI.

What exactly is meant by "performing services as an employee?"

Well, for starters the treatment of an employee by an employer as anything other than an employee for Federal employment tax purposes is immaterial. Thus, if a worker should be properly classified as an employee, it is of no consequence that the employee is treated as a non-employee by the employer for Federal employment tax purposes.

For purposes of 199A, there is a **presumption** that former employees who continue to offer the same services on a contract basis to their former employer are considered to be performing services as an employee. This presumption **lasts three years** after ceasing to be treated as an employee for Federal employment tax purposes and applies regardless of whether the individual provides services directly or indirectly through an entity or entities.

> **EXAMPLE:** Allen is employed by PRS, a partnership for Federal tax purposes, as a fulltime employee and is treated as such for Federal employment tax purposes. Allen quits his job for PRS and enters into a contract with PRS under which Allen provides substantially the same services that Allen previously provided to PRS in Allen's capacity as an employee. Because Allen was treated as an employee for services he provided to PRS, and now is no longer treated as an employee with regard to such services, Allen is presumed (solely for purposes of section 199A) to be in the trade or business of performing services as an employee with regard to his services performed for PRS. Any amounts paid by PRS to Allen with respect to such services will not be QBI for purposes of section 199A. The presumption would apply even if, instead of contracting directly with PRS, Allen formed a disregarded entity or a pass-through entity, and the entity entered into the contract with PRS.

Upon notice from the IRS, an individual may **rebut the presumption** by providing records, such as contracts or partnership agreements, that provide sufficient evidence to corroborate the individual's status as a non-employee under Federal tax law, regulations, and principles (including the common-law employee classification rules).

> **EXAMPLE:** Kristina is a financial advisor employed by a financial advisory firm, Bay Hill Advisors, a partnership for Federal tax purposes, as a fulltime employee and is treated as such for Federal employment tax purposes. Kristina has taxable income below the threshold amount. Bay Hill is a partnership and offers Kristina the opportunity to be admitted as a partner. Kristina elects to be admitted as a partner to Bay Hill and is admitted as a partner to Bay Hill. As a partner in Bay Hill, Kristina shares in the net profits of Bay Hill, is obligated to Bay Hill in ways that Kristina was not previously obligated as an employee, is no longer entitled to certain benefits available only to employees of Bay Hill, and has materially modified her relationship with Bay Hill. Kristina's share of net profits is not subject to a floor or capped at a dollar amount. Kristina is presumed (solely for purposes of section 199A) to be in the trade or business of performing services as an employee with respect to the services Kristina provides to Bay Hill. However, Kristina is able to rebut the presumption by showing that Kristina became a partner in Bay Hill by sharing in the profits of Bay Hill, materially modifying Kristina's relationship with Bay Hill, and otherwise satisfying the requirements under Federal tax law, regulations, and principles (including common-law employee classification rules) to be respected as a partner.

SPECIFIED SERVICE TRADE OR BUSINESS (SSTB)

The 199A deduction may be reduced or completely eliminated for certain types of businesses when income exceeds the threshold amount based on filing status. This is because income from a specified service trade or business is not income for QBI purposes when the taxable income of the taxpayer exceeds the threshold.

TIP: If taxable income does not exceed the threshold amount, the nature of the taxpayer's business is irrelevant for purposes of the deduction.

A specified service trade or business is any trade or business involving the **performance of services** in the fields of:

- **Health**, including physicians, nurses, dentists, veterinarians, physical therapists, psychologists, and other similar healthcare professionals. However, it excludes services not directly related to a medical services field, such as the operation of health clubs or spas; payment processing; or the research, testing, manufacture, and sale of pharmaceuticals or medical devices;

- **Law**, including lawyers, paralegals, legal arbitrators, mediators, and similar professionals. However, it excludes services that do not require skills unique to the field of law such as services by printers, delivery services, or stenography services;

- **Accounting**, including accountants, enrolled agents, return preparers, financial auditors, and similar professionals;

  TIP: This category is not limited to services requiring state licensure as a certified public accountant (CPA). This category includes tax return and bookkeeping services but does not include payment processing and billing analysis.

- **Actuarial science**, including actuaries, and similar professionals;

- **Performing arts**, including actors, directors, singers, musicians, entertainers, and similar professionals. However, it excludes services that don't require skills unique to the creation of performing arts, such as the maintenance and operation of equipment or facilities for use in the performing arts or the provision of services by persons who broadcast video or audio of performing arts to the public;

- **Consulting**, including providing advice and counsel with the intention of influencing decisions made by a government or governmental agency and all attempts to influence legislators and other government officials on behalf of a client by lobbyists, and other similar professionals. However, it excludes the performance of services other than advice or counsel, such as sales, training or educational courses. It also excludes embedded or ancillary services that are otherwise not SSTBs, if there is no separate payment for the services;

- **Athletics**, including athletes, coaches, and managers in sports such as baseball, basketball, football, soccer, hockey, martial arts, boxing, bowling, tennis, golf, snowboarding, track and field, billiards, racing, and other athletic performance. However, it excludes services that do not require skills unique to athletic competition, such as the maintenance and operation of equipment or facilities for use in athletic events or the provision of services by persons who broadcast video or audio of athletic events to the public;

- **Financial services**, including managing wealth, advising clients with respect to finances, developing retirement plans, developing wealth transition plans, the provision of advisory and other similar services regarding valuations, mergers, acquisitions, dispositions, restructuring (including in title 11 or similar cases), and raising financial capital by underwriting, or acting as a client's agent in the issuance of securities, and similar services. This includes services provided by financial advisors, investment bankers, wealth planners, retirement advisors, and other similar professionals. However, it excludes taking deposits or making loans, but does include arrange lending transactions between a lender and borrower;

- **Brokerage services**, including services in which a person arranges transactions between a buyer and a seller with respect to securities for a commission or fee including services provided by stockbrokers and other similar professionals. However, it excludes services provided by real estate agents and brokers, or insurance agents and brokers;

- **Investing and investment management**, in which a fee is received for providing investing, asset management, or investment management services, including providing advice with respect to buying and selling investments. However, it excludes the service of directly managing real property;

- **Trading securities, commodities, or partnership interests;**

- **Dealing in securities, commodities, or partnership interests;**

- **Any trade or business where the principal asset is the reputation or skill of one or more of its employees or owners**, as demonstrated by:

    ○ Receiving fees, compensation, or other income for endorsing products or services;

    ○ Licensing or receiving fees, compensation or other income for the use of an individual's image, likeness, name, signature, voice, trademark, or any other symbols associated with the individual's identity; or

    ○ Receiving fees, compensation, or other income for appearing at an event or on radio, television, or another media format (including fees or income to reality performers performing as themselves on television, social media, or other forums, radio, television, and other media hosts, and video game players).

TIP: If you think about it, most small service businesses rely on the "reputation or skill" of one or more employees or owners. The final regulations provide a narrow definition to businesses—where **reputation or skill is the principal asset**—generating income through licensing, endorsements and appearance fees.

> **EXAMPLE:** Gordon is a well-known chef and the sole owner of multiple restaurants each of which is owned in a disregarded entity. Due to Gordon's skill and reputation as a chef, Gordon receives an endorsement fee of $500,000 for the use of his name on a line of cooking utensils and cookware. Gordon is in the trade or business of being a chef and owning restaurants and such trade or business is not an SSTB. However, he is also in the trade or business of receiving endorsement income. Gordon's trade or business consisting of the receipt of the endorsement fee for his skill and/or reputation is an SSTB.

DE MINIMIS RULE

A trade or business is <u>not</u> an SSTB if <u>less</u> than **10 percent** of the gross receipts (5 percent if gross receipts are greater than $25 million) of the trade or business are attributable to the performance of specified services.

> **EXAMPLE:** Landscape LLC sells lawn care and landscaping equipment and also provides advice and counsel on landscape design for large office parks and residential buildings. The landscape design services include advice on the selection and placement of trees, shrubs, and flowers and are considered to be the performance of services in the field of consulting. Landscape LLC separately invoices for its landscape design services and does not sell the trees, shrubs, or flowers it recommends for use in the landscape design. Landscape LLC maintains one set of books and records and treats the equipment sales and design services as a single trade or business for purposes of sections 162 and 199A. Landscape LLC has gross receipts of $2 million. $250,000 of the gross receipts is attributable to the landscape design services, an SSTB. Because the gross receipts from the consulting services exceed 10 percent of Landscape LLC's total gross receipts, the entirety of Landscape LLC's trade or business is considered an SSTB.

> **EXAMPLE:** Animal Care LLC provides veterinarian services performed by licensed staff and also develops and sells its own line of organic dog food at its veterinarian clinic and online. The veterinarian services are considered to be the performance of services in the field of health. Animal Care LLC separately invoices for its veterinarian services and the sale of its organic dog food. Animal Care LLC maintains separate books and

records for its veterinarian clinic and its development and sale of its dog food. Animal Care LLC also has separate employees who are unaffiliated with the veterinary clinic and who only work on the formulation, marketing, sales, and distribution of the organic dog food products. Animal Care LLC treats its veterinary practice and the dog food development and sales as separate trades or businesses for purposes of section 162 and 199A. Animal Care LLC has gross receipts of $3,000,000. $1,000,000 of the gross receipts is attributable to the veterinary services, an SSTB. Although the gross receipts from the services in the field of health exceed 10 percent of Animal Care LLC's total gross receipts, the dog food development and sales business is not considered an SSTB due to the fact that the veterinary practice and the dog food development and sales are separate trades or businesses under section 162.

COMPONENTS OF THE DEDUCTION

As previously mentioned, a taxpayer **other than a corporation** generally may deduct:

- **20 percent** of *qualified business income (QBI)*, plus
- **20 percent** of qualified REIT dividends and qualified PTP income.

These components are calculated independently and added together to arrive at the deduction before applying the 20% of taxable income limitation. If either component is a loss it will not reduce the other, rather, the loss will carry forward and offset income from the same component in future years.

QBI COMPONENT

QBI is the **net amount** of qualified items of income, gain, deduction and loss from a *qualified trade or business*. QBI includes income earned through a business operated as a sole proprietorship or through a partnership, S corporation, and certain trusts or estates.

QBI does not include items such as:

- Items that are not properly includable in taxable income
- Investment items such as capital gains or losses or dividends
- Interest income not properly allocable to a trade or business
- Wage income
- Income that is not effectively connected with the conduct of business within the United States
- Commodities transactions or foreign currency gains or losses
- Certain dividends and payments in lieu of dividends
- Income, loss, or deductions from notional principal contracts
- Annuities, unless received in connection with the trade or business
- Amounts received as reasonable compensation from an S corporation
- Amounts received as guaranteed payments from a partnership
- Payments received by a partner for services other than in a capacity as a partner
- Qualified REIT dividends
- PTP income

QBI is **separately determined** for each qualified trade or business of the taxpayer. A qualified trade or business means any trade or business other than a *specified service trade or business (SSTB)* and other than the trade or business of performing services as an employee.

> **EXCEPTION:** The SSTB exclusion from the definition of a qualified trade or business phases-in when taxable income exceeds the threshold amount. A taxpayer with taxable income below the threshold may consider income from the SSTB as QBI for purposes of the deduction.

For purposes of section 199A, deductions are considered attributable to a trade or business to the extent that the individual's gross income from the trade or business is taken into account in calculating the allowable deduction.

> **EXAMPLE:** In a taxable year, if a qualified trade or business has $100,000 of ordinary income from inventory sales and makes an expenditure of $25,000 that is required to be capitalized and amortized over five years under applicable Federal income tax rules, QBI is $100,000 minus $5,000 (current-year ordinary amortization deduction), or $95,000. QBI is not reduced by the entire amount of the capital expenditure, but rather only by the amount allowed as a deduction in determining taxable income for the year under the qualified trade or business's method of accounting.

Qualified items of gain or loss are taken into account to determine QBI only to the extent **included or allowed in the determination of taxable income for the year.** To determine the total amount of QBI, the taxpayer must consider all items that are related to the trade or business including, but not limited to, charitable contributions, unreimbursed partnership expenses, business interest expense, deductible part of self-employment tax, self-employment health insurance deduction, and self-employed SEP, SIMPLE, and qualified plan deductions.

QBI does not include any losses or deductions disallowed under the basis, at-risk, passive loss, or section 461(l) limitations, as they aren't included or allowed in determining taxable income for the year. Instead, these losses and deductions are taken into account in the tax year they are included in determining taxable income.

> **EXCEPTION:** Disallowed losses or deductions allowed in the taxable year are generally taken into account for purposes of computing QBI except to the extent the losses or deductions were disallowed, suspended, limited, or carried over from taxable years ending **before January 1, 2018.**

> **EXAMPLE:** Assume a qualified trade or business has a passive loss that is not allowable for taxable year 2019 in the amount of $50,000, and that the loss is attributable to a qualified trade or business. Assume further that $20,000 of the 2019 loss is allowed for the taxable year 2020. The 2019 loss of $20,000 allowed in 2020 is taken into account in determining the taxpayer's QBI from the qualified trade or business in 2020.

Domestic business items are treated as qualified items of income, gain, deduction, and loss only to the extent they are **effectively connected** with the conduct of a trade or business within the **United States.**

TIP: In the case of an individual with QBI from sources within the Commonwealth of Puerto Rico, if all such income for the taxable year is taxable under section 1 (income tax rates for individuals), then the term "United States" is considered to include the Commonwealth of Puerto Rico for purposes of determining the individual's QBI.

QBI of the taxpayer does not include any amount paid by an S corporation that is treated as **reasonable compensation** of the taxpayer. Similarly, QBI does not include any **guaranteed payment** for services rendered with respect to the trade or business, and, to the extent provided in regulations, does not include any amount paid or incurred by a partnership to a partner, acting other than in his or her capacity as a partner, for services.

Qualified Business Loss Carryover

If the net amount of QBI from all qualified trades or businesses during the taxable year is a loss, the qualified business loss is carried over for purposes of calculating the deduction under section 199A and in the next taxable year is treated as a loss from a qualified trade or business. The qualified business loss carryover continues to carry forward, reduced by any qualified business income in subsequent years, until the taxpayer has a taxable year with net qualified business income.

REIT/PTP COMPONENT

The qualified REIT/PTP component is the sum of qualified real estate investment trust dividends and the net amount of qualified publicly traded partnership income earned directly or through a relevant passthrough entity (RPE).

A taxpayer may claim the 20% deduction for this component even if there is no QBI from a qualified trade or business. Also, unlike the QBI component, the qualified REIT/PTP component is not subject to the W-2 UBIA limitation (unless PTP income is generated by an SSTB).

Qualified REIT Dividends

Certain entities that engage in real estate activities and meet the requirements of section 856 may elect special treatment as a *real estate investment trust (REIT)*.

REITs are often listed publicly on a stock exchange or sold directly to investors and have become a popular option for investors seeking a steady stream of income. The reason, REITs are required to distribute at least 90 percent of their taxable income to shareholders annually in the form of dividends.

A qualified REIT dividend for purposes of section 199A is generally a dividend from a REIT received during the tax year that is not a **capital gain dividend** or considered **qualified dividend income.** You may note that these excluded dividends are taxed at preferential rates, which is why the 20% deduction does not apply.

There is a **45-day holding period requirement**. A qualified REIT dividend does not include any REIT dividend received with respect to any share of REIT stock that is held for 45 days or less during the 91-day period beginning on the date that is 45 days before the date on which such share became ex-dividend with respect to the dividend.

TIP: When counting the number of days the recipient held the stock, include the day the recipient disposed of the stock, but do not include the day the recipient acquired the stock or certain days during which the recipient's risk of loss was diminished.

In addition, a qualified REIT dividend does not include any dividend on shares of REIT stock to the extent the recipient is under an obligation (whether pursuant to a short sale or otherwise) to make related payments with respect to positions in substantially similar or related property.

TIP: The amount of Section 199A dividends paid by the REIT should be included in the amount reported in box 5 of Form 1099-DIV. This amount may include REIT dividends for which it is impractical for the REIT to determine whether the recipient has met the holding period requirement.

Qualified Publicly Traded Partnership Income

Interests in certain partnerships are traded like stocks on an established securities market, or readily tradable on a secondary market. The taxpayer treats income from a publicly traded partnership (PTP) separately from partnerships that are part of the QBI component.

In general, the term qualified PTP income means the net amount of such taxpayer's allocable share of income, gain, deduction, and loss from a PTP that is not taxed as a corporation, plus gain or loss attributable to assets of the PTP giving rise to ordinary income under section 751(a) or (b) that is considered attributable to the trades or businesses conducted by the partnership.

Negative Combined Qualified REIT Dividends/Qualified PTP Income

If the combined amount of REIT dividends and qualified PTP income is less than zero, the portion of the individual's section 199A deduction related to qualified REIT dividends and qualified PTP income is zero for the taxable year. The negative combined amount must be **carried forward** and used to offset the combined amount of REIT dividends/qualified PTP income in the succeeding taxable years of the individual for purposes of section 199A.

CALCULATING THE 199A DEDUCTION

TAXABLE INCOME BELOW THRESHOLD

In general, the amount of the QBI deduction equals the QBI component plus the qualified **REIT/PTP component.**

There are a number of rules that limit the deduction, so let's run through a few basic scenarios, starting with the simplest application of the rules, and then we will work our way through a few of the more difficult examples.

The three limits you need to be aware of (and the order in which they apply) are:

1. SSTB limitation
2. W-2 Wages / UBIA limitation
3. Taxable income limitation

The first two limits affect only the **QBI component** and apply only if taxable income exceeds the threshold amount. Taxpayers must compare 2020 taxable income to a threshold amount that is indexed annually for inflation.

Filing Status	Threshold Amount	Full Phase-in
MFJ	$326,600	$426,600
MFS	$163,300	$213,300
S / HH	$163,300	$213,300

Therefore, the logical first step for a taxpayer with QBI is a quick peek at the taxpayer's taxable income. Is it more than the 2020 threshold amount?

If the answer is NO, the calculation is simple.

20% QBI + 20% REIT/PTP = QBI deduction before the taxable income limitation.

> The overall 199A deduction cannot exceed **20% of taxable income**, calculated before the QBI deduction, minus **net capital gain.**

EXAMPLE 1: Alfonso, an unmarried individual, owns and operates a computer repair shop as a sole proprietorship. The business generated $100,000 in net taxable income from operations. Alfonso has no capital gains or losses. After allowable deductions not relating to the business, Alfonso's total taxable income is $81,000.

The business's QBI is $100,000, the net amount of its qualified items of income, gain, deduction, and loss. Alfonso's Section 199A deduction is equal to $16,200, the <u>lesser</u> of 20% of Alfonso's QBI from the business ($100,000 QBI × 20% = $20,000) or 20% of Alfonso's total taxable income ($81,000 taxable income × 20% = $16,200).

EXAMPLE 2: Assume the same facts as in Example 1, except that Alfonso also has $7,000 in net capital gain and that, after allowable deductions not relating to the business, Alfonso's total taxable income is $74,000.

Alfonso's total taxable income minus net capital gain is $67,000 ($74,000 taxable income – $7,000 net capital gain). Alfonso's section 199A deduction is equal to $13,400, the <u>lesser</u> of 20% of Alfonso's QBI from the business ($100,000 QBI × 20% = $20,000) or 20% of Alfonso's total taxable income minus net capital gain ($67,000 taxable income net of capital gain × 20% = $13,400).

TAXABLE INCOME ABOVE THRESHOLD

The following limitations do <u>not</u> apply to any taxpayer whose taxable income is <u>not</u> more than the threshold amount, nor do they impact the qualified REIT/PTP component of the deduction.

A **full reduction** is completely phased-in when the taxpayer has taxable income in excess of the threshold amount plus $50,000 ($100,000 joint return). The <u>full</u> reduction is as follows:

- The taxpayer is unable to consider <u>any</u> QBI, W-2 wages, and UBIA from an SSTB (the "SSTB limitation")
- The maximum QBI component is limited to 50% of W-2 wages, or, if greater, 25% of W-2 wages + 2.5% of the ***unadjusted basis immediately after acquisition (UBIA)*** of qualified property (the "W-2 UBIA limitation")

There is a small window (called a **phase-in** range) where the limitations are not fully applied. If taxable income before the QBI deduction is more than $163,300 but not $213,300 for single filers ($326,600 and $426,600 if MFJ), an applicable percentage of any SSTB is treated as a qualified trade or business and the W-2 UBIA limitation phases-in.

The ***phase-in percentage*** is equal to the ratio that the excess of the taxable income of the taxpayer for the taxable year over the threshold amount bears to $50,000 ($100,000 joint return), up to a maximum of 100%.

Phase-in Percentage

$$\frac{\textit{Taxable Income} - \textit{Threshold Amount}}{\textit{\$50,000 (or \$100,000 joint return)}}$$

EXAMPLE: A single taxpayer has taxable income of $183,300.

$183,300 – $163,300 threshold = $20,000 excess taxable income.

$20,000 ÷ $50,000 = **40% phase-in percentage**.

The applicable percentage is the amount of SSTB income, wages, and UBIA to consider <u>before</u> applying the W-2 UBIA limitation. The ***applicable percentage*** starts at 100% (because all SSTB items are considered below the threshold) and is reduced by the phase-in percentage. The calculation of the applicable percentage for an SSTB is done on Schedule A (Form 8995-A).

Applicable Percentage
100% – Phase-in Percentage

TIP: A question this complex is unlikely to appear on the exam. Don't worry about calculating phased-in reductions.

SSTB LIMITATION

The SSTB limitation is irrelevant when taxable income does <u>not</u> exceed the threshold amount. There is a small window (called a phase-in range) where a portion of the SSTB income, wages, and UBIA is eliminated for purposes of the 199A deduction.

A taxpayer with taxable income in excess of the threshold amount plus $50,000 ($100,000 joint return) is unable to consider <u>any</u> items (including income) from an SSTB.

EXAMPLE: David is single and has 2020 taxable income of $220,000 from his law firm. He has W-2 wages of $80,000.

STEP 1: Compare taxable income to the threshold for is filing status.

$220,000	taxable income
– $163,300	threshold amount (single)
$56,700	excess taxable income

David's law firm is an SSTB and he has more than $50,000 of excess taxable income. David is unable to consider any income or wages from this business for QBI purposes. His deduction is **$0**.

For a taxpayer with taxable income within the phase-in range, the computation of QBI with respect to an SSTB takes into account only the applicable percentage of qualified items of income, gain, deduction, or loss, and of allocable W-2 wages and UBIA.

W-2 UBIA LIMITATION

The 199A deduction is subject to the W-2 UBIA limitation, which is the <u>greater</u> of:

- 50% of the W-2 wages paid with respect to the qualified trade or business, or
- The sum of 25% of the W-2 wages + 2.5% of the unadjusted basis of qualified property

The determination of **W-2 wages and UBIA** is made <u>separately</u> for each trade or business. Under certain circumstances, an individual may aggregate businesses together before applying the limits (discussed later).

A pass-through entity is required to report QBI information (including allocable share of W-2 wages and UBIA) to owners.

Unreported W-2 wages or UBIA is **presumed to be zero** if <u>not</u> determined and reported for each trade or business (or aggregated trade or business). This information should appear on a K-1 provided by the RPE.

DETERMINING W-2 WAGES

W-2 wages generally include amounts paid to employees for the performance of services, plus elective deferrals (for example, contributions to 401(k) plans), deferred compensation, and Roth IRA contributions.

Wages paid to a statutory employee are not included when the "Statutory Employee" box on Form W-2 is checked. Only W-2 wages that are properly allocable to QBI may be taken into account in computing the W-2 UBIA limitations.

TIP: Unlike an S corporation, a sole proprietor or partnership with no employees does not have W-2 wages.

DETERMINING UBIA

UBIA stands to the unadjusted basis, immediately after acquisition, of all *qualified property* held for use in the trade or business.

In order to understand UBIA, we need to define a few things.

The *unadjusted basis immediately after acquisition* means the basis on the **placed-in-service date**. The basis of the property is not adjusted (reduced) by depreciation. Improvements to property are treated as separate qualified property.

Qualified property is **depreciable tangible property** that is held by, and available for use in, the qualified trade or business at the close of the taxable year, that is used at any point during the taxable year in the production of qualified business income, and for which the depreciable period has not ended before the close of the taxable year.

The depreciable period ends on the later of 10 years after the property is placed-in-service or the last day of the full year for the applicable recovery period under section 168. Additional first-year depreciation, such as bonus depreciation, doesn't affect the applicable recovery period.

Property acquired within 60 days of the year-end that is disposed within 120 days without being used by the trade or business for at least 45 days generally isn't qualified property.

APPLYING THE W-2 UBIA LIMITATION

Like the SSTB limitation, the W-2 UBIA limitation does not apply unless the taxpayer has taxable income in excess of the threshold amount.

TIP: If the amount of a taxpayer's QBI deduction is less than 50% of W-2 wages it isn't necessary to calculate the phased-in reduction since it will only be higher than 50% of W-2 wages. In that case, the QBI deduction is allowed in full, subject to the 20% of taxable income limit.

A taxpayer with taxable income that exceeds the threshold amount plus $50,000 ($100,000 MFJ) is subject to the full phased-in reduction. This means that the QBI component is limited to 50% of W-2 wages, or, if greater, 25% of W-2 wages + 2.5% of UBIA of qualified property.

> **EXAMPLE:** A single taxpayer has a sole proprietorship that manufactures widgets and QBI of $70,000. The taxpayer has taxable income that is more than $50,000 above the threshold amount. The business buys a widget-making machine for $100,000 and places it in service in the current year. The business has one employee with W-2 wages of $20,000.
>
> **STEP 1:** Calculate the 20% QBI deduction before the W-2 UBIA limitation.
>
> $$\$70,000 \text{ QBI} \times 20\% = \mathbf{\$14,000}$$
>
> **STEP 2:** Calculate the W2 UBIA limitation which is the greater of:

$10,000   **50% W-2 Wages** (50% × $20,000)

$7,500   **25% W-2 Wages** (25% × $20,000) **+ 2.5% UBIA** (2.5% × $100,000)

NOTE: It isn't necessary to calculate a phase-in percentage because this taxpayer is subject to the full phased-in reduction.

STEP 3: The QBI deduction is $10,000, which is the <u>lesser</u> of $14,000, or $10,000 W-2 wage and UBIA limitation.

Phased-in Reduction

A phased-in reduction applies when taxable income exceeds the threshold amount by less than $50,000 ($100,000 MFJ). The ***excess amount*** is the amount by which 20% QBI is greater than the W-2 UBIA limitation. For a full reduction (like the prior example) the entire excess amount is disallowed because the phase-in percentage is 100%. In a phased-in reduction, the phase-in percentage reduces the 20% QBI deduction by a portion of the excess amount.

Phased-in Reduction

Excess Amount × Phase-in Percentage

EXAMPLE: A single taxpayer has a sole proprietorship that manufactures widgets and QBI of $70,000. The taxpayer has taxable income that is **$30,000** above the threshold amount. The business buys a widget-making machine for $100,000 and places it in service in the current year. The business has one employee with W-2 wages of $20,000.

STEP 1: Calculate the 20% QBI deduction <u>before</u> the W-2 UBIA limitation.

$70,000 QBI × 20% = **$14,000**

STEP 2: Calculate the W2 UBIA limitation which is the <u>greater</u> of:

$10,000   **50% W-2 Wages** (50% × $20,000)

$7,500   **25% W-2 Wages** (25% × $20,000) **+ 2.5% UBIA** (2.5% × $100,000)

STEP 3: Calculate the phased-in reduction.

$4,000   **Excess amount** ($14,000 – $10,000)

× 60%   **Phase-in percentage** ($30,000 ÷ $50,000)
_____

$2,400   **Phased-in reduction**

STEP 4: Reduce $14,000 (20% QBI) by the $2,400 phased-in reduction to arrive at **$11,600** QBI component.

AGGREGATION RULES

A taxpayer may be engaged in more than one trade or business. In general, each trade or business is a **separate trade or business** for purposes of applying the limitations. An individual <u>may</u> aggregate trades or businesses, treating the aggregate as a **single trade or business** for purposes of applying the limitations. This may be helpful if a business does <u>not</u> have W-2 wages and the other does.

A business may be aggregated only if an individual can demonstrate <u>all</u> the following:

- The same person or group of persons, directly or indirectly, owns **50 percent** or more of each trade or business to be aggregated, and

- The ownership exists for a majority of the taxable year in which the items attributable to each trade or business to be aggregated are included in income, and
- All of the items attributable to each trade or business to be aggregated are reported on returns with the same taxable year, not taking into account short taxable years, and
- None of the trades or businesses to be aggregated is an **SSTB**, and
- At least **two of the following factors** apply:

  1. The trades or businesses provide products and services that are the same or customarily offered together.

  2. The trades or businesses share facilities or share significant centralized business elements, such as personnel, accounting, legal, manufacturing, purchasing, human resources, or information technology resources.

  3. The trades or businesses are operated in coordination with, or reliance upon, one or more of the businesses in the aggregated group (for example, supply chain interdependencies).

If an individual chooses to aggregate trades or businesses, the individual must **combine the QBI, W-2 wages, and UBIA** of qualified property of each trade or business within an aggregated trade or business prior to applying the W-2 wages and UBIA of qualified property limitations.

FORM 8995 AND FORM 8995-A

A taxpayer **does not need to itemize** deductions to claim this deduction. The taxpayer claims the 199A deduction after calculating adjusted gross income (AGI).

Taxpayers use *Form 8995-A Qualified Business Income Deduction* to claim the qualified business income deduction.

A one-page simplified version (Form 8995) is available if:

- The taxpayer's 2020 taxable income is not more than the threshold amount.
- The taxpayer is not using the aggregation rules.
- The taxpayer is not a patron of an agricultural or horticultural cooperative.

Form 8995-A is filed if a taxpayer does not qualify to file the simplified Form 8995.

LESSON 7

Taxes

TAX CALCULATIONS

Income tax is a percentage of **taxable income**. Tax rates vary according to the amount of taxable income.

U.S. income tax is a **progressive tax**, whereby rates increase as taxable income increases. The IRS has established **tax brackets** at various income levels. Taxable income within each bracket is taxed at the corresponding tax rate. For tax year 2020, the top rate is 37 percent. The **marginal tax rate** is the rate at which the last dollar of income is taxed.

Upon determining the amount of income tax and any **alternative minimum tax (AMT)**, subtract any **non-refundable tax credits** (non-refundable credits only reduce tax, the taxpayer does not receive a refund of any excess) and add any **other taxes** owed (discussed later). The result is the taxpayer's **total tax**.

Compare the total tax with **total payments** (including **refundable credits**) to determine whether a refund or additional tax payment is due. The IRS treats refundable credits the same as payments of tax. If the total payments (the sum of refundable credits, withheld federal income tax, estimated tax payments and amount applied from prior year return, and any amount paid with request for an extension to file) are more than the total tax, the taxpayer can receive a refund of the excess.

Most taxpayers use either the **Tax Table** or the **Tax Computation Worksheet** to figure their income taxes. However, there are special methods if income includes any of the following items:

- Net capital gain
- Qualified dividends taxed at the same rates as a net capital gain
- Lump-sum distributions
- Farming or fishing income
- Investment income more than $2,200 in 2020 for certain children (Form 8615 Tax for Certain Children Who Have Unearned Income)
- Parents' election to report a child's investment income (Form 8814 Parents' Election To Report Child's Interest and Dividends)
- Foreign earned income exclusion or the housing exclusion

OTHER TAXES

A taxpayer must complete Schedule 2 and attach certain forms to report additional taxes. These taxes include the following:

- Alternative minimum tax (Form 6251)
- Excess advance premium tax credit repayment (Form 8962)
- Self-employment tax (Schedule SE)
- Unreported social security and Medicare tax (Form 4137 for tips, Form 8919 for wages)
- Additional Taxes on Qualified Retirement Plans, IRAs, and Other Tax-Favored Accounts (Form 5329)
- Household employment taxes (Schedule H)
- Repayment of first-time homebuyer credit (Form 5405)
- Additional Medicare Tax (Form 8959)
- Net Investment Income Tax (Form 8960)

Use **Form 5329** to report additional taxes on IRAs, other qualified retirement plans, modified endowment contracts, Coverdell ESAs, QTPs, Archer MSAs, HSAs or ABLE accounts.

ALTERNATIVE MINIMUM TAX

Taxpayers with certain income or expenses that receive special treatment under the regular tax system may be subject to an additional tax known as the *alternative minimum tax (AMT)*. AMT is a separate tax that is imposed in addition to the regular tax. Use *Form 6251, Alternative Minimum Tax—Individuals*, to figure AMT separately, after eliminating certain deductions and credits, to arrive at *alternative minimum taxable income (AMTI)*. AMT liability exists if taxable income for regular tax purposes, combined with *adjustments* and *tax preference items*, is more than the *AMT exemption* amount.

For taxable years beginning in 2020, the **AMT exemption** amounts are:

- $113,400 Joint Returns or Surviving Spouses
- $72,900 Unmarried Individuals (other than Surviving Spouses)
- $56,700 Married Individuals Filing Separate

For taxable years beginning in 2020, the amounts used to determine the **phaseout of the exemption** amounts are (the exemption amounts above reduce by 25% of AMTI in excess of the following):

- $1,036,800 Joint Returns or Surviving Spouses
- $518,400 Unmarried Individuals (other than Surviving Spouses)
- $518,400 Married Individuals Filing Separate

For taxable years beginning in 2020, the excess taxable income above which the 28 percent tax rate applies is:

- $98,950 Married Individuals Filing Separate Returns
- $197,900 Joint Returns, Surviving Spouses, and Unmarried Individuals

For 2020, the **alternative minimum tax brackets** are:

Filing Status	26% AMT Tax Rate	28% AMT Tax Rate
Married filing separately	AMTI up to $98,950	AMTI above $98,950
All other filers	AMTI up to $197,900	AMTI above $197,900

The AMT exemption amount is subtracted from AMTI <u>before</u> calculating the tax. For 2020, apply a flat tax rate of **26%** up to $197,900 ($98,950 for MFS). A **28%** tax rate applies to the excess. This is the *tentative minimum tax*. If the tentative minimum tax exceeds normal income tax liability the taxpayer reports the difference as AMT on the tax return.

ADJUSTMENTS AND TAX PREFERENCE ITEMS

AMT is caused by two types of adjustments and preferences—deferral items and exclusion items. Deferral items (for example, depreciation) generally do not cause a permanent difference in taxable income over time. Exclusion items (for example, the standard deduction) do cause a permanent difference. The more common adjustments and tax preference items include the following:

- **Adjustments** – The first step to determine AMTI is adjusting the taxpayer's taxable income:
  1. Add the amount claimed for the standard deduction <u>or</u> the amount claimed for state, local, and foreign taxes as an itemized deduction.
  2. Subtract any refund of state, local, and foreign taxes included in gross income

- **Preference Items** – The tax code provides preferential treatment to certain income and deduction items. Under AMT rules, these items do not receive special treatment, thus increasing tax liability for an individual who would otherwise pay less tax. The following list includes the more common preference items that increase AMTI:

  1. Tax-exempt interest from **specified private activity municipal bonds**
  2. Difference between depreciation allowed for regular tax purposes and depreciation allowed for AMT purposes
  3. Difference between gain or loss on the sale of property reported for regular tax purposes and gain or loss reported for AMT purposes
  4. Addition of certain income from incentive stock options
  5. Change in certain passive activity loss deductions
  6. Depletion that is more than the adjusted basis (not applicable to independent producers)
  7. Deduction for excess intangible drilling costs not amortized over a 60-month period

CREDIT FOR PRIOR YEAR MINIMUM TAX

A taxpayer with AMT liability in the current year may recapture that amount in future years in the form of a credit. This **non-refundable credit** can offset future tax liability only to the extent prior AMT tax paid was due to **deferral items**. The credit <u>cannot</u> reduce tax below the *tentative minimum tax* for the year.

SELF-EMPLOYMENT TAX

A self-employed taxpayer does <u>not</u> have wages, and unlike an employee, amounts are <u>not</u> withheld from wages to pay social security or Medicare taxes. Instead, a self-employed taxpayer uses *Schedule SE* to figure *self-employment tax* due on *net earnings from self-employment*.

SELF-EMPLOYMENT INCOME

The IRS defines net earnings from self-employment as the gross income from a trade or business, less business deductions. A partner's distributive share of ordinary income or loss is also self-employment income.

TIP: Certain deductions which are no longer deductible by employees as an itemized deduction (for example, car expenses) may be deductible by a self-employed taxpayer on Schedule C. Details of these expenses are found in *Expenses and Deductions* in Part 2 Businesses.

The Internal Revenue Code lists income from the following sources as specifically <u>not</u> income from self-employment:

- Income earned as an employee
- Income from rental real estate (unless a real estate dealer)
- Dividends from stocks or bonds (unless a securities dealer)
- Payments to a retired partner that continue after death
- Income received for services as an employee of a state (one example is a notary)

TIP: A taxpayer with *net earnings from self-employment* of at least **$400** in 2020 must file a tax return to report the income.

SELF-EMPLOYMENT TAX

Self-employment tax under the *Self Employed Contributions Act (SECA)* is a Social Security and Medicare tax primarily for individuals who work for themselves. Income earned as an employee or as a notary is not subject to SECA tax. Payments of SECA tax contribute to coverage under the Social Security system. Social Security coverage provides the taxpayer with retirement benefits, disability benefits, survivor benefits, and hospital insurance

(Medicare) benefits. An individual may deduct a portion of SECA tax as an adjustment to income on Form 1040. The self-employed <u>must</u> pay SECA tax and file Schedule SE if either of the following applies:

- Net earnings from self-employment were **$400** or more
- Had church employee income of **$108.28** or more

A self-employed taxpayer pays self-employment tax on net earnings from self-employment by attaching Schedule SE to the return. This tax is the equivalent of social security and Medicare tax. For 2020, the self-employment tax rate is **15.3%** (12.4% social security and 2.9% Medicare). For 2020, all net earnings are subject to Medicare tax but social security tax applies only to the first **$137,700** ($142,800 in 2021) of net earnings.

A tax rate of **2.9%** (Medicare tax) applies to the excess. For higher-income taxpayers, a **.9%** *Additional Medicare Tax* applies when income exceeds one of the following threshold amounts (based on filing status):

- Married filing jointly—$250,000
- Married filing separately—$125,000
- Single, Head of household, or Qualifying widow(er)—$200,000

A taxpayer with both wages and self-employment income reduces the threshold amount for applying the Additional Medicare Tax on the self-employment income (but <u>not</u> below zero) by the amount of wages subject to Additional Medicare Tax.

> Before applying the tax rates, a self-employed taxpayer reduces income from self-employment by the percentage of tax that employers normally pay for their employees (50%).

> **EXAMPLE:** Peter has $100,000 income from self-employment. If Peter were an employee, his employer would pay $7,650 (7.65%). He subtracts this portion from his self-employment income to determine his **net earnings from self-employment** of $92,350 ($100,000 – $7,650). His SECA tax is $14,129.55 ($92,350 × 15.3%).

ADDITIONAL TAXES ON TAX-FAVORED ACCOUNTS

EXCESS CONTRIBUTIONS

> Contributions above the allowed limits are *excess contributions*. A **6% excise tax** applies if the taxpayer does <u>not</u> withdraw excess contributions (and interest or other income resulting from the contribution) by the due date of the return (including extensions).

This tax applies <u>each</u> year on excess amounts that remain in the following account types:

- Traditional IRA
- Roth IRA
- Coverdell Education Savings Account (ESA)
- Archer Medical Savings Account (MSA)
- Health Savings Account (HSA)
- Achieving a Better Life Experience (ABLE) Account

The taxpayer will include the interest or other income that was earned on the excess contribution in gross income on the return for the year in which the excess contribution was made. The withdrawal of interest or other income may be subject to an additional 10% tax on early distributions.

TIP: You can't apply an excess contribution to an earlier year even if you contributed less than the maximum amount allowable for the earlier year. However, you may be able to apply it to a later year if the contributions for that later year are less than the maximum allowed for that year.

> **EXAMPLE 1:** Maria, age 35, made an excess contribution in 2020 of $1,000, which she withdrew by April 15, 2021, the due date of her return. At the same time, she also withdrew the $50 income that was earned on the $1,000. She must include the $50 in her gross income for 2020 (the year in which the excess contribution was made). She must also pay an additional tax of $5 (the 10% additional tax on early distributions because she isn't yet 59.5 years old), but she doesn't have to report the excess contribution as income or pay the 6% excise tax. Maria receives a Form 1099-R showing that the earnings are taxable for 2020.

> **EXAMPLE 2:** For 2020, Paul Jones is 45 years old and single, his compensation is $31,000, and he contributed $6,500 to his traditional IRA. Paul has made an excess contribution to his IRA of $500 ($6,500 minus the $6,000 limit). The contribution earned $5 interest in 2020 and $6 interest in 2021 before the due date of the return, including extensions. He doesn't withdraw the $500 or the interest it earned by the due date of his return, including extensions.
>
> Paul figures his additional tax for 2020 by multiplying the $500 excess contribution by 6%, giving him an additional tax liability of $30. He enters the tax on Form 5329, and on Schedule 2 (Form 1040).

> **EXAMPLE 3:** Sam is 40 years old and files jointly with his spouse. His MAGI for 2020 is $200,000. He contributes $6,000 to his Roth IRA on July 1, 2020, which grows to $7,000. He does not contribute to any other retirement plans. He has excess income of $4,000 ($200,000 - $196,000) and must reduce his maximum contribution and any earnings by 40% ($4,000 ÷ $10,000). His excess contribution is $2,400 ($6,000 contribution × 40%) and earnings on his excess contribution are $400 ($1,000 earnings × 40%). He must remove $2,800 ($2,400 excess contribution <u>and</u> $400 earnings on excess contribution) from the account by the due date for his return or he is liable for the 6% excise tax.

TIP: For purposes of determining excess contributions, any contribution that is withdrawn on or before the due date (including extensions) for filing the tax return for the year is treated as an amount not contributed. This treatment only applies if any earnings on the contributions are also withdrawn. The earnings are considered earned and received in the year the excess contribution was made.

AGE 59.5 RULE RETIREMENT ACCOUNTS

Generally, a taxpayer younger than age 59.5 pays a **10% additional tax** on the distribution of any assets from a qualified plan or IRA (traditional IRAs and Roth IRAs). This additional tax applies to the part of the distribution the taxpayer must include in gross income and is in addition to any regular income tax on that amount.

TIP: Early withdrawals generally are subject to a 10% additional tax penalty. However, the additional tax penalty is 25% (instead of 10%) if funds are withdrawn within 2 years of beginning participation in a SIMPLE IRA.

Generally, the amounts a taxpayer withdraws from a retirement plan before reaching age 59.5 are called "early" or "premature" distributions. To discourage the use of retirement funds for purposes other than normal retirement, the law imposes an additional 10% tax on certain early distributions from certain retirement plans. The additional tax is equal to 10% of the portion of the distribution that is includible in income. Distributions that aren't taxable, such as distributions that are rolled over to another qualified retirement plan, aren't subject to this additional 10%

tax. Generally, early distributions are those received from a qualified retirement plan or deferred annuity contract before reaching age 59.5. Taxpayers must pay an additional 10% early withdrawal tax unless an exception applies. There are certain exceptions to this additional 10% tax.

EXCEPTIONS FOR ANY QUALIFIED PLAN OR IRA

The following exceptions apply to distributions from any qualified plan or IRA (traditional IRA and Roth IRA):

- Distributions made to a beneficiary or estate on or after owner's death
- Distributions made because the taxpayer is totally and permanently disabled
- Distributions made as part of a series of substantially equal periodic payments over taxpayer's life expectancy or the life expectancies of taxpayer and taxpayer's designated beneficiary (if these distributions are from a qualified plan other than an IRA, the taxpayer must separate from service with this employer before the payments begin for this exception to apply)
- Distributions to the extent taxpayer has deductible medical expenses that exceed **7.5%** of adjusted gross income for 2020 whether or not they itemize deductions for the year

  TIP: A taxpayer does not have to itemize deductions to take advantage of this exception to the additional tax. However, a taxpayer can only take into account unreimbursed medical expenses that would be able to include in figuring a deduction for medical expenses on Schedule A. The exception amount is the amount paid for unreimbursed medical expenses during 2020, minus 7.5% of 2020 AGI.

- Distributions made due to an IRS levy of the plan
- Distributions that are qualified military reservist distributions (generally, these are distributions made to individuals called to active duty for at least 180 days after September 11, 2001)
- Distributions that are excepted from the additional income tax by federal legislation relating to certain emergencies and disasters. Made as a qualified disaster distribution related to certain federally declared disasters (limited to $100,000 for qualified hurricane distributions and a separate $100,000 for qualified wildfire distributions)

  TIP: Participants taking a qualified disaster distribution can include it in income in equal amounts over three years, beginning with the year that includes the distribution date. Participants may also repay qualified disaster distributions within three years of receiving a distribution by making one or more contributions to an eligible retirement plan. Any repayment is treated as a trustee-to-trustee transfer.

- Distributions up to **$5,000** if the distribution is a qualified birth or adoption distribution:
  1. Up to $5,000 for the birth or adoption of child (**each parent** can receive up to $5,000 for the same child and can receive up to $5,000 for **each child** if multiple births and/or adoptions)
  2. Must include the name, age, and TIN of such child or eligible adoptee on the taxpayer's return
  3. An eligible adoptee is any individual (other than a child of the taxpayer's spouse) who has not attained age 18 or is physically or mentally incapable of self-support
  4. A qualified distribution is made during the 1-year period beginning on the date on which a child of the individual is born or on which the legal adoption by the individual of an eligible adoptee is finalized

EXCEPTIONS FOR QUALIFIED PLAN ONLY

The following additional exceptions apply only to distributions from a qualified plan but not an IRA:

- Distributions made to the taxpayer after taxpayer **separated from service** with this employer if the separation occurred in or after the year taxpayer reached **age 55**, or distributions made from a qualified governmental benefit plan if the taxpayer were a qualified public safety employee (federal, state, or local government, including specified law enforcement officers, customs, and border protection officers, firefighters, emergency medical services, and air traffic controllers) who separated from service in or after the year taxpayer reached age 50

- Distributions made to an alternate payee under a qualified domestic relations order (QDRO)
- Distributions of dividends from employee stock ownership plans
- Corrective distributions (and associated earnings) of excess contributions, excess aggregate contributions, and excess deferrals (if made timely)

EXCEPTIONS FOR IRA ONLY

The following additional exceptions apply only to distributions from an IRA (traditional IRA and Roth IRA) but not a qualified plan:

- Qualified first-time homebuyer distributions, if the distribution is to buy, build, or rebuild a first home:
  1. Up to **$10,000** for qualified acquisition costs if used within 120 days of distribution
  2. $10,000 for **each spouse** if both are first-time homebuyers (a first-time homebuyer cannot own a main home during the two-year period ending on the date of acquisition of the home)
  3. Must be used for qualified acquisition costs for the main home of a taxpayer, spouse, child, grandchild, parent, or other ancestors
- Distributions are not in excess of taxpayer's qualified higher education expenses (the education must be for the taxpayer, taxpayer's spouse, or the children or grandchildren of the taxpayer or taxpayer's spouse)
- Distributions are not in excess of certain health insurance premiums paid while unemployed
- Returned IRA contributions (and associated earnings) if withdrawn by extended due date of return (Note: the exception to the additional tax does not apply to the earnings on these returned contributions)

TIP: Distributions that are rollovers or transfers to another IRA or qualified retirement plan aren't subject to this additional 10% tax. This is true as long as the taxpayer follows the one IRA-to-IRA rollover per year rule.

CARES ACT UPDATE: The CARES Act **waives the 10% early withdrawal penalty for up to $100,000** of **coronavirus-related distributions** from **eligible retirement plans** on or after January 1, 2020, and before December 31, 2020. The CARES Act also waives the 20% mandatory federal withholding requirement for qualified plan distributions.

The term eligible retirement plan is defined in 402(c)(8)(B) and includes defined contributions plans such as a 401(k), as well as 403(b), 457, and IRAs. Money purchase pension plans and defined benefit plans also became eligible for this treatment with the passage of the **Consolidated Appropriations Act, 2021**.

This treatment is available if a taxpayer, spouse, or dependent is diagnosed with COVID-19 or SARS by the Center for Disease Control and Prevention. It is also available to an individual who experiences adverse financial consequences as a result of quarantine, layoff or reduced hours, inability to work due to lack of childcare due to the virus, or business closure or reduced business hours due to the virus.

Contributions (up to the amount of the coronavirus-related distribution) made **within 3 years** to eligible retirement plans are treated as if the taxpayer made a direct trustee to trustee transfer within 60 days of the distribution. In other words, the taxpayer can contribute the money back into the plan for a period of 3 years beginning the day after the contribution without penalty or tax consequences.

Unless the taxpayer elects otherwise, any amount required to be included in gross income for a taxable year is **spread over the 3-taxable-year period** beginning with such taxable year.

Exceptions to 10% Additional Tax		
Type of Distribution	401(k) and Other Qualified Retirement Plans	IRA / SEP, SIMPLE IRA and SARSEP Plans
After participant/IRA owner reaches age 59.5	Yes	Yes
After the death of the participant/IRA owner	Yes	Yes
Total and permanent disability of the participant/IRA owner	Yes	Yes
Series of substantially equal payments	Yes	Yes
Separation from service during or after year employee reaches age 55 (age 50 for public safety employees)	Yes	**No**
Dividend pass through from an ESOP	Yes	N/A
Because of an IRS levy of the plan	Yes	Yes
Amount of your unreimbursed medical expenses (>7.5% AGI)	Yes	Yes
To an alternate payee under a Qualified Domestic Relations Order	Yes	**No**
Payment of health insurance premiums paid while unemployed	**No**	Yes
Qualified higher-education expenses	**No**	Yes
Qualified first-time homebuyers up to $10,000	**No**	Yes
Qualified birth or adoption expenses up to $5,000	Yes	Yes
Certain distributions to qualified military reservists called to active duty	Yes	Yes
Corrective distributions (and associated earnings) of excess deferrals, excess contributions, and excess aggregate contributions made timely	Yes	N/A
Excess IRA contributions if withdrawn by extended due date of return	N/A	Yes
Earnings on excess IRA contributions distributed	N/A	**No**
Permissive withdrawals from a plan with auto-enrollment features	Yes	Yes for SIMPLE IRAs and SARSEPs
Rollovers	Yes	Yes
Governmental 457(b) distributions are not subject to the 10% additional tax except for distributions attributable to rollovers from another type of plan or IRA		

DISTRIBUTIONS FROM A ROTH IRA

Qualified distributions from a *Roth IRA* may be **tax-free**. A qualified distribution meets both of the following requirements:

- Made after the **five-year** period beginning with the first year a contribution was made, and
- Meets one of the following criteria:
  1. Made on or after the date the taxpayer reaches **age 59.5**
  2. Meets one of the exceptions to distributions from an IRA (traditional IRA and Roth IRA) listed previously under *Age 59.5 Rule Retirement Accounts*

If a taxpayer receives a distribution that is not a *qualified distribution*, they may have to pay the 10% additional tax on early distributions. The 5-year period used for determining whether the 10% early distribution tax applies to a distribution from a conversion or rollover contribution is separately determined for each conversion and rollover and is not necessarily the same as the 5-year period used for determining whether a distribution is a qualified distribution.

> **EXAMPLE:** For example, if a calendar-year taxpayer makes a conversion contribution on February 25, 2021, and makes a regular contribution for 2020 on the same date, the 5-year period for the conversion begins January 1, 2021, while the 5-year period for the regular contribution begins on January 1, 2020.

ORDERING RULES

If a distribution from a Roth IRA is not a qualified distribution, part of it may be taxable. There is a set order in which contributions (including conversion contributions and rollover contributions from qualified retirement plans) and earnings are considered to be distributed from the Roth IRA. For these purposes, disregard the withdrawal of excess contributions and the earnings on them. Order the distributions as follows:

- **Regular contributions** – This portion is not included in gross income or subject to the 10% early distribution tax.
- **Conversion and rollover contributions** – On a first-in, first-out basis (generally, total conversions and rollovers from the earliest year first). Take these conversion and rollover contributions into account as follows:
  1. **Taxable portion** – This is the amount that was previously required to be included in gross income because of the conversion or rollover. The 10% early distribution tax applies to this amount.
  2. **Nontaxable portion** – This amount reflects basis in the converted account and was not included in gross income. The 10% early distribution tax does not apply to this amount.
- **Earnings on contributions** – The portion of the distribution allocable to earnings should be included in gross income and is subject to the 10% early distribution tax.

AGE 72 RULE (FORMERLY AGE 70.5 RULE) RETIREMENT ACCOUNTS

Generally, a taxpayer must make annual withdrawals from a qualified retirement plan when reaching age 72 (or age 70.5 if turned 70.5 prior to January 1, 2020). If distributions are less than the *required minimum distribution (RMD)* for the year, taxpayers may have to pay a **50% excise tax on the amount not distributed as required.**

For a *Roth* retirement plan, amounts can remain in the account until the taxpayer dies (**no RMD**). Mandatory distributions are not required when attaining age 72 (or 70.5) for a Roth account.

TIP: The penalty may be waived if the account owner establishes that the shortfall in distributions was due to reasonable error and that reasonable steps are being taken to remedy the shortfall. In order to qualify for this relief, the taxpayer must file *Form 5329* and attach a letter of explanation.

CARES ACT UPDATE: The IRS **waived** the mandatory distribution requirement for taxpayers subject to the required minimum distribution (RMD) rules in 2020. The waiver applies to defined contribution plans and IRAs, as well as 403(b) and 457 plans. This waiver is for 1 year only, and the RMD rules return to normal in 2021.

Money cannot remain in a retirement plan indefinitely (except for a Roth), and eventually, a taxpayer must take a *required minimum distribution (RMD)*. The taxpayer generally must make annual withdrawals from a traditional IRA, SIMPLE IRA, SEP IRA, or retirement plan when reaching age 72 (or 70.5).

A taxpayer may defer the first-year distribution to April 1 of the year following the year in which the taxpayer reaches age 72 (or 70.5). This is referred to as the *required beginning date*. The taxpayer must withdraw the RMD for any year after the year attaining age 72 (or 70.5) by December 31 of that later year.

TIP: For 401(k), profit-sharing, 403(b), or other defined contribution plans the required beginning date may be **delayed** until April 1 following the year the participant **retires** from the employer sponsoring the plan.

A taxpayer reaches age 70.5 on the date that is 6 calendar months after their 70th birthday.

EXAMPLE 1: You are retired and your 70th birthday was June 30, 2019. You reached age 70.5 on December 30, 2019. You must take your first RMD (for 2019) by April 1, 2020, and your second RMD (for 2020) by December 31, 2020.

EXAMPLE 2: You are retired and your 70th birthday was July 1, 2019. You reached age 70.5 on January 1, 2020. You do not have an RMD for 2019. You must take your first RMD for 2021, when you turn 72, by April 1, 2022.

Figure the RMD for each year by dividing the IRA account balance as of the close of business on December 31 of the preceding year by the applicable distribution period or life expectancy. To calculate the divisor, compare the taxpayer's age at the end of the year to the corresponding number in the *Uniform Lifetime Table*, or the *Joint Lifetime Table* if a spouse is more than 10 years younger. Both tables are published in Pub 590-B.

EXAMPLE 3: Laura was born on October 1, 1948. She reaches age 70.5 in 2019. Since she turned 70.5 prior to January 1, 2020, her required beginning date is April 1, 2020. As of December 31, 2018, her IRA account balance was $26,500. No rollover or recharacterization amounts were outstanding. Using the Uniform Lifetime Table, the applicable distribution period for someone her age (71) is 26.5 years. Her required minimum distribution for 2019 is $1,000 ($26,500 ÷ 26.5). That amount is distributed to her by April 1, 2020. If Laura had been born in 1949, she would turn 70.5 after January 1, 2020, and would be subject to the new RMD rules and her first distribution (age 72 in 2021) wouldn't be until April 1, 2022 (the year after she turns 72).

TIP: The first year following the year a taxpayer reaches age 72 (or 70.5), a taxpayer will generally have two required distribution dates: the first withdrawal by April 1 for the year the taxpayer turns 72 (or 70.5), and an additional withdrawal by December 31 for the current year. To avoid having both of these amounts included in income in the same year, the taxpayer can make the first withdrawal by December 31 of the year of the first distribution instead of waiting until April 1 of the following year.

EXAMPLE 4: John reached age 70.5 on August 2, 2019. Since John had reached age 70.5 before 2020, he must receive his 2019 RMD by April 1, 2020, based on his 2018 year-end balance. John has until December 31, 2020, to receive his 2020 RMD, based on his 2019 year-end balance.

If John receives his initial RMD for 2019 on April 1, 2020, then both his 2019 and 2020 distributions will be included in income on his 2020 income tax return.

EXAMPLE 5: Paul reached age 70.5 on January 28, 2020. Since Paul had not reached age 70.5 before 2020, his first RMD is due for 2021, the year he turns 72. Paul's first RMD is due by April 1, 2022, based on his 2020 year-end balance. Paul must receive his 2022 required minimum distribution by December 31, 2022, based on his 2021 year-end balance.

REPORTING ADDITIONAL TAXES ON TAX-FAVORED ACCOUNTS

Use *Form 5329 Additional Taxes on Qualified Plans (Including IRAs) and Other Tax-Favored Accounts* to calculate the additional tax on:

- Early Distributions (taxpayers may also have to complete Form 5329 to indicate that they qualify for an exception to the additional tax on early distributions).
- Excess Contributions
- Excess Accumulation in Qualified Retirement Plans

TIP: A taxpayer that only owes the additional 10% tax on early distributions may be able to report this tax directly on Schedule 2 (Form 1040), without filing Form 5329. Form 5329 is also used to calculate additional tax on certain distributions from education accounts and ABLE accounts, but that is beyond the scope of this lesson.

TAXES FOR HOUSEHOLD EMPLOYEES

A taxpayer has a household employee if hiring someone to do household work in or around the taxpayer's home and that worker is their *employee*. The worker is an employee if the taxpayer controls the work performed and how the worker performs the duties. If the worker controls how duties are performed, the worker is not the taxpayer's employee but is considered *self-employed*.

While popularly referred to as a "Nanny Tax", other household employees are also subject to these rules. Other examples of workers who do household work are babysitters, cleaning people, drivers, domestic workers, butlers, cooks, private nurses, yard workers, etc. Services not of a household nature, such as services performed as a private secretary, tutor, or librarian, even though performed in taxpayer's home, aren't considered household work.

Household work is work done in or around the taxpayer's home. A worker who performs childcare services for a taxpayer in the worker's home (outside the taxpayer's home) generally is not an employee of the taxpayer. If an agency provides the worker and controls the work performed and how duties are performed, the worker is not an employee of the taxpayer. Other individuals specifically excluded are the taxpayer's parents (unless caring for the taxpayer's child under age 18 and the taxpayer is divorced or widowed), spouse, child under age 21, or anyone under age 18 whose principal occupation is not household employment (for example, a student).

PAYING

A taxpayer (employer) is not responsible for withholding *federal* income tax for household employees unless the employee asks and the taxpayer agrees; however, the employer must report and pay the following taxes when applicable:

- **Social Security and Medicare taxes** – If a *household employee* is paid cash wages of **$2,200** or more in 2020, the employer must pay their share of Social Security (6.2%) and Medicare (1.45%) taxes, totaling 7.65% of wages. The *employer's* share is not withheld from the employee's pay. The employer may either pay or withhold the *employee's* share, which is also 7.65%. A total of 15.3% is paid for the employer's and employee's share of Social Security and Medicare taxes. The maximum amount of wages subject to the 6.2% *Social Security tax* is **$137,700** in 2020. There is no wage limit for the 1.45% *Medicare tax*. In addition, an employer is required to withhold an *additional 0.9% Medicare tax* from wages paid to an employee in **excess of $200,000** in a calendar year.

- **Federal unemployment tax (FUTA)** – If the combined cash wages of all household employees is **$1,000** or more in any calendar quarter of 2019 or 2020, the employer must pay FUTA tax. The **first $7,000 of wages paid to each household employee** in 2020 is FUTA wages and is subject to FUTA tax. The 2020 FUTA tax rate is 6.0% of FUTA wages. The $7,000 is the *federal* wage base. The *state* wage base may be different. Federal wages more than $7,000 per employee in 2020 are not taxed. The employer may also owe *state unemployment tax (SUTA)*. Generally, the employer takes a credit against FUTA tax for amounts paid into state unemployment funds. The credit may be as much as 5.4% against the FUTA tax rate. If entitled to the maximum credit, the 6.0% FUTA tax rate after the 5.4% credit, results in a net FUTA tax rate of 0.6%. Only the employer pays FUTA and SUTA taxes; it is not withheld from the employee's wages.

REPORTING

A taxpayer with a household employee files *Schedule H* to report the tax with their personal tax return by the due date plus extensions of filing their personal tax return. In general, the amount of tax attributed to household employees increases the tax due on the taxpayer's personal return (Form 1040). A household employer needs an employer identification number (EIN) and must provide a 2020 Form W-2 no later than January 31, 2021, to all household employees with cash wages of **$2,200** or more, or if they withheld taxes, in 2020.

NET INVESTMENT INCOME TAX

The *Net Investment Income Tax (NIIT)* applies at a rate of **3.8%** to certain net investment income of individuals, estates, and trusts that have income above the statutory threshold amounts. Individuals, estates, and trusts will use *Form 8960 Net Investment Income Tax—Individuals, Estates, and Trusts* to compute their Net Investment Income Tax.

In general, investment income includes, but is not limited to interest, dividends, capital gains, rental and royalty income, non-qualified annuities, income from businesses involved in trading of financial instruments or commodities and businesses that are passive activities to the taxpayer (within the meaning of Section 469). The taxpayer may reduce investment income by certain expenses properly allocable to the income.

For purposes of the Net Investment Income Tax (NIIT), net investment income does not include distributions from a qualified retirement plan (for example, 401(a), 403(a), 403(b), 457(b) plans, and IRAs). However, these distributions are taken into account when determining the modified adjusted gross income threshold. Distributions from a nonqualified retirement plan are included in net investment income.

An *individual* taxpayer with net investment income will owe the NIIT if modified adjusted gross income exceeds one of the following thresholds:

Filing Status	Threshold Amount
Married filing jointly	$250,000
Married filing separately	$125,000
Single	$200,000
Head of household (with qualifying person)	$200,000
Qualifying widow(er) with dependent child	$250,000

For an *individual*, the NIIT is 3.8% on the lesser of:

- the net investment income, or
- the excess of modified adjusted gross income over the threshold amounts above

Janine, a single filer, has $180,000 of wages. Janine also received $90,000 from a passive partnership interest, which is considered Net Investment Income. Janine's modified adjusted gross income is $270,000.

Janine's modified adjusted gross income exceeds the threshold of $200,000 for single taxpayers by $70,000. Janine's Net Investment Income is $90,000.

The Net Investment Income Tax is based on the lesser of $70,000 (the amount that Janine's modified adjusted gross income exceeds the $200,000 threshold) or $90,000 (Janine's Net Investment Income). Janine owes NIIT of $2,660 ($70,000 x 3.8%).

An *estate or trust* with **undistributed** net investment income will owe the NIIT if adjusted gross income exceeds **$12,950** for 2020.

For an *estate or trust*, the NIIT is 3.8% on the lesser of:

- the undistributed net investment income, or
- the excess of the adjusted gross income over the dollar amount at which the highest tax bracket begins for an estate or trust for the tax year (for estates and trusts, the 2020 threshold amount is $12,950)

TIP: The Net Investment Income Tax does not apply to any amount of gain that is excluded from gross income for regular income tax purposes. For example, Section 121 exempts the first $250,000 ($500,000 in the case of a married couple) of gain recognized on the sale of a principal residence from gross income for regular income tax purposes and, thus, from the NIIT.

TAX ON UNEARNED INCOME OF CERTAIN CHILDREN ('KIDDIE TAX')

When certain children have more than **$2,200** of *unearned income* in 2020, part of that income may be taxed at the **parent's tax rates** instead of the child's tax rates. The parents may **be able to elect** to report the child's interest, dividends, and capital gain distributions on the parent's return, otherwise, all the child's net unearned income over $2,200 for 2020 is taxed using the parent's brackets and rates if the parent's rate is higher than the child's rate.

TIP: This rule has been in place since the 1980s in order to prevent parents from shifting portfolio income to children for the purpose of reducing taxes.

PARENTAL ELECTION

Parents **can elect to include a child's income from interest, dividends, and capital gain distributions on the parent's return** under certain circumstances. Parents making the election file *Form 8814 Parents' Election To Report Child's Interest and Dividends*, with the parent's return. If making this election, the child does not have to file a return.

Parents making the election file *Form 8814 Parents' Election To Report Child's Interest and Dividends*, with the parent's return. If making this election, the child does not have to file a return.

The **parent** can make the election only if the **child** meets all of the following conditions:

- The child was under age 19 (or under age 24 if a full-time student) at the end of the year
- The child's **only income** was from *interest* and *dividends* (including *capital gain distributions* and Alaska Permanent Fund dividends)
- The child's *gross income* is less than **$11,000** in 2020
- The child is required to file a return (the child's *gross income* is more than **$1,100** in 2020) unless the parent makes this election
- The child does not file a joint return for the year
- There were no estimated tax payments for the tax year, and no overpayment of tax from the previous tax year applied to the current tax year estimated tax under the child's name and Social Security number
- There was no federal income tax withheld from the child's income

The **parent must also qualify to make the election**. The **parent** qualifies if any of the following apply:

- The parent is filing a joint return for the year with the child's other parent.
- The parent and the child's other parent were married to each other but file separate returns for the year and the parent making the election had the higher taxable income.
- The parent was unmarried, treated as unmarried for federal income tax purposes, or separated from the child's other parent by a divorce or separate maintenance decree. The child must have lived with the parent for most of the year (the parent was the custodial parent). If the custodial parent remarried, the custodial parent can make the election on a joint return with the new spouse. But if the custodial parent and the new spouse do not file a joint return, the custodial parent qualifies to make the election only if the custodial parent had higher taxable income than the new spouse.

TIP: If the parent and the child's other parent were not married but lived together during the year with the child, only the parent with the higher taxable income, qualifies to make the election.

Parents use Form 8814 if they elect to report the child's income on their return. If elected, the child will not have to file a return. A separate Form 8814 must be filed for each child whose income the parent chooses to report. To make the election, complete and attach Form(s) 8814 to the parent's tax return and file return by the due date (including extensions).

NO PARENTAL ELECTION

If the parents **can't elect** or **don't elect** to include a child's income from interest, dividends, and capital gain distributions on the parent's return, on the child's return, all the child's net *unearned income* over $2,200 for 2020 is **taxed using the parent's brackets and rates if the parent's rate is higher than the child's rate.**

Parents <u>not</u> making the election file *Form 8615 Tax for Certain Children Who Have Unearned Income*, with the **child's return**.

TIP: For tax years after 2019, the SECURE Act has changed the tax rate back to the parent's tax rates (instead of the trust and estate's tax rates).

For *Form 8615*, "*unearned income*" includes all taxable income other than earned income. Unearned income includes taxable interest, ordinary dividends, capital gains (including capital gain distributions), rents, royalties, etc. It also includes taxable social security benefits, pension and annuity income, taxable scholarship and fellowship grants not reported on Form W-2, unemployment compensation, alimony, and income (other than earned income) received as the beneficiary of a trust.

Form 8615 must be filed for any **child** who meets <u>all</u> of the following conditions:

- The child had <u>more than</u> **$2,200** of *unearned income* in 2020
- The child is required to file a return (the child's *gross income* is <u>more than</u> **$1,100** in 2020) unless the parent makes the election to report the child's interest, dividends, and capital gain distributions
- The child <u>either</u>:
  1. Was under age 18 at the end of the year,
  2. Was age 18 at the end of the year and didn't have earned income that was more than half of the child's support, or
  3. Was a full-time student at least age 19 and under age 24 at the end of the year and didn't have earned income that was more than half of the child's support
- At least one of the child's parents was alive at the end of the year
- The child doesn't file a joint return for the year

For these rules, the term "child" includes a legally adopted child and a stepchild. These rules apply whether or not the child is a dependent.

The parent may be able to elect to report the child's interest, dividends, and capital gain distributions on the parent's return if <u>both</u> the child <u>and</u> the parent meet certain conditions. One of the conditions is, the child's <u>only</u> income was from *interest* and *dividends* (including *capital gain distributions* and Alaska Permanent Fund dividends). If the parent makes this election, the child won't have to file a return <u>or</u> Form 8615.

LESSON 8

Credits

HEALTH INSURANCE PREMIUM TAX CREDIT (REFUNDABLE)

PREMIUM TAX CREDIT (PTC)

Individuals and families can take a premium tax credit to help them afford health insurance coverage **purchased through an Affordable Insurance Exchange** (also known as a Health Insurance Marketplace). The premium tax credit is **refundable** so taxpayers who have little or no income tax liability can still benefit. The credit also can be paid in advance to a taxpayer's insurance company to help cover the cost of premiums.

Premium tax credits are available only to individuals and families with household incomes of **at least 100— but no more than 400—percent of the federal poverty level.**

POVERTY GUIDELINES FOR THE 48 CONTIGUOUS STATES AND THE DISTRICT OF COLUMBIA	
PERSONS IN FAMILY/HOUSEHOLD	POVERTY GUIDELINE
For families/households with more than 8 persons, add $4,420 for each additional person.	
1	$12,490
2	$16,910
3	$21,330
4	$25,750
5	$30,170
6	$34,590
7	$39,010
8	$43,430

Household income includes the income of the taxpayer and any dependents who reside with the taxpayer. Furthermore, individuals who meet this income level are only eligible for the premium tax credit if they purchase coverage through the Health Insurance Marketplace, sometimes referred to as the Health Insurance Exchange, or simply the "Exchange". **The credit is not available for the purchase of insurance outside of the Exchange.**

A taxpayer <u>cannot</u> receive the credit if he or she files a **married filing separate** return or if he or she can be **claimed as a dependent of another taxpayer.**

Also, no credit is available with respect to a taxpayer or family member who is able to obtain affordable coverage through an eligible employer-sponsored plan that provides minimum value or through a government program, like Medicaid, Medicare, CHIP or TRICARE.

The Exchanges are responsible for the initial determination of eligibility for the premium tax credit. During enrollment through the Exchange, the Exchange will also determine if the taxpayer is eligible for advance payments of the premium tax credit. Advance credit payments are amounts paid directly to the insurance company on the taxpayer's behalf; the taxpayer is responsible for paying the balance of the premium, if any.

If a taxpayer is eligible for, and chooses to receive the benefit of, an advance credit payment, the taxpayer must file a tax return to reconcile the amount of advance credit payments (which is always based on an estimate made by the Exchange) with the amount of the actual premium tax credit allowable determined at the end of the tax year. **A taxpayer must file an income tax return for this purpose even if he or she is not otherwise required to file a return.**

The Exchange will issue the taxpayer a Health Insurance Marketplace Statement, **Form 1095-A**, by January 31 following the tax year. This form shows the amount of the premiums for the health care plan or plans the taxpayer and their family members enrolled in and certain other information that is needed to compute the premium tax credit. Form 1095-A also reports any advance credit payments made on the taxpayer's behalf.

Form 8962 Premium Tax Credit (PTC), is filed with the taxpayer's return and is used to reconcile the amount of the advance credit payments to the amount of the actual premium tax credit allowable to the taxpayer. If the actual allowable premium tax credit computed on the return is more than the advance credit payments made during the year, the difference will be listed on the tax return as an additional tax payment (thereby increasing the refund or decreasing the amount of tax owed). If the advance credit payments are more than the amount of the actual allowable premium tax credit, the difference is reflected on the return as an additional tax amount. However, if the taxpayer's household income is below 400 percent of the poverty level, limitations as to the amount of the excess credit that has to be repaid are applicable.

AFFORDABLE CARE ACT (ACA) PROVISIONS

INDIVIDUAL SHARED RESPONSIBILITY PAYMENT

The individual shared responsibility provision of the Affordable Care Act requires everyone on the individual income tax return to have qualifying health care coverage for each month of the year or have a coverage exemption. Otherwise, the IRS may require the taxpayer to make an *individual shared responsibility payment*.

> The TCJA reduces the individual responsibility payment for failing to maintain minimum essential coverage, enacted as part of the Affordable Care Act, to **$0**. The provision is effective with respect to health coverage status for months beginning after December 31, 2018.

TIP: The TCJA does not change the requirement that individuals must be covered by a health plan that provides at least minimum essential coverage.

Depending upon the circumstances, the Health Insurance Marketplace, health coverage providers, and certain employers may provide information forms to the taxpayer and the IRS.

- **Form 1095-A, Health Insurance Marketplace Statement** – The Health Insurance Marketplace sends this form to individuals who enrolled in coverage there, with information about the coverage, who was covered, and when. The deadline for the Marketplace to provide Form 1095-A is **February 1**.
- **Form 1095-B, Health Coverage** – Health insurance providers send this new form to individuals they cover, with information about who was covered and when. The deadline for coverage providers to provide Form 1095-B is **March 31**.
- **Form 1095-C, Employer-Provided Health Insurance Offer and Coverage** – Certain employers send this new form to certain employees, with information about what coverage the employer offered. The deadline for employers to provide Form 1095-C is **March 31**.

TIP: Some taxpayers may not receive a Form 1095-B or Form 1095-C by the time they are ready to file their tax return. It is not necessary to wait for Forms 1095-B or 1095-C in order to file. Taxpayers may instead rely on other information about their health coverage to prepare their returns. These forms should not be attached to the income tax return.

CHILD AND DEPENDENT CARE CREDIT (NON-REFUNDABLE)

To qualify for the **nonrefundable** child and dependent care credit, a taxpayer must meet <u>all</u> the following tests:

- The filing status must be single, head of household, qualifying widow(er) with dependent child, or married filing jointly. Married couples <u>must</u> file a joint return unless an exception exists.
- The care must be for one or more *qualifying person(s)*.
- The taxpayer (<u>and</u> spouse if married) <u>must</u> have earned income during the year.
- The taxpayer <u>must</u> pay the expenses so the taxpayer (<u>and</u> spouse if married) can work or look for work.
- Payments cannot go to the following individuals:
  1. A spouse
  2. A person who is a dependent of the taxpayer, or the taxpayer's child if under age 19 at the end of the year (even if not a dependent)
  3. The parent of the qualifying person if the qualifying person is the taxpayer's child (under age 13)
- The taxpayer must identify the care provider on the tax return (name, address, TIN).
- If a taxpayer excludes dependent care benefits provided by a dependent care benefits plan, the total exclusion must be less than the dollar limit for qualifying expenses (generally **$3,000** if one qualifying person was cared for or **$6,000** if two or more qualifying persons were cared for).

> **EXAMPLE:** Randall is married and both he and his wife are employed. Each has earned income in excess of $6,000. They have two children, Anne and Andy, ages 2 and 4, who attend a daycare facility licensed and regulated by the state. Randall's work-related expenses are $6,000 for the year.
>
> Randall's employer has a dependent care assistance program as part of its cafeteria plan, which allows employees to make pre-tax contributions to a dependent care flexible spending arrangement. Randall has elected to take the maximum $5,000 exclusion from his salary to cover dependent care expenses through this program.
>
> Although the dollar limit for his work-related expenses is $6,000 (two or more qualifying persons), Randall figures his credit on only $1,000 of the $6,000 work-related expense paid. This is because his dollar limit is reduced as shown next.
>
> | | |
> |---|---:|
> | Maximum allowable expenses for two qualifying persons | $6,000 |
> | Dependent care benefits cafeteria plan and excluded from income | –5,000 |
> | Reduced work-related expenses Randall can use for the credit | **$1,000** |

QUALIFYING PERSON TEST

For purposes of the *child and dependent care credit*, a "qualifying person" is:

- A dependent who was **under age 13** when the care was provided.
- An individual living with a taxpayer for more than half of a year who is physically or mentally unable to care for himself, if he is:
  1. A spouse
  2. A dependent
  3. Would have been a dependent except for one of the following:
     A. He received gross income of $4,300 or more in 2020

B. He filed a joint return

C. Another person could claim the taxpayer or the taxpayer's spouse as a dependent

In determining whether a person is a qualifying person, treat a person who is born or dies as living with the taxpayer for the entire year if he lived in the taxpayer's home the entire time he was alive.

An individual is considered physically or mentally incapable if the person is incapable of caring for his or her hygiene or nutritional needs or requires the full-time attention of another person for his or her own safety or the safety of others. An individual's inability to engage in any substantial gainful activity or to perform the normal household functions does not of itself establish physical or mental incapability. The status of whether a person is a qualifying individual is determined on a daily basis.

TIP: A qualifying person for this credit must meet different requirements than a qualifying person for purposes of a dependent or the EIC.

JOINT RETURN TEST

Generally, married couples must file a joint return to take the credit. However, those legally separated or living apart from a spouse may be able to file a separate return and still take the credit. Only the custodial parent can claim the credit. A married taxpayer living apart from a spouse is not considered married, and he can take the credit if all the following apply:

- Taxpayer files a separate return
- Taxpayer's home is the home of a qualifying person for more than half the year
- Taxpayer paid more than half of the cost of keeping up a home for the year
- Spouse did not live in the taxpayer's home for the last six months of the year

HOW TO FIGURE THE CREDIT

The credit is a percentage of *work-related expenses,* which allow the taxpayer to work or look for work.

> To claim the credit, the taxpayer (and spouse if filing jointly) **must have earned income** during the year. Child and dependent care **expenses must be work-related** to qualify for the credit. To be work-related, expenses must allow the taxpayer to work or look for work. If married, generally both spouses must work or look for work. One spouse is treated as working during any month he is a full-time student or isn't physically or mentally able to care for himself. Work also includes actively looking for work. However, if you don't find a job and have no earned income for the year, you can't take this credit.

The expenses to figure the credit on *Form 2441 Child and Dependent Care Expenses* cannot be more than any one of the following:

- **$3,000** if one qualifying person or **$6,000** if more than one qualifying person
- If single at the end of the year, the taxpayer's earned income for the year
- If married at the end of the year, the smaller of the taxpayer or a spouse's earned income for the year

TIP: A spouse who is a full-time student or incapable of self-care is treated as having earned income of at least $250/month if there is one qualifying person in the taxpayer's home or at least $500/month for two or more.

The credit is available only for employment-related expenses. The amount of employment-related expenses is capped to $3,000 for one qualifying individual or $6,000 for two or more qualifying individuals. The taxpayer may apply the limitations for two or more qualifying individuals in unequal proportions.

> **EXAMPLE:** Ida had employment-related expenses of $4,000 for her dependent young son Jimmy and $1,500 for her dependent elderly mother Jane (both are qualifying individuals). Ida may take the aggregate payment of $5,500 ($4,000 + $1,500) into account when determining the credit, even though the expenses related to one of the qualifying individuals exceeded $3,000.

To qualify for the credit, a taxpayer must have one or more qualifying persons. However, it is possible a qualifying child could have no expenses and a second qualifying child could have expenses exceeding $3,000. Since there are two qualifying children, the $6,000 limit would still be used to compute the credit. The taxpayer can use both qualifying children and the $6,000 limit to figure the credit. On Form 2441, list zero for the one child and the actual amount for the second child.

To determine the credit amount, multiply work-related expenses (after applying the earned income and dollar limits) by a percentage (based on AGI). The applicable percentage begins at **35%** for taxpayers with AGI less than $15,000 and decreases by 1% for each $2,000 increase in AGI. Taxpayers with AGI more than $43,000 receive the **minimum percentage of 20%**.

TIP: In figuring each $2,000 increase, treat any excess as a full $2,000. For example, a $9,000 increase is a 5% reduction.

> The **maximum amount of this credit** is **$1,050** (35% of $3,000) for one qualifying person or **$2,100** (35% of $6,000) for more than one qualifying person.

EDUCATION CREDITS

There are two tax credits available to persons who pay expenses for higher (postsecondary) education. They are as follows:

- The *Lifetime Learning credit*
- The *American Opportunity credit*

Generally, a taxpayer may claim a credit if he meets <u>all</u> of the following three requirements:

- He pays *qualified education expenses* of higher education
- He pays the education expenses for an *eligible student*
- The student is the taxpayer, a spouse, or a dependent

A taxpayer <u>cannot</u> claim a credit if <u>any</u> of the following applies:

- Filing status is married filing separately (MFS)
- The person qualifies as a dependent of another taxpayer
- Modified adjusted gross income (MAGI) is above the phase-out limit
- Taxpayer (or spouse) is a nonresident alien for any part of the year and did not elect to be treated as a resident alien for tax purposes
- The taxpayer claims another education credit or the tuition and fees deduction for the same student in the same year

A taxpayer cannot claim multiple credits for the same student in the same year. The American opportunity credit will always be greater than or equal to the lifetime learning credit for any student who is eligible for both credits. A taxpayer who is eligible for more than one credit can choose to claim either credit, but not both. A taxpayer with education expenses for more than one student in the same year can choose to take the credits on a per-student, per-year basis.

> **EXAMPLE:** A taxpayer can claim the American Opportunity credit for one student and the Lifetime Learning credit for another student in the same year. A taxpayer can claim both the American Opportunity credit and the Lifetime Learning credit—but not for the same student.

A taxpayer uses *Form 8863 Education Credits (American Opportunity and Lifetime Learning Credits)* to figure and claim their education credits. Taxpayers must complete a separate Part III on page 2 for each student for whom they are claiming either the American opportunity credit or lifetime learning credit before completing either Part I or Part II (use additional copies of page 2 as needed for each student).

2020 Education Credits

	American Opportunity Credit	**Lifetime Learning Credit**
Maximum credit	$2,500 credit **per eligible student**	$2,000 credit **per return**
Limit on MAGI	$180,000 MFJ and $90,000 S, HH, or QW (NOT indexed for inflation)	$138,000 if MFJ and $69,000 if S, HH, or QW (2020 inflation amounts)
Refundable	**40% refundable**	**Non-refundable** credit limited to the amount of tax liability
Availability	Available **ONLY** for the **first 4 years**	Available **ALL years AND** for courses to acquire or improve job skills
Number of tax years' credit available	Available **ONLY** for **4 tax years** per eligible student	Available for an **UNLIMITED** number of years
Type of degree required	Student must be pursuing an undergraduate degree or other recognized education credential	Student does **not** need to be pursuing a degree or other recognized education credential
Number of courses	Student enrolled at least half-time for at least one academic period beginning in the tax year	Available for one or more courses
Felony drug conviction	**No felony** drug convictions on student's records	**Felony** drug convictions **permitted**
Qualified expenses	Books, supplies, and equipment **do not** need to be purchased from the institution in order to qualify	Tuition and required enrollment fees, including required amounts paid to the institution for course-related books, supplies, and equipment

QUALIFIED EDUCATION EXPENSES

For purposes of the education credits, consider only *qualified education expenses* in determining the credit amount. Qualified education expenses **must be required for enrollment or attendance** at an *eligible educational institution* and include tuition and required enrollment fees. Expenses include amounts paid to the institution for course-related books, supplies, and equipment.

- Only certain expenses for course-related books, supplies, and equipment qualify:
    1. **American Opportunity credit** – Qualified education expenses include amounts spent on books, supplies, and equipment needed for a course of study, whether or not the taxpayer purchases materials from the educational institution as a condition of enrollment or attendance.
    2. **Lifetime Learning credit** – Qualified education expenses include **only** amounts for books, supplies, and equipment **required to be paid to the institution as a condition of enrollment or attendance**.
- Qualified education expenses do <u>not</u> include amounts paid for:
    1. **Room and board**, insurance, medical expenses (including student health fees), transportation, or other similar personal, living, or family expenses.
    2. Any course or other education involving sports, games, or hobbies, or any noncredit course, unless such course or other education is part of the student's degree program or (for the Lifetime Learning credit only) helps the student acquire or improve job skills.
    3. Nonacademic fees, such as student activity fees, athletic fees, insurance expenses, or other expenses unrelated to the academic course of instruction.

TIP: Expenses paid or deemed paid by a dependent are considered paid by the taxpayer. Someone other than the taxpayer, spouse, or dependent (such as a relative or former spouse) may make a payment directly to an eligible educational institution to pay for an eligible student's qualified education expenses. In this case, treat the student as receiving the payment from the other person and, in turn, paying the institution. If the taxpayer is eligible to claim the student as a dependent on his tax return, he is considered to have paid the expenses.

AMERICAN OPPORTUNITY CREDIT (PARTIALLY REFUNDABLE)

The American Opportunity Tax Credit replaces the Hope credit. Students must attend at least half-time for one academic period.

- The credit is available for the **first four years** of postsecondary education, and **40% of the credit is refundable** for most taxpayers (up to a maximum of $1,000).
- The **maximum credit per student is $2,500** (100% of first $2,000 and 25% of the next $2,000).
- The threshold before the reduction of the credit is <u>more</u> than that for the Lifetime Learning credit. The amount of the American Opportunity credit phases out based on a taxpayer's modified adjusted gross income (MAGI). The phase-out begins if MAGI is between $80,000 and $90,000 ($160,000 and $180,000 MFJ). A taxpayer cannot claim a credit if MAGI is $90,000 or more ($180,000 or more MFJ). These phase-out levels are <u>not</u> indexed for inflation.

A taxpayer may <u>not</u> claim the American Opportunity credit if **convicted of a drug-related felony** before the end of the taxable year.

Paid preparers of federal income tax returns or claims for refund involving the American Opportunity Tax Credit (AOTC) <u>must</u> meet the due diligence requirements in determining if the taxpayer is eligible for, or the amount of, the AOTC. Failure to do so for a return filed in 2021 (generally 2020 tax returns filed in 2021) shall pay a penalty of **$540** for each failure (IRC Section 6695(g) Failure to be diligent in determining eligibility for certain tax benefits). A tax preparer can use *Form 8867 Paid Preparer's Due Diligence Checklist* to document due diligence.

LIFETIME LEARNING CREDIT (NON-REFUNDABLE)

A Lifetime Learning credit of **up to $2,000** is available for *qualified education expenses* paid for students enrolled in *eligible educational institutions*. The Lifetime Learning credit is computed on a family-wide basis. The amount of the Lifetime Learning credit is 20% of the first $10,000 of qualified education expenses paid for all eligible students. Differences from other credits include the following:

- Student does not need to pursue a degree or other credentials
- Available for an **unlimited number of years**
- Used for courses to acquire or improve job skills and all years of postsecondary education
- No half-year requirement for eligible students, available for one or more courses
- Felony drug conviction rule does not apply

The amount of the Lifetime Learning credit phases out based on a taxpayer's modified adjusted gross income (MAGI). For 2020, the phase-out begins if MAGI is between $59,000 and $69,000 ($118,000 and $138,000 MFJ). A taxpayer cannot claim a credit if 2020 MAGI is $69,000 or more ($138,000 or more MFJ).

> **CONSOLIDATED APPROPRIATIONS ACT UPDATE:** The Consolidated Appropriations Act, 2021 repeals the deduction for qualified tuition and fees and increases the phaseout limits for the lifetime learning credit, effective for taxable years beginning after December 31, 2020, as a transition from the tuition and fees deduction to an increased income limitation on lifetime learning credit.
>
> Beginning in 2021, the phaseout limits for the Lifetime Learning credit will be the same as the phaseout limits for the American Opportunity credit (phaseout begins if MAGI is between $80,000 and $90,000 ($160,000 and $180,000 MFJ) and no credit if MAGI is $90,000 or more ($180,000 or more MFJ)). Also, like the American Opportunity credit, beginning in 2021 the Lifetime Learning credit phaseout limits will no longer adjust for inflation. This change is testable on exams administered starting May 1, 2022.

ADOPTION CREDIT (NON-REFUNDABLE)

A **nonrefundable** credit is available for *qualified expenses* paid to adopt an *eligible child* (under age 18 or with special needs). The maximum adoption credit is **$14,300 per child** in 2020.

- The credit is limited to the amount of qualified expenses and is reduced by any qualified expenses claimed for the same child in a prior year.

> **EXAMPLE:** Paul paid $30,000 in qualified adoption expenses to adopt an eligible foreign child, and the adoption became final in 2020. Under a qualified adoption assistance program, Paul's employer reimbursed him for $14,300 of those expenses. Paul may exclude the $14,300 reimbursement from his income. The remaining $15,700 of expenses ($30,000 - $14,300) continue to be qualified adoption expenses that are eligible for the credit. However, Paul's credit is dollar-limited to $14,300. The remaining $1,400 ($30,000 - $14,300 - $14,300) may never be claimed as a credit or excluded from gross income.

- The full credit of $14,300 in 2020 may be allowed for the adoption of a child with special needs even if there are no qualified expenses.

- The credit begins to phase out for taxpayers with MAGI in excess of $214,520 and is completely phased out for taxpayers with MAGI of $254,520 or more

The adoption credit is <u>not</u> refundable but the taxpayer may carry forward any unused credit amounts to future tax years.

- **Qualified adoption expenses** are reasonable and necessary expenses directly related to, and whose principal purpose is for, the legal adoption of an eligible child. These expenses include the following:
  - Adoption fees
  - Court costs
  - Attorney fees
  - Travel expenses (including meals and lodging) while away from home
  - Re-adoption expenses to adopt a foreign child
- **Nonqualified expenses** are expenses that meet the following criteria:
  - Expenses that violate state or federal law
  - Expenses for carrying out any surrogate parenting arrangement
  - Expenses for the adoption of a spouse's child
  - Expenses for which the taxpayer received funds under any federal, state, or local program
  - Expenses allowed as a credit or deduction under any other federal income tax rule
  - Expenses paid or reimbursed by an employer or any other person or organization
  - Expenses paid before 1997

WHEN TO CLAIM THE CREDIT

If the eligible child is a U.S. citizen or resident, a taxpayer may claim the adoption credit even if the adoption never became final. A taxpayer may claim expenses paid prior to finalization in the year following the year of payment. Expenses paid in the year the adoption becomes final are included in that year. A taxpayer may claim expenses paid after the adoption becomes final in the year of payment. If the eligible child is <u>not</u> a U.S. citizen or resident, a taxpayer cannot take the adoption credit or exclusion unless the adoption becomes final.

SUBSTANTIATION REQUIREMENTS

Taxpayers must include *Form 8839 Qualified Adoption Expenses* along with their tax return to claim the adoption credit. Taxpayers should keep documentation to support their claim for the adoption credit, but do not need to include any documentation when they file their tax return. Adoption-related documents taxpayers should keep include:

- **Domestic or foreign adoption finalized in the United States** – an adoption order or decree
- **Domestic adoptions that are not final** – an adoption taxpayer identification number, obtained for the child, or one of the following documents:
  1. A home study completed by an authorized placement agency
  2. A placement agreement with an authorized placement agency
  3. A document signed by a hospital official authorizing the release of a newborn child from the hospital to the taxpayer for legal adoption
  4. A court document ordering or approving the placement of the child for legal adoption
  5. An original affidavit or a notarized statement, from an adoption attorney, government official, or other person, stating that he placed or is placing a child with the taxpayer for legal adoption or is facilitating the adoption process for the taxpayer in an official capacity
- **Adoptions of special needs children** – the state determination of special needs

EARNED INCOME CREDIT (REFUNDABLE)

The *earned income tax credit (EIC or EITC)* is a **refundable tax credit** for certain people who work and have *earned income*.

The maximum amount of the EIC in 2020 is:

Qualifying Children	Maximum Credit
0	$538
1	$3,584
2	$5,920
3 +	$6,660

Earned income includes all of the following:

- Wages, salaries, and tips
- Union strike benefits
- Long-term disability benefits received prior to minimum retirement age
- Net earnings from self-employment
- Non-taxable combat pay (only if elected and included in taxable income)

Earned income does not include:

- Interest and dividends
- Pensions
- Social Security
- Unemployment benefits
- Alimony
- Child support
- Pay received for work while in jail

A taxpayer will base the credit on AGI if lower than earned income.

CONSOLIDATED APPROPRIATIONS ACT UPDATE: The Consolidated Appropriations Act, 2021 provides a temporary special rule for the determination of **earned income** for the *earned income credit*. This special rule applies only to 2020.

If the earned income of the taxpayer for the taxpayer's first taxable year beginning in 2020 is less than the earned income of the taxpayer for the preceding taxable year (2019), the *earned income credit* may, at the **election** of the taxpayer, be determined using 2019 earned income.

TIP: The taxpayer should elect to use 2019 earned income if it is more than 2020 earned income and if the taxpayer's EIC is greater using 2019 earned income versus 2020 earned income.

WHO MAY CLAIM THE EIC?

To claim the EIC, taxpayers must meet <u>all</u> of the following rules:

- Investment income <u>must</u> be **$3,650 or less** for 2020
- Married taxpayers <u>must</u> file a **joint return (MFJ)**
- Taxpayer(s) and <u>all</u> qualifying children must have a valid Social Security number
- Taxpayer <u>must</u> be a U.S. citizen or resident alien all year, or a nonresident alien married to a U.S. citizen or resident alien and filing a joint return
- Taxpayer <u>cannot</u> file Form 2555 related to foreign-earned income
- Taxpayer <u>cannot</u> be the *qualifying child* of another person
- Taxpayer <u>must</u> have earned income; however, 2020 earned income <u>and</u> AGI **cannot be more than:**

Qualifying Children	S, QW, HH	MFJ
0	$15,820	$21,710
1	$41,756	$47,646
2	$47,440	$53,330
3 +	$50,954	$56,844

Taxpayers with **no qualifying children** <u>must</u> meet the following criteria:

- Be age 25 but younger than 65 at the end of the year
- Live in the United States for more than half of the year
- Not qualify as a dependent of another person

Taxpayers with a qualifying child <u>must</u> meet the *relationship*, *age*, and *residency tests*:

- **Relationship Test** – To be a qualifying child, a child must fall into one of the following categories:
  1. Son, daughter, stepchild, foster child, adopted child, or a descendant of any of them (for example, a grandchild)
  2. Brother, sister, half-brother, half-sister, stepbrother, stepsister, or a descendant of any of them (for example, a niece or nephew)
- **Age Test** – A qualifying child must be as follows:
  1. Younger than the taxpayer <u>or</u> taxpayer's spouse if filing a joint return, and
     A. Under age 19 at the end of the year, or
     B. A full-time (five months or more) student under age 24 at the end of the year
  2. Permanently and totally disabled at any time during the year, regardless of age
- **Residency Test** – Child must have lived with the taxpayer in the U.S. for more than half of the tax year

Sometimes a child meets the rules to be a qualifying child of more than one person. However, only one person can treat that child as a qualifying child and claim the EIC using that child. Taxpayers can choose which person will claim the EIC. If the taxpayers do not reach an agreement and more than one person claims the EIC using the same child, the tiebreaker rule applies, and the parent with whom the child lived the longest during the year receives the credit. If the child lived with each parent the same amount of time, the parent with the higher AGI receives the credit.

A taxpayer uses *Schedule EIC Earned Income Credit, Qualifying Child Information* to give the IRS information about their qualifying child(ren).

> Paid preparers of federal income tax returns or claims for refund involving the Earned Income Credit <u>must</u> meet the due diligence requirements in determining if the taxpayer is eligible for, or the amount of, the EIC. Failure to do so for a return filed in 2021 (generally 2020 tax returns filed in 2021) shall pay a penalty of **$540** for each failure. See IRC Section 6695(g). A tax preparer can use *Form 8867 Paid Preparer's Due Diligence Checklist* to document due diligence.

DISALLOWANCE OF THE EIC AND CERTAIN OTHER CREDITS

Certain errors may cause the IRS to deny a taxpayer the EIC. If the denial is because of taxpayer error due to reckless or intentional disregard of the rules, the taxpayer cannot claim the EIC for the next two years. If the error is due to fraud, the taxpayer cannot claim the EIC for the next 10 years. A taxpayer who wants (and meets the requirements) to claim the EIC must attach *Form 8862* to his return if the EIC was reduced or disallowed for any reason other than a math or clerical error for a year after 1996.

A taxpayer can claim the credit without filing Form 8862 if he meets all the eligibility requirements and either of the following applies:

- After the credit was reduced or disallowed in an earlier year:
  1. The taxpayer filed Form 8862 (or other documents) and the credit was then allowed, and
  2. The credit was not reduced or disallowed again for any reason other than a math or clerical error.
- The taxpayer is taking the EIC without a qualifying child and the only reason the EIC was disallowed in the earlier year was that a child listed on Schedule EIC was not his qualifying child.

TIP: These rules also apply to taxpayers who are denied the American Opportunity Tax Credit (AOTC), Child Tax Credit (CTC), Additional Child Tax Credit (ACTC), and Credit for Other Dependents (ODC).

CHILD TAX CREDIT AND CREDIT FOR OTHER DEPENDENTS

CHILD TAX CREDIT (PARTIALLY REFUNDABLE AS ADDITIONAL CHILD TAX CREDIT)

A *child tax credit* is available for <u>each</u> *qualifying child*.

> Effective for tax years 2018 through 2025, the TCJA temporarily increases the child tax credit to **$2,000 per qualifying child** and provides a $500 non-refundable credit for qualifying dependents <u>other</u> than qualifying children.

TIP: The child tax credit **(CTC) is <u>not</u> refundable**, only the portion that is designated as the additional child tax credit **(ACTC) is refundable**. Thus, for 2020, per qualifying child, up to $1,400 is refundable as the ACTC.

> To receive the CTC or the ACTC, a taxpayer <u>must</u> include a **Social Security number** for each qualifying child for whom the credit is claimed.

A **qualifying child** for purposes of the child tax credit is a child who meets <u>all</u> the following criteria:

- Is the taxpayer's son, daughter, stepchild, foster child, adopted child, brother, sister, stepbrother, stepsister, or a descendant of any of them (a grandchild, niece, or nephew)
- Was <u>younger</u> than **age 17** at the end of the tax year <u>and</u> younger than the taxpayer (or spouse)

- Did not provide <u>more</u> than half of his own support for the year
- Lived with the taxpayer for more than half of the year
- Is claimed as a dependent on the return
- Is a U.S. citizen, a U.S. national, or a resident of the United States

TIP: Treat a person who was born or died as having lived with the taxpayer for the entire tax year if the taxpayer's home was the person's home the entire time he was alive. Temporary absences for special circumstances, such as school, vacation, business, medical care, military service, or detention in a juvenile facility, count as time the child lived with the taxpayer.

> A **qualifying child** is an individual who has <u>not</u> attained **age 17** during the taxable year. A child who is not a citizen, national, or resident of the United States <u>cannot</u> be a qualifying child.

ADDITIONAL CHILD TAX CREDIT

If a taxpayer cannot claim the full amount ($2,000) of the Child Tax Credit (CTC), a **refundable** *additional child tax credit (ACTC)* may be available. The portion refundable as the ACTC is up to **15%** of earned income (including tax-free combat pay) that exceeds **$2,500,** up to a <u>maximum</u> of **$1,400** per qualifying child in 2020.

To claim the ACTC credit, the taxpayer must attach *Schedule 8812 Additional Child Tax Credit* to their tax return. A taxpayer filing Form 2555 (relating to foreign earned income) <u>cannot</u> claim the ACTC.

> **EXAMPLE:** May and Bob file as Married Filing Jointly and have two children who qualify for the child tax credit. Their MAGI is $56,000 and their tax liability is $954. They can only claim $954, reducing their tax to zero. As they could not claim the maximum child tax credit, May and Bob may also be eligible for the additional child tax credit.
>
> Because their tax liability is less than the full amount of the child tax credit (in their case $4,000), they may be able to take the additional child tax credit of $2,800 ($4,000 – $954 = $3,046 but, limited to $1,400 per child).

> **CONSOLIDATED APPROPRIATIONS ACT UPDATE:** The Consolidated Appropriations Act, 2021 provides a temporary special rule for the determination of **earned income** for the *additional child tax credit.* This special rule applies <u>only</u> to 2020.
>
> If the earned income of the taxpayer for the taxpayer's first taxable year beginning in 2020 is <u>less</u> than the earned income of the taxpayer for the preceding taxable year (2019), the *additional child tax credit* may, at the **election** of the taxpayer, be determined using 2019 earned income.
>
> **TIP:** The taxpayer should elect to use 2019 earned income if it is more than 2020 earned income and if the taxpayer's ACTC is <u>greater</u> using 2019 earned income versus 2020 earned income.

LIMITS ON THE CREDITS

The TCJA also modifies the adjusted gross income phaseout thresholds. The credit begins to phase out for taxpayers with adjusted gross income in excess of **$400,000** (married taxpayers filing a joint return) and **$200,000** (for all other taxpayers). These phase-out thresholds are <u>not</u> indexed for inflation.

Round income above these levels up to the nearest thousand and multiply by 5% ($50 per $1,000). Subtract the result from the maximum child tax credit.

ADDITIONAL $500 CREDIT FOR OTHER DEPENDENTS (NON-REFUNDABLE)

The TCJA also temporarily enhances the child tax credit by allowing an additional **$500 non-refundable credit** for qualifying dependents other than qualifying children. The new provision generally retains the present-law definition of dependent. Examples of a qualified dependent include dependents over age 17, such as children in college or a dependent parent. The $500 non-refundable credit may be claimed only with respect to any dependent who is a citizen, national, or resident of the United States. Thus, non-U.S. citizens living in Canada and Mexico do not qualify for the $500 non-refundable credit.

> **EXAMPLE:** Your 10-year-old nephew lives in Mexico and qualifies as your dependent. He is not a U.S. citizen, U.S. national, or U.S. resident alien. You cannot use him to claim the credit for other dependents (ODC).

The Social Security number requirement, for the child tax credit, does not apply to a non-child dependent for whom the $500 non-refundable credit is claimed. In order to claim the $500 non-refundable credit with respect to any individual, however, the taxpayer must include such individual's **TIN** (SSN, ITIN, or ATIN) on the tax return.

> **EXAMPLE:** Robert and Susan file a joint return and they both have SSNs. Their tax liability is $2,000. They have three qualifying dependents. Tom is their 18-year-old son, has an SSN, and meets the qualifying child dependent test. Jill is their 17-year-old adopted child, has an ATIN, and meets the qualifying child dependent test. Robert's mother, Esther, is 65 years old, has an ITIN, and meets the qualifying relative test. They are all U.S. residents. Tom, Jill, and Esther are all qualifying dependents for the credit for other dependents.

FOREIGN TAX CREDIT (NON-REFUNDABLE)

If a taxpayer paid income tax to a foreign country, he can choose to take a **nonrefundable credit** against his U.S. income tax or an itemized **deduction.** He cannot take a credit (or deduction) for foreign income taxes paid on the income he excludes from U.S. tax under any of the following:

- Foreign earned income exclusion
- Foreign housing exclusion
- Income from Puerto Rico exempt from U.S. tax
- Possession exclusion

The taxpayer must file *Form 1116 Foreign Tax Credit* to take the credit unless all of the following apply:

- All of the foreign source income is passive income, which generally includes interest and dividends
- The taxpayer reported all of his foreign source income and the foreign tax paid on it on a qualified payee statement, which includes Forms 1099-INT and 1099-DIV
- The total of creditable foreign taxes was not more than **$300** ($600 if married filing jointly)
- The taxpayer elects this procedure for the tax year

SAVER'S CREDIT (NON-REFUNDABLE)

A taxpayer may claim the **nonrefundable** *saver's credit* (formerly retirement savings contributions credit) for qualified contributions or deferrals made to certain retirement plans. The credit amount begins at 50% of the taxpayer's contributions to the plan, contributions up to $2,000 ($4,000 MFJ), and is reduced depending on taxpayer's adjusted gross income (AGI) and filing status. The maximum credit is $1,000 ($2,000 MFJ).

2020 Saver's Credit			
Credit Rate	Married Filing Jointly	Head of Household	All Other Filers
50%	AGI not more than $39,000	AGI not more than $29,250	AGI not more than $19,500
20%	$39,001 – $42,500	$29,251 – $31,875	$19,501 – $21,250
10%	$42,501 – $65,000	$31,876 – $48,750	$21,251 – $32,500
0%	more than $65,000	more than $48,750	more than $32,500

EXAMPLE: Jill, who works at a retail store, is married and earned $38,500 in 2020. Jill's husband was unemployed in 2020 and didn't have any earnings. Jill contributed $1,000 to her IRA for 2020. After deducting her IRA contribution, the adjusted gross income shown on her joint return is $37,500. Jill may claim a 50% credit of $500, for her $1,000 IRA contribution.

- A taxpayer may not take the credit if one of the following is true:
    1. 2020 AGI is more than $32,500 ($48,750 HH, $65,000 MFJ)
    2. Someone else claimed the taxpayer as a dependent
    3. The taxpayer is younger than **age 18**
    4. The taxpayer is a full-time student
- Contributions which are eligible include:
    1. Contributions to a traditional or Roth IRA
    2. Elective deferrals to a 401(k), Simple IRA, SARSEP, 403(b) annuity, governmental 457(b) plan
    3. Contributions to a 501(C)(18) plan
    4. Voluntary after-tax **employee contributions** to a qualified retirement or 403(b) annuity; employee contributions will be voluntary as long as they are not a condition of employment
    5. Contributions to an ABLE account if you're the designated beneficiary

Employer contributions under 414(h)(2) are not voluntary employee contributions and do not qualify for the credit. Rollover contributions (money the taxpayer moves from another retirement plan or IRA) are not eligible for the Saver's Credit. Also, eligible contributions may be reduced by any recent distributions received from a retirement plan or IRA.

The amount of retirement distributions from a qualified retirement plan as defined in section 4974(c) must be reported by the taxpayer using *Form 8880 Credit for Qualified Retirement Savings Contributions*. The following payments are not reported: loans from a qualified employer plan, tax-exempt distributions, and military retirement plan.

CREDIT FOR EXCESS SOCIAL SECURITY AND RRTA TAX WITHHELD (REFUNDABLE)

Most employers must withhold social security tax from employee wages. Certain government employers (some federal, state and local governments) don't have to withhold social security tax.

A railroad employer must withhold Tier 1 Railroad Retirement Tax Act (RRTA) tax and Tier 2 RRTA tax. Tier 1 RRTA provides social security and Medicare equivalent benefits, and Tier 2 RRTA provides a private pension benefit.

A taxpayer that has **more than one employer** during the taxable year may have excess social security tax withheld if total wages and compensation were over **$137,700** (the 2020 wage base limit) for the year. This could result in withheld taxes that exceed the maximum amount due for the tax year. The taxpayer can receive a **refundable credit** for the excess withholding by filing Schedule 3.

All wages are subject to Medicare tax withholding.

TIP: A taxpayer with one employer that withheld too much social security or RRTA tax, can't claim the excess as a credit against income tax. The employer should adjust the excess. If the employer doesn't adjust the overcollection, the taxpayer can use Form 843, Claim for Refund and Request for Abatement to claim a refund.

LESSON 9

Filing Considerations

FILING DEADLINES AND EXTENSIONS

FILING DEADLINES

The income tax return is due by the 15th day of the 4th month after the close of the tax year. Usually, this falls on April 15. If the due date falls on a Saturday, Sunday, or legal holiday, the due date is delayed until the next business day. The IRS considers a paper return "on time" when it arrives with a proper address and sufficient postage and bears a postmark on or before the due date. A return sent using IRS e-file is on time if the *authorized electronic return transmitter* postmarks the transmission by the due date.

EXTENSIONS

AUTOMATIC 6-MONTH EXTENSION TO FILE

A taxpayer may request an *automatic six-month extension* by filing Form 4868 (via paper or electronically) by the due date of the return or by paying all or part of the income tax due using a credit or debit card. For most taxpayers, this extends the due date until October 15.

Please note that this is **not an extension of time to pay** taxes. The taxpayer must estimate the taxes due and can submit the payment with the extension request.

SERVING IN A COMBAT ZONE

Deadlines are extended for certain taxpayers serving in a combat zone or a contingency operation in support of the Armed Forces. When individuals serve in a qualified combat zone, the deadline for **filing and payment** increases by **180 days** after the latter of the last day in a qualified combat zone or the last day of a continuous hospitalization related to injury from service. In addition to the 180 days, a service member in a qualified combat zone can receive a deadline extension of up to three and a half months, based on the number of days remaining to file upon entering the combat zone. This period is representative of the time normally allotted for filing taxes (January 1–April 15). If entering the combat zone before the first of the year, the servicemember may add the entire three and a half months to the 180-day extension.

EXAMPLE: Captain Margaret Jones, a resident of Maryland, entered Saudi Arabia on December 1, 20X1. She remained there through March 31, 20X3, when she departed for the United States. She wasn't injured and didn't return to the combat zone. The deadlines for filing Captain Jones' 20X1, 20X2, and 20X3 returns are figured as follows. Note: For simplification purposes, this example assumes all months have 30 days.

The 20X1 tax return. The deadline is January 15, 20X4. This deadline is 285 days (180 plus 105) after Captain Jones' last day in the combat zone (March 31, 20X3). The 105 additional days are the number of days in the 3½ month filing period that were left when she entered the combat zone (January 1–April 15, 20X2).

The 20X2 tax return. The deadline is January 15, 20X4. The deadline is 285 days (180 plus 105) after Captain Jones' last day in the combat zone (March 31, 20X3). The 105 additional days are the number of days in the 3½ month filing period that were left when she entered the combat zone (January 1–April 15, 20X3).

The 20X3 tax return. The deadline is April 15, 20X4. The deadline isn't extended because the 180-day extension period after March 31, 20X3, plus the number of days left in the filing period when she entered the combat zone (105) ends on January 15, 20X4, which is before the due date for her 20X3 return (April 15, 20X4).

The term *combat zone* is a general term that includes all of the following hostile areas where the military may serve—actual combat areas, direct combat support areas, and contingency operations areas. A *contingency operation* is a military operation that is designated by the Secretary of Defense or results in calling members of the uniformed services to active duty (or retains them on active duty) during a war or a national emergency declared by the President or Congress.

There are multiple classes that qualify for the same treatment:

- Armed forces such as the Army, Navy, Air Force, Marine Corps, and Coast Guard
- Uniformed services, which includes the armed forces, and the commissioned corps of the National Oceanic and Atmospheric Administration (NOAA) and the Public Health Service
- Support personnel, such as the Red Cross

INDIVIDUALS OUTSIDE THE UNITED STATES

A taxpayer who is a U.S. citizen (or resident) may receive an **automatic two-month extension to file a return and pay** any federal income tax due if—on the due date of the return—he is in the military or naval service on duty outside the United States and Puerto Rico, or lives and maintains a main place of business outside the United States and Puerto Rico. Interest applies from the due date until paid. The taxpayer must attach a statement to their return explaining which situation applies.

TAX WITHHOLDING AND ESTIMATED TAX

Federal income tax is a "pay-as-you-go" system. Failure to pay or a significant under-estimation of the amount owed may lead to the assessment of penalties and interest. There are two payment methods—withholding and estimated tax.

WITHHOLDING

An employer withholds income tax from an employee's pay and deposits with the IRS in the name of the employee. In order to determine the proper amount of withholding, an employee completes *Form W-4, Employee's Withholding Certificate*.

TIP: Allowances are no longer used for the redesigned Form W-4.

Individuals may withhold tax on income sources like pensions, bonuses, commissions, and gambling winnings. Recipients of pensions, annuities (including commercial annuities), and certain other deferred compensation will use *Form W-4P, Withholding Certificate for Pension or Annuity Payments* to tell payers the correct amount of federal income tax to withhold, to choose not to have any federal income tax withheld, or to have an additional amount of tax withheld. The withholding agent does not send these forms to the IRS unless there is a written request.

ESTIMATED TAX

Income from dividends, interest, capital gains, rent, royalties, and self-employment is not subject to withholding. A taxpayer with income from these sources must make estimated quarterly payments.

An individual with no tax liability in the previous full year is not required to pay estimated tax. Estimated tax liability exists when both of the following conditions exist:

- An individual will owe at least **$1,000** in tax, after subtracting withholding and credits, and
- Withholding and credits will be less than the smaller of one of the following:
  1. **90%** of the tax to be shown on **this year's tax return**, or
  2. **100%** of the tax shown on **last year's tax return** (110% if AGI more than $150,000).

EXAMPLE: Jason earns $130,000, and his tax liability for the current year is $10,000, double what it was the prior year. He can avoid a penalty if his combined payments are at least $5,000 (100% of prior year liability).

The IRS may issue a penalty even if a refund is due when a sufficient amount of tax is unpaid by the due date for each of the periods as indicated in the following table (next business day if on Saturday, Sunday, or legal holiday). Non-business taxpayers use Form 1040-ES to make estimated payments to the IRS.

Estimated Tax Due Dates for Individuals	
For the period:	**Due date:**
Jan. 1 – Mar. 31 (3 months)	April 15 (fourth month)
Apr. 1 – May 31 (2 months)	June 15 (sixth month)
Jun. 1 – Aug. 31 (3 months)	September 15 (ninth month)
Sep. 1 – Dec. 31 (4 months)	January 15 (first month following tax year)*
*The January 15 installment is not required for a taxpayer who pays all tax due and files Form 1040 by January 31.	

EXAMPLE: Janet does not pay any estimated tax for 2020. She files her 2020 income tax return and pays the balance due shown on her return on January 26, 2021. Janet's estimated tax for the fourth payment period is considered to have been paid on time. However, she may owe a penalty for not making the first three estimated tax payments, if required. Any penalty for not making those payments will be figured up to January 26, 2021.

EXAMPLE: Margaret sold an investment property in July. She has no other income and did not owe taxes the prior year. She estimates owing $25,000 in taxes because of the transaction. If she is required to pay estimated tax, she must make her first payment by September 15. However, she had no tax liability in the prior year and is not required to make estimated payments.

Certain taxpayers may request a waiver from the penalty. A taxpayer requesting a complete waiver can elect to have the IRS calculate the penalty, while a taxpayer requesting a partial waiver must calculate the penalty on *Form 2210*. The taxpayer must attach Form 2210 and a statement to their tax return explaining the reasons for not meeting the estimated tax requirements and the period for the waiver request.

TAX PAYMENTS AND REFUNDS

TAX DUE

A taxpayer with tax due from a tax return can pay by check, money order, credit card, debit card, or cash (at a retail partner). If you're an individual taxpayer, IRS Direct Pay offers you a free, electronic payment method directly from a bank account at no cost. Online payments are available at https://www.irs.gov/payments.

Checks should be made payable to the "United States Treasury". The IRS instructs taxpayers to write identifying information on the check, including the first SSN used on the return and the year and from number. Payment by mail should include a *Form 1040-V Payment Voucher*, although it is not a requirement.

INSTALLMENTS

A taxpayer may request a monthly installment plan if they are unable to pay the full amount of tax owed. Before applying for any payment agreement, a taxpayer must file all required tax returns. Installment agreements generally provide up to **72 months** to pay the tax. In certain circumstances, the payment period could be longer or the amount agreed to could be less than the amount of tax owed. An installment plan is not valid unless accepted by the IRS. However, if a taxpayer **owes $10,000 or less** and meets certain other criteria, **the IRS must accept the request**. Those requirements are:

- During the past five tax years, the taxpayer (and spouse if filing jointly) has timely filed all income tax returns and paid any tax due, and has not entered into an installment agreement for payment of income tax.
- The taxpayer agrees to pay the full amount owed within three years and to comply with the tax laws while the agreement is in effect.
- The taxpayer is financially unable to pay the liability in full when due.

An *installment agreement* generally requires equal monthly payments, and the taxpayer must fully pay all of the tax owed within the time left in the 10-year period during which the IRS can collect the tax. If a taxpayer cannot pay in full by the end of the collection period, but can pay some of the tax owed, they may qualify for a partial payment installment agreement. To request an installment agreement a taxpayer can attach *Form 9465 Installment Agreement Request* to the front of their tax return, or—in cases where the return is already filed—mail it directly to the IRS.

If the IRS approves a request, they send a notice detailing the terms of the agreement and request a user fee to establish the plan. The user fee is reduced if the taxpayer is able to apply online.

If the balance due is **$50,000 or less**, the taxpayer can apply for an installment agreement online instead of filing Form 9465. To do that, go to IRS.gov/opa.

2020 Long-term Agreement User Fees (paying in more than 120 days)			
Long-term Payment Plan Installment Agreement	Apply online	Apply by phone, mail, or in-person	Low income: Apply online, by phone, mail, or in-person
Automatic Withdrawal / Direct Debit	$31	$107	$31 fee waived
Non-Direct Debit	$149	$225	$43*

*$43 setup fee may be reimbursed if certain conditions are met

A taxpayer whose adjusted gross income is at or below 250% of the applicable federal poverty level (low-income taxpayer) that enters into long-term payment plans may qualify to pay the low income reduced fee. The IRS will waive or may reimburse the user fee for *low-income taxpayers* only, for installment agreements entered into on or after April 10, 2018. The IRS will waive the user fee if the low-income taxpayer agrees to make electronic debit payments by entering into a direct debit installment agreement. The IRS will reimburse the user fee that was paid for the installment agreement upon completion for low-income taxpayers who are unable to make electronic debit payments through a direct debit installment agreement.

A taxpayer that can pay the full amount owed within **120 days** should not request an installment agreement on Form 9465. Instead, they can call or apply online to establish a request to pay in full. A taxpayer who can pay within the 120-day period can avoid paying the fee to set up the agreement.

Once approved, a taxpayer may submit a request to modify or terminate the installment agreement. This request will not suspend the statute of limitations on collection. While the IRS considers a request to modify or terminate the installment agreement, the taxpayer **must comply with the existing agreement.**

A taxpayer with outstanding tax liability (including penalties and interest) of $50,000 or less may file Form 9465. This is known as a *streamlined installment agreement* because the IRS **does not require a financial statement** (Form 433-F, Collection Information Statement) or substantial disclosure of financial information. A liability greater than $50,000 can be considered if the taxpayer pays down the liability to $50,000 or less prior to the agreement being granted. Generally, a taxpayer must pay off the balance due on a streamlined installment agreement within a 72-month period.

If the total amount the taxpayer owes is **greater than $25,000 but not more than $50,000**, the taxpayer must agree to a Direct Debit Installment Agreement (DDIA) or make payments by payroll deduction **to request an installment agreement without completing a financial statement** (Form 433-F, Collection Information Statement).

> The taxpayer will be charged interest and late payment penalties on any tax not paid by its due date, even if a request to pay in installments is granted. Interest and any applicable penalties will be charged until the balance is paid in full. To limit interest and penalty charges, the taxpayer should file the return on time and pay as much of the tax as possible with the return.

The IRS generally may not levy against property:

- While a request for an installment agreement is being considered,
- While an installment agreement is in effect,
- For 30 days after a request for an agreement has been rejected,
- For 30 days after termination of an installment agreement (due to taxpayer default), or
- While the IRS Office of Appeals is evaluating an appeal of the rejection or termination.

However, the IRS may file a Notice of Federal Tax Lien to secure the government's interest against other creditors. Termination of an installment agreement may cause the filing of a Notice of Federal Tax Lien and/or an IRS levy action.

OVERPAYMENT

A taxpayer who has an overpayment of tax may apply their overpayment to their estimated tax liability for the following tax year or request a refund. The IRS can mail a refund check; however, the fastest way to receive a refund is through direct deposit. *Form 8888* is necessary when the taxpayer wants the refund to go into more than one account or wants to buy up to $5,000 in paper series I savings bonds. Otherwise, a taxpayer may enter routing and account information for their financial institution or bank directly on their tax return. The taxpayer can have their refund (or part of it) deposited directly to a traditional IRA, Roth IRA, or SEP-IRA, but not a SIMPLE IRA. The taxpayer must establish the IRA at a bank or other financial institution before requesting the direct deposit. The IRS can also send a refund to a TreasuryDirect® online account to buy U.S. Treasury marketable securities and savings bonds.

FILING A CLAIM FOR REFUND

> The normal deadline for filing a claim for refund or credit is **three years from the date for filing the original return or two years after paying the tax**, whichever is later. The IRS treats payments or returns made before the due date—without regard to extensions—as received on the due date.

EXAMPLE: The return of a taxpayer filed on March 1 is considered filed on the due date of April 15. However, if he had an extension to file (for example, until October 15) but files earlier and the IRS receives it July 1, the return is considered filed on July 1.

If a claim is filed within three years after the date of filing the return, the credit or refund cannot be more than the part of the tax paid within the three-year period—plus any extension of time for filing the return—immediately before the claim was filed. If a claim is filed after the 3-year period, but within two years from the time the tax is paid, the credit or refund cannot be more than the tax paid within the two years immediately before filing the claim.

EXAMPLE: You made estimated tax payments of $1,000 and got an automatic extension of time from April 15, 2021, to October 15, 2021, to file your 2020 income tax return. When filing your return on the extended due date, you pay an additional $200 tax. Three years later, on October 15, 2024, you file an amended return and claim a refund of $700. Because you filed within 3 years after filing your return, you could get a refund of any tax paid after April 15, 2021.

EXAMPLE: The situation is the same as in the prior example, except that you file your return on October 31, 2021, after the extension period ends. You paid an additional $200 on that date. Three years later, on October 27, 2024, you file an amended return and claim a refund of $700. Although you filed your claim within 3 years from the date you filed your original return, the refund is limited to $200. The estimated tax of $1,000 was paid before the 3 years plus the 6-month extension period.

EXCEPTION: A notable exception to the 3-year rule is an amended return based on a bad debt or worthless security, which a taxpayer generally must file within **seven years** after the due date of the return for the tax year in which the debt or security became worthless.

A taxpayer generally files *Form 1040-X* with the IRS center determined by where they live at the time. A taxpayer may use Form 1040-X to do the following:

- Correct Forms 1040, 1040-SR, 1040-NR, or 1040-NR-EZ (**Note:** As of 2020, Form 1040-NR-EZ is not in use; however, prior year 1040-NR-EZ can be amended)
- Make certain elections after the prescribed deadline
- Change amounts previously adjusted by the IRS
- Make a claim for a carryback due to a loss or unused credit

A taxpayer files Form 1040-X only after filing the original return, and before the expiration of the deadline. The taxpayer files a separate form for each year or period involved and includes an explanation of each item of income, deduction, or credit used as a basis for the claim. The taxpayer must attach all appropriate forms and schedules to Form 1040-X or it will be returned. A taxpayer who files an erroneous refund claim may be subject to a penalty of 20% of the disallowance.

LIABILITY AND RELIEF

JOINT AND SEVERAL LIABILITY

A married taxpayer is *jointly and severally liable* for the tax and any additions to tax, interest, or penalties that arise because of a joint return, even after divorce. Joint and several liability means that **each taxpayer is legally responsible for the entire liability.** One spouse may be held responsible for all the tax due, even if the other spouse earned all the income or claimed improper deductions or credits. Relief from **joint liability**, such as *innocent spouse relief*, is different from *injured spouse relief*.

RELIEF FROM JOINT AND SEVERAL LIABILITY

There are three types of relief available to married persons who filed joint returns:

- **Innocent spouse relief** – A taxpayer may be **relieved of responsibility** for paying tax, interest, and penalties because a spouse or former spouse failed to report income, reported income improperly, or claimed improper deductions or credits. A taxpayer will use *Form 8857* to request relief, provided he meets all of the following conditions to qualify:
  1. The spouses must have filed a joint return with an understatement of tax directly related to the spouse's erroneous items.
  2. The taxpayer seeking relief can establish that at the time he signed the joint return, he did not know and had no reason to know, that there was an understatement of tax.
  3. Taking into account all the facts and circumstances, it would be unfair to hold taxpayer liable for the understatement of tax.
- **Separation of liability relief** – For those who are no longer married, widowed, or legally separated and have not been members of the same household for a 12-month period. The understated tax (plus interest and penalties) on the joint return is allocated between spouses (or former spouse). The tax allocated is generally the amount the taxpayer is responsible to pay. This type of relief is available only for unpaid liabilities resulting from the understated tax. Refunds are not allowed.
- **Equitable relief** – For a properly stated but underpaid tax. If a taxpayer does not qualify for other forms of relief, the taxpayer may still be relieved of responsibility for tax, interest, and penalties.

INJURED SPOUSE RELIEF

Relief from a **separate liability** of the other spouse on a joint tax return. **Injured spouse relief** is when one spouse's individual liability, if collected, would harm the other spouse.

Sometimes a liability belongs only to one spouse. A taxpayer is an *"injured spouse"* if he files a joint return and all or part of his **share of the refund** was, or will be, applied against the **separate** past-due federal tax, state tax, child support, or federal non-tax debt (such as a student loan) of his spouse with whom he filed the joint return. An injured spouse may be entitled to recoup their share of the refund.

The injured spouse files *Form 8379* with a jointly filed tax return when the joint overpayment was—or is expected to be—applied to a past-due obligation of the other spouse. By filing Form 8379, the injured spouse may be able to get back his share of the joint refund. The taxpayer may file form 8379 with a joint return, with an amended return, or by itself at a later time.

EXAMPLE: Tom and Lucy expect a refund of $5,000 when they jointly file their tax return. Tom has $60,000 in past-due taxes that he accumulated prior to getting married. To prevent the entire refund from being applied against his past-due obligation, they can file Form 8379, to protect Lucy's share of the refund.

LESSON 10

Specialized Returns

ESTATE TAX (FORM 706)

APPLICABLE CREDIT AND APPLICABLE EXCLUSION

The tax code imposes additional federal taxes on certain transfers of property (including money). Property transferred or given away during a lifetime may be subject to *gift tax*. Property owned at death (*estate*) may be subject to *estate tax*, and the gross income of the estate may be subject to *income tax*. Lifetime gifts or *bequests* (gifts after death from taxpayer's estate) also may become subject to an additional *generation skipping transfer (GST)* tax. This occurs when the gifts or bequests are to a person, such as a grandchild, who is more than one generation younger than the taxpayer is. The GST tax rate is **40%** for 2020.

TIP: Most gifts are <u>not</u> subject to the gift tax and most estates are <u>not</u> subject to the estate tax. For example, there is usually no tax on transfers to a spouse or to a charity. The gift tax usually does not apply until the value of the gifts to that person exceeds the *annual exclusion* for the year. Even if tax applies to gifts or the estate, it may be eliminated by the *applicable credit* (formerly called the unified credit).

The *applicable credit* reduces or eliminates <u>both</u> the *gift tax* and the *estate tax*. During the life of the taxpayer, the applicable credit offsets gift tax due. Any applicable credit used against gift tax reduces the amount of credit that the taxpayer can use in a later year. The total amount used during life against gift tax reduces the credit available to use against the estate tax. The sunset provision within the *Economic Growth and Tax Relief Reconciliation Act of 2001 (EGTRRA)* repeals the estate tax in 2010; however, it was to reappear in 2011 with applicable exclusions reverting to substantially lower levels (same as 2002). The *2010 Tax Relief Act* revives the estate tax for those dying after 2009.

> The Tax Cuts and Jobs Act doubled the estate and gift tax exemption for estates of decedents dying in 2020. The top estate tax rate is **40%**. There is an **$11.58 million** *applicable exclusion* (also called the basic exclusion) amount in 2020, and beneficiaries receive a stepped-up basis. The *applicable credit* for taxable gifts and estates is **$4,577,800**, exempting $11.58 million from gift and estate tax in 2020.

The following table shows the applicable credit and applicable exclusion amount for the calendar years in which a gift is made or a *decedent* dies.

Applicable Credit for Gift and Estate Tax Purposes		
Year	Applicable Credit	Applicable Exclusion
2020	$4,577,800	$11,580,000
2021	$4,625,800	$11,700,000

A *taxable estate* in excess of the *applicable exclusion* ($11.58 million for 2020) may be subject to the estate tax. The taxable estate is the *gross estate* less allowable deductions. The *executor* of a decedent's estate uses *Form 706* to figure the estate tax. This tax is levied on the entire taxable estate and not just on the share received by a particular beneficiary. Form 706 also calculates the *generation skipping transfer (GST)* tax on *direct skips* (transfers of property included in the decedent's gross estate to persons more than one generation younger). For transfers to unrelated persons, a *direct skip* occurs if the recipient is more than **37.5 years younger** than the decedent.

PORTABILITY OF DECEASED SPOUSAL UNUSED EXCLUSION (PORTABILITY ELECTION)

The *2010 Tax Relief Act* has a new twist that allows the executor of a deceased spouse's estate to transfer any unused exclusion (*deceased spousal unused exclusion (DSUE)* amount) to the surviving spouse. The exclusion becomes available to the surviving spouse and is in addition to any applicable exclusion to which the survivor is entitled. In the past, only effective estate planning could preserve this benefit.

TIP: There is a catch—the executor of the estate of the deceased spouse <u>must</u> timely file an estate tax return on which such amount is computed, and make an election on the return, regardless of the size of the decedent's gross estate. Such election, once made, shall be irrevocable.

GROSS ESTATE

The gross estate includes the ***fair market value (FMV)*** of all property in which the taxpayer **had an interest at the time of death** (or an ***alternate valuation date***, if elected).

> The ***gross estate*** also <u>includes</u> the following:
>
> - The value of property transferred before death where the decedent held a ***retained life estate***
> - Certain property transferred before death where the decedent held a ***reversionary interest***
> - Property transferred before death where the transfer was revocable
> - Transfers taking effect at death
> - Life insurance proceeds **payable to the estate** <u>or</u> if **taxpayer owned the policy**
> - Certain gifts made within three years of death regarding the above-mentioned property
> - The value of certain annuities payable to taxpayer's estate or heirs
> - The includible portion of joint estates with right of survivorship
> - The includible portion of tenancies by the entirety
> - Property over which the decedent possessed a general power of appointment
> - Qualified terminable interest property (QTIP)
> - Dower or curtsey (or statutory estate) of the surviving spouse
> - Community property to the extent of the decedent's interest as defined by applicable law

ALTERNATE VALUATION DATE

The alternate valuation date is **6 months** from the date of death. Any property <u>not</u> sold within that time is valued at the FMV on the alternate valuation date.

Any property distributed, sold, exchanged, or otherwise disposed of or separated or passed from the gross estate by any method within 6 months after the decedent's death is valued on the date of distribution, sale, exchange, or other disposition. Value this property on the date it ceases to be a part of the gross estate; for example, on the date the title passes as the result of its sale, exchange, or other disposition.

TIP: Any property which is affected by mere lapse of time is valued as of the date of the decedent's death, but adjusted for any difference in its value not due to mere lapse of time as of the date 6 months after the decedent's death, or as of the date of its distribution, sale, exchange, or other disposition, whichever date first occurs.

> The executor can make this election <u>only</u> if it **reduces both the gross estate and estate tax due.**

TAXABLE ESTATE

The allowable deductions from the gross estate used in determining the ***taxable estate*** include:

- Funeral expenses paid out of the estate
- Debts owed at the time of death and other claims against the estate

- Administrative expenses such as court costs, executor fees, and professional fees
- The *marital deduction* (generally, the value of the property that passes to the surviving spouse)
  1. The marital deduction is generally not allowed if the surviving spouse is not a U.S. citizen unless passing to such a surviving spouse in a *qualified domestic trust (QDOT)*
- The *charitable deduction* (generally, the value of the property that passes from the estate to a qualifying charity for exclusively charitable purposes)
- The state death tax deduction (generally any estate, inheritance, legacy, or succession taxes paid as the result of the decedent's death to any state or the District of Columbia)
- Losses incurred during the settlement of estates arising from fires, storms, shipwrecks, or other casualties, or from theft, when such losses are not compensated for by insurance or otherwise

APPLYING THE APPLICABLE CREDIT TO ESTATE TAX

The *tentative tax base* includes the taxable estate plus taxable gifts made after 1976. Apply estate tax rates to determine the *tentative estate tax*. The following credits reduce the tax:

- The applicable credit
- Credit for foreign death taxes paid
- Credit for federal gift taxes on pre-1977 gifts
- **Credit for tax on prior transfers** – If the decedent's estate includes property received from a person who died within 10 years before or two years after the decedent received the gift, the decedent's estate may receive a credit for estate taxes previously paid on the property.

If the combined credits are more than the tentative estate tax, there is no estate tax liability. Otherwise, deduct the credits from the tentative estate tax to arrive at *net estate tax due*.

FILING AN ESTATE TAX RETURN (FORM 706)

An estate tax return, **Form 706**, must be filed for decedents who were citizens or residents of the United States at the time of death and the gross estate, plus any adjusted taxable gifts (post-1976 gifts), is more than the filing requirement for the year of death (same as the applicable exclusion amount). For 2020, a return is not necessary if gross estate plus adjusted taxable gifts are less than $11.58 million.

> The executor must file Form 706, Estate (and Generation-Skipping Transfer) Tax Return, to report estate and/or GST tax **within nine months** after the date of the decedent's death, plus extension. Use Form 4768, Application for Extension of Time To File a Return and/or Pay U.S. Estate (and Generation-Skipping Transfer) Taxes, to apply for an automatic 6-month extension of time to file Form 706.

Under certain circumstances, the IRS may grant an extension of time to pay (up to 10 years) if the executor can show reasonable cause.

TIP: Estates with **gross income of more than $600** or a beneficiary who is a **nonresident alien** must file *Form 1041 U.S. Income Tax Return for Estates and Trusts.* The due date for filing Form 1041 for estates that use a calendar year accounting period is generally **April 15**. An estate may choose either a calendar or a fiscal year to report income. If on a fiscal year, Form 1041 is due by the **15th day of the fourth month** after the end of the tax year. If the due date is a Saturday, Sunday, or legal holiday, the form must be filed by the next business day. The personal representative can request an automatic **5 1/2 month extension** of time to file Form 1041. Estates with tax years ending two or more years after the date of the decedent's death must pay estimated tax in the same manner as individuals. Note: This should be the extent of what is tested regarding estate income tax on the Part 1 Individuals exam, but additional information is in Part 2 Businesses under Specialized Returns (as it is a topic within Part 2).

GIFT TAX (FORM 709)

The gift tax applies to transfers by gift of property. A *gift* is made when taxpayers give property (including money), or the use of (or income from) property, without expecting to receive something of at least equal value in return. The IRS may also consider property sold at less than full value or interest-free or reduced-interest loans to be gifts. The general rule is that any gift is a taxable gift. However, there are many exceptions to this rule. Generally, the following gifts are <u>not</u> taxable gifts:

- Gifts, excluding gifts of future interests, that are not more than the annual exclusion for the year
- Tuition or medical expenses paid <u>directly</u> to a **medical or educational institution** for anyone
- Gifts subject to the *marital deduction* (to a spouse)
- Gifts to a political organization for its use
- Gifts to charities

The *gift tax* is a tax on the transfer of property made during the life of the donor. The **gift tax is filed and paid by the donor** of the gift, <u>not</u> the recipient, using IRS Form 709.

There is an **$11,580,000** *applicable exclusion* amount in 2020. The *applicable credit* for taxable gifts is **$4,577,800**, exempting $11.58 million from gift tax in 2020.

TIP: For 2021, the applicable credit for taxable gifts is $4,625,800, exempting $11.7 million from gift tax.

ANNUAL EXCLUSION

A separate *annual exclusion* applies each year to each person to whom a gift is made. The gift tax annual exclusion is subject to cost-of-living increases.

> For 2020, a taxpayer generally can give a gift valued at up to **$15,000** (same in 2021) each, to any number of people, and none of the gifts will be taxable. Any amounts given above the $15,000 annual gift tax exclusion can be offset using the Applicable Credit.

TIP: Married taxpayers can each give gifts valued at up to $15,000 to the same person in 2020 without making a taxable gift. If one spouse gives more than the $15,000 annual exclusion to a person in 2020, the spouses can treat the gift as made one-half by each spouse. This is *gift splitting*. Both must consent to split the gift and <u>all</u> other gifts for the year. In 2020, gift splitting allows married couples to give up to $30,000 to a person without making a taxable gift. Taxpayers who wish to split gifts <u>must</u> file a *gift tax return (Form 709)*. Each spouse <u>must</u> file a **separate Form 709**, as a joint form does not exist.

A gift tax return, *Form 709* <u>must</u> be filed for any reportable gift over $15,000 in 2020, even if no tax is due.

EXEMPTIONS AND DEDUCTIONS

Certain gifts are exempt from the $15,000 (2020) annual exclusion. A donor can make **unlimited transfers without having to pay tax** in the following situations:

- **Medical exemption** – Amounts paid on behalf of others directly to a **medical care provider**. The recipient of this money does not need to be a relative, but the money needs to be paid **directly to the medical care provider**.

- **Education exemption** – Amounts paid on behalf of others directly to a **qualified university for tuition**. The recipient of this money does not need to be a relative, but the money needs to be paid **directly to the university**.
- **Political contributions** made to a political organization that will use the money for its own purposes (i.e. not acting as an intermediary to distribute money to a third party).

> These transfers are <u>not</u> "gifts" as that term is used on Form 709 and are <u>not</u> reportable gifts. A taxpayer is **not required to file a Form 709 gift tax return to report these transfers**.

In addition, a donor may claim a deduction for gifts in excess of the $15,000 (2020) annual exclusion to the following recipients:

- **Marital deduction** – Transfers made **between spouses** are usually exempt from taxation. There are some specific types of property transfers to spouses that may not be fully exempt. Also, 2020 transfers to **non-U.S. citizen spouses** over $157,000 ($159,000 for 2021) are **taxable**.
- **Charitable contributions** to qualified charity. A taxpayer does not need to report the following deductible gifts made to charities if he does not have other reportable gifts:
  1. The taxpayer's entire interest in property, if no other interest has been transferred for less than adequate consideration or for other than a charitable use
  2. A qualified conservation contribution (perpetual restriction on the use of real property)

> If a taxpayer is required to file a return to report noncharitable gifts <u>and</u> made gifts to charities, the taxpayer <u>must</u> **include all charitable gifts on Form 709**. The taxpayer can claim a deduction for charitable gifts on the return.

EXAMPLE: In 2020, you give your niece, Mary, a cash gift of $8,000. You pay the $15,000 college tuition of your friend, David, directly to his school. You give your 25-year-old daughter, Lisa, $25,000. You also give your 27-year-old son, Ken, $25,000. Before 2020, you had never given a taxable gift. You apply the exceptions to the gift tax and the applicable credit as follows:

- Apply the **educational exemption**. Payment of tuition expenses directly to the school is not subject to the gift tax. Therefore, the gift for David is <u>not</u> taxable.
- Apply the **annual exclusion**. The first $15,000 you give someone during 2020 is not a taxable gift. Therefore, your $8,000 gift to Mary, the first $15,000 of your gift to Lisa, and the first $15,000 of your gift to Ken are <u>not</u> taxable gifts. $20,000 of the gifts will be taxable. This amount includes $10,000 remaining from your gift to Lisa plus $10,000 remaining from your gift to Ken.
- Apply the **applicable credit** against the tax computed on the total taxable gifts (after the annual exclusion). The gift tax on $20,000 in taxable gifts is $3,800. The applicable credit amount in 2020 is $4,577,800. The applicable credit is reduced to $4,574,000 after applying $3,800 to offset the computed tax.

You do not have to pay any gift tax for 2020. However, you do have to file Form 709.

GIFTS OF FUTURE INTERESTS

A taxpayer cannot exclude gifts of *future interests* under an annual exclusion provision. A gift of a future interest is a gift that is limited so that its use, possession, or enjoyment will begin at some point in the future. <u>Any</u> gifts of future interest are reportable on Form 709, gift tax return.

A contribution to a Qualified Tuition Program (QTP), such as a 529 Plan, can be treated as a completed gift of a present interest to the designated beneficiary. A special rule allows a donor to front-load a QTP with 5-years worth of the annual exclusion for a total of **$75,000** ($15,000 annual exclusion × 5 years of annual exclusions) in 2020, $150,000 for a married couple gift splitting in 2020. This amount is excluded from gift tax if the donor elects to account for the gift ratably over a 5-year period. The election allows a taxpayer to apply the annual exclusion to a portion of the contribution in each of the 5 years, beginning in the year of contribution.

GENERATION-SKIPPING TRANSFER (GST) TAX

A taxpayer must report on Form 709 the GST tax imposed on *inter vivos* direct skips. An inter vivos direct skip is a transfer of property during the donor's lifetime that is subject to the gift tax and made to a *skip person*. A "skip person" is someone two or more generations below the donor **or** if the recipient is not related to the giver, they are 37½ years younger than the giver.

Like the gift tax, each individual taxpayer has a lifetime GST exemption to exclude a certain amount of assets from the tax. For 2020, the effective GST exemption is $11.58 million ($11.7 million in 2021), on lifetime transfers or distributions (directly or in trust) to a skip person.

FILING A GIFT TAX RETURN (FORM 709)

A gift tax return, **Form 709**, is generally due the year following a taxable gift, at the same time as the federal income tax return. Extensions for the federal income tax return automatically extend the time to file the gift tax return. For 2020, the top tax rate on taxable gifts is **40%**. The taxpayer also reports GST tax on Form 709.

- Generally, a taxpayer must file a gift tax return on Form 709, Gift (and Generation-Skipping Transfer) Tax Return, if any of the following apply:
  1. Gifts to a person (other than a spouse) are more than the annual exclusion for the year
  2. The taxpayer and his spouse are splitting a gift
  3. The taxpayer makes the gift to someone (other than a spouse) of a *future interest* that the recipient cannot actually possess, enjoy, or receive income from until some time in the future
  4. The taxpayer gave his spouse an interest in property that some future event will end
- A taxpayer does not have to file a gift tax return to report gifts to (or for the use of) political organizations and gifts made by paying someone's tuition or medical expenses directly.
- A taxpayer does not have to file a gift tax return to report deductible gifts made to charities if he does not have other reportable gifts. If a taxpayer is required to file a gift tax return to report other reportable gifts, must **include all charitable gifts on return** and can claim a deduction for the charitable gifts.

THE FINAL RETURN (DECEDENT'S FINAL FORM 1040)

An income tax return must be filed for a *decedent* (a person who died) if the decedent met the filing requirements at the time of his death. Should death occur during the filing season (i.e., Jan 1–April 15) and before filing a prior year return, the normal deadline for filing (usually April 15) applies to that return. The individual responsible for filing the return may be a surviving spouse, relative, executor, administrator, or legal representative. This is not the final return, as the decedent was alive for several months into a new tax year.

The final income tax return is due at the same time the decedent's return would have been due had death not occurred. A final return for a decedent who was a calendar year taxpayer is generally due on April 15 following the year of death, regardless of when during that year death occurred.

If the decedent is married at the time of death, the decedent and surviving spouse are considered married for the whole year for filing status purposes.

- A surviving spouse who does <u>not</u> remarry before the end of the tax year in which the decedent died may file a joint return with the decedent. If otherwise applicable, the return can include the full standard deduction based on filing status for the decedent.

- If the surviving spouse remarries during the year, they <u>must</u> file apart from the decedent. The decedent must file separately (MFS); however, the surviving spouse can file a joint return with the new spouse.

- A court-appointed personal representative may revoke an election to file a joint return that the surviving spouse previously made alone. The representative does this by filing a separate return for the decedent within one year from the due date of the return (including any extensions). The joint return made by the surviving spouse will then be regarded as the separate return of that spouse by excluding the decedent's items and refiguring the tax liability.

INCOME TO INCLUDE

The decedent's income includible on the final return is generally determined as if the person were still alive except that the taxable period is usually shorter because it ends on the date of death. All income the decedent would have received had death not occurred that was <u>not</u> properly includible on the final return is *income in respect of a decedent (IRD)* and taxable to the estate or person who receives it. The method of accounting used by the decedent also determines the income and expenses includible on the final return.

- **Cash method** – The final return includes items actually or *constructively received* before death.

  1. The decedent constructively received interest from coupons on bonds if the coupons matured in the decedent's final tax year but had not been cashed. Include the interest on the final return.

  2. Generally, the decedent constructively received a dividend if it was available for use by the decedent without restriction. If the corporation customarily mailed its dividend checks, the dividend was includible when received. If the individual died between the time the corporation declared the dividend and the time it arrived in the mail, the decedent did not constructively receive it before death. Do not include the dividend in the final return.

- **Accrual method** – Generally, under an accrual method of accounting, report income when earned. If the decedent used an accrual method, only the income items normally accrued before death are included in the final return.

EXAMPLE: Frank Johnson owned and operated an apple orchard. He used the cash method of accounting. He sold and delivered 1,000 bushels of apples to a canning factory for $2,000, but didn't receive payment before his death. The proceeds from the sale are income in respect of a decedent. When the estate was settled, payment had not been made and the estate transferred the right to the payment to his widow. When Frank's widow collects the $2,000, she must include that amount in her return. It isn't reported on the final return of the decedent or on the return of the estate.

EXAMPLE: Assume the same facts, except that Frank used the accrual method of accounting. The amount accrued from the sale of the apples would be included on his final return. Neither the estate nor the widow would realize income in respect of a decedent when the money is later paid.

INCOME IN RESPECT OF A DECEDENT (IRD)

Certain types of property, such as capital assets, receive a step-up in basis when included in the decedent's estate and transferred to a beneficiary due to death. Other assets, for example, traditional IRAs, are transferred in-kind to the beneficiary and do not receive a basis adjustment. The beneficiary is responsible for paying tax on income from these assets. All income the decedent would have received had death not occurred that was not properly includible on the final return, discussed earlier, is income in respect of a decedent. Income in respect of a decedent is included in the income of one of the following:

- The decedent's estate, if the estate receives it
- The beneficiary, if the right to income is passed directly to the beneficiary and he receives it
- Any person to whom the estate properly distributes the right to receive it

> The character of the IRD is the same as it would be to the decedent if he were alive. If the income would have been a capital gain to the decedent, it will be a capital gain to the taxpayer.

If an executor filed an estate tax return (Form 706) for the decedent, the taxpayer who must include IRD in his gross income may be able to claim a deduction for the estate tax paid on that income.

EXAMPLE: On February 1, George High, a cash method taxpayer, sold his tractor for $3,000, payable March 1 of the same year. His adjusted basis in the tractor was $2,000. George died on February 15, before receiving payment. The gain to be reported as income in respect of a decedent is the $1,000 difference between the decedent's basis in the property and the sale proceeds. In other words, the income in respect of a decedent is the gain the decedent would have realized had he lived.

EXAMPLE: Cathy O'Neil was entitled to a large salary payment at the date of her death. The amount was to be paid in five annual installments. The estate, after collecting two installments, distributed the right to the remaining installments to you, the beneficiary. The payments are income in respect of a decedent. None of the payments were includible on Cathy's final return. The estate must include in its income the two installments it received, and you must include in your income each of the three installments as you receive them.

MEDICAL EXPENSE DEDUCTIONS

- Medical expenses paid <u>before</u> death by the decedent are deductible, subject to limits, on the final income tax return if deductions are itemized. This includes expenses for the decedent, as well as for the decedent's spouse and dependents.
- Medical expenses that were <u>not</u> paid before death are liabilities of the estate and appear on the federal estate tax return (Form 706). If the estate pays medical expenses for the decedent during the one-year period beginning with the day after death, the executor may elect to treat all or part of the expenses as paid by the decedent at the time the decedent incurred them. An executor making this election may claim all or part of the expenses on the decedent's income tax return as an itemized deduction, rather than on the federal estate tax return (Form 706).

LOSS DEDUCTIONS

A decedent's **net operating loss** deduction from a prior year and any capital losses (including **capital loss carryovers**) can be deducted only on the decedent's final income tax return. An unused net operating loss or capital loss is not deductible on the estate's income tax return.

CREDITS

The individual filing a decedent's tax return may claim any tax credits that applied to the decedent before death on the decedent's final income tax return. Certain credits, like the EIC or the child tax credit, still apply even though the return covers a period of fewer than 12 months.

TERRORIST OR MILITARY ACTION RELATED FORGIVENESS

Terrorist or military action related forgiveness occurs when an individual meets both of the following criteria.

- Is a member of the U.S. Armed Forces at death.
- Dies from wounds or injury incurred while a member of the U.S. Armed Forces in a terrorist or military action.

In general, forgiveness applies to:

- The tax year death occurred, and
- Any earlier tax year in the period beginning with the year before the year in which the wounds or injury occurred.

The beneficiary or trustee of the estate of a deceased service member doesn't have to pay tax on any amount received that would have been included (had the servicemember not died) in the deceased member's gross income for the year of death.

> **EXAMPLE:** Army Private John Kane died in 2020 of wounds incurred in a terrorist attack in 2019. His income tax liability is forgiven for all tax years from 2018 through 2020.

FILING THE RETURN

If the court has appointed a personal representative, that person must sign the return. If it is a joint return, the surviving spouse must also sign it. If the court has not appointed a personal representative, the surviving spouse (on a joint return) signs the return and writes in the signature area "Filing as surviving spouse." If the court has not appointed a personal representative and there is no surviving spouse, the person in charge of the decedent's property must file and sign the return as "personal representative". A surviving spouse filing jointly with the decedent may submit a claim for refund by filing the return.

TIP: Write the word "DECEASED", the decedent's name, and the date of death across the top of the tax return.

FOREIGN TAXPAYERS AND ACCOUNTS

RESIDENT ALIEN OR NONRESIDENT ALIEN

Each year, thousands of nonresident aliens are gainfully employed in the United States. Thousands more own rental property or earn interest or dividends from U.S. investments. Most **U.S. source income** a nonresident alien receives is subject to withholding with a tax rate of **30%**. A nonresident who receives U.S. income must file a return (Form 1040-NR) if additional taxes are due or if conducting a business in the U.S. A nonresident alien who is married to a U.S. citizen or resident at the end of the year can choose tax treatment as a U.S. resident.

> A taxpayer who is not a citizen of the United States must determine if he is a resident alien or a nonresident alien for tax purposes. **Resident aliens** must file a tax return following the same rules that apply to U.S. citizens. This means that a resident alien's worldwide income is subject to U.S. tax and is reported on Form 1040. **Nonresident aliens** must file special forms and adhere to different rules.

Generally, the IRS considers a person a *resident alien* if they meet either the *green card test* or the *substantial presence test*.

- **Green Card Test** – A lawful permanent resident of the United States at any time during 2020 and took no steps to be a resident of a foreign country under an income tax treaty. In most cases, the taxpayer is a lawful permanent resident if issued an alien registration card, also known as a green card.

- **Substantial Presence Test** – You are considered a U.S. resident if you meet the substantial presence test. You meet this test if you were physically present in the United States for at least:

  1. 31 days during 2020, and

  2. 183 days during the 3-year period that includes 2020, 2019, and 2018, counting:

     A. All of the days present in 2020

     B. One-third of the days present in 2019

     C. One-sixth of the days present in 2018

For purposes of the substantial presence test, the term "United States" includes all 50 states and the District of Columbia, territorial waters, and the seabed and subsoil of those submarine areas that are adjacent to U.S. territorial waters and over which the United States has exclusive rights under international law to explore and exploit natural resources. The term does not include U.S. possessions and territories or U.S. airspace.

> **EXAMPLE:** You were physically present in the U.S. on 120 days in each of the years 2018, 2019, and 2020. To determine if you meet the substantial presence test for 2020, count the full 120 days of presence in 2020, 40 days in 2019 (1/3 of 120), and 20 days in 2018 (1/6 of 120). Since the total for the 3-year period is 180 days, you are not considered a resident under the substantial presence test for 2020.

The United States has income tax treaties with a number of foreign countries. For nonresident aliens, these treaties can often reduce or eliminate U.S. tax on various types of personal services and other income, such as pensions, interest, dividends, royalties, and capital gains. Each individual treaty must be reviewed to determine whether specific types of income are exempt from U.S. tax or taxed at a reduced rate.

TIP: Generally, the IRS considers a taxpayer a nonresident alien for the year if he is not a U.S. resident under either of these tests. However, a taxpayer may still qualify as a nonresident alien if he is a resident of a treaty country within the meaning of an income tax treaty between the United States and that country. The complete text of most U.S. tax treaties is available on the IRS website.

ELECTION TO BE TAXED AS A RESIDENT ALIEN

Generally, a taxpayer cannot file as married filing jointly if either spouse was a nonresident alien at any time during the tax year. However, nonresident aliens married to U.S. citizens or residents can choose to be treated as U.S. residents and file joint returns. A nonresident alien can elect taxation as a U.S. resident for the whole year if all of the following apply:

- Taxpayer is married
- Taxpayer's spouse was a U.S. citizen or resident alien on the last day of the tax year
- Taxpayer files a joint return for the year of the election using Form 1040

A resident alien must include **worldwide** income for the whole year on the return, subjecting the entire amount to taxation under U.S. tax laws. The taxpayer must agree to keep the records, books, and other information needed to figure the tax. A taxpayer who made the election in an earlier year can file a joint return or separate return for 2020.

DUAL-STATUS TAX YEAR

A dual-status year is one in which you change status between nonresident and resident alien. Different U.S. income tax rules apply to each status. Most dual-status years are the years of arrival or departure. Before you arrive in the United States, you are a nonresident alien. After you arrive, you may or may not be a resident, depending on the circumstances. If you become a U.S. resident, you stay a resident until you leave the United States.

NONRESIDENT INCOME TAXES AND WITHHOLDING

NONRESIDENT ALIEN WITHHOLDING (NRA WITHHOLDING)

Aliens must report certain income on a U.S tax return. For *resident aliens*, this includes income from sources both within and outside the United States. *Nonresident aliens (NRA)* are generally subject to U.S. income tax only on their U.S. source income. They are subject to two different tax rates, one for *effectively connected income (ECI)*, and one for fixed or determinable, annual, or periodic (*FDAP*) income.

Effectively connected income is earned in the U.S. from the operation of a business in the U.S. or is personal service income earned in the U.S. (such as wages or self-employment income). It is taxed for a nonresident at the **same graduated rates** as for a U.S. person.

FDAP income is defined very broadly and generally includes all **U.S. source income** except gains derived from the sale of real or personal property and income specifically excluded from gross income such as tax-exempt interest. FDAP income generally includes any noneffectively connected U.S. source income earned by a foreign person.

Independent personal services (a term commonly used in tax treaties) are personal services performed by an independent nonresident alien contractor as contrasted with those performed by an employee. This category of pay includes payments for professional services, such as fees of an attorney, physician, or accountant made directly to the person performing the services.

TIP: A direct payment to a nonresident alien performing independent personal services outside the United States is foreign (not U.S.) source income.

Common forms of FDAP income include passive income such as interest, dividends, rents, and royalties. This income is taxed at a **flat 30% rate**, unless a tax treaty specifies a lower rate.

> Generally, a foreign person is subject to U.S. tax on U.S. source income. Most types of U.S. source income received by a foreign person are subject to U.S. tax at a rate of 30%. A reduced rate, including exemption, may apply if there is a tax treaty between the foreign person's country of residence and the United States. The tax is generally withheld from the payment made to the foreign person.

The term *NRA withholding* refers to withholding required under sections 1441, 1442, and 1443 of the Internal Revenue Code. Generally, NRA withholding describes the withholding regime that requires withholding on a payment of **U.S. source income**. Payments to foreign persons, including nonresident alien individuals, foreign entities, and governments, may be subject to NRA withholding. Generally, the U.S. person who pays an amount subject to NRA withholding is the person responsible for withholding, also known as the *withholding agent*. **The withholding agent is personally liable for any tax required to be withheld**. This liability is independent of the tax liability of the foreign person to whom the payment is made. If the withholding agent fails to withhold and the foreign payee fails to satisfy its U.S. tax liability, then both are liable for the tax, as well as interest and any applicable penalties.

ILLEGAL ALIENS

Foreign workers who are illegal aliens are subject to U.S. taxes in spite of their illegal status. U.S. employers or payers who hire illegal aliens may be subject to various fines, penalties, and sanctions imposed by U.S. Immigration and Customs Enforcement. If such employers or payers choose to hire illegal aliens, the payments made to those aliens are subject to the same tax withholding and reporting obligations that apply to other classes of aliens. Illegal aliens who are nonresident aliens and who receive income from performing independent personal services are subject to 30% withholding unless exempt under some provision of law or a tax treaty. Illegal aliens who are resident aliens and who receive income from performing dependent personal services are subject to the same reporting and withholding obligations that apply to U.S. citizens who receive the same kind of income.

EFFECTIVELY CONNECTED INCOME (ECI)

If you are engaged in a U.S. trade or business, all income, gain, or loss for the tax year that you get from sources within the United States (other than certain investment income) is treated as effectively connected income. This applies whether or not there is any connection between the income and the trade or business being carried on in the United States during the tax year.

Generally, you can receive effectively connected income only if you are a nonresident alien engaged in trade or business in the United States during the tax year. However, the income you receive from the sale or exchange of property, the performance of services, or any other transaction in another tax year is treated as effectively connected in that year if it would have been effectively connected in the year the transaction took place or you performed the services.

Whether a taxpayer is engaged in a trade or business in the United States depends on the nature of their activities. A taxpayer who performs personal services in the United States is usually considered to be engaged in a U.S. trade or business. Certain kinds of investment income are treated as ECI if they pass either of the two following tests:

- **Business Activities Test** – Usually applies when income, gain, or loss comes directly from the active conduct of the trade or business. Under this test, if the conduct of the U.S. trade or business was a material factor in producing the income, the income is effectively connected.
- **Asset Use Test** – The income must be associated with U.S. assets used (or held for use) in the conduct of a U.S. trade or business.

SOURCE OF INCOME

All profits or losses from U.S. sources that are from the operation of a business in the United States are effectively connected with a trade or business in the United States. For example, profit from the sale in the United States of inventory property purchased either in this country or in a foreign country is effectively connected trade or business income. A share of U.S. source profits or losses of a partnership that is engaged in a trade or business in the United States is also effectively connected with a trade or business in the United States. A nonresident alien usually is subject to U.S. income tax only on U.S. source income. The general rules for determining U.S. source income that applies to most nonresident aliens are shown in the following table:

Summary of Source Rules for Income of Nonresident Aliens	
Item of Income:	**Factor Determining Source:**
Salaries, wages, other compensation	Where services performed
Business income: Personal services	Where services performed
Business income: Sale of inventory - purchased	Where sold
Business income: Sale of inventory - produced	Where produced (allocation may be necessary §1.863-3(f))
Interest	Residence of payer
Dividends	Whether a U.S. or foreign corporation*
Rents	Location of property
Royalties: Natural resources	Location of property
Royalties: Patents, copyrights, etc.	Where property is used
Sale of real property	Location of property
Sale of personal property	Seller's tax home (Publication 519, for exceptions)
Pensions	Where services were performed that earned the pension
Scholarships - Fellowships	Generally, the residence of the payer

*Exceptions include: a) Dividends paid by a U.S. corporation are foreign source if the corporation elects the Puerto Rico economic activity credit or possessions tax credit. b) Part of a dividend paid by a foreign corporation is U.S. source if at least 25% of the corporation's gross income is effectively connected with a U.S. trade or business for the 3 tax years before the year in which the dividends are declared

FORM 1040-NR

WHO MUST FILE

In general, a nonresident alien who receives U. S. source income must file a return (Form 1040-NR) if additional taxes are due or if conducting a business in the United States. A nonresident alien who is married to a U.S. citizen or resident at the end of the year can choose tax treatment as a U.S. resident.

A taxpayer must file Form 1040-NR if any of the following conditions apply:

- A nonresident alien engaged in a trade or business in the United States during 2020 must file even if they do not receive income from the trade or business, has no U.S. source income, or receives income exempt from U.S. tax. However, a nonresident alien taxpayer with no gross income does not complete the schedules for Form 1040-NR. Instead, they should attach a list of the kinds of exclusions claimed and the amount of each.
- A nonresident alien not engaged in a trade or business in the United States during 2020 who received income from U.S. sources reportable on *Schedule NEC, Tax on Income Not Effectively Connected with a U.S. Trade or Business* and not all of the U.S. tax owed was withheld from that income.
- Received HSA, Archer MSA, or Medicare Advantage MSA distributions.
- Had net earnings from self-employment of at least $400 and are a resident of a country with whom the United States has an international social security agreement.
- Advance payments of the premium tax credit were made for the taxpayer, spouse, or a dependent who enrolled in coverage through the Marketplace.

- Advance payments of the health coverage tax credit were made for the taxpayer, spouse, or a dependent.
- The taxpayer represents a deceased person who would have had to file Form 1040-NR.
- The taxpayer represents an estate or trust that has to file Form 1040-NR.

A nonresident alien must also file a return if owing any special taxes, including any of the following:

- Alternative minimum tax.
- Additional tax on a qualified plan, including an individual retirement arrangement (IRA), or other tax-favored accounts. However, if this is the only tax owed, the taxpayer can file Form 5329 by itself.
- Household employment taxes. If this is the only tax owed, the taxpayer can file Schedule H by itself.
- Social security and Medicare tax on tips not reported to the employer or on wages received from an employer who did not withhold these taxes.
- Recapture of first-time homebuyer credit.
- Write-in taxes or recapture taxes, including uncollected social security and Medicare or RRTA tax on tips reported to an employer or on group-term life insurance and additional taxes on HSAs.

A nonresident alien does not need to file Form 1040-NR in 2020 if they meet one of the below exceptions:

- The only U.S. trade or business was the performance of personal services – **this filing exception is not available for 2018 through 2025**, since under the TCJA for taxable years 2018 through 2025 the amount of a personal exemption is zero.
- The taxpayer is a nonresident alien student, teacher, or trainee temporarily present in the United States under an "F," "J," "M," or "Q" visa, and has no income that is subject to tax under section 871.
- The taxpayer is a student or business apprentice who was eligible for the benefits of Article 21(2) of the U.S.-India Income Tax Treaty, is single or a qualifying widow(er), and gross income for 2020 was less than or equal to $12,400 if single ($24,800 if a qualifying widow(er)).
- The taxpayer is a partner in a U.S. partnership that was not engaged in a trade or business in the United States during the tax year and Schedule K-1 (Form 1065) includes only income from U.S. sources reportable on Schedule NEC.
- The taxpayer's gross income was less than $5.

NONRESIDENT FILING STATUS

One key difference between Form 1040-NR and Form 1040 is filing status. A taxpayer that is a nonresident alien at any time during the tax year cannot file as head of household. The only filing status available for nonresidents from most countries (except Canada, Mexico, and South Korea) is:

- **Single** – The rate schedule for single filers is more favorable than for married filing separately.
- **Married Filing Separately** – A married nonresident alien who is not married to a US citizen or resident generally must use the tax rate schedule for married filing separate returns when determining the tax on income effectively connected with a US trade or business. The taxpayer normally cannot use the tax rate schedule for single individuals.
- **Qualifying Widow(er)** – A QW nonresident alien who meets the same eligibility requirements as taxpayers filing Form 1040, can use the qualifying widow(er) filing status and use the joint return tax rate schedule.

EXEMPTIONS

The *Tax Cuts and Jobs Act* repealed the deduction for exemptions. Beginning in 2018, and continuing through 2025, taxpayers can **no longer deduct personal exemptions or exemptions for dependents**.

DEDUCTIONS

Nonresident aliens (other than those covered by the United States-India Income Tax Treaty) cannot claim the standard deduction. A nonresident alien generally cannot claim deductions related to income that is not connected with their U.S. business activities. A nonresident alien can deduct certain itemized deductions if they receive income effectively connected with their U.S. trade or business. These deductions include state and local income taxes, charitable contributions to U.S. organizations, casualty and theft losses, and miscellaneous deductions. Use Schedule A of Form 1040-NR to claim itemized deductions.

FORM 1040-NR-EZ

Beginning with tax year 2020, taxpayers will no longer use Form 1040-NR-EZ. Instead, the redesigned Form 1040-NR will be used by all nonresident alien taxpayers with a US filing requirement. The lines on Form 1040-NR have been rearranged so that, in most instances, they are for the same tax items as the lines on 2020 Form 1040 or 1040-SR.

DUE DATE

- **Individuals:**
  1. If were an employee and received wages subject to U.S. income tax withholding, file Form 1040-NR by the 15th day of the 4th month after your tax year ends. A return for a calendar year is due by April 15.
  2. If did not receive wages as an employee subject to U.S. income tax withholding, file Form 1040-NR by the 15th day of the 6th month after your tax year ends. A return for a calendar year is due by June 15.
- **Estates and trusts:**
  1. If filing for a nonresident alien estate or trust that has an office in the United States, file the return by the 15th day of the 4th month after the tax year ends.
  2. If filing for a nonresident alien estate or trust that does not have an office in the United States, file the return by the 15th day of the 6th month after the tax year ends.
- **Extension of time to file** – If cannot file the return by the due date, file Form 4868 to get an automatic 6-month extension of time to file. Must file Form 4868 by the regular due date of the return.

FOREIGN ACCOUNT AND ASSET REPORTING

FATCA REQUIREMENTS

The *Foreign Account Tax Compliance Act (FATCA)* is a tax law addressing tax non-compliance by U.S. taxpayers with foreign accounts by focusing on reporting by U.S. taxpayers and foreign financial institutions.

In general, federal law requires U.S. citizens and resident aliens to report any worldwide income, including income from foreign trusts and foreign bank and securities accounts. In most cases, affected taxpayers need to complete and attach Schedule B to their tax returns. Part III of Schedule B asks about the existence of foreign accounts, such as bank and securities accounts, and generally requires U.S. citizens to report the country in which each account is located.

In addition, certain taxpayers may also have to complete and attach to their return *Form 8938 Statement of Special Foreign Financial Assets*.

Generally, U.S. citizens, resident aliens and certain nonresident aliens must report specified foreign financial assets on Form 8938 if the aggregate value of those assets exceeds $50,000 on the last day of the tax year or $75,000 at any time during the tax year (higher threshold amounts apply to married individuals filing jointly and individuals living abroad).

The FATCA Form 8938 requirement does <u>not</u> replace or otherwise affect a taxpayer's obligation to file an FBAR Form 114.

FBAR REQUIREMENTS

FBAR refers to *Form 114, Report of Foreign Bank and Financial Accounts*, that must be filed with the Financial Crimes Enforcement Network (FinCEN), which is a bureau of the Treasury Department. *FinCEN Form 114* is used to report a **financial interest in or signature authority over a foreign financial account**. The due date for filing the FBAR is **April 15**. FinCEN will grant filers failing to meet the FBAR annual due date of April 15 an automatic six-month extension to **October 15** each year. Accordingly, specific requests for this extension are <u>not</u> required.

> A United States person that has a financial interest in or signature authority over foreign financial accounts must file an FBAR if the aggregate value of the foreign financial accounts **exceeds $10,000** at any time during the calendar year.

GENERAL FBAR DEFINITIONS

- **Financial Account** – A financial account includes, but is not limited to, securities, brokerage, savings, demand, checking, deposit, time deposit, or other account maintained with a financial institution (or other person performing the services of a financial institution). A financial account also includes a commodity futures or options account, an insurance policy with a cash value (such as a whole life insurance policy), an annuity policy with a cash value, and shares in a mutual fund or similar pooled fund (i.e., a fund that is available to the general public with a regular net asset value determination and regular redemptions).

- **Joint Account** – A financial account type listed above owned jointly by two or more persons.

- **Foreign Financial Account** – A foreign financial account is a financial account located outside of the United States. For example, an account maintained with a branch of a United States bank that is physically located outside of the United States is a foreign financial account. An account maintained with a branch of a foreign bank that is physically located in the United States is not a foreign financial account.

- **Financial Interest** – A United States person has a financial interest in a foreign financial account for which:

  1. The United States person is the owner of record or holder of legal title, regardless of whether the account is maintained for the benefit of the United States person or for the benefit of another person; or

2. The owner of record or holder of legal title is one of the following:

    A. An agent, nominee, attorney, or a person acting in some other capacity on behalf of the United States person with respect to the account;

    B. A corporation in which the United States person owns directly or indirectly: (i) more than 50 percent of the total value of shares of stock or (ii) more than 50 percent of the voting power of all shares of stock;

    C. A partnership in which the United States person owns directly or indirectly: (i) an interest in more than 50 percent of the partnership's profits (e.g., distributive share of partnership income taking into account any special allocation agreement) or (ii) an interest in more than 50 percent of the partnership capital;

    D. A trust of which the United States person: (i) is the trust grantor and (ii) has an ownership interest in the trust for United States federal tax purposes. See 26 U.S.C. sections 671-679 to determine if a grantor has an ownership interest in a trust;

    E. A trust in which the United States person has a greater than 50 percent present beneficial interest in the assets or income of the trust for the calendar year; or

    F. Any other entity in which the United States person owns directly or indirectly more than 50 percent of the voting power, the total value of equity interest or assets, or interest in profits.

- **Person** – A person means an individual (including a minor child) and legal entities including, but not limited to, a limited liability company, corporation, partnership, trust, and estate. *Generally, a child is responsible for filing their own FBAR report. If a child cannot file their own FBAR for any reason, such as age, the child's parent, guardian, or another legally responsible person must file it for the child. If the child cannot sign the FBAR, a parent or guardian <u>must</u> electronically sign the child's FBAR.

- **Signature Authority** – Signature authority is the authority of an individual (alone or in conjunction with another individual) to control the disposition of assets held in a foreign financial account by direct communication (whether in writing or otherwise) to the bank or other financial institution that maintains the financial account. Certain exceptions apply.

- **United States** – For FBAR purposes, the United States includes the States, the District of Columbia, all United States territories and possessions (e.g., American Samoa, the Commonwealth of the Northern Mariana Islands, the Commonwealth of Puerto Rico, Guam, and the United States Virgin Islands), and the Indian lands as defined in the Indian Gaming Regulatory Act. References to the laws of the United States include the laws of the United States federal government and the laws of all places listed in this definition.

- **United States Person** – United States person means United States citizens (including minor children); United States residents; entities, including but not limited to, corporations, partnerships, or limited liability companies created or organized in the United States or under the laws of the United States; and trusts or estates formed under the laws of the United States.

> The federal tax treatment of an entity does not determine whether the entity has an FBAR filing requirement. For example, an entity that is disregarded for purposes of Title 26 of the United States Code must file an FBAR, if otherwise required to do so. Similarly, a trust for which the trust income, deductions, or credits are taken into account by another person for purposes of Title 26 of the United States Code must file an FBAR, if otherwise required to do so.

FBAR FILING CONSIDERATIONS

The FBAR is an annual report and must be filed on or before April 15th of the year following the calendar year being reported. The FBAR must be filed electronically through FinCEN's BSA E-Filing System.

FinCEN will grant filers failing to meet the FBAR annual due date of April 15 an automatic six-month extension to October 15 each year. Accordingly, specific requests for this extension are not required.

Persons required to file an FBAR must retain records that contain the name in which each account is maintained, the number or other designation of the account, the name and address of the foreign financial institution that maintains the account, the type of account, and the maximum account value of each account during the reporting period.

The records must be retained for a period of **5 years** from April 15th of the year following the calendar year reported and must be available for inspection as provided by law.

An officer or employee who files an FBAR to report signature authority over an employer's foreign financial account is not required to personally retain records regarding these accounts.

EXCEPTIONS TO FBAR FILING

- **Certain Accounts Jointly Owned by Spouses** – The spouse of an individual who files an FBAR is not required to file a separate FBAR if the following conditions are met:
  1. All the financial accounts that the non-filing spouse is required to report are jointly owned with the filing spouse;
  2. The filing spouse reports the jointly owned accounts on a timely filed FBAR electronically signed; and
  3. The filers have completed and signed *Form 114a, Record of Authorization to Electronically File FBARs* (maintained with the filers' records).

  Otherwise, both spouses are required to file separate FBARs, and each spouse must report the entire value of the jointly owned accounts.

- **Consolidated FBAR** – If a United States person that is an entity is named in a consolidated FBAR filed by a greater than 50 percent owner, such entity is not required to file a separate FBAR.

- **Correspondent/Nostro Account** – Correspondent or Nostro accounts (which are maintained by banks and used solely for bank-to-bank settlements) are not required to be reported.

- **Governmental Entity** – A foreign financial account of any governmental entity of the United States (as defined above) is not required to be reported by any person. For purposes of this form, a governmental entity includes a college or university that is an agency of, an instrumentality of, owned by, or operated by a governmental entity. For purposes of this Form 114, a governmental entity also includes an employee retirement or welfare benefit plan of a governmental entity.

- **International Financial Institution** – A foreign financial account of any international financial institution (if the United States government is a member) is not required to be reported by any person.

- **IRA Owners and Beneficiaries** – An owner or beneficiary of an IRA is not required to report a foreign financial account held in the IRA.

- **Participants in and Beneficiaries of Tax-Qualified Retirement Plans** – A participant in or beneficiary of a retirement plan described in Internal Revenue Code section 401(a), 403(a), or 403(b) is not required to report a foreign financial account held by or on behalf of the retirement plan.

- **Signature Authority** – An individual who has signature authority over, but no financial interest in, a foreign financial account is not required to report the account in the following situations:
  1. An officer or employee of a bank that is examined by the Office of the Comptroller of the Currency, the Board of Governors of the Federal Reserve System, the Federal Deposit Insurance Corporation, the Office of

Thrift Supervision, or the National Credit Union Administration is not required to report signature authority over a foreign financial account owned or maintained by the bank.

2. An officer or employee of a financial institution that is registered with and examined by the Securities and Exchange Commission or Commodity Futures Trading Commission is not required to report signature authority over a foreign financial account owned or maintained by the financial institution.

3. An officer or employee of an Authorized Service Provider is not required to report signature authority over a foreign financial account that is owned or maintained by an investment company that is registered with the Securities and Exchange Commission. Authorized Service Provider means an entity that is registered with and examined by the Securities and Exchange Commission and provides services to an investment company registered under the Investment Company Act of 1940.

4. An officer or employee of an entity that has a class of equity securities listed (or American depository receipts listed) on any United States national securities exchange is not required to report signature authority over a foreign financial account of such entity.

5. An officer or employee of a United States subsidiary is not required to report signature authority over a foreign financial account of the subsidiary if its United States parent has a class of equity securities listed on any United States national securities exchange and the subsidiary is included in a consolidated FBAR report of the United States parent.

6. An officer or employee of an entity that has a class of equity securities registered (or American depository receipts in respect of equity securities registered) under section 12(g) of the Securities Exchange Act is not required to report signature authority over a foreign financial account of such entity.

- **Trust Beneficiaries** – A trust beneficiary with a financial interest described in section (2)(e) of the financial interest definition is not required to report the trust's foreign financial accounts on an FBAR if the trust, trustee of the trust, or agent of the trust: (1) is a United States person and (2) files an FBAR disclosing the trust's foreign financial accounts.

- **United States Military Banking Facility** – A financial account maintained with a financial institution located on a United States military installation is not required to be reported, even if that military installation is outside of the United States.

FATCA vs. FBAR

	Form 8938, Statement of Specified Foreign Financial Assets	FinCEN Form 114, Report of Foreign Bank and Financial Accounts (FBAR)
Who Must File?	Specified individuals, which include U.S citizens, resident aliens, and certain non-resident aliens that have an interest in specified foreign financial assets and meet the reporting threshold	U.S. persons, which include U.S. citizens, resident aliens, trusts, estates, and domestic entities that have an interest in foreign financial accounts and meet the reporting threshold
Does the United States include U.S. territories?	No	Yes, resident aliens of U.S territories and U.S. territory entities are subject to FBAR reporting
Reporting Threshold (Total Value of Assets)	$50,000 on the last day of the tax year or $75,000 at any time during the tax year (higher threshold amounts apply to married individuals filing jointly and individuals living abroad)	$10,000 at any time during the calendar year
When do you have an interest in an account or asset?	If any income, gains, losses, deductions, credits, gross proceeds, or distributions from holding or disposing of the account or asset are or would be required to be reported, included, or otherwise reflected on your income tax return	Financial interest: you are the owner of record or holder of legal title; the owner of record or holder of legal title is your agent or representative; you have a sufficient interest in the entity that is the owner of record or holder of legal title Signature authority: you have authority to control the disposition of the assets in the account by direct communication with the financial institution maintaining the account
What is Reported?	Maximum value of specified foreign financial assets, which include financial accounts with foreign financial institutions and certain other foreign non-account investment assets	Maximum value of financial accounts maintained by a financial institution physically located in a foreign country
When Due?	By due date, including extension, if any, for income tax return	Received by April 15th (automatic six-month extension until October 15th)
Where to File?	File with income tax return pursuant to instructions for filing the return	File electronically through FinCEN's BSA E-Filing System. The FBAR is not filed with a federal tax return
Penalties	Up to $10,000 for failure to disclose and an additional $10,000 for each 30 days of non-filing after IRS notice of a failure to disclose, for a potential maximum penalty of $60,000; criminal penalties may also apply (adjusted annually for inflation)	If non-willful, up to $10,000; if willful, up to the greater of $100,000 or 50 percent of account balances; criminal penalties may also apply (adjusted annually for inflation)

BUSINESSES

SEE EXAM PART 2

LESSON 1

Business Entities

BUSINESS ENTITY OVERVIEW

COMMON TYPES OF BUSINESS ENTITIES

- **Sole Proprietor** – An unincorporated business that is owned by one individual.
  1. The business does not exist separately from the owner.
  2. The owner personally accepts the risks of business to the extent of all the owner's assets, whether the owner uses them in the business or uses them personally.
  3. The owner includes business income and expenses on his personal tax return (Schedule C).
- **Partnership** – A relationship between **two or more people** who join to carry on a business.
  1. Each partner contributes money, property, labor, or skill, and shares in business profits and losses. Partners, other than limited partners, are personally liable for company debts.
  2. Partners can be individuals, corporations, trusts, estates, or other partnerships.
  3. Partnerships must file an annual information return to report operational income, deductions, gains, losses, etc., but do not pay income tax. Instead, any profits or losses "pass through" to its partners. Partners include their respective shares of the partnership items on their tax returns.
- **Qualified Joint Venture** – An unincorporated business jointly owned by a married couple is generally classified as a partnership for federal tax purposes. Previously, married individuals in a business together were considered partners and required to file an annual Form 1065 Partnership Return.
  1. A *qualified joint venture*, whose only members are a married couple filing a joint return, can elect <u>not</u> to be treated as a partnership for federal tax purposes. Each spouse is treated as a sole proprietor and claims a share of the income and expenses of the business on the appropriate form (e.g., Schedule C) based on their respective interest in the business, with the combined interest totaling 100%. The allocation is 50/50 in community property states.
  2. A qualified joint venture conducts a trade or business where all the following exist:
     A. The only members of the joint venture are a married couple who file a joint return.
     B. Both spouses materially participate in the trade or business (mere joint ownership of property is not enough).
     C. Both spouses elect not to be treated as a partnership.
     D. The business is co-owned by both spouses (and not in the name of a state law entity, such as a partnership or LLC).
- **Corporation** – A person or group of people incorporated by charter from the Secretary of State.
  1. This includes associations, joint stock companies, insurance companies, and trusts and partnerships that operate as associations or corporations.
  2. The profit is taxed to the corporation when earned <u>and</u> then is taxed to the shareholders when distributed as dividends. Shareholders cannot deduct any loss of the corporation.
  3. An eligible domestic corporation can avoid *double taxation* by electing treatment as an *S corporation*. Generally, an S corporation is exempt from federal income tax other than tax on certain capital gains and passive income. On their tax returns, the S corporation's shareholders include their shares of the corporation's separately stated items of income, deduction, loss, and credit, and their shares of non-separately stated income or loss.
- **Limited Liability Company** – A limited liability company (LLC) is an entity formed under state law by filing articles of organization as an LLC. (see additional discussion on LLCs)
  1. LLC members are <u>not</u> personally liable for its debts.

2. For federal income tax purposes (<u>not</u> legal):

    A. The IRS considers a single-member LLC to be a ***disregarded entity*** by default, but the LLC can elect to be classified as an association taxable as a corporation.

    B. The IRS considers a multi-member LLC to be a partnership by default, but the LLC can elect to be classified as an association taxable as a corporation.

- **Trust** – A trust (excluding a grantor trust) is a separate legal entity for federal tax purposes. A taxpayer may create a trust while alive or upon death by means of a will.

- **Estate** – An estate comes into being upon the death of an individual.

    1. A decedent's estate is a separate legal entity for federal tax purposes.

    2. An estate consists of real and/or personal property of the deceased person.

LIMITED LIABILITY COMPANIES (LLC)

A ***Limited Liability Company (LLC)*** is a business structure that is allowed and governed by state statute. This means that different states may have different laws and requirements for LLCs.

Owners of an LLC are called ***members***. Most states do not restrict ownership, and so members may include individuals, corporations, other LLCs and foreign entities. There is no maximum number of members, and most states also permit "single-member" LLCs having only one owner.

> **EXCEPTION:** A few types of businesses generally cannot be LLCs, such as banks and insurance companies.

The LLC is a popular choice for business owners who desire to limit personal liability, but also prefer not to deal with double taxation and all the formalities of forming a corporation. The members of the LLC can benefit from the IRS treating the business like a corporation for tax purposes, without the additional administrative burden of actually being a corporation.

Unlike a partnership, all members of the LLC are protected from personal liability without any restriction on their participation in the business. An LLC member is typically liable only to the extent of his investment in the business. This is a big advantage over a partnership, where at least one partner is personally liable for the debts of the company.

Unlike a corporation, the LLC is not taxed as a separate business entity (unless otherwise elected). Instead, all profits and losses pass through to each member to report on his personal federal tax return, just like the partners of a partnership would.

Unlike an S corporation, an LLC can have more than 100 members, including other businesses such as partnerships and corporations.

TAX TREATMENT

The election made for federal tax purposes does not impact the limited liability protection provided to LLC members under state law. For federal tax purposes, the IRS will tax the LLC as either:

- A corporation
- A partnership
- A part of the owner's tax return (called a **disregarded entity**)

Default Treatment

The way the LLC is taxed at the federal level is determined by decisions that the LLC makes. If the taxpayer does not inform the IRS of a desire to be taxed in another manner, the default entity classification for federal tax purposes will be as follows:

- An LLC with **two or more members** will be classified as a **partnership.**
- An LLC with only **one member** will be **disregarded** as an entity separate from its owner.

Alternate Election

The members of the LLC can benefit from the IRS treating the business like a corporation for tax purposes, without the additional administrative burden of actually being a corporation. The check-the-box regulations under IRC section 7701, allow an LLC to **choose its classification.**

> The LLC may elect an alternative treatment no more than **75 days** after the beginning of the tax year the election is to take effect, or **anytime in the preceding tax year.**
>
> - The LLC may elect treatment as a **corporation** by filing Form 8832.
> - The LLC may elect treatment as an **S corporation** by filing Form 2553.

TIP: The LLC must meet certain requirements prior to making an S election. No more than 100 members who are individuals, estates, exempt organizations or certain trusts. Non-resident alien shareholders are also not allowed.

> **60-month limitation rule** – Once an eligible entity makes an election to change its classification, the entity generally <u>cannot</u> change (without IRS permission) its classification by election again during the 60 months after the effective date. The 60-month limitation does not apply if a newly formed eligible entity made the previous election and the election was effective on the date of formation.

TIP: The owner's tax return should reflect the activities of a disregarded entity. When an individual owns 100% of the LLC, income is reported on Schedules C, E, and F of form 1040. If a corporation owns the LLC, income is reported on the appropriate part of the corporate tax return. A disregarded entity does not file its own income tax return; however, the LLC will be treated as its own entity for employment taxes and certain excise taxes.

EMPLOYER IDENTIFICATION NUMBER (EIN)

A business must obtain an *employer identification number (EIN)* by filing *Form SS-4* if the business meets one of the following conditions:

- Has one or more employees
- Files returns for employment or excise taxes
- Maintains a qualified retirement plan
- Operates as a corporation, partnership, is a non-profit, estate, or trust (not grantor trust)

RECORDKEEPING

In order to deduct business expenses, a taxpayer must be able to prove certain elements of expense. The taxpayer can prove them by maintaining *adequate evidence* that substantiates the expense and receipts when required. Written evidence is more reliable than oral evidence alone. A taxpayer must generally prepare a written or electronic record for it to be considered adequate. A taxpayer should maintain an account book, diary, log, statement of expense, trip sheets, or similar record.

A taxpayer cannot approximate or estimate deductions, and generally must have **documentary evidence**, such as receipts, canceled checks, or bills, to support expenses. Documentary evidence should show the amount, date, place, and essential character of the expense.

Documentary evidence is <u>not</u> needed if the expense, other than lodging, is less than **$75** or for a transportation expense for which a receipt is not readily available.

PROVING EXPENSES

The taxpayer must generally provide a written statement of the **business purpose** of an expense. A written explanation is unnecessary if the business purpose of an expense is clear from the surrounding circumstances. A canceled check, together with a bill from the payee, ordinarily establishes the cost. However, a canceled check by itself does not prove a business expense without other evidence to show that it was for a business purpose.

TIP: The taxpayer should record the elements of an expense or of a business use at or near the time of the expense or use and support it with sufficient documentary evidence. A timely-kept record has more value than a statement prepared later when generally there is a lack of accurate recall. The taxpayer does not need to write down the elements of every expense on the day of the expense. A weekly log that accounts for use during the week is considered a timely-kept record.

To prove certain business expenses you must keep records that show details of the following elements:

Expense Type	Amount	Time	Description	Business Purpose and Relationship
Travel	Cost of each separate expense for travel, lodging, and meals. Incidental expenses may be totaled in reasonable categories such as taxis, fees, and tips, etc.	Dates you left and returned for each trip and number of days spent on business.	Destination or area of your travel (name of city, town, or other designation).	Purpose: Business purpose for the expense or the business benefit gained or expected to be gained. Relationship: N/A
Gifts	Cost of the gift.	Date of the gift.	Description of the gift.	Purpose: Business purpose for the expense or the business benefit gained or expected to be gained. Relationship: Occupations or other information (such as names, titles, or other designations) about the recipients that shows their business relationship to you.
Transportation	Cost of each separate expense. For car expenses, the cost of the car and any improvements, the date you started using it for business, the mileage for each business use, and the total miles for the year.	Date of the expense. For car expenses, the date of the use of the car.	Your business destination.	Purpose: Business purpose for the expense. Relationship: N/A

RECORD RETENTION

A business taxpayer must keep records as long as needed for the administration of any provision of the Internal Revenue Code. Generally, this means keeping records that support items shown on the return until the *period of limitations* for that return expires.

The period of limitations is the period of time in which the taxpayer can amend a return to claim a credit or refund, or the IRS can assess additional tax. This is generally 3 years from the date the taxpayer files the return. Returns filed before the due date are treated as filed on the due date.

A taxpayer must keep records relating to property until the period of limitations expires for the year he/she sells the property. A taxpayer who receives property in a nontaxable exchange must keep records for the original property until the period of limitations expires for the year he/she sells the replacement property. These records are necessary to figure any depreciation, amortization, or depletion deduction, and to figure basis for computing gain or loss when sold.

A taxpayer with employees must keep all employment tax records for at least 4 years after the date the tax becomes due or is paid, whichever is later.

Period of Limitations:

IF you...	THEN the period is...
1 Owe additional tax and (2), (3), and (4) do not apply	3 years
2 Do not report income and it is more than 25% of the gross income shown on return	6 years
3 File a fraudulent return	No limit
4 Do not file a return	No limit
5 File a claim for credit or refund after filing return	Later of 3 years or 2 years after tax was paid
6 File a claim for a loss from worthless securities	7 years

TIP: The IRS does not require taxpayers to maintain records in a particular way. If using a computerized system, individuals must be able to produce legible records of the information needed to determine the correct tax liability. In addition, the taxpayer must keep proof of payment, receipts, and other documents to prove the amount shown. Paper records, such as receipts and invoices, support information summarized in a computer program or in a paper ledger or checkbook. A business should keep each supporting document for as long as is necessary and the length necessary will vary depending on the item the record supports. Documents that support expenditures for capital improvements or depreciable business assets, for example, should be kept until the asset is disposed of and the tax consequences of the disposition have been reported and are closed. Documents that support other shorter-lived expenditures or income items do not have to be kept for as long a period of time.

EMPLOYEES

WHO ARE EMPLOYEES?

Before an employer can know how to treat payments made to workers for services, the employer must first know the business relationship that exists between the employer and worker. The person performing the services may be one of the following:

- **Independent contractor** – An independent contractor is self-employed and the earnings of a person who is working as an independent contractor are subject to Self-employment tax. People such as doctors, dentists, veterinarians, lawyers, accountants, contractors, subcontractors, public stenographers, or auctioneers who are in an independent trade, business, or profession in which they offer their services to the general public are typically not employees. However, whether these people are independent contractors or employees depends on the facts in each case.

An individual is usually an independent contractor if the employer, the person for whom the individual performs the services, has the right to control or direct only the **result** of the work and not the **means and methods** of accomplishing the result.

- **Common-law employees** – Under common-law rules, anyone who performs services for a person is an employee of that person if the employer has the right to control what will be done and how it will be done. This is true even when an employer gives the employee freedom of action. What matters is the **right to control** the details of how the employee performs the services.

1. It does not matter whether the individual is employed full time or part-time.
2. An **officer** of a corporation is generally an employee; however, an officer who performs no services or only minor services, and neither receives nor is entitled to receive any pay, is not considered an employee.
3. A corporate **director** is not an employee with respect to services performed as a director.
4. Employers generally must withhold and pay income, Social Security, and Medicare taxes on wages paid to common-law employees.

- **Statutory employees** – If someone who works for an individual is not an employee under the common law rules discussed above, the employer must not withhold federal income tax from the employee's pay, unless backup withholding applies. Although the following persons may not be common law employees, they may be considered employees by statute for Social Security, Medicare, and FUTA tax purposes under certain conditions.

1. A commission (or agent) driver who delivers beverages (not milk), food, laundry, or dry cleaning.
2. A full-time life insurance sales agent who sells primarily for one life insurance company.
3. A home worker who works by guidelines of the person for whom the work is done, with materials furnished by and returned to that person or to someone that person designates.
4. A full-time traveling or city salesperson that works on an individual's behalf and turns in orders to the latter from wholesalers, retailers, contractors, or operators of hotels, restaurants, or other similar establishments. The goods sold must be merchandise for resale or supplies for use in the buyer's business operation. The work performed must be the salesperson's principal business activity.

- **Statutory nonemployees** – Direct sellers, qualified real estate agents and certain companion sitters are—by law —considered nonemployees. They are treated generally as self-employed for all federal tax purposes, including income and employment taxes.

TAX WITHHOLDING AND REPORTING

SELF-EMPLOYMENT TAX

Self-employment tax under the **Self Employed Contributions Act (SECA)** is a Social Security and Medicare tax primarily for individuals who work for themselves. Income earned as an employee or as a notary is not subject to SECA tax. Payments of SECA tax contribute to coverage under the Social Security system. Social Security coverage provides the taxpayer with retirement benefits, disability benefits, survivor benefits, and hospital insurance (Medicare) benefits. An individual may deduct a portion of SECA tax as an adjustment to income on Form 1040. The self-employed must pay SECA tax and file Schedule SE (Form 1040) if either of the following applies:

- Net earnings from self-employment were **$400** or more
- Had church employee income of **$108.28** or more

In 2020, a tax rate of **15.3%** applies to the first **$137,700** ($142,800 in 2021) of income from self-employment. A tax rate of **2.9%** applies to the excess. For higher-income taxpayers, a **.9% Additional Medicare Tax** applies when income exceeds one of the following threshold amounts (based on filing status):

- Married filing jointly—$250,000
- Married filing separately—$125,000
- Single, Head of household, or Qualifying widow(er)—$200,000

A taxpayer with both wages and self-employment income reduces the threshold amount for applying the Additional Medicare Tax on the self-employment income (but not below zero) by the amount of wages subject to Additional Medicare Tax.

Before applying the tax rates, a self-employed taxpayer reduces income from self-employment by the percentage of tax that employers normally pay for their employees.

> **EXAMPLE:** Peter has $100,000 income from self-employment. If Peter were an employee, his employer would pay $7,650 (7.65%). He subtracts this portion from his self-employment income to determine his net earnings from self-employment of $92,350 ($100,000 – $7,650). His SECA tax is $14,129.55 ($92,350 × 15.3%).

PAYROLL TAXES

Employment taxes include Social Security, Medicare, federal income tax withholding, and federal unemployment (FUTA) tax. Generally, taxpayers do not pay or withhold tax on payments to independent contractors. The general rule is that an individual is an independent contractor if the person for whom the services are performed has the right to control or direct only the result of the work and not the means and methods of accomplishing the result.

- **Income tax** – Employers generally must withhold federal income tax from wages. They use Form W-4 to figure how much federal income tax to withhold from each wage payment.

- **FICA taxes** – Social Security and Medicare taxes pay for benefits that workers and their families receive under the *Federal Insurance Contributions Act (FICA)*. Social Security tax pays for benefits under the old age, survivors, and disability insurance part of FICA. Medicare tax pays for benefits under the hospital insurance part of FICA. Employers must withhold part of these taxes from their employee's wages and must pay a matching amount. The employee tax rate for social security is 6.2%. The employer tax rate for social security remains unchanged at 6.2%. The Medicare tax rate is 1.45% each (2.9% total) for employers and employees, and an additional Medicare tax of 0.9% applies to certain high-income employees. Employers are responsible for withholding the 0.9% Additional Medicare Tax on an individual's wages paid in excess of $200,000 in a calendar year, without regard to filing status. An employer is required to begin withholding Additional Medicare Tax in the pay period in which it pays wages in excess of $200,000 to an employee and continues to withhold it each pay period until the end of the calendar year. There is no employer match for Additional Medicare Tax. The Social Security wage base limit to which Social Security tax applies is **$137,700** for 2020. There is no wage base limit for Medicare tax; all covered wages are subject to Medicare tax.

Report FICA taxes or current period adjustments on **Form 941**, Employer's Quarterly Federal Tax Return. An employer who is required or has elected to File 941, Employer's Quarterly Federal Tax Return, must file Form 941 for each calendar quarter regardless of whether the employer paid wages or not. Some taxpayers may qualify to file **Form 944**, Employer's ANNUAL Federal Tax Return. This form is designed so the smallest employers (those whose annual liability for social security, Medicare, and withheld federal income taxes is $1,000 or less) will file and pay these taxes only once a year instead of every quarter.

TIP: Corrections to a previously filed Form 941 or Form 944 are to be made on Form 941-X or Form 944-X.

- **FUTA taxes** – This tax is part of the federal and state program under the *Federal Unemployment Tax Act (FUTA)* that pays unemployment compensation to workers who lose their jobs. Employers must report and pay FUTA tax separately from Social Security and Medicare taxes and withheld income tax. The employer must pay FUTA tax only from separate funds. Employees do not pay this tax or have it withheld from their pay. If a company pays **$1,500 or more** in wages to employees during any calendar quarter during 2019 or 2020, or employs one or more employees for at least some part of a day in any 20 or more different weeks during the year, it must pay Federal Unemployment Taxes (FUTA). Employers must report federal unemployment tax on **Form 940**, Employer's Annual Federal Unemployment (FUTA) Tax Return. Unemployment taxes also include payments made to a state unemployment compensation fund or to a state disability benefit fund. Employers also need to pay State Unemployment Taxes (SUTA), employers must report state unemployment tax on a state unemployment tax return.

SPECIAL CIRCUMSTANCES FOR FAMILY MEMBERS

Employment tax requirements for family employees may vary from those that apply to other employees.

- **Child employed by parents** – Payments for the services of a child under age 18 who works for his or her parent in a trade or business are <u>not</u> subject to social security and Medicare taxes if the trade or business is a sole proprietorship or a partnership in which each partner is a parent of the child. Payments for the services of a child under age 21 who works for his or her parent in a trade or business are <u>not</u> subject to **FUTA** tax. Payment for the services of a child is **subject to income tax withholding, regardless of age**.

  The wages for the services of a child are subject to income tax withholding as well as social security, Medicare, and FUTA taxes if he or she works for:

  1. A corporation, even if it is controlled by the child's parent,

  2. A partnership, even if the child's parent is a partner, unless each partner is a parent of the child, or

  3. An estate, even if it is the estate of a deceased parent.

- **One spouse employed by another** – The wages for the services of an individual who works for his or her spouse in a trade or business are subject to income tax withholding and social security and Medicare taxes, but <u>not</u> to **FUTA** tax.

  The wages for the services of a spouse are subject to income tax withholding as well as social security, Medicare, and FUTA taxes if he or she works for:

  1. A corporation, even if it is controlled by the individual's spouse, or

  2. A partnership, even if the individual's spouse is a partner.

- **Parent employed by child** – The wages for the services of a parent employed by his or her child in a trade or business are subject to income tax withholding and social security and Medicare taxes. Wages paid to a parent employed by his or her child are <u>not</u> subject to **FUTA** tax, regardless of the type of services provided.

ESTIMATED TAXES

Generally, estimated tax payments are required to pay employment tax obligations.

- **Sole proprietors, partners, and S corporation shareholders** – When the owner(s) of such a business expect to owe $1,000 or more in taxes, those individuals generally make estimated tax payments. Individual taxpayers use Form 1040-ES to figure and pay estimated tax.

- **Corporations** – Generally, a corporation must make estimated tax payments (via EFTPS or Form 1120-W) if expecting to owe tax of $500 or more when filing a return.

- **When to pay estimated tax** – Installment payments are due by the 15th day of the 4th, 6th, 9th, and 12th months of the corporate tax year. The due date is different for individuals who must make payments by the 15th day of the 4th, 6th, 9th, and 1st month.

ELECTRONIC DEPOSIT OF EMPLOYMENT TAXES

All taxpayers must use electronic funds transfer to make all federal tax deposits (such as deposits of employment tax, excise tax, and corporate income tax). Generally, electronic funds transfers are made using the *Electronic Federal Tax Payment System (EFTPS).* A taxpayer who does not want to use EFTPS can arrange for an authorized financial institution to make deposits on his behalf with **Form 941**. The penalty for failure to use EFTPS when required is **10%** of the amounts subject to electronic deposit requirements but not deposited using EFTPS.

There are two deposit schedules—monthly and semi-weekly. Employers determine the required deposit schedule before the beginning of each calendar year by calculating prior employment tax liability within a look back period (begins July 1 and ends June 30).

- **Monthly deposit schedule** – tax liability during look back period was $50,000, or less.
- **Semi-weekly deposit schedule** – tax liability during look back period was more than $50,000.

TRUST FUND RECOVERY PENALTY

The person responsible for withholding, accounting for, or depositing or paying specified taxes including NRA withholding and employment taxes, and willfully fail to do so, can be held personally liable for a penalty equal to the **full amount of the unpaid trust fund tax**, <u>plus</u> **interest**. A responsible person for this purpose can be an officer of a corporation, a partner, a sole proprietor, or an employee of any form of business. A trustee or agent with authority over the funds of the business can also be held responsible for the penalty. Willfully, in this case, means voluntarily, consciously, and intentionally.

REQUIRED FORMS

Employers are required to collect Form I-9 and Form W-4 from employees.

- **Form I-9** – The employer must verify that each new employee is legally eligible to work in the United States. The taxpayer must complete the U.S. Citizenship and Immigration Services *Form I-9, Employment Eligibility Verification* and maintain in records.
- **Form W-4** – Employers use the filing status and withholding allowances shown on this form to calculate the amount of income tax to withhold from the employee's wages.

INFORMATIONAL RETURNS

An information return is a tax document that businesses are required to file in order to report certain business transactions to the Internal Revenue Service. Any person, including a corporation, partnership, individual, estate, and trust, with reportable transactions during the calendar year must file information returns to report those transactions to the IRS. Persons required to file must also furnish statements to the recipients of the income. Filers who have 250 or more returns must file the returns electronically.

TIP: The recipient of an informational return does not send copies to the IRS unless required. A taxpayer must attach Form W-2 to the front of their Form 1040 series tax return. A taxpayer should also attach Forms W-2G and 1099-R, but <u>only</u> if federal income tax was withheld.

- **Form W-2, Wage and Tax Statement** – After the calendar year is over, each employer must furnish copies of Form W-2 to each employee who earned wages during the year. The employer must also send a copy to the Social Security Administration.
- **Form W-2G, Certain Gambling Winnings** – An organization conducting gaming activities must report certain gambling transactions to taxpayers and the IRS. Form W-2G reflects winnings and federal tax withholding. In general, the gambling organization must use Form W-2G if any tax is withheld or the taxpayer has winnings equivalent to the following:
  1. Bingo or slot machine – $1,200 or more (<u>not</u> reduced by wager)
  2. Keno –$1,500 (reduced by wager)
  3. Poker – More than $5,000 (reduced by wager)
  4. All others – $600 or more <u>and</u> at least 300 times the amount of the wager
- **Form 1098, Mortgage Interest Statement** – A person (or organization) engaged in a trade or business that receives at least $600 of mortgage interest (including certain points) on any mortgage in the calendar year must

report the mortgage interest on Form 1098 to the payor and the IRS. Report prepaid interest (other than points) only in the year in which it properly accrues. The form is not filed if the interest is received from a corporation, partnership, trust, estate, association, or company other than a sole proprietor.

- **Form 1098-E, Student Loan Interest Statement** – A person (including a financial institution, a governmental unit, and an educational institution) that receives interest payments of $600 or more during the year on one or more qualified student loans must furnish this statement to each student.

- **Form 1098-T, Tuition Statement** – An eligible educational institution must provide each enrolled student with reportable transactions on this form in order to report certain amounts billed or payments received by the institution for qualified tuition and related expenses. The institution also reports scholarships or grants using this form.

- **Form 1099-B, Proceeds from Broker and Barter Exchange Transactions** – In general, a securities broker must report and provide a Form 1099-B for each person for whom the broker has sold (including short sales) stocks, bonds, commodities, regulated futures contracts, foreign currency contracts, forward contracts, debt instruments, etc., for cash. Recent legislation now requires brokers to report cost basis in addition to proceeds from these transactions. Cost basis information makes the calculation of gains and losses easier for taxpayers.

- **Form 1099-C, Cancellation of Debt** – Certain entities must issue a Form 1099-C to each borrower for canceled debts in excess of $600 on secured property. Under certain circumstances, a borrower may recognize taxable income because of a debt that is canceled.

- **Form 1099-DIV, Dividends and Distributions** – A corporation must generally send Forms 1099-DIV to the IRS with Form 1096 **by February 28** of the year following the year of a distribution. Generally, a corporation must furnish Forms 1099-DIV to shareholders **by January 31** of the year following the close of the calendar year during which the corporation made the distributions. It is necessary to file a *Form 1099-DIV* with the IRS for each person the corporation:

  1. Paid dividends (including capital gain dividends) and other distributions on stock of **$10 or more**,
  2. Withheld and paid any foreign tax on dividends and other distributions on stock,
  3. Withheld any federal income tax on dividends under the backup withholding rules, or
  4. Paid **$600 or more** as part of a liquidation.

- **Form 1099-G, Certain Government Payments** – This form reports certain payments that exceed $10, such as unemployment compensation and state or local income tax refunds.

- **Form 1099-INT, Interest Income** – Financial institutions that pay interest must report details regarding those payments in the following circumstances:

  1. The interest payments are at least $10. Certain types of interest, such as interest on delayed death benefits paid by a life insurance company or interest on a state or federal tax refund have a higher threshold of $600.
  2. If the institution withheld and paid any foreign tax on interest.
  3. If the institution withheld (and did not refund) any federal income tax under the backup withholding rules regardless of the amount of the payment.

- **Form 1099-MISC, Miscellaneous Income** – A business taxpayer uses Form 1099-MISC to report certain business payments. These payments include the following items:

  1. Rent payments of $600 or more, other than rents paid to real estate agents.
  2. Prizes and awards of $600 or more (not for services), such as winnings on radio shows.
  3. Royalty payments of $10 or more.
  4. Payments to certain crew members by operators of fishing boats.

Form 1099-MISC is no longer used to report **nonemployee compensation**. Form **1099-NEC** is now used for this purpose.

- **Form 1099-NEC, Nonemployee Compensation** – A business taxpayer uses Form 1099-NEC to report payments of **$600 or more** (and the amount is fixed and determinable) for services performed for one's business by people not treated as employees, such as vendors, subcontractors, independent contractors, attorneys, accountants, or directors. Generally, payments to a corporation are excluded from this reporting requirement.

- **Form 1099-OID, Original Issue Discount** – Original issue discount (OID) is the difference between the purchase price of a debt instrument and its maturity value. Each year, a portion of the discount accrues as income to the recipient. A financial institution must report OID if it amounts to $10 or more.

- **Form 1099-R, Distributions from Pensions, Annuities, Retirement or Profit-Sharing Plans, IRAs, Insurance Contracts, etc.** – Form 1099-R communicates reportable distributions of $10 or more from retirement accounts, insurance contracts, and annuities. In addition to the amount distributed, a number or letter code in box 7 tells the taxpayer details about the type of distribution they received.

- **Form 8300** – Generally, a taxpayer in a trade or business that receives more than **$10,000 in cash** in a single transaction or in related transactions, must file *Form 8300, Report of Cash Payments Over $10,000 in a Trade or Business.* The form provides valuable information to the IRS and the Financial Crimes Enforcement Network (FinCEN) in their efforts to combat money laundering. The form is due by the **15th day** after the date the cash transaction occurred and may be filed electronically using FinCEN's BSA E-Filing System. Besides filing Form 8300, the taxpayer must provide a written statement to each party included on the Form 8300 by **January 31** of the year following the reportable transaction. This statement must include the name, address, contact person and business telephone number, and the aggregate amount of reportable cash. The statement must also indicate that the information was provided to the IRS.

BACKUP WITHHOLDING

A business taxpayer reporting payments made to a U.S. person must withhold **24%** (backup withholding rate) from a payment that is subject to Form 1099 reporting if one of the following conditions exists:

- The person does not provide its *taxpayer identification number (TIN)* in the manner required. Generally, a person provides a TIN on *Form W-9*.
- The IRS provides notification that the TIN furnished by the payee is incorrect.
- There has been a notified payee underreporting.
- There has been a payee certification failure.

REGULAR GAMBLING WITHHOLDING

Regular gambling withholding is **24%**. Regular gambling withholding is applicable when gambling winnings exceed $5,000 for sweepstakes, wagering pools, or lotteries. Poker tournaments are "wagering pools" according to IRS Rev. Proc. 2007-57. For other wagering transactions (for example blackjack, or similar table games), regular gambling withholding does not apply unless winnings are at least $600 and 300 times the amount wagered. If withholding applies, a taxpayer who does not provide a SSN or TIN is subject to backup withholding.

Certain Informational Returns

Form	Title	What to Report	Amounts to Report	Due Date to IRS	Due Date to Recipient
1095-C	Employer-Provided Health Insurance Offer and Coverage	Offers of health coverage and enrollment in health coverage for employees.	See form instructions	February 28*	January 31
1098	Mortgage Interest Statement	Mortgage interest (including points) and certain mortgage insurance premiums you received in the course of your trade or business from individuals and reimbursements of overpaid interest.	$600 or more	February 28*	January 31
1098-E	Student Loan Interest Statement	Student loan interest received in the course of your trade or business.	$600 or more	February 28*	January 31
1098-T	Tuition Statement	Qualified tuition and related expenses, reimbursements or refunds, and scholarships or grants (optional).	See form instructions	February 28*	January 31
1099-B	Proceeds from Broker and Barter Exchange Transactions	Sales or redemptions of securities, futures transactions, commodities, and barter exchange transactions.	All amounts	February 28*	February 15
1099-C	Cancellation of Debt	Cancellation of a debt owed to the Federal Government or any organization having a significant trade or business of lending money.	$600 or more	February 28*	January 31
1099-DIV	Dividends and Distributions	Distributions, such as dividends, capital gain distributions, or nontaxable distributions, that were paid on stock and liquidation distributions.	$10 or more, except $600 or more for liquidations	February 28*	January 31
1099-G	Certain Government Payments	Unemployment compensation, state and local income tax refunds, agricultural payments, and taxable grants.	$10 or more for refunds and unemployment	February 28*	January 31
1099-INT	Interest Income	Interest income.	$10 or more ($600 or more in some cases)	February 28*	January 31
1099-MISC (Also for direct sales of $5,000 or more of consumer goods for resale.)	Miscellaneous Income	Rent or royalty payments; prizes and awards that are not for services, such as winnings on TV or radio shows.	$600 or more, except $10 or more for royalties	February 28	January 31
1099-NEC	Nonemployee Compensation	For services performed by someone not employed by the business, like vendors, independent contractors, and attorneys	$600 or more	January 31	January 31
1099-OID	Original Issue Discount	Original issue discount.	$10 or more	February 28*	January 31

1099-R	Distributions from Pensions, Annuities, Retirement or Profit-Sharing Plans, IRAs, Insurance Contracts, etc.	Distributions from retirement or profit-sharing plans, any IRA, insurance contracts, and IRA recharacterization.	$10 or more	February 28*	January 31
W-2G	Certain Gambling Winnings	Gambling winnings from horse racing, dog racing, jai alai, lotteries, keno, bingo, slot machines, sweepstakes, wagering pools, poker tournaments, etc.	Generally, $600 or more; $1,200 or more from bingo or slot machines; $1,500 or more from keno	February 28*	January 31
W-2	Wage and Tax Statement	Wages, value of healthcare benefits, tips, other compensation; social security, Medicare, and withheld income taxes. Include bonuses, vacation allowances, severance pay, certain moving expense payments, some kinds of travel allowances, and third-party payments of sick pay.	See form instructions	To SSA January 31	January 31

*The due date is March 31 if filed electronically

ACCOUNTING PERIODS AND METHODS

ACCOUNTING PERIODS

Taxpayers must use a **tax year** to figure taxable income. A tax year is an annual accounting period for keeping records and reporting income and expenses. Taxpayers may use a calendar year or a fiscal year (including a 52-53-week tax year). All books, records, income, and expenses must reflect the same tax year. Unless a taxpayer has a **required tax year**, the taxpayer must adopt a tax year by filing the first income tax return using that tax year. A required tax year is a tax year required under the Internal Revenue Code or the Income Tax Regulations.

- A corporation establishes a tax year when filing the first income tax return.
- Partnerships, S corporations, or Personal Service Corporations (PSC) may adopt a fiscal year by filing:
  1. Form 1128 (2553 S corps). Must establish the business purpose for the election, or
  2. Form 8716, if they otherwise qualify to make a Section 444 election

FISCAL YEAR AND CALENDAR YEAR

A **fiscal year** is 12 consecutive months ending on the last day of any month except December 31. A calendar year is 12 consecutive months beginning on January 1 and ending on December 31.

A calendar year taxpayer must maintain books and records, and report income and expenses, from January 1 through December 31 of each year. If the taxpayer filed the first tax return using the calendar tax year, and later starts a business as a sole proprietor, becomes a partner in a partnership, or becomes a shareholder in an S corporation, the taxpayer must continue to use the calendar year on subsequent returns unless the IRS grants approval to change it. Generally, anyone can adopt the calendar year. However, the taxpayer must adopt the calendar year if:

- The taxpayer did not keep books or records,

- An annual accounting period does not exist,
- The tax year does not qualify as a fiscal year, or
- A provision in the Internal Revenue Code requires the taxpayer to use a calendar year.

52-53 WEEK TAX YEAR

A taxpayer can elect to use a 52-53-week tax year if the taxpayer keeps books and records and reports income and expenses on that basis. If the taxpayer adopts this method, the 52-53-week tax year <u>must</u> **always end on the same day of the week**. The 52-53-week tax year must always end on:

- Whatever date this same day of the week last occurs in a calendar month, or
- Whatever date this same day of the week occurs that is closest to the last day of the calendar month.

> **EXAMPLE:** If the taxpayer elects a tax year that always ends on the last Monday in February, the 2020 taxable year will end on February 22, 2021.

Taxpayers elect a 52-53-week tax year by attaching a statement to the tax return that includes the following:

- The month in which the new 52-53-week tax year ends
- The day of the week on which the tax year always ends
- The date on which the tax year ends

For purposes of depreciation or amortization, a 52-53-week tax year is considered 12 calendar months. The IRS may consent to a change in the tax year, provided the business files Form 1128.

ACCOUNTING METHODS

An accounting method is a set of rules that determine when and how taxpayers report income and expenses. A taxpayer should choose a method when filing his first tax return. The taxpayer must use the same accounting method from year to year. The taxpayer <u>must</u> seek IRS approval to change an accounting method. The IRS does not require a single accounting method for all taxpayers. The system must clearly reflect all income and expenses. Careful records must validate the information on the return. An accounting method clearly reflects income only if all items of gross income and expenses are treated the same from year to year. Permissible methods include the following:

- Cash method
- Accrual method
- Special methods of accounting for certain items of income and expenses
- Combination (hybrid) method using elements of two or more of the above

TIP: A **$26 million** "small business taxpayer" exception applies to various accounting requirements. In general, when average annual gross receipts exceed this threshold, the taxpayer cannot use the cash method, must capitalize inventory and certain expenses, and must use the percentage-of-completion method to account for long-term contacts. The threshold adjusts annually for inflation and remains at $26 million for 2021.

CASH METHOD

Most individuals and many small businesses use the cash method of accounting.

- Under the cash method, a taxpayer includes in gross income all items of income actually or *constructively* received during the tax year. Taxpayers must include in income the value of property or services received at fair market value (FMV).

Constructive receipt occurs when an amount is credited to an account or made available to the taxpayer **without restriction**. Possession is not a requirement. If an agent of the taxpayer receives income, the taxpayer is considered to receive it when the agent receives it. The taxpayer does not constructively receive income if control of its receipt is subject to substantial restrictions or limitations.

- The taxpayer deducts expenses in the tax year actually paid. However, a taxpayer can only deduct an expense paid in advance in the year to which it applies, unless the expense qualifies for the *12-month rule*.

Under the **12-month rule**, a taxpayer is not required to capitalize amounts paid to create certain rights or benefits for the taxpayer that do not extend beyond the earlier of:

- Twelve months after the right or benefit begins, or
- The end of the tax year following the tax year in which payment occurred

The following entities cannot use the cash method or any combination that includes it:

- A corporation (not SCORP or qualified PSC) with average annual gross receipts more than **$26 million** for 2020.
- A partnership with a corporation (other than SCORP) as a partner, and with the partnership having average annual gross receipts exceeding **$26 million** for 2020
- A tax shelter

ACCRUAL METHOD

A corporation (not a qualified PSC) must use the *accrual method* of accounting if average annual gross receipts exceed **$26 million** for 2020.

TCJA: The gross receipts test allows taxpayers with annual average gross receipts that do not exceed **$26 million** for 2020 for the three prior taxable-year periods (the "gross receipts test") to use the cash method. This includes any farming C corporation (or farming partnership with a C corporation partner). The provision exempts taxpayers that meet the $26 million gross receipts test (2020) from the requirement to keep inventories.

Under the accrual method, an amount is **includable in income when all events occur that fix the right to receive the income**, which is the earliest of the date when:

- The required performance takes place
- Payment is due
- The corporation receives payment, and the amount can be determined with reasonable accuracy

Generally, an accrual basis taxpayer can deduct accrued expenses in the tax year when the following conditions exist:

- All events that determine the liability have occurred.
- The amount of the liability can be figured with reasonable accuracy.
- The *economic performance* takes place with respect to the expense.

A taxpayer reports an *advance payment* for services to be performed in a later tax year as income in the year he/she receives payment. The taxpayer can elect to postpone including the advance payment in income until the next tax year. However, recognition may not go beyond the next year.

PERCENTAGE OF COMPLETION METHOD

The taxpayer must account for long-term contracts (excluding certain real property construction contracts) by using the *percentage of completion* method described in IRC Sec. 460. Under this method, record gross income from the contract as the taxpayer completes the work.

> **TCJA:** For contracts entered into after 2017, the provision expands the exception for small construction contracts from the requirement to use the percentage-of-completion method. Under the provision, contracts within this exception are those contracts for the construction or improvement of real property if the contract is expected (at the time such contract is entered into) to be **completed within two years** of commencement of the contract and is performed by a taxpayer that (for the taxable year in which the contract was entered into) meets the **$26 million gross receipts test** for 2020.

COMBINATION (HYBRID) METHOD

Generally, a taxpayer can use any combination of cash, accrual, and special methods of accounting, as long as the combination clearly reflects income and is consistent. The following restrictions apply:

- If an inventory is necessary to account for income, the taxpayer must use an accrual method for purchases and sales. Generally, a taxpayer can use the cash method for other items.
- Taxpayers who use the cash method to report income must also use it for expenses.
- Taxpayers who use an accrual method for reporting expenses must also use it to figure income.
- Taxpayers must treat any combination that includes the cash method as the cash method.

BUSINESS AND PERSONAL ITEMS

A taxpayer can account for business and personal items using different accounting methods. For example, an individual may determine business income and expenses under an accrual method, even if the individual uses the cash method to figure personal items.

MULTIPLE BUSINESSES

A taxpayer who operates multiple separate and distinct businesses may use a different accounting method for each. The taxpayer must maintain a complete and separate set of books and records for each business in order for those businesses to be considered truly separate and distinct.

INVENTORY

An inventory is necessary to clearly show income when the production, purchase, or sale of merchandise is an income-producing factor. In order for a business to account for an inventory, the business must use the *accrual method* of accounting for purchases and sales. To figure taxable income, the inventory must be valued at the beginning and end of each tax year. The rules for valuing inventory are not the same for all businesses. The method used must conform to the generally accepted accounting principles for similar businesses and must clearly reflect income. The inventory practices must be consistent from year to year.

> **TCJA:** A provision exempts certain taxpayers from the requirement to keep inventories. Specifically, taxpayers that meet the gross receipts test (**$26 million** for 2020) are not required to account for inventories under section 471 but rather may use a method of accounting that either treats inventories as **non-incidental materials and supplies** or conforms to the taxpayer's financial accounting treatment of inventories.

Each test period for gross receipts is three consecutive years prior to the tax year. For example, the average of the test period for the year 2020 equals the sum of gross receipts for (2017 + 2018 + 2019) divided by 3. If the average receipts for any of the periods tested are more than the stated limit (**$26 million** for 2020), the business may <u>not</u> use the cash method to value inventory.

WHAT CONSTITUTES INVENTORY

Inventory includes the following:

- Merchandise or stock in trade.
- Purchased merchandise if title has passed to an individual, even if the merchandise is in transit or the owner does not have physical possession for another reason.
- Goods under contract for sale that are not segregated and applied to the contract.
- Goods out on consignment.
- Goods held for sale in display rooms, merchandise mart rooms, or booths located away from the place of business.
- Raw materials, work in process, and finished product.
- Supplies that physically become a part of the item intended for sale.
- When selling merchandise by mail and receiving payment upon delivery (*COD*), the title passes when the buyer makes payment. Include the merchandise in closing inventory until the buyer pays for it
- Include containers (kegs, bottles, and cases) in inventory if the title has not passed to the buyer of the contents whether they are on hand or returnable. If the title has passed to the buyer, exclude the containers from inventory. Under certain circumstances, some containers can be depreciated.

Inventory does <u>not</u> include the following:

- Certain merchandise
  1. Goods sold, but only if the title has passed to the buyer
  2. Goods consigned to the person
  3. Goods ordered for future delivery if a person does not yet have the title
- Certain assets
  1. Land, buildings, and equipment used in business
  2. Notes, accounts receivable, and similar assets
  3. Real estate held for sale by a real estate dealer in the ordinary course of business
  4. Supplies that do not physically become part of the item intended for sale

IDENTIFYING INVENTORY COST

An individual can use any of the following methods to identify the cost of items in inventory:

- **Specific identification method** – Use this method if the actual cost of items in inventory is identified and matched.
- **FIFO (first-in first-out) or LIFO (last-in first-out) method** – Use this method if specific identification is not possible, or the same type of goods are intermingled in the inventory and the individual cannot identify them with specific invoices.
  1. The **FIFO** method assumes the items purchased or produced first are the first items sold, consumed, or otherwise disposed of. Match the items in inventory at the end of the tax year with the costs of similar items most recently purchased or produced.

2. The **LIFO** method assumes the items of inventory purchased or produced last are the first items sold. Items included in closing inventory are considered to be from the opening inventory in the order of acquisition and from those acquired during the tax year. Taxpayers must file Form 970 (or statement) with the tax return for the year in which the taxpayer first uses LIFO. The rules for this method are very complex.

INVENTORY VALUATION

The value of the inventory is a major factor in figuring taxable income. There are several valuation methodologies for inventory, but for exam purposes, we will focus on the *cost method*.

- **Cost method** – To properly value inventory at cost include all associated direct and indirect costs. The following rules apply:

  1. For merchandise on hand at the beginning of the tax year, cost means the ending inventory price of the goods.

  2. For merchandise purchased during the year, cost means the invoice price less appropriate discounts plus transportation or other charges incurred in acquiring the goods. It can also include other costs that the business must capitalize under the uniform capitalization rules.

  3. For merchandise produced during the year, cost means all direct and indirect costs that the business must capitalize under the uniform capitalization rules.

EXAMPLE: Calculate the cost of goods sold using the cost method. ****Most likely to appear on the exam.**

Jack Roston operates a small manufacturing business as a sole proprietorship. His business, Roston Rubber, manufactures industrial rubber seals and makes rubber bands used in packaging. He uses the accrual method of accounting. He incurred the following expenses during the year.

Beginning inventory, raw materials	$14,000
Beginning inventory, work in process	$20,000
Beginning inventory, finished goods	$100,000
Ending inventory, raw materials	$15,000
Ending inventory, work in process	$12,000
Ending inventory, finished goods	$110,000
Purchases	$2,000,000
Salaries, factory	$200,000
Salaries, sales	$50,000
Chemicals used in manufacturing process	$10,000
Office supplies	$5,000
Freight-in on raw material purchases	$3,000

What was his cost of goods sold? (Disregard uniform capitalization rules for this computation.)

A. $2,210,000
B. $2,207,000
C. $2,268,000
D. $2,265,000

ANSWER: If a business manufactures products or purchases them for resale, it generally must value inventory at the beginning and end of each tax year to determine the cost of goods sold. Deduct the cost of goods sold from gross receipts to figure gross profit for the year. Selling or administrative salaries and office supplies do not directly relate to the cost of the manufactured product and are not part of the cost of goods sold. The following are types of expenses that figure into the cost of goods sold—the cost of products or raw materials (including freight), storage, direct labor (include contributions to retirement plans) for workers who produce the products, and factory overhead.

Beginning Inventory	$134,000	($100,000 + $20,000 + $14,000)
+ Purchases	$2,000,000	
+ Factory Salaries	$200,000	
+ Chemicals	$10,000	
+ Freight	$3,000	
– Ending Inventory	$137,000	($110,000 + $12,000 + $15,000)
Cost of Goods Sold	**$2,210,000**	

UNIFORM CAPITALIZATION RULES

Under Section 263A (the *uniform capitalization rules)*, capitalize the direct costs and part of the indirect costs for production or resale activities. Include these costs in the basis of property produced or acquired for resale, rather than claiming them as a current deduction. Costs are recovered through depreciation, amortization, or cost of goods sold when the property is used, sold or disposed of.

> **TCJA:** Beginning in 2018, any producer or reseller that meets the **gross receipts test ($26 million** for 2020) is exempted from the application of section 263A. The provision retains the exemptions from the uniform capitalization rules that are not based on a taxpayer's gross receipts.

An individual is subject to the uniform capitalization rules if he does any of the following:

- Acquires for resale or produces real or tangible personal property
  1. An individual produces property if he constructs, builds, installs, manufactures, develops, improves, creates, raises, or grows the property.
  2. Tangible personal property includes films, sound recordings, videotapes, books, artwork, photographs, or similar property containing words, ideas, concepts, images, or sounds.

The uniform capitalization rules do not apply to the following:

- Small resellers of personal property with average annual gross receipts of **$26 million or less** for 2020
- Property produced to use as personal or non-business property or for uses not connected with a trade or business or an activity conducted for profit
- Research and experimental expenditures deductible under Section 174
- Intangible drilling and development costs of oil, gas, or geothermal wells or any amortization deduction allowable under Section 59(e) for intangible drilling, development, or mining expenditures
- Property produced under a long-term contract, except for certain home construction contracts
- Timber and certain ornamental trees raised, harvested, or grown, and the underlying land
- Qualified creative expenses paid or incurred as a freelance (self-employed) writer, photographer, or artist that are otherwise deductible on the tax return

- Costs allocable to natural gas acquired for resale to the extent these costs would otherwise be allocable to cushion gas stored underground
- Property produced if substantial construction occurred before March 1, 1986
- Property provided to customers in connection with providing services (It must be *de minimis* in amount and not included in inventory in the hands of the service provider.)
- Loan origination
- Costs of producers using a simplified production method with indirect costs of $200,000 or less

LESSON 2

Business Taxation

EXPENSES AND DEDUCTIONS

BUSINESS START-UP AND ORGANIZATIONAL COSTS

Business start-up and organizational costs are generally *capital expenditures*. However, a taxpayer may elect (on the tax return) to deduct up to $5,000 of business start-up costs and $5,000 of organizational costs as an expense in the initial year. For each category, reduce the deduction by the amount of costs that exceed $50,000. The taxpayer must amortize any remaining costs over a 180-month period, beginning with the **initial month of operation**. If the total costs are $55,000 or more, the initial deduction is reduced to zero, but the company may still amortize its organizational and start-up costs over 15 years (180 months).

Business start-up costs include amounts paid or incurred for (1) creating an active trade or business, or (2) investigating the creation or acquisition of an active trade or business.

- To qualify as a start-up cost it must meet <u>both</u> of the following:

  1. A cost that could be deducted if paid or incurred to operate an existing active trade or business (in the same field as the one entered into), and

  2. A cost **paid <u>or</u> incurred before** the day the active trade or business begins

- Start-up costs include the following:

  1. Analysis or survey of potential markets, products, labor supply, transportation facilities, etc.

  2. Advertisements for business opening

  3. Salaries and wages for employees who are being trained and their instructors

  4. Travel and other necessary costs for securing prospective distributors, suppliers, or customers

  5. Salaries and fees for executives and consultants, or for similar professional services

Start-up costs do <u>not</u> include deductible interest, taxes, or research and experimental costs.

Organizational costs include the direct costs of creating a corporation or a partnership.

- To qualify as an organizational cost it must meet <u>all</u> of the following:

  1. For the creation of the corporation or the partnership

  2. Chargeable to a capital account

  3. Could be amortized over the life of the corporation or the partnership if the corporation or the partnership had a fixed life, and

  4. Cost incurred:

     ○ **Corporation – Incurred before the end of the first tax year** in which the corporation is in business. A corporation using the *cash method* of accounting can deduct organizational costs **incurred within the first tax year**, even if it does <u>not</u> pay them in that tax year.

     ○ **Partnership – Incurred by the due date of the partnership return** (excluding extensions) for the first tax year in which the partnership is in business. A partnership using the *cash method* of accounting can deduct an organizational cost <u>only</u> if it has been **paid by the end of the tax year**. However, any cost the partnership could have deducted as an organizational cost in an earlier tax year (if it had been paid that year) can be deducted in the tax year of payment.

- Organizational costs include costs of temporary directors, organizational meetings, state filing fees, and legal and accounting fees for services incident to the incorporation of the corporation or organization of the partnership.

The following items are capital expenses that <u>cannot</u> be amortized, and are therefore <u>not</u> organizational costs or start-up costs:

- Costs for issuing and selling stock, securities, or partnership interests, such as commissions, professional fees, and printing costs (these costs are <u>not</u> deductible or amortizable)
- Costs associated with acquiring assets or transferring assets to the corporation or partnership (these costs need to be included in the basis of the asset)

A business elects to deduct the start-up and/or organizational costs by claiming the deduction on their tax return (filed by the due date including extensions) for the tax year in which the active trade or business begins. A business that intends to amortize the organizational and/or start-up costs must file Form 4562 with their tax return in the initial year of operation.

GIFTS

A deduction is **not available for business gifts made in excess of $25** to a person during the tax year. If a taxpayer gives a gift to a member of a customer's family, the gift is generally considered an indirect gift to the customer. This rule does <u>not</u> apply if the taxpayer has a bona fide, independent business connection with that family member and the gift is not intended for the customer's eventual use.

If the taxpayer and the taxpayer's spouse <u>both</u> give gifts, the IRS treats them as one taxpayer. It does not matter whether they have separate businesses, are separately employed, or whether they each have an independent connection with the recipient. If a partnership gives gifts, the IRS treats the partnership and the partners as one taxpayer.

EXAMPLE: Bob Jones sells products to Local Company. He and his wife, Jan, gave Local Company three gourmet gift baskets to thank them for their business. They paid $80 for each gift basket, or $240 total. Three of Local Company's executives took the gift baskets home for their families' use. Bob and Jan have no independent business relationship with any of the executives' other family members. They can deduct a total of $75 ($25 limit × 3) for the gift baskets.

Incidental costs, such as engraving on jewelry, or packaging, insuring, and mailing, are generally <u>not</u> included in determining the cost of a gift for purposes of the $25 limit.

A cost is incidental only if it doesn't add substantial value to the gift. For example, the cost of gift wrapping is an incidental cost. However, the purchase of an ornamental basket for packaging fruit isn't an incidental cost if the value of the basket is substantial compared to the value of the fruit.

EXCEPTION: The following items are <u>not</u> considered gifts for purposes of the $25 limit.

- An item that costs $4 or less and has the business name clearly and permanently imprinted on the gift, and is one of a number of identical items you widely distribute. Examples include pens, desk sets, and plastic bags and cases.
- Signs, display racks, or other promotional material to be used on the business premises of the recipient.

RENTAL EXPENSES

Rent is any amount paid for the use of property not owned by the individual. In general, a taxpayer may deduct rent as an expense only if the rent is for the use of property in the taxpayer's business. If the taxpayer has or will receive equity in or title to the property, the rent is not deductible. The taxpayer may not take a rental deduction for unreasonable rent. Ordinarily, the issue of reasonableness arises only if the taxpayer and the lessor are related. If an individual rents his home and uses part of it as a place of business, the individual may be able to deduct the rent paid for that part. The taxpayer must meet the requirements for business use of the home. Generally, rent paid because of one's business is deductible in the year paid or accrued. The 12-month rule prevents a cash basis taxpayer from deducting a payment of rent more than 12 months in advance. Deduct the remainder in the period to which it applies.

EXPENSES ON LEASED PROPERTY

The IRS treats lease payments, including taxes on leased property, as payments of rent. Amortize costs to acquire a lease over the remaining term of the lease. A taxpayer must depreciate permanent improvements to leased property, such as buildings, using the modified accelerated cost recovery system (MACRS) over an appropriate recovery period, not the remaining term of the lease.

INTEREST EXPENSE

- **Deductible interest** – A taxpayer may generally deduct as a business expense all interest paid or accrued during the tax year on debts related to his business. Interest relates to business if the taxpayer uses the proceeds of the loan for a business expense. It does not matter what type of property secures the loan. A taxpayer may deduct interest on a debt only if all the following requirements are met:
  1. The taxpayer is legally liable for the debt. If liable for part of a business debt, the taxpayer may deduct his share of the total interest paid or accrued.
  2. Both the taxpayer and the lender intend that the taxpayer will repay the debt.
  3. The taxpayer and the lender have a true debtor-creditor relationship.
- **Capitalized interest** – Under the uniform capitalization rules, a taxpayer generally must capitalize interest on debt to produce (construct, build, demolish, install, manufacture, develop, improve, create, raise, or grow) real property or certain tangible personal property. Add the interest (and points) to the basis of the property. Designated property is any of the following:
  1. Real property
  2. Tangible personal property with a class life of 20 years or more
  3. Tangible personal property with an estimated production period of more than two years
  4. Tangible personal property with an estimated production period of more than one year if the estimated cost of production is more than $1 million

TCJA: A limitation on the deduction for **business interest** applies to taxable years beginning after December 31, 2017, for certain taxpayers with more than $25 million of average annual gross receipts. This limit is indexed for inflation and is **$26 million** for 2020.

For all taxpayers, the deduction for business interest is limited to the sum of:

1. business interest income of the taxpayer for the taxable year, and
2. 30 percent of the adjusted taxable income of the taxpayer for the taxable year (not less than zero), and
3. the floor plan financing interest (i.e., automotive dealership interest on floor plan financing indebtedness) of the taxpayer for the taxable year.

The limitation applies at the taxpayer level (i.e., the entity level—C corporation, partnership, S corporation, sole proprietorship).

Business interest means any interest paid or accrued on indebtedness properly allocable to a trade or business. Business interest income means the amount of interest includible in the gross income of the taxpayer for the taxable year which is properly allocable to a trade or business. Business interest does <u>not</u> include investment interest, and business interest income does <u>not</u> include investment income, within the meaning of §163(d).

A deduction for business interest is permitted to the full extent of business interest income and any floor plan financing interest. The deduction for any remaining business interest is limited to 30 percent of adjusted taxable income. The amount of any business interest not allowed as a deduction for any taxable year is treated as business interest paid or accrued in the succeeding taxable year. The amount of any business interest <u>not</u> allowed as a deduction for any taxable year may be **carried forward indefinitely**.

EXCEPTION: The limitation does <u>not</u> apply to any taxpayer that meets the **$26 million gross receipts test** (2020) of §448(c) (i.e., if the average annual gross receipts for the three-taxable-year period ending with the prior taxable year does <u>not exceed</u> $26 million). Aggregation rules apply to determine the amount of a taxpayer's gross receipts under the $26 million gross receipts test.

INSURANCE PREMIUMS

A deduction may be available for certain premiums paid for insurance related to a business, which includes the following:

- Insurance that covers fire, storm, theft, accident, or similar losses.
- Credit insurance that covers losses from business bad debts.
- Group hospitalization and medical insurance for employees, including long-term care insurance:
  1. If a partnership pays accident and health insurance premiums for its partners, it generally may deduct them as guaranteed payments to partners.
  2. If an S corporation pays accident and health insurance premiums for its more-than-2% shareholder-employees, it generally may deduct them, but it must also include the amount in the shareholder's wages subject to federal income tax withholding.
- Liability insurance.
- Malpractice insurance that covers the taxpayer's personal liability for professional negligence resulting in injury or damage to patients or clients.
- Workers' compensation insurance set by state law that covers any claims for bodily injuries or job-related diseases suffered by employees in the taxpayer's business, regardless of fault:
  1. If a partnership pays workers' compensation premiums for its partners, it generally may deduct them as guaranteed payments to partners.
  2. Workers' compensation premiums paid by S corporation for its more-than-2% shareholder-employees are generally deductible but must be included in the shareholder's wages.
- Contributions to a state unemployment insurance fund are deductible as taxes if they are considered taxes under state law.
- Overhead insurance that pays for business overhead expenses incurred during long periods of disability caused by injury or sickness.

- Car and other vehicle insurance that covers vehicles used in business for liability, damages, and other losses. If taxpayer operates a vehicle partly for personal use, deduct only the part of the insurance premium applied to the business use of the vehicle. If using the standard mileage rate to figure car expenses, the taxpayer may <u>not</u> deduct any car insurance premiums.
- Life insurance covering officers and employees if the taxpayer is not a beneficiary under the contract.
- Business interruption insurance for lost profits if the business closes due to a fire or other cause.

A taxpayer may <u>not</u> deduct premiums on the following kinds of insurance:

- Self-insurance reserve funds.
- Premiums for a policy that pays for the company's lost earnings due to sickness or disability.
- Certain life insurance and annuities.
- Insurance to secure a loan. If a taxpayer insures his life or the life of another person with a financial interest in the business to get or protect a business loan, the taxpayer may not deduct the premiums as a business expense. The taxpayer may not deduct the premiums as interest on business loans or as an expense of financing loans. In the event of death, the proceeds of the policy are generally not taxed as income even if the beneficiary uses them to liquidate the debt.

SELF-EMPLOYED HEALTH INSURANCE DEDUCTION

Premiums paid for medical and dental insurance and qualified long-term care insurance may be deductible provided they are for the taxpayer, his spouse, or his dependents, and the taxpayer is:

- A self-employed individual with a net profit reported on Schedule C Profit or Loss from Business or Schedule F Profit or Loss from Farming, or
- A partner with net earnings from self-employment reported on Schedule K-1 (Form 1065), or
- A shareholder owning more than 2% of the outstanding stock of an S corporation with wages from the corporation reported on Form W-2, Wage and Tax Statement.

The taxpayer <u>must</u> establish the insurance plan under the taxpayer's business; however, the policy may be either in the name of the business or in the name of the individual.

- **A self-employed** individual filing a Schedule C or F can have the policy in his name or under the business.
- **Partners** may pay the premiums themselves, or the partnership may pay the premiums and report the premium amounts on Schedule K-1 (Form 1065) as guaranteed payments to be included in the taxpayer's gross income. However, if the policy is in the taxpayer's name and the taxpayer pays the premiums, the partnership must reimburse the taxpayer and report the premium amounts on Schedule K-1 (Form 1065) as guaranteed payments to be included in gross income. Otherwise, the insurance plan is not considered established under the business.
- **More-than-2% shareholders** may pay their own premiums or the SCORP may pay them and report the premium amounts on Form W-2 as wages to be included in taxpayer's gross income. However, if the policy is in the taxpayer's name and he/she pays the premiums, the SCORP must reimburse the taxpayer and report the amount on Form W-2 as wages included in gross income. Otherwise, the insurance plan is not considered as established under the business.

TIP: Partners and more-than-2% shareholders may be able to amend prior year returns to claim self-employed health insurance deductions allowable under the rules explained above. Shareholders should write "Filed Pursuant to Notice 2008-1" at the top of any amended return.

TRAVEL

An individual is traveling away from home if duties require him to be away from the general area of his tax home for a period substantially longer than an ordinary day's work, and he/she needs to get sleep or rest to meet the demands of work while away. Generally, a tax home is the entire city or general area where the main place of business or work is located, regardless of where the individual maintains a family home.

> **EXAMPLE:** A person lives with family in Florida but works in Boston where he stays in a hotel and eats in restaurants. He returns to Florida every weekend. The taxpayer may not deduct any of the travel, meals, or lodging in Boston because it is his tax home. The travel to the family home in Florida is not for work, so these expenses are also not deductible. If a person regularly works in more than one place, the person's tax home is the general area where the main place of business or work is located.

Deductible travel expenses while away from home include the costs of the following:

- Travel by airplane, train, bus, or car between home and business destination
- Using a personal car while at a business destination
- Fares for taxis or between the airport or train station and the hotel, the hotel and the work location, and from one customer to another, or from one place of business to another
- Lodging
- Tips paid for services related to any of these expenses
- Dry cleaning and laundry
- Business calls while on a business trip. This includes business communications by fax machine or other communication devices.
- Other similar ordinary and necessary expenses related to business travel. These expenses might include transportation to and from a business meal, public stenographer's fees, computer rental fees, and operating and maintaining a house trailer.
- A taxpayer may deduct 50% of meals when traveling in 2020 if he must stop for substantial sleep or rest to perform his duties properly while traveling away from home on business. The taxpayer may not deduct expenses for meals that are lavish or extravagant. An expense is not considered lavish or extravagant if it is reasonable based on the facts and circumstances.

TRAVEL IN THE UNITED STATES

- Taxpayers may deduct all travel expenses if the trip is entirely business related.
- If the trip is primarily for business and, while at the business destination, the taxpayer extends his stay for a vacation, makes a personal side trip, or has other personal activities, the taxpayer may deduct only business-related travel expenses.
- If the trip is primarily for personal reasons, such as a vacation, the entire cost of the trip is a nondeductible personal expense. However, a taxpayer may deduct any expenses while at a destination directly related to business.

TRAVEL OUTSIDE THE UNITED STATES

- A taxpayer may deduct 100% of travel expenses if traveling outside the United States and spends the entire time on business activities:
  1. Even if the taxpayer does not spend the entire time on business activities, the trip is considered entirely for business if the taxpayer meets <u>any</u> of the following exceptions:
     A. Did not have substantial control over arranging the trip

B. The taxpayer is outside the United States for a week or less, combining business and non-business activities

C. The taxpayer spends less than 25% of the total time the taxpayer was outside the United States on non-business activities

D. The taxpayer can establish that a personal vacation is not a major consideration, even if the taxpayer has substantial control over arranging the trip

- If the trip is primarily for business but the taxpayer spends time on other activities, the taxpayer generally may not deduct all of the travel expenses. Only the business portion of the cost of getting to and from the destination is deductible. Individuals must allocate costs between business and other activities to determine the deductible amount.

- If the trip is primarily for vacation or for investment purposes, the entire cost of the trip is a non-deductible personal expense. If a taxpayer spends time attending brief professional seminars or a continuing education program, the taxpayer may deduct registration fees and other expenses directly related to business.

CAR EXPENSES

A taxpayer can deduct car expenses for vehicles used exclusively in a trade or business. If using a car for both business and personal purposes, the taxpayer must divide expenses based on actual mileage. Generally, commuting expenses between the taxpayer's home and a business location, within the area of the taxpayer's tax home, are not deductible.

A taxpayer can deduct actual car expenses, which include depreciation (or lease payments), gas and oil, tires, repairs, tune-ups, insurance, and registration fees. Or, instead of figuring the business part of these actual expenses, may be able to use the standard mileage rate to figure the deduction.

For 2020, the rate is **57.5 cents per mile** on business miles driven (56 cents in 2021). To qualify, the taxpayer must use this method for the first year placing the vehicle in service. A taxpayer may not use the business standard mileage rate for a vehicle after using any depreciation method other than straight-line, or after claiming a Section 179 deduction for that vehicle. The taxpayer cannot claim the business standard mileage rate for more than four vehicles used simultaneously. A taxpayer may use the business standard mileage rate for vehicles used for hire, such as taxicabs unless the standard mileage rate is otherwise not allowed.

The taxpayer can also deduct the business part of the interest on the car loan, state and local personal property tax on the car, parking fees, and tolls, whether or not claiming the standard mileage rate.

MEALS AND ENTERTAINMENT

A taxpayer may deduct (within limits) certain meals if the expense is **ordinary, necessary,** and **incurred in a trade or business.**

The TCJA provides that **no deduction** is allowed with respect to:

- An activity generally considered to be entertainment, amusement, or recreation,
- Membership dues with respect to any club organized for business, pleasure, recreation, or other social purposes, or
- A facility or portion thereof used in connection with any of the above items.

The **TCJA repeals the deduction for entertainment**, amusement, or recreation that is directly related to (or, in certain cases, associated with) the active conduct of the taxpayer's trade or business (and the related rule applying a 50 percent limit to such deductions).

EXCEPTION: A business may continue to deduct expenses for recreational, social, or similar activities (including facilities) primarily for the benefit of **employees** (other than employees who are highly compensated employees).

UPDATE IR-2018-195, Oct. 3, 2018

The TCJA eliminated the deduction for any expenses related to activities generally considered entertainment, amusement or recreation.

Taxpayers may continue to **deduct 50 percent of the cost of business meals** if the taxpayer (or an employee of the taxpayer) is present and the food or beverages are <u>not</u> considered lavish or extravagant. The meals may be provided to a current or potential business customer, client, consultant or similar business contact.

Food and beverages that are provided during entertainment events will not be considered entertainment if purchased separately from the event.

Prior to 2018, a business could deduct up to 50 percent of entertainment expenses directly related to the active conduct of a trade or business or, if incurred immediately before or after a bona fide business discussion, associated with the active conduct of a trade or business.

The Department of the Treasury and the IRS expect to publish proposed regulations clarifying when business meal expenses are deductible and what constitutes entertainment. Until the proposed regulations are effective, taxpayers can rely on guidance in Notice 2018-76.

Under this notice, taxpayers may deduct 50 percent of an otherwise allowable business meal expense if:

1. The expense is an ordinary and necessary expense under §162(a) paid or incurred during the taxable year in carrying on any trade or business;
2. The expense is not lavish or extravagant under the circumstances;
3. The taxpayer, or an employee of the taxpayer, is present at the furnishing of the food or beverages;
4. The food and beverages are provided to a current or potential business customer, client, consultant, or similar business contact; and
5. In the case of food and beverages provided during or at an entertainment activity, the food and beverages are purchased separately from the entertainment, or the cost of the food and beverages is stated separately from the cost of the entertainment on one or more bills, invoices, or receipts. The entertainment disallowance rule may not be circumvented through inflating the amount charged for food and beverages.

For each example, assume that the food and beverage expenses are **ordinary and necessary expenses** under §162(a) paid or incurred during the taxable year in carrying on a trade or business and are **not lavish or extravagant** under the circumstances. Also, assume that the taxpayer and the business contact are not engaged in a trade or business that has any relation to the entertainment activity.

EXAMPLE 1

Taxpayer A invites B, a business contact, to a baseball game. A purchases tickets for A and B to attend the game. While at the game, A buys hot dogs and drinks for A and B.

The baseball game is entertainment as defined in §1.274-2(b)(1)(i) and, thus, the cost of the game tickets is an entertainment expense and is not deductible by A. The cost of the hot dogs and drinks, which are purchased separately from the game tickets, is not an entertainment expense and is not subject to the §274(a)(1) disallowance. Therefore, A may deduct 50 percent of the expenses associated with the hot dogs and drinks purchased at the game.

EXAMPLE 2

Taxpayer C invites D, a business contact, to a basketball game. C purchases tickets for C and D to attend the game in a suite, where they have access to food and beverages. The cost of the basketball game tickets, as stated on the invoice, includes the food and beverages.

The basketball game is entertainment as defined in §1.274-2(b)(1)(i) and, thus, the cost of the game tickets is an entertainment expense and is not deductible by C. The cost of the food and beverages, which are not purchased separately from the game tickets, is not stated separately on the invoice. Thus, the cost of the food and beverages also is an entertainment expense that is subject to the §274(a)(1) disallowance. Therefore, C may not deduct any of the expenses associated with the basketball game.

EXAMPLE 3

Assume the same facts as in Example 2, except that the invoice for the basketball game tickets separately states the cost of the food and beverages.

As in Example 2, the basketball game is entertainment as defined in §1.274-2(b)(1)(i) and, thus, the cost of the game tickets, other than the cost of the food and beverages, is an entertainment expense and is not deductible by C. However, the cost of the food and beverages, which is stated separately on the invoice for the game tickets, is not an entertainment expense and is not subject to the §274(a)(1) disallowance. Therefore, C may deduct 50 percent of the expenses associated with the food and beverages provided at the game.

> Taxpayers may still generally deduct **50 percent** of the **food and beverage expenses** associated with **operating their trade or business** (e.g., meals consumed by employees on work travel).

For amounts incurred and paid after December 31, 2017, and until December 31, 2025, the provision expands this 50 percent limitation to expenses of the employer associated with providing food and beverages to employees through an eating facility that meets requirements for de minimis fringes and for the convenience of the employer. Such amounts incurred and paid after December 31, 2025, are <u>not</u> deductible.

TIP: The *Consolidated Appropriations Act, 2021* provides a 100% deduction for business food or beverages provided by a restaurant in 2021 and 2022. Keep in mind, exams prior to May 1, 2022 test the 2020 tax year so this temporary rule should not appear on earlier exams.

M&E paid or incurred <u>after</u> December 31, 2017	
Entertainment expenses	0% deductible
Business meals (<u>not</u> separately paid or identified) during entertainment activity with current or prospective customers	0% deductible
Business meals (separately paid or identified) during entertainment activity with current or prospective customers	50% deductible
Business meals with employees, stockholders, agents, or directors	50% deductible
Business meals with current or prospective customers	50% deductible
Employee meals while traveling	50% deductible
Employee meals provided for employer's convenience	50% deductible
Company holiday party	100% deductible

CASUALTY AND THEFT

If a taxpayer has business or income-producing property, such as rental property, and it is stolen or completely destroyed, the decrease in FMV is <u>not</u> considered. The loss is the taxpayer's adjusted basis in the property minus the salvage value, insurance, and other reimbursements. There are two methods to deduct a casualty or theft loss of inventory, including items held for sale to customers:

- Deduct the loss through the increase in the cost of goods sold by properly reporting opening and closing inventories. Taxpayers must not claim this loss again as a casualty or theft loss. If a taxpayer takes the loss through the increase in the cost of goods sold, the taxpayer should include any insurance or reimbursement in gross income.

- Deduct the loss separately. If deducted separately, a taxpayer must eliminate the affected inventory items from the cost of goods sold by making a downward adjustment to opening inventory or purchases. The taxpayer must reduce the loss by the reimbursement received and must not include the reimbursement in gross income. If the taxpayer does not receive reimbursement by the end of the year, the taxpayer may not claim a loss to the extent the taxpayer has a reasonable prospect of recovery.

TIP: Losses on business property (other than employee property) and income-producing property are <u>not</u> subject to the same limitations as personal-use property. Taxpayers generally must deduct a casualty loss in the year it occurs. However, if there is a casualty loss from a federally declared disaster, a taxpayer may choose to deduct that loss on his return or amended return for the **tax year immediately preceding the tax year of the disaster**. Claiming the loss on the previous year's return may result in a lower tax for that year, often producing or increasing a cash refund.

BAD DEBTS

If an individual owes a taxpayer money that the taxpayer is unable to collect, then the taxpayer has a bad debt. The taxpayer does not have to wait until a debt is due to determine whether it is worthless. A debt becomes worthless when there is no longer any chance the debtor will pay the amount owed. Generally, a **business bad debt** is one that comes from operating a business. A taxpayer may claim a bad debt deduction only if the amount owed to the taxpayer was previously included in gross income. This applies to amounts owed to the taxpayer from all sources of taxable income, including sales, services, rents, and interest. Business bad debts are mainly the result of **credit sales** to customers. In the books, record goods that have been sold, but not paid for, and services that have been performed, but not paid for, as either accounts receivable or notes receivable. After a reasonable period, if a taxpayer has tried to collect the amount due but is unable to do so, the uncollectible part becomes a business bad debt.

- A taxpayer who uses the accrual method of accounting should claim a bad debt deduction only if the entire uncollectible amount was previously included in income.
- If a taxpayer uses the cash method of accounting, the taxpayer may not claim a bad debt deduction for amounts owed because the amounts were never included in income.
- Taxpayers who claim a deduction for a bad debt and later recover (collect) all or part of it may have to include the recovery in gross income. The amount to include is limited to the amount actually deducted. However, taxpayers can exclude the amount deducted that did not reduce their tax. Report the recovery as "Other income" on the appropriate business form or schedule.

TAXES

The following taxes are deductible:

- **Employment taxes** – A deduction is allowed for FICA and FUTA taxes paid out of company funds as an employer. Deductible taxes also include payments made to a state unemployment compensation fund or to a state disability benefit fund (SUTA).
- **Self-employment tax** – A self-employed taxpayer can deduct a portion of self-employment tax paid on his personal return.
- **Personal property tax** – Tax imposed by a state or local government on personal property used in a business. Registration fees for the right to use property within a state or local area are deductible.
- **Real estate taxes** – A deduction is allowed for real estate taxes paid on business property. Deductible real estate taxes are any state, local, or foreign taxes on real estate levied for the general public welfare. The taxing authority must base the taxes on the assessed value of the real estate and charge them uniformly against all property under its jurisdiction. Add property assessments for improvements that increase the value of the property assessed to basis. Do not deduct these as taxes. Examples of assessments include roads, sidewalks, water connections, and extending utility service lines to the property.
- **Sales tax** – Sales tax paid on a service or on the purchase or use of property as part of the cost of the service or property. If the service or the cost or use of the property is a deductible business expense, the business can deduct the tax as part of that service or cost. If the property is merchandise bought for resale, the sales tax is part of the cost of the merchandise. If the property is depreciable, add the sales tax to the basis for depreciation.
- **Excise taxes** – A deduction is allowed for excise taxes that are ordinary and necessary expenses of carrying on a business. Taxpayers who owe excise taxes are required to file a **quarterly Form 720 Federal Excise Tax Return**. The person who receives payment for these items is responsible for collection and payment of the tax. Items subject to excise taxes include:
  1. Fuel taxes

2. Environmental taxes

3. Communications and air transportation taxes

4. Manufacturers taxes

5. Retail tax on heavy trucks, trailers, and tractors

6. Ship passenger taxes

7. Foreign insurance taxes

8. Obligations not in registered form

- **Heavy highway use vehicle tax** – The tax applies to highway motor vehicles with a taxable gross weight of 55,000 pounds or more. Vans, pickup trucks, panel trucks, and similar trucks generally are not subject to this tax. The taxpayer who acquires the vehicle for use must report and pay the tax monthly on **Form 2290,** separate from the other excise taxes. A taxpayer may receive a credit or request the suspension of this tax if the vehicle is driven less than 5,000 miles (7,500 if an agricultural vehicle) during a one-month tax period.

MISCELLANEOUS EXPENSES

Business taxpayers may deduct certain expenses that relate directly to the conduct of business as Miscellaneous Expenses. These expenses include the following:

- Advertising
- Expenses for operation of vehicles used in business
- Credit card fees
- Franchise fees
- Internet-related expenses
- Legal and professional fees
- Tax preparation fees
- License and regulatory fees
- Costs of moving machinery
- Penalties paid for late performance or nonperformance of a contract
- Repairs
- Supplies and materials
- Utilities, and telephone

NONDEDUCTIBLE BUSINESS EXPENSES

Not all business expenses are deductible. The following are examples of nondeductible expenses:

- Anticipated liabilities
- Bribes and kickbacks
- Charitable contributions (except for C corporation, all others pass through and claim on personal return)
- 100% of entertainment expenses
- 50% of business meals
- Lobbying expenses
- Political contributions
- Penalties or fines for violation of the law
- Demolition expenses

• Club dues and membership fees incurred for any club organized for business, pleasure, recreation, or any other social purpose. Certain exceptions are made for chambers of commerce, boards of trade, business leagues, professional associations, and trade associations.

EMPLOYEE COMPENSATION

TEST FOR DEDUCTING PAY

The employer may deduct employee pay that is an ordinary and necessary expense, provided it is both reasonable and for services performed.

> **EXCEPTION:** The otherwise allowable deduction for compensation (including commissions and performance-based compensation) with respect to a *covered employee* of a **publicly held corporation** is limited to no more than **$1 million** per year.
>
> The definition of covered employee includes both the **Principal Executive Officer** (PEO) and the **Principal Financial Officer** (PFO) and the **three most highly compensated officers** for the taxable year (other than the PEO and PFO) who are required to be reported on the company's proxy statement for the taxable year (if such a statement is necessary).
>
> Further, an individual is a covered employee if the individual holds one of these positions at any time during the taxable year. An individual remains a covered employee with respect to compensation otherwise deductible for subsequent years, including for years during which the individual is no longer employed by the corporation and years after the individual has died.

Wages subject to federal employment taxes generally include all payments to an employee for services performed. Payment may be in cash or in other forms. Wages include salaries, vacation pay, bonuses, commissions, and fringe benefits.

EMPLOYEE BUSINESS EXPENSE REIMBURSEMENTS

A reimbursement or allowance arrangement is a system by which an employer pays the advances, reimbursements, and charges for employees' business expenses. How the employer reports a payment depends on whether the employer has an *accountable* or a *non-accountable plan*. If a single payment includes both wages and an expense reimbursement, the employer must specify the amount of the reimbursement. These rules apply to all ordinary and necessary employee business expenses that would otherwise qualify for a deduction by the employee.

• **Accountable plan** – Amounts paid under an *accountable plan* are not **wages** and are not subject to the withholding and payment of FICA, FUTA, and income taxes. An *accountable plan* reimbursement or allowance arrangement must meet all three of the following rules:

1. The employee must pay or incur deductible expenses while performing services as an employee. The reimbursement or advance must be paid for the expense and must not be an amount that would have otherwise been paid by the employee.
2. The employee must substantiate these expenses to the employer within a reasonable period.
3. The employee must return any unsubstantiated expenses within a reasonable period.

> **EXAMPLE:** Jade learns that she must attend a conference for her employer. She charges the cost of her hotel and airline tickets to her personal credit card. During her trip, she incurs various meals and expenses related to her job. When she returns, she submits her receipts to her employer who reimburses her for her business-

related costs. Her employer reimburses her for expenses on her next check but does not withhold or pay any taxes on the amount of the reimbursement.

- **Reasonable period of time** – The definition of a reasonable period of time depends on the facts and circumstances of your situation. However, regardless of the facts and circumstances of the situation, actions that take place within the times specified in the following list will be treated as taking place within a reasonable period of time.
  1. The employee receives an advance within 30 days of the time of the expense.
  2. The employee adequately accounts for expenses within 60 days after they were paid or incurred.
  3. The employee returns any excess reimbursement within 120 days after the expense was paid or incurred.
  4. The employee is given a periodic statement (at least quarterly) that asks him to either return or adequately account for outstanding advances and the employee complies within 120 days of the statement.
- **Nonaccountable plan** – Payments to an employee for travel and other necessary expenses of the business under a nonaccountable plan are **wages** and are treated as supplemental wages and subject to the withholding and payment of FICA, FUTA, and income taxes. The payments are treated as paid under a nonaccountable plan if:
  1. An employee is not required to, or does not, substantiate expenses to the employer with receipts or other documentation,
  2. The employer advances an amount to the employee for business expenses, and the employee is not required to, or does not, return in a timely manner any amount not used for business expenses,
  3. The employer advances or pays an amount to the employee regardless of whether the employer reasonably expects the employee to incur business expenses related to the business, or
  4. The employer pays a reimbursement that he would have otherwise paid as wages.

  TIP: Under the TCJA employee expenses are no longer deductible on an individual income tax return. Reimbursements under a nonaccountable plan are therefore less desirable from the employee's perspective.
- **Per diem or other fixed allowance** – An employer may reimburse employees by travel days, miles, or other fixed allowance. In these cases, the employee is considered to have accounted to the employer if the reimbursement does not exceed rates established by the federal government. The standard mileage rate for 2020 is **57.5 cents per mile.**

WAGES NOT PAID IN MONEY

If in the course of business, an employer pays employees in a medium that is neither cash nor a readily negotiable instrument, such as a check, the employer has paid them "in kind." Payments in kind may be in the form of goods, lodging, food, clothing, or services. Generally, the FMV of such payments at the time that the employer provides them is subject to employment taxes and withholding. If the property is a capital asset, the difference between the FMV and the adjusted basis of the property is taxable income (capital gain) to the business.

MOVING EXPENSES

Nonqualified moving expense reimbursements or payments are includible in an employee's gross income and are subject to employment taxes and withholding.

Qualified moving expense reimbursements are excluded from an employee's gross income. Qualified moving expenses are defined as any amount received (directly or indirectly) from an employer as payment for (or reimbursement of) expenses which would be deductible as moving expenses if directly paid or incurred by the employee. However, any such amount actually deducted by the individual is not eligible for this exclusion.

The TCJA **repeals the exclusion of qualified moving expense reimbursements** from gross income and wages (except for members of the Armed Forces) for taxable years beginning after December 31, 2017, and before January 1, 2026. All moving expenses paid or reimbursed for taxable years 2018 through 2025, will be taxable to the employee (except for members of the Armed Forces) and subject to tax withholding.

The TCJA also **suspends the employee's deduction for moving expenses** (except for members of the Armed Forces) for taxable years 2018 through 2025. Employee (except for members of the Armed Forces) moving expenses for taxable years 2018 through 2025, are not deductible as an above the line deduction on the employee's individual income tax return.

DE MINIMIS MEALS

The employer may exclude from wages any meal or meal money provided to an employee if it has so little value (taking into account how frequently the employer provides meals to employees) that accounting for it would be unreasonable or administratively impracticable. The exclusion applies, for example, to the following items:

- Coffee, doughnuts, or soft drinks
- Occasional meals or meal money provided to enable an employee to work overtime (does not apply to meal money figured on the basis of hours worked)
- Occasional parties or picnics for employees and their guests

This exclusion also applies to meals provided at an employer-operated eating facility for employees if the annual revenue from the facility equals or exceeds the direct costs of the facility. If food or beverages furnished to employees qualify as a de minimis benefit, employers may deduct their full cost.

MEALS ON BUSINESS PREMISES

The de minimis meals exclusion also applies to meals provided at an employer-operated eating facility for employees if the annual revenue from the facility equals or exceeds the direct operating costs of the facility.

The value of meals provided by the employer, furnished on the business premises, for the **employer's convenience** are generally <u>not</u> taxable income and are <u>not</u> subject to income tax withholding, FICA, or FUTA taxes. This exclusion does not apply if employees may choose additional pay instead of meals.

- **Food service employees** – Meals furnished to a restaurant or other food service employee during, or immediately before or after, his shift are furnished for employer's convenience.
- **Employees available for emergency calls** – Meals furnished during working hours so an employee will be available for emergency calls during the meal period are furnished for employer's convenience. Employers must have a reasonable expectation for calls to occur.

TCJA: For amounts incurred or paid after 2017 and before 2026, the **50% limit on deductions** for food or beverage expenses also applies to food or beverage expenses excludable from employee income as a de minimis fringe benefit. However, food or beverage expenses related to employee recreation, such as holiday parties or annual picnics, aren't subject to the 50% limit on deductions when made primarily for the benefit of your employees other than employees who are officers, shareholders or other owners who own a 10% or greater interest in your business, or other highly compensated employees. **While the business deduction may be limited, the rules that allow the taxpayer to exclude certain de minimis meals and meals on the business premises from the employee's wages still apply.**

TIP: The *Consolidated Appropriations Act, 2021* provides a 100% deduction for business food or beverages provided by a restaurant in 2021 and 2022. Keep in mind, exams prior to May 1, 2022 test the 2020 tax year so this temporary rule should not appear on earlier exams.

LODGING ON BUSINESS PREMISES

Employers may exclude the value of lodging from wages if it meets the following tests:

- It is furnished on employer's business premises
- It is furnished for employer's convenience
- The employee must accept it as a condition of employment

Different tests may apply to lodging furnished by educational institutions. The exclusion does not apply if the employee can choose to receive additional pay instead of lodging.

HEALTH INSURANCE PLANS

If the employer pays the cost of an accident or health insurance plan for company employees, including an employee's spouse and dependents, the payments are not wages and are not subject to FICA and FUTA taxes, or federal income tax withholding. Under the recently enacted *Affordable Care Act*, health coverage provided for children of employees who are under age 27 is now generally tax-free to the employee. Generally, this exclusion also applies to qualified long-term care insurance contracts. For income tax withholding include the value of health insurance benefits in the wages of S corporation employees who own more than 2% of the S corporation (2% shareholders). For FICA and FUTA tax purposes, exclude the health insurance benefits from the wages only for employees and their dependents or for a class or classes of employees and their dependents.

EMPLOYER RETIREMENT PLAN CONTRIBUTIONS

Eligible employer contributions to retirement plans are deductible by the employer and are not gross income for the employee.

HEALTH SAVINGS ACCOUNTS AND MEDICAL SAVINGS ACCOUNTS

Employer contributions to an employee's Health Savings Account (HSA) or Archer medical savings account (MSA) are not subject to FICA or FUTA taxes, or federal income tax withholding if it is reasonable to believe at the time of the contributions that they will be excludable from the income of the employee. To the extent that it is not reasonable to believe that they will be excludable, the contributions are subject to these taxes. Employee contributions to HSAs or MSAs through a payroll deduction plan must be included in wages and are subject to FICA, FUTA, and income tax withholding. However, HSA contributions made under a salary reduction arrangement in a *Section 125-cafeteria plan* are not **wages** and are not **subject to employment taxes or withholding**.

CAFETERIA PLAN

A cafeteria plan is a separate written plan maintained by an employer for employees that meets the specific requirements of and regulations of section 125 of the Internal Revenue Code. It provides participants an opportunity to receive certain benefits on a pretax basis. Participants in a cafeteria plan must be permitted to choose among at least one taxable benefit (such as cash) and one qualified benefit.

A qualified benefit is a benefit that does not defer compensation and is excludable from an employee's gross income under a specific provision of the Code, without being subject to the principles of constructive receipt. Qualified benefits include the following:

- Accident and health benefits (but not Archer medical savings accounts or long-term care insurance)
- Adoption assistance
- Dependent care assistance

- Group-term life insurance coverage
- Health savings accounts, including distributions to pay long-term care services
- The written plan must specifically describe all benefits and establish rules for eligibility and elections.

A section 125 plan is the only means by which an employer can offer employees a choice between taxable and nontaxable benefits without the choice causing the benefits to become taxable. A plan offering only a choice between taxable benefits is not a section 125 plan.

MEDICAL CARE REIMBURSEMENTS

Generally, medical care reimbursements paid to employees under an employer's self-insured reimbursement plan are <u>not</u> **wages** and are <u>not</u> **subject to employment taxes or withholding**.

FRINGE BENEFITS

Employers generally <u>must</u> **include fringe benefits in an employee's gross income**. The benefits are subject to income tax withholding and employment taxes. Fringe benefits include employer-provided cars or aircraft flights, free or discounted commercial flights, vacations, discounts on property or services, memberships in country clubs or other social clubs, and tickets to entertainment or sporting events. In general, the amount that the employer must include is the amount by which the fair market value of the benefits is more than the sum of what the employee paid for it plus any amount that the law excludes.

NON-TAXABLE FRINGE BENEFITS

The following fringe benefits are not taxable (or are minimally taxable, as noted below):

- Services provided to employees at no additional cost to the employer.
- Qualified employee discounts.
- *Working condition fringes* of property or services that the employee could deduct as a business expense if the employee had paid for it. Examples include a company car for business use, subscriptions to business magazines, and the value of an employer-provided cell phone, provided primarily for noncompensatory business reasons.
- *Holiday gifts* – If an employer gives employees turkeys, hams, or other items of nominal value at Christmas or other holidays, the value of the gift should not be included in the employees' wages. However, if the employer gives an employee cash, gift certificates, or similar items that may easily be exchanged for cash, the employer should include the value of that gift as extra salary or wages to the employee, regardless of the amount involved.
- The use of on-premises athletic facilities, if substantially <u>all</u> of the use is by employees, their spouses, and their dependent children.
- A qualified tuition reduction an educational organization provides to employees for education.
- Certain *minimal value fringes* (including an occasional cab ride when an employee must work overtime, local transportation benefits provided because of unsafe conditions and unusual circumstances, and meals that the employer provides at eating places that the employer runs for the employees if the meals are not furnished at below cost).
- *Transportation* – Employer-provided qualified transportation fringe benefits are excluded from employee wages, within limits. Qualified transportation fringe benefits include the following for 2020 (and 2021):
  1. Transit passes and commuter highway vehicle transportation – Up to $270 per month for combined commuter highway vehicle transportation and transit passes.
  2. Qualified parking – Up to $270 per month for qualified parking.

TCJA: For tax years beginning after December 31, 2017, the act suspends the exclusion from gross income and wages for qualified bicycle commuting reimbursements.

TCJA: The TCJA also **disallows a deduction** for any expense incurred for providing any transportation fringe, or any payment or reimbursement, for commuting between the employee's residence and place of employment, except as necessary for **ensuring the safety** of an employee.

AWARDS

Generally, if tangible personal property is received (other than cash, a gift certificate, or an equivalent item) as an award for length of service or safety achievement, its value may be excluded from the taxpayer's income.

The Tax Cuts and Jobs Act adds a definition of "tangible personal property" that may be considered a deductible employee achievement award. It provides that tangible personal property shall not include cash, cash equivalents, gift cards, gift coupons or gift certificates (other than arrangements conferring only the right to select and receive tangible personal property from a limited array of such items preselected or preapproved by the employer), or vacations, meals, lodging, tickets to theater or sporting events, stocks, bonds, other securities, and other similar items.

- **Achievement awards** – Tangible personal property that meets all the following requirements:
  1. The employer gives the award to an employee for length of service or safety achievement.
  2. The employer gives the award as part of a meaningful presentation.
  3. The employer gives the award under conditions that do not create a significant likelihood of disguised pay.
- **Length-of-service award** – An award where either of the following applies:
  1. The employee receives the award after five years of employment.
  2. The employee did not receive another length-of-service award (other than one of very small value) during the same year or in any of the prior four years.
- **Safety achievement award** – An award for safety achievement will qualify unless:
  1. Given to a manager, administrator, clerical employee, or other professional employees
  2. During the tax year, more than 10% of employees, excluding those listed in (1), have already received a safety achievement award (other than one of very small value)
- The deduction for awards given to any one employee during the tax year is limited to:
  1. $400 for awards that are not qualified plan awards, or
  2. $1,600 for all awards, whether or not qualified plan awards

A *qualified plan award* is an achievement award given as part of an established written plan or program that does not favor highly compensated employees as to eligibility or benefits. A highly compensated employee for 2020 (and 2021) is an employee who meets either of the following tests:

- The employee was a 5% owner at any time during the year or the preceding year.
- The employee received more than $130,000 in pay for the preceding year.

EXAMPLE: Ben Green received three employee achievement awards during the year: a nonqualified plan award of a watch valued at $250, and two qualified plan awards of a stereo valued at $1,000 and a set of golf clubs valued at $500. Assuming that the requirements for qualified plan awards are otherwise satisfied, each award by itself would be excluded from income. However, because the $1,750 total value of the awards is more than $1,600, Ben must include $150 ($1,750 − $1,600) in his income.

GENERAL BUSINESS CREDITS

OVERVIEW OF FORM 3800

Taxpayers group most available business credits into a *general business credit*, and report on *Form 3800*. The general business credit for the year consists of any carryforward of business credits from prior years plus the total current year business credits. In addition, the general business credit for the current year may increase later by the carryback of business credits from later years.

> The general business credit is <u>not</u> refundable. A taxpayer can only subtract the credit directly from tax liability. The general business credit cannot reduce tax liability <u>below</u> the *tentative minimum tax* <u>or</u> 25% of the regular tax in excess of $25,000, whichever is greater. Any unused credit may be **carried back one year then forward for up to 20 years**.

The following credits are part of the general business credit (** indicates common topic on past exams):

- **Alternative fuel vehicle refueling property** – This credit applies to the cost of any qualified fuel vehicle refueling property placed in service during the business's tax year.

- **Alternative motor vehicle credit ** – Unless otherwise indicated, the maximum tentative credit is based on year, make, model, and type of <u>new</u> qualifying alternative motor vehicle purchased, which may be a qualified fuel cell vehicle or a qualified plug-in electric drive motor vehicle.

- **Biodiesel and renewable diesel fuels credit** – This credit applies to certain fuels sold or used in a business. The amount of credit that the taxpayer can claim depends on the type of eligible fuels involved and how many gallons of each the taxpayer sold or used.

- **Biofuel Producer credit** – This credit is for producers of certain biofuels. The credit amount will vary based on the number of gallons and type(s) of fuels involved.

- **Carbon oxide sequestration credit** – This credit is for carbon oxide, which is captured at a qualified facility and disposed of in a secure geological storage or used in a qualified enhanced oil or natural gas recovery project.

- **Credit for employer Social Security and Medicare taxes paid on certain employee tips** – This credit is generally equal to the employer's portion of Social Security and Medicare taxes paid on tips received by employees of a food and beverage establishment where tipping is customary.

- **Credit for employer differential wage payments** – This credit provides certain small businesses with an incentive to continue to pay wages to an employee performing services on active duty in the uniformed services of the United States for a period of more than 30 days.

- **Credit for employer-provided childcare facilities and services ** – The credit is 25% of the qualified childcare facility expenditures <u>plus</u> 10% of the qualified child care resource and referral expenditures paid or incurred during the tax year. The credit limit is $150,000 per year.

- **Credit for increasing research activities ** – This credit is designed to encourage businesses to increase the amounts they spend on research and experimental activities, including energy research. The regular credit is 20% of the **increase** in research activities.

- **Credit for small employer health insurance premiums** – The credit is generally **50% of premiums** paid by the employer. The employer must have fewer than 25 full-time equivalent employees (FTEs) for the tax year and pay average annual wages for the tax year of <u>less</u> than **$56,000 per FTE** in 2020. The employer must be required under a qualifying arrangement to pay a uniform percentage (not less than 50%) of the premium cost for each enrolled employee's health insurance coverage.

- **Credit for small employer pension plan start-up costs **** – This credit applies to pension plan start-up costs of a new qualified defined benefit or defined contribution plan (including a 401(k) plan), SIMPLE plan, or simplified employee pension. The credit equals 50% of the startup costs paid or incurred during the tax year to establish and administer the plan and educate employees about the plan, up to a maximum of **$5,000** per year. The credit is available for each of the first three years of the plan. Taxpayers can choose to start claiming the credit in the tax year prior to the tax year in which the plan becomes effective.

   TIP: The Secure Act of 2019 increased the credit from $500 to a maximum of **$5,000 per year in 2020**.

- **Disabled access credit **** – This credit is for an eligible small business that pays or incurs expenses to provide access to persons who have disabilities. The credit is 50% of the first $10,000.

- **Distilled spirits credit** – This credit is available to distillers and importers of distilled spirits and eligible wholesalers of distilled spirits.

- **Empowerment zone employment credit** – This credit is for employers who have employees in and engage in business in an empowerment zone for which the credit is available. For tax years that include December 31, 2020, the credit is 20% of the employer's qualified wages (up to $15,000) paid or incurred during calendar year 2020 on behalf of qualified empowerment zone employees.

- **Energy efficient home credit** – This credit is available for eligible contractors of certain homes sold for use as a residence. The allowable credit is $2,000 for each home meeting the 50% energy efficient standard, and for those that meet the 30% energy efficient standard, the allowable credit is $1,000.

- **Indian employment credit** – This credit applies to qualified wages and health insurance costs paid or incurred for qualified (American Indian) employees. Credit is up to 20% of expenses.

- **Investment credit **** – The investment credit is the total of the following credits:
   1. Rehabilitation credit (**20%** if a certified historic structure)
   2. Energy credit
   3. Qualifying advanced coal project credit
   4. Qualifying gasification project credit
   5. Qualifying advanced energy project credits

- **Low sulfur diesel fuel production credit** – This credit is for the production of low sulfur diesel by a qualified small business. The credit generally is 5 cents for every gallon of low sulfur diesel fuel produced by a qualified small business refiner during the tax year.

- **Low-income housing credit** – This credit generally applies to each new qualified low-income building placed in service after 1986. Generally, it is taken over a 10-year credit period.

- **New markets credit** –This credit is for qualified equity investments made in qualified community development entities. The primary mission is serving or providing investment capital, for low-income communities or persons.

- **Nonconventional source fuel credit** (carryforward only) – This credit is allowed for qualified coke or coke gas produced and sold to an unrelated person during the tax year.

- **Orphan drug credit**– This credit applies to qualified expenses incurred in testing certain drugs for rare diseases and conditions. The credit is 50% of qualified clinical testing expenses paid or incurred during the tax year.

- **Qualified railroad track maintenance credit** – This credit applies to certain regional and switching railroads that may be able to claim a credit for expenses made to upgrade their railroad tracks (including roadbed, bridges, and related track structures).

- **Renewable electricity, refined coal, and Indian coal production credit** – This credit is for the sale of electricity, refined coal, or Indian coal produced in the United States or U.S. possessions from qualified energy resources at a qualified facility.

- **Work opportunity credit **** – This credit is for qualified first- or second-year wages paid to *targeted group* employees during the tax year. In general, the amount of **qualified wages** that may be taken into account for an employee is **limited to $6,000**, except for certain targeted groups. These employees have a high unemployment rate or other special employment needs. The business does not have to be in an empowerment zone, renewal community, or rural renewal county to qualify for this credit. The credit is 25% of qualified first-year wages of employees working more than 120 but less than 400 hours in the year, plus 40% of qualified first-year wages for employees working more than 400 hours in the year, plus 50% of qualified second-year wages of employees certified as long-term family assistance recipients. The *Consolidated Appropriations Act, 2021* extends the WOTC through 2025.

An employee is a member of a targeted group if he is a:

1. Qualified long-term unemployment recipient,
2. Long-term family assistance recipient,
3. Qualified recipient of Temporary Assistance for Needy Families (TANF),
4. Qualified veteran,
5. Qualified ex-felon,
6. Designated community resident (i.e., lives in empowerment zones),
7. Vocational rehabilitation referral,
8. Summer youth employee,
9. SNAP recipient, or
10. SSI recipient.

LOSS LIMITATIONS

A taxpayer may not take a deduction against ordinary income for a loss if the loss is in *excess of basis*, if the amount is not *at-risk*, or if the loss is the result of a *passive activity*.

There are four potential limitations on S corporation and partnership losses. These limitations, in the order in which they apply, are the *basis rules*, the *at-risk limitations*, the *passive activity limitations,* and the *excess business loss limitations* (**suspended** for 2018, 2019, and 2020 by the *CARES Act*).

CARES ACT UPDATE: The TCJA introduced the *excess business loss* limitation by creating a provision, section 461(l), for taxable years beginning after 2017 and before 2026. However, the CARES Act **retroactively suspends** the provision by amending section 461(l) to restrict the limitation on excess business losses of noncorporate taxpayers to tax years beginning after 2020 and before 2026. The CARES Act **repealed** the excess business loss limitation for tax years 2018, 2019, and 2020. A taxpayer who filed a return for tax years 2018, 2019, or 2020 subject to the limitation can file an amended return to claim a refund.

BASIS RULES

Generally, a taxpayer may not claim a loss greater than the adjusted basis of his S corporation or partnership interest. The taxpayer may carry forward disallowed losses and deductions due to the basis limit **indefinitely** and deduct them subject to the basis limit for that year.

AT-RISK LIMITS

Generally, any loss from an activity subject to the at-risk rules is allowed <u>only</u> to the extent of the total amount at risk in the activity at the end of the tax year. Losses disallowed because of the at-risk limits are deductions from the **same activity** in the next tax year. The at-risk rules generally limit the amount of loss and other deductions to the amount the taxpayer could actually lose in the activity.

The amount at-risk refers to the money and adjusted basis of property contributed to the activity, plus amounts borrowed for use in the activity if the taxpayer is personally liable for repayment or pledges other property (other than property used in the activity) as security for the loan.

Generally, a taxpayer is <u>not</u> **at risk** for amounts such as the following:

- Nonrecourse loans that are <u>not</u> secured by the taxpayer's own property
- Cash, property, or borrowed amounts used in the activity that are **protected against loss** by a guarantee, stop-loss agreement, or other similar arrangements (excluding casualty insurance and insurance against tort liability)
- Amounts borrowed for use in the activity from a person (or relative of that person) that has an interest in the activity, other than as a creditor

> **EXAMPLE:** Jim contributes $50,000 to a partnership that limits his liability. He also personally guarantees a recourse loan of $25,000 made to the partnership to purchase equipment. He is "at risk" for $75,000.

PASSIVE ACTIVITIES

A taxpayer with a loss from a passive activity can offset the loss with income from other passive activities. Generally, a taxpayer is **unable to deduct a loss from a passive activity.** Carry forward any excess *passive activity loss (PAL)* or credit to the next tax year and use to offset only passive income.

The passive activity rules apply to:

- Individuals
- Estates
- Trusts (other than grantor trusts)
- Personal service corporations
- Closely held corporations

TIP: Even though the rules don't apply to grantor trusts, partnerships, and S corporations directly, they do apply to the owners of these entities.

For a **closely held corporation**, the passive activity loss is the excess of passive activity deductions over the sum of passive activity gross income <u>and</u> **net active income**.

There are two kinds of passive activities:

- Business activities in which the taxpayer does not *materially* participate during the year
- Rental activities (even with material participation, unless the taxpayer is a real estate professional)

MATERIAL PARTICIPATION

The IRS will consider participation to be material if the taxpayer can satisfy any of the following tests:

- The taxpayer participated in the activity for **more than 500** hours during the tax year.

- The taxpayer's participation was substantially **all of the participation** in the activity of all individuals for the tax year, including the participation of individuals who did not own any interest in the activity.
- The taxpayer participated in the activity for **more than 100** hours during the tax year, and at least as much as <u>any</u> other individual for the year.

RENTAL REAL ESTATE PROFESSIONAL EXCEPTION

A loss from rental real estate may offset ordinary income if under one of the following exceptions:

- A *Real Estate Professional* may deduct losses against ordinary income, when:
  1. More than half of work is involved in real property trades or businesses in which the person *materially participates*, and
  2. More than **750 hours** of material participation is in real property trades or businesses.
- If rental losses are not more than **$25,000**, and the taxpayer or spouse actively participates in the rental activity, the passive activity limits may not apply. *Active participation* is a less stringent standard than material participation. Active participation includes management decisions such as approving tenants, deciding rental terms, approving expenditures, etc.
  1. If a taxpayer (S or MFJ) has modified adjusted gross income (MAGI) of $100,000 or less, the loss is deductible up to the $25,000 special allowance. If MAGI is more than $100,000, the $25,000 special allowance is limited to 50% of the difference between $150,000 and MAGI. There is no allowance if MAGI is more than **$150,000**.

> If a taxpayer or spouse actively participated in a passive rental real estate activity, they may be able to **deduct up to $25,000** of loss from the activity from their nonpassive income. This special allowance is an exception to the general rule disallowing losses in excess of income from passive activities.

NOT-FOR-PROFIT ACTIVITIES

If the intention of the business is not to make a profit, there is a limit on the deductions allowed. The taxpayer cannot use a loss from the activity to offset other income. Hobby, sport, or recreation activities fall under this limit. The limit on not-for-profit losses applies to individuals, partnerships, estates, trusts, and S corporations. It does not apply to corporations other than S corporations. If a partnership or S corporation carries on a not-for-profit activity, these limits apply at the partnership or S corporation level. They are reflected in the individual shareholder's or partner's distributive shares.

> An activity is **presumed carried on for profit** if it:
>
> - Produced a profit in at least **three of the last five** tax years, including the current year, or
> - Produced a profit in at least two of the last seven tax years, including the current year if the activities consist primarily of breeding, training, showing, or racing horses

LIMIT ON DEDUCTIONS

If the taxpayer does <u>not</u> carry on the activity for profit, deductions occur in the following order and only to the extent stated in the three categories.

- **Category 1** – First, deductions a taxpayer can take for personal as well as for business activities are allowed in full. For individuals, all nonbusiness deductions, such as those for home mortgage interest, taxes, and casualty losses, may also be deducted on the appropriate lines of Schedule A (Form 1040).

- **Category 2** – Next, deduct expenses that would be allowable if the activity were to be engaged in for profit. For example, rent, labor, wages, travel, transportation, etc. These expenses are limited to the amount of gross income less the expenses in Category 1.

- **Category 3** – Then, allow deductions which lead to basis adjustments (e.g. depreciation, amortization and the portion of casualty losses that is not deductible in Category 1). These expenses are limited to the amount of gross income from the activity less the expenses in Categories 1 and 2. If there is any gross income remaining after Category 1 and 2 items, the depreciation must be allocated to each depreciable asset.

For individuals, the allowed expenses are reported as itemized deductions on Schedule A but keep in mind that a taxpayer can no longer claim any miscellaneous itemized deductions that are subject to the 2%-of-adjusted-gross-income limitation.

AFFORDABLE CARE ACT

IMPORTANT TERMS

- **Applicable Large Employer (ALE)** – An ALE is, for a particular calendar year, any single employer, or group of employers treated as an Aggregated ALE Group, that employed an average of at least **50 full-time employees** (including full-time equivalent employees) on business days during the preceding calendar year. All types of employers can be ALEs, including tax-exempt organizations and government entities.

- **Full-time Employee** – An employee who is employed an average of at least **30 hours** of service per week with the employer for a calendar month. For this purpose, 130 service hours in a calendar month is treated as the monthly equivalent of at least 30 hours per week.

- **Full-time employee equivalent (FTE)** – Add up the total hours of service for which the employer pays wages to employees during the year (but not more than 2,080 hours for any employee), and divide that amount by 2,080. If the result is not a whole number, round to the next lowest whole number. (If the result is less than one, however, round up to one FTE.)

EMPLOYER SHARED RESPONSIBILITY PROVISION

Under the Affordable Care Act's employer shared responsibility provisions, certain employers (called applicable large employers or ALEs) must either offer minimum essential coverage that is "affordable" and that provides "minimum value" to their full-time employees (and their dependents), or potentially make an employer shared responsibility payment to the IRS. The employer shared responsibility provisions are sometimes referred to as "the employer mandate" or "the pay or play provisions."

> The vast majority of employers fall below the ALE threshold of 50 full-time employees and are <u>not</u> subject to the employer shared responsibility provisions.

An ALE member may choose either to offer affordable minimum essential coverage that provides minimum value to its full-time employees (and their dependents) or potentially owe an employer shared responsibility payment to the IRS. Depending on its decisions about offering minimum essential coverage to its full-time employees and their dependents, an ALE member may be subject to one of two potential employer shared responsibility payments, but not both, and the two types of payments are calculated differently:

- ALE **does <u>not</u> offer minimum essential coverage** to at least **95 percent** of its full-time employees (and their dependents) – On an annual basis, this payment is equal to **$2,570** (in 2020, as adjusted for inflation each year) for each full-time employee in the calendar year, with the first 30 employees excluded from the calculation. This calculation is based on all full-time employees (minus 30), including full-time employees who have minimum essential coverage under the employer's plan or from another source.

- ALE **does offer minimum essential coverage** to at least **95 percent** of its full-time employees (and their dependents) – On an annual basis, this payment is equal to **$3,860** (in 2020, as adjusted for inflation each year) but only for each full-time employee who receives the premium tax credit. The total payment in this instance cannot exceed the amount the employer would have owed had the employer not offered minimum essential coverage to at least 95 percent of its full-time employees (and their dependents).

For either type of employer shared responsibility payment to apply to an ALE member, at least one full-time employee must receive the premium tax credit for purchasing coverage through the Marketplace.

ANNUAL REPORTING REQUIREMENT

ALEs must report to the IRS information about the health care coverage, if any, they offered to full-time employees. ALEs also must furnish to employees a statement that includes the same information provided to the IRS. Employees may use this information to determine whether, for each month of the calendar year, they may claim the premium tax credit on their individual income tax returns.

- **Form 1095-C, Employer-Provided Health Insurance Offer and Coverage** – Form 1095-C is filed and furnished to any employee of an ALE member who is a full-time employee for one or more months of the calendar. ALE Members must report that information for all twelve months of the calendar year for each employee.

Generally, you must file Forms 1094-C and 1095-C by February 28 if filing on paper (or March 31 if filing electronically) of the year following the calendar year to which the return relates.

Anyone required to file 250 or more information returns, must file them electronically. This requirement applies separately for each type of return and separately for each type of corrected return.

LESSON 3

Business Property

PROPERTY TYPES

Generally, the sale or trade of an asset will result in a *capital gain* or loss. The sale or trade of a non-capital asset will generally result in *ordinary gain* or loss. In some situations, part of the gain or loss may be a capital gain or loss and part may be an ordinary gain or loss. Determining the character of the resulting gain or loss depends on the classification of the property.

CAPITAL ASSETS

Rather than defining capital assets, the law provides a list of properties that are not capital assets:

- Intangibles such as a patent, invention, model or design (whether or not patented), secret formula or process, copyright, and a composition (literary, musical, or artistic) **created by the efforts of the taxpayer** or having a substituted or **transferred basis** from the taxpayer who created the property (or for whom the property was created).
- Supplies regularly used or consumed in the ordinary course of a taxpayer's trade or business
- Accounts or notes receivable acquired in the ordinary course of a trade or business for services rendered or from the sale of property held mainly for sale to customers
- Inventory or property held mainly for sale to customers or property that will physically become a part of the merchandise that is for sale to customers
- Depreciable property and real property (real estate) used in the taxpayer's trade or business

TIP: Use the acronym "I SAID" to help remember what is not a capital asset.

TIP: The TCJA amends section 1221(a)(3) for dispositions after 2017 adding to the list a patent, invention, model or design (whether or not patented), and a secret formula or process.

In general, ordinary income tax rates apply when selling assets other than capital assets. Capital assets receive preferential tax treatment. Taxpayers generally hold capital assets for business or investment purposes (for example, stocks or copyrights acquired for investment).

SECTION 1231 PROPERTY

Certain business property **held for more than 1 year** that is **used in the trade or business** and is either **depreciable property** or **real property** (including land) is classified as *Section 1231 property*.

TIP: Generally, property held for the production of rents or royalties is considered to be used in a trade or business.

Section 1231 also applies to the involuntary conversion (but not sale or exchange) of capital assets held for more than 1 year in connection with a trade or business or a transaction entered into for profit. This property does not need to be used in the business.

The following transactions result in gain or loss subject to section 1231 treatment:

- **Sales or exchanges of real property or depreciable personal property** – This property must be used in a trade or business and held longer than 1 year. Generally, property held for the production of rents or royalties is considered to be used in a trade or business. This property must also be either **real property** or of a kind that is **subject to depreciation** under section 167 of the Internal Revenue Code. Depreciable personal property includes amortizable section 197 intangibles.

- **Sales or exchanges of leaseholds** – The leasehold must be used in a trade or business and held longer than 1 year.
- **Sales or exchanges of cattle and horses** – The cattle and horses must be held for draft, breeding, dairy, or sporting purposes and held for 2 years or longer.
- **Sales or exchanges of other livestock** – This livestock does not include poultry. It must be held for draft, breeding, dairy, or sporting purposes and held for 1 year or longer.
- **Sales or exchanges of unharvested crops** – The crop and land must be sold, exchanged, or involuntarily converted at the same time and to the same person and the land must be held longer than 1 year. The taxpayer cannot keep any right or option to directly or indirectly reacquire the land (other than a right customarily incident to a mortgage or other security transaction). Growing crops sold with a lease on the land, though sold to the same person in the same transaction, are not included.
- **Cutting of timber or disposal of timber, coal, or iron ore** – The cutting or disposal must be treated as a sale, as described in chapter 2 under Timber and Coal and Iron Ore.
- **Condemnations** – The condemned property must have been held longer than 1 year. It must be business property or a capital asset held in connection with a trade or business or a transaction entered into for profit, such as investment property. It cannot be property held for personal use.
- **Casualties and thefts** – The casualty or theft must have affected business property, property held for the production of rents and royalties, or investment property (such as notes and bonds). The taxpayer must have held the property longer than 1 year. However, if casualty or theft losses are more than casualty or theft gains, neither the gains nor the losses are taken into account in the section 1231 computation.

TIP: Section 1231 property does <u>not</u> include property held mainly for sale to customers (**inventory**) and patents or **copyrights created** through the personal efforts of the taxpayer.

Section 1231 property receives special treatment when sold. All current year Section 1231 gains and losses are netted to determine if there is a net gain or loss. Net Section 1231 gain is taxed at favorable **long-term capital gain** rates while a loss is an **ordinary loss**.

EXCEPTION: A taxpayer with current year net Section 1231 gain must recapture Section 1231 losses claimed in the five prior years as ordinary gain before the capital gain rates apply.

In addition to having the character of Section 1231, any gain on property that is subject to the allowance for depreciation may <u>also</u> be subject to the recapture provisions of *Section 1245* or *Section 1250*.

SECTION 1245 RECAPTURE

Any property (other than real property) that is or has been subject to an allowance for depreciation or amortization is subject to *Section 1245 recapture* rules. The taxpayer recaptures a portion of the gain from the disposition of the property due to depreciation as ordinary income.

TIP: Section 1245 property does <u>not</u> include buildings and structural components. The term "building" includes a house, barn, warehouse, or garage. The term "structural component" includes walls, floors, windows, doors, central air conditioning systems, light fixtures, etc.

SECTION 1250 RECAPTURE

All real property that is subject to an allowance for depreciation and has <u>never</u> been Section 1245 property is subject to *Section 1250 recapture* rules. It includes leasehold of land or Section 1250 property subject to an allowance for depreciation. A fee simple interest in land is not included because it is not depreciable.

A **maximum tax rate of 25%** applies to depreciation up to the amount of **straight-line depreciation**. This portion is *unrecaptured Section 1250 gain*.

Any amount of *additional depreciation* is **taxed as ordinary income** and is recaptured as *Section 1250 gain*. Additional depreciation is the actual depreciation that is <u>more</u> than the depreciation figured using the straight-line method. If a taxpayer holds Section 1250 property for one year or less, all the depreciation is additional depreciation.

EXAMPLE: Christine is in the 35% tax bracket. She purchased a rental property several years ago for $100,000. She sells the property for $150,000. The depreciation taken under ACRS was $41,840, but if she had used the straight-line method, the depreciation would have been $37,970.

Total gain is $91,840 ($150,000 sales price – $100,000 purchase price + $41,840 depreciation taken).

Christine used a method of accelerated depreciation (ACRS) and has a Section 1250 gain. Section 1250 gain is $3,870 ($41,840 ACRS – $37,970 straight-line), the difference between ACRS depreciation taken and the straight-line depreciation method. Ordinary income tax rates apply to Section 1250 gain.

Unrecaptured Section 1250 gain is $37,970, the amount of straight-line depreciation taxed as a capital gain at a maximum 25% rate.

The remaining $50,000 gain ($91,840 total gain – $3,870 Section 1250 gain – $37,970 unrecaptured Section 1250 gain) is taxable as a long-term capital gain at a maximum rate of 20%.

DEPRECIATION

There are two basic types of property:

1. **Tangible property** – Is physical in nature. Includes land, structures, equipment, natural resources, etc. Tangible property is further divided into:
   - *Real property* – Real estate including land, houses, buildings, etc.
   - *Personal property* – Any tangible property other than real property
2. **Intangible property** – Does not have a physical presence. Includes computer software, patents, goodwill, stocks, and bonds.

Expenditures that do not have a useful life beyond one year are *expenses*, which are generally deductible in the year incurred. Property acquired with a useful life greater than one year or *improvements* that increase the value of the property, lengthen its life, or adapt it to a different use are *capital expenditures*. An item of capital expenditure is *capitalized* (added to capital), and the cost is systematically *recovered* (written off) each year, in various ways, depending on the type of property. Depreciation reduces the basis for figuring gain or loss on a later sale or exchange.

The methods for recovering the cost of an asset over its useful life include the following:

- **Depreciation** – For tangible income producing property, other than natural resources

- **Depletion** – For assets that diminish over time, such as oil, gas, and other natural resources
- **Amortization** – For intangible assets, such as patents and goodwill

The taxpayer recovers the cost of tangible income-producing property through yearly tax deductions by depreciating the property, that is, by deducting some of the cost each year on the tax return. Three basic factors determine how much depreciation the taxpayer may deduct:

- The basis in the property
- The recovery period for the property
- The depreciation method used

A taxpayer cannot simply deduct mortgages, principal payments, or the cost of furniture, fixtures, or equipment as an expense. The taxpayer may deduct depreciation <u>only</u> on the part of the property **used for a business or income-producing activity**. A taxpayer cannot depreciate personal-use property. Depreciation reduces the basis for figuring gain or loss on a later sale or exchange.

WHAT PROPERTY CAN BE DEPRECIATED

- Property may be depreciated if it meets <u>all</u> the following requirements:
  1. The taxpayer owns the property
  2. The taxpayer uses the property in business or income-producing activity (e.g., rental property)
  3. The property has a determinable useful life
  4. The taxpayer expects the property to last more than one year
- Certain property <u>cannot</u> be depreciated:
  1. Land (land preparation costs, such as landscaping costs are depreciable)
  2. Property placed in service and disposed of in the same year
  3. Equipment used to build capital improvements
  4. *Section 197 intangibles* – The following assets are Section 197 intangibles and must be amortized over 180 months:
     A. Goodwill
     B. Going concern value
     C. Workforce in place
     D. Business books and records, operating systems, or any other information base, including lists or other information concerning current or prospective customers
     E. A patent, copyright, formula, process, design, pattern, know-how, format, or similar item
     F. A customer-based intangible
     G. A supplier-based intangible
     H. Any item similar to items (C) through (G)
     I. A license, permit, or other right granted by a governmental unit or agency
     J. A covenant not to compete in connection with the acquisition of a business
     K. Any franchise, trademark, or trade name
     L. A contract for the use of, or a term interest in, any item in this list

A taxpayer cannot amortize any of the intangibles listed in items (A) through (H) that he creates rather than acquires unless he creates them in acquiring assets that make up a trade or business or a substantial part of a trade or business.

TIP: A taxpayer **cannot depreciate personal-use property**. The depreciation deduction is allowed <u>only</u> on the part of the property **used for a business or income-producing activity**. If the property is also used for personal use, that part <u>cannot</u> receive a deduction. A farmer can elect to claim 75% business use without records if using the vehicle in farming business most of the normal business day.

DEPRECIATION METHODS

Generally, a taxpayer must use the *Modified Accelerated Cost Recovery System (MACRS)* to depreciate residential rental property placed in service after 1986. MACRS consists of two systems that determine how property may be depreciated:

- **General Depreciation System (GDS)** – Generally, taxpayers must use GDS for property used in most rental activities. Recovery periods generally are shorter than under ADS.
- **Alternative Depreciation System (ADS)** – ADS uses the **straight-line** method of depreciation. A taxpayer electing to use ADS may not change the election, which applies to all property in the same class that is placed in service during the tax year of the election. However, the election applies on a property-by-property basis for residential rental property and nonresidential real property.

Taxpayers must continue to use the same depreciation method unless the IRS grants approval to change accounting methods. The methods under MACRS for depreciating property are as follows:

- **Straight-line depreciation** – Deduct equal amounts throughout the recovery period.
  1. A taxpayer <u>must</u> use the straight-line method and a mid-month convention for residential rental property. In the first year of claiming depreciation for residential rental property, take depreciation only for the number of months the property is in use.

> **EXAMPLE:** Saul purchases a $2,000 computer for his business that has a useful life of 5-years. He uses the computer exclusively for business. He can claim $400 in annual depreciation until he no longer has a basis in the computer. If he uses the half-year convention (discussed later), he claims $200 in the first year.

- **200% or 150% declining balance** – Allows for greater depreciation percentages in early years. Use the straight-line method in place of accelerated depreciation in the first tax year it provides an equal or larger deduction than either the 200% or 150% declining balance (DB) method.

Upon sale or other disposition, certain nonresidential real estate may be subject to **recapture of excess depreciation** *(un-recaptured Section 1250 gain)* if a method other than straight-line depreciation was used. The recaptured amount is the excess depreciation amount **above what would have been claimed using the straight-line method.**

RECOVERY PERIODS

Under regular MACRS (GDS), depreciable property generally falls into one of the following classes:

- **5-year property** – Computers and peripheral equipment, office machinery (typewriters, calculators, copiers, etc.), automobiles, light trucks, appliances, carpeting, furniture, etc., used in a residential rental real estate activity. Depreciation on automobiles and light trucks is limited. Taxpayers may use 200% or 150% DB.
- **7-year property** – Office furniture and fixtures (desks, file cabinets, etc.). This class also includes any property that does not have a class life and that has not been designated by law as being in any other class. Taxpayers may use 200% or 150% DB.
- **15-year property** – Roads, fences, and shrubbery. Taxpayers may use 150% DB.
- **20-year property** – Includes improvements such as utilities and sewers.

- **Residential rental property (27.5-year property)** – Real property that is a rental building or structure (including mobile homes) for which 80% or more of the gross rental income for the tax year is from dwelling units. It does not include a unit in a hotel, motel, inn, or other establishments where more than half of the units are used on a transient basis. Depreciate additions or improvements to the structure over the same period. In a case like this, the straight-line method is necessary along with a mid-month convention. For the first year, take depreciation only for the number of months the property was in use.

- **Non-residential real property (39-year property)** – Commercial buildings and structures. Includes Section 1250 property. Must use the straight-line method and mid-month convention.

CONVENTIONS

Depreciation begins when the taxpayer places the property in service for the production of income. Depreciation ends when either the taxpayer fully recovers the cost, or the property is retired from service, whichever happens first. Property is placed in service in a rental activity when it is ready and available for a specific use in that activity. Even if unused, it is in service when it is ready and available for its specific use. A *convention* is a method established under MACRS to set the beginning and end of the recovery period. The convention used determines the number of months that the taxpayer may claim as depreciation in the year the property was placed in service and in the year disposed. Use the mid-month convention for residential rental property and nonresidential real property. For all other property, use the half-year or mid-quarter convention, as appropriate.

- **Mid-month convention** – Use a mid-month convention for all residential rental property and nonresidential real property. Treat all property placed in service, or disposed of, during the month as placed in service, or disposed of, at the midpoint of that month.

- **Mid-quarter convention** – Use a mid-quarter convention if the mid-month convention does not apply and the total depreciable basis of MACRS property placed in service in the last three months of a tax year is more than 40% of the total basis of all such property placed into service during the year. For this convention, the MACRS property excludes nonresidential real property, residential rental property, and property placed in service and disposed of in the same year. Under this convention, treat all property placed in service, or disposed of, during any quarter of a tax year as placed in service, or disposed of, at the midpoint of the quarter.

- **Half-year convention** – Use the half-year convention if neither the mid-quarter convention nor the mid-month convention applies. Under this convention, treat all property placed into service, or disposed of, during a tax year as being placed into service, or disposed of, at the midpoint of that tax year. If this convention applies, the taxpayer may deduct a half year of depreciation for the first year and the last year that the taxpayer depreciates the property. The taxpayer may deduct a full year of depreciation for any other year during the recovery period.

TIP: The half-year convention applies to most transactions. Under this convention, all property transactions are considered to occur at the **midpoint of the year**.

SECTION 179 DEDUCTION

In 2020, the maximum deduction under Section 179 increases to **$1,040,000**, and the phaseout threshold amount increases to **$2,590,000** for qualifying property placed in service during the year.

The Section 179 deduction applies to tangible personal property such as machinery and equipment purchased from an **unrelated party** for use in a trade or business, and if the taxpayer elects, qualified real property.

Section 179 applies to both **new and used equipment**. If a taxpayer buys qualifying property with cash and a trade-in, its cost for purposes of the Section 179 deduction includes only the cash paid. This deduction is not allowed for property held for the production of income, such as rental property. Instead of depreciating property over time, a taxpayer may elect to claim as an expense up to **$1,040,000** in 2020.

EXCEPTION: You <u>cannot</u> claim a Section 179 deduction of more than **$25,900** of the cost of a sport utility vehicle (SUV) placed in service during 2020.

Section 179 deduction limits apply to <u>both</u> the partnership and its partners. The partnership determines its Section 179 deduction subject to the limits. It then allocates the deduction among its partners. The same is true for an S corporation and its shareholders.

The property must be placed in service during the tax year, and must be one of the following types of depreciable property:

- Tangible personal property
- Machinery and equipment
- Property contained in or attached to a building (not structural components), such as office equipment, refrigerators, grocery store counters, printing presses, testing equipment, and signs
- Gasoline storage tanks and pumps at retail service stations
- Livestock, including horses, cattle, hogs, sheep, goats, and mink and other fur-bearing animals
- Other tangible property (<u>except</u> buildings and their structural components) used as:
  1. An integral part of manufacturing, production, or extraction; or as an integral part of furnishing transportation, communications, electricity, gas, water, or sewage disposal services,
  2. A research facility used in connection with any of the activities in (1) above, or
  3. A facility used in any of the activities in (1) for the bulk storage of fungible commodities
- Single purpose agricultural (livestock) or horticultural structures
- Petroleum storage or distribution facilities (except buildings and their structural components)
- Off-the-shelf computer software

TCJA: For property placed in service in taxable years beginning after December 31, 2017, a provision expands the definition of qualified real property eligible for Section 179 expensing to include any of the following improvements to nonresidential real property—roofs, HVAC, fire protection and security systems.

A taxpayer may <u>not</u> claim a Section 179 deduction for land or land improvements, property leased to another taxpayer, and property used outside the United States.

REDUCED SECTION 179 DEDUCTION

Under certain conditions, the amount of the Section 179 deduction may be reduced or eliminated:

- If the cost of the qualifying Section 179 property placed in service in 2020 is **more than $2,590,000**, the taxpayer generally <u>must</u> reduce the dollar limit (but <u>not</u> below zero) by the amount of cost more than $2,590,000. If the cost of Section 179 property placed in service during 2020 is $3,630,000 or more, the taxpayer cannot take a Section 179 deduction.
- Married taxpayers who file separately in 2020 must combine all purchases as if they are filing jointly to determine the allowable Section 179 deduction; otherwise, the deduction is $520,000 each.
- The taxpayer <u>must</u> use the property **more than 50%** for business in the year placed in service. The Section 179 deduction is allowed only for the business use portion of the property. If the property is also for personal use, that part cannot receive a deduction. If the business use falls below 50% in future years, the taxpayer <u>must</u> include a portion of the Section 179 deduction in income (***Section 179 recapture***).

- Limitations apply to *listed property* (see listed property for details).

SPECIAL DEPRECIATION ALLOWANCE (BONUS DEPRECIATION)

A business taxpayer may take an additional **100% *special depreciation allowance***, often referred to as "bonus depreciation" on certain qualified property. The special depreciation allowance applies only for the first year the property is in service. The allowance is an additional deduction taken after any Section 179 expense deduction and before the taxpayer figures regular depreciation under MACRS. Qualified property includes tangible property depreciated in **20 years or less under MACRS.**

TCJA: The 100% special depreciation allowance now applies to both **new and used property.**

- For the 100% special depreciation allowance, the qualified property must be acquired and placed in service after September 27, 2017, and before January 1, 2023 (January 1, 2024, for longer production period property and certain aircraft).
- A taxpayer **may elect out** of the Section 168(k) additional first-year depreciation deduction with respect to any class of property that is qualified property placed in service during the taxable year.
- Limitations apply to *listed property* (see listed property for details).

LISTED PROPERTY

The listed property rules are designed to keep people from claiming tax deductions for the personal use of the property while claiming it is used in a trade or business.

Listed property is any of the following:

- Passenger automobiles (cars, trucks, vans, and SUVs) **weighing 6,000 pounds or less**
- Any other property used for transportation, unless it is an excepted vehicle
- Property generally used for entertainment, recreation, or amusement (including photographic, phonographic, communication, and video-recording equipment)

TIP: The TCJA removes computer or peripheral equipment from the definition of listed property.

A taxpayer can claim the Section 179 deduction and a special depreciation allowance (bonus depreciation) for listed property and depreciate listed property using GDS and a declining balance method if the property meets the business-use requirement. To meet this requirement, listed property must be **used predominantly for qualified business use (more than 50%** of its total use). If this requirement is not met, the following rules apply:

- Property not used predominantly for qualified business use during the year it is placed in service does not qualify for the *Section 179 deduction*.
- Property not used predominantly for qualified business use during the year it is placed in service does not qualify for a *special depreciation allowance*.
- Any depreciation deduction under MACRS for property not used predominantly for qualified business use during any year must be figured using the *straight-line method over the ADS recovery period*. This rule applies each year of the recovery period.
- *Excess depreciation* on property previously used predominantly for qualified business use must be *recaptured* (included in income) in the first year in which it is no longer used predominantly for qualified business use.

DEPRECIATION OF PASSENGER AUTOMOBILES

Section 280F(a) limits the annual cost recovery deduction with respect to certain **passenger automobiles** (cars, trucks, vans, and SUVs **weighing 6,000 pounds or less**). This limitation is commonly referred to as the *luxury automobile depreciation limitation* or the *Section 280F limitation*.

The depreciation limitations under Section 280F that apply to passenger automobiles placed in service in 2020, and for which the additional first-year depreciation deduction under Section 168(k) is not claimed (elected out), the maximum amount of allowable depreciation is:

- $10,100 for the first year,
- $16,100 for the second year,
- $9,700 for the third year, and
- $5,760 for each later taxable year in the recovery period.

These limitations are indexed for inflation.

Under Section 280F, the depreciation limitation increases by **$8,000** for the additional first-year depreciation deduction under Section 168(k) for passenger automobiles placed in service in 2020. With the **additional first-year depreciation** deduction under Section 168(k), the maximum amount of allowable depreciation for a vehicle is:

- $18,100 for the first year,
- $16,100 for the second year,
- $9,700 for the third year, and
- $5,760 for each later taxable year in the recovery period.

These limits assume that the vehicle is used 100% for business. If the use of the vehicle is not 100% for business, these limits are reduced and the deductible depreciation is even less. The reduction is based on the percentage used for business. If the vehicle is used 75% for business, the allowable depreciation is 75% of the limited amount. If **business use is less than 50%** the alternative depreciation system must be used, which is essentially straight-line spread out over a longer period.

The limits for "clean fuel", hybrid cars, and electric cars are roughly three times higher than above.

VEHICLES NOT SUBJECT TO LIMITS

The following vehicles are not **considered passenger automobiles** and are not subject to the deduction limit:

- Ambulance or hearse
- Taxis, transport vans, and other vehicles that transport people or property for hire
- Qualified nonpersonal use vehicles specifically modified for business

TIP: Passenger automobiles (cars, trucks, vans, and SUVs **weighing more than 6,000 pounds**) are not subject to the Section 280F(a) limits. Vehicles not subject to the Section 280F(a) limits and that meet the business-use requirement (must be used predominantly for qualified business use, more than 50% of its total use), qualify for the 100% special depreciation allowance (bonus depreciation).

DE MINIMIS SAFE HARBOR

The *de minimis safe harbor election* eliminates the burden of determining whether every small dollar expenditure for the acquisition of property is properly deductible or capitalizable under the more detailed acquisition and improvement rules. This election allows taxpayers to follow financial accounting treatment of these expenditures for tax purposes, provided the amounts deducted under their financial accounting policies adhere to specific dollar limitations.

The regulations provide a de minimis safe harbor limit of **$5,000** per invoice (or per item substantiated by invoice) for taxpayers that have an *Applicable Financial Statement (AFS)*. This limit is **$2,500** for taxpayers that do not have an AFS.

A larger safe harbor limitation is reasonable for a taxpayer with an AFS because an AFS provides independent assurance that the taxpayer's de minimis policies are consistent with the requirement of generally accepted accounting principles and do not materially distort the taxpayer's financial statement income.

It is important to note that the $2,500/$5,000 limit operates as a "cliff". Taxpayers <u>cannot</u> deduct a portion of an item up to this limitation amount. In other words, a taxpayer cannot deduct $2,500 of an item costing $3,000. This entire item does not qualify for the safe harbor.

A taxpayer electing the safe harbor may deduct and may <u>not</u> capitalize or treat as materials or supplies amounts paid to acquire or produce a unit of tangible property, if:

- The taxpayer has, at the beginning of the taxable year, accounting procedures treating as an expense for non-tax purposes:
  1. Amounts paid for property costing less than a certain dollar amount; or
  2. Amounts paid for property with an economic useful life of 12 months or less;
- The taxpayer treats the amounts paid for the property as an expense on its books and records in accordance with its accounting procedures

EXAMPLE: In 2020, you do not have an applicable financial statement and you purchase five laptop computers for use in your trade or business. You paid $2,000 each for a total cost of $10,000 and these amounts are substantiated in an invoice. You had an accounting procedure in place at the beginning of 2020 to expense the cost of tangible property if the property costs $2,000 or less. You treat each computer as an expense on your books and records for 2020 in accordance with this policy. If you elect the de minimis safe harbor in your tax returns for your 2020 tax year, you can deduct the cost of each $2,000 computer.

The de minimis safe harbor is an **annual election** that applies only to the tax year for which it is made. A taxpayer may choose to apply the safe harbor in one year, but not in the next. A taxpayer must consistently apply the safe harbor to all amounts paid during an election year for the acquisition or improvement of tangible property, including the acquisition of materials and supplies that also meet the safe harbor requirements. A taxpayer cannot choose to apply the safe harbor to some items and not to others.

TIP: The de minimis election is made by attaching a statement to a timely filed original federal tax return (including extensions) for the tax year in which the amounts are paid. The statement must be titled "Section 1.263(a)-1(f) de minimis safe harbor election" and include the taxpayer's name, address, and taxpayer identification number, and a statement that the taxpayer is making the de minimis safe-harbor election under Reg. 1.263(a)-1(f). Each member of a consolidated group makes its own election. In the case of a partnership or S-Corporation, the entity makes the election, not the partners or shareholders.

REPAIRS AND IMPROVEMENTS

Modifications to property have traditionally been categorized as either **improvements** that <u>must</u> be capitalized or **repairs** that are currently deductible and do not affect basis.

Improvement means an addition to or partial replacement of property that is a *betterment* to the property, restores the property, or adapts it to a new or different use.

Expenses that may result in a betterment to the property include expenses for fixing a pre-existing defect or condition, enlarging or expanding the property, or increasing the capacity, strength, or quality of the property.

Expenses that may be for restoration include expenses for replacing a substantial structural part of the property, repairing damage to the property, or rebuilding the property to a like-new condition.

A taxpayer treats each improvement as <u>separate</u> depreciable property. Annual deductions for depreciation are determined by class life of the property.

MACRS recovery periods apply to property used in rental activities. Using the General Depreciation System (GDS), appliances, carpeting, and furniture used in a rental real estate activity can be depreciated over a 5-year recovery period. Land improvements, such as roads, shrubbery, and fences can be depreciated over a 15-year recovery period.

Additions and improvements, such as a new roof use the same recovery period as that of the property to which the addition or improvement is made, determined as if the property were placed in service at the same time as the addition or improvement (generally, 27.5 years residential real property or 39 years for nonresidential real property).

Common Examples of Improvements to Real Property

Additions	**Miscellaneous**	**Plumbing**
Bedroom	Storm windows, doors	Septic system
Bathroom	New roof	Water heater
Deck	Central vacuum	Soft water system
Garage	Wiring upgrades	Filtration system
Porch	Satellite dish	
Patio	Security system	**Interior Improvements**
		Built-in appliances
Lawn & Grounds	**Heating & Air Conditioning**	Kitchen modernization
Landscaping	Heating system	Flooring
Driveway	Central air conditioning	Wall-to-wall carpeting
Walkway	Furnace	
Fence	Duct work	**Insulation**
Retaining wall	Central humidifier	Attic
Sprinkler system	Filtration system	Walls, floor
Swimming pool		Pipes, duct work

Generally, the taxpayer may deduct the cost of repairing business property in the same way as any other business expense. This generally includes the costs of routine repairs and maintenance to the property that result from use of the property and that keep the property in an ordinary efficient operating condition.

EXAMPLE: Deductible repairs include costs such as painting exteriors or interiors of business buildings, repairing broken window panes, replacing worn-out minor parts, sealing cracks and leaks, and changing oil or other fluids to maintain business equipment.

However, if the cost is for a betterment to the property, to restore the property, or to adapt the property to a new or different use, you must treat it as an improvement and depreciate it.

EXAMPLE: You repair a small section on one corner of the roof of a rental house. You deduct the cost of the repair as a rental expense. However, if you completely replace the roof, the new roof is an improvement because it is a restoration of the building. You depreciate the cost of the new roof.

Costs Incurred During an Improvement

A taxpayer must capitalize both the direct and indirect costs of an improvement. Indirect costs include repairs and other expenses that directly benefit or are incurred by reason of the improvement.

EXAMPLE: if you improve the electrical system in your building, you must also capitalize the costs of repairing the holes that you made in walls to install the new wiring. This rule applies even if this work, performed by itself, would otherwise be treated as currently deductible repair costs.

TIP: A unit of property with an acquisition cost of $200 or less is generally not required to be capitalized and is treated instead as materials and supplies. All costs to improve eight specified building systems must be treated as capital expenditures. Those systems are HVAC, plumbing, electrical, escalators, elevators, fire protection and alarm, security, and gas distribution.

In addition to the de minimis safe harbor election, there are two additional elections that allow the taxpayer to deduct rather than capitalize costs for improvements.

Safe Harbor for Small Taxpayers

A small taxpayer is defined as average annual gross receipts of no more than **$10 million** during the preceding three years. Specifically, **with respect to buildings** that have an unadjusted basis (i.e., original cost) of **$1 million or less**, a taxpayer with no more than $10 million in annual gross receipts may be able to elect to treat expenditures as deductible repairs, regardless of their nature.

Under this provision, a small taxpayer is not required to capitalize expenditures (even if they would otherwise meet the definition of improvements) if the total amount expended during the year does not exceed the lesser of **$10,000** or **2% of the unadjusted basis** of the building.

Qualifying lessees may also take advantage of this safe harbor with respect to leasehold improvements. A lessee with annual gross receipts of no more than $10 million applies the safe harbor by substituting the total amount of rent due over the lease term for the unadjusted basis of the building.

EXAMPLE: Assume a taxpayer has annual gross receipts of less than $10 million and owns an office building that was purchased for $750,000. In 2020, the taxpayer pays $5,500 for improvements to the building. As long as these expenses are no more than the lesser of 2% of the original cost (in this case, $15,000) or $10,000, the taxpayer can immediately deduct all of the costs, regardless of their nature. Because the $5,500 meets these criteria, the small taxpayer safe harbor applies. Now assume the same facts except that the taxpayer spends $10,500 for costs related to the building during 2020. Since $10,500 exceeds the lesser of 2% of the original cost or $10,000, the small taxpayer safe harbor is not available and the taxpayer must capitalize any expenditures that qualify as improvements.

Note that the availability of the safe harbor is an "all or nothing" proposition as to each building owned by the taxpayer; that is, if the expenditure limits are exceeded, the safe harbor does not apply at all with respect to that building. There is no "pro rata" application of the safe harbor permitting a portion of the costs (i.e., the first

$10,000) to be immediately expensed. Note also that amounts deducted under the general overall de minimis safe harbor or the safe harbor for routine maintenance are counted toward the expenditure limit.

Routine Maintenance Safe Harbor

In addition to the small taxpayer safe harbor, there is a *routine maintenance safe harbor* that applies to all taxpayers. The safe harbor for routine maintenance permits a deduction for any expenditures that the taxpayer reasonably expects to be **required more than once** during an asset's class life (or over 10 years in the case of buildings). It is not essential that the maintenance activities, in fact, be performed more than once during the class life.

Routine maintenance for a building includes the recurring activities that a taxpayer expects to perform as a result of the taxpayer's use of any of the property to keep the building structure (including its structural components) or each building system in its ordinarily efficient operating condition.

The term "structural components" includes such parts of a building as walls, partitions, floors, and ceilings, as well as any permanent coverings therefor such as paneling or tiling; windows and doors; all components (whether in, on, or adjacent to the building) of a central air conditioning or heating system, including motors, compressors, pipes and ducts; plumbing and plumbing fixtures, such as sinks and bathtubs; electric wiring and lighting fixtures; chimneys; stairs, escalators, and elevators, including all components thereof; sprinkler systems; fire escapes; and other components relating to the operation or maintenance of a building.

Routine maintenance activities include, for example, the inspection, cleaning, and testing of the building structure or each building system, and the replacement of damaged or worn parts with comparable and commercially available replacement parts.

The safe harbor is still applicable if the taxpayer can substantiate that, at the time the property was placed in service, there was a reasonable expectation that the activities would be performed more than once. The specific form of substantiation will vary from asset to asset, but documentation from the seller or manufacturer recommending a maintenance schedule consistent with the safe harbor would be optimal.

If a cost was for an improvement to a building or equipment, under the routine maintenance safe harbor, the taxpayer can deduct the amounts that meet all of the following criteria:

- The cost is paid for recurring activities performed on tangible property.
- The cost arises from the use of the property in the taxpayer's trade or business.
- The cost keeps the property in an ordinarily efficient operating condition.
- The taxpayer reasonably expects, at the time the property is placed in service, to perform the activity:
  1. **For buildings and building systems** – more than once during the 10-year period beginning when placed in service, or
  2. **For other property** – more than once during the class life of the particular type of property.

The routine maintenance safe harbor does not apply to amounts paid for **betterments**, amounts paid to adapt a unit of property to a new or different use, and most **restorations**. See § 1.263(a)-3(i)(3). However, the routine maintenance safe harbor may apply to certain restoration costs (i.e., qualifying routine maintenance that includes the costs of replacing major components/substantial structural parts or the costs of rebuilding a unit of property to a like-new condition after the end of its class life).

TIP: A taxpayer may make an irrevocable election to capitalize, rather than deduct, all costs for repairs and maintenance consistent with its books and records.

BASIS OF PROPERTY

COST BASIS

Basis is the amount of a taxpayer's investment in a property for tax purposes. A gain or loss is determined by subtracting the adjusted basis from the proceeds of the sale, exchange, or other disposition of property. Use basis to figure deductions for depreciation, amortization, depletion, and casualty losses. If a taxpayer uses property for both business and investment purposes and for personal purposes, the taxpayer must properly allocate basis according to percentage of use. The taxpayer can depreciate only the basis allocated to the business or investment use of the property. The basis of property is usually its cost. The cost is the amount paid in cash, debt obligations, other property, or services. A taxpayer's cost basis also includes (but is not limited to) amounts paid for the following:

- Commissions
- Sales tax, freight, installation, and testing
- Legal and accounting fees (when they must be capitalized)
- Excise taxes, revenue stamps, recording fees, and real estate taxes (if assuming seller's liability)

Certain events may adjust (increase or decrease) an original basis in property:

- Improvements to a property will increase basis
- Deductions for depreciation, casualty losses, or claiming certain credits will reduce basis

REAL PROPERTY

Real property, also called real estate, is land and generally anything built on, growing on, or attached to the land. Certain fees and other expenses are part of the cost basis of the property. If a taxpayer buys buildings and the land on which the buildings stand for a lump sum, allocate the cost basis among the land and the buildings. Allocate the cost basis according to the respective FMV of the land and buildings at the time of purchase. Calculate the basis of each asset by multiplying the lump sum by a fraction. The numerator is the FMV of that asset, and the denominator is the FMV of the whole property at the time of purchase. If the FMV of the land and buildings is unknown, a taxpayer can allocate the basis using the assessed values for real estate tax purposes. If a taxpayer buys property and assumes an existing mortgage on the property, the basis includes the amount paid for the property plus the amount outstanding on the mortgage. Adjust the basis by certain settlement costs as described below:

- A taxpayer's basis includes the **settlement fees** and **closing costs** paid for buying the property. A fee for buying property is a cost that the taxpayer must pay even if the taxpayer buys the property with cash. Do not include fees and costs for getting a loan on the property in the basis.
    1. Taxpayers may add the following settlement fees or closing costs to the basis:
        A. Abstract fees (abstract of title fees)
        B. Charges for installing utility services
        C. Legal fees (fees for the title search and preparation of the sales contract and deed)
        D. Recording fees
        E. Survey fees
        F. Transfer taxes
        G. Owner's title insurance
        H. Any amounts the buyer agrees to pay for the seller, such as back taxes or interest, recording or mortgage fees, cost of improvements or repairs, and sales commissions

2. Taxpayers may not add the following settlement fees and closing costs to basis:
   A. Casualty insurance premiums
   B. Rent for occupancy of the property before closing
   C. Charges for utilities or other services related to the property before closing
   D. Charges connected with getting a loan, such as points (discount points, loan origination fees), mortgage insurance premiums, loan assumption fees, cost of a credit report, and fees for an appraisal required by a lender
   E. Fees for refinancing a mortgage. If a taxpayer pays points to get a loan (including a mortgage, second mortgage, line of credit, or a home equity loan), the points may not be added to the basis of the related property. Generally, the points are deducted over the term of the loan.
   F. Amounts placed in escrow for the future payment of taxes and insurance

BASIS ALLOCATION

If a taxpayer acquires a trade or business for a lump sum, allocate the consideration paid to the various assets acquired. Generally, the purchaser will reduce the amount paid by any cash and general deposit accounts (including checking and savings accounts) received. Allocate the remaining consideration to the other business assets received in proportion to (but not more than) their fair market value. Any amount remaining (not allocated to assets) is goodwill.

EXAMPLE: Setting Sun Partnership purchased a business, Family Dry Cleaners, for $750,000. Family Dry Cleaners assets consist of: $50,000 in cash, equipment with a fair market value of $200,000, and land and building with a fair market value of $450,000.

For real estate tax purposes, the city assessed the value of the land at $100,000 and the building at $200,000. The buyer and seller did not enter into an allocation agreement for this transaction. What basis must Setting Sun Partnership use for the land, building, and intangible asset "goodwill"?

A. Land $100,000, Building $200,000, and Goodwill $150,000
B. Land $150,000, Building $300,000, and Goodwill $0
C. Land $150,000, Building $300,000, and Goodwill $50,000
D. Land $100,000, Building $350,000, and Goodwill $50,000

ANSWER: Basis for cash is always the amount received. Allocate basis to the equipment up to the FMV of the equipment. If a person purchases a building and land in a single transaction, allocate the cost between each. Figure the basis of each asset by multiplying the lump sum by a fraction. The numerator is the FMV of that asset, and the denominator is the FMV of the whole property at the time of purchase. If you are not certain of the FMV of the land and buildings, you can allocate the basis using the assessed values for real estate tax purposes. The building's assessed value is two-thirds of the total assessed value. Allocate two-thirds of the current FMV of the combined real estate to the building. The remainder is goodwill. *The correct answer is C.*

Cash	$50,000	
Equipment	$200,000	
Property	$450,000	($300,000 Building, $150,000 Land)
Goodwill	$50,000	($750,000 purchase price - $700,000 FMV of assets received)
Total	**$750,000**	

ADJUSTED BASIS

Before figuring the gain or loss on a sale, exchange, or other disposition of property or figuring the allowable depreciation, depletion, or amortization, a taxpayer must usually make certain adjustments (increases and decreases) to the cost of the property. The result is the adjusted basis.

- **Increase** the basis of any property by all items properly added to a capital account. These include (but are not limited to) the following items:

  1. **Capital improvements** – Costs of improvements having a useful life of more than one year, which increase the value of the property, lengthen its life, or adapt it to a different use.

  2. **Assessments for local improvements** – Increase basis by property assessments for improvements that increase the value of the property. Do not deduct these as taxes. Examples of assessments are as follows:

     A. Roads

     B. Sidewalks

     C. Water connections

     D. Extending utility service lines to the property

- **Decrease** the basis of any property by all items that represent a return of capital for the period during which the taxpayer held the property. Items that decrease basis include (but are not limited to) the following:

  1. **Non-taxable corporate distributions** – Also known as non-dividend distributions. This amount reflects a return of capital and reduces basis.

  2. **Casualty and theft losses** – Decrease the basis of a taxpayer's property by any insurance proceeds or other reimbursement and by any deductible loss not covered by insurance. Increase the basis in the property by the amount spent on repairs that restore the property to its pre-casualty condition.

  3. **Depreciation and Section 179 deduction** – The basis of a taxpayer's qualifying business property will be decreased by any Section 179 deductions taken and the depreciation deducted, or could have been deducted (including any special depreciation allowance), on the taxpayer's returns under the chosen method of depreciation.

  4. **Easements** – The amount received for granting an easement is considered proceeds from the sale of an interest in real property. It reduces the basis of the affected part of the property.

  5. **Certain credits** – Basis may be reduced by the amount of credits received for the following:

     A. Alternative motor vehicle credit

     B. Alternative fuel vehicle refueling property credit

     C. Residential energy efficient property credit

PROPERTY RECEIVED FOR SERVICES

If a taxpayer receives property for services rendered, its FMV must be included in income. The amount included in income becomes the basis. If the taxpayer performed the services for a price agreed on beforehand, it will be accepted as the FMV of the property if there is no evidence to the contrary. If the property is subject to certain restrictions, the basis in the property is its FMV when it substantially vests. However, this rule does not apply if the taxpayer makes an election to include in income the FMV of the property at the time it is transferred, less any amount the taxpayer paid for it. Property is substantially vested when it is transferable or when it is not subject to a substantial risk of forfeiture.

BARGAIN PURCHASES

A bargain purchase is the purchase of an item for less than its FMV. If a taxpayer buys goods or other property at less than FMV as compensation for services, include the difference between the purchase price and the property's FMV in income. The basis in the property is its FMV (the purchase price plus the amount included in income).

INVOLUNTARY CONVERSIONS

Condemnation is the process by which private property is legally taken for public use without the owner's consent. A *threat of condemnation* exists if a taxpayer learns of a decision to acquire his property for public use through a report in a newspaper or other news medium, and this report is confirmed by a representative of the government body or public official involved. The taxpayer must have reasonable grounds to believe that, if he does not sell voluntarily, his property will be condemned. A threat of condemnation is sufficient to commence the condemnation process for tax purposes.

TIP: The government does not have to actually take the property to begin the process. However, the government must have decided to acquire it. The fact that the government is merely considering a property is not sufficient. And the property must be condemned so that it can be used for a public purpose not because it is unsafe or in violation of the building codes.

If a taxpayer receives replacement property because of an *involuntary conversion*, such as a casualty, theft, or condemnation, calculate the basis of the replacement property by using the basis of the converted property.

- **Similar or related property** – If a taxpayer receives replacement property similar or related in service or use to the converted property, the replacement property's basis is the same as the converted property's basis on the date of the conversion, with the following adjustments:

    1. Basis decreases by the following:

        A. Any loss recognized on the involuntary conversion, and

        B. Any money received that the taxpayer does not spend on similar property

    2. Basis increases by the following:

        A. Any gain recognized on the involuntary conversion, and

        B. Any cost of acquiring the replacement property

- **Money or property not similar or related** – If a taxpayer receives money or property not similar or related in use to the converted property, and he buys replacement property similar or related in use to the converted property, the basis of the replacement property is its cost decreased by the gain not recognized on the conversion.

INHERITED PROPERTY

The basis of an inherited capital asset is generally the FMV of the property on the date of death or an alternate valuation date if elected by the personal representative. A *step-up* in basis occurs when the FMV is greater than the decedent's basis. Gain on inherited property is always long-term.

PROPERTY CHANGED FROM PERSONAL TO BUSINESS OR RENTAL USE

If a taxpayer holds property for personal use and then changes it to business use or uses it to produce rent, the taxpayer may begin to depreciate the property at the time of the change. To do so, calculate the property's basis for depreciation. An example of changing property held for personal use to business or rental use would be renting a former personal residence. The basis for depreciation is the lesser of the following:

- The FMV of the property on the date of the change
- The adjusted basis on the date of the change

EXAMPLE: Several years ago, you paid $160,000 to have your home built on a lot that cost $25,000. You paid $20,000 for permanent improvements to the house and claimed a $2,000 casualty loss deduction for damage to the house before changing the property to rental use last year. Because land isn't depreciable, you include only the cost of the house when figuring the basis for depreciation.

Your adjusted basis in the house when you changed its use was $178,000 ($160,000 + $20,000 − $2,000). On the same date, your property had an FMV of $180,000, of which $15,000 was for the land and $165,000 was for the house. The basis for figuring depreciation on the house is its FMV on the date of change ($165,000) because it's less than your adjusted basis ($178,000).

If the taxpayer sells the property at a profit, the original basis (with adjustments) is used.

> **EXAMPLE:** Assume the same facts as in the previous example except that you sell the property at a gain after being allowed depreciation deductions of $37,500. Your adjusted basis for figuring gain is $165,500 ($178,000 + $25,000 (land) − $37,500).

If the taxpayer sells the property at a loss, the cost for purposes of determining basis is the FMV on the date of conversion (with adjustments). This rule prevents a taxpayer from shifting nondeductible losses on personal property to deductible losses on business property.

> **EXAMPLE:** Assume the same facts as in the previous example, except that you sell the property at a loss after being allowed depreciation deductions of $37,500. In this case, you would start with the FMV on the date of the change to rental use ($180,000) because it's less than the adjusted basis of $203,000 ($178,000 + $25,000) on that date. Reduce that amount ($180,000) by the depreciation deductions to arrive at a basis for loss of $142,500 ($180,000 − $37,500).

SECURITIES

The following rules apply to most investors. Day-traders and dealers in securities may utilize different methods to account for their transactions.

- **Stocks or bonds** – The basis of purchased stocks or bonds is generally the purchase price plus any costs of purchase, such as commissions and recording or transfer fees.
  1. **Nontaxable stock dividends or stock splits** – Total basis and percentage ownership do not change. Allocate the total adjusted basis of all shares *pro rata* to each share. Reduce the basis of existing shares by the amount of basis allocated to the new shares. This rule applies only when the additional stock received is identical to the stock held.
  2. **Return of capital** – Also known as non-dividend distributions. This amount reflects a return of capital and reduces basis.

LIKE-KIND EXCHANGES OF REAL PROPERTY

Nonrecognition of gain under Section 1031 in the case of like-kind exchanges completed after December 31, 2017, shall apply only to **real property** that is not held primarily for sale. A taxpayer can no longer defer gain on tangible personal property held for use in a trade or business or held for investment.

In general, for tax purposes, like-kind properties are real properties used in a trade or business or held for investment. If a taxpayer trades *business or investment real property* for other business or investment real property it's a *like-kind exchange (Section 1031 Exchange)*, and the taxpayer does not pay tax on any gain or get a tax deduction on any loss until he sells or disposes of the property received. Property used primarily for personal use, like a primary residence or a second home or vacation home, does not qualify for like-kind exchange treatment.

Most real estate will be like-kind to other real estate. For example, the following transactions involve real property of a like-kind:

- Trade of land improved with an apartment house for land improved with a store building
- City property for farm property
- Improved property for unimproved property
- Real property improved with a residential rental house for vacant land
- Real estate owned by a taxpayer for a real estate lease that runs 30 years

One exception for real estate is that real property within the United States is not like-kind to real property outside the United States. Also, improvements that are conveyed without land are not of like-kind to land.

TIP: In a like-kind exchange, the taxpayer must hold both the property transferred and the property received for investment or productive use in a trade or business. Buildings, land, and rental houses are examples of real property that may qualify.

The **replacement property** must be **identified within 45 days** and **received** by the earliest of the **180th day** after the date on which the property given up in the exchange transfers, or the due date of the tax return, including extensions, for the tax year in which the transfer of the property given up occurs.

After December 31, 2017, only real property qualifies as exchange property under Section 1031, personal property no longer qualifies. Can no longer defer gain on tangible personal property held for use in a trade or business or held for investment.

> The like-kind exchange rules do not apply to property held for **personal use**, stocks, bonds, notes, certificates of trust, beneficial interests, or partnership interests.

GAIN RECOGNITION

The general rule is that if the properties in an exchange are **"like-kind" real properties**, and the properties are held either for productive use in a trade or business or for investment, then **no gain or loss** will be recognized on the transaction by either party.

> The *amount realized* from a sale or trade of property is everything received for the property. This includes the money, the fair market value of any property or services, and debt or other liabilities assumed by the buyer. The taxpayer may subtract exchange expenses from the consideration received to figure the amount realized on the exchange. The difference between the adjusted basis of the property plus liabilities assumed by the taxpayer and the amount realized in a sale or trade is the *realized gain (or loss)* on the transaction. The amount of income or loss *recognized* is the amount a taxpayer includes in taxable income for the tax year. A taxpayer must **recognize** the gain up to the **amount of boot received** (less exchange expenses) or the amount of **realized gain**, whichever is less. If the taxpayer realizes a loss on the like-kind exchange, **no loss is recognized**. A taxpayer may recognize a loss only on transfers of unlike property.

BOOT

Transactions such as *like-kind exchanges* may defer or partially defer recognition of gain. A taxpayer may have a *partially nontaxable* exchange and may recognize gain if he receives property that is not like-kind, known as *boot.* The taxpayer treats boot the same as if money is received upon the exchange.

Boot is the <u>total</u> amount received for the following:

- Any money received from the other party
- The FMV of other (not like-kind) property received
- Net liabilities assumed by the other party (<u>after</u> subtracting liabilities the taxpayer assumes, cash paid to the other party, and the FMV of other property given up)

EXAMPLE: Adam, who is not a dealer in real estate, exchanges real estate held for investment, which he purchased in 1990 for $50,000, for other real estate (to be held for productive use in trade or business) which has a fair market value of $60,000, and $20,000 in cash. The gain from the transaction is $30,000 but is recognized only to the extent of the cash received of $20,000.

If, in addition to like-kind property, the taxpayer **gives up** unlike property (other property), the taxpayer must recognize gain or loss on the unlike property. The gain or loss is equal to the difference between the fair market value of the unlike property and the adjusted basis of the unlike property.

EXCHANGE EXPENSES

Exchange expenses are generally the closing costs paid by the taxpayer such as brokerage commissions, attorney fees, and deed preparation fees. Subtract these expenses from the consideration received to figure the amount realized on the exchange.

Exchange expenses the taxpayer pays **reduce boot received**, but <u>not</u> below zero, before determining the *realized* gain. Exchange expenses **increase the basis** of the like-kind property received.

ASSUMPTION OF LIABILITIES

<u>Add</u> liabilities the **other party assumes** to determine the **amount realized**. <u>Subtract</u> liabilities the **taxpayer assumes** to calculate the **realized gain**.

EXAMPLE: Adam owns an apartment house with an FMV of $220,000, an adjusted basis of $100,000, and subject to a mortgage of $80,000. Bill owns an apartment house with an FMV of $250,000, an adjusted basis of $175,000, and subject to a mortgage of $150,000. Adam transfers his apartment house to Bill and receives in exchange Bill's apartment house plus $40,000 in cash. Adam assumes the mortgage on the apartment house received from Bill, and Bill assumes the mortgage on the apartment house received from Adam. Bill pays $10,000 in exchange expenses.

Adam's realized gain is $120,000. Calculated as follows:

FMV of like-kind property received from Bill	$250,000
Cash received from Bill	+ 40,000
Liabilities Bill assumes	+ 80,000
Amount realized	**$370,000**
less: Adjusted basis of property Adam transfers	– 100,000
less: Mortgage Adam assumes	– 150,000
Realized gain	**$120,000**

Bill's realized gain is $65,000. Calculated as follows:

FMV of like-kind property received from Adam	$220,000
Cash received from Adam	+ 0
Liabilities Adam assumes	+ 150,000
less: Exchange expenses paid	– 10,000
Amount realized	**$360,000**
less: Adjusted basis of property Bill transfers	– 175,000
less: Mortgage Bill assumes	– 80,000
less: Cash paid to Adam	– 40,000
Realized gain	**$65,000**

Recognized gain is limited to the lesser of the **gain realized** or **boot received**. Boot is the sum of cash received, the FMV of other property received, and the net liabilities that the other party assumes. The taxpayer subtracts exchange expenses paid from boot received.

Adam must recognize $40,000 of his $120,000 realized gain. Calculated as follows:

Money received (cash)	$40,000
Net liability other party assumes ($80,000 – $150,000)	+ 0
Total money and unlike property received	$40,000
less: Exchange expenses paid	– 0
Recognized gain	**$40,000**

Bill must recognize $20,000 of his $65,000 realized gain. Calculated as follows:

Money received (cash)	$0
Net liability other party assumes ($150,000 – $80,000 – $40,000)*	+ 30,000
Total money and unlike property received	$30,000
less: Exchange expenses paid	– $10,000
Recognized gain	**$20,000**

*The excess of the $150,000 of liabilities assumed by Adam minus the total ($120,000) of the $80,000 of liabilities Bill assumed and the $40,000 cash Bill paid.

BASIS OF PROPERTY RECEIVED

If a taxpayer acquires property in a like-kind exchange, the basis of the replacement (like-kind) property is generally the **same as the basis of the property transferred**, with the following adjustments:

- **Increase** basis by the total amount of:
  1. Boot paid (money, *basis* of other property transferred, net liabilities the taxpayer assumes)
  2. Exchange expenses the taxpayer pays
  3. Any **gain recognized** on the exchange
- **Decrease** basis by the amount of:
  1. Boot received (money, *FMV* of other property received, net liabilities the other party assumes)
  2. Any **loss recognized** on the exchange

Allocate this basis first to the unlike property received, other than money, up to its fair market value on the date of the exchange. The rest is the basis of the like-kind property.

EXAMPLE: A taxpayer exchanges land with a basis of $2,000 and a fair value of $10,000 for nearby land worth $13,000. To make up the difference, the taxpayer also transfers other property worth $3,000 that has a basis of $7,000.

To determine the basis of the replacement property, start with the $2,000 basis of the property transferred and add the $7,000 basis of other (unlike) property transferred for a total of $9,000. The taxpayer must recognize gain or loss on the unlike property. In this case, the recognized loss on the replacement property is $4,000 ($7,000 basis – $3,000 FMV). The recognized loss reduces basis to $5,000 ($9,000 – $4,000).

In situations where a taxpayer receives multiple like-kind replacement properties, the basis is allocated between the properties (other than money) received in proportion to its relative FMV on the date of the exchange.

EXAMPLE: A taxpayer exchanges real estate held for investment with an adjusted basis of $8,000 for real estate he now holds for investment. The fair market value (FMV) of the real estate received is $14,000. The taxpayer also receives $1,000 in cash and pays $500 in exchange expenses. The property the taxpayer gave up was subject to a $3,000 mortgage for which he was personally liable. The other party in the trade agreed to pay off the mortgage. The property received is subject to a $4,000 mortgage that the taxpayer assumes.

FMV of like-kind property received	$14,000
Cash	+ 1,000
Mortgage assumed by other party	+ 3,000
Total received	$18,000
less: Exchange expenses	– 500
Amount realized	**$17,500**
less: Adjusted basis of property transferred	– 8,000
less: Mortgage taxpayer assumed	– 4,000
Realized gain	**$5,500**

The realized gain is <u>recognized</u> (taxable) up to $500, figured as follows:

Money received (cash)	$1,000
Net liability other party assumes ($3,000 – $4,000)	+ 0
Total money and unlike property received	$1,000
less: Exchange expenses paid	– 500
Recognized gain	**$500**

The <u>basis</u> for the property received is increased by $1,000:

Basis of transferred property	$8,000
Net liability taxpayer assumes ($4,000 – $3,000)	+ 1,000
Exchange expenses	+ 500
Recognized gain	+ 500
less: Boot received	– 1,000
Adjusted basis	**$9,000**

RELATED PARTY

If a taxpayer and a *related party* enter into a like-kind exchange and either party disposes of the like property within two years, <u>both</u> **parties must report any unrecognized gain or loss from the original trade** on the return for the year the disposition occurs.

A taxpayer may <u>not</u> **deduct a loss** (other than a distribution in complete liquidation of a corporation) if the transaction involves the following related parties:

- Family members. This includes <u>only</u> brothers and sisters, half-brothers and half-sisters, spouse, ancestors (parents, grandparents, etc.), and lineal descendants (children, grandchildren, etc.)
- A partnership or corporation with **more than 50%** directly or indirectly owned by taxpayer

- A tax-exempt charitable or educational organization controlled by the taxpayer or family member

LESSON 4

Corporations

BUSINESSES TAXED AS CORPORATIONS

The following businesses formed after 1996 are taxed as corporations:

* A business formed under a federal or state law that refers to it as a corporation, body corporate, body politic, joint-stock company, or joint-stock association
* An insurance company
* Certain banks
* A business wholly owned by a state or local government
* A business specifically required to be taxed as a corporation by the Internal Revenue Code (for example, certain publicly traded partnerships)
* Certain foreign businesses
* Any other business that elects taxation as a corporation (for example, an LLC) by filing Form 8832, Entity Classification Election

PERSONAL SERVICE CORPORATIONS

A flat **21% tax rate** now applies to all corporations, including a *personal service corporation (PSC)* and a *qualified personal service corporation*.

A corporation is a **personal service corporation** if it meets all of the following requirements:

* Its principal activity during the "testing period" (generally the prior tax year) is performing personal services in the fields of accounting, actuarial science, architecture, consulting, engineering, health (including veterinary services), law, and the performing arts
* Its employee-owners substantially perform the services
* Employee-owners own more than **10%** of FMV of outstanding stock on the last day of the testing period:
  1. A person is an employee-owner of a personal service corporation if he is an employee of the corporation or performs personal services for, or on behalf of, the corporation on any day of the testing period, and owns any stock in the corporation.
  2. Furthermore, the PSC may be a **qualified personal service corporation** if current (or retired) employees performing the personal services, their estates, or their beneficiaries own at least **95%** of the corporation's stock, by value, directly or indirectly.

CLOSELY HELD CORPORATIONS

A corporation (other than a personal service corporation) is closely held if at any time during the last half of the tax year, more than **50%** of the value of its outstanding stock is owned (directly or indirectly) by or for **five or fewer** individuals, including certain trusts and private foundations.

A closely held corporation is subject to additional limitations in the tax treatment of items such as passive activity losses, at-risk rules, and compensation paid to corporate officers.

AFFILIATED GROUP

An affiliated group is one or more chains of includible corporations connected through stock ownership with a common parent corporation. The parent corporation must directly own stock equal to at least **80%** of the **total voting power** of the stock of such corporation, with a value equal to at least **80%** of the **total value** of the stock of such corporation.

PROPERTY EXCHANGED FOR STOCK

TIP: Many of the questions on the exam regarding corporate funding transactions test the concepts of basis on contributed property, gain recognition, and contribution of services in exchange for ownership

IRC SECTION 351 EXCHANGE

The transfer of property (or money and property) to a corporation in exchange for stock in that corporation (other than nonqualified preferred stock) is usually <u>not</u> taxable if immediately afterward the taxpayer is in *control* of the corporation.

This type of nontaxable *§351 exchange* applies both to individuals and to groups who transfer property to a corporation. Both the corporation and any person involved in a nontaxable exchange of property for stock must attach to their income tax returns a complete statement of all facts pertinent to the exchange. It is important to recognize when a taxpayer has control. Without control, treat a contribution of property like a purchase and sale. Sometimes this can result in a loss.

A shareholder that owns—directly or indirectly—<u>more</u> than **50%** of the corporation's stock **cannot deduct the loss.** Any gain the corporation realizes on the sale of the property is recognized only to the extent that it exceeds the previously disallowed loss. If the property is sold at a loss, no benefit is received for the loss previously disallowed. *See Related Persons, later.*

Control of Corporation – To be in control of a corporation the transferors <u>must</u> own at least **80%** of the total combined voting power of all classes of stock, and at least **80%** of the outstanding shares of each class of nonvoting stock, **immediately after the exchange**. This does not apply if the corporation is an investment company, in a bankruptcy or similar proceeding in exchange for stock used to pay creditors, or if the taxpayer receives the stock in exchange for the corporation's debt that accrued while the taxpayer held the debt.

EXAMPLE 12-1: You and Bill Jones buy property for $100,000. You both organize a corporation when the property has a fair market value of $300,000. You transfer the property to the corporation for all its authorized capital stock, which has a par value of $300,000. No gain is recognized by you, Bill, or the corporation.

EXAMPLE 12-2: You and Bill transfer the property with a basis of $100,000 to a corporation in exchange for stock with a fair market value of $300,000. This represents only 75% of each class of stock of the corporation. The other 25% was already issued to someone else. You and Bill recognize a taxable gain of $200,000 on the transaction.

• **Services rendered** – The term "property" does <u>not</u> include services rendered to the issuing corporation. The value of stock received for services is income to the recipient. The basis of stock received for services is the amount the shareholder includes in income. If a shareholder performs services in exchange for stock, the control requirement for §351 can be lost. Only the shares attributed to the exchange of "property" count toward the control requirement.

EXAMPLE 12-3: You transfer property worth $35,000 and render services valued at $3,000 to a corporation in exchange for stock valued at $38,000. Right after the exchange, you own 85% of the outstanding stock. No gain is recognized on the exchange of property. However, you recognize ordinary income of $3,000 as payment for services you rendered to the corporation.

- **Money or property received** – A taxpayer may need to recognize gain if money or property other than stock is received during the exchange. The taxpayer recognizes gain only up to the amount of money <u>plus</u> the FMV of the other property received.
- **Liabilities** – If the corporation assumes taxpayer liabilities, the exchange generally is <u>not</u> treated as if the taxpayer received money or other property. There are two exceptions:
  1. If liabilities assumed are more than the taxpayer's adjusted basis in the property, the taxpayer recognizes gain up to the difference. However, if the liabilities assumed give rise to a deduction when paid, such as a trade account payable or interest, no gain is recognized.
  2. If there is no good business reason for the corporation to assume the liabilities, or if the main purpose in the exchange is to avoid federal income tax, treat the assumption as if the taxpayer receives money in the amount of the liabilities.

EXAMPLE 12-4: You transfer property to a corporation for stock. Immediately after the transfer, you control the corporation. You also receive $10,000 in the exchange. Your adjusted basis in the transferred property is $20,000. The stock you receive has a fair market value (FMV) of $16,000. The corporation also assumes a $5,000 mortgage on the property for which you are personally liable. Gain is realized as follows.

FMV of stock received	$16,000
Cash received	10,000
Liability assumed by corporation	5,000
Total received	$31,000
Minus: Adjusted basis of property transferred	20,000
Realized gain	$11,000

The liability assumed is not treated as money or other property. The recognized gain is limited to $10,000, the cash received.

- The **basis of the stock received by the shareholder** is generally the adjusted basis of the property transferred.
  1. Increase basis by any amount treated as a dividend and by any gain recognized.
  2. Decrease basis by any cash received (other than payment for services), the FMV of any other property received, and any loss recognized on the exchange. Also, decrease basis by the amount of liability the corporation or another party to the exchange assumed unless payment of the liability gives rise to a deduction when paid.
- The **basis of any other property received by the shareholder** is its **FMV** on the date of the trade.
- A **corporation's basis of property** transferred in exchange for its stock is the same as the basis the shareholder had in the property <u>increased</u> by any gain the shareholder recognized on the exchange.

> • A special rule limits basis to FMV on certain *loss importation transactions*. If the property has a built-in loss (FMV of the property is lower than the shareholder's basis) the corporation's basis is equal to the **value of the property immediately after the transaction.**

- **Paid-in-capital** – Contributions to the capital of a corporation, whether or not by shareholders, are paid-in-capital. These contributions are <u>not</u> taxable to the corporation. The corporation's basis of property contributed by a shareholder is the same as the basis the shareholder had in the property, increased by any gain the shareholder recognized on the exchange. The basis of property contributed to capital by a person other than a shareholder is **$0**.

- **Election to reduce basis** – In a Section 351 transaction, if the basis of the property transferred exceeds the property's FMV (a built-in loss), the parties may irrevocably **elect** under §362(e)(2)(C) to treat the basis of the stock received by the shareholder as having a basis equal to the FMV of the property transferred. The basis of the property received by the corporation is the same as the basis the shareholder had in the property. Note: This is the exact opposite of the general rule.

DETAILED EXAMPLES OF CORPORATE TRANSACTIONS

Two shareholders each contribute property to a corporation in exchange for stock with a net fair market value (FMV) of $50,000. 100% of the stock was exchanged for $100,000 in property. Each shareholder now owns 50% of the corporation.

Shareholder A – Contributes $30,000 cash and a trailer with $15,000 basis and $20,000 FMV.

Shareholder B – Contributes a tractor with $20,000 basis and $60,000 FMV. The corporation pays $10,000 to Shareholder B in the transaction.

When applying the principle of control consider all shares of the transferors even if they are not related parties. The combined ownership of these shareholders is more than 80% immediately after the transaction. They have control, and the transaction is a §351 exchange. The exchange is non-taxable unless the shareholder receives money, property, or a relief of liabilities.

Shareholder A – Does not receive any property or recognize gain. The basis of stock for this shareholder is $45,000, the adjusted basis of property and money transferred to the corporation.

Shareholder B – Must recognize gain up to the amount of property received of $10,000. The basis of stock for this shareholder is $20,000. Basis is unchanged because it increases by the $10,000 gain recognized by the shareholder and decreases by the $10,000 payment to the shareholder.

Corporation – Contributions to the capital of a corporation, whether or not by shareholders, are paid-in-capital. These contributions are not taxable to the corporation. The corporation's basis of property contributed by a shareholder is the same as the basis the shareholder had in the property, increased by any gain the shareholder recognized on the exchange. The corporation has a $15,000 basis in the trailer and an adjusted basis of $30,000 in the tractor.

Alternate Scenario #1 – Shareholder A contributes $10,000 in services, $20,000 in cash, and a trailer with a basis of $15,000 and FMV of $20,000. Shareholder A must recognize income of $10,000; the value of stock received for services. Shareholder A's stock basis is $45,000, the adjusted basis of property and money transferred to the corporation <u>plus</u> value of stock received for services. The corporation still has a $15,000 basis in the trailer as this nontaxable exchange qualifies under §351.

Alternate Scenario #2 – Shareholder A contributes $30,000 in services and a trailer with a basis of $15,000 and FMV of $20,000. This is no longer a nontaxable exchange under §351. The combined stock exchanged for property is only 70% and 30% is for contributed services. Shareholder A must recognize income of $30,000 for services performed and $5,000 in gain on the trailer. Shareholder B must recognize the entire gain of $40,000 on the tractor. The corporation now has a basis of $20,000 in the trailer and a basis of $60,000 for the tractor. Each shareholder has a basis of $50,000 in the stock.

FILING AND PAYING INCOME TAXES

A corporation generally must make estimated tax payments as it earns or receives income during its tax year. After the end of the tax year, the corporation must file an income tax return.

INCOME TAX RETURN

Unless exempt under Section 501 of the Internal Revenue Code, all domestic corporations in existence for any part of a tax year (including corporations in bankruptcy) <u>must</u> file an income tax return whether or not they have taxable income. A corporation generally must file *Form 1120* to report its income, gains, losses, deductions, and credits and to figure its income tax liability.

- **When to file** – A corporation must file its income tax return by the **15th day of the 4th month** after the end of its tax year (April 15 for a calendar year corporation). A new corporation filing a short-period return must generally file by the 15th day of the 4th month after the short period ends. A corporation that has dissolved must generally file by the 15th day of the fourth month after the date it dissolved.

> **EXCEPTION:** A corporation with a fiscal tax year ending June 30 must file by the 15th day of the 3rd month after the end of its tax year. The filing deadline for an S corporation is also the 15th day of the 3rd month after the end of its tax year.

- **Extension of time to file** – A corporation uses *Form 7004* to request an automatic six-month extension of time to **file** a corporate income tax return. The extension is seven months if the fiscal year ends in June. The IRS will grant the extension if the form is completed properly, filed timely, and any tax due is paid by the due date for the return. Form 7004 does <u>not</u> extend the time for **paying the tax** due on the return.
- A corporation must pay tax in full no later than the 15th day of the fourth month after the end of its tax year.
- All deposits (including Social Security, Medicare, withheld income, excise, and corporate income taxes) <u>must</u> be made by **electronic funds transfer**. Generally, electronic fund transfers are made using the *Electronic Federal Tax Payment System (EFTPS).*

PENALTIES

A corporation that is without reasonable cause, for each month or part of a month the corporation:

- **Does not file** its tax return by the due date, including extensions, it may be penalized **5%** of the unpaid tax, up to a maximum of **25%** of the unpaid tax. The minimum penalty for a return that is more than **60 days late** is the <u>smaller</u> of the **tax due** or **$435** for returns required to be filed in 2021 (generally 2020 tax year).
- **Does not pay** the tax when due, it may be penalized **one-half of 1%** of the unpaid tax, up to a maximum of **25%** of the unpaid tax.

If a corporation is granted an extension of time to file a corporation income tax return, it will not be charged a late payment penalty if the tax shown (or the amount of tax paid by the regular due date of the return), is **at least 90%** of the tax shown on the total tax line of your return, and the balance due shown on the return is paid by the extended due date.

ESTIMATED TAX

Generally, a corporation <u>must</u> make installment payments if it expects tax for the year to be **$500 or more**. If the corporation does not pay the installments when they are due, it could be subject to an underpayment penalty.

Installment payments are due by the 15th day of the fourth, sixth, ninth, and 12th months of the corporation's tax year. If any due date falls on a Saturday, Sunday, or legal holiday, the installment is due on the next business day.

REGULAR METHOD

For a corporation, the **required annual payment** is generally the lesser of—

- **100%** of the tax shown on the return for the taxable year (or, if no return is filed, 100% of the tax for such year), or

- **100%** of the tax shown on the return of the corporation for the preceding taxable year. The return must cover a full 12-month period and show a positive tax liability (not $0). This option is not available for a large corporation (i.e., taxable income of $1,000,000 or more in any of the three prior tax years).

Under the regular method, **each required installment is 25% of the required annual payment.**

OTHER METHODS

If a corporation's income is expected to vary during the year because, for example, its business is seasonal, it may be able to lower the amount of one or more required installments by using one or both of the following methods:

- The annualized income installment method
- The adjusted seasonal installment method

Quick refund of overpayments – A corporation that has overpaid its estimated tax for the tax year may be able to apply for a quick refund if the overpayment is at least 10% of its expected tax liability and at least $500. The corporation must file *Form 4466, Corporation Application for Quick Refund of Overpayment of Estimated Tax* before the 16th day of the fourth month after the end of the tax year, and before the corporation files its income tax return. Do not file Form 4466 before the end of the corporation's tax year. The IRS will act on the form within 45 days from the date filed.

FORM 1120 SCHEDULES

A corporation with total receipts for the tax year and total assets at the end of the tax year of **less than $250,000** is not required to complete Schedules L, M-1, and M-2. All others must report the required information on the appropriate schedules.

SCHEDULE L, BALANCE SHEET PER BOOKS

The balance sheet should agree with the corporation's books and records. Schedule L is a statement of the assets, liabilities, and capital at the beginning and end of the tax year. Total assets should equal the sum of total liabilities and shareholders' equity.

SCHEDULE M-1, RECONCILIATION OF INCOME PER BOOKS WITH INCOME PER RETURN

Taxpayers have different objectives when they prepare the financial statements and when they complete their tax return. The financial statements are prepared with an objective of maximizing income and thus increasing the net worth of the shareholders, while maintaining conformity with accounting principles. The tax return is prepared with the objective of minimizing taxable income and thus reducing taxes paid, while maintaining compliance with tax law. The books and records of a corporation are kept in accordance with accounting principles and not in accordance with tax law. The result of these differing objectives is a large disparity between book income and taxable income.

A corporation uses Schedule M-1 of Form 1120 to reconcile book income with the income it reports on its tax return. Book income includes certain items that are not deductions for tax purposes (e.g. nondeductible meals and entertainment expenses). To reconcile with income for tax reporting purposes, the corporation adds these nondeductible amounts to book income. Book income also includes certain items <u>not</u> recognized for tax purposes (e.g. tax-exempt interest). Subtract these items from book income to arrive at the corporation's income per return.

A corporation (or S corporation) that has $250,000 in total receipts <u>or</u> $250,000 in total assets ($1,000,000 in assets for a partnership) at the end of the tax year is <u>required</u> to complete **Schedule M-1.**

Schedule M-1 filing threshold		
Entity	Total Receipts	Total Assets
Corporation	$250,000	$250,000
S Corp	$250,000	$250,000
Partnership	$250,000	$1,000,000

SCHEDULE M-2

Tracks the adjusted items of income (loss), deductions, and distributions. Schedule M-2 provides insight into the taxation of distributions to shareholders.

- Analysis of Unappropriated Retained Earnings per Books (C corporation) – This reflects the amount available to shareholders as dividends.
- Analysis of Accumulated Adjustments Account, Other Adjustments Account, and Shareholders' Undistributed Taxable Income Previously Taxed (S Corporation) – These accounts influence the taxation of distributions to shareholders.

SCHEDULE M-3

A business with total assets of **$10 million or more** on the last day of the tax year must complete Schedule M-3 instead of Schedule M-1.

A taxpayer uses schedule M-1 or M-3 to make differences between financial accounting net income and taxable income more transparent. Schedule M-3 is more detailed and requires a separate reporting of income and expense differences (unlike M-1). Schedule M-3 also requires the taxpayer to identify the differences as temporary or permanent.

PERMANENT OR TEMPORARY DIFFERENCES

As mentioned previously, there are different rules for determining the taxpayer's financial income per books and for determining taxable income.

These rules result in differences that can be:

- Timing differences that are reported for tax purposes in a different accounting period, and
- Permanent differences that are never reported for tax purposes.

Timing Differences

Timing differences occur because tax laws require the recognition of some income and expenses in a different period than that required for book purposes. Timing differences originate in one period and reverse or terminate in one or more subsequent periods. There are four basic categories of timing differences:

- Income recognized in financial statements before it is taxable;
- Income taxable before it is recognized in financial statements;
- Expenses recognized in financial statements before they are deducted on the tax return; and
- Expenses deductible on the tax return before they are recognized on financial statements.

Permanent Differences

Permanent differences between book and tax income result from transactions that (under applicable tax laws and regulations) will not be offset by any corresponding differences in other periods. Permanent differences apply only for the tax year in which they occur.

Common Items That Cause Permanent Differences			
Item	Book Treatment	Tax Return Treatment	Adjustment
Tax-exempt interest	Include in Income	Exclude from Income	Decrease Book Income
Nontaxable life insurance proceeds on officers	Include in Income	Exclude from Income	Decrease Book Income
Dividends that qualify for dividends received deduction	Include in Income	Deduct from Income	Decrease Book Income*
50% business meals	Deduct from Income	Not Deductible	Increase Book Income
100% entertainment expenses	Deduct from Income	Not Deductible	Increase Book Income
Fines and penalties	Deduct from Income	Not Deductible	Increase Book Income
Lobbying and political expenses	Deduct from Income	Not Deductible	Increase Book Income
Premiums paid on life insurance policies on officers	Deduct from Income	Not Deductible	Increase Book Income

*Form 1120, Schedule M-1 reconciles to taxable income before deductions for net operating loss and special deductions. Do not include net operating losses or the dividends-received deduction as part of the M-1 reconciliation.

It is important to remember that timing differences will reverse in subsequent periods, and permanent differences do not.

SCHEDULE M-1 RECONCILIATION

DIFFERENCES BETWEEN BOOKS AND TAX RETURN

If an income or expense is treated the same way for tax purposes, no adjustment is necessary. However, if there are differences between the books and the tax return an adjustment is made to offset book income.

Reconciliation of Book Income (Loss) with Income (Loss) per Return			
Item	On Books	On Tax Return	M-1 Treatment
Income	Yes	No	Decrease Book Income
Expenses	Yes	No	Increase Book Income
Income	No	Yes	Increase Book Income
Deductions	No	Yes	Decrease Book Income

M-1 adjustments fall into four general categories:

- Income recorded on the books this year but not included on this return
- Expenses recorded on the books this year but not deducted on this return
- Income subject to tax but not recorded on the books this year
- Deductions on the tax return but not charged against book income this year

For a corporation (the entity that is most often tested) the reconciliation starts with Net income (loss) per books, proceeds backward through the financial statement and ends with Taxable income <u>before</u> **net operating loss deduction** and **special deductions**.

Summary Table of the M-1, Form 1120
Net income (loss) per BOOKS (start)
Add to Book Income
Federal income tax Net capital loss Taxable income not on the books Book expenses not on tax return
Subtract from Book Income
Book income not on tax return Deductions on tax return not charged to book income
Income (loss) per TAX RETURN (end)

The following adjustments are not a complete list of every event that creates a timing difference between taxable and book income. These are the items that are more commonly tested. For questions about **M-1** or **M-3** you need to remember how the item is accounted for book purposes and how that might be different than for tax purposes.

M-1 ADJUSTMENTS THAT INCREASE BOOK INCOME

Add these categories to book income on Schedule M-1.

Federal Income Tax

Schedule M-1 starts with the net income per books (after the deduction for income tax expense) as shown in the corporation's profit or loss account. The amount to add back on Schedule M-1 includes current and deferred taxes.

Net Capital Loss

This represents a timing difference since capital losses can be deducted on the books. Under IRC section 1211, capital losses can only be deducted to the extent of capital gains. The excess capital loss can be carried back three years and forward five years for tax purposes. There is no limitation on losses expensed for book purposes.

Income on Tax Return NOT Included on Books

These are items that because of timing or other generally accepted accounting provisions, have either:

- Been previously reported,
- Been used to reduce a balance sheet item, or
- Will be reported in some subsequent period.

Examples include:

- Gain recognized in subsequent years on an installment sale.
- Tax gain in excess of book gain on sale or disposal of assets. (Due to depreciation differences for book and tax purposes.)
- Prepaid rental income. Advanced rents are timing differences, which, for tax purposes, are included in taxable income in the year of receipt, but are reported in the period earned for book purposes.

Expenses on Books NOT Included on Tax Return

This category contains both permanent and timing differences. Some expenses are not deductible for tax purposes or temporarily deferred until some future event occurs. These expenses decrease book income on the financial statements but do not affect taxable income in the current year.

Some of the more common items include:

- Fines and penalties.
- Political contributions.
- Business gifts that exceed $25.
- 50% of business meals.
- 100% of entertainment expenses (entertainment is no longer deductible).
- Book depreciation exceeding the amount allowed for tax.
- Business interest expense exceeding the amount allowed for tax.
- Reserves for future expenses, which are not currently deductible for tax.
- Expenses incurred to earn tax-exempt income are not allowed as a deduction in the computation of taxable income.
- Charitable contributions in excess of the 10% of taxable income limitation.
- Provisions for estimated expenses are established for book purposes as contingencies, but they are not allowed for tax purposes until they become fixed and determinable.

The **conservatism principle** in accounting requires companies to recognize liabilities when they become probable.

- Officer's life insurance premiums are not allowed as a deduction for tax purposes in certain situations but would be reflected as a book deduction.

EXAMPLE: A company may maintain a life insurance policy on the life of its CEO and other top management in which the company is named as beneficiary. For book purposes, the premiums are expensed as incurred (usually as insurance expense). If the policy provides for a cash surrender value, the portion of the premium that relates to cash surrender value is recorded as an asset. For tax purposes, no deduction is allowed for premiums paid on any life insurance policy covering the life of any officer/employee when the company is directly or indirectly the beneficiary of the policy.

M-1 ADJUSTMENTS THAT REDUCE BOOK INCOME

Subtract these categories from book income on Schedule M-1.

Income on Books NOT Included on Tax Return

The books may reflect current income for financial reporting while deferring the item for tax purposes. This category also includes financial income not subject to tax. These income items increase book income on the financial statements but do not affect taxable income in the current year.

Examples include:

- Tax-exempt interest on municipal bonds,
- Officer's life insurance proceeds (since the premiums are not deductible, income from the policy is exempt from tax), and
- Installment receipts, which show up as deferred gross profit.

Deductions on Tax Return NOT Included on Books

This includes all deductions claimed for tax purposes that are not recorded in the corporation's books.

Examples include:

- The excess charitable contribution carryover (not allowed as a deduction for tax purposes in prior years) appears here as a timing difference.
- Depreciation is the most common example. Tax depreciation often exceeds the amount allowed for books.

> Generally, taxpayers are allowed to use accelerated depreciation for tax purposes while using the straight-line method for book purposes.

SPECIAL PROVISIONS

Rules on income and deductions that apply to individuals also apply, for the most part, to corporations. The following special provisions apply to corporations.

RELATED PERSONS

> A corporation that uses an accrual method of accounting **cannot deduct business expenses** and interest owed to a related person who uses the cash method of accounting <u>until</u> the corporation makes the payment and the corresponding amount is **includible in the related person's gross income.**

TIP: Section 267(a)(2) prevents <u>all</u> related parties (not just corporations) from using different accounting methods to claim a current deduction and defer recognizing the income.

Determine the relationship, for this rule, as of the end of the tax year for which the expense or interest would otherwise be deductible. If the IRS denies a deduction, the rule will continue to apply even if the corporation's relationship with the person ends before the expense or interest is includible in the gross income of that person. These rules also **deny the deduction of losses on the sale or exchange** of property between related persons.

- **Related persons** – For purposes of this rule, the following persons are related to a corporation:

  1. Another corporation that is a member of the same controlled group

  2. An individual who owns, directly or indirectly, more than 50% of the value of the outstanding stock of the corporation

  3. A trust fiduciary when the trust or the grantor of the trust owns, directly or indirectly, more than 50% in value of the outstanding stock of the corporation

  4. An S corporation if the same persons own more than 50% in value of the outstanding stock of each corporation

  5. A partnership if the same persons own more than 50% in value of the outstanding stock of the corporation and more than 50% of the capital or profits interest in the partnership

  6. Any employee-owner if the corporation is a personal service corporation, regardless of the amount of stock owned by the employee-owner

- **Ownership of stock** –The following rules determine whether an individual directly or indirectly owns any of the outstanding stock of a corporation:

  1. Stock owned, directly or indirectly, by a corporation, partnership, estate, or trust is treated as being owned proportionately by or for its shareholders, partners, or beneficiaries.

  2. Treat an individual as owning the stock owned, directly or indirectly, by or for the individual's family. Family includes only brothers and sisters (including half-brothers and half-sisters), a spouse, ancestors, and lineal descendants.

  3. Any individual owning (other than by applying rule 2) any stock in a corporation is treated as owning the stock owned directly or indirectly by that individual's partner.

CAPITAL LOSSES

A corporation can deduct capital losses only up to the amount of its capital gains. A corporation **cannot deduct excess capital loss** in the current tax year. Instead, it carries the loss to other tax years and deducts it from any net capital gains that occur in those years. The character of a net capital loss carried to another tax year is always **short-term.**

A corporation may not carry a capital loss (or a net operating loss) from, or to, a year for which it is an **S corporation** other than as a deduction against the net recognized *built-in gain* of the S corporation for the taxable year. Built-in gain is the excess of the book value of the contributed property over the adjusted tax basis in the property upon the contribution.

Capital losses that are not used to offset capital gains in the current period may be **carried back for three periods then forward for five years** to offset capital gains in those periods. Any capital losses that have not been used for five years after they occurred are lost forever to the corporation.

- Carryback three years prior to the loss year
- Carryback two years prior to the loss year
- Carryback one year prior to the loss year
- Carryforward any remaining loss for five years

EXAMPLE 12-5: A calendar year corporation has a net short-term capital gain of $3,000 and a net long-term capital loss of $9,000. The short-term gain offsets some of the long-term loss, leaving a net capital loss of $6,000. The corporation treats this $6,000 as a short-term loss when carried back or forward.

The corporation carries the $6,000 short-term loss back 3 years. In year 1, the corporation had a net short-term capital gain of $8,000 and a net long-term capital gain of $5,000. It subtracts the $6,000 short-term loss first from the net short-term gain. This results in a net capital gain for year 1 of $7,000. This consists of a net short-term capital gain of $2,000 ($8,000 − $6,000) and a net long-term capital gain of $5,000.

When carrying a capital loss from one year to another, the following rules apply:

- When figuring the current year's net capital loss, the taxpayer cannot combine it with a capital loss carried from another year. In other words, carry capital losses only to years that would otherwise have a total net capital gain.
- If the taxpayer carries capital losses from 2 or more years to the same year, deduct the loss from the earliest year first.
- The taxpayer cannot use a capital loss carried from another year to produce or increase a net operating loss.

NET OPERATING LOSSES

A corporation figures a *net operating loss (NOL)* in the same way it figures taxable income. It starts with its gross income and subtracts its deductions. If a corporation's annual business deductions are more than its annual business income, the corporation has an NOL. A net operating loss may be **carried forward indefinitely** and used as a deduction in the future period.

Figuring the NOL – If deductions are more than its gross income, the corporation has an NOL. The following rules apply when calculating NOL:

- NOL <u>cannot</u> increase because of carryovers from other years (including NOL, capital loss, and charitable contribution carryovers).
- A corporation <u>cannot</u> consider the domestic production activities deduction.
- A corporation can take the deduction for dividends received without regard to the aggregate limits (based on taxable income) that normally apply.
- A corporation can figure the deduction for dividends paid on certain preferred stock of public utilities without limiting it to its taxable income for the year.

TIPS:

- Capital losses may <u>not</u> offset net capital gains in the carryover year if that deduction creates or increases a net operating loss.
- Normally <u>no</u> deduction for charitable contributions is allowed in a loss year because charitable contributions are limited to a percentage of net income.
- Casualty or theft losses <u>may be included</u> as part of the net operating loss.

TCJA: The TCJA introduced new rules for NOLs arising in taxable years beginning after December 31, 2017. The general 2-year NOL carryback rule does <u>not</u> apply and the taxpayer may carry the loss forward indefinitely. Exceptions apply to certain farming losses (2-year carryback) and NOLs of property and casualty insurance companies. There is also a provision that <u>limits</u> the NOL deduction to **80% of taxable income** (determined without regard to the deduction). These rules are **temporarily suspended** by the *CARES Act*.

TIP: NOLs arising in taxable years beginning <u>before</u> 2018 remain subject to **prior law**. Accordingly, such NOLs are <u>not</u> subject to the 80-percent limitation and remain subject to the prior law carryback rules (generally 2-year carryback) and the 20-year carryover limitation.

CARES ACT UPDATE: As authorized by the CARES Act, the IRS issued Revenue Procedure 2020-24 providing guidance on procedures for **carrying back NOLs arising in taxable years 2018, 2019, or 2020** to each of the **five preceding tax years.** As a result of this amendment, taxpayers take into account such NOLs in the earliest taxable year in the carryback period, carrying forward unused amounts to each succeeding taxable year. Also, for losses arising in 2018, 2019, or 2020 taxable years the NOL deduction is <u>not</u> limited to 80% of taxable income.

If a taxpayer chooses to carry back an NOL, they must first carry the entire NOL back 5 years. Carry back the entire NOL to the 5th tax year before the loss year. Any NOL not used in the 5th preceding year is then carried to the 4th preceding year, and so on. Any NOL not applied in the 5 preceding years can be carried forward to tax years following the year of loss. Any NOL not carried back may be carried forward indefinitely and used as a deduction in the future period it is carried to.

A taxpayer within the scope of this revenue procedure may **elect to waive** the carryback period in the case of a net operating loss arising in a taxable year beginning after December 31, 2017, and before January 1, 2021. Such an election must be made no later than the due date, including extensions, for filing the taxpayer's income tax return for the first taxable year ending after March 27, 2020.

TIP: The CARES Act provisions could be of substantial benefit for taxpayers with losses in 2018, 2019, or 2020. Taxpayers with an NOL in those tax years have the ability to carry the NOL back five years and the NOL deduction is not limited to 80% of taxable income for NOLs arising in those years.

SPECIAL DEDUCTIONS

DIVIDENDS-RECEIVED DEDUCTION

A corporation can deduct a percentage of the dividends received from another domestic corporation, within certain limits. This amount is determined by the amount of ownership the corporation has in the corporation paying the dividend.

TCJA: The act reduced the 70% dividends received deduction to 50% and the 80% dividends received deduction to 65% for taxable years beginning after December 31, 2017.

Dividends Received Deduction	
Ownership	Deduction Percentage
Less than 20% ownership	**50%** of the dividends received
20-79% ownership	**65%** of the dividends received
80% and more ownership	**100%** of the dividends received

Small business investment companies and *affiliated corporations* can deduct **100%** of the dividends received from taxable domestic corporations. An affiliated corporation possesses at least 80 percent of the total voting power of the stock of such corporation.

Corporations <u>cannot</u> take a deduction for dividends received from the following entities:

- A real estate investment trust (REIT)
- A corporation exempt from tax under Section 501 or 521 of the Internal Revenue Code either for the tax year of the distribution or the preceding tax year
- A corporation whose stock was held less than 46 days during the 91-day period, beginning 45 days before the stock became *ex-dividend* (when the holder has no rights to the dividend)
- A corporation whose preferred stock was held less than 91 days during the 181-day period, beginning 90 days before the stock became ex-dividend with respect to the dividend if the dividends received are for a period or periods totaling more than 360 days
- Any corporation, if the taxpayer is under an obligation to make related payments with respect to positions in substantially similar or related property

The deduction for dividends received is generally **limited to 65% (or 50%) of taxable income**. If taxable income is less than the amount of dividends received use taxable income to calculate the deduction.

The taxable income limit does not apply if a corporation has a **net operating loss** for the tax year. To determine whether a corporation has an NOL, figure the dividends-received deduction <u>without</u> the 65% (or 50%) taxable income limit.

EXAMPLE 12-8: A corporation loses $40,000 from operations. It receives $100,000 in dividends from a 20%-owned corporation.

Operating Income	($40,000)
Dividend Income	$100,000
Taxable Income	$60,000

Taxable income is $60,000 ($100,000 – $40,000) before the deduction for dividends received. The limit based on taxable income is $39,000 ($60,000 × 65%) and the maximum deduction based on the dividends received is $65,000 ($100,000 × 65%). The taxable income limit does not apply if a corporation has a net operating loss for the tax year, determined without considering the taxable income limit.

Operating income	($40,000)
Dividend income	$100,000
Maximum dividends received deduction	($65,000)
Taxable income after maximum deduction	($5,000)

If the corporation claims the 65% deduction against on the dividends received it will have an NOL of $5,000. As a result, the 65% of taxable income limitation does not apply. The corporation can deduct the full $65,000.

EXAMPLE 12-9: Assume the same facts, except that the corporation only loses $15,000 from operations.

After claiming the dividends-received deduction of $65,000 ($100,000 × 65%), its taxable income is $20,000. Because the corporation will not have an NOL after applying a full dividends-received deduction, its allowable dividends-received deduction is limited to 65% of its taxable income, or $55,250 ($85,000 × 65%).

Operating income	($15,000)
Dividend income	$100,000
Taxable income	$85,000

Taxable income is $85,000 ($100,000 – $15,000) before the deduction for dividends received. The limit based on taxable income is $55,250 ($85,000 × 65%) and the maximum deduction based on the dividends received is $65,000 ($100,000 × 65%). The taxable income limit does not apply if a corporation has a net operating loss for the tax year, determined without considering the taxable income limit.

Operating income	($15,000)
Dividend income	$100,000
Maximum dividends received deduction	($65,000)
Taxable income after maximum deduction	$20,000

If the corporation claims the maximum deduction on the dividends received it will have taxable income of $20,000. The taxable income limitation applies because the result is not a loss. The corporation may deduct only $55,250 of the $100,000 dividends received.

Operating income	($15,000)
Dividend income	$100,000
Limited dividends received deduction	($55,250)
Taxable income after limited deduction	$29,750

CHARITABLE CONTRIBUTIONS

CARES ACT UPDATE: The CARES Act temporarily increases the limit on **qualified cash contributions** made in 2020. A corporation may deduct qualified contributions of cash up to **25 percent of its taxable income**. Contributions that exceed that amount can carry over to the next tax year. This relief also applies to qualified cash contributions made in 2021, as the relief was extended by the *Consolidated Appropriations Act, 2021*.

To qualify, the contribution must be:

- a **cash** contribution
- made to a qualifying organization
- made during the calendar year 2020 or 2021

Contributions of non-cash property do not qualify for this relief. Taxpayers may still claim non-cash contributions as a deduction, subject to the normal limits.

A corporation can claim a limited deduction for charitable contributions made in cash or other property. The contribution is deductible if made to, or for the use of, a qualified organization. The corporation cannot take a deduction if any of the net earnings of an organization receiving contributions benefit any private shareholder. A corporation cannot deduct charitable contributions that **exceed 10%** of its taxable income for the tax year. Figure taxable income for this purpose without the following:

- The deduction for charitable contributions

- The dividends-received deduction
- The deduction allowed under Section 249 (premium on bond repurchase) of the Internal Revenue Code

A corporation may **carry forward to each of the subsequent five years** any charitable contributions made during the current year that exceed the 10% limit.

For a contribution of property, the corporation must reduce the contribution by the sum of the following:

- The ordinary income and short-term capital gain that would result if the property is sold at FMV, and
- For certain contributions, the long-term capital gain that would result if the property were sold at its FMV. The reduction for the long-term capital gain applies to the following:

  1. Contributions of tangible personal property for use by an exempt organization for a purpose or function unrelated to the basis for its exemption
  2. Contributions of any property to or for the use of certain private foundations (except for stock)
  3. Contributions of any patent, certain copyrights, trademark, trade name, trade secret, know-how, software (that is a Section 197 intangible), or similar property, or applications or registrations of such property

A corporation (other than an S corporation) may be able to claim a deduction equal to the lesser of:

- Basis of the donated inventory or property plus one-half of the property's appreciation gain if the donated inventory or property was sold at fair market value on the date of the donation, or
- Two times basis of the donated inventory or property.

This deduction may be allowed for certain contributions of:

- Inventory and other property made to a donee organization and used solely for the care of the ill, the needy, and infants.
- Scientific property constructed by the corporation (other than an S corporation, personal holding company, or personal service corporation) and donated no later than 2 years after substantial completion of the construction.
- Computer technology and equipment acquired or constructed and donated no later than 3 years after either acquisition or substantial completion of construction to an educational organization for educational purposes within the United States.

FIGURING TAX

TCJA: Corporations (including personal service corporations) are taxed at a flat **21% corporate rate.**

ALTERNATIVE MINIMUM TAX (AMT)

TCJA: A new provision **repeals** the corporate alternative minimum tax for taxable years beginning after December 31, 2017.

ACCUMULATED EARNINGS TAX

While corporations are not required to distribute income, the law discourages them from building an investment portfolio subject only to the corporate income tax. A corporation can accumulate its earnings for a possible expansion or other bona fide business reasons. Earnings accumulate beyond the reasonable needs of the business may be subject to an accumulated earnings tax of **20%**. To determine if the corporation is subject to this tax, treat an accumulation of $250,000 ($150,000 for PSC) or less generally as within the reasonable needs of most businesses. Reasonable needs of the business include the following:

- Specific, definite, and feasible plans for use of the earnings accumulation in the business, or
- The amount necessary to redeem stock included in a deceased shareholder's gross estate.

PERSONAL HOLDING COMPANY TAX

A tax rate of **20%** may apply to undistributed *personal holding company* (PHC) income. This tax discourages using closely held corporations to attempt to avoid personal income taxes on investment income. Generally, a corporation is a PHC if it meets both of the following requirements:

- **Stock ownership requirement** – At any time during the last half of the tax year, more than 50% in value of the corporation's stock is owned—directly or indirectly—by five or fewer individuals.
- **PHC income test** – At least 60% of the corporation's adjusted ordinary gross income for the tax year is PHC income. PHC income includes income from dividends, interest, rents, and certain royalties.

SHAREHOLDER EARNINGS AND PROFITS (E&P)

The *earnings and profits* of a corporation determine the character of distributions paid to shareholders. If a corporation's E&P for the year (figured as of the close of the year without reduction for any distributions made during the year) is more than the total amount of distributions made during the year, all distributions made during the year are treated as dividends (distributions of *current year E&P*). Shareholders of a corporation receive dividend tax treatment for a distribution of E&P regardless of whether the source of E&P is taxable or tax-free income. If the distributions exceed current year E&P, the distribution may still be a dividend, provided the corporation has accumulated E&P. If the corporation has no E&P, the distribution is not a dividend and may be a tax-free return of capital or a capital gain. E&P is taxable income, plus or minus certain adjustments. Items the corporation must add back to taxable income to calculate E&P include the following:

- Muni bond interest
- Excluded life insurance proceeds
- Federal income tax refunds
- Dividends received deduction

ACCUMULATED E&P

If a corporation's current year E&P is less than the total distributions made during the year, treat part or all of each distribution as a distribution of *accumulated E&P*. Accumulated E&P is earnings and profits the corporation accumulated (did not distribute) in previous years.

- If the corporation **has current year E&P**, figure the use of E&P as follows:
  1. Divide the current year E&P by the total distributions made during the year.
  2. Multiply each distribution by the percentage to get the amount treated as a distribution of current year E&P.
  3. Start with the first distribution, and treat the part of each distribution greater than the allocated current year E&P figured in (2) as a distribution of accumulated E&P.
  4. If accumulated E&P is reduced to $0, the remaining part of each distribution is applied against, and reduces, the adjusted basis of the stock in the hands of the shareholders. To the extent that the balance is more than the adjusted basis of the stock, treat it as a gain from the sale or exchange of property.

EXAMPLE 12-6: You are the only shareholder of a corporation that uses the calendar year as its tax year. In January, you figure your corporation's current year earnings and profits for the previous year. At the beginning of the year, the corporation's accumulated earnings and profits balance was $20,000. During the year, the corporation made four $4,000 distributions to you ($4,000 × 4 = $16,000). At the end of the year (before subtracting distributions made during the year), the corporation had $10,000 of current year earnings and profits.

Since the corporation's current year earnings of $10,000 are less than distributions made during the year of $16,000, treat part of each distribution as a distribution of accumulated earnings and profits. Divide the $10,000 by $16,000 and the result is .625. Multiply each $4,000 distribution by .625 to get $2,500, which is the amount of each distribution treated as a distribution of current year earnings and profits. Treat the remaining $1,500 of each distribution as a distribution from accumulated earnings and profits. The corporation distributed $6,000 ($1,500 × 4) of accumulated earnings. The remaining $14,000 ($20,000 – $6,000) of accumulated earnings is available for use in the following year.

- If there is **no current year E&P** (a loss), figure the use of accumulated E&P as follows:
  1. Prorate the current year loss to the date of each distribution made during the year.
  2. Figure the available accumulated E&P balance on the date of each distribution by subtracting the prorated amount of current year E&P from the accumulated balance.
  3. Treat each distribution as a distribution of the adjusted accumulated E&P.
  4. If adjusted accumulated E&P is reduced to $0, the remaining distributions are applied against, and reduce, the adjusted basis of the stock in the hands of the shareholders. Treat any balance that is more than the adjusted basis of the stock as a gain from the sale or exchange of property.

EXAMPLE: 12-7: Same circumstances as the prior example, except at the end of the year (before subtracting distributions made during the year), the corporation had a **negative $10,000 current year E&P** balance. The distributions occur on March 31, June 30, September 30, and December 31.

Since the corporation had no current year E&P, treat all of the distributions as distributions of accumulated E&P. **Prorate the negative current year E&P balance to the date of each distribution** made during the year. Spread the negative $10,000 evenly by prorating a negative $2,500 to each distribution.

March 31 Distribution	
Accumulated earnings and profits	$20,000
Prorated current year earnings and profits	($2,500)
Accumulated earnings and profits available	$17,500
Amount of distribution treated as a dividend	($4,000)

June 30 Distribution	
Accumulated earnings and profits	$13,500
Prorated current year earnings and profits	($2,500)
Accumulated earnings and profits available	$11,000
Amount of distribution treated as a dividend	($4,000)

September 30 Distribution	
Accumulated earnings and profits	$7,000
Prorated current year earnings and profits	($2,500)
Accumulated earnings and profits available	$4,500
Amount of distribution treated as a dividend	($4,000)

December 31 Distribution	
Accumulated earnings and profits	$500
Prorated current year earnings and profits	($2,500)
Accumulated earnings and profits available	($2,000)
Amount of distribution treated as a dividend	$0
Nondividend amount*	$4,000
Year-end accumulated earnings and profits	($2,000)

*The nondividend amount is a reduction of stock basis or gain from sale/exchange of property.

The corporation issues a Form 1099-DIV to report **$12,000** (the March 31, June 30, and September 30 distributions had positive E&P) of the $16,000 distributed as dividends, and **$4,000** as a nondividend distribution (after prorating the current year loss, the corporation did not have enough E&P for the Dec 31 distribution to be classified as a dividend).

DISTRIBUTIONS

In general, treat corporate distributions to a shareholder as:

- **Dividends** – If the distribution is from current or accumulated E&P
- **Non-dividend distribution** – Any part of a distribution that is not from E&P is applied against and reduces the adjusted basis of the stock in the hands of the shareholder
- **Gain** – To the extent the distribution is more than the adjusted basis of the stock, the shareholder has a gain (usually a capital gain) from the sale or exchange of property

Most distributions are in money, but they may also be in stock or other property. If distributions of property occur, other than stock dividends or rights, the amount of the distribution is generally the amount of any money paid to the shareholder plus the FMV of the property, reduced by any liabilities assumed. The basis of the property to the shareholder is the FMV of the property. In general, distributions are **taxable as dividends** to the extent of E&P.

GAIN FROM PROPERTY DISTRIBUTIONS

A corporation will recognize a gain on the distribution of property to a shareholder if the FMV of the property is more than its adjusted basis. This treatment is similar to a sale of property by the corporation. If the property was depreciable or amortizable, the corporation may have to treat all or part of the gain as ordinary income from depreciation recapture. For this purpose, the FMV of the property is the greater of the following amounts:

- The actual FMV
- The amount of any liabilities a shareholder assumed connected to the distribution of property

TIP: A corporation does <u>not</u> recognize a loss for a nonliquidating distribution of property that has declined in value below its adjusted basis.

DISTRIBUTIONS OF STOCK OR STOCK RIGHTS

Distributions by a corporation of its stock are stock dividends. Stock rights (stock options) are distributions by a corporation of rights to acquire its stock. Distributions of stock dividends and stock rights are generally tax-free to shareholders. The shareholder's holding period begins the day after the distribution date. Treat the distribution of stock or stock rights the same as other property if any of the following apply:

- Any shareholder has the choice to receive cash or other property instead of stock or stock rights.
- The distribution gives cash or other property to some shareholders and an increase in the percentage interest in the corporation's assets or E&P to other shareholders.
- The distribution is in convertible preferred stock and has the same result as previous rule.
- The distribution gives preferred stock to some shareholders and common stock to others.
- The distribution is on preferred stock.

DEEMED DISTRIBUTIONS

The following events may be treated as a distribution to a shareholder:

- **Below-market loans** – If a corporation gives a shareholder a loan on which no interest is charged or on which interest is charged at a rate below the applicable federal rate, the interest not charged may be treated as a distribution to the shareholder.
- **Corporation cancels shareholder's debt** – If a corporation cancels a shareholder's debt without repayment by the shareholder, treat the amount canceled as a distribution.
- **Transfers of property to shareholders for less than FMV** – A sale or exchange of property by a corporation to a shareholder may be treated as a distribution to the shareholder. If a shareholder is not a corporation and the FMV of the property on the date of sale or exchange exceeds the price paid by the shareholder, the excess may be treated as a distribution.
- **Unreasonable rents** – If a corporation rents property from a shareholder at above market rates, the excessive part of the rent may be treated as a distribution to the shareholder.
- **Unreasonable salaries** – If a corporation pays an employee who is also a shareholder a salary that is unreasonably high considering the services actually performed by the shareholder-employee, the excessive part of the salary may be treated as a distribution.

FORM 1099-DIV

The corporation must generally send Forms 1099-DIV to the IRS with Form 1096 **by February 28** (March 31 if filing electronically) of the year following the year of the distribution. Generally, a corporation must furnish Forms 1099-DIV to shareholders by **January 31** of the year following the close of the calendar year during which the corporation made the distributions. It is necessary to file a *Form 1099-DIV* with the IRS for each person the corporation:

- Paid dividends (including capital gain dividends) and other distributions on stock of **$10** or more,
- Withheld and paid any foreign tax on dividends and other distributions on stock,
- Withheld any federal income tax on dividends under the backup withholding rules, or
- Paid **$600** or more as part of a liquidation

REDEMPTION OF STOCK

A stock redemption is the acquisition of corporate stock from a shareholder in exchange for money or property. Treat stock redemptions as a **distribution**, in part or full payment, **in exchange for stock**. The transaction is a sale or trade and is subject to the capital gain or loss provisions unless considered a dividend or other distribution on the stock.

Treat the redemption as a **sale or trade** of stock if <u>any</u> of the following are true:

- The redemption is not essentially equivalent to a dividend.
- The redemption is substantially disproportionate and is a distribution in partial liquidation:
  1. Immediately after the redemption, the shareholder owns less than 50% of the total combined voting power of all classes of stock entitled to vote, and
  2. The ratio of ownership is less than 80% of the ratio of ownership prior to the redemption.
- There is a complete redemption of all the stock of the corporation owned by the shareholder.

Whether the redemption is treated as a sale, trade, dividend, or other distribution depends on the circumstances in each case. Both direct and indirect ownership of stock is considered.

LIQUIDATING DISTRIBUTIONS

Liquidating distributions are distributions received during a partial or complete liquidation of a corporation. These distributions are, at least in part, one form of a return of capital. The corporation may pay them in one or more installments.

A liquidating distribution is <u>not</u> taxable until the taxpayer recovers the basis of the stock. After the basis of the stock is reduced to $0, the liquidating distribution is a capital gain, either long-term or short-term depending on how long the taxpayer held the stock.

If the total liquidating distributions are less than the basis of the stock, the shareholder has a capital loss, reportable only after receipt of the final distribution in liquidation that results in the redemption or cancellation of the stock. The disallowance of losses from the sale or exchange of property between related persons does <u>not</u> apply to liquidating distributions.

S CORPORATIONS (FORM 1120S)

An eligible domestic corporation can avoid double taxation by electing treatment as an *S corporation (S corp)*. Like a partnership, an S corp is a flow-through entity.

Generally, an S corp is exempt from federal income tax other than tax on certain capital gains and passive income. On their tax returns, the S corp shareholders include their share of the corporation's separately stated items of income, deduction, loss, and credit, and their share of non-separately stated ordinary business income or loss reported to them on *Schedule K-1 (Form 1120S)*.

SEPARATELY STATED ITEMS

Some of the items stated separately on *Schedule K-1 (Form 1120S)* include the following:

- Net rental real estate income (loss)

- Other net rental income (loss)
- Interest income (loss)
- Ordinary and qualified dividends
- Royalties
- Capital gains and losses (LTCG, STCG, 1250, and 1231)
- Collectibles (28%) gains (loss)
- Section 179 deduction
- Foreign transactions
- AMT items
- Items affecting shareholder basis (including drilling costs)
- Charitable contributions
- Credits
- Starting with tax year 2018, S corporations report each shareholder's share of qualified business income, W-2 wages, and other information on Schedule K-1 so the shareholders may determine their deduction for 20 percent of qualified business income (Section 199A qualified business income deduction).

> **TCJA:** As part of the reporting requirements for passthrough entities imposed by the regulations, a pass-through entity is required to allocate and disclose Qualified Business Income, W-2 wages, and the unadjusted basis of property. If any one item is <u>not</u> allocated, that item is **presumed to be zero**. There is no exception for pass-through entities that know that all of its owners have taxable income below the thresholds. In addition, a pass-through entity is required to disclose whether it has multiple trades or businesses, and if any of those businesses are Specified Service Trades or Businesses.

TAXES

The income tax filing deadline is the **15th day of the third month** after the end of its tax year (March 15 for a calendar year S corp). This deadline is unchanged from years past, but it is no longer the same as C corp (April 15 for a calendar year C corp). An S corp can obtain an automatic six-month extension of time to file by filing Form 7004. In most cases, all items pass through to S corp shareholders; however, there are circumstances where the S corp may have income tax liability if the S corp was previously a C corp and has:

- **Built-in gains** – If S corp has a net recognized built-in gain on assets held when it was a C corp
- **Excess net passive income** – An S corp with accumulated E&P that has passive investment income exceeding 25% of gross receipts must pay tax on excess net passive income
- **LIFO recapture tax** – If C corp had LIFO inventory and changed (or transferred it) to an S corp
- **Investment Credit Recapture** – The S corp may need to recapture certain credits allowed for periods it was not an S corp

S CORPORATION FILING PENALTIES

A penalty is assessed against the S corporation if it is required to file a return and it (a) fails to file the return by the due date, including extensions, or (b) files a return that fails to show all the information required, unless such failure is due to reasonable cause. In the absence of reasonable cause, the applicable penalties for returns required to be filed in 2021 (generally 2020 tax returns filed in 2021) are:

- **Late or incomplete filing** (§6699) – **$210** for **each month** or part of a month (for a maximum of 12 months) the failure continues, **multiplied by the total number of shareholders** in the S corporation during <u>any</u> part of the S corporation's tax year for which the return is due.

- **Failure to furnish K-1 to shareholder** (§6722) – A **$280** penalty may be imposed for **each failure** to furnish Schedule K-1 to a shareholder when due and each failure to include on Schedule K-1 all the information required to be shown (or the inclusion of incorrect information). If the taxpayer intentionally disregards the requirement to furnish or report correct information the penalty increases to $560 or, if greater, 10% of the amount required to be reported.

THE "S" ELECTION

The eligible corporation must make the election to become an S corporation and **all shareholders (and former shareholders from that year) must agree** to that election to be an S corporation. This election is done on Form 2553 and it must be signed by all shareholders.

To receive S corporation treatment, a domestic corporation or other domestic entity eligible to elect to be treated as a corporation (such as LLC) must make the election on *Form 2553*. The corporation must file Form 2553 no more than **two months and 15 days** after the beginning of the tax year the election is to take effect, or in the year prior.

To be an S corporation, the entity must meet all the following tests:

- It must be a small business corporation:
  1. It has no more than **100** shareholders.
  2. All shareholders are individuals, estates, exempt organizations, or certain trusts (not **partnerships** or **corporations**).
  3. It has no **nonresident alien shareholders**.
  4. It has only **one class of stock**.
- It is not one of the following ineligible corporations:
  1. A bank or thrift institution that uses the reserve method of accounting
  2. An insurance company subject to tax
  3. A corporation that has elected to be treated as a possessions corporation
  4. A domestic international sales corporation (DISC) or former DISC

The Tax Cuts and Jobs Act (TCJA) expands qualifying beneficiaries of an electing small business trust (ESBT), effective January 1, 2018. An ESBT may be a shareholder of an S corporation. Generally, the eligible beneficiaries of an ESBT include individuals, estates, and certain charitable organizations eligible to hold S corporation stock directly. A nonresident alien individual may not be a shareholder of an S corporation, but the TCJA, allows a nonresident alien individual to be a potential current beneficiary of an ESBT.

TIP: Members of a family are treated as 1 shareholder. This includes a husband and wife, and all members of a family that share a common ancestor, and their respective estates.

A parent S corporation can elect to treat an eligible wholly-owned subsidiary as a qualified subchapter S subsidiary. If the corporation makes this election, the subsidiary's assets, liabilities, and items of income, deduction, and credit generally are treated as those of the parent.

TIP: An entity intending to be classified as an S corporation that fails to make a timely "S" election may qualify for late election relief under Revenue Procedure 2013-30. There must be reasonable cause, and generally, less than 3 years and 75 days have passed since the effective date of the election.

TERMINATION OF ELECTION

Once the corporation makes the election it stays in effect until terminated. If the corporation terminates the election, the corporation (or a successor corporation) can make another election on Form 2553 only with IRS consent for any tax year before the **fifth** tax year after termination. An election terminates automatically in any of the following cases:

- The corporation is no longer a small business corporation.
- The corporation, for each of three consecutive tax years, has accumulated earnings and profits and derives more than 25% of its gross receipts from passive investment income.
- The election is revoked with the consent of shareholders who hold more than 50% of the number of issued and outstanding shares of stock (including non-voting stock).

INCOME AND EXPENSES

An S corporation allocates income (or loss) and separately stated items **in proportion** to the shareholder's percentage of ownership. This is in contrast to a partnership, which is not required to allocate items based on the partner's percentage of ownership. Ownership is determined for each day of the year.

A shareholder cannot deduct a loss that exceeds the basis of his stock increased by any loans the shareholder made to the S corp. The amount of a shareholder's stock and debt basis is very important. Unlike a C corporation, the stock and/or debt basis of an S corporation goes up and/or down each year based on the S corporation's operations.

Shareholder losses are subject to the following limitations, in the order in which they apply, the **basis rules**, the **at-risk limitations**, the **passive activity limitations,** and the **excess business loss limitations** (**suspended** for 2018, 2019, and 2020 by the **CARES Act**). Additional details on these limitations appear in the section on Loss Limitations.

> **CARES ACT UPDATE:** The CARES Act **repealed** the excess business loss limitation for tax years 2018, 2019, and 2020. The limitation on excess business losses returns for tax years beginning after 2020 and before 2026.

DISTRIBUTIONS

The earnings and profits of an S corp are taxable to its shareholders, whether distributed or not. The taxable amount of distribution is contingent on the shareholder's stock basis. It is not the corporation's responsibility to track a shareholder's stock and debt basis; rather it is the shareholder's responsibility. Treat a distribution to shareholders from an S corp that does not have accumulated E&P as a **return of capital** up to the shareholders' basis and as **gain** from the sale or exchange of property on the excess. Generally, the S corporation has accumulated E&P only if it has not distributed E&P accumulated in prior years when the S corporation was a C corporation. Treat the portion of a distribution attributed to accumulated E&P as a dividend. If the S corporation has AE&P it must maintain the following accounts to determine taxable dividends:

- **Accumulated Adjustments Account (AAA)** – The accumulated adjustments account (AAA) is an account of the S corporation that generally reflects the accumulated undistributed net income after 1982.
- **Accumulated Earnings and Profits Account (AE&P)** – Generally, S corporation accumulated E&P is from undistributed E&P accumulated in prior years when the S corporation was a C corporation.
- **Other Adjustments Account (OAA)** – The OAA tracks tax-exempt income if the S corporation has AE&P. Tax-exempt income increases shareholder basis. Treat OAA as non-taxable distribution to the shareholder, reducing the shareholder's basis.

Ordering rules determine the taxation of distributions:

1	Accumulated Adjustments Account (AAA)	Not Taxable
2	Accumulated Earnings and Profits (AE&P)	Taxable Dividend
3	Other Adjustments Account (OAA)	Not Taxable
4	Stock Basis/Return of Capital	Not Taxable
5	In Excess of Stock Basis	Capital gain

ACCUMULATED ADJUSTMENTS ACCOUNT

S corporations with accumulated E&P must maintain the AAA to determine the tax effect of distributions. On the first day of the corporation's first tax year as an S corporation, the balance of the AAA is $0. At the end of the tax year, adjust the AAA for the items as explained below:

- Increase the AAA by income (other than tax-exempt income).
- Decrease the AAA by deductible losses and expenses, and nondeductible expenses (other than expenses related to tax-exempt income).
- Decrease AAA (but not below $0) by distributions (other than dividends from accumulated E&P).

TIP: AAA is increased for the same items that increase basis except for capital contributions and tax-exempt income. AAA is decreased for the same items that decrease basis except for nondeductible expenses related to tax-exempt income. Unlike stock basis, the AAA may be reduced below zero, but only by losses and **not** by distributions.

With the consent of all its affected shareholders, an S corp can make an election to distribute accumulated E&P before the AAA, or they can elect to distribute all or part of the accumulated E&P with a deemed dividend. Otherwise, apply property distributions (including cash) in the following order (to reduce accounts of the S corp to figure the tax effect of distributions made to its shareholders):

- Reduce the AAA by the amount of the distribution, but not below $0. Distributions from this account are a **return of capital** and reduce the shareholders' basis.
- Reduce the *previously taxed income (PTI)* account by any remaining amount, but not below $0. This account is for income prior to 1983. It is reduced only if there is a balance. Like the AAA, distributions from this account are tax-free to the extent of the shareholders' basis.
- Reduce accumulated E&P by any amount remaining, but not below $0. Treat distributions from accumulated E&P as **dividends**.
- The remaining distributions are a return of capital, up to the shareholders' basis. If the shareholders' basis is reduced to $0, the remainder is a capital gain.

For simplification purposes, this guide does not show these rules in their entirety.

Distributions of appreciated property are valued at FMV. The S corp will recognize a gain (but not a loss) on the property to the extent that FMV of the property exceeds its basis. The gain will pass through to the shareholders on the K-1.

SHAREHOLDER STOCK BASIS IN S CORPORATION

In computing stock basis, the shareholder starts with the initial capital contribution to the S corporation or the initial cost of the stock purchased (the same as a C corporation). That amount is then increased and/or decreased based on the flow-through amounts from the S corporation. An income item will increase stock basis, while a loss, deduction, or distribution will decrease stock basis.

The order in which stock basis is increased or decreased is important. Since both the taxability of a distribution and the deductibility of a loss are dependent on stock basis, there is an **ordering rule** in computing stock basis. Stock basis adjusts annually, as of the last day of the S corporation year, in the following order:

- Increased for income items and excess depletion;
- Decreased for distributions;
- Decreased for non-deductible, non-capital expenses and depletion; and
- Decreased for items of loss and deduction.

EXAMPLE 12-10: Sigma Corp, an S corporation, has accumulated earnings and profits of $1,000 and a balance in the AAA of $2,000 on January 1, 20X1. Sigma's sole shareholder Bella holds 100 shares of stock with a basis of $20 per share as of January 1, 20X1. On April 1, 2001, Sigma makes a distribution of $1,500 to Bella. Bella's pro rata share of the income earned by Sigma during 20X1 is $2,000 and Bella's pro rata share of Sigma's losses is $1,500. For the taxable year ending December 31, 20X1, Sigma does not have a net negative adjustment as defined in section 1368(e)(1)(C). Sigma does not make the election under section 1368(e)(3) to distribute its earnings and profits before its AAA.

The AAA is increased from $2,000 to $4,000 for the $2,000 of income earned during the 20X1 taxable year. The AAA is decreased from $4,000 to $2,500 for the $1,500 of losses. The AAA is decreased from $2,500 to $1,000 for the portion of the distribution ($1,500) to Bella that does not exceed the AAA.

	AAA	AE&P
Jan 1 beginning balance	$2,000	$1,000
Income	+ 2,000	
Losses	– 1,500	
Balance before distribution	$2,500	$1,000
Shareholder distribution	– 1,500	
Dec 31 ending balance	**$1,000**	**$1,000**

Bella holds 100 shares of stock with a basis of $20 per share as of January 1, 20X1 ($2,000 basis in stock). As of December 31, 20X1, Bella's basis in the stock is $1,000 ($10 per share), calculated as follows:

Jan 1 beginning basis	$2,000
Income	+ 2,000
Shareholder distribution	– 1,500
Losses	– 1,500
Dec 31 ending basis	**$1,000**

If a shareholder receives a non-dividend distribution from an S corporation, the distribution is tax-free to the extent it does not exceed the shareholder's stock basis. A shareholder treats a non-dividend distribution in excess of stock basis as a capital gain (usually LTCG) on the shareholder's personal return.

- Shareholder basis is **increased** by the total of:
  1. Separately stated Items of income (including tax-exempt)

2. Non-separately computed income

3. The excess of the deductions for depletion over the basis of the property

- Shareholder basis is **decreased** by:

    1. Distributions by the corporation not includible in the income of the shareholder

    2. Separately stated loss items

    3. Non-separately computed loss

    4. Any expense of the corporation not deductible in computing its taxable income and not properly chargeable to capital account

    5. The shareholder's deduction for depletion for any oil and gas property held by the S corp

LESSON 5

Partnerships

FORMING A PARTNERSHIP

An unincorporated organization formed after 1996 with two or more members is generally classified as a partnership. This organization is formed to carry on a trade or business, with each person contributing money, property, labor, or skill, and each expecting to share in the profits and losses of the business, whether or not a formal partnership agreement is made. Certain organizations are not partnerships:

- An organization formed under a federal or state law that refers to it as incorporated or as a corporation, body corporate, or body politic
- An organization formed under a state law that refers to it as a joint-stock company or joint-stock association
- An insurance company
- Certain banks
- An organization wholly owned by a state or local government
- An organization specifically required to be taxed as a corporation by the IRS
- Certain foreign organizations
- A tax-exempt organization
- A real estate investment trust
- An organization classified as a trust
- Any other organization that elects classification as a corporation

PARTNERSHIP AGREEMENT

The partnership agreement includes the original agreement and any modifications. All partners must agree to any modifications, or the partnership must adopt any modifications in any other manner provided by the partnership agreement. The agreement or modifications can be oral or written. Partners can modify the partnership agreement for a particular tax year after the close of the year but not later than the date for filing the partnership return for that year. This filing date does not include any extension of time. If the partnership agreement or any modification is silent on any matter, treat the provisions of local law as part of the agreement.

EXCLUSION FROM PARTNERSHIP RULES

Certain partnerships that do not actively conduct business can choose complete or partial exclusion from treatment as a partnership for federal income tax purposes. All partners must agree to make the choice, and the partners must be able to compute their own taxable income without computing the partnership's income. An eligible organization that desires exclusion from the partnership rules must make the election on *Form 1065* no later than the time for filing the partnership return for the first tax year for which the organization desires exclusion, including extensions.

FAMILY PARTNERSHIP

Members of a family can be partners. The IRS will only recognize family members (or any other persons) as partners if one of the following is true:

- If capital is a *material* income-producing factor, they acquired their capital interest in a bona fide transaction (including gift or purchase), and actually own and control the partnership interest. Capital is a material income-producing factor if a substantial part of the gross income of the business comes from the use of capital.
- If capital is not a material income-producing factor, they joined in good faith to conduct business. They agreed that contributions of each entitle them to a share in the profits, and some capital or service has been (or is) provided by each partner. Capital is not a material income-producing factor if business income consists primarily of fees, commissions, or other compensation for personal services performed by members or employees of the partnership.

If a family member receives a gift of a capital interest in a partnership, in which capital is a *material* income-producing factor, the donee's distributive share of partnership income is subject to <u>both</u> of the following restrictions:

- It must be figured by reducing the partnership income by reasonable compensation for services the donor renders to the partnership.
- The donee's distributive share of partnership income attributable to donated capital must not be proportionately greater than the donor's share attributable to the donor's capital.

For purposes of determining a partner's distributive share, an **interest purchased by one family member from another family member is considered a gift from the seller**. The fair market value of the purchased interest is considered donated capital. For this purpose, members of a family include only spouses, ancestors, and lineal descendants (or a trust for the primary benefit of those persons).

> **EXAMPLE 13-1:** A father sold 50% of his business to his son. The resulting partnership had a profit of $60,000. Capital is a material income-producing factor. The father performed services worth $24,000, which is reasonable compensation, and the son performed no services. The $24,000 must be allocated to the father as compensation. Of the remaining $36,000 of profit due to capital, at least 50%, or $18,000, must be allocated to the father since he owns a 50% capital interest. The son's share of partnership profit cannot be more than $18,000.

If spouses carry on a business together and share in the profits and losses, they may be partners whether or not they have a formal partnership agreement. A **married couple** can elect not to treat the joint venture as a partnership if they meet each of the following requirements:

- The only members of the joint venture are a married couple who file a joint return.
- The filing status of the married couple is married filing jointly.
- Both spouses materially participate in the trade or business.
- Both spouses elect this treatment.

If both spouses elect this treatment, all income, gains, losses, deductions, and credits are divided based on each spouse's interest in the joint venture, and both spouses are treated as *sole proprietors* for income and self-employment tax. If the spouses do <u>not</u> make this election, they should carry their respective shares of the partnership income or loss from Schedule K-1 to their joint or separate Form(s) 1040. Each spouse should include his respective share of self-employment income on a separate Schedule SE. This generally does not increase the total tax on the return, but it does give each spouse credit for Social Security earnings on which retirement benefits are based.

LIMITED PARTNERSHIP

A limited partnership is formed under a state limited partnership law and composed of at least one general partner and one or more limited partners.

- A general partner is personally liable for partnership debts.
- A limited partner's liability for partnership debts is limited to the amount of money or other property that the partner contributed or is required to contribute to the partnership.

LIMITED LIABILITY COMPANY

A limited liability company (LLC) is an entity formed under state law by filing articles of organization as an LLC. LLC owners are called members. Unlike a partnership, LLC members are not personally liable for company debts. An LLC may be classified for federal income tax purposes as either a partnership, a corporation (including an S corporation), or for a single-member LLC, an entity disregarded as an entity separate from its owner. By default, a multi-member LLC is taxed as a partnership. The LLC may elect treatment as a corporation by filing **Form 8832** (Form 2553 for S Corporation).

TERMINATING A PARTNERSHIP

> **TCJA:** An existing partnership shall be considered as continuing if it is <u>not</u> terminated. A partnership shall be considered as terminated <u>only</u> if no part of any business, financial operation, or venture of the partnership continues to be carried on by any of its partners in a partnership. The TCJA repeals the rule providing for technical terminations of partnerships resulting from a sale or exchange of 50% of the interest in partnership capital and profits for taxable years beginning after December 31, 2017.

The partnership's tax year ends on the date of termination. If a partnership terminates before the end of the tax year or changes tax years, the partnership must file Form 1065 for the **short period**, which is the period from the beginning of the tax year through the date of termination or change. The return is due the **15th day of the third month** following the date of termination.

PARTNERSHIP RETURN (FORM 1065)

Form 1065 is an information return used to report income, gains, losses, deductions, credits, etc., from the operation of a partnership. The partnership does not pay taxes; instead, income or loss items "pass through" to its partners. *Schedule K-1* states each partner's **distributive share** of these items for partners to include on their own tax returns:

- Income (loss) items
    1. Ordinary business income (loss)
    2. Net rental real estate income (loss)
    3. Other net rental income (loss)
    4. Guaranteed payments
- Portfolio income
    1. Interest income
    2. Ordinary and qualified dividends
    3. Royalties
    4. Net short-term and long-term capital gain (loss)
    5. Collectibles (28%) gain (loss)
    6. Unrecaptured Section 1250 gain
    7. Net Section 1231 gain (loss)
- Deductions
    1. Section 179 deduction
    2. Other deductions (charitable contributions, intangible drilling costs, pensions, etc.)
- Self-employment earnings (loss)
- Credits
- Foreign transactions
- Alternative Minimum Tax (AMT) items
- Tax-exempt income and nondeductible expenses
- Distributions

- Starting with tax year 2018, partnerships report each partner's share of qualified business income, W-2 wages, and other information on Schedule K-1 so the partners may determine their deduction for 20 percent of qualified business income (Section 199A qualified business income deduction).

> **TCJA:** As part of the reporting requirements for passthrough entities imposed by the regulations, a pass-through entity is required to allocate and disclose Qualified Business Income, W-2 wages, and the unadjusted basis of property. If any one item is not allocated, that item is **presumed to be zero**. There is no exception for pass-through entities that know that all of its owners have taxable income below the thresholds. In addition, a pass-through entity is required to disclose whether it has multiple trades or businesses, and if any of those businesses are Specified Service Trades or Businesses.

If a limited liability company is treated as a partnership, it must file Form 1065. A partnership is not considered to engage in a trade or business and is not required to file a *Form 1065*, for any tax year in which it neither receives income nor pays or incurs any expenses treated as deductions or credits for federal income tax purposes.

The partnership return must be signed by a partner. Any partner of a partnership or any member of a limited liability company may sign the return.

PARTNER LOSSES

Partner losses are subject to the following limitations, in the order in which they apply, the *basis rules*, the *at-risk limitations*, the *passive activity limitations,* and the *excess business loss limitations* (**suspended** for 2018, 2019, and 2020 by the *CARES Act*). Additional details on these limitations appear in the section on Loss Limitations.

> **CARES ACT UPDATE:** The CARES Act **repealed** the excess business loss limitation for tax years 2018, 2019, and 2020. The limitation on excess business losses returns for tax years beginning after 2020 and before 2026.

WHEN TO FILE

A domestic partnership must file Form 1065 by the **15th day of the third month** following the date its tax year ended (March 15 for a calendar year partnership). Taxpayers who need more time to file a partnership return may file Form 7004 to request an automatic six-month extension of time to file. A penalty is assessed against the partnership if it is required to file a partnership return and it fails to file the return by the due date or files a return that fails to show all the information required unless such failure is due to reasonable cause.

REQUIRED TAX YEAR

A partnership must conform its tax year to its partners' tax years unless any of the following apply.

- The partnership can establish a **business purpose** for a different tax year
- The partnership elects under **Section 444** to have a tax year other than a required tax year. The *deferral period* of the taxable year elected cannot be longer than 3 months
- The partnership elects to use a 52-53-week tax year that ends with reference to either its required tax year or a tax year elected under Section 444

TIP: The term "deferral period" means, with respect to any taxable year of the entity, the months between the beginning of such year, and the close of the 1st required taxable year ending within such year. A partnership can select a tax year that is different from what is required, but only if the deferral period of the selected tax year is no more than **three months** different from the tax year that should be used.

The rules for the *required tax year* for partnerships are as follows.

- If one or more partners having the same tax year own a **majority interest** (more than 50% interest) in partnership profits and capital, the partnership <u>must</u> use the tax year of those partners.
- If there is <u>no</u> majority interest, the partnership <u>must</u> use the tax year common to <u>all</u> principal partners (5% or more interest)
- If there is <u>no</u> majority interest tax year and the principal partners do <u>not</u> have the same tax year, the partnership generally <u>must</u> use the tax year that results in the **least aggregate deferral** of income

FILING PENALTIES

In the case of any return required to be filed in 2021 or furnished in 2021 (generally 2020 tax returns filed in 2021), a partnership that is without reasonable cause is subject to penalties for the following failures:

- **Late or incomplete filing** (§6698) – **$210** for **each month** or part of a month (for a maximum of 12 months) the failure continues, **multiplied by the total number of partners** in the partnership during <u>any</u> part of the partnership's tax year for which the return is due.
- **Failure to furnish K-1 to partner** (§6722) – A **$280** penalty may be imposed for **each failure** to furnish Schedule K-1 to a partner when due and each failure to include on Schedule K-1 all the information required to be shown (or the inclusion of incorrect information). If the taxpayer intentionally disregards the requirement to furnish or report correct information the penalty increases to $560 or, if greater, 10% of the amount required to be reported.

PARTNERSHIP CENTRALIZED AUDIT

The *Bipartisan Budget Act of 2015 (BBA)* created a centralized partnership audit regime that applies to all partnerships <u>unless</u> the partnership is an eligible partnership and **elects out** by making a valid election using *Schedule B-2 (Form 1065)*.

Under the BBA, the IRS generally assesses and collects any understatement of tax (called an *imputed underpayment* or IU) **at the partnership level**. Partnerships may request to modify the IU and may elect to push out the adjustments underlying the IU instead of paying. Partners have no participation right to challenge partnership adjustment.

A partnership <u>must</u> designate a partnership representative on its tax return for each taxable year <u>unless</u> it makes a valid election out of the centralized partnership audit regime. The designation of a partnership representative for one taxable year is effective <u>only</u> for that taxable year. The partnership representative must have a substantial presence in the United States.

There can only be one partnership representative at any time during the tax year. The designated partnership representative remains in effect until the designation is terminated by a valid revocation, a valid resignation, or a determination by the IRS that the designation is not in effect.

Partnerships with 100 or fewer partners for the taxable year can elect out of the centralized partnership audit regime if all partners are eligible partners. Eligible partners are:

- Individuals
- C corporations
- Foreign entities that would be treated as a C corporation if it were domestic
- S corporations
- Estates of deceased partners

To calculate the number of eligible partners, add the number of Schedules K-1 the partnership is required to issue to partners and include all shareholders for any partner that is an S corporation.

All elections out are valid unless the IRS determines otherwise.

Partnerships are <u>not</u> eligible to elect out of the centralized partnership audit regime if they are required to issue a Schedule K-1 to partners that are:

- Partnerships
- Trusts
- Foreign entities that would not be treated as a C corporation were it a domestic entity
- Disregarded entities
- Estates of individuals other than deceased partners
- People who hold an interest in the partnership on behalf of another person

TRANSACTIONS BETWEEN PARTNERSHIP AND PARTNERS

For the situations listed below, treat a partner as <u>not</u> being a member of the partnership.

- Performing services for, or transferring property to, a partnership if:
  1. There is a related allocation and distribution to a partner.
  2. The entire transaction, when viewed together, is properly characterized as occurring between the partnership and a partner not acting in the capacity of a partner.
- Transferring money or other property to a partnership if:
  1. There is a related transfer of money or other property by the partnership to the contributing partner or another partner.
  2. The transfers together are properly characterized as a sale or exchange of property.

GUARANTEED PAYMENTS

Guaranteed payments are those made by a partnership to a partner determined **without regard to the partnership's income.**

A partnership treats guaranteed payments for services, or for the use of capital, as if the partnership had made them to a person who is not a partner. This treatment is for purposes of determining gross income and deductible business expenses only. For other tax purposes, treat guaranteed payments as a partner's distributive share of ordinary income. Guaranteed payments are included in income in the partner's tax year in which the partnership's tax year ends. Guaranteed payments are <u>not</u> subject to income tax withholding.

- The partnership generally deducts guaranteed payments as a business expense on Form 1065. However, the partnership capitalizes guaranteed payments made to partners for organizing the partnership or syndicating interests in the partnership. A **guaranteed payment** is deducted before calculating the distributive share of partnership ordinary business income (loss).
- If a partner is to receive a **minimum payment** from the partnership, the guaranteed payment is the amount by which the minimum payment is more than the partner's distributive share of the partnership income before taking into account the guaranteed payment.

EXAMPLE 13-2: Under a partnership agreement, Divya is to receive 30% of the partnership income, but not less than $8,000 (minimum payment). The partnership has net income of $20,000. Divya's distributive share, without regard to the minimum guarantee, is $6,000 (30% × $20,000). The guaranteed payment that can be deducted by the partnership is $2,000 ($8,000 Divya's minimum payment − $6,000 Divya's distributive share). Divya's income from the partnership is $8,000 ($6,000 distributive share and $2,000 guaranteed payment), and the remaining $12,000 of partnership income ($20,000 net income – $2,000 guaranteed payment – $6,000 Divya's distributive share = $12,000) will be reported by the other partners in proportion to their shares under the partnership agreement.

If the partnership net income had been $30,000, there would have been no guaranteed payment since her share, without regard to the guarantee, would have been greater than the guarantee.

- If guaranteed payments to a partner result in a partnership loss in which the partner shares, the partner must report the full amount of the guaranteed payments as ordinary income. The partner separately takes into account his distributive share of the partnership loss, to the extent of the adjusted basis of the partner's partnership interest.
- Treat premiums for health insurance paid by a partnership on behalf of a partner, for services as a partner, as guaranteed payments. The partnership can deduct the payments as a business expense, and the partner must include them in gross income. However, if the partnership accounts for insurance paid for a partner as a reduction in distributions to the partner, the partnership cannot deduct the premiums.

SALE OR EXCHANGE OF PROPERTY

Losses are <u>not</u> allowed from the sale or exchange of property directly or indirectly between a partnership and a person whose direct or indirect interest in the capital or profits of the partnership is **more than 50%**. The basis of each partner's interest in the partnership is decreased (not below zero) by the partner's share of the disallowed loss.

Gain is **ordinary income** in a sale or exchange of property directly or indirectly between a person and a partnership, or between two partnerships, if <u>both</u> of the following tests hold true:

- More than 50% of the capital or profits interest in the partnership(s) is directly or indirectly owned by the same person.
- The property in the hands of the transferee immediately after the transfer is not a capital asset:
  1. Accounts receivables
  2. Inventory
  3. Stock-in-trade
  4. Depreciable or real property used in a trade or business

To determine if there is more than 50% ownership in capital or profits, the following rules apply:

- An interest directly or indirectly owned by, or for, a corporation, partnership, estate, or trust is considered to be owned by, or for its shareholders, partners, or beneficiaries.
- An individual is considered to own the interest directly or indirectly owned by, or for, the individual's family. For this rule, "family" includes only brothers, sisters, half-brothers, half-sisters, spouses, ancestors, and lineal descendants. **This information frequently appears on the test.

EXAMPLE 13-3: Individuals A and B and Trust T are equal partners in Partnership ABT. A's husband, AH, is the sole beneficiary of Trust T. Trust T's partnership interest will be attributed to AH only for further attributing the interest to A. As a result, A is a more-than-50% partner. This means that any deduction for losses on transactions between her and ABT will not be allowed, and gain from property that in the hands of the transferee is not a capital asset is treated as ordinary gain, rather than capital gain.

CONTRIBUTION OF PROPERTY

The general rule is that neither the partner nor the partnership recognizes a gain or loss when a person contributes property to the partnership in exchange for a partnership interest.

EXCEPTION: There is an exception under §721(b) where [nonrecognition]...shall **not** apply to gain realized on a transfer of property to a partnership which would be treated as an investment company (within the meaning of section 351) if the partnership were incorporated.

For tax purposes, a partnership takes a carryover basis in contributed property equal to the contributing partners' adjusted bases in the property at the time of the contribution, **plus** any gain recognized by the partner at the time of the contribution. The partnership's tax basis in its assets is known as *inside basis*.

A contribution of money or other property to the partnership followed by a distribution of different property from the partnership to the partner (disguised sale) is treated not as a contribution and distribution, but as a sale of the property if both of the following tests are true:

- The distribution would not have been made but for the contribution.
- The partner's right to the distribution does not depend on the success of the partnership operations.

The following rules apply to property contributions:

- If a partner contributes property to a partnership, the partnership's basis for determining depreciation, depletion, gain, or loss for the property is the **same as the partner's adjusted basis** for the property when the partner contributed the property, increased by any **gain recognized** by the partner at the time of contribution.
- If the contributed property is subject to a debt, or if the partnership assumes a partner's liabilities, the basis of that partner's interest is reduced by the **liability assumed** by the other partners. If the liabilities assumed exceed the partner's basis in the property, the partner must recognize a gain for the excess liabilities assumed.

EXAMPLE 13-4: Ivan acquired a 20% interest in a partnership by contributing property that had an adjusted basis to him of $8,000 and a $4,000 mortgage. The partnership assumed payment of the mortgage. The basis of Ivan's interest is:

Adjusted basis of contributed property	$8,000
Minus: Part of mortgage assumed by other partners (80% × $4,000)	3,200
Basis of Ivan's partnership interest	$4,800

If, as an alternative, the contributed property had a $12,000 mortgage, the basis of Ivan's partnership interest would be zero. The $1,600 difference between the mortgage assumed by the other partners, $9,600 (80% × $12,000), and his basis of $8,000 would be treated as capital gain from the sale or exchange of a partnership interest. However, this gain wouldn't increase the basis of his partnership interest.

- A partner generally must recognize gain on the distribution of property (other than money) if the partner contributed appreciated property to the partnership during the 7-year period before the property is distributed to another partner, other than a partner who owns more than 50% of the partnership. This is called a *net precontribution gain*. The amount of gain recognized by the contributing partner is the difference between the FMV of the property and the adjusted basis of his interest in the partnership immediately before the distribution, reduced (but not below zero) by any money received in the distribution.

ALLOCATIONS TO ACCOUNT FOR BUILT-IN GAIN OR LOSS

The fair market value of property at the time it is contributed may be different from the partner's adjusted basis. The partnership must allocate among the partners any income, deduction, gain, or loss on the property in a manner that will account for the difference. This rule also applies to contributions of accounts payable and other accrued but unpaid items of a cash basis partner.

The partnership can use different allocation methods for different items of contributed property. A single reasonable method must be consistently applied to each item, and the overall method or combination of methods must be reasonable.

If the partnership sells contributed property and recognizes gain or loss, built-in gain or loss is allocated to the contributing partner. If contributed property is subject to depreciation or other cost recovery, the allocation of deductions for these items takes into account built-in gain or loss on the property. However, the total depreciation, depletion, gain, or loss allocated to partners cannot be more than the depreciation or depletion allowable to the partnership or the gain or loss realized by the partnership.

> **EXAMPLE 13-5:** Areta and Sofia formed an equal partnership. Areta contributed $10,000 in cash to the partnership and Sofia contributed depreciable property with a fair market value of $10,000 and an adjusted basis of $4,000. The partnership's basis for depreciation is limited to the adjusted basis of the property in Sofia's hands, $4,000.
>
> In effect, Areta purchased an undivided one-half interest in the depreciable property with her contribution of $10,000. Assuming that the depreciation rate is 10% a year under the General Depreciation System (GDS), she would have been entitled to a depreciation deduction of $500 per year, based on her interest in the partnership, if the adjusted basis of the property equaled its fair market value when contributed. To simplify this example, the depreciation deductions are determined without regard to any first-year depreciation conventions.
>
> However, since the partnership is allowed only $400 per year of depreciation (10% of $4,000), no more than $400 can be allocated between the partners. The entire $400 must be allocated to Areta.

CONTRIBUTION OF SERVICES

A partner can acquire an interest in partnership capital or profits as compensation for services performed or to be performed.

- A *capital interest* is an interest that would give the holder a share of the proceeds if the partnership sold its assets at fair market value and the proceeds were distributed in a complete liquidation of the partnership. The **fair market value** of such an interest received by a partner as compensation for services must generally be **included in the partner's gross income** in the first tax year in which the partner can transfer the interest, or the interest is not subject to a substantial risk of forfeiture.

- A *profits interest* is a partnership interest other than a capital interest. If a person receives a profits interest for providing services to, or for the benefit of, a partnership in a partner capacity or in anticipation of being a partner, the receipt of such an interest is <u>not</u> a taxable event for the partner or the partnership. However, this does not apply in any of the following situations:

  1. The profits interest relates to a substantially certain and predictable stream of income from partnership assets, such as income from high-quality debt securities or a net lease.

  2. Within two years of receipt, the partner disposes of the profits interest.

  3. The profits interest is a limited partnership interest in a publicly traded partnership.

BASIS IN PARTNERSHIP

An individual partner's adjusted basis in his *partnership interest* is known as *outside basis*. In general, a partner's outside basis is his separate tax capital account, which reflects adjusted basis, plus his share of the partnership's debt.

Initially, outside basis is determined by including the amount of the **adjusted basis in the property contributed** plus any **cash contributed by the partner**. If the partner must recognize gain because of the contribution, this gain is included in the basis of his interest. If there are liabilities, outside basis **includes the partner's share of all liabilities assumed**. In subsequent years, the outside basis is increased and decreased by partnership operations.

Outside basis is maintained by each individual partner outside of the partnership books. Outside basis is the computation that most examiners are concerned with because it is the basis that the taxpayer uses to limit losses, determine the taxability of partnership distributions, and compute gain/loss on the disposition of their partnership interest. Outside basis is calculated at the end of the partnership tax year.

Increases – A partner's basis is increased by the following items:

- Additional contributions to the partnership (includes assumption of partnership liabilities)
- The partner's distributive share of taxable and nontaxable partnership income
- The partner's distributive share of the excess of the deductions for depletion over the basis of the property, unless the property is oil or gas wells and the partnership allocates basis to partners

Decreases – The partner's basis is decreased (but never below zero) by the following items:

- The money (including a decreased share of partnership liabilities or an assumption of the partner's individual liabilities by the partnership) and adjusted basis of property distributed to the partner by the partnership
- The partner's distributive share of the partnership losses, including capital losses
- The partner's share of nondeductible partnership expenses that are not capital expenditures
- The partner's deduction for depletion for any partnership oil and gas wells, up to the proportionate share of the adjusted basis of the wells allocated to each partner

EFFECT OF PARTNERSHIP LIABILITIES

A partner's basis in a partnership includes his share of a partnership liability if the liability:

- Creates or increases the partnership's basis in any of its assets,
- Gives rise to a current deduction to the partnership, or
- Is a nondeductible, noncapital expense of the partnership

If a property transfer occurs between a partner and a partnership and the property is subject to a liability, treat the transferee as having assumed the liability to the extent it does not exceed the FMV of the property. Liabilities assumed by either party receive the same treatment as a transfer of money:

- If a partner's share of partnership liabilities **increases** or a partner's individual liabilities increase because said partner assumes partnership liabilities, treat this increase as a *contribution* of money by the partner to the partnership.

- If a partner's share of partnership liabilities **decreases** or a partner's individual liabilities decrease because said partnership assumes his individual liabilities, treat this decrease as a *distribution* of money to the partner by the partnership.

Consider a partner or *related person* to assume partnership liability only to the extent that:

- He is personally liable for it (i.e., recourse liability),
- The creditor knows that the liability was assumed by the partner or related person,
- The creditor can demand payment from the partner or related person, and
- No other partner or person related to another partner will bear the economic risk of loss on that liability immediately after the assumption.

RELATED PERSON

Related persons, for these purposes (different for a corporation), include all the following:

- An individual and:
  1. His spouse, ancestors, and lineal descendants (not brothers and sisters)
  2. A corporation if it directly or indirectly owns **80%** of the value of outstanding stock
  3. A tax-exempt educational or charitable organization controlled directly or indirectly by the person or by members of the person's family (not brothers and sisters)
- A fiduciary of a trust and:
  1. A grantor of any trust
  2. A beneficiary of the same trust
  3. A fiduciary of a separate trust if the same person is the grantor of both trusts
  4. A corporation if the trust or the grantor of the trust directly or indirectly owns 80% of the value of outstanding stock
- A corporation and:
  1. A different corporation if members of the same controlled group
  2. A partnership if the same persons own **80%** or more in value of the outstanding stock and interest in the partnership
  3. An S corporation if the same persons own **80%** of the value of outstanding stock of each corporation
- An executor and a beneficiary of an estate
- A partnership and:
  1. A person owning, directly or indirectly, **80%** or more interest in the partnership, or
  2. Another partnership if the same persons, directly or indirectly, own **80%** interest

RECOURSE LIABILITY

A partnership liability is a *recourse liability* to the extent that any partner or a related person, defined earlier, has an economic risk of loss for that liability. A partner's share of a recourse liability equals his *economic risk of loss* for that liability. A partner has an economic risk of loss if that partner or a related person would be obligated—whether by agreement or law—to make a net payment to the creditor or a contribution to the partnership with respect to the liability if the partnership were constructively liquidated.

The partners who are responsible to repay the debt bear the economic risk of loss. These are usually the general partners who are jointly and severally liable for partnership debt. If a limited or general partner guarantees the recourse debt, there would be no special allocation of debt to that partner's basis because the guaranteeing partner could still pursue the general partners for reimbursement. This holds true unless the guarantor waives all rights of subrogation, and then the liability may be allocated to that partner.

> A partner's **outside basis** and amount **at-risk** increases by his/her share of recourse liabilities.

NONRECOURSE LIABILITY

A partnership liability is a *nonrecourse liability* if no partner or related person has an economic risk of loss for that liability. If a partnership fails to repay a nonrecourse liability, the lender can foreclose on the property but cannot take collection action against the partners individually. In this case, the creditor can only hope for the partnership to be profitable so the debt will be repaid. **The creditor bears the economic risk of loss**. None of the partners bear the economic risk of loss. If the partnership is not profitable and cannot repay the loan, then the partners are not obligated to take cash out of their pocket to repay the loan.

If a partner guarantees the non-recourse debt or makes a direct loan to the partnership, they would ultimately be economically at-risk because there would be no chance of reimbursement by the other partners. This is barring any side agreement with another partner for reimbursement. The liability would be allocated in its entirety, for outside basis purposes, to the partner guaranteeing the loan.

A partner's share of nonrecourse liabilities is generally **proportionate to his share of partnership profits**.

> A partner's **outside basis** increases by his/her share of nonrecourse liabilities. A nonrecourse liability generally does not increase the amount at risk because the partner is not personally liable.

> **EXCEPTION:** Certain nonrecourse loans, called *qualified nonrecourse financing*, do increase amount at-risk. These loans must be secured by the real estate used in the activity and loaned or guaranteed by any government agency (federal, state, or local) or loaned from a qualified person regularly engaged in the business of lending money, such as a bank or savings. No person may be personally liable for repayment.

UNREALIZED RECEIVABLES AND INVENTORY

The income or a portion of the income generated from the use or sale of *unrealized receivables* and *inventory items* is generally taxed as **ordinary income** rather than capital gain. Property of this type is known as a *hot asset* (or Section 751 property).

> The identification of IRC section 751 assets is critical to both the sale or exchange of a partnership interest, a partner receiving retirement payments for property, and disproportionate distributions.

UNREALIZED RECEIVABLES

The basis for any unrealized receivables includes all costs or expenses for the receivables that were paid or accrued but not previously taken into account under the partnership's method of accounting. The basis of unrealized receivables is $0 for partnerships that use the cash method of accounting.

> An unrealized receivable has not been included in income. An accrual-basis taxpayer includes a receivable in income before payment is received (generally when providing goods or services); therefore, an accrual-basis taxpayer typically does not have unrealized receivables.

Unrealized receivables include any right to be paid for services or goods which are not capital assets. The following are examples of unrealized receivables:

- Goods delivered if payment would be treated as received for property other than a capital asset
- Services rendered or to be rendered
- Other items of potential gain that would be ordinary income if the following partnership property were sold at its fair market value on the date of the payment:
  1. Mining property for which exploration expenses were deducted
  2. Stock in a Domestic International Sales Corporation (DISC)
  3. Certain farmland if costs for soil and water conservation or land clearing were deducted
  4. Franchises, trademarks, or trade names
  5. Oil or gas property for which intangible drilling and development costs were deducted
  6. Stock of certain controlled foreign corporations
  7. Market discount bonds and short-term obligations
  8. Property subject to recapture of depreciation under Sections 1245 and 1250
- The term unrealized receivables also covers potential depreciation recapture.

INVENTORY ITEMS

Inventory includes the following property:

- Property that would properly be included in the partnership's inventory if on hand at the end of the tax year or that is held primarily for sale to customers
- Property that, if sold or exchanged by the partnership, would not be a capital asset or Section 1231 property
- Property held by the partnership that would be considered inventory if held by the partner selling the partnership interest or receiving the distribution

Inventory is **substantially appreciated** if, at the time of the distribution, the FMV of the inventory is more than **120%** of the partnership's adjusted basis for the property.

PARTNERSHIP DISTRIBUTIONS TO PARTNERS

Distributions fall into two categories—*current distributions* and *liquidating distributions*.

In a current distribution, the partnership is simply distributing money or property to a continuing partner. On the other hand, a liquidating distribution completely terminates the partner's interest in the partnership. A single distribution or a series of distributions can liquidate the interest.

It is important to remember that the reporting of partnership income and the actual distribution of cash may not occur simultaneously. A partner must report his **distributive share** of partnership income in his taxable year in which the partnership's taxable year ends. That may or may not be the same year in which he or she receives a distribution of partnership profits.

> A partner reports his share of income, regardless of distributions, and does <u>not</u> recognize income simply because a distribution occurs.

As with sales of partnership interests, distributions can be complicated by the presence of hot assets which have ordinary income potential. Whether or not this complication must be considered depends on whether the partner receives a proportionate or disproportionate share of these assets. If the distribution does not upset the partners' original share of the partnership's ordinary income assets, it is a proportionate distribution and the regular distribution rules apply. If, on the other hand, a partner receives more or less than his or her share of hot assets, the transaction will be treated as a sale or exchange. IRC section 751 must be considered for both current and liquidating distributions. The determination of a proportionate share is determined based on the fair market value of the assets instead of the bases of the assets.

For exam purposes, we are only concerned with proportionate (pro rata) distributions. These are distributions in which the partner's share of hot assets and Non-IRC section 751 assets remain unchanged after the distribution. The regular distribution rules will apply in these instances.

In general, a distribution is a tax-free return of capital to the partner, and **neither the partner nor the partnership recognizes any gain or loss**. A partner's adjusted basis in his partnership interest decreases (but not below zero) by the money and adjusted basis of property distributed.

EXAMPLE 13-6: The adjusted basis of Jo's partnership interest is $14,000. She receives a distribution of $8,000 cash and land that has a basis of $2,000 and FMV of $3,000. Because the cash received does not exceed the basis of her partnership interest, Jo does not recognize any gain on the distribution. She will recognize any gain on the land when she sells or otherwise disposes of it. The distribution decreases the adjusted basis of Jo's partnership interest to $4,000 [$14,000 − ($8,000 + $2,000)].

WHEN A PARTNER RECOGNIZES A GAIN

Although the general rule aims to treat partnership distributions as nontaxable events, the exceptions can quickly overshadow the general rule. The possibility of moving property in and out of partnerships unimpeded by tax considerations creates potential for abuse. Transactions, which are essentially sales, can masquerade as tax-free distributions. To prevent income or basis shifting among partners, several provisions track property movements. It is not possible, for example, for partners to use their partnership as a device to "swap" appreciated or depreciated property among themselves.

Partners generally do not recognize gain or loss when they receive distributions from a partnership. **A partner will recognize gain only if money included in the distribution exceeds his outside basis.** If the partnership distributes property to a partner, that partner generally does not recognize any gain until the sale or other disposition of the property. **A partner will never recognize a loss on a current distribution.**

TIP: Treat any discharge of partnership liabilities as a distribution of money to the partner. A distribution of marketable securities to a partner receives the same treatment as a distribution of money in determining whether the partner will recognize a gain on the distribution. This treatment does not apply if that partner contributed the security to the partnership or an investment partnership made the distribution to an eligible partner.

In general, treat a recognized gain as a **capital gain** from the sale of the partnership interest on the date of the distribution. A distribution that alters a partner's share of unrealized receivables or substantially appreciated inventory receives ordinary income treatment.

EXAMPLE 13-7: The adjusted basis of Jesse's partnership interest is $10,000. He receives a distribution of $12,000 cash. Because the money received exceeds the basis of his partnership interest, Jesse will recognize a gain on the distribution. The distribution decreases the adjusted basis of Jesse's partnership interest to $0 [$10,000 − $12,000], as it cannot be less than zero. The remaining $2,000 is a capital gain.

PARTNER'S BASIS FOR DISTRIBUTED PROPERTY

The basis of property distributed to the partner by a partnership is its adjusted basis to the partnership immediately before the distribution. However, the basis of the property to the partner cannot be more than the adjusted basis of his interest in the partnership, reduced by any money received in the same transaction. A partner's holding period for property distributed to the partner includes the period the partnership held the property. If a partner contributed the property to the partnership, then the period that partner held the property is also included.

> **EXAMPLE 13-8:** The adjusted basis of Steve's partnership interest is $10,000. He receives a distribution of $4,000 cash and property that has an adjusted basis to the partnership of $8,000. His basis for the distributed property is limited to $6,000 ($10,000 − $4,000, the cash he receives).

> **EXAMPLE 13-9:** The adjusted basis of Jason's partnership interest is $6,000. He receives a distribution of $7,000 cash and a laptop computer that has an adjusted basis of $2,000 and FMV of $4,000. Because the cash received exceeds the basis of his partnership interest, Jason will recognize a capital gain on the excess money received of $1,000 [$7,000 − $6,000]. The distribution decreases the adjusted basis of Jason's partnership interest to $0 [$6,000 − ($7,000 + $2,000)], as it cannot be less than zero. Since Jason does not have a basis in his partnership interest, the basis of the laptop is $0. He will recognize any gain on the laptop when he sells or otherwise disposes of it.

LIQUIDATING DISTRIBUTIONS

Unlike current distributions, **the partner can recognize a loss on a liquidating distribution**. This can happen only if the partner receives no property other than money, unrealized receivables, or inventory. In other words, the receipt of a capital asset will prevent the recognition of loss.

A partner does not **recognize a loss** on a distribution unless **all the following** requirements exist:

- The adjusted **basis of the partner's interest** in the partnership **exceeds the distribution**.
- The partner's **entire interest** in the partnership is **liquidated**.
- The distribution is **only in money, unrealized receivables, or inventory items**. No loss is recognized if any other property is received.

The amount of any loss recognized is the difference between the partner's outside basis in his partnership interest before the distribution and the sum of money and the partnership's adjusted basis of distributed receivables and inventory.

BASIS ALLOCATION

The determination of basis in the distributed property in a liquidating distribution is somewhat different than in a current distribution because the partner is exiting the partnership and will no longer have any outside basis. In a liquidating distribution, the exiting partner is said to take a substituted basis in the property distributed. **Outside basis must be $0 after the distribution of property.**

After the liquidating partner's outside basis is allocated to cash and ordinary income assets, any remaining basis is allocated to other property received.

Allocate the basis using the following rules:

- **Allocate the basis first to unrealized receivables and inventory items** included in the distribution by assigning a basis to each item equal to the partnership's adjusted basis in the item immediately before the distribution. If the total assigned basis exceeds the allocable basis, decrease the assigned basis by the amount of the excess.
- Allocate any remaining basis to properties other than unrealized receivables and inventory items by assigning a basis to each property **equal to the partnership's adjusted basis in the property**. If the allocable basis exceeds the total assigned basis, increase the assigned basis by the amount of the excess. The remaining outside basis is first allocated to properties with unrealized appreciation. Any remaining outside basis is then allocated among all properties in proportion to their fair market values. If the total assigned basis exceeds the allocable basis, decrease the assigned basis by the amount of the excess.

EXAMPLE 13-10: Eun's basis in her partnership interest is $55,000. In a distribution in liquidation of her entire interest, she receives properties A and B, neither of which is inventory or unrealized receivables.

Property A has an adjusted basis to the partnership of $5,000 and a fair market value of $40,000. Property B has an adjusted basis to the partnership of $10,000 and a fair market value of $10,000.

	Property A	Property B
Basis	$5,000	$10,000
FMV	$40,000	$10,000

To figure her basis in each property, Eun first assigns basis of $5,000 to property A and $10,000 to property B (the partnership's inside basis). At this point, Eun has assigned $15,000 of her $55,000 allocable basis, so Eun will assign an additional $35,000 from allocable basis to Property A (its unrealized appreciation).

	Property A	Property B	Total Allocated
Assigned from basis	$5,000	$10,000	$15,000
Assigned from unrealized appreciation	$35,000	$0	$35,000
Total	$40,000	$10,000	$50,000

Eun has $5,000 of allocable basis remaining ($55,000 – $15,000 – $35,000 = $5,000). She allocates the remaining $5,000 between the properties based on their fair market values: $4,000 ($40,000 ÷ $50,000) to property A and $1,000 ($10,000 ÷ $50,000) to property B.

	Property A	Property B	Total Allocated
Assigned from basis	$5,000	$10,000	$15,000
Assigned from unrealized appreciation	$35,000	$0	$35,000
Assigned in proportion to FMV	$4,000	$1,000	$5,000
Total	$44,000	$11,000	$55,000

Eun's basis in property A is $44,000 and her basis in property B is $11,000. Her outside basis is reduced to $0.

EXAMPLE 13-11: Armando's basis in his partnership interest is $20,000. In a distribution in liquidation of his entire interest, he receives properties C and D, neither of which is inventory or unrealized receivables.

Property C has an adjusted basis to the partnership of $15,000 and a fair market value of $15,000. Property D has an adjusted basis to the partnership of $15,000 and a fair market value of $5,000.

	Property C	Property D
Basis	$15,000	$15,000
FMV	$15,000	$5,000

To figure his basis in each property, Armando first assigns $15,000 basis to property C and $15,000 to property D (the partnership's inside basis). This amount is more than his outside basis, so Arnaldo must assign a $10,000 basis decrease ($30,000 – $20,000 allocable basis). He assigns the entire $10,000 to property D (its unrealized depreciation).

	Property C	Property D	Total Allocated
Assigned from basis	$15,000	$15,000	$30,000
Assigned from unrealized depreciation	$0	($10,000)	($10,000)
Total	$15,000	$5,000	$20,000

Armando's basis in property C is $15,000, and his basis in property D is $5,000. His outside basis is reduced to $0.

DISPOSITION OF PARTNER'S INTEREST

SALE, EXCHANGE, OR OTHER TRANSFER

The sale or exchange of a partner's interest in a partnership usually results in **capital gain or loss**. This gain or loss is the difference between the amount realized and the adjusted basis of the partner's interest in the partnership. If the selling partner is relieved of any partnership liabilities, that partner must include the liability relief as part of the amount realized for his or her interest.

EXAMPLE 13-12: Kumar became a limited partner in the ABC Partnership by contributing $10,000 in cash on the formation of the partnership. The adjusted basis of his partnership interest at the end of the current year is $20,000, which includes his $15,000 share of partnership liabilities. The partnership has no unrealized receivables or inventory items. Kumar sells his interest in the partnership for $10,000 in cash. He had been paid his share of the partnership income for the tax year.

Kumar realizes $25,000 from the sale of his partnership interest ($10,000 cash payment + $15,000 liability relief). He reports $5,000 ($25,000 realized – $20,000 basis) as a capital gain.

As an alternative, assume the facts are the same except that Kumar withdraws from the partnership when the adjusted basis of his interest in the partnership is zero. He is considered to have received a distribution of $15,000, his relief of liability. He reports a capital gain of $15,000.

PAYMENTS TO PARTNER FOR UNREALIZED RECEIVABLES AND INVENTORY ITEMS

If a partner receives money or property in exchange for any part of a partnership interest, the amount due to his share of partnership unrealized receivables or inventory items results in **ordinary** income or loss. Treat this amount as if the partner receives it for the sale or exchange of property that is not a capital asset. The income or loss realized by a partner is the amount allocable to the partner if the partnership had sold all of its property for cash at FMV—in a taxable transaction—immediately prior to the partner's transfer of interest in the partnership.

EXAMPLE 13-13: You are a partner in ABC Partnership. The adjusted basis of your partnership interest at the end of the current year is zero. Your share of potential ordinary income from partnership depreciable property is $5,000. The partnership has no other unrealized receivables or inventory items. You sell your interest in the partnership for $10,000 in cash, and you report the entire amount as a gain since your adjusted basis in the partnership is zero. For your $10,000 gain, you report as ordinary income your $5,000 share of potential ordinary income from the partnership's depreciable property and the remaining $5,000 gain is a capital gain.

LIQUIDATION AT PARTNER'S RETIREMENT OR DEATH

Payments made by the partnership to a retiring partner or successor in interest of a deceased partner in return for the partner's entire interest in the partnership may be allocated between payments in liquidation of the partner's interest in partnership property and other payments. Treat payments that include an assumption of the partner's share of partnership liabilities as a distribution of money.

A payment made in liquidation of the interest of a retiring or deceased partner:

- In exchange for his interest in partnership property is a **distribution**, not a distributive share or guaranteed payment that could give rise to a deduction for the partnership.
- Not made in exchange for an interest in partnership property is a **distributive share** of partnership income or guaranteed payment.

Recognize a gain – Upon receipt of the distribution, the retiring partner or successor in interest of a deceased partner will recognize gain only to the extent that any money distributed is more than the partner's adjusted basis in the partnership.

Recognize a loss – The partner will recognize a loss only if the distribution is in money, unrealized receivables, and inventory items. The partner will recognize no loss if any other property is received.

For income tax purposes, treat a retiring partner or successor in interest of a deceased partner as a partner until the complete liquidation of his interest in the partnership.

Inventory received in the dissolution of the partnership and sold within **5 years** of the date of dissolution will result in ordinary income or loss; not a capital gain or loss.

LESSON 6

Retirement Plans

OVERVIEW OF RETIREMENT PLANS

COMMON TERMS

- **Highly compensated employees** – A *highly compensated employee (HCE)* is one who:
  1. Owned **more than 5%** of the interest in the business at any time during the current or preceding year, regardless of compensation, or
  2. Received compensation from the employer in excess of the threshold amount during the look-back year, and if the employer so elects, was in the **top 20 percent** of employees when ranked by compensation.

The dollar threshold on 2020 compensation that is used to determine whether or not a taxpayer is a highly compensated employee is **$130,000**. Under the *look-back rule*, an individual earning more than $130,000 in 2020 is a highly compensated employee for 2021 plan calculations. If the employer elects the top 20 percent rule, some individuals with compensation above the limit may not be considered highly compensated.

- **Excludable employees** – Employers are not required to cover the following employees under a SIMPLE or SEP IRA plan:
  1. Employees who are covered by a union agreement and whose retirement benefits were bargained for in good faith by the employees' union and employer
  2. Nonresident alien employees who have received no U.S. source wages, salaries, or other personal services compensation from employer
- **Compensation** – Compensation for plan allocations is the pay a participant received from the employer for personal services for a year. Compensation includes all of the following payments:
  1. Wages and salaries
  2. Fees for professional services
  3. Other amounts received (cash or noncash) for personal services actually rendered by an employee, including, but not limited to commissions, tips, fringe benefits, and bonuses
- **Compensation for the self-employed** – A self-employed taxpayer must make a special computation to determine compensation for purposes of retirement plan contributions and deductions for his own account. Compensation is net earnings from self-employment, <u>reduced</u> by the total of:
  1. The deduction for the employer-equivalent portion of self-employment tax
  2. The deduction for contributions on own behalf to the plan
- **Annual compensation limit** – The maximum amount of compensation the employer may consider when determining contributions and benefits for an employee in 2020 is **$285,000**.
- **Catch-up contribution** – A plan can permit participants who are age 50 or older at the end of the calendar year to make catch-up contributions in addition to elective deferrals and SIMPLE plan salary reduction contributions.
  1. The 2020 catch-up contribution limitation for defined contribution plans **other than** SIMPLE plans is **$6,500**.
  2. The catch-up contribution limitation for **SIMPLE** plans is **$3,000** for 2020.
- **Loans** – Loans are <u>not</u> permitted from IRAs or from IRA-based plans such as SEPs, SARSEPs and SIMPLE IRA plans. Loans are only possible from qualified plans that satisfy the requirements of §401(a), from annuity plans that satisfy the requirements of §403(a) or 403(b), and from governmental plans. (Code §72(p)(4); Reg. § 1.72(p)-1, Q&A-2)

COLA INCREASES FOR DOLLAR LIMITATIONS ON BENEFITS AND CONTRIBUTIONS

The tax law places limits on the dollar amount of contributions to retirement plans and IRAs and the amount of benefits under a pension plan. IRC Section 415 requires the limits to be adjusted annually for cost-of-living increases (COLA).

	2020	2021
SEP		
SEP Minimum Compensation	600	650
SEP Maximum Contribution	57,000	58,000
SEP Maximum Compensation	285,000	290,000
SIMPLE Plans		
SIMPLE Maximum Contributions	13,500	13,500
Catch-up Contributions	3,000	3,000
401(k), 403(b), Profit-Sharing Plans, etc.		
Annual Compensation	285,000	290,000
Elective Deferrals	19,500	19,500
Catch-up Contributions	6,500	6,500
Defined Contribution Limits	57,000	58,000
Other		
Highly Compensated Employee Threshold	130,000	130,000
Defined Benefit Limits	230,000	230,000
Key Employee	185,000	185,000
457 Elective Deferrals	19,500	19,500

SEP IRA

Simplified Employee Pensions (SEP) provide a simplified method for employers to contribute to a retirement plan for themselves and employees. Under a SEP, the employer can contribute to a traditional individual retirement arrangement (called a SEP-IRA) set up by or for each eligible employee. A SEP cannot be a Roth IRA. A SEP-IRA is one that the employee owns and controls; the **employer contributes** to the financial institution that maintains the SEP-IRA.

ESTABLISHING A SEP PLAN

Employers can establish a SEP for any year as late as the due date (including extensions) of the income tax return for that year. There are three basic steps in setting up a SEP:

- The employer must execute a formal written agreement to provide benefits to all eligible employees. The employer can satisfy the written agreement requirement by adopting an IRS model SEP using *Form 5305-SEP*.
- Each eligible employee must receive certain information about the SEP.
- A SEP-IRA must be set up by or for each eligible employee.

ELIGIBLE EMPLOYEES

The employer will establish participation requirements for employees in the plan. Employees who satisfy the requirements must be included in the plan. The requirements may be less restrictive, but not more than the following:

- Employee is age 21 or older.
- Employee has worked for the employer in at least **three of the last five** years.
- Employee has received at least **$600** in compensation from the employer in 2020.

HOW CONTRIBUTIONS ARE MADE

Employees cannot contribute to a SEP IRA (other than SAR SEP, which was discontinued in 1997). Annual employer contributions are not mandatory. If contributing, the employer must base all contributions on a written allocation formula and must not discriminate in favor of highly compensated employees. When the employer contributes, the employer must contribute to the SEP-IRAs of all participants who actually performed personal services during the year for which the contributions are made, including employees who die or terminate employment before contributions are made. Contributions are made as a percentage of each employee's compensation. The percentage must be the same for all employees.

ANNUAL CONTRIBUTION LIMIT

The SEP rules permit an employer to contribute a limited amount of money each year to each employee's SEP-IRA. A self-employed taxpayer can contribute to a SEP-IRA established on his own behalf. Contributions must be in the form of **money** (cash, check, or money order), not **property**.

> Contributions made by the employer for 2020 to a common-law employee's SEP-IRA cannot exceed the lower of **25% of the employee's compensation** or $57,000. Compensation generally does not include the employer's contributions to the SEP.

- **Compensation** – Compensation for plan allocations is the pay a participant received from the employer for personal services for a year. Compensation includes all of the following payments:
  1. Wages and salaries
  2. Fees for professional services
  3. Other amounts received (cash or noncash) for personal services actually rendered by an employee, including, but not limited to commissions, tips, fringe benefits, and bonuses

- **Compensation for the self-employed** – Those who are self-employed must make a special computation to determine contributions for their own accounts. The deduction for contributions to the SEP-IRA and net earnings depend on each other. For this reason, a self-employed individual determines the deduction for contributions to his SEP-IRA indirectly by reducing the contribution rate called for in the plan. The formula to determine contribution percentage is *rate/(1+rate).*

When figuring the deduction made to one's own SEP-IRA, compensation is **net earnings from self-employment** (provided that personal services are a material income-producing factor), reduced by the total of:

1. The deduction for the deductible part of self-employment tax.
2. The deduction for contributions to his own SEP-IRA.

EXAMPLE: Peter is a sole proprietor with $100,000 net income on his Schedule C. His deduction for self-employment tax on Form 1040 is $7,650. Peter subtracts the deductible part of self-employment tax, arriving at $92,350. The contribution rate for his SEP plan for employees is 25%. Peter needs to adjust the contribution percentage for his own contribution .25 ÷ 1.25 =.20. His SEP contribution is $18,470 ($92,350 × 20%).

Compensation, after deducting his own contribution, is $73,880 ($92,350 – $18,470).

There is a simple way to quickly verify the accuracy of his contribution/deduction amount:

	$100,000	Schedule C net profit
–	$7,650	Deductible part of self-employment tax
–	$18,470	Deduction for contributions to his own SEP
=	$73,880	Compensation subject to plan's **full** rate
×	25%	Plan's full rate
=	$18,470	Deduction for contributions to his own SEP

For SEP and qualified plans, net earnings from self-employment is gross income from a trade or business (provided personal services are a material income-producing factor) <u>minus</u> allowable business deductions. Allowable deductions include contributions to SEP and qualified plans for common-law employees and the deduction allowed for the deductible part of self-employment tax.

Net earnings from self-employment don't include items excluded from gross income (or their related deductions) other than foreign earned income and foreign housing cost amounts.

Net earnings include a partner's distributive share of partnership income or loss (other than separately stated items, such as capital gains and losses). It doesn't include income passed through to shareholders of S corporations. Guaranteed payments to limited partners are net earnings from self-employment if they are paid for services to or for the partnership. Distributions of other income or loss to limited partners aren't net earnings from self-employment.

EMPLOYER/EMPLOYEE CONTRIBUTION LIMITS

An employer <u>cannot</u> consider the part of an employee's compensation above the 2020 *annual compensation limit* of **$285,000** when figuring the contribution limit for an employee. However, **$57,000** in 2020 is the maximum contribution for an eligible employee under §415(c)(1)(A). Excess contributions are included in the employee's income for the year and are treated as contributions by the employee to his SEP-IRA. SEP contributions are not included on an employee's Form W-2 unless contributions were made under a salary reduction arrangement. Additionally, if the employer maintains another *defined contribution* plan for employees, the *annual additions* to an account are limited to the <u>lesser</u> of **$57,000** or **100% of the participant's compensation**. When figuring this limit, the employer must combine contributions to <u>all</u> defined contribution plans. Because a SEP is considered a defined contribution plan for this limit, employer contributions to a SEP must be added to employer contributions to other defined contribution plans. Contributions are 100% immediately vested to the employee.

SAR SEP

A *Salary Reduction Simplified Employee Pension (SAR SEP)* is a SEP set up before 1997 that includes a salary reduction arrangement. Under a SAR SEP, employees can choose to have the employer contribute part of their pay to their SEP-IRAs rather than receive it in cash. This contribution is an *elective deferral* because an employee chooses (elects) to contribute the money and tax is deferred until it is distributed.

SIMPLE PLANS

Generally, an employer with **100 or fewer** employees making at least $5,000 in compensation last year can set up a *Savings Incentive Match Plan for Employees (SIMPLE)*. The employer <u>cannot</u> maintain another qualified plan unless the other plan is for collective bargaining (union) employees. Under a SIMPLE plan, **employees** can choose to make salary reduction contributions rather than receiving these amounts as part of their regular pay. In addition, the **employer** will contribute <u>either</u> matching or non-elective contributions.

In order to avoid additional tax, the participant must maintain a SIMPLE IRA for at least two years from the date of initial contribution. If a withdrawal, rollover distribution, or transfer from a SIMPLE IRA does not satisfy the 2-year rule and is otherwise an early distribution, the additional tax imposed because of the early distribution increases from 10% to 25% of the amount distributed.

The two types of SIMPLE plans are the SIMPLE IRA plan and the SIMPLE 401(k) plan. A SIMPLE plan cannot be a Roth IRA. Contribution methods and limits of a SIMPLE IRA and SIMPLE 401(k) are the same. Unlike the IRA version, the SIMPLE 401(k) is a *qualified plan* and is subject to those rules (under certain conditions, a SIMPLE 401(k) plan is not subject to the nondiscrimination and top-heavy rules).

ESTABLISHING A SIMPLE PLAN

An employer can set up a SIMPLE IRA plan effective on any date from January 1 through October 1 of a year, provided the employer did not previously maintain a SIMPLE IRA plan. A new employer that comes into existence after October 1 may set up a SIMPLE IRA plan as soon as administratively feasible after the business comes into existence. If the employer previously maintained a SIMPLE IRA plan, he can establish a SIMPLE IRA plan effective only on January 1 of a year.

- **Notification requirement** – The employer must notify each employee of the following information before the beginning of the election period:
  1. The employee's opportunity to make or change a salary reduction choice
  2. The employer's contribution method
  3. A summary description provided by the financial institution
  4. Written notice that the employee can transfer his balance without cost or penalty if he uses a designated financial institution
- **Election period** – The election period is generally the **60-day period** immediately preceding January 1 of a calendar year (November 2 to December 31 of the preceding calendar year). However, the dates of this period are modified if the plan is established mid-year.

Employers must adopt a written plan to establish a SIMPLE 401(k) or SIMPLE IRA. For a SIMPLE IRA <u>only</u>, the employer may establish the plan and notify employees with a model plan document:

- **Form 5304-SIMPLE** – To allow each plan participant to choose his own financial institution, or
- **Form 5305-SIMPLE** – If the employer requires an initial designated financial institution

ELIGIBLE EMPLOYEES

Any employee who received **at least $5,000** in compensation during any two years preceding the current calendar year and who can reasonably expect to receive at least $5,000 during the current calendar year is eligible to participate. The term "employee" includes a self-employed individual who received earned income. Employers may use less restrictive eligibility requirements (but not more restrictive ones) by eliminating or reducing the prior year compensation requirements, the current year compensation requirements, or both.

CONTRIBUTION DEADLINE

The employer must make the salary reduction contributions to the SIMPLE IRA within 30 days after the end of the month in which the amounts would otherwise have been payable to the employee in cash. Matching contributions or non-elective contributions are due by the due date (including extensions) for filing the employer's federal income tax return for the year. Certain plans subject to Department of Labor rules may have an earlier due date for salary reduction contributions.

EMPLOYER/EMPLOYEE CONTRIBUTION LIMITS

- **Salary reduction contributions** – Employees may contribute to the SIMPLE IRA through salary reductions up to **$13,500** for 2020. These contributions must be expressed as a percentage of the employee's compensation unless the employer permits the employee to express them as a specific dollar amount. Employers cannot place restrictions on the contribution amount (such as limiting the contribution percentage), except to comply with the $13,500 limit. The maximum percentage an employee may contribute is 100% of his compensation up to the dollar limit.

- **Multiple plans** – If an employee participates in any other employer plan during the year and has elective salary reductions under those plans, the total amount of the salary reduction contributions that an employee can make to all the plans is limited to **$19,500** in 2020.

- **Catch-up contribution** – Participants who are age 50 or older at the end of the year can make catch-up contributions in addition to elective deferrals and SIMPLE plan salary reduction contributions. The additional catch-up contribution limitation for **SIMPLE** plans is **$3,000** for 2020.

The employer <u>must</u> also contribute using one of two methods:

- **3% matching contribution** – The employer must **match** each employee's salary reduction contribution on a dollar-for-dollar basis **up to 3%** of the employee's compensation (<u>not</u> limited by the annual compensation limit).
  1. The employer can reduce the 3% match, but not lower than 1%, and it cannot be for more than two years during the five-year period ending with the calendar year the reduction is effective. The employer must notify employees of the lower match before the 60-day election period for the calendar year.
  2. The maximum matching contribution is always based on the employees' compensation for the entire calendar year.

  EXAMPLE: Bob's annual salary is $50,000 and he starts contributing to his employer's SIMPLE IRA plan on September 1. He contributes $1,536 through December 31. Bob's employer must match Bob's contributions up to 3% of Bob's calendar-year compensation, or $1,500 (3% of $50,000). It doesn't matter that Bob only contributed to the plan during the last 4 months of the calendar year.

- **2% nonelective contribution** – The employer must make nonelective contributions of **2%** of the employee's compensation up to the annual limit of $285,000 for 2020 for <u>all</u> eligible employees, regardless of whether or not the employee chooses to make salary reduction contributions.

Contributions are 100% immediately vested to the employee.

An employer deducts contributions for employees on its tax return, and employees can exclude these contributions from their gross income. However, salary reduction contributions are subject to FICA and federal unemployment (FUTA) taxes. Matching and non-elective contributions are not subject to these taxes. Contributions are not subject to federal income tax withholding.

TIP: A sole proprietor or partner cannot deduct contributions made to a retirement plan for himself as a business expense, only those made for his common-law employees. Sole proprietors and partners deduct contributions on Form 1040.

403(B) PLANS

A 403(b) plan, often called a tax-sheltered annuity (TSA), is a retirement plan for certain employees of public schools, tax-exempt organizations, and certain ministers. A 403(b) has similar contribution limits and features of qualified plans, such as the ability to borrow against a balance; however, a 403(b) is not necessarily a qualified plan for ERISA purposes. Employees cannot set up their own 403(b) account. Only employers can set up 403(b) accounts.

Any eligible employee may participate. The following employees are able to participate:

- Employees of tax-exempt organizations established under Section 501(c)(3)
- Employees of public school systems who are involved in the daily operations of a school
- Employees of cooperative hospital service organizations
- Civilian faculty and staff of the Uniformed Services University of the Health Sciences (USUHS)
- Employees of public school systems organized by Indian tribal governments
- Certain ministers

Individual accounts in a 403(b) plan can be any of the following types:

- An annuity contract, which is a contract provided through an insurance company
- A custodial account, which is an account invested in mutual funds
- A retirement income account set up for church employees. Generally, retirement income accounts can invest in either annuities or mutual funds.

Generally, the maximum amount contributable (MAC) to a 403(b) account in 2020 is limited to the lesser of:

- **The annual additions limit** – $57,000 or **100% of compensation** for the most recent year, whichever is less. This is a limit on the total contributions (elective deferrals, nonelective contributions, and after-tax contributions) that can be made to a 403(b) account.
- **The elective deferral limit** – An employee may generally contribute up to **$19,500**. A participant with at least 15 years of service can contribute up to **$3,000** more. Participants older than 50 are eligible for an additional catch-up contribution of up to **$6,500** more.

TIP: An employee may contribute the smaller of the elective deferral limit or 100% of compensation. If the employer makes nonelective contributions (matching contributions, discretionary contributions and certain mandatory contributions) the MAC is the limit on annual additions.

If, for any year, elective deferrals are contributed to multiple retirement accounts for the same taxpayer (whether or not with the same employer), consider all contributions to determine whether the total is more than the limit for that year. The limit on elective deferrals applies to amounts contributed to:

- 401(k) plans, to the extent excluded from income
- Section 501(c)(18) plans, to the extent excluded from income
- SIMPLE plans
- SEP plans
- All 403(b) plans

A taxpayer may convert distributions from tax-qualified retirement plans and tax-sheltered annuities by making a rollover into a Roth IRA, subject to the restrictions that currently apply to rollovers from a traditional IRA into a Roth IRA.

QUALIFIED PLANS

A *qualified plan* is a retirement plan that offers a tax-favored way to save for retirement. Employers may deduct contributions made to the plan for employees. A qualified plan for a self-employed taxpayer is called a *Keogh plan*, and generally follows the same rules for contributions and benefits. Earnings on these contributions are generally tax-free until distributed at retirement. Profit sharing, money purchase, and defined benefit plans are qualified plans. A *401(k) plan* is also a qualified plan. The qualified plan rules are more complex than the SEP plan and SIMPLE plan rules. However, there are advantages to qualified plans, such as increased flexibility in designing plans and increased contribution and deduction limits in some cases. There are two basic kinds of qualified plans —*defined contribution* plans and *defined benefit* plans—and different rules apply to each. An employer can have more than one qualified plan, but contributions to all plans must not total more than the overall limits.

DEFINED CONTRIBUTION PLAN

A defined contribution plan has an individual account for each participant in the plan. It provides benefits largely based on the amount contributed to that participant's account. Any income, expense, gain, loss, and forfeiture of other accounts that may be allocated to an account also affect benefits. A defined contribution plan can be either a *profit-sharing plan* or a *money purchase pension plan*.

- **Profit-sharing plan (PSP)** – Although it is called a profit-sharing plan, employers do not actually have to make a business profit for the year in order to contribute (except for the self-employed). A PSP can be set up to allow for discretionary employer contributions, meaning the amount contributed each year to the plan is not fixed. An employer may even not contribute to the plan for a given year. The plan must provide a definite formula for allocating the contribution among the participants and for distributing the accumulated funds to the employees after they reach a certain age, after a fixed number of years, or upon certain other occurrences. In general, the employer can be more flexible in contributing to a PSP than to a money purchase pension plan or a defined benefit plan.

- **Money purchase pension plan (MPPP)** – Contributions to a money purchase pension plan are fixed and are not based on business profits. For example, if the plan requires that contributions be 10% of the participants' compensation without regard to whether the employer has profits (or the self-employed person has earned income), the plan is a money purchase pension plan. This applies even though the compensation of a self-employed individual as a participant depends on earned income derived from business profits.

DEFINED BENEFIT PLAN

A defined benefit plan is any plan that is not a defined contribution plan. Contributions to a defined benefit plan are based on what is needed to provide definitely determinable benefits to plan participants. Actuarial assumptions and computations are required to figure these contributions. Generally, continuing professional help is necessary to have a defined benefit plan.

QUALIFIED PLAN RULES

To qualify for the tax benefits available to qualified plans, a plan must meet certain requirements (qualification rules) of the tax law. Generally, unless an employer writes his own plan, the financial institution that provided the plan will take the continuing responsibility for meeting qualification rules that are later changed. Some of the important rules include the following:

- The employer must adopt a written plan.

- The employer must use plan assets only for the benefit of employees or their beneficiaries.
- The plan must, at a minimum, cover at least the lesser of the following:
  1. 50 employees, or
  2. The greater of:
     A. 40% of all employees, or
     B. Two employees. If there is only one employee, the plan must benefit that employee.
- Contributions or benefits must not discriminate in favor of highly compensated employees.
- The plan must meet minimum vesting standards.
- In general, an employee who meets both the following requirements <u>must</u> be allowed to participate:
  1. Has reached age 21, and
  2. Has at least one year of service (1,000-hour rule). The requirement is two years if the plan is not a 401(k) plan and provides that after not more than two years the employee has a non-forfeitable right to all accrued benefits.

> **SECURE ACT:** Effective for plan years beginning after December 31, 2020, 401(k) plans must cover part-time workers with at least 500 hours of service for 3 consecutive years. The employer may elect to exclude such employees from testing under the nondiscrimination and coverage rules, and from the application of the top-heavy rules.

ESTABLISHING A PLAN

To take a deduction for contributions for a tax year, the plan must be set up (adopted) by the **last day of that year** (December 31 for calendar year employers).

MINIMUM FUNDING REQUIREMENT

In general, if the plan is an MPPP or a defined benefit plan, the employer must pay enough into the plan to satisfy the minimum funding standard each year. The amount depends on the plan formula using actuarial assumptions and formulas.

- **Quarterly installments of required contributions** – If the plan is a defined benefit plan subject to the minimum funding requirements, the employer must make quarterly payments of the required contributions.
- **Due dates** – Installments are due **15 days** after the end of each quarter.
- **Installment percentage** – Quarterly installments must be 25% of the required annual payment.
- **Extended period for making contributions** – The employer must make contributions required to satisfy the minimum funding requirement for a plan year by **8.5 months** after the end of that year.

CONTRIBUTIONS

Employer contributions generally fund a qualified plan. However, employees participating in the plan may be permitted to contribute, and the employer may be permitted to contribute on its own behalf. The employer may make deductible contributions for a tax year up to the due date of its tax return (plus extensions) for that year.

LIMITS ON CONTRIBUTIONS AND BENEFITS

The plan must provide that contributions or benefits cannot exceed certain limits. The limits differ depending on whether a plan is a defined contribution plan or a defined benefit plan.

Defined benefit plan – For 2020, the annual benefit for a participant under §415(b)(1)(A) for a defined benefit plan cannot exceed the lesser of the following amounts:

- 100% of the participant's average compensation for his highest three consecutive calendar years
- $230,000

Defined contribution plan – For 2020, under §415(c)(1)(A) a defined contribution plan's annual contributions and other additions (excluding earnings) to the account of a participant cannot exceed the lesser of the following amounts:

- 100% of the participant's compensation
- $57,000

EMPLOYER DEDUCTION LIMITS

Employers can usually deduct, subject to limits, contributions made to a qualified plan, including those made for their own retirements. The contributions (and earnings and gains on them) are generally tax-free until distributed by the plan. The deduction limit for employer contributions to a qualified plan depends on the kind of plan the employer has.

- **Defined contribution plans** – The deduction for contributions to a defined contribution plan (PSP or MPPP) cannot be more than 25% of the compensation paid (or accrued) during the year to eligible employees participating in the plan. The following rules apply:
  1. Elective deferrals (discussed later) are not subject to the limit.
  2. Compensation includes elective deferrals.
  3. The maximum compensation taken into account for each employee in 2020 is **$285,000**.
- **Defined benefit plans** – The deduction for contributions to a defined benefit plan is based on actuarial assumptions and computations. An actuary must figure the deduction limit.

401(K) PLAN ELECTIVE DEFERRALS

A qualified plan can include a cash or deferred arrangement under which a participant can choose to have the employer contribute part of his before-tax compensation to the plan rather than receive the compensation in cash. A plan with this type of arrangement is a ***401(k) plan***. This contribution is an ***elective deferral*** because participants choose (elect) to defer receipt of the money. In general, a qualified plan can include a cash or deferred arrangement only if the qualified plan is one of the following ***defined contribution plans***:

- A profit-sharing plan
- A money purchase pension plan in existence on June 27, 1974, that included a salary reduction arrangement on that date

The plan <u>cannot</u> require, as a condition of participation, that an employee complete **more than one** year of service. There is a limit on the amount an employee can defer each year under these plans. The plan must provide that employees cannot defer more than the limit that applies for a particular year. For 2020, the basic limit of §402(g)(1) on elective deferrals (employee contributions) is **$19,500**, plus the additional catch-up contribution amount of **$6,500** if the employee is older than age 50. This limit applies to all salary reduction contributions and elective deferrals. If considering the plan in conjunction with other plans, the employee has exceeded the deferral limit, include the difference in gross income.

Employer contributions to a 401(k) plan are generally deductible by the employer for the year the employer contributes to the plan. Matching or non-elective contributions made to the plan are also deductible by the employer in the year of contribution. The employees' elective deferrals other than designated Roth contributions are not taxed until distributed from the plan. Elective deferrals are included in wages for FICA and federal unemployment (FUTA) tax. Employers report the total amount of elective deferrals to employees on Form W-2.

DISTRIBUTIONS

Generally, an employer cannot make distributions until one of the following occurs:

- The employee retires, dies, becomes disabled, or otherwise severs employment.
- The plan ends, and the employer does not establish or continue another defined contribution plan.
- In the case of a 401(k) plan that is part of a profit-sharing plan, the employee reaches age 59.5 or suffers financial hardship.
- The employee becomes eligible for a qualified reservist distribution.

ROLLOVERS

Distributions from a qualified plan minus a prorated part of any cost basis are subject to income tax in the year they are distributed. Since most recipients have no cost basis, a distribution is taxable. An exception is a distribution that is properly rolled over. The recipient of an *eligible rollover distribution* from a qualified plan can defer the tax on it by rolling it over into a traditional IRA or another eligible retirement plan. An eligible rollover distribution is a distribution of all or any part of an employee's balance in a qualified retirement plan that is not any of the following:

- A required minimum distribution
- A series of substantially equal payments made at least once a year over any of the following periods:
    1. The employee's life or life expectancy
    2. The joint lives or life expectancies of the employee and beneficiary
    3. A period of 10 years or longer
- A hardship distribution
- The portion of a distribution that represents the return of an employee's nondeductible contributions to the plan
- Loans treated as distributions
- Dividends on employer securities
- The cost of any life insurance coverage provided under a qualified retirement plan

If during a year, a qualified plan pays **to a participant** one or more eligible rollover distributions that are reasonably expected to total $200 or more, the payor must withhold 20% of each distribution for federal income tax. If the participant chooses to have the plan pay it directly to an IRA or another eligible retirement plan (a direct rollover), no withholding is required.

TAX ON EARLY DISTRIBUTIONS

Generally, a taxpayer younger than age 59.5 pays a **10% additional tax** on the distribution of any assets from a qualified retirement plan (including a traditional IRA). The tax applies to the part of the distribution the taxpayer must include in gross income and is in addition to any regular income tax due.

Exceptions to this rule include the following:

- Qualified retirement plan distributions (doesn't apply to IRAs) are received after **separation from service** when the separation from service occurs in or after the year the taxpayer reaches **age 55** (age 50 for qualified public safety employees including specified law enforcement officers, customs and border protection officers, firefighters, emergency medical services, and air traffic controllers).

- The taxpayer has unreimbursed medical expenses that are more than **7.5% of AGI** in 2020.

  TIP: A taxpayer does not have to itemize deductions to take advantage of this exception to the additional tax. However, a taxpayer can only take into account unreimbursed medical expenses that would be able to include in figuring a deduction for medical expenses on Schedule A. The exception amount is the amount paid for unreimbursed medical expenses during 2020, minus 7.5% of 2020 AGI.

- The distributions are not more than the cost of medical insurance for certain unemployed taxpayers
- The taxpayer is disabled
- The taxpayer is the beneficiary of a deceased IRA owner
- Made as part of a *series of substantially equal periodic payments* (SOSEPP under IRS Rule 72t) beginning after separation from service and made at least annually for the life or life expectancy of the employee or the joint lives or life expectancies of the employee and his designated beneficiary. (Payments, except in the case of death or disability, must continue for at least five years or until the employee reaches age 59.5, whichever is longer.)
- The distributions are not more than the taxpayer's qualified higher education expenses. The education must be for the taxpayer, taxpayer's spouse, or the children or grandchildren of the taxpayer or taxpayer's spouse. (Not available for qualified plan distributions)
- The distribution is to buy, build, or rebuild a first home (Not available for qualified plan distributions):
  1. Up to $10,000 for qualified acquisition costs if used within 120 days of distribution.
  2. $10,000 for each spouse if both are *first-time homebuyers.* A first-time homebuyer cannot own a main home during the two-year period ending on the date of acquisition of the home.
  3. Must be used for qualified acquisition costs for the main home of a taxpayer, spouse, child, grandchild, parent, or other ancestors.
- The distribution is due to an IRS levy on the plan
- The distribution is a qualified reservist distribution
- Made to an alternate payee under a QDRO
- Timely made to reduce excess contributions under a 401(k) plan
- Timely made to reduce excess employee or matching employer contributions
- Timely made to reduce excess elective deferrals
- The amount is rolled into another retirement plan within **60 days**

- Made as a qualified disaster distribution related to certain federally declared disasters (limited to $100,000 for qualified hurricane distributions and a separate $100,000 for qualified wildfire distributions)

  TIP: Participants taking a qualified disaster distribution can include it in income in equal amounts over three years, beginning with the year that includes the distribution date. Participants may also repay qualified disaster distributions within three years of receiving a distribution by making one or more contributions to an eligible retirement plan. Any repayment is treated as a trustee-to-trustee transfer.

- Up to **$5,000** for the birth of child or adoption
  1. Must include the name, age, and TIN of such child or eligible adoptee on the taxpayer's return
  2. An eligible adoptee is any individual (other than a child of the taxpayer's spouse) who has not attained age 18 or is physically or mentally incapable of self-support.
  3. A qualified distribution is made during the 1-year period beginning on the date on which a child of the individual is born or on which the legal adoption by the individual of an eligible adoptee is finalized.

TIP: The Secure Act of 2019 amended section 72(t) is amended to allow for up to $5,000 in penalty-free withdrawals from retirement plans for individuals in case of the birth of child or adoption.

CARES ACT UPDATE: The CARES Act **waives the 10% early withdrawal penalty for up to $100,000** of *coronavirus-related distributions* from *eligible retirement plans* on or after January 1, 2020, and before December 31, 2020. The CARES Act also waives the 20% mandatory federal withholding requirement for qualified plan distributions.

The term eligible retirement plan is defined in 402(c)(8)(B) and includes defined contributions plans such as a 401(k), as well as 403(b), 457, and IRAs. No provision is made for defined benefit plans.

This treatment is available if a taxpayer, spouse, or dependent is diagnosed with COVID-19 or SARS by the Center for Disease Control and Prevention. It is also available to an individual who experiences adverse financial consequences as a result of quarantine, layoff or reduced hours, inability to work due to lack of childcare due to the virus, or business closure or reduced business hours due to the virus.

Contributions (up to the amount of the coronavirus-related distribution) made **within 3 years** to eligible retirement plans are treated as if the taxpayer made a direct trustee to trustee transfer within 60 days of the distribution. In other words, the taxpayer can contribute the money back into the plan for a period of 3 years beginning the day after the contribution without penalty or tax consequences.

Unless the taxpayer elects otherwise, any amount required to be included in gross income for a taxable year is **spread over the 3-taxable-year period** beginning with such taxable year.

TIP: We anticipate that taxpayers will need to file amended tax returns to claim a refund of the overpayment for years they recognize income and subsequently repay coronavirus-related distributions within the allowable 3-year period.

LOANS

A qualified plan may, but is not required to, provide for loans. If a plan provides for loans, the plan may limit the amount available as a loan. The maximum amount that a plan can permit as a loan is the greater of **$10,000** or **50%** of the vested account balance, but the loan may not exceed **$50,000**.

> **EXAMPLE:** If a participant has an account balance of $40,000, the maximum amount that he or she can borrow from the account is $20,000.

A plan that provides for loans must specify the procedures for applying for a loan and the repayment terms for the loan. The employee must repay the loan within five years and make payments in substantially equal payments that include principal and interest and that are paid at least quarterly. Loan repayments are not considered plan contributions. A loan for purchasing the employee's principal residence may be paid back over a period of more than five years.

Loans are not taxable distributions unless they fail to satisfy the plan loan rules of the regulations with respect to the amount, duration, and repayment terms. In addition, a loan that is not paid back according to the repayment terms is treated as a distribution from the plan and is taxable as such.

CARES ACT UPDATE: The loan amount for certain qualified plans has increased to the lesser of **$100,000** or **100%** of the participant's account balance (from $50,000 / 50% previously). Participants may delay the repayment period for an existing loan with due dates in 2020 for 1 year.

PROHIBITED TRANSACTIONS

Prohibited transactions are transactions between the plan and a ***disqualified person*** that are prohibited by law. A disqualified person who takes part in a prohibited transaction must pay a tax. Prohibited transactions generally include the following transactions:

- A transfer or use of plan income or assets to, or for the benefit of, a disqualified person
- Any act of a fiduciary that deals with plan income or assets in his own interest
- The receipt of consideration by a fiduciary for his own account from any party dealing with the plan in a transaction that involves plan income or assets
- Any of the following acts between the plan and a disqualified person:
  1. Selling, exchanging, or leasing property
  2. Lending money or extending credit
  3. Furnishing goods, services, or facilities

DISQUALIFIED PERSON

A disqualified person is any of the following:

- A fiduciary of the plan
- A person providing services to the plan
- An employer, any of whose employees are covered by the plan
- An employee organization, any of whose members are covered by the plan
- Any direct or indirect owner of 50% or more of any of the following:
  1. The combined voting power of all classes of stock entitled to vote, or the total value of shares of all classes of stock of a corporation that is an employer or employee organization
  2. A partnership that is an employer or employee organization described previously
  3. The beneficial interest of a trust or unincorporated enterprise that is an employer or an employee organization described previously
- A member of the family of any individual described previously. A member of a family is the spouse, ancestor, lineal descendant, or any spouse of a lineal descendant
- A corporation, partnership, trust, or estate of which (or in which) any direct or indirect owner is a disqualified person and holds 50% or more of any of the following:
  1. The combined voting power of all classes of stock entitled to vote, or the total value of shares of all classes of stock of a corporation
  2. The capital interest or profits interest of a partnership
  3. The beneficial interest of a trust or estate
- An officer, director, a 10% or more shareholder, or highly compensated employee
- A 10% or more (in capital or profits) partner

TAX ON PROHIBITED TRANSACTION

The initial tax on a prohibited transaction is **15%** of the amount involved for each year (or part of a year) in the taxable period. If the person does not correct the transaction within the taxable period, the IRS will impose an additional tax of **100%** of the amount involved.

REPORTING REQUIREMENTS

An annual return form is **due by the last day of the seventh month after the plan year ends**. Taxpayers who are required to file must use one of the following forms:

- **Form 5500-SF** – This new simplified form is filed if a plan meets all the following conditions:
  1. The plan is a small plan (less than 100 participants at the beginning of the plan year).
  2. The plan meets the conditions for being exempt from the requirements for an independent qualified public accountant audit of the plan's books and records.
  3. Plan assets are 100% invested in secure investments with a readily determinable fair value.
  4. The plan holds no employer securities.
  5. The plan is not a multiemployer plan.
- **Form 5500-EZ** – This form is for a one-participant plan only, as described below:
  1. The plan is a one-participant plan if either of the following is true:
  2. The plan covers only the business owner (or the owner and his spouse), and the owner (or his spouse) owns the entire business (whether incorporated or unincorporated).
  3. The plan covers only one or more partners in a business partnership.
  4. A one-participant plan may <u>not</u> file an annual return on Form 5500. Every one-participant plan required to file an annual return must file either Form 5500-EZ or, if eligible, Form 5500-SF.
  5. A one-participant plan (or plans) with total assets of **$250,000** or less at the end of the plan year does not have to file Form 5500-EZ for that plan year. All plans should file a Form 5500-EZ for the final plan year to show that all plan assets have been distributed.
- **Form 5500** – All qualified plans that are not eligible for the forms above must prepare the annual report on Form 5500.

Table 14-1. Key Retirement Plan Rules for 2020

Type of Plan	Last Date for Contribution	Maximum Contribution	Maximum Deduction	When to Set Up Plan
SEP	Due date of employer's return (including extensions)	Smaller of $57,000 or 25% of participant's compensation	25% of all participants' compensation	Any time up to the due date of employer's return (including extensions)
SIMPLE IRA and SIMPLE 401(k)	**Salary reduction contributions:** 30 days after the end of the month for which the contributions are to be made **Matching or nonelective contributions:** Due date of employer's return (including extensions)	**Employee contribution:** Salary reduction contribution up to $13,500, $16,500 if age 50 or older **Employer contribution:** *Either* dollar-for-dollar matching contributions up to 3% of employee's compensation (not limited by the annual compensation limit), *or* fixed non-elective contributions of 2% of compensation	Same as maximum contribution	Any time between 1/1 and 10/1 of the calendar year For a new employer coming into existence after 10/1, as soon as administratively feasible
Qualified Plan: Defined Contribution Plan	**Elective deferral:** Due date of employee's return (including extensions) **Employer contribution:** Money Purchase or Profit-Sharing: Due date of employer's return (including extensions)	**Employee contribution:** Elective deferral up to $19,500, $26,000 if age 50 or older **Employer contribution:** Money Purchase or Profit-Sharing: Smaller of $57,000 or 100% of participant's compensation	25% of all participants' compensation, plus amount of elective deferrals made	By the end of the tax year
Qualified Plan: Defined Benefit Plan	Contributions must be paid in quarterly installments depending on the plan year, due 15 days after the end of each quarter	Amount needed to provide an annual benefit no larger than the smaller of $230,000 or 100% of the participant's average compensation for his highest three consecutive calendar years	Based on actuarial assumptions and computations	By the end of the tax year

LESSON 7

Specialized Returns

DECEDENT'S FINAL INCOME TAX RETURN

An income tax return must be filed for a *decedent* (a person who died) if the decedent met the filing requirements at the time of his death. Should death occur during the filing season (i.e., Jan 1–April 15) and before filing a prior year return, the normal deadline for filing (usually April 15) applies to that return. The individual responsible for filing the return may be a surviving spouse, relative, executor, administrator, or legal representative. This is not the final return, as the decedent was alive for several months into a new tax year.

> The final income tax return is due at the same time the decedent's return would have been due had death not occurred. A final return for a decedent who was a calendar year taxpayer is generally due on April 15 following the year of death, regardless of when during that year death occurred.

If the decedent is married at the time of death, the decedent and surviving spouse are considered married for the whole year for filing status purposes.

- A surviving spouse who does not remarry before the end of the tax year in which the decedent died may file a joint return with the decedent. If otherwise applicable, the return can include the full standard deduction based on filing status for the decedent.

- If the surviving spouse remarries during the year, they must file apart from the decedent. The decedent must file separately (MFS); however, the surviving spouse can file a joint return with the new spouse.

- A court-appointed personal representative may revoke an election to file a joint return that the surviving spouse previously made alone. The representative does this by filing a separate return for the decedent within one year from the due date of the return (including any extensions). The joint return made by the surviving spouse will then be regarded as the separate return of that spouse by excluding the decedent's items and refiguring the tax liability.

INCOME TO INCLUDE

The decedent's income includible on the final return is generally determined as if the person were still alive except that the taxable period is usually shorter because it ends on the date of death. All income the decedent would have received had death not occurred that was not properly includible on the final return is *income in respect of a decedent (IRD)* and taxable to the estate or person who receives it. The method of accounting used by the decedent also determines the income and expenses includible on the final return.

- **Cash method** – The final return includes items actually or *constructively received* before death.
  1. The decedent constructively received interest from coupons on bonds if the coupons matured in the decedent's final tax year but had not been cashed. Include the interest on the final return.
  2. Generally, the decedent constructively received a dividend if it was available for use by the decedent without restriction. If the corporation customarily mailed its dividend checks, the dividend was includible when received. If the individual died between the time the corporation declared the dividend and the time it arrived in the mail, the decedent did not constructively receive it before death. Do not include the dividend in the final return.

- **Accrual method** – Generally, under an accrual method of accounting, report income when earned. If the decedent used an accrual method, only the income items normally accrued before death are included in the final return.

INCOME IN RESPECT OF A DECEDENT (IRD)

Certain types of property, such as capital assets, receive a step-up in basis when included in the decedent's estate and transferred to a beneficiary due to death. Other assets, for example, traditional IRAs, are transferred in-kind to the beneficiary and do not receive a basis adjustment. The beneficiary is responsible for paying tax on income from these assets. All income the decedent would have received had death not occurred that was not properly includible on the final return, discussed earlier, is income in respect of a decedent. Income in respect of a decedent is included in the income of one of the following:

- The decedent's estate, if the estate receives it
- The beneficiary, if the right to income is passed directly to the beneficiary and he receives it
- Any person to whom the estate properly distributes the right to receive it

> The character of the IRD is the same as it would be to the decedent if he were alive. If the income would have been a capital gain to the decedent, it will be a capital gain to the taxpayer.

If an executor filed an estate tax return (Form 706) for the decedent, the taxpayer who must include IRD in his gross income may be able to claim a deduction for the estate tax paid on that income.

MEDICAL EXPENSE DEDUCTIONS

- Medical expenses paid <u>before</u> death by the decedent are deductible, subject to limits, on the final income tax return if deductions are itemized. This includes expenses for the decedent, as well as for the decedent's spouse and dependents.
- Medical expenses that were <u>not</u> paid before death are liabilities of the estate and appear on the federal estate tax return (Form 706). If the estate pays medical expenses for the decedent during the one-year period beginning with the day after death, the executor may elect to treat all or part of the expenses as paid by the decedent at the time the decedent incurred them. An executor making this election may claim all or part of the expenses on the decedent's income tax return as an itemized deduction, rather than on the federal estate tax return (Form 706).

LOSS DEDUCTIONS

A decedent's **net operating loss** deduction from a prior year and any capital losses (including **capital loss carryovers**) can be deducted only on the decedent's final income tax return. An unused net operating loss or capital loss is not deductible on the estate's income tax return.

CREDITS

The individual filing a decedent's tax return may claim any tax credits that applied to the decedent before death on the decedent's final income tax return. Certain credits, like the EIC or the child tax credit, still apply even though the return covers a period of fewer than 12 months.

FILING THE RETURN

If the court has appointed a personal representative, that person must sign the return. If it is a joint return, the surviving spouse must also sign it. If the court has not appointed a personal representative, the surviving spouse (on a joint return) signs the return and writes in the signature area "Filing as surviving spouse." If the court has not appointed a personal representative and there is no surviving spouse, the person in charge of the decedent's property must file and sign the return as "personal representative". A surviving spouse filing jointly with the decedent may submit a claim for refund by filing the return.

TIP: Write the word "DECEASED", the decedent's name, and the date of death across the top of the tax return.

ESTATE INCOME TAX

PERSONAL REPRESENTATIVE

A *personal representative* of an estate is an executor, administrator, or anyone who is in charge of the decedent's property. Generally, a decedent's will names an *executor* (or *executrix*) to administer the estate and distribute properties as the decedent has directed. The court usually appoints an *administrator* (or *administratrix*) if no will exists, if no executor was named in the will, or if the named executor cannot or will not serve. The personal representative has a fiduciary responsibility to the ultimate recipients of the income and the property of the estate.

When a person dies a probate proceeding <u>may</u> be opened. Depending on state law, probate will generally open within 30 to 90-days from the date of death.

One of the probate court's first actions will be to appoint a legal representative for the decedent and his or her estate. The legal representative may be a surviving spouse, other family member, executor named in the decedent's will or an attorney. The probate court will issue *Letters Testamentary* authorizing the estate administrator of the decedent to act on the decedent's behalf. The administrator will need the Letters Testamentary to handle the decedent's tax and other matters.

For estate tax purposes, if there is no executor or administrator appointed, qualified, and acting within the United States, the term "executor" includes anyone in actual or constructive possession of any property of the decedent. It includes, among others, the decedent's agents and representatives; safe-deposit companies, warehouse companies, and other custodians of property in this country; brokers holding securities of the decedent as collateral; and the debtors of the decedent who are in this country.

DUTIES

The primary duties of a personal representative are to collect all the decedent's assets, pay his or her creditors, and distribute the remaining assets to the heirs or other beneficiaries.

The personal representative also <u>must</u> perform the following duties:

- Apply for an employer identification number (EIN) for the estate if required to file a return.
- File all tax returns, including income, estate, and gift tax returns, when due.
- Pay the tax determined up to the date of discharge from duties.

TIP: The first action you should take if you are the personal representative for the decedent is to apply for an EIN for the estate. You should apply for this number as soon as possible because you need to enter it on returns, statements, and other documents you file concerning the estate. You also must give the identification number to payers of interest and dividends and other payers who must file a return concerning the estate.

FILING REQUIREMENTS

A decedent and their estate are separate taxable entities. So if filing requirements are satisfied, an estate administrator may have to file different types of tax returns.

First, the personal representative may need to file income tax returns for the decedent (Form 1040 series). The decedent's Form 1040 for the year of death, and for any preceding years for which a return was not filed, are required if the decedent's income for those years was above the filing requirement.

Second, the personal representative may need to file income tax returns for the estate (Form 1041). To file this return the personal representative will need to get a new EIN. An estate is required to file an income tax return if assets of the estate generate more than $600 in annual income. For example, if the decedent had interest, dividend or rental income when alive, then after death that income becomes income of the estate and may trigger the requirement to file an estate income tax return.

If the estate operates a business after the owner's death, the estate administrator is required to secure a new employer identification number for the business, report wages or income under the new EIN and pay any taxes that are due.

Third, the personal representative may need to file an estate tax return (Form 706). Estate tax is a tax on the transfer of assets from the decedent to their heirs and beneficiaries. In general, estate tax only applies to large estates.

An estate is a taxable entity separate from the decedent and comes into being with the death of the individual. It exists until the final distribution of its assets to the heirs and other beneficiaries. The estate must report income earned by the assets during this period on **Form 1041**. The tax generally is figured in the same manner and on the same basis as for individuals, with certain differences in the computation of deductions and credits.

2020 Tax Rate Schedule for Estates and Trusts	
If taxable income is:	**Then income tax equals:**
Not over $2,600	10% of the taxable income
Over $2,600 but not over $$9,450	$260 plus 24% of the excess over $2,600
Over $9,450 but not over $12,950	$1,904 plus 35% of the excess over $9,450
Over $12,950	$3,129 plus 37% of the excess over $12,950

TIP: Estates and Trusts reach the top marginal rate at a lower income level than an individual taxpayer.

The estate reports its income, like an individual reports income, annually on either a calendar or a fiscal year basis. The estate's first tax year can be any period that ends on the last day of a month and does not exceed 12 months. The personal representative chooses the estate's accounting period and method to report income (cash, accrual, or other) when filing its first Form 1041. The tax year and accounting method generally cannot change without IRS approval.

Every domestic estate with gross income of **$600 or more** during a tax year must file a Form 1041. If one of the beneficiaries of the domestic estate is a nonresident alien, the personal representative must file Form 1041, even if the gross income of the estate is less than $600.

INCOME IN RESPECT OF A DECEDENT

Certain types of property, such as capital assets, receive a step-up in basis when included in the decedent's estate and transferred to a beneficiary due to death. Other assets, for example, traditional IRAs, are transferred in-kind to the beneficiary and do not receive a basis adjustment. The beneficiary is responsible for paying tax on income from these assets. All income the decedent would have received had death not occurred that was not properly includible on the final return, discussed earlier, is *income in respect of a decedent (IRD).* Income in respect of a decedent is included in the income of one of the following:

• The decedent's estate, if the estate receives it

• The beneficiary, if the right to income is passed directly to the beneficiary and he receives it

• Any person to whom the estate properly distributes the right to receive it

The character of the IRD is the same as it would be to the decedent if he were alive. If the income would have been a capital gain to the decedent, it will be a capital gain to the taxpayer. If an executor filed an estate tax return (Form 706) for the decedent, the taxpayer who must include IRD in his gross income may be able to claim a deduction for the estate tax paid on that income.

EXEMPTION AND DEDUCTIONS ON FORM 1041

In figuring taxable income on Form 1041, an estate is generally allowed the same deductions as an individual. Special rules, however, apply to some deductions for an estate. This section includes discussions of those deductions affected by the special rules.

- **Exemption deduction** – An estate is allowed an exemption deduction of $600 in figuring its taxable income. An estate cannot claim an exemption for dependents.
- **Charitable contributions** – An estate qualifies for a deduction for amounts of gross income paid or permanently set aside for qualified charitable organizations. The adjusted gross income limits for individuals do not apply. However, to make a contribution deductible by his estate, the decedent must specifically provide for that contribution in his will. If there is no will, or if the will makes no provision for the payment to a charitable organization, then a deduction will not be allowed even though all of the beneficiaries may agree to the gift.
  1. An estate cannot deduct any contribution from income not included in the estate's gross income. If the will specifically provides that the estate is to pay contributions out of its gross income, the contributions are fully deductible.
  2. An estate cannot deduct a qualified conservation easement granted after the date of death and before the due date of the estate tax return. A contribution deduction is allowed to the estate for estate tax purposes.
- **Losses** – Generally, an estate can claim a deduction for a loss it sustains on the sale of property. An estate and a beneficiary of that estate are generally treated as related persons for purposes of the disallowance of a loss on the sale of an asset between related persons.
- **Casualty and theft losses** – The estate can deduct losses incurred from casualties and thefts during the administration of the estate only if the estate has not claimed them on the federal estate tax return (Form 706). The personal representative must file a statement with the estate's income tax return waiving the deduction for estate tax purposes.
- **Net operating loss deduction** – An estate can claim a net operating loss deduction, figured in the same way as an individual's, except that it cannot deduct any distributions to beneficiaries or the deduction for charitable contributions in figuring the loss or the loss carryover.
  1. The estate <u>cannot</u> deduct carryover losses resulting from net operating losses or capital losses sustained by the decedent before death on the estate's income tax return.
- **Administration expenses** – Expenses of administering an estate can be deducted either from the gross estate in figuring the federal estate tax on Form 706 or from the estate's gross income in figuring the estate's income tax on Form 1041. However, the estate cannot claim these expenses for both estate tax and income tax purposes. The personal representative must file a statement with the estate's income tax return waiving the deduction for estate tax purposes.
- **Depreciation and depletion** – The executor must apportion the allowable deductions for depreciation and depletion that accrue after the decedent's death between the estate and the beneficiaries, depending on the income of the estate that is allocable to each.
- **Distribution deduction** – An estate is allowed a deduction for the tax year for any income that the estate must distribute currently and for other amounts that are properly paid, credited, or required to be distributed to beneficiaries. The deduction is limited to the distributable net income of the estate.

DUE DATE AND ESTIMATED TAX

The estate must pay its income tax liability in full when it files the return. Estates with tax years ending two or more years after the date of the decedent's death must pay estimated tax in the same manner as individuals. The due date for filing Form 1041 for estates that use a calendar year accounting period is generally April 15. An estate may choose either a calendar or a fiscal year to report income. If on a fiscal year, Form 1041 is due by the **15th day of the fourth month** after the end of the tax year. If the due date is a Saturday, Sunday, or legal holiday, the form must be filed by the next business day. The personal representative can request an automatic **5 1/2 month extension** of time to file Form 1041.

DISTRIBUTIONS TO BENEFICIARIES FROM AN ESTATE

- The beneficiaries of an estate that must distribute all of its income currently must report their share of the distributable net income whether or not they actually received it.
- The beneficiaries of an estate that does not have to distribute all of its income currently must report all income that must be distributed to them (whether or not actually distributed) plus all other amounts paid, credited, or required to be distributed, up to their share of distributable net income.

REQUEST FOR PROMPT ASSESSMENT OF TAX

The IRS ordinarily has 3 years from the date an income tax return is filed, or its due date, whichever is later, to charge any additional tax due. A personal representative may request a prompt assessment of tax after the return has been filed. This reduces the time for making the assessment to 18 months from the date the written request for prompt assessment was received. This request can be made for any tax return (except the estate tax return) of the decedent or the decedent's estate. This may permit a quicker settlement of the tax liability of the estate and an earlier final distribution of the assets to the beneficiaries.

TRUSTS

A trust is a legal arrangement whereby one party (the trustee) manages property for the benefit of another (beneficiary). Federal laws govern the income tax treatment of trusts; however, many of the legal aspects fall under the laws of the state in which the trust was executed. An *inter vivos trust*, more commonly referred to as a *living trust*, is a trust that takes effect during the lifetime of the grantor. A *testamentary trust* is created at death by instructions in the decedent's will and is funded with property from the probate estate. The primary parties to a trust are as follows:

- **Grantor** – The person who creates and usually contributes property to the trust. Also called a trustor or settlor.
- **Beneficiary** – The individuals or entities named in the trust that benefit from trust property.
- **Trustee** – The fiduciary responsible for assets within the trust who assumes legal title to trust property and is accountable for administering the provisions of the trust on behalf of the beneficiaries. The trustee also is responsible for the payment of trust taxes and accounting for trust income, assets, and distributions.

A *grantor trust* is a trust in which the grantor retains control or has an interest as beneficiary. Circumstances under which income of a trust is taxed to a grantor are in general as follows—

- The grantor has a *reversionary interest* in either trust property or the income therefrom that exceeds **5%** of the value of that portion of the trust.
- The grantor has beneficial enjoyment of trust property.
- The grantor retains certain administrative powers, such as disposing of property for less than adequate consideration, borrowing trust funds, and general powers of administration (such as controlling investments, substituting property, or the power to direct the voting of securities).
- The grantor or a nonadverse party has the power to **revoke** the trust or return trust property to the grantor.

- The grantor or a nonadverse party has the power to distribute income to or for the benefit of the grantor or the grantor's spouse.

> Income from a grantor trust is **taxed to the grantor** as if no trust existed.

The property owned by the trust is the *Corpus* (also called principal). The character of distributions from a trust may be either principal or income, or both. For trust accounting purposes, such factors as income type, the trust document, and local law determine this classification. This classification is important because it can determine who is entitled to the income and the distribution amount. There are various types of trusts, all with different intents and purposes. All trusts fall into one of the following categories:

- **Simple trust** – A simple trust is one that is <u>required</u> to **distribute all income** currently. The trust may not use any amount of trust assets for charitable purposes. No distributions may occur in excess of the *fiduciary accounting income (FAI)* as determined by applicable law (i.e., a simple trust may <u>not</u> distribute amounts allocated to principal).
- **Complex trust** – Any trust that does not meet the definition of a simple trust is a complex trust.

ALLOCATING EXPENSES AGAINST INCOME

A distribution to a beneficiary is not always taxable income. To determine the appropriate character of a distribution, and the *distribution deduction* for the trust, the trustee must allocate a portion of trust expenses to its various sources of income. No deduction is available for direct or indirect expenses related to tax-exempt income. All deductible items directly attributable to one class of income must reduce that class. For example, fees to manage a municipal bond portfolio reduce tax-exempt income, while the expenses of managing a rental property reduce rental income.

> The trustee may allocate expenses not attributable to a specific class of income (such as trustee fees or legal expenses) to any item of income **included in computing Distributable Net Income (DNI).**

The calculation considers all expenses, including those charged to principal for trust accounting purposes. The trustee has some discretion on which class of income he will apply the indirect expenses against; however, if the trust has tax-exempt income, he must allocate a portion of the expenses against it. In general, indirect expenses reduce tax-exempt income according to the ratio of tax-exempt income to all other income included in DNI (not capital gains allocated to corpus). Calculate this ratio before deducting direct expenses. The trustee must utilize a method that will allocate a "reasonable proportion" of indirect expenses to tax-exempt income.

EXAMPLE 15-1: Trust A (simple trust) has $8,000 in taxable interest and $2,000 in tax-exempt interest. The trust paid $500 in trustee fees. What is the taxable amount of income to the beneficiary?

All expenses in this example are indirect costs. Reduce tax-exempt interest by a pro-rata share of expenses of $100 ($500 in fees multiplied by 20%, the ratio of tax-exempt income to total income). Net taxable income is gross taxable interest less $400 in allocable indirect expenses (80% pro-rata share).

Net taxable income of trust	$7,600
Net tax-exempt income of trust	+ 1,900
DNI of trust	**$9,500**

Because this is a simple trust, all income must be distributed currently. DNI is composed of 80% taxable and 20% tax-exempt income. The beneficiary has $7,600 in taxable income. The trust may claim a distribution deduction for the taxable amount of the distribution to the beneficiary.

EXAMPLE 15-2: Trust B (simple trust) has $15,000 in tax-exempt interest and $5,000 in taxable interest. The trust paid $1,000 in commissions to purchase tax-free municipal bonds and $2,000 in attorney fees. What amount of income is tax-free to the beneficiary?

First, allocate the $2,000 of indirect expenses to income. The tax-exempt portion of income is 75% of the total (gross) income included in DNI. Allocate $1,500 of the attorney fees to tax-exempt interest and $500 to taxable interest. The trustee must also decrease tax-exempt income by $1,000 of direct expenses. The total required distribution to the beneficiary is $17,000, of which $4,500 is taxable.

Net taxable income of trust	$4,500
Net tax-exempt income of trust	+ 12,500
DNI of trust	**$17,000**

DISTRIBUTABLE NET INCOME (DNI)

Trusts and estates must calculate DNI each year to determine the maximum amount of income distributions for which a distribution deduction is available. A trust may not deduct distributions in excess of the taxable amount of DNI. DNI with respect to any taxable year is the taxable income (before the distribution deduction) of the estate or trust computed with the following modifications:

- **Deduction for distributions** – No deduction for income distributions (paid, credited, or required)
- **Deduction for personal exemption** – The trust shall take no deduction for personal exemptions
- **Capital gains and losses** – The trust shall exclude gains from the sale or exchange of capital assets from DNI to the extent that the trust allocates such gains to *corpus* (trust principal) and does not pay them, credit them, or require that they are distributed to any beneficiary during the taxable year.
- **Extraordinary dividends and taxable stock dividends** – (For simple trusts only.) A fiduciary, acting in good faith, who determines such dividends are allocable to *corpus* under the terms of the governing instrument and applicable local law, may exclude these items from DNI, provided the dividends are not paid or credited to any beneficiary.
- **Tax-exempt income** – Add net tax-exempt income to DNI. To arrive at *net tax-exempt income*, reduce the total amount of tax-exempt income by any expenses that relate directly to the tax-exempt income and a pro-rata share of expenses that are not attributable to a specific class of income (such as trustee fees).

TAXABLE INCOME

Income from an estate or trust (other than a grantor trust) is taxable to the entity unless distributions are made (or required to be made) to beneficiaries. The **entity must pay tax on undistributed income**, and the **beneficiary will pay tax on actual (or required) distributions**.

TIP: Estates and trusts are subject to the highest marginal tax rate 37% and the 3.8% tax on Net Investment Income Tax (NIIT) when taxable income exceeds **$12,950** in 2020. The tax impact of retaining capital gains in a trust is generally less favorable than distributing the income to its beneficiaries. This is a planning opportunity if the fiduciary has discretion.

The income distributed to the beneficiary retains the same character in the hands of the beneficiary as in the hands of the estate or trust. The formula to determine the **taxable income of the estate or trust** is:

Gross Income received by the estate/trust from all taxable sources (includes capital gains or losses)

. . .*less* deductions and expenses (excluding expenses credited to tax-exempt income)

The result is the taxable income of the estate/trust **before** the distribution deduction.

. . .*less* the *distribution deduction* (limited to the taxable portion of DNI)

. . .*less* the exemption amount ($300 simple trust, $100 complex trust, and $600 estate)

The result is the *taxable income* of the trust or estate.

EXAMPLE 15-3: Trust C (a simple trust) receives long-term capital gains on stock sales of $15,000, dividends of $50,000, rents of $25,000, and tax-exempt interest of $25,000. The terms of the trust require the trustee to allocate all gains to principal and distribute all income equally between two beneficiaries. The trust expenses include taxes on the rental property of $5,000 and the trustee's commissions of $3,900 (the trustee allocates $1,300 to principal and $2,600 to income). Determine the amount of income taxable to each beneficiary and the amount taxable to the trust.

Dividends	$50,000	
Rents	+ 25,000	
Tax-exempt interest	+ 25,000	
Total		$100,000
Deductions:		
Rental expenses	$5,000	
Trustee's commissions allocable to income	+ 2,600	
		– $7,600
Fiduciary accounting income (FAI)		$92,400

Fiduciary accounting income (FAI) is the amount of income (after expenses allocable to income) the trustee will use to determine distributions for beneficiaries. A simple trust is required to distribute all FAI currently. For purposes of FAI, the trustee may allocate certain items of income or expense to either the principal or the income accounts, according to the trust document under state law. For this example, the trust allocates capital gains to corpus. As a result, gains are not part of FAI. The capital expenses are also not a deduction for FAI. FAI is a separate calculation from net taxable income or DNI. Just like with FAI, DNI does not include gains allocated to principal. Before calculating the DNI of the trust, the trustee must apportion expenses that do not directly relate to a specific item of income between tax-exempt and taxable income sources. The total amount of expenses in this example are $3,900. The trustee did allocate a portion of the commissions to principal; however, that is only important for FAI. For DNI purposes, all indirect expenses are applicable. The trustee will allocate indirect expenses to tax-exempt according to its percentage of all income included in the calculation for DNI. In this example, $25,000 in tax-exempt income represents 25% of total gross income included in DNI. Capital gains are generally not income for DNI purposes because the trust allocates them to principal.

Dividends		$50,000
Rents		+ 25,000
Tax-exempt interest	$25,000	
less: Commissions (tax-exempt)	– 975	
		+ 24,025
Total		$99,025
Deductions:		
Rental expenses	$5,000	
Trustee's commissions (on taxable)	+ 2,925	
		– $7,925
Distributable Net Income (DNI)		$91,100

DNI determines the maximum distribution deduction a trust may use to reduce trust income. The trust cannot claim a deduction for distributions that exceed the taxable amount of DNI. The taxable amount of DNI is $67,075 ($75,000 taxable income – $7,925 deductions), which is 73.6% of DNI. Accordingly, the distributions in the hands of each beneficiary will retain the same character of taxable and tax-exempt income. The trust must consider all income from taxable sources in the calculation of net income. The trustee will not include income or expenses (either direct or indirect) that relate to tax-exempt income in the calculation of net income. For more information, see IRC §265, 26 CFR §1.652(b)-3, and §1.265-1.

Capital Gains	$15,000	
Dividends	+ 50,000	
Rents	+ 25,000	
Gross Income		$90,000
Deductions:		
Rental expenses	$5,000	
Trustee's commissions on taxable income	+ 2,925	
Distributions to beneficiaries	+ 67,075	
Personal exemption	+ 300	
		– $75,300
Trust Taxable Income		$14,700

DEPRECIATION

Trust may not allocate depreciation to principal unless the specific provisions in the trust permit the trustee to maintain a depreciation reserve. If a trust does not allocate depreciation to principal, the deduction for depreciation passes through to the income beneficiaries and does not affect the calculation of DNI or the net income of the trust. An estate or trust may not make an election under Section 179 to expense certain tangible property.

REQUIREMENTS FOR TRUST TAX RETURNS

Trusts, similar to estates, use Form 1041 to report income tax liability. Unlike an estate, a trust cannot use a fiscal year. The due date for filing Form 1041 for a trust is April 15. The IRS will grant an automatic **5 1/2 month extension** of time to file Form 1041 at the request of the trustee (Form 7004). Trusts must pay estimated tax in the same manner as individuals. A trust (also for an estate) may be subject to AMT. If applicable, the trust (or estate) files *Schedule I* along with Form 1041 to compute the following:

- Alternative minimum taxable income
- The income distribution deduction on a minimum tax basis, and
- AMT for the trust (or estate)

FARMERS

SCHEDULE F

Farmers use *Schedule F* (Form 1040) to figure the net profit or loss from **regular farming operations**. This includes **farm products raised for sale** or **products bought for resale**. Income from farming includes amounts received from cultivating, operating, or managing a farm for gain or profit, as either owner or tenant.

Schedule F includes income from **operating** a stock, dairy, poultry, fish, fruit, or truck (vegetable) farm and income from operating a plantation, ranch, range, or orchard. It also includes income from the sale of crop shares if the taxpayer materially participates in producing the crop. Income received from operating a nursery, which specializes in growing ornamental plants, is considered income from farming. **Livestock held primarily for sale is a farm product, is included in inventory, and reported on Schedule F.** When a farmer sells farm products bought for resale, his profit or loss is the difference between the selling price and the basis in the item (usually the cost).

Income reported on Schedule F does not include gains or losses from sales or other dispositions of the following farm assets:

- Land (§1231 property)
- Depreciable land improvements (§1250 property)
- Depreciable farm equipment (§1245 property)
- Depreciable buildings and structures (§1250 property)
- Depreciable livestock held for draft, breeding, sport, or dairy purposes (§1245 property)
- Raised livestock (no depreciable basis) held for draft, breeding, sport, or dairy purposes (§1231 property)

Land and depreciable property (including not held for resale) used in farming are not capital assets. Farmers generally use Form 4797 to report these transactions as ordinary income or capital gain under the rules for §1231 transactions.

Most property held more than one year is §1231 property. In addition to having the character of §1231, property that is subject to the allowance for depreciation is also subject to the provisions of either §1245 or §1250.

LIVESTOCK USED IN BUSINESS

Livestock **used in the farm business** must either be **depreciated** (recovery period is 5-year GDS or 7-year ADS) unless *raised livestock* which has no depreciable basis, or included in **inventory.** Examples include livestock held primarily for draft (working animals), breeding, dairy, or sporting purposes. Treat the sale of livestock **used in the business** the same as other depreciable business property (§1245). The result of the sale is either ordinary or capital gain or loss, depending on the circumstances. In either case, farmers should always report these sales on **Form 4797.**

Sale or exchange of this livestock used in the business may qualify as a **Section 1231** gain or loss. For Section 1231 transactions, livestock includes cattle and horses (held at least 24 months) and hogs, mules, donkeys, sheep, goats, fur-bearing animals, and other mammals (held at least 12 months). Livestock does not include chickens, turkeys, pigeons, geese, emus, ostriches, rheas, or other birds, fish, frogs, reptiles, etc.

A farmer who sells depreciable property (§1245 property or §1250 property) at a gain, may have to recognize all or part of the gain as ordinary income under the depreciation recapture rules. A gain on the disposition of §1245 property is treated as ordinary income to the extent of depreciation allowed or allowable. Any gain remaining after applying the depreciation recapture rules is a §1231 gain, which may be taxed as a capital gain. Net §1231 gains are ordinary gains up to the amount of non-recaptured §1231 losses from the five prior years; the rest is a **long-term capital gain.** Losses from §1231 property are **ordinary losses.** If the property is not held for the required holding period (generally 12 months), the transaction is not subject to §1231 treatment, and any gain or loss is ordinary income reported in Part II of Form 4797.

Gain on the sale of *raised livestock* is generally the gross sales price reduced by any expenses of the sale. Expenses of the sale include sales commissions, freight or hauling, and other similar expenses. The basis of the animal sold is zero if the taxpayer deducted the costs of raising it during the years the taxpayer raised the animal. Gain on the sale of *purchased livestock* is generally the gross sales price minus the *adjusted basis* and any expenses.

Where to Report Sales of Farm Product		
Item Sold	**Schedule F**	**Form 4797**
Farm products raised for sale, including crops and livestock	X	
Farm products bought for resale, including crops and livestock	X	
Farm products not held primarily for sale, such as livestock held for draft, breeding, sport, or dairy purposes (bought or raised)		X

SALES CAUSED BY WEATHER-RELATED CONDITIONS

If a farmer sells or exchanges more livestock, including poultry, than he normally would in a year because of a drought, flood, or other weather-related condition, he may be able to postpone reporting the gain from the additional animals until the next year.

The farmer must meet all of the following conditions to qualify:

- Their principal trade or business is farming.
- They use the cash method of accounting.
- They can show that, under their usual business practices, they would not have sold or exchanged the additional animals this year except for the weather-related condition.
- The weather-related condition caused the federal government to designate an area as eligible for assistance.

CROP INSURANCE AND CROP DISASTER PAYMENTS

Farmers must include in income any crop insurance proceeds they receive as the result of crop damage. The income is generally recognized in the year received. Farmers treat the crop disaster payments received from the federal government as crop insurance proceeds. The government provides crop disaster payments to a farmer as the result of destruction or damage to crops, or the inability to plant crops, due to drought, flood, or any other natural disaster. Farmers can **postpone** reporting crop insurance proceeds as income until **the year following the year the damage occurred** if they meet all the following conditions:

- They use the cash method of accounting.
- They receive the crop insurance proceeds in the same tax year the crops are damaged.
- Under normal business practices, they would have included income from the damaged crops in any tax year following the year the damage occurred.

EXAMPLE: A December 2020 cold spell in Florida froze the entire Florida Citrus temple orange crop, scheduled for February harvest. The entire 2020 crop was declared a disaster, and Florida Citrus received a crop disaster payment in December 2020. Florida Citrus uses the accrual method of accounting and—unlike farmers using the cash method—cannot postpone reporting the payment.

INCOME AVERAGING FOR FARMERS

Taxpayers who are engaged in a farming business may be able to average all or some of their farm income by allocating it to the **three prior years** (base years).

Only a taxpayer engaged in a farming business as an individual, a partner in a partnership, or a shareholder in an S corporation may use income averaging. Corporations, partnerships, S corporations, estates, and trusts cannot use income averaging.

ESTIMATED TAXES

Estimated tax payments are not required for a taxpayer with at least **two-thirds of gross income from farming** who pays the entire tax liability by **March 1** following the tax year. Otherwise, to avoid a penalty, the taxpayer must make one estimated tax payment by **January 15** (following the tax year) equaling the lesser of **66 2/3%** of the tax due, or **100%** of the prior year tax liability.

Gross income from farming is the total of the following amounts from the tax return:

- Gross farm income from Schedule F (Form 1040)
- Gross farm rental income from Form 4835
- Gross farm income from Schedule E (Form 1040)
- Gains from the sale of livestock used for draft, breeding, sport, or dairy purposes (Form 4797)

Gross income from farming does not include:

- Wages as a farm employee
- Income from contract grain harvesting and hauling with workers and machines furnished by the taxpayer
- Gains from the sale of farmland or depreciable farm equipment

EXEMPT ORGANIZATIONS

Certain organizations receive an exemption from federal income taxes. In general, these exempt organizations must apply for recognition of their tax-exempt status and submit annual informational returns to the IRS. Contributions to domestic tax-exempt organizations, except organizations testing for public safety, are deductible as charitable contributions on the donor's federal income tax return. An organization may qualify for exemption from federal income tax if it is organized and operated exclusively for one or more of the following purposes:

- Religious
- Charitable
- Scientific
- Testing for public safety
- Literary
- Educational (includes public daycare for children to enable parents to work)
- Fostering national or international amateur sports competition (but only if none of its activities involve providing athletic facilities or equipment)
- The prevention of cruelty to children or animals

To qualify, the organization must be a corporation, community chest, fund, foundation, or trust. An individual or a partnership will <u>not</u> qualify. Qualifying organizations include the following:

- Nonprofit old-age homes
- Parent-teacher associations
- Charitable hospitals or other charitable organizations
- Alumni associations
- Schools
- State schools, universities, or hospitals
- Chapters of the Red Cross or Salvation Army
- Boys' or Girls' Clubs
- Churches

FORM 1023 – RECOGNITION OF EXEMPTION

The IRS will <u>not</u> treat most tax-exempt organizations as tax-exempt unless the organization applies for recognition of exemption by filing *Form 1023.*

If the organization files for tax-exemption within **27 months** of its formation, the tax-exempt status will be effective from its formation date. If the organization files more than 27 months after its formation, the tax-exempt status will start from the filing date.

Some organizations are <u>not</u> required to file Form 1023. The following organizations are **exempt automatically** if they meet the requirements of Sec. 501(c)(3):

- Churches, interchurch organizations of local units of a church, conventions or associations of churches, or integrated auxiliaries of a church, such as a men's or women's organization, religious school, mission society, or youth group.
- Any organization (other than a private foundation) normally having annual gross receipts of **$5,000** or less.
  1. **Gross receipts test** – For purposes of the gross receipts test, an organization normally does not have more than $5,000 annually in gross receipts if:
     A. During its first tax year, the organization received gross receipts of $7,500 or less,
     B. During its first two years, it had a total of $12,000 or less in gross receipts, and
     C. If in existence for at least three years, the total gross receipts received by the organization during the immediately preceding two years, plus the current year, are $15,000 or less

An organization with gross receipts more than the amounts in the gross receipts test, unless otherwise exempt from filing Form 1023, must file a Form 1023 within 90 days after the end of the period in which the gross receipts exceeded the amounts in the test.

FORM 990 INFORMATIONAL RETURNS

All private foundations exempt under Section 501(c)(3) must file *Form 990-PF.* Exempt organizations, other than private foundations, must file annual information returns on *Form 990* or *Form 990-EZ (*short version). Form 990-EZ is designed for use by small exempt organizations and nonexempt charitable trusts. An organization may file Form 990-EZ instead of Form 990 if it meets both of the following requirements:

- Gross receipts during the year were <u>less</u> than **$200,000.**
- Total assets at the end of the year were <u>less</u> than **$500,000.**

Most tax-exempt organizations whose gross annual receipts are normally $50,000 or less can file the e-Postcard (**Form 990-N**). These returns are due by the **15th day of the fifth month** after the end of the organization's accounting period. Thus, for a calendar year taxpayer, the informational return is due May 15 of the following year. A taxpayer may use **Form 8868** to request an automatic **six-month** extension until November 15th.

FORM 990-T UNRELATED BUSINESS TAXABLE INCOME (UBTI)

Even though an organization is recognized as tax exempt, it still may be liable for tax on its **unrelated business taxable income (UBTI)**. Unrelated business taxable income is income from a trade or business, regularly carried on, that does not substantially relate to the charitable, educational, or another purpose that is the basis for the organization's exemption. An exempt organization that has **$1,000** or more of gross income from an unrelated business must file **Form 990-T** in addition to the obligation to file the annual information return, Form 990, 990-EZ, or 990-PF. Organizations <u>must</u> make quarterly payments of estimated tax on **UBTI** if expecting tax for the year to be **$500** or more.

FAILURE TO FILE FORM 990 PENALTIES

Generally (for 2020 returns required to be filed in 2021), an exempt organization that, without reasonable cause, fails to file a required return must pay a penalty of **$20** a day for each day the failure continues. The same penalty will apply if the organization does not give all the information required on the return or does not give the correct information. The maximum penalty for any single return is the smaller of **$10,500 or 5%** of the organization's gross receipts for the year. For an organization that has gross receipts of more than $1,084,000, the penalty is **$105** a day up to a maximum of **$54,000** for any single return.

EMPLOYMENT TAX RETURNS

Every employer, including an organization exempt from federal income tax, who pays wages to employees is responsible for withholding, depositing, paying, and reporting federal income tax, Social Security and Medicare (FICA) taxes, and federal unemployment tax (FUTA), unless that employer is specifically exempted by law from those requirements or if the taxes clearly do not apply. Payments for services performed by a minister of a church in the exercise of the ministry, or a member of a religious order performing duties required by the order, are generally not subject to FICA or FUTA taxes. Churches and qualified church-controlled organizations can elect exemption from employer FICA taxes by filing Form 8274.

Organization Reference Chart

Description of organization	General nature of activities	Application Form	Annual Return required
501(c)(1) Corporations Organized under Act of Congress (including Federal Credit Unions)	Instrumentalities of the United States	No Form	None
501(c)(2) Title Holding Corporation For Exempt Organization	Holding title to property of an exempt organization and distributing net income to it	1024	990 (or EZ)
501(c)(3) Religious, Educational, Charitable, Scientific, Literary, Testing for Public Safety, to Foster National or International Amateur Sports Competition, or Prevention of Cruelty to Children or Animals Organizations	Activities of nature implied by description of class of organization	1023 (or EZ)	990 (or EZ), or 990-PF
501(c)(4) Civic Leagues, Social Welfare Organizations; and Local Associations of Employees	Promotion of community welfare; charitable, educational, or recreational	Must provide notice on 8976; may also submit 1024-A	990 (or EZ)
501(c)(5) Labor, Agricultural, and Horticultural Organizations	Educational or instructive, the purpose being to improve conditions of work, and to improve products and/or efficiency	1024	990 (or EZ)
501(c)(6) Business Leagues, Chambers of Commerce, Real Estate Boards, etc.	Improvement of business conditions of one or more lines of business	1024	990 (or EZ)
501(c)(7) Social and Recreational Clubs	Pleasure, recreation, social activities	1024	990 (or EZ)
501(c)(8) Fraternal Beneficiary Societies and Associations	Providing for payment of life, sickness, accident or other benefits to members within a lodge system	1024	990 (or EZ)
501(c)(9) Voluntary Employees Beneficiary Associations	Employee association providing for payment of life, sickness, accident, or other benefits to members	1024	990 (or EZ)
501(c)(10) Domestic Fraternal Societies and Associations	Earnings devoted to charitable, fraternal, and other specified purposes within a domestic lodge system. No benefits to members	1024	990 (or EZ)
501(c)(11) Teachers' Retirement Fund Associations	Teachers' association for payment of retirement benefits	Letter	990 (or EZ)

Organization Reference Chart

Description of organization	General nature of activities	Application Form	Annual Return required
501(c)(12) Benevolent Life Insurance Associations, Mutual Ditch or Irrigation Companies, Mutual or Cooperative Telephone Companies, and Like Organizations	Activities of a mutual or cooperative nature	1024	990 (or EZ)
501(c)(13) Cemetery Companies	Burials and incidental activities	1024	990 (or EZ)
501(c)(14) State-Chartered Credit Unions, Mutual Reserve Funds	Loans to members	Letter	990 (or EZ)
501(c)(15) Mutual Insurance Companies or Associations	Providing insurance to members substantially at cost	1024	990 (or EZ)
501(c)(16) Cooperative Organizations to Finance Crop Operations	Financing crop operations in conjunction with activities of a marketing or purchasing association	1120-C, Letter	990 (or EZ)
501(c)(17) Supplemental Unemployment Benefit Trusts	Provides for payment of supplemental unemployment compensation benefits	1024	990 (or EZ)
501(c)(18) Employee Funded Pension Trust (created before June 25, 1959)	Payment of benefits under a pension plan funded by employees	Letter	990 (or EZ)
501(c)(19) Post or Organization of Past or Present Members of the Armed Forces	Activities implied by nature of organization	1024	990 (or EZ)
501(c)(21) Black Lung Benefit Trusts	Funded by coal mine operators to satisfy their liability for disability or death due to black lung diseases	Letter	990-BL
501(c)(22) Withdrawal Liability Payment Fund	To provide funds to meet the liability of employers withdrawing from a multi-employer pension fund	Letter	990 (or EZ)
501(c)(23) Veterans' Organization (created before 1880)	To provide insurance and other benefits to veterans	Letter	990 (or EZ)
501(c)(25) Title Holding Corporations or Trusts with Multiple Parent Corporations	Holding title and paying over income from real property to 35 or fewer parents or beneficiaries	1024	990 (or EZ)
501(c)(26) State-Sponsored Organization Providing Health Coverage for High-Risk Individuals	Provides health care coverage to high-risk individuals	Letter	990 (or EZ)
501(c)(27) State-Sponsored Workers' Compensation Reinsurance Organization	Reimburses members for losses under workers' compensation acts	Letter	990 (or EZ)

Organization Reference Chart

Description of organization	General nature of activities	Application Form	Annual Return required
501(c)(28) National Railroad Retirement Investment Trust	Manages and invests the assets of the Railroad Retirement Account	No Form	990
501(c)(29) CO-OP health insurance issuers	A qualified health insurance issuer which has received a loan or grant under the CO-OP program	Letter and Form 8718	990
501(d) Religious and Apostolic Associations	Regular business activities; Communal religious community	No Form	1065
501(e) Cooperative Hospital Service Organizations	Performs cooperative services for hospitals	1023	990 (or EZ)
501(f) Cooperative Service Organizations of Operating Educational Organizations	Performs collective investment services for educational organizations	1023	990 (or EZ)
501(k) Child Care Organizations	Provides care for children	1023	990 (or EZ)
501(n) Charitable Risk Pools	Pools certain insurance risks of sec. 501(c)(3) organizations	1023	990 (or EZ)
501(q) Credit Counseling Organization	Credit counseling services	1023	990
521(a) Farmers' Cooperative Associations	Cooperative marketing and purchasing for agricultural procedures	1028	1120-C
527 Political organizations	A party, committee, fund, association, etc., that directly or indirectly accepts contributions or makes expenditures for political campaigns	8871	1120-POL, 990 (or EZ)

REPRESENTATION

SEE EXAM PART 3

LESSON 1

Preparing Returns

RETURN PREPARERS

The term *tax return preparer* means any person who **prepares for compensation**, or who employs one or more persons to prepare for compensation, any return of tax or any claim for refund of tax. A person may be a preparer without regard to professional status, educational qualifications, nationality, residence, or business location. It is not necessary to prepare the entire return; a person is considered a preparer as long as he prepares a substantial portion of the return.

- A person shall <u>not</u> be a tax return preparer merely because such person:
    1. furnishes typing, reproducing, or other mechanical assistance,
    2. provides tax assistance under a Volunteer Income Tax Assistance (VITA) program established by the IRS,
    3. prepares a return for an employer (or of an officer or employee of the employer) by whom he is regularly and continuously employed,
    4. prepares as a fiduciary a return or claim for refund for any person, or
    5. prepares a claim for refund for a taxpayer in response to any notice of deficiency or in response to any waiver of restriction after the commencement of an audit.

DUTIES FOR HANDLING RETURNS

A tax return preparer <u>must</u>:

- Sign the return (if paid preparer) unless not required by instruction or code of law.
- Indicate their identifying number on the return. All paid tax return preparers (including attorneys, CPAs, and enrolled agents) <u>must</u> apply for a *Preparer Tax Identification Number (PTIN)*—if they already have one, they <u>must</u> annually renew—before preparing any federal tax returns. Anyone who prepares federal tax returns for compensation must have a valid PTIN before preparing returns.
- Provide a copy of the return to the taxpayer no later than the time the original return is presented for signature to the taxpayer.
- Keep the following records for a period of three years after the close of the return period during which the return or claim for refund was presented for signature to the taxpayer:
    ◦ Retain a completed copy of the return or claim for refund, or
    ◦ Retain a record of the name, taxpayer ID number, and taxable year of the taxpayer for whom was prepared, and the type of return or claim for refund prepared. Also, retain a record of the name of the individual tax return preparer required to sign.

PREPARER TAX IDENTIFICATION NUMBER

All paid tax return preparers (including attorneys, CPAs, and enrolled agents) must have a *Preparer Tax Identification Number (PTIN)* before preparing any federal tax returns. A PTIN is a number issued by the IRS to paid tax return preparers. It is the tax preparer's identification number and, when applicable, must be placed in the paid preparer section of a tax return. Any individual who, for compensation, prepares all or substantially all of a tax return or claim for refund—including making determinations that affect tax liability—needs a PTIN.

> Preparing or signing a tax return or claim for refund without a valid PTIN is a violation of regulations.

PREPARER PENALTIES

Return preparers are responsible for taking a reasonable position on a tax return. To be reasonable, there must be *substantial authority* for the position, or in the case of a disclosed position, a *reasonable basis* for the treatment of such item on the return. The return cannot contain *frivolous positions*, which have no basis for validity in existing law or which have been deemed frivolous by the U.S. Tax Court or another federal court. The IRS may assess penalties within three years after the taxpayer files the return. No proceeding in court without assessment for the collection of such tax shall begin after the expiration of such period. There is no statute of limitations for fraudulent returns.

The substantial authority standard is an objective standard involving an analysis of the law and application of the law to relevant facts. It is less stringent than the *more likely than not* standard (the standard that is met when there is a greater than 50% likelihood of the position being upheld) but more stringent than the reasonable basis standard. There is substantial authority for the tax treatment of an item only if the weight of the authorities supporting the treatment is substantial in relation to the weight of authorities supporting contrary treatment. All authorities relevant to the tax treatment of an item, including the authorities contrary to the treatment, are taken into account in determining whether substantial authority exists. The weight of authorities is determined in light of the pertinent facts and circumstances.

Reasonable basis is a relatively high standard of tax reporting that is significantly higher than not frivolous or not patently improper. The reasonable basis standard is not satisfied by a return position that is merely arguable. If a return position is reasonably based on one or more of the authorities set forth in §1.6662–4(d)(3)(iii) (taking into account the relevance and persuasiveness of the authorities, and subsequent developments), the return position will generally satisfy the reasonable basis standard even though it may not satisfy the substantial authority standard.

A *tax shelter*, for purposes of the substantial understatement portion of the accuracy-related penalty, is a partnership or other entity, plan, or arrangement, with a significant purpose to avoid or evade federal income tax. Tax shelters have a higher standard and must have a confidence level of at least *more likely than not* (greater than 50% likelihood) that one or more significant tax issues would be resolved in the taxpayer's favor.

Taxpayers and tax return preparers who wish to avoid certain penalties can use **Form 8275** (Disclosure Statement), Form **8275-R** (Regulation Disclosure Statement), or by following revenue procedure to disclose items or positions that are not otherwise adequately disclosed on a tax return (use Form 8275-R to disclose items or positions taken contrary to a regulation).

TIP: Guidance is published annually in a revenue procedure in the Internal Revenue Bulletin that identifies circumstances when an item reported on a return is considered adequate disclosure for purposes of the substantial understatement aspect of the accuracy-related penalty and for avoiding the preparer's penalty relating to understatements due to unreasonable positions. A preparer does not have to file Form 8275 for items that meet the requirements of the revenue procedure.

> **EXAMPLE:** Generally, you will have met the requirements for adequate disclosure of a charitable contribution deduction if you complete the contributions section of Schedule A (Form 1040), supply all required information, and attach all related forms required pursuant to statute or regulation.

Form 8275 is filed in order to avoid the portions of the accuracy-related penalty due to disregard of rules or to a substantial understatement of income tax for **non-tax shelter items** if the return position has a reasonable basis. It also is used for disclosures relating to preparer penalties for understatements due to unreasonable positions or disregard of rules.

The portion of the accuracy-related penalty attributable to the following types of misconduct cannot be avoided by disclosure on Form 8275:

- Negligence
- Disregard of regulations
- Any substantial understatement of income tax on a tax shelter item

- Any substantial valuation misstatement under chapter one of the Internal Revenue Code
- Any substantial overstatement of pension liabilities
- Any substantial estate or gift tax valuation understatements
- Any claim of tax benefits from a transaction lacking economic substance (§7701(o))
- Any otherwise undisclosed foreign financial asset understatement
- Any inconsistent estate basis

AVOIDANCE VS. EVASION

- **Avoidance** of tax is <u>not</u> a criminal offense. Taxpayers have the right to reduce, avoid, or minimize their taxes by legitimate means. One who avoids tax does not conceal or misrepresent but shapes and preplans events to reduce or eliminate tax liability within the parameters of the law.
- **Evasion** involves some affirmative act to evade or defeat a tax, or payment of tax. Examples of affirmative acts are deceit, subterfuge, camouflage, concealment, attempts to color or obscure events, or make things seem other than they are. Common evasion schemes include:
  1. Intentional understatement or omission of income
  2. Claiming fictitious or improper deductions
  3. False allocation of income
  4. Improper claims, credits, or exemptions
  5. Concealment of assets

FRAUD

Negligence is a failure to make a reasonable attempt to comply with the provisions of the tax code or a failure to exercise the ordinary and reasonable care that a reasonable person would exercise when completing a tax return. Unlike negligence, fraud is a willful attempt to evade or defeat a lawful tax. Affirmative acts of fraud are actions taken by the taxpayer, return preparer and/or promoter to deceive or defraud.

INDICATORS OF FRAUD

Signs of fraud, known as first indicators (or badges) of fraud:

- **Income**
  1. Omitting specific items where similar items are included.
  2. Omitting entire sources of income.
  3. Failing to report or explain substantial amounts of income identified as received.
  4. Inability to explain substantial increases in net worth, especially over a period of years.
  5. Substantial personal expenditures exceeding reported resources.
  6. Inability to explain sources of bank deposits substantially exceeding reported income.
  7. Concealing bank accounts, brokerage accounts, and other property.
  8. Inadequately explaining dealings in large sums of currency or the unexplained expenditure of currency.
  9. Consistent concealment of unexplained currency, especially in a business not routinely requiring large cash transactions.
  10. Failing to deposit receipts in a business account, contrary to established practices.
  11. Failing to file a tax return, especially for a period of several years, despite evidence of receipt of substantial amounts of taxable income.
  12. Cashing checks, representing income at check-cashing services and at banks where the taxpayer does not maintain an account.

13. Concealing sources of receipts by a false description of the source of disclosed income, and/or nontaxable receipts.

- **Expenses or Deductions**

    1. Claiming fictitious or substantially overstated deductions.

    2. Claiming substantial business expense deductions for personal expenditures.

    3. Claiming dependency exemptions for nonexistent, deceased, or self-supporting persons. Providing false or altered documents, such as birth certificates, lease documents, school/medical records, for the purpose of claiming the education credit, additional child tax credit, earned income tax credit (EITC), or other refundable credits.

    4. Disguising trust fund loans as expenses or deductions.

- **Books and Records**

    1. Multiple sets of books or no records.

    2. Failure to keep adequate records, concealment of records, or refusal to make records available.

    3. False entries, or alterations made on the books and records; back-dated or post-dated documents; false invoices, false applications, false statements, or other false documents or applications.

    4. Invoices are irregularly numbered, unnumbered or altered.

    5. Checks made payable to third parties that are endorsed back to the taxpayer. Checks made payable to vendors and other business payees that are cashed by the taxpayer.

    6. Variances between the treatment of questionable items as reflected on the tax return, and representations within the books.

    7. Intentional under- or over-footing of columns in journal or ledger.

    8. Amounts on tax return not in agreement with amounts in books.

    9. Amounts posted to ledger accounts not in agreement with source books or records.

    10. Journalizing questionable items out of correct account.

    11. Recording income items in suspense or asset accounts.

    12. False receipts to donors by exempt organizations.

- **Allocations of Income**

    1. Distribution of profits to fictitious partners.

    2. Inclusion of income or deductions in the tax return of a related taxpayer, when tax rate differences are a factor.

- **Conduct of Taxpayer**

    1. False statement about a material fact pertaining to the examination.

    2. Attempt to hinder or obstruct the examination. For example, failure to answer questions, repeated canceled or rescheduled appointments, refusal to provide records, threatening potential witnesses (including the examiner) or assaulting the examiner.

    3. Failure to follow the advice of accountant, attorney, or return preparer.

    4. Failure to make full disclosure of relevant facts to the accountant, attorney or return preparer.

    5. The taxpayer's knowledge of taxes and business practices where numerous questionable items appear on the tax returns.

    6. Testimony of employees concerning irregular business practices by the taxpayer.

    7. Destruction of books and records, especially if just after an examination was started.

    8. Transfer of assets for purposes of concealment, or diversion of funds and/or assets by officials or trustees.

    9. Pattern of consistent failure over several years to report income fully.

10. Proof that the tax return was incorrect to such an extent and in respect to items of such magnitude and character as to compel the conclusion that the falsity was known and deliberate.

11. Payment of improper expenses by or for officials or trustees.

12. Willful and intentional failure to execute pension plan amendments

13. Backdated applications and related documents.

14. False statements on Tax Exempt/Government Entity (TE/GE) determination letter applications.

15. Use of false social security numbers.

16. Submission of false Form W–4.

17. Submission of a false affidavit.

18. Attempt to bribe the examiner.

19. Submission of tax returns with false claims of withholding (Form 1099-OID, Form W-2) or refundable credits (Form 4136, Form 2439) resulting in a substantial refund.

20. Intentional submission of a bad check resulting in erroneous refunds and releases of liens.

21. Submission of false Form W-7 information to secure Individual Taxpayer Identification Number (ITIN) for self and dependents.

- **Methods of Concealment**

  1. The inadequacy of consideration.

  2. Insolvency of the transferor.

  3. Asset ownership placed in other names.

  4. Transfer of all or nearly all of the debtor's property.

  5. Close relationship between parties to the transfer.

  6. Transfer made in anticipation of a tax assessment or while the investigation of a deficiency is pending.

  7. Reservation of any interest in the property transferred.

  8. Transaction not in the usual course of business.

  9. Retention of possession or continued use of an asset.

  10. Transactions surrounded by secrecy.

  11. False entries in books of transferor or transferee.

  12. Unusual disposition of the consideration received for the property.

  13. Use of secret bank accounts for income.

  14. Deposits into bank accounts under nominee names.

  15. Conduct of business transactions in false names.

PREPARER PENALTIES FOR FRAUD

- **IRC §7206 Fraud and false statements** – A preparer who willfully performs any of the following acts is guilty of a **felony** and, upon conviction, a fine of not more than **$250,000** ($500,000 in the case of a corporation), **imprisonment** of not more than **3 years**, or both (together with the costs of prosecution).

  1. Makes and subscribes any return, statement, or other documents, under a written declaration that it is made under the **penalties of perjury**, and which he does not believe to be true and correct as to every material matter.

  2. Aids or assists in, or procures, counsels, or advises the preparation or presentation under, or in connection with any matter arising under, the internal revenue laws, of a return, affidavit, claim, or other document, which is fraudulent or is false as to any material matter, whether or not such falsity or fraud is with the

knowledge or consent of the person authorized or required to present such return, affidavit, claim, or document.

3. Simulates or falsely or fraudulently executes or signs any bond, permit, entry, or other document required by the provisions of the internal revenue laws, or by any regulation made in pursuance thereof, or procures the same to be falsely, or fraudulently executed, or advises, aids in, or connives at such execution thereof.

4. Conceals property with intent to defraud or in connection with any compromise or closing agreement.

5. Withholding, falsifying, and destroying records or making any false statement relating to the estate or financial condition of the taxpayer.

- **IRC §7207 Fraudulent returns, statements, or other documents** – A preparer who willfully gives information to the Secretary known by him to be fraudulent or to be false regarding any material matter is guilty of a **misdemeanor** and, upon conviction, a fine of not more than **$10,000** ($50,000 in the case of a corporation), **imprisonment** of not more than **1 year**, or both.

UNDERSTATEMENT OF LIABILITY §6694

Circular 230 §10.34 outlines standards with respect to tax returns and documents, affidavits and other papers. A practitioner must not sign a tax return or claim for refund that the practitioner knows or reasonably should know contains an unreasonable position. Preparer penalties under §6694 apply to the following circumstances:

- **Unreasonable positions** – A penalty of **$1,000 or 50% of preparer's fee**, whichever is greater.
  1. A position lacking substantial authority is unreasonable if the preparer knew (or should have known) of the position, and
     A. For **undisclosed positions** – The position does not have *substantial authority*.
     B. For **disclosed positions** – The position does not have a *reasonable basis*.
     C. For **tax shelters** – There was not a reasonable belief that the position would *more likely than not* be sustained on its merits.
  2. If a return preparer understates tax liability on a return, the IRS will not impose a penalty if the preparer shows that there is a *reasonable cause* and the tax return preparer acted in *good faith*.
- **Willful or reckless conduct** – A penalty of **$5,000 or 75% of preparer's fee**, whichever is greater.
  1. Willful or reckless conduct is conduct by the tax return preparer that is a willful attempt in any manner to understate the liability for tax on the return or a reckless (or intentional) disregard of rules or regulations.
  2. The amount of any penalty payable for willful misconduct is reduced by any penalty for an unreasonable position.

AIDING AND ABETTING UNDERSTATEMENT OF TAX LIABILITY

IRC 6701 is the penalty for aiding and abetting understatement of tax liability. In general, tax counselors who advise clients to take unsupported filing positions or to file false or fraudulent returns are subject to the penalty. The authors of legal opinions made available to promoters of tax shelters may also be liable for the penalty. The penalty may be imposed even if the opinion does not contain any false advice if the writer knows that the opinion is based on inaccurate assumptions and/or knows of other facts which render the legal advice false.

> The penalty is **$1,000**, however, if the return, affidavit, claim or other document relates to a corporation, the penalty is $10,000.

The penalty is for any person who does the following:

- Aids or assists in, procures, or advises with respect to, the preparation or presentation of any portion of a return, affidavit, claim, or other document;

- Knows (or has reason to believe) that such portion will be used in connection with any material matter arising under the internal revenue laws; and
- Knows that such portion (if so used) would result in an understatement of the liability for tax of another person.

In order to aid in the understatement of another's tax, it is not necessary to actually prepare the tax return or document that leads to the understatement. A person who controls the activities of subordinates and either orders the subordinates to act, or does not prevent their participation in actions that person knows will produce an understatement, is subject to the penalty under IRC 6701.

The burden of proof for this penalty lies with the government. Most court decisions hold that the government need only establish its proof by a preponderance of evidence rather than the clear and convincing evidence standard.

There is **no statute of limitation** on assessment of penalties under IRC 6701 because the penalty does not depend on the filing of a return.

FAILURES UNDER §6695

Any tax return preparer who fails to take certain actions may be assessed other penalties with respect to the preparation of tax returns for other persons. In the case of any failure relating to a return or claim for refund **filed in 2021** (generally 2020 tax returns filed in 2021), the penalty amounts under §6695 are:

- A penalty of **$50 for each occurrence** up to a maximum of **$27,000 a year** unless it is shown that such failure is due to reasonable cause and not willful neglect:
  1. **§6695(a) Failure to furnish copy of return to taxpayer** – The tax preparer must furnish a completed copy of the return or claim for refund to the taxpayer no later than the time it is presented for the taxpayer's signature.
  2. **§6695(b) Failure to sign return** – The tax preparer must sign a tax return or claim for refund if the tax preparer has primary responsibility for the overall substantive accuracy of the preparation of the tax return or claim for refund.
  3. **§6695(c) Failure to furnish identifying number** – A tax return preparer must obtain and exclusively use a PTIN, rather than a social security number (SSN), as the identifying number to be included with the tax return preparer's signature on a tax return or claim for refund.
  4. **§6695(d) Failure to retain copy or list** – A tax return preparer must keep a copy of the tax return, or retain, on a list, the name and taxpayer identification number of the taxpayer for whom the return was prepared. The records must be available for inspection for the 3-year period following the close of the return period during which the return or claim for refund was presented for signature to the taxpayer. A "return period" is the 12-month period beginning on July 1 of each year and ending on June 30.
  5. **§6695(e) Failure to file correct information returns** – Each person who employs (or engages) one or more income tax return preparers to prepare any return of tax is responsible for retaining a record of the name, taxpayer identification number, and principal place of work during the return period of each income tax return preparer employed (or engaged) by the person at any time during that period. The record must be available for inspection upon request by the district director for the 3-year period following the close of the return period. (A penalty of $50 per return <u>and</u> $50 per item in return.)
- **§6695(f) Negotiation of check** – Any tax return preparer who endorses or otherwise negotiates (directly or through an agent) a refund check (including an electronic version of a check) issued to a taxpayer (other than the preparer), shall pay a penalty of **$540** with respect to each check. The penalty does not vary based on how much compensation the preparer receives from the taxpayer, the amount of the refund check, or the direct deposit. The penalty applies to a tax return preparer who directs the IRS to deposit a taxpayer's refund into a bank account in the preparer's name or into a bank account under the preparer's control. The preparer may not

endorse or negotiate a check for a taxpayer even though the preparer was designated as the taxpayer's representative on a Form 2848, Power of Attorney. A tax return preparer may deposit a refund check **into the taxpayer's account**. (A penalty of $540 per check, with no limit to a maximum penalty.)

> A tax return preparer will not be considered to have endorsed or otherwise negotiated a check as a result of having affixed the taxpayer's name to a refund check for the purpose of depositing the check into an account in the name of the taxpayer or in the joint names of the taxpayer and one or more other persons (excluding the tax return preparer). See Treas. Reg. 1.6695-1(f)(1).

TIP: Taxpayers sometimes request that their refunds be direct deposited into a bank account in the preparer's name or into a bank account under the preparer's control when taxpayers do not have their own bank account. Even if a taxpayer has requested the direct deposit to be made in this manner, the preparer is still subject to the IRC 6695(f) penalty for complying with the request.

- **§6695(g) Failure to be diligent in determining eligibility for certain tax benefits** – Any return preparer who fails to comply with due diligence requirements imposed to determine eligibility for, or the amount of, the credit allowable shall pay a penalty of **$540** for each failure. Those who prepare returns that claim *Earned Income Credit (EIC), American Opportunity Tax Credit (AOTC), Child Tax Credit (CTC)* (including the *Additional Child Tax Credit (ACTC)* and the *Credit for Other Dependents (ODC)*), and *Head of Household (HOH)* filing status must not only ask all the questions required on *Form 8867, Paid Preparer's Due Diligence Checklist,* but must also ask additional questions when information seems incorrect, inconsistent or incomplete. In addition, the preparer must verify identity, prepare a computational checklist (Form 8867 or equivalent), and meet a recordkeeping requirement. Form 8867 is filed with the tax return. (A penalty of $540 per failure, with no limit to a maximum penalty.)

> A **separate penalty applies** with respect to each eligibility for, and amount of, credit claimed on a return or claim for refund for which the due diligence requirements are not satisfied. The $540 penalty applies to each failure.

To meet the due diligence requirements, a tax preparer must retain records for **three years** from the latest of the following dates:

- The due date of the tax return (not including extensions).
- The date the return was filed (for a signing tax return preparer electronically filing the return).
- The date the return was presented to the taxpayer for signature (for a signing tax return preparer not electronically filing the return).
- The date a nonsigning tax return preparer submits the part of the return he is responsible for to the signing tax return preparer.

SAFEGUARDING TAXPAYER INFORMATION

> A taxpayer <u>must</u> provide **written consent** <u>before</u> a tax return preparer **uses the taxpayer's tax return information.** Additionally, a tax return preparer may <u>not</u> request a taxpayer's consent to use tax return information for purposes of solicitation after the tax return preparer provides a completed tax return to the taxpayer for signature.

Internal Revenue Code §7216 **is a criminal provision** that prohibits preparers of tax returns from **knowingly or recklessly** disclosing or using tax return information. A convicted preparer may be fined **not more than $1,000 or imprisoned not more than one year or both, for each violation.**

In addition to criminal penalties, a **civil penalty** for unauthorized disclosure or use of tax return information by a tax return preparer is imposed by **§6713**. The penalty is **$250 for each unauthorized disclosure or use.** The maximum penalty on any person **shall not exceed $10,000 in a calendar year**. Internal Revenue Code §6713 imposes a penalty on any person who is engaged in the business of preparing, or providing services in connection with the preparation of returns of tax, or any person who for compensation prepares a return for another person, and who:

- Discloses any information furnished to him for, or in connection with, the preparation of any such return, or
- Uses any such information for any purpose other than to prepare, or assist in preparing any such return.

The §6713 penalty does not require that the disclosure to be knowing or reckless as it does under §7216. Generally, unless otherwise specified, a written consent is **effective for a period of one year** from the date the taxpayer signs the consent. Disclosing tax return information to another tax preparer within the United States that is assisting in the preparation of the return generally does not require the consent of the taxpayer.

PAYMENT

The tax preparer has **30 days** to pay the penalty upon receipt of a demand for payment from the IRS. The preparer may elect to pay at least **15%** of the amount of the penalty and file a claim for refund. If the claim for refund is denied (or six months have passed), the preparer has **30 more days** to begin a proceeding in the appropriate U.S. district court for the determination of liability.

TAXPAYER SUPPORTING DOCUMENTATION

A taxpayer must keep records as long as needed for the administration of any provision of the Internal Revenue Code. Generally, this means keeping records that support items shown on the return until the *period of limitations* for that return expires.

The period of limitations is the period of time in which the taxpayer can amend a return to claim a credit or refund, or the IRS can assess additional tax. This is generally 3 years from the date the taxpayer files the return. Returns filed before the due date are treated as filed on the due date.

A taxpayer must keep records relating to property until the period of limitations expires for the year he sells the property. A taxpayer who receives property in a nontaxable exchange must keep records for the original property until the period of limitations expires for the year he sells the replacement property. These records are necessary to figure any depreciation, amortization, or depletion deduction, and to figure basis for computing gain or loss when sold.

A taxpayer with employees must keep all employment tax records for at least 4 years after the date the tax becomes due or is paid, whichever is later.

Period of Limitations	
IF you...	**THEN the period is...**
1 Owe additional tax and (2), (3), and (4) do not apply	3 years
2 Do not report income and it is more than 25% of the gross income shown on return	6 Years
3 File a fraudulent return	No limit
4 Do not file a return	No limit
5 File a claim for credit or refund after filing return	Later of 3 years or 2 years after tax was paid
6 File a claim for a loss from a bad debt or worthless securities	7 years

TIP: It is good practice for taxpayers to maintain records, both basic and specific. Records do not need to be required to be of benefit. For example, a taxpayer who receives a Form W-2 should keep a copy until he begins receiving Social Security benefits. This will help protect his benefits in case there is a question about his work record or earnings in a particular year. The IRS does not require taxpayers to maintain records in a particular way. If using a computerized system, individuals must be able to produce legible records of the information needed to determine the correct tax liability. In addition, the taxpayer <u>must</u> keep proof of payment, receipts, and other documents to prove the amount shown.

APPLYING TO BECOME AN AUTHORIZED E-FILE PROVIDER

An *Authorized IRS E-File Provider* is a business or organization authorized by the IRS to participate in *IRS e-file.* It may be a sole proprietorship, partnership, corporation, or other entity. The firm submits an e-file application, meets the eligibility criteria, and must pass a suitability check before the IRS assigns an *Electronic Filing Identification Number (EFIN).* To register for e-file, the preparer must first register for e-services.

- **Step 1: Choose provider options** – Applicants determine the type of provider they are:
  1. **Electronic Return Originator (ERO)** – originates the electronic submission of tax returns
  2. **Intermediate service provider** – assists with processing between ERO and transmitter
  3. **Transmitter** – sends the electronic return data directly to the IRS
  4. **Online provider** – allows taxpayers to self-prepare returns by entering return data directly on commercially available software
  5. **Software developer**
  6. **Reporting agent** – originates the electronic submission of certain returns for its clients and/or transmits the returns to the IRS. A Reporting Agent must be an accounting service, franchiser, bank, or other approved entity.
- **Step 2: Complete and submit the IRS E-File Application** – The IRS E-File Application is available on the IRS Web site. Each individual who is a principal or responsible official must register for e-services on the IRS Web site, if not already registered, prior to submitting the IRS E-File Application to the IRS. Principals and responsible officials must submit either fingerprint cards or evidence of professional status as an attorney, certified public accountant, enrolled agent, an officer of a publicly held corporation, or banking official.
- **Step 3: Pass a suitability check** – The IRS conducts a suitability check on the applicant, and on all principals and responsible officials listed on e-file applications, to determine the applicant's suitability to be an Authorized IRS

E-File Provider. The IRS does not complete suitability checks on applicants applying only as a software developer.

DENIAL TO PARTICIPATE IN IRS E-FILE

The IRS notifies the applicant of denial to participate in IRS e-file and the date on which the applicant may re-apply. In most circumstances, the denied applicant may appeal the decision through an Administrative Review. If the denial expires or reverses, the applicant may reapply to participate in IRS e-file. The IRS reviews each firm or organization, Principal, and Responsible Official listed on the IRS E-File Application. The IRS may deny an applicant participation in IRS e-file for a variety of reasons that include but are not limited to the following:

- An indictment or conviction of any criminal offense under the laws of the United States or of a state or other political subdivision, or an active IRS criminal investigation
- Failure to file timely and accurate federal, state, or local tax returns
- Failure to timely pay any federal, state, or local tax liability
- Assessment of penalties
- Suspension/disbarment from practice before the IRS or before a state or local tax agency
- Disreputable conduct or other facts that may adversely impact IRS e-file
- Misrepresentation on an IRS E-File Application
- Unethical practices in return preparation
- Assessment against the applicant for not meeting the due diligence requirements of §6695(g)
- Stockpiling returns prior to official acceptance to participate in IRS e-file
- Knowingly and directly or indirectly employing or accepting assistance from any firm, organization, or individual denied participation in IRS e-file, or suspended or expelled from participating in IRS e-file
- Subject of a court injunction or prohibited from filing returns by any federal or state legal action that prohibits them from participation

ACCEPTANCE

After an applicant passes the suitability check and the IRS completes processing the application, the IRS notifies the applicant of acceptance to participate in IRS e-file. Transmitters and software developers must complete testing before acceptance. The IRS assigns an Electronic Filing Identification Number (EFIN) to all providers and assigns an Electronic Transmission Identification Number (ETIN) to transmitters. A provider must update his application information within 30 days of the date of any changes to the information on his current application.

THE E-FILE PROCESS

Tax preparers may file returns electronically through a system known as *IRS e-file* through *electronic return originators* who are authorized e-file providers.

- Modernized E-File (MeF) accepts tax returns for the current year and two prior years. The IRS accepts an electronic version of Form 4868 for the current tax year.
- In prior years, a taxpayer could not e-file an individual income tax return after October 15, even if the IRS granted an extension to file beyond that date. MeF now accepts electronic returns year round.
- All prescribed due dates for filing of returns apply to e-file returns. An electronically filed return is not considered filed until the IRS acknowledges acceptance of the electronic portion of the tax return for processing. The IRS accepts individual income tax returns electronically only if the taxpayer signs the return using a Personal Identification Number (PIN).

- The receipt of an *electronic postmark* provides taxpayers with confidence that they have filed their returns timely. The date of the postmark is **considered the date of filing** when the date of electronic postmark is on or before the prescribed due date even if the return is received by the IRS after the prescribed due date for filing. All requirements for signing the return and completing a paper declaration, if required, as well as for timely resubmitting of a rejected timely filed return must be adhered to for the electronic postmark to be considered the date of filing.

E-FILE MANDATE

Paid preparers—or the preparer's firm in the aggregate—who prepare and expect to file **11 or more** income tax returns for individuals, trusts and estates are **required to file these returns electronically.**

ELECTRONIC RETURN ORIGINATOR (ERO)

An Electronic Return Originator (ERO) originates the electronic submission of returns for taxpayers who want to e-file their returns. An ERO originates the electronic submission of a return after the taxpayer authorizes (Form 8879) the filing of the return via IRS e-file. The ERO must have either prepared the return or collected it from a taxpayer. Duties of the ERO include the following:

- **Safeguarding IRS *e-file* from fraud and abuse** – An ERO who is also the paid preparer should exercise due diligence in the preparation of returns involving the Earned Income Tax Credit (EITC) because it is a popular target for fraud and abuse. EROs must not electronically file individual income tax returns **prior to receiving Forms W-2, W-2G or 1099-R.**
- **Verifying Taxpayer Identification Numbers (TIN)** – Confirm identities on the return.
- **Be aware of non-standard information documents** – Look for suspicious or altered documents.
- **Be careful with addresses** – Verify the taxpayer's address has not changed.
- **Avoiding refund delays** – Recommend taxpayers supply current information and check their return.

RETURNS NOT ELIGIBLE FOR IRS E-FILE

Taxpayers may file both state and federal returns using the IRS e-file system. However, e-file is not available for the following individual income tax returns and related conditions:

- Prior year tax returns more than two prior years
- Tax returns for fiscal year tax periods
- Amended returns other than 2019 Forms 1040 and 1040-SR. The IRS announced on August 17, 2020 that taxpayers can now submit Form 1040-X electronically. Only tax year **2019** Forms 1040 and 1040-SR returns are eligible, additional improvements are planned for the future.
- Returns containing forms or schedules that cannot be processed by IRS e-file other than those forms and schedules that are required to be submitted with Form 8453
- Tax returns with a Taxpayer Identification Number (TIN) beginning with **9**. This does not apply to certain Adopted Taxpayer Identification Numbers (ATIN) and Individual Taxpayer Identification Numbers (ITIN).
- The IRS cannot electronically process tax returns with rare or unusual processing conditions or that exceed the specifications for returns allowable in IRS e-file

FORM 8453

IRS e-file returns must contain all of the same information as paper returns. Not all forms are eligible to transmit electronically. In such cases, the ERO must submit to the IRS all paper documents required to complete the filing of returns by attaching them to *Form 8453* and sending them to the IRS.

LENGTH OF TIME TO KEEP RECORDS

The ERO must retain the following material **until the end of the calendar year** at the business address from which it originated the return or at a location that allows the ERO access the material because it must be available at the time of IRS request. An ERO may retain the required records at the business address of the responsible official or at a location that allows the responsible official to access the material during any period of time the office is closed because it must be available at the time of IRS request through the end of the calendar year. The ERO must maintain the following records:

- A copy of *Form 8453, U.S. Individual Income Tax Transmittal for an IRS e-file Return,* and supporting documents that are not included in the electronic records submitted to the IRS
- Copies of Forms W-2, W-2G, and 1099-R
- A copy of signed IRS *e-file* consent to disclosure forms
- A complete copy of the electronic portion of the return that can be readily and accurately converted into an electronic transmission that the IRS can process
- The acknowledgment file for IRS accepted returns

> IRS e-file Signature Authorization Forms 8879 and 8878 <u>must</u> be available to the IRS for three years from the due date of the return or the IRS received date, whichever is later.

EROs may electronically image and store all paper records they are required to retain for IRS e-file. This includes Forms 8453 and paper copies of Forms W-2, W-2G, and 1099-R, as well as any supporting documents not included in the electronic record and Forms 8879 and 8878. In brief, the electronic storage system must ensure an accurate and complete transfer of the hard copy to the electronic storage media. The ERO must be able to reproduce all records with a high degree of legibility and readability (including the taxpayers' signatures).

PROVIDING INFORMATION TO THE TAXPAYER

The ERO must provide a complete copy of the return to the taxpayer. EROs may provide this copy in any media, including electronic, that is acceptable to both the taxpayer and the ERO. A complete copy of a taxpayer's return includes Form 8453 and other documents that the ERO cannot electronically transmit, when applicable, as well as the electronic portion of the return. The ERO must, at the request of the taxpayer, provide the Declaration Control Number (DCN) and the date the IRS accepted the electronic individual income tax return data. The ERO must also, if requested, supply the electronic postmark if the Transmitter provided one for the return.

The ERO should also advise taxpayers that, if needed, they must file an amended return as a paper return and mail it to the processing center that would handle the taxpayer's paper return (currently only 2019 Forms 1040 and 1040-SR returns can be amended electronically).

RULES FOR RETURNING RECORDS

In general, at the request of a client, a practitioner <u>must</u> promptly **return all records** of the client that are necessary for the client to comply with his federal tax obligations. The practitioner may retain copies of the records returned to a client. The existence of a **dispute** over fees generally does <u>not</u> relieve the practitioner of his responsibility under this section. Nevertheless, if applicable state law allows or permits the retention of a client's records in the case of a dispute over fees for services rendered, the practitioner need only return those records that must be attached to the taxpayer's return. The practitioner must provide the client with reasonable access to review and copy any additional records of the client retained by the practitioner that are necessary for the client to comply with his federal tax obligations.

Per Circular 230 §10.28 records of the client include **all documents or written or electronic materials** provided to the practitioner, or obtained by the practitioner in the course of the practitioner's representation of the client, **that preexisted the retention of the practitioner by the client**. The term also includes materials that were prepared by the client or a third party (not including an employee or agent of the practitioner) at any time and provided to the practitioner with respect to the subject matter of the representation. The term also includes any return, claim for refund, schedule, affidavit, appraisal or any other document prepared by the practitioner, or his or her employee or agent, that was presented to the client with respect to a prior representation if such document is necessary for the taxpayer to comply with his or her current Federal tax obligations. The term does not include any return, claim for refund, schedule, affidavit, appraisal or any other document **prepared by the practitioner** or the practitioner's firm, employees or agents if the practitioner is withholding such document pending the client's performance of its contractual obligation to pay fees with respect to such document.

ELECTRONIC SIGNATURE REQUIREMENTS

As with an income tax return submitted to the IRS on paper, the taxpayer and paid preparer must sign an electronic income tax return. Electronic signatures are required for returns using e-file.

Taxpayers must sign and date the Declaration of Taxpayer to authorize the origination of the electronic submission of the return to the IRS prior to the transmission of the return to the IRS. The Declaration of Taxpayer includes the taxpayer's declaration under penalties of perjury that the return is true, correct and complete, as well as the taxpayer's Consent to Disclosure. The Consent to Disclosure authorizes the IRS to disclose information to the taxpayer's providers. Taxpayers authorize Intermediate Service Providers, Transmitters and EROs to receive from the IRS an acknowledgment of receipt or reason for rejection of the electronic return, an indication of any refund offset, and the reason for any delay in processing the return or refund and the date of the refund.

There are currently two methods for signing individual income tax returns electronically. Both methods allow taxpayers to use a Personal Identification Number (PIN) to sign the return and the *Declaration of Taxpayer*. The Declaration of Taxpayer includes the taxpayer's declaration under penalties of perjury that the return is true, correct and complete, as well as the taxpayer's *Consent to Disclosure*, authorizing the IRS to disclose information to the taxpayer's providers.

- The *Self-select PIN* method requires a taxpayer to provide his **prior year Adjusted Gross Income** (AGI) amount or prior year PIN for use by the IRS to authenticate the taxpayer. This method may be completely paperless if taxpayers enter their own PIN directly into the electronic return record using keystrokes after reviewing the completed return. Taxpayers may also authorize the ERO to enter the PIN on their behalf, in which case the taxpayers must review and sign a completed signature authorization form (Form 8879) after reviewing the return.

- The *Practitioner PIN* method does not require the taxpayer to provide their **prior year AGI** amount or prior year PIN. When using the Practitioner PIN method, a taxpayer must sign a completed **signature authorization** form (Form 8879). A taxpayer, who uses the Practitioner PIN method and enters his own PIN in the electronic return record using keystrokes after reviewing the completed return, must still appropriately sign the signature authorization form.

- Regardless of the method of electronic signature used a taxpayer may enter his own PIN, the ERO may select and enter the taxpayer's PIN, or the software may generate the taxpayer's PIN in the electronic return.

IRS E-FILE SIGNATURE AUTHORIZATION

When a taxpayer is unable to enter his PIN directly in the electronic return, a taxpayer may authorize the ERO to enter his PIN in the electronic return record by signing the appropriate completed IRS e-file signature authorization form. *Form 8879, IRS E-File Signature Authorization*, authorizes an ERO to enter the taxpayer's PIN on

Individual Income Tax Returns, and *Form 8878, IRS E-File Authorization for Application of Extension of Time to File*, authorizes an ERO to enter the taxpayer's PIN on Forms 4868 and 2350.

The ERO may enter the taxpayer's PIN in the electronic return record before the taxpayer signs Form 8879 or 8878, but the taxpayer must sign and date the appropriate form <u>before</u> the ERO originates the electronic submission of the return. The taxpayer must sign and date Form 8879 or Form 8878 after reviewing the return and ensuring the tax return information on the form matches the information on the return. The ERO may sign Forms 8879 and 8878 by rubber stamp, mechanical device (such as signature pen), or computer software program. Taxpayers e-filing their returns through an ERO have the option to electronically sign Forms 8878 and 8879 if the ERO uses software that provides identity verification and e-signature. Otherwise, the taxpayer signs these forms by handwritten signature.

ELECTRONIC SIGNATURES FOR EROS

The ERO must also sign with a PIN. The ERO should use the same PIN for the entire tax year. The ERO may manually input his PIN, or the software can generate the PIN in the electronic record in the location designated for the ERO Electronic Filing Identification Number (EFIN)/PIN. By entering a PIN in the ERO EFIN/PIN field, the ERO is attesting to the ERO Declaration. For returns prepared by the ERO firm, return preparers are declaring under the penalties of perjury that they reviewed the returns and they are true, correct, and complete. An ERO may authorize members of the firm or designated employees to sign for them, but the ERO is still responsible.

REJECTED RETURNS AND RESOLUTION

The IRS electronically acknowledges the receipt of all transmissions. Returns in each transmission are either accepted or rejected for specific reasons. Accepted returns meet the processing criteria and IRS considers them "filed" as soon as the return is signed electronically or through the receipt by the IRS of a paper signature. Rejected returns fail to meet processing criteria and the IRS considers them "not filed."

If the IRS rejects the electronic portion of a taxpayer's individual income tax return for processing, and the ERO cannot rectify the reason for the rejection, the ERO must take reasonable steps to inform the taxpayer of the rejection **within 24 hours**.

The ERO may resubmit, without additional signatures, a return where the amounts do not differ by **more than** $50 to *Total Income* or *AGI*, <u>or</u> $14 to Total Tax, Federal Income Tax Withheld, or Amount You Owe.

When the ERO advises the taxpayer of an unfiled return, the ERO must provide the taxpayer with the reject code(s) accompanied by an explanation. If the taxpayer chooses not to have the electronic portion of the return corrected and transmitted to the IRS, or if the IRS cannot accept the return for processing, the taxpayer must file a paper return. In order to timely file the return, the taxpayer must file the paper return by the later of the due date of the return or **10 calendar days** after the date the IRS gives notification that it rejected the electronic portion of the return or that the return cannot be accepted for processing. A taxpayer should include an explanation in the paper return as to why he is filing the return after the due date.

PAYMENTS

Taxpayers who owe additional tax must pay their balances due by the original due date of the return or be subject to interest and penalties. An extension of time to file may be filed electronically by the original return due date, but it is an extension of time to file the return, not an extension of time to pay a balance due. Taxpayers can e-file and, at the same time, authorize an electronic fund withdrawal (EFW). Taxpayers who choose this option must provide account numbers and routing transit numbers for qualified savings, checking, or share draft accounts. In addition, taxpayers may make payments through the Electronic Federal Tax Payment System (EFTPS), by check, electronically using a credit or debit card, or by filing an installment agreement request.

REFUNDS

> A provider must never charge a separate fee for direct deposit and must accept any direct deposit election by a taxpayer to any eligible financial institution designated by the taxpayer.

The taxpayer may designate refunds for direct deposit to qualified accounts in the taxpayer's name. Qualified accounts include savings, checking, share draft, or consumer asset accounts (for example, IRA or money market accounts). Providers should caution taxpayers that some financial institutions do not permit the deposit of joint income tax refunds into individual accounts. The IRS is not responsible if the financial institution refuses direct deposits for this reason. The provider must advise taxpayers that they cannot rescind a direct deposit election and they cannot make changes to routing transit numbers of financial institutions or to their account numbers after the IRS has accepted the return.

ADVERTISING STANDARDS

IRS e-file is a brand name. Firms accepted for participation in IRS e-file as EROs are *Authorized IRS E-File Providers*. All providers must abide by the following advertising standards:

- A provider must comply with the advertising and solicitation provisions of Treasury Department Circular No. 230. This circular prohibits the use or participation in the use of any form of public communication containing a false, fraudulent, misleading, deceptive, unduly influencing, coercive, or unfair statement of claim.
- The provider must not use improper or misleading advertising in relation to IRS e-file.
- A provider must not use the IRS name, "Internal Revenue Service," or "IRS" within a firm's name. However, once accepted to participate in IRS e-file, a firm may represent itself as an "Authorized IRS E-File Provider." If promotional materials or logos provided by the IRS are used, the provider must comply with all IRS instructions pertaining to their use. Advertising materials must not carry the FMS, IRS, or other Treasury Seals.
- If a provider uses radio, television, Internet, signage, or other methods of communication to advertise IRS e-file, the provider must keep a copy of the text or, if prerecorded, the recorded advertisement. The provider must retain copies until the end of the calendar year following the last transmission or use. The records must be made available to the IRS upon request.
- If a provider uses direct mail, e-mail, fax communications, or other distribution methods to advertise, the provider must retain a copy, as well as a list or other description of the firms, organizations, or individuals to whom the provider sent the communication. The provider must retain the records until the end of the calendar year following the date sent.
- A provider must not advertise that individual income tax returns may be electronically filed prior to the receipt of Forms W-2, W-2G, and 1099-R.
- Providers must not use improper or misleading advertising in relation to IRS e-file, including the periods for refunds and tax refund-related products including *Refund Anticipation Loans (RALs)*. Any claims by providers concerning faster refunds by virtue of electronic filing must be consistent with the language in official IRS publications. If providers advertise the availability of a RAL or other tax refund-related product, the provider and financial institution must clearly refer to or describe the funds as a loan or other financial product, not as a **refund**. The advertisement of a RAL or other tax refund-related product must be easy to identify and in readable print. That is, it must make clear in the advertising that the taxpayer is borrowing against the anticipated refund or receiving another tax refund-related product and is not obtaining the refund itself.

SANCTIONING

A sanction is an action taken by the IRS to reprimand, suspend or expel from participation in IRS e-file, an Authorized IRS e-file Provider based on the level of infraction.

Violations of IRS e-file requirements may result in warning or sanctioning Principals, Responsible Officials and the Provider. Before sanctioning, the IRS may issue a warning letter that describes specific corrective action the Provider must take. The IRS may also sanction without issuance of a warning letter.

Sanctioning may be a written reprimand, suspension or expulsion from participation from IRS e-file, or other sanctions, depending on the seriousness of the infraction. The IRS categorizes the seriousness of infractions as Level One, Level Two and Level Three.

- **Level One** – violations of the rules governing IRS e-file Program that have little or no adverse impact on the quality of electronically filed returns or IRS e-file. A Provider may receive a letter of reprimand for a Level One infraction.
- **Level Two** – violations of the rules governing IRS e-file that have an adverse impact upon the quality of electronically filed returns or on IRS e-file. Depending on the infractions, the IRS may either restrict participation in IRS e-file or suspend the Authorized IRS e-file Provider from participation in IRS e-file for one year and the remainder of the current year.
- **Level Three** – violations of the rules governing IRS e-file that have a significant adverse impact on the quality of electronically filed returns or on IRS e-file. Depending on the infractions, the IRS may suspend the Provider from participation in IRS e-file for two years and the remainder of the current year, or depending on the severity of the infraction, i.e., fraud or criminal conduct, could result in expulsion of the Provider from participating in IRS e-file without the opportunity for future participation.

The firm, Principal or Responsible Official may appeal sanctions through the Administrative Review Process. Suspended Providers and individuals are usually ineligible to participate in IRS e-file for a period of either one or two years from the effective date of the sanction, but they may reapply after resolution of suitability issues. Individuals of firms expelled from participation may be eligible for reconsideration after a five-year waiting period.

In most circumstances, a sanction is effective 30 days after the date of the letter informing of the sanction or the date the reviewing offices or the Office of Appeals affirms the sanction, whichever is later. In certain circumstances, the IRS can immediately suspend or expel a Provider, Principal or Responsible Official without warning or notice. If a firm, Principal or Responsible Official is suspended or expelled from participation in IRS e-file, every related entity, including those that listed the suspended or expelled Principal or Responsible Official on its IRS e-file Application, may also be suspended or expelled.

DATA PROTECTION AND IDENTITY THEFT

DATA PROTECTION

Every tax professional in the United States—whether a member of a major accounting firm or an owner of a one-person storefront—is a potential target for highly sophisticated, well-funded and technologically adept cybercriminals around the world.

Their objective: to steal your clients' data so they can file fraudulent tax returns that better impersonate their victims and are harder to detect. Their tactics: using email, the phone or other means to trick you into giving up computer passwords, e-Services passwords, to steal your EFINs or CAF numbers or even to take remote control of your entire computer system.

Protecting client data also is the law. Federal Trade Commission regulations require professional tax preparers to create and enact security plans to protect client data. Also, see IRS Publication 5293, Data Security Resource Guide for Tax Professionals

FTC SAFEGUARDS RULE (16 CFR PART 314)

This *Federal Trade Commission (FTC)* Rule, (otherwise known as the *Safeguards Rule*) requires financial institutions, as defined, which includes professional tax preparers, data processors, affiliates and service providers to ensure the security and confidentiality of customer records and information. It protects against any anticipated threats or hazards to the security or integrity of such records. In addition, it protects against unauthorized access to or use of such records or information which could result in substantial harm or inconvenience to any customer.

> This Safeguards Rule <u>requires</u> that financial institutions develop, implement and maintain an *Information Security Program*.

The plan should be written in one or more accessible parts and contain administrative, technical and physical safeguards that are appropriate to the business' size and complexity, nature, and scope of activities and sensitivity of customer information handled.

A checklist available in IRS Publication 4557 includes many activities that can be included in an information security program.

FTC PRIVACY OF CONSUMER FINANCIAL INFORMATION RULE (16 CFR PART 313)

This rule (otherwise known as the *Financial Privacy Rule*) aims to protect the privacy of the consumer by requiring financial institutions, as defined, which includes professional tax preparers, data processors, affiliates and service providers to **give their customers privacy notices** that explain the financial institution's information collection and sharing practices. In turn, customers have the right to limit some sharing of their information. Also, financial institutions and other companies that receive personal financial information from a financial institution may be limited in their ability to use that information.

SECURITY BEST PRACTICES

If you handle taxpayer information, you may be subject to the Gramm-Leach Bliley Act (GLB Act) and the Federal Trade Commission (FTC) Financial Privacy and Safeguards Rules. Whether you are subject to the GLB Act and the FTC Rules or not, you could benefit from implementing the general processes and best practices outlined in FTC information privacy and safeguards guidelines. Financial institutions, as defined by FTC, include professional tax preparers, data processors, their affiliates and service providers who are significantly engaged in providing financial products or services. They must take the following steps to protect taxpayer information. Other businesses, organizations and individuals handling taxpayer information should also follow these steps because they represent best practices for all.

- Take responsibility or assign an individual or individuals to be responsible for safeguards;
- Assess the risks to taxpayer information in your office, including your operations, physical environment, computer systems and employees, if applicable. Make a list of all the locations where you keep taxpayer information (computers, filing cabinets, bags, and boxes taxpayers may bring you);
- Write a plan of how you will safeguard taxpayer information.
- Put appropriate safeguards in place;
- Use only service providers who have policies in place to also maintain an adequate level of information protection defined by the Safeguards Rule; and
- Monitor, evaluate and adjust your security program as your business or circumstances change.

To safeguard taxpayer information, you must determine the appropriate security controls for your environment based on the size, complexity, nature and scope of your activities. Security controls are the management, operational, and technical safeguards you may use to protect the confidentiality, integrity and availability of your customers' information. Examples of security controls are:

- Locking doors to restrict access to paper or electronic files;
- Requiring passwords to restrict access to computer files;
- Encrypting electronically stored taxpayer data;
- Keeping a backup of electronic data for recovery purposes;
- Shredding paper containing taxpayer information before throwing it in the trash;
- Do not email unencrypted sensitive personal information.

The FTC has fact sheets and guidelines on privacy and safeguards for businesses on their Web site at www.ftc.gov. In addition, you may seek outside professional help to assess your information security needs.

IRS E-FILE SECURITY AND PRIVACY STANDARDS

Authorized IRS e-file Providers that participate in the role as an Online Provider must follow the IRS six security, privacy, and business standards to better serve taxpayers and protect their individual income tax information collected, processed, and stored. Compliance with these standards is mandatory. The standards are based on industry best practices and are intended to supplement the Gramm-Leach-Bliley Act and the implementing rules and regulations promulgated by the Federal Trade Commission.

- **Extended Validation SSL Certificate.** This standard applies to Authorized IRS e-file Providers participating in online filing of individual income tax returns that collect taxpayer information via the Internet. These Providers must possess a valid and current Extended Validation Secure Socket Layer ("SSL") certificate using SSL 3.0 / TLS 1.0 or later and minimum 1024-bit RSA/128-bit AES.

- **External Vulnerability Scan.** This standard applies to Providers participating in online filing of individual income tax returns that collect, transmit, process or store taxpayer information. These Providers must contract with an independent third-party vendor to run **weekly external network vulnerability scans** of all their "system components" in accordance with the applicable requirements of the Payment Card Industry Data Security Standards ("PCIDSS"). A scanning vendor certified by the Payment Card Industry Security Standards Council and listed on their current list of Approved Scanning Vendors must perform all scans. In addition, Providers whose systems are hosted must ensure that their host complies with all applicable requirements of the PCIDSS. For purposes of this standard, "system components" are defined as any network component, server or application that is included in or connected to the taxpayer data environment. The taxpayer data environment is that part of the network that possesses taxpayer data or sensitive authentication data. If scan reports reveal vulnerabilities, action must be taken to address the vulnerabilities in line with the scan report's recommendations. Providers must retain weekly scan reports for at least one year. The ASV and the host (if present) must be located in the United States.

- **Information Privacy and Safeguard Policies.** Applies to Providers participating in online filing of individual income tax returns that own or operate a Web site through which taxpayer information is collected, transmitted, processed or stored. These Providers must have a written information privacy and safeguard policy consistent with the applicable government and industry guidelines and include the following statement: "We maintain physical, electronic and procedural safeguards that comply with applicable law and federal standards." In addition, a privacy seal vendor acceptable to the IRS shall certify Providers' compliance with these policies.

- **Web Site Challenge-Response Test.** This standard applies to Providers participating in online filing of individual income tax returns that own or operate a Web site through which taxpayer information is collected, transmitted, processed or stored. These Providers must implement an effective challenge-response protocol (e.g., CAPTCHA) to protect their Web site against malicious bots. Taxpayer information must not be collected, transmitted, processed or stored unless the user successfully completes this challenge-response test.

- **Public Domain Name Registration.** Applies to Providers participating in online filing of individual income tax returns that own or operate a Web site through which taxpayer information is collected, transmitted, processed or stored. These Providers must have their Web site's domain name registered with a domain name registrar that is located in the United States and accredited by the Internet Corporation for Assigned Names and Numbers ("ICANN"). The domain name must be locked and not be private.

- **Reporting of Security Incidents.** This standard applies to Providers participating in online filing of individual income tax returns that collect, transmit, process or store taxpayer information. These Providers must report security incidents to the IRS as soon as possible but no later than the next business day after confirmation of the incident. For purposes of this standard, an event that can result in an unauthorized disclosure, misuse, modification or destruction of taxpayer information must be considered a reportable security incident. In addition, if the Provider's Web site is the proximate cause of the incident, the Provider must cease collecting taxpayer information via their Web site immediately upon detection of the incident and until the underlying causes of the incident are successfully resolved.

IDENTITY THEFT

Tax preparers play a critical role in assisting clients, both individuals and businesses, who are victims of tax-related identity theft. The IRS is working hard to prevent and detect identity theft as well as reduce the time it takes to resolve these cases. Tax-related identity theft occurs when someone uses a stolen social security number to file a tax return claiming a fraudulent refund. Thieves may also use a stolen EIN from a business client to create false Forms W-2 to support refund fraud schemes.

Preparers and taxpayers should be aware that the IRS does not initiate contact with taxpayers by email, text messages or social media channels to request personal or financial information. This includes requests for PIN numbers, passwords or similar access information for credit cards, banks or other financial accounts. The IRS does not call taxpayers with threats of lawsuits or arrests.

Phishing is a scam typically carried out through unsolicited email and/or websites that pose as legitimate sites and lure unsuspecting victims to provide personal and financial information. Taxpayers and preparers should report all unsolicited email claiming to be from the IRS or an IRS-related function to: phishing@irs.gov.

IDENTITY PROTECTION PIN

An *Identity Protection PIN (IP PIN)* is a six-digit number that prevents someone else from filing a tax return using a taxpayer's Social Security number. The IRS mails confirmed victims of identity theft a CP01A Notice with the IP PIN each year. The taxpayer will provide the IP PIN to the IRS with the tax return. The IRS uses the IP PIN to verify identity when a taxpayer files an electronic or paper tax return.

Starting in 2021, taxpayers may voluntarily opt into the IP PIN program as a proactive way to protect against tax-related identity theft. These taxpayers must pass a rigorous identity verification process. Spouses and dependents are eligible for an IP PIN if they can pass the identity proofing process.

An incorrect or missing IP PIN will result in the rejection of an e-filed return or a delay of a paper return until it can be verified.

A taxpayer should not reveal the IP PIN to anyone other than a trusted tax professional before signing and submitting the tax return. **The IRS will never ask for an IP PIN.** Phone calls, email or texts asking for an IP PIN are scams.

SIGNS OF TAX-RELATED IDENTITY THEFT

- More than one tax return was filed using your client's SSN,
- Your client has a balance due, refund offset or a collection action taken for a year in which your client did not file a tax return,
- IRS records indicate your client received wages from an unknown employer,
- A business client may receive an IRS letter about an amended tax return, fictitious employees or about a defunct, closed or dormant business.

WHAT TO DO IF YOUR IDENTITY IS STOLEN

The Federal Trade Commission (FTC), the lead federal agency on general identity theft issues, has recommended steps identity theft victims should take to protect their credit. See identitytheft.gov for general recommendations for your clients. The FTC recommends these steps for victims of identity theft:

- File a complaint with the FTC at identitytheft.gov.
- Contact financial institutions, and close any financial or credit accounts opened without permission or tampered with by identity thieves.

TIP: Contact one of the three major credit bureaus to place a fraud alert on your credit records:

- **Equifax** www.Equifax.com, 1-800-525-6285
- **Experian** www.Experian.com, 1-888-397-3742
- **TransUnion** TransUnion.com, 1-800-680-7289

If your client's SSN has been compromised, whether from a data breach, computer hack or stolen wallet, and they have reason to believe they are at risk for tax-related identity theft, you should take these steps:

- If your client received an IRS notice, respond immediately to the telephone number provided.
- Complete *Form 14039, Identity Theft Affidavit*. Fax or mail to the IRS according to the instructions.
- To inquire about specific client's return information, you must have a power of attorney on file, and you must authenticate your identity with the IRS customer service representative.

A victim of identity theft or a person authorized to obtain the identity theft victim's tax information may request a redacted copy (one with some information blacked-out) of a fraudulent return that was filed and accepted by the IRS using the identity theft victim's name and SSN. Due to federal privacy laws, the victim's name and SSN must be listed as either the primary or secondary taxpayer on the fraudulent return; otherwise, the IRS cannot disclose the return information. For this reason, the IRS cannot disclose return information to any person listed only as a dependent. Visit irs.gov for more information on how to make this request.

BUSINESS IDENTITY THEFT

Business identity theft happens when someone creates, uses, or attempts to use, the identifying information of a business, without authority, to obtain tax benefits. Business identity thieves file fraudulent business returns to receive refundable business credits or to perpetuate individual identity theft.

Sometimes the identity theft incident is related to tax administration and sometimes it's not. The incident may surface in different ways.

Business identity theft is more complex than individual identity theft. Many of the same indicators that signify simple filing or processing errors also hint at business identity theft. While on the surface these occurrences may appear to indicate business identity theft, they may also stem from something as simple as transposed numbers.

Signs of identity theft related to tax administration

- Your client receives IRS notices about fictitious employees.
- Your client notices activity related to or receives IRS notices regarding a defunct, closed or dormant business after all account balances have been paid.
- Your client's return is accepted as an amended return, but the taxpayer has not filed a return for that year.

If these things occur, the IRS and the taxpayer will need to do some research before determining the incident is a result of identity theft. Identity theft not related to tax administration should be reported to the Federal Trade Commission.

Signs of identity theft not related to tax administration

- Receive bills for business lines of credit or credit cards they do not have.
- Notice that a credit report indicates credit or other open accounts they did not authorize.
- See unexplained bank account withdrawals.
- Don't get their bills or other mail.
- Find unfamiliar accounts or charges on their credit report.
- Get a notice that information was compromised by a data breach at a company where they do business or have an account.

Protective actions to take if business information is compromised

Respond immediately to any notices from the IRS. If there is a reason to believe someone fraudulently used the business Employer Identification Number, notify the IRS immediately using the contact information on the notice or letter.

- File a police report with the local police department.
- Carefully review and reconcile account statements as soon as they receive them.
- Regularly review business registration information online (for all active and closed businesses).
- Monitor credit reports for suspicious activity every 12 months.
- Close any accounts that have been tampered with or opened without their permission.
- File a complaint with the Federal Trade Commission.
- Update virus, malware, and other security software programs on their computers.
- Remain vigilant and be alert for suspicious or unusual activity.

TIP: Place a fraud alert on credit reports by contacting any one of the four nationwide credit reporting companies:

- **Dun & Bradstreet** www.smallbusiness.dnb.com 800-234-3867
- **Equifax** www.equifax.com 800-525-6285
- **Experian** www.experian.com 888-397-3742
- **Trans Union** www.transunion.com 800-916-8800

LESSON 2

Practice Before the IRS

PRACTICE BEFORE THE IRS

IRS RETURN PREPARER OFFICE

The IRS *Return Preparer Office* (RPO) is responsible for implementing the new requirements and oversight of the IRS return preparer program. It will work in partnership with the Office of Professional Responsibility, which is responsible for the enforcement of Circular 230 conduct issues.

DIRECTOR OF THE OFFICE OF PROFESSIONAL RESPONSIBILITY

The duties of the Director of the *Office of Professional Responsibility* (OPR) include the following:

- Acting on applications for enrollment to practice before the IRS
- Inquiries on matters under the Director's jurisdiction
- Institutes' disciplinary proceedings related to practitioners

UNENROLLED TAX RETURN PREPARER

An unenrolled return preparer is an individual other than an attorney, CPA, enrolled agent, or enrolled actuary who prepares and signs a taxpayer's return as the preparer, or who prepares a return but is <u>not</u> required (by the instructions to the return or regulations) to sign the return. The unenrolled return preparer designation includes individuals who passed the IRS registered tax return preparer competency test that was offered between November 2011 and January 2013. Unenrolled return preparers may only represent taxpayers before revenue agents, customer service representatives, or similar officers and employees of the Internal Revenue Service. Unenrolled return preparers cannot represent taxpayers, regardless of the circumstances requiring representation, before appeals officers, revenue officers, attorneys from the Office of Chief Counsel, or similar officers or employees of the Internal Revenue Service or the Department of Treasury. Unenrolled return preparers cannot execute closing agreements, extend the statutory period for tax assessments or collection of tax, execute waivers, execute claims for refund, or sign any document on behalf of a taxpayer.

- An unenrolled return preparer may not sign documents for a taxpayer and may only represent taxpayers in limited situations. An unenrolled return preparer <u>cannot</u>:
  1. Represent a taxpayer before other offices of the IRS, such as Collection or Appeals
  2. Execute closing agreements
  3. Extend the statutory period for tax assessments or collection of tax
  4. Execute waivers
  5. Execute claims for refund
  6. Receive refund checks

DEFINITION OF PRACTICE BEFORE THE IRS

Practice before the IRS comprehends all matters connected with a presentation to the IRS relating to a taxpayer's rights, privileges, or liabilities under laws or regulations administered by the IRS. Such presentations include but are not limited to the following:

- Preparing documents (this does NOT include preparing a tax return)
- Filing documents
- Corresponding and communicating with the IRS
- Representing a taxpayer at conferences, hearings, or meetings with the IRS
- Rendering written advice with respect to any entity, transaction, plan, or arrangement

TIP: Certain tasks, which anyone may perform, do not constitute practice before the IRS. These tasks include appearing as a witness for a taxpayer or furnishing information at the request of the IRS.

WHO MAY PRACTICE

Any of the following individuals may practice before the IRS, with the assumption that they are not currently under suspension or disbarred:

- **Attorneys** – Any attorney who is a member in good standing of the bar of the highest court of any state, possession, territory, commonwealth, or the District of Columbia
- **Certified public accountants (CPAs)** – Any CPA who is duly qualified to practice as a CPA in any state, possession, territory, commonwealth, or the District of Columbia
- **Enrolled agents** – Any enrolled agent in active status
- **Enrolled retirement plan agents** – Any enrolled retirement plan agent in active status
- **Enrolled actuaries** – Any individual enrolled as an actuary by the Joint Board for the Enrollment of Actuaries
- **IRS Annual Filing Season Program (AFSP)** – A non-credentialed preparer that has a record of completion for the IRS Annual Filing Season Program has *limited representation rights*. Representation is limited to examinations of the taxable period covered by the tax return he prepared and signed.

Practice for *enrolled retirement plan agents* and *enrolled actuaries* is limited to certain Internal Revenue Code sections that relate to their area of expertise, principally those governing retirement plans.

Individuals placed in inactive status and individuals ineligible to practice before the Internal Revenue Service may not state or imply that they are eligible to practice before the Internal Revenue Service, or use the terms enrolled agent, enrolled retirement plan agent, the designation "EA" or other forms of reference to eligibility to practice before the IRS.

OTHER UNENROLLED INDIVIDUALS

Because of their special relationship with a taxpayer, the following unenrolled individuals may represent the specified taxpayers before the IRS, provided they present satisfactory identification and proof of authority to represent the taxpayer:

- *Individuals* may represent themselves and members of their immediate family. Immediate family means a spouse, child, parent, brother, or sister of the individual.
- An *officer* of a corporation may represent the corporation.
- A *general partner* may represent the partnership before the IRS.
- A regular full-time *employee* may represent his employer.
- A *fiduciary* (trustee, executor, administrator, receiver, or guardian) stands in the position of a taxpayer and acts as the taxpayer, not as a representative.
- Any individual may represent an individual or entity, located outside the United States, before personnel of the IRS when such representation takes place <u>outside</u> the United States.

THOSE WHO MAY NOT PRACTICE

In general, individuals who are not eligible or who have lost the privilege may not practice before the IRS. Corporations, associations, partnerships, and other non-individuals are not eligible to practice before the IRS.

A valid PTIN does not provide any representation rights. The IRS will <u>not</u> grant limited representation rights to an unenrolled preparer without an AFSP Record of Completion for the tax year of any tax return he prepares and signs after December 31, 2015. Attorneys, CPAs, and enrolled agents will continue to have unlimited representation rights and can represent clients before any office of the IRS.

ENROLLED AGENTS

The EA designation is the highest credential issued by the IRS (technically, the United States Department of the Treasury issues the enrollment card). Enrolled Agents, along with Attorneys and CPAs, are the only tax professionals with unlimited representation rights, meaning they can represent any client on any matter before the IRS. This is true even if the EA did not preparer the tax return involved.

The United States Tax Court was established by Congress to provide a forum in which people can dispute tax issues. Most tax disputes never reach the courthouse steps. An EA does <u>not</u> handle criminal matters or represent clients in tax court unless the EA also happens to be an attorney or is one of the few non-attorneys admitted to practice before the tax court. What you may find interesting is that docketed tax court cases represent only 3% of cases annually. That means an EA is able to handle 97% of the issues that arise.

Simply put, an enrolled agent can perform all of the same functions as a CPA or Attorney before any office of the IRS. The role of an enrolled agent extends beyond simply preparing tax returns. Enrolled agents can charge a fee for tax advice, help taxpayers navigate audits, request payment agreements with the IRS, settle tax debts and various collection issues, and handle taxpayer appeals.

IRS DIVISION	WHAT CAN AN EA DO?
Examinations – When the IRS is investigating the facts and trying to determine if a taxpayer owes money. This is called an "audit." • **2,644,059** taxpayer delinquency investigations in 2019.	• Represent the taxpayer before the IRS. • Corresponding and communicating with the IRS. • Representing a taxpayer at conferences, hearings, or meetings with the IRS.
Collections – When the IRS is attempting to collect a tax debt that is enforceable. • **543,604** notices of Federal tax liens filed in 2019. • **782,735** levies requested on third parties in 2019.	• Offer in compromise – Offer to pay less. • Executing installment agreements (payment plan) on behalf of client. • Extending the collection period. • Abatements, releasing liens, preventing a levy (seizure of property).
Office of Appeals Appealing an IRS enforcement decision.	• Collection Due Process (CDP). • Collection Appeals Program (CAP).

ENROLLMENT PROCESS AND MAINTAINING ENROLLMENT

THE ENROLLMENT PROCESS

The Office of Professional Responsibility (OPR) may grant enrollment to practice before the IRS to an applicant who demonstrates special competence in tax matters by passing a written examination administered by the IRS. In addition, applicants may qualify because of past service and technical experience in the IRS. In either case, the applicant must file certain forms.

- Applicants apply to take the *special enrollment examination* by filing **Form 2587.**
- Individuals, who have passed the examination or are applying based on past service and technical experience with the IRS, may apply for enrollment by filing **Form 23,** *Application for Enrollment to Practice before the Internal Revenue Service.* This can be done online at pay.gov.
  1. The application must include a check or money order.
  2. If an application is denied, the OPR must inform the applicant of the reason in a notice of denial, which may be appealed within 30 days of receipt.

Once enrolled, practitioners must renew enrollment as required under a *three-year enrollment cycle.* The year of renewal depends on the last digit of the SSN or EIN a practitioner uses to enroll, regardless of whether or not the practitioner was enrolled for a full three years. The IRS processes applications for renewal between **November 1 and January 31**. Renewed enrollments are **effective as of April 1** following the period of application.

MAINTAINING ENROLLMENT

All tax return preparers must annually renew their preparer tax identification number (PTIN). Certain requirements are necessary in order to continue registration. These include, but are not limited to, *continuing professional education (CPE)* and the avoidance of actions that can subject a practitioner to censure, suspension, or disbarment.

The IRS requires an EA to complete a minimum of **16 hours** of CPE annually, and at least **2 hours** (of the 16-hour minimum requirement) must be for **ethics or professional conduct.** The minimum amount will not satisfy the total requirement for the three-year enrollment cycle, which is **72 hours** (24 hours per year). The continuing education requirements are pro-rated if enrollment occurs in the middle of an enrollment cycle, at a rate of two hours of required education for each month or part of a month enrolled.

TIP: We recommend taking 24 hours annually to avoid a large deficit in year 3.

To qualify for continuing education credit, a course of learning must be a qualifying continuing education program designed to enhance professional knowledge in Federal taxation or Federal tax related matters (programs comprised of current subject matter in Federal taxation or Federal tax related matters, including accounting, tax return preparation software, taxation, or ethics); and be a qualifying continuing education program consistent with the Internal Revenue Code and effective tax administration.

- All continuing education programs are measured in terms of *contact hours*. A contact hour is 50 minutes of continuous participation in a program. The IRS only grants credit for a full contact hour, i.e., 50 minutes or multiples thereof.
- Qualifying CPE programs must meet certain standards. A qualified sponsor must run all CPE programs. They must require attendance and issue a certificate of attendance. The instructor's background, experience,

education, and training should be appropriate for the subject matter. The course must provide a written outline, textbook, or suitable electronic educational materials. Self-study courses (including online, correspondence, and taped program courses) meet this standard if they require registration by the participant, provide a means of measuring completion such as a written test, provide a certification of successful test completion, and provide a written outline, textbook, or acceptable electronic substitutes.

- Keep records of completed CPE for **four years** following the date of renewal of enrollment.

DUTIES AND RESTRICTIONS

DUTIES

Practitioners must promptly submit records or information requested by officers or employees of the IRS. When the Office of Professional Responsibility requests information concerning possible violations of the regulations by other parties, the practitioner must provide the information and be prepared to testify in disbarment or suspension proceedings. The IRS may exempt a practitioner from these rules if the information requested is privileged or the request is of doubtful legality. When making this determination, the practitioner must be acting in good faith and on reasonable grounds.

COMPETENCE

A practitioner must possess the necessary competence to engage in practice before the Internal Revenue Service. Competent practice requires the appropriate level of knowledge, skill, thoroughness, and preparation necessary for the matter for which the practitioner is engaged. A practitioner may become competent for the matter for which the practitioner has been engaged through various methods, such as consulting with experts in the relevant area or studying the relevant law.

CONTINGENT FEES

A fee that is based on whether or not a position on a tax return is **challenged** by the IRS is known as a contingent fee. A practitioner may not charge a contingent fee for services in connection with any matter before the IRS, except:

- Services related to an IRS examination or challenge of:
  1. An original tax return, or
  2. An amended tax return filed within 120 days of a taxpayer receiving a notice of examination
- For services rendered in connection with a claim for credit or refund filed solely in connection with the determination of statutory interest or penalties assessed by the IRS
- Services connected to a judicial proceeding

TIP: The IRS lost a case in Federal District Court regarding the ability to charge a contingent fee in *Ridgely v. Lew, 55 F. Supp. 3 d 89*. The IRS did not acquiesce.

CONFIDENTIALITY PRIVILEGE

The confidentiality protection of certain communications between a taxpayer and an attorney (privileged communications) applies to similar communications between a taxpayer and any *federally authorized tax practitioner*.

- One may not invoke this confidentiality privilege in any administrative proceeding with an agency other than the IRS.

- The protection of this privilege applies only to tax advice given to the taxpayer by any individual who is a federally authorized tax practitioner. The confidentiality protection applies to communications that would be considered privileged if they were between the taxpayer and an attorney and that relate to:

    1. Noncriminal tax matters before the IRS, or
    2. Noncriminal tax proceedings brought in federal court by or against the United States.

- The confidentiality privilege does not apply to the following:

    1. Communications made prior to the enactment date (7/22/1998).
    2. Information disclosed to a tax practitioner for the purpose of preparing a return.
    3. Written communications between the tax practitioner and a director, shareholder, officer, employee, agent, or representative of a corporation that promotes the direct or indirect participation of the corporation in any tax shelter.
    4. Information that is also available from non-privileged sources.
    5. Communication between the taxpayer's tax practitioner and a third-party who provides information about the taxpayer to the practitioner.

CLIENT OMISSIONS – DUTY TO ADVISE

A practitioner generally may rely in good faith on information furnished by the client. The practitioner may not, however, ignore the implications of information furnished and must make reasonable inquiries if it appears to be incorrect or inconsistent. A practitioner who is aware the client has not complied with the rules and regulations of the IRS or knows of any error or omission must promptly **advise the client** concerning the existence of the error or omission and of the consequences of allowing them to remain uncorrected. If not corrected, the practitioner **cannot sign the return**. A practitioner may not advise a client to take a frivolous position on a return.

ADVERTISING AND SOLICITATION

The practitioner may advertise using any method(s) he chooses. A practitioner may not make any advertising statement that is in any way false, fraudulent, coercive, misleading, or deceptive or that violates any state, federal, or other applicable rules. A practitioner may not use the word "certified" or otherwise imply an employment relationship with the IRS.

> **EXAMPLE:** Examples of acceptable descriptions for enrolled agents are "enrolled to practice before the IRS," "admitted to practice before the IRS" or "enrolled to represent taxpayers before the IRS."

If the practitioner publishes a schedule of fees, he must adhere to the schedule for at least **30 days** from the last date of publication. Such a schedule must include fixed fees for specific routine services, hourly rates, a range of fees for particular services and any fees charged for an initial consultation.

In the case of radio and television broadcasting **containing fee information**, the broadcast must be recorded and the practitioner must retain a recording of the actual transmission. In the case of direct mail and e-commerce communications, the practitioner must retain a copy of the actual communication, along with a list or other description of persons to whom the communication was mailed or otherwise distributed. The copy must be retained by the practitioner for a period of at least **36 months** from the date of the last transmission or use.

DILIGENCE AS TO ACCURACY

A practitioner must exercise due diligence in preparing, approving, and filing tax returns and all other documents, as well as any oral statements relating to IRS or Treasury Department matters. The practitioner must use the same diligence in determining the correctness of oral or written statements made to clients with reference to any matter administered by the Internal Revenue Service. A practitioner will be presumed to have exercised due diligence if the practitioner relies on the work product of another person and the practitioner used reasonable care in engaging, supervising, training, and evaluating the person.

CONFLICT OF INTEREST

A conflict of interest exists if the representation of one client is directly adverse to another client or if there is a significant risk that the representation of one or more clients will be materially limited by the practitioner's responsibilities to another client, to a former client or a third person, or by a personal interest of the practitioner. Practitioners may not represent a client if such representation causes or appears to cause a conflict of interest unless:

- The practitioner reasonably believes that he will be able to provide competent and diligent representation to each affected client,
- The representation is not prohibited by law, and
- Each affected client waives the conflict of interest **in writing** at the time the practitioner knows of the existence of the conflict of interest. The confirmation may be made within a reasonable period of time, but in no event later than 30 days after the practitioner becomes aware of the conflict.

REFUND CHECK NEGOTIATION

A practitioner may <u>not</u> endorse or otherwise negotiate any check issued to a client by the government in respect of a Federal tax liability. This includes directing or accepting payment by any means, electronic or otherwise, into an account owned or controlled by the practitioner or any firm or other entity with whom the practitioner is associated.

A penalty may be imposed, per IRC §6695(f), on a return preparer who endorses or negotiates a refund check issued to any taxpayer other than the return preparer. The prohibition on return preparers negotiating a refund check is limited to a refund check for returns they prepared.

Under Treas. Reg. 1.6695-1(f), a tax preparer, however, may affix the taxpayer's name to a check for the purpose of **depositing the check into the account in the name of the taxpayer** or in joint names of the taxpayer and one or more persons (excluding the tax return preparer) if authorized by the taxpayer or the taxpayer's recognized representative. The IRS may sanction any income tax return preparer that violates this provision.

TAX PREPARER-BANK

A preparer that is also a financial institution, but has <u>not</u> made a loan to the taxpayer on the basis of the taxpayer's anticipated refund, may

- cash a refund check and remit all of the cash to the taxpayer
- accept a refund check for deposit in full to a taxpayer's account provided the bank does not initially endorse or negotiate the check, or
- endorse a refund check for deposit in full to a taxpayer's account pursuant to a written authorization of the taxpayer.

A preparer bank may also subsequently endorse or negotiate a refund check as part of the check-clearing process through the financial system after initial endorsement.

PERFORMANCE AS A NOTARY

A practitioner who is a notary public and has an interest in a matter before the IRS may <u>not</u> engage in any notary activities related to that matter.

REQUIREMENTS FOR WRITTEN ADVICE

A Federal tax matter is any matter concerning the application or interpretation of at least one of the following:

- A revenue provision as defined in section 6110(i)(1)(B) of the Internal Revenue Code,
- Any provision of law impacting a person's obligations under the internal revenue laws and regulations, including but not limited to the person's liability to pay tax or obligation to file returns, or
- Any other law or regulation administered by the Internal Revenue Service.

A practitioner providing written advice concerning Federal tax matters must follow certain requirements. The practitioner must:

- Base the written advice on reasonable factual and legal assumptions (including assumptions as to future events),
- Reasonably consider all relevant facts and circumstances that the practitioner knows or reasonably should know,
- Use reasonable efforts to identify and ascertain the facts relevant to written advice on each Federal tax matter,
- Not rely upon representations, statements, findings, or agreements (including projections, financial forecasts, or appraisals) of the taxpayer or any other person if reliance on them would be unreasonable
- Relate applicable law and authorities to facts, and
- Not take into account the possibility that a tax return will not be audited or that a matter will not be raised on audit.

In evaluating whether a practitioner giving written advice concerning one or more Federal tax matters complied with the requirements, the Commissioner, or delegate, will apply a reasonable practitioner standard, considering all facts and circumstances, including, but not limited to, the scope of the engagement and the type and specificity of the advice sought by the client.

Reliance on representations, statements, findings, or agreements is unreasonable if the practitioner knows, or reasonably should know, that one or more representations or assumptions on which any representation is based are incorrect, incomplete, or inconsistent. A practitioner may only rely on the advice of another person if the advice was reasonable and the reliance is in good faith considering all the facts and circumstances. Reliance is not reasonable when:

- The practitioner knows or reasonably should know that the opinion of the other person should not be relied on,
- The practitioner knows or reasonably should know that the other person is not competent or lacks the necessary qualifications to provide the advice, or
- The practitioner knows or reasonably should know that the other person has a conflict of interest in violation of the rules described in this part.

TIP: Continuing education presentations provided to an audience solely for the purpose of enhancing practitioners' professional knowledge on Federal tax matters are not considered written advice on a Federal tax matter.

PRACTICE OF LAW

Nothing in the regulations in this part may be construed as authorizing those who are not members of the bar to practice law.

ASSISTANCE FROM OR TO DISBARRED PERSONS

A practitioner may not, knowingly and directly or indirectly **accept assistance** from <u>or</u> **assist** any person who is under disbarment or suspension from practice before the IRS if the assistance relates to a matter or matters constituting practice before the IRS.

BEST PRACTICES FOR TAX ADVISORS

Practitioners should provide clients with the highest quality representation concerning federal tax issues by adhering to best practices in providing advice and in preparing or assisting in the preparation of a submission to the Internal Revenue Service. Best practices include the following:

- Communicating clearly with the client regarding the terms of the engagement
- Establishing the facts, determining which facts are relevant, evaluating the reasonableness of any assumptions or representations, relating the applicable law to the relevant facts, and arriving at a conclusion supported by the law and the facts. The practitioner generally may rely in good faith without verification upon information furnished by the client. The practitioner may not, however, ignore the implications of information furnished to, or actually known by, the practitioner, and must make reasonable inquiries if the information as furnished appears to be incorrect, inconsistent with an important fact or another factual assumption, or incomplete.
- Advising the client on the importance of the conclusions reached—for example—whether a taxpayer may avoid accuracy-related penalties under the Internal Revenue Code if a taxpayer acts in reliance on the advice
- Acting fairly and with integrity in practice before the Internal Revenue Service

RECORDKEEPING

In general, practitioners must keep records for a period of three years. They <u>must</u>:

- Keep records of completed CPE for **four years** following the date of renewal of enrollment.
- Keep written consents due to conflicts of interest for at least 36 months from the date of the conclusion of the representation of the affected clients.
- Maintain copies of any direct mail, internet, or radio/television advertising for at least 36 months from date of last publication or transmission.
- The tax return preparer <u>must</u> either **retain a completed copy** of the return or claim for refund—or as an alternative—a **list showing the name, taxpayer identification number, and taxable year of the taxpayer for whom was prepared, and the type of return or claim for refund prepared** for each return or claim for refund prepared. The records <u>must</u> indicate the **name of the individual tax return preparer required to sign the return or claim for refund** and be available for inspection for **three years** following the close of the *return period* in which the return or claim for refund was presented to the taxpayer for signature (or the date the return becomes due for an extended return). A *"return period"* is the 12-month period beginning on **July 1** of each year.

CONDUCT SUBJECT TO SANCTION

The Secretary of the Treasury, or delegate, after notice and an opportunity for a proceeding, may censure, suspend, or disbar any practitioner from practice before the Internal Revenue Service if the practitioner is shown to be incompetent or disreputable, fails to comply with the prohibited conduct standards of §10.52 (not best practices), or with intent to defraud, willfully and knowingly misleads or threatens a client or prospective client.

Circular 230 discipline includes **Censure** (essentially a public reprimand), **Suspension** of practice privileges and **Disbarment**. A suspension can be for a fixed term or may be indefinite, and a practitioner must request and be granted reinstatement by the OPR before practice privileges are restored. When a practitioner is suspended for a fixed term, the individual may not petition to be reinstated to practice before the end of the term. When a practitioner is disbarred, he may not petition for reinstatement for five years. The OPR also may propose a monetary penalty on any practitioner who engages in conduct subject to sanction. The monetary penalty may be proposed against the individual or a firm, or both, and can be in addition to any Censure, Suspension or Disbarment. The amount of the penalty may be up to the amount of gross income derived or to be derived from the conduct giving rise to the penalty.

The practitioner (or firm) is provided with notice and an opportunity for a conference and an opportunity for a formal proceeding before any sanctions are imposed.

If formal discipline is not appropriate, the OPR may issue a private reprimand or a cautionary "soft letter." The "soft letter" typically advises a practitioner of allegations and warns against noncompliance with obligations under Circular 230, but does not reach a conclusion as to whether a violation was actually committed.

> A practitioner may face a monetary penalty if engaging in conduct subject to sanction. The amount of the penalty shall not exceed the gross income derived (or to be derived) from the conduct giving rise to the penalty. The Secretary of the Treasury, or delegate, may impose a monetary penalty on an employer, firm, or entity if it knew, or reasonably should have known of such conduct of a preparer acting on its behalf. Any monetary penalty imposed on an employer, firm or other entity may be in addition to or in lieu of penalties imposed on the practitioner.

INCOMPETENCE AND DISREPUTABLE CONDUCT

Incompetence and disreputable conduct for which the IRS may sanction a practitioner includes, but is not limited, to the following:

- Conviction of any criminal offense under the Federal tax laws
- Conviction of any criminal offense involving dishonesty or breach of trust
- Conviction of any felony under federal or state law for which the conduct involved renders the practitioner unfit to practice before the Internal Revenue Service
- Giving false or misleading information, or participating in any way in the giving of false or misleading information to the Department of the Treasury or any officer or employee thereof, or to any tribunal authorized to pass upon federal tax matters in connection with any matter pending or likely to be pending before them
- Solicitation of employment as prohibited under §10.30, the use of false or misleading representations with intent to deceive a client or prospective client in order to procure employment, or intimating that the practitioner is able to improperly obtain special consideration or action from the IRS or any officer or employee thereof
- Willfully failing to make a federal tax return in violation of the federal tax laws, or willfully evading, attempting to evade, or participating in any way in evading or attempting to evade any assessment or payment of any federal tax
- Willfully assisting, counseling, or encouraging a client or prospective client in violating, or suggesting to a client or prospective client to violate any Federal tax law, or knowingly counseling or suggesting to a client or prospective client an illegal plan to evade federal taxes
- Misappropriation of, or failure to properly or promptly remit funds received from a client for the purpose of payment of taxes or other obligations due the United States
- Directly or indirectly attempting to influence, or offering or agreeing to attempt to influence, the official action of any officer or employee of the IRS by the use of threats, false accusations, duress, or coercion by the offer of any special inducement or promise of an advantage or by the bestowing of any gift, favor, or item of value

- Disbarment or suspension from practice as an attorney, certified public accountant, public accountant, or actuary by any duly constituted authority of any state, territory, or possession of the United States, including a commonwealth, the District of Columbia, any federal court of record, or any federal agency, body, or board
- Knowingly aiding and abetting another person to practice before the Internal Revenue Service during a period of suspension, disbarment, or ineligibility of such other person
- Contemptuous conduct in connection with practice before the IRS, including the use of abusive language, making false accusations or statements, knowing them to be false, or circulating or publishing malicious or libelous matter
- Giving a false opinion, knowingly, recklessly, or through gross incompetence, including an opinion that is intentionally or recklessly misleading, or engaging in a pattern of providing incompetent opinions on questions arising under the federal tax laws
- Willfully failing to sign a tax return prepared by the practitioner when federal tax laws require the signature unless the failure is due to reasonable cause and not due to willful neglect
- Willfully disclosing or otherwise using a tax return or tax return information in a manner not authorized by the Internal Revenue Code, contrary to the order of a court of competent jurisdiction, or contrary to the order of an administrative law judge in a proceeding instituted under the Circular 230 instructions for sanction proceedings

VIOLATIONS SUBJECT TO SANCTION

The IRS may sanction a practitioner if the practitioner willfully violates any of the regulations (not best practices), recklessly or through gross incompetence violates Circular 230 directives relating to standards with respect to tax returns and documents, affidavits and other papers, requirements for covered opinions, procedures to ensure compliance, and requirements for other written advice.

Any individual who has **principal authority** and responsibility for overseeing a firm's practice must take reasonable steps to ensure that the firm has adequate procedures in effect for all members, associates, and employees for purposes of complying with Circular 230. In the absence of a person or persons identified by the firm as having the principal authority and responsibility, the IRS may identify one or more individuals responsible for compliance.

Any individual with principal authority will be subject to discipline if—through willfulness, recklessness, or gross incompetence—he does not take reasonable steps to ensure that the firm has adequate procedures in place (and that they are followed) <u>and</u> a member, associate, or employee (in connection with their practice with the firm) is in violation of Circular 230. If an individual with principal authority becomes aware of such violations he can also face discipline for failing to take prompt action to correct the noncompliance.

DISCIPLINARY PROCEEDINGS

Whenever the Director of the OPR determines a practitioner violated any provision of the laws governing practice before the IRS, that official may *reprimand* the practitioner <u>or</u> *institute a proceeding* for a sanction. An official institutes a proceeding by filing a complaint. Except in certain unusual circumstances, the director will not institute a proceeding for censure, suspension, or disbarment against a practitioner until the facts (or conduct) that may warrant such action have been given in writing to that practitioner, and the practitioner has been given the opportunity to demonstrate or achieve compliance with the rules.

CONFERENCES

The Director of the OPR may confer with a practitioner concerning allegations of misconduct irrespective of whether a proceeding has been instituted. If the conference results in a stipulation in connection with an ongoing proceeding in which the practitioner is the respondent, either party may enter the stipulation in the record to the proceeding. In lieu of a proceeding being instituted or continued, a practitioner may offer consent to be sanctioned.

CONTENTS OF COMPLAINT

- There are three <u>required</u> components of a complaint:
  1. **Charges** – A complaint must name the respondent, provide a clear and concise description of the facts and law that constitute the basis for the proceeding, and be signed by the Director of the OPR or a person representing that official.
  2. **Specification of sanction** – The complaint must specify the sanction sought by the Director of the OPR against the practitioner or appraiser.
  3. **Demand for answer** – The Director of the OPR must notify the respondent of the following:
     A. The time for answering the complaint (which may not be less than 30 days from the date of service of the complaint)
     B. The name and address of the Administrative Law Judge with whom the answer must be filed
     C. The name and address of the person representing the Director of the OPR to whom a copy of the answer must be served
     D. That a decision by default may be rendered against the respondent in the event an answer is not filed as required
- The complaint must be properly served by either hand delivery, dropping off at the respondent's place of business, or by certified or first class mail to the respondent's last known address.

TIME TO ANSWER, DEFAULT

The respondent must file an answer with the Administrative Law Judge and serve it on the Director of the OPR within the time specified in the complaint.

- The answer must be written and contain a statement of facts that constitute the respondent's grounds of defense. General denials are not permitted. The respondent must specifically admit or deny each allegation set forth in the complaint, except that the respondent may state that the respondent is without sufficient information to admit or deny a specific allegation.
- Every allegation in the complaint that is not denied in the answer is deemed admitted and will be considered proved; no further evidence for such allegation need be adduced at a hearing.
- Failure to file an answer within the time prescribed constitutes an admission of guilt to the allegations of the complainant and a waiver of hearing, and the Administrative Law Judge may make the decision by default without a hearing or further procedure.

SUPPLEMENTAL CHARGES

The Director of the OPR may amend the complaint with the permission of the Administrative Law Judge in order to file supplemental charges against the respondent if it appears that the respondent:

- In the answer, falsely and in bad faith, denies a material allegation of fact in the complaint or states that the respondent has insufficient knowledge to form a belief, when the respondent possesses such information, or
- Has knowingly introduced false testimony during proceedings against the respondent

REPLY TO ANSWER

The Director of the OPR may file a reply to the respondent's answer, but unless otherwise ordered by the Administrative Law Judge, no reply to the respondent's answer is required. If the director does not file a reply, any new matter in the answer is deemed denied.

PROOF

In the case of a difference between the charges and the evidence provided, the Administrative Law Judge, at any time before decision, may authorize amendment of the pleadings to conform to the evidence. The Administrative Law Judge must give the party to whom the amendment would adversely affect a reasonable opportunity to address the allegations as amended, and the Administrative Law Judge must make findings on any issue presented by the pleadings as amended.

MOTIONS AND REQUESTS

At any time after the filing of the complaint, any party may file a motion with the Administrative Law Judge. A motion must concisely specify its grounds and the relief sought and, if appropriate, must contain a memorandum of facts and law in support. The Administrative Law Judge should issue written orders disposing of any motion or request and any response thereto.

ADMINISTRATIVE LAW JUDGE

An Administrative Law Judge (ALJ) conducts proceedings on complaints for the sanction of a practitioner, employer, firm or other entity, or appraiser. The ALJ has the authority, in connection with any proceeding above assigned or referred, to do the following:

- Administer oaths and affirmations
- Make rulings on motions and requests, which rulings may not be appealed prior to the close of a hearing except in extraordinary circumstances and at the discretion of the ALJ
- Determine the time and place of hearing and regulate its course and conduct
- Adopt or modify rules of procedure as needed for the orderly disposition of proceedings
- Rule on offers of proof, receive relevant evidence, and examine witnesses
- Take or authorize the taking of depositions or answers to requests for admission
- Receive and consider oral or written argument on facts or law
- Hold or provide for the holding of conferences for the settlement or simplification of the issues with the consent of the parties
- Perform such acts and take such measures as are necessary or appropriate to the efficient conduct of any proceeding
- Make decisions

DISCOVERY

The ALJ may permit discovery, at his discretion, only upon written motion demonstrating the relevance, materiality, and reasonableness of the requested discovery. Within 10 days of receipt of the answer, the ALJ will notify the parties of the right to request discovery and the timeframe for filing a request. In response to a request for discovery, the ALJ may order depositions upon oral examination, or answers to requests for admission.

HEARINGS

An ALJ will preside at all hearings for the sanction of a practitioner. The hearing must occur within 180 days of the date for filing the answer unless the ALJ determines that a later date better serves the interests of justice.

REPRESENTATION

A respondent may appear in person, be represented by a practitioner, or be represented by an attorney. A practitioner, the attorney, or the proposed respondent may sign the answer or any other document required to be filed in the proceeding on behalf of the respondent.

EVIDENCE

The rules of evidence common in courts of law are not controlling in hearings or proceedings conducted under this part. The ALJ may exclude evidence that is irrelevant, immaterial, or unduly repetitious. Any depositions taken as noted above are allowable as evidence as is any matter requested under the discovery process above. Any statements made are applicable to the hearing in-process only and may not be used in any other proceeding. Official documents, records, and papers in the possession of the IRS or the OPR are always admissible as evidence.

TRANSCRIPT

Transcripts of the proceedings, as well as copies of any presented evidence such as documents or affidavits, must be made available to the respondent upon request. The costs (if any) are based upon the nature of the items sought.

PROPOSED FINDINGS AND CONCLUSIONS

Except in cases where the respondent has failed to answer the complaint or where a party has failed to appear at the hearing, the parties must have a reasonable opportunity to submit proposed findings and conclusions and their supporting reasons to the ALJ.

DECISIONS OF THE ADMINISTRATIVE LAW JUDGE

- **Hearings** – Within 180 days after the conclusion of a hearing, the ALJ should enter a decision in the case. The decision must include a statement of findings and conclusions, as well as the reasons or basis for making such findings and conclusions, and an order of censure, suspension, disbarment, monetary penalty, disqualification, or dismissal of the complaint.
- **Summary adjudication** – In the event that a party files a motion for summary adjudication, the ALJ should rule on the motion for summary adjudication within 60 days after the party in opposition files a written response or, if no written response is filed, within 90 days after the party files a motion for summary adjudication.
- **Returns and return information** – In the decision, the Administrative Law Judge should redact any information that could identify third parties and replace it with a code, provide a key to the code to the IRS and the involved practitioner, and remind all parties of the penalties for disclosure of such information to uninvolved third parties.
- **Standard of proof** – If the sanction is censure or suspension of fewer than six months duration the ALJ, in rendering findings and conclusions, will consider an allegation of fact to be proven if it is established by the party who is alleging the fact by a preponderance of the evidence in the record. If the sanction is a monetary penalty, disbarment, or a suspension of six months or longer duration, the party alleging a fact that is necessary for a finding against the practitioner must prove the allegation by clear and convincing evidence in the record.
- **Copy of decision** – The ALJ will provide the decision to the Director of the OPR, with copies to the director's authorized representative and to the respondent or the respondent's authorized representative.
- **When final** – In the absence of an appeal to the Secretary of the Treasury or delegate, the decision of the ALJ will become the decision of the agency 30 days after the date of the ALJ's decision without further proceedings.

APPEALS

Any party to such a proceeding may file an appeal of the decision of the ALJ with the Secretary of the Treasury, or delegate. The appeal must include a brief that states exceptions to the decision of the ALJ and supporting reasons for such exceptions. The practitioner must file the appeal and brief, in duplicate, with the Director of the OPR **within 30 days** of the date that the decision of the ALJ is served on the parties. The Director of the OPR will immediately furnish a copy of the appeal to the Secretary of the Treasury or delegate who decides appeals.

DECISION TO REVIEW

On appeal from or review of the decision of the Administrative Law Judge, the Secretary of the Treasury or associated delegate will make the agency decision. The Secretary of the Treasury or associated delegate should make the agency decision within 180 days after receipt of the appeal.

DISBARMENT, SUSPENSION, CENSURE

The Secretary of the Treasury, after notice and an opportunity for a proceeding, may censure, suspend, or disbar any practitioner from practice before the IRS if the practitioner is shown to be incompetent or disreputable, fails to comply with any regulation in Circular 230, or with intent to defraud, willfully and knowingly misleads or threatens a client or prospective client.

NOTICE

On the issuance of a final order censuring, suspending, or disbarring a practitioner or a final order disqualifying an appraiser, the Director of the OPR may give notice of the censure, suspension, disbarment, or disqualification to appropriate officers and employees of the Internal Revenue Service and to interested departments and agencies of the federal government. The Director of the OPR may determine the manner of giving notice to the proper authorities of the state that licensed the censured, suspended, or disbarred person to practice.

PETITION FOR REINSTATEMENT

The Director of the OPR may entertain a petition for reinstatement from any person disbarred from practice before the Internal Revenue Service or any disqualified appraiser after the expiration of **five years** following such disbarment or disqualification. Reinstatement will not be granted unless the Internal Revenue Service is satisfied that the petitioner is not likely to engage thereafter in conduct contrary to the regulations and that granting such reinstatement would not be contrary to the public interest.

EXPEDITED SUSPENSION

The Director of the OPR may expedite a proceeding to suspend the practitioner from practice before the IRS, when the practitioner has:

- Had a license to practice as an attorney, certified public accountant, or actuary suspended or revoked for cause
- Been convicted of a tax-related crime, any crime involving dishonesty or breach of trust, or any felony, which renders the practitioner unfit to practice before the IRS
- Violated conditions imposed on the practitioner pursuant items covered in the section on disbarment, suspension, and censure above
- Been sanctioned by a court of competent jurisdiction, whether in a civil or criminal proceeding (including suits for injunctive relief), relating to any taxpayer's tax liability or relating to the practitioner's own tax liability, for:
  1. Instituting or maintaining proceedings primarily for delay,
  2. Advancing frivolous or groundless arguments, or
  3. Failing to pursue available administrative remedies

A proceeding under this section is instituted by a complaint, which must give a plain and concise description of the allegations that constitute the basis for the proceeding. The complaint must notify the respondent of the following information:

- The place and due date for filing an answer
- That a decision by default may be rendered if the respondent fails to file an answer as required
- That the respondent may request a conference with the Director of the OPR to address the merits of the complaint and that any such request must be made in the answer

- That the respondent may be suspended either immediately following the expiration of the period within which an answer must be filed or, if a conference is requested, immediately following the conference

The respondent must file an answer to a complaint described in this section no later than **30 calendar days** following the date the complaint is served <u>unless</u> the Director of the OPR extends the time for filing. If the respondent does not make a request for a conference in the answer or does not timely file the answer, the respondent will be deemed to have waived his right to a conference, and the Director of the OPR may suspend such respondent at any time following the date on which the answer was due. If a conference is held, it will be held at a place and time selected by the Director of the OPR, but no sooner than **14 calendar days** after the date by which the answer must be filed with the Director of the OPR, unless the respondent agrees to an earlier date.

LESSON 3

Representation Before the IRS

THIRD PARTY AUTHORIZATION

POWER OF ATTORNEY

Individuals may represent themselves before the IRS or grant another the legal authority to represent them with a *power of attorney*. The representative must be a person eligible to practice before the IRS. A power of attorney authorizes an individual to act in place of a taxpayer in tax matters. If the authorization is not limited, the individual may generally perform the following acts:

• Represent a taxpayer before any office of the IRS

• Record the interview

• Sign an offer or a waiver of restriction on assessment or collection of a tax deficiency, or a waiver of notice of disallowance of claim for credit or refund

• Sign consent to extend the statutory period for assessment or collection of a tax

• Sign a closing agreement

• Receive, but <u>not</u> endorse or cash, a refund check drawn on the U.S. Treasury

A power of attorney is most often required when authorizing another individual to perform at least one of the following acts on behalf of a taxpayer:

• Represent a taxpayer at a conference with the IRS

• Prepare and file a written response to the IRS

A newly filed power of attorney concerning the same matter will revoke a previously filed power of attorney.

FIDUCIARY

A power of attorney does not establish a *fiduciary relationship*. An individual uses *Form 56, Notice Concerning Fiduciary Relationship*, to notify the IRS of the existence of a fiduciary relationship. A fiduciary (trustee, executor, administrator, receiver, or guardian) stands in the position of a taxpayer and **acts as the taxpayer**, <u>not</u> as a representative.

A fiduciary is treated by the IRS as if he or she is actually the taxpayer. Upon appointment, the fiduciary automatically has both the right and the responsibility to undertake all actions the taxpayer is required to perform. For example, the fiduciary must file returns and pay any taxes due on behalf of the taxpayer.

An authorized representative is treated by the IRS as the agent of the taxpayer. He or she can only perform the duties authorized by the taxpayer, as indicated on Form 2848. An authorized representative is <u>not</u> required nor permitted to do anything other than the actions explicitly authorized by the taxpayer.

A fiduciary may authorize an individual to represent or perform certain acts on behalf of the person or entity by filing a power of attorney that names the eligible individual(s) as representative(s) for the person or entity. Because the fiduciary stands in the position of the person or entity, the fiduciary must sign the power of attorney on behalf of the person or entity. A fiduciary can also perform certain acts a representative cannot, for example, cashing a refund check (see 31 CFR § 240.14).

SIGNATURE AUTHORITY

The representative named under a power of attorney may <u>not</u> sign a tax return on behalf of a taxpayer unless the Internal Revenue Code (IRC) permits the signature and the power of attorney specifically authorizes it. The IRC permits this in situations where the person liable for the return is unable to make it due to disease, injury, or prolonged absence from the United States for a period of at least **60 days** prior to the due date of the return.

FORM 2848 POWER OF ATTORNEY AND DECLARATION OF REPRESENTATIVE

Form 2848 appoints a representative admitted to practice before the IRS to act on a taxpayer's behalf. Specific authorization on the form is necessary to authorize:

- A *durable power of attorney*; otherwise, the powers terminate if a taxpayer becomes incapacitated or incompetent.

- Signing the return for a taxpayer, if permitted.

- Receiving a refund check. If a representative is to receive a refund check on a taxpayer's behalf, it must specifically authorize this in the power of attorney. However, those permitted to practice before the IRS may <u>not</u> endorse or otherwise cash a refund check.

- Substitution or delegation of authority under the power of attorney to another recognized representative.

    1. Under a substitution, the IRS recognizes only the newly recognized representative as the taxpayer's representative.

    2. Under a delegation, the IRS recognizes both representatives as authorized to represent the taxpayer.

- Disclosure of returns to a third party. A representative may not execute consents that will allow the IRS to disclose tax return information to a third party unless this authority is specifically delegated to the representative.

- Sending a representative a copy of all notices and communications sent to the taxpayer by the IRS. The taxpayer must check the box that is provided under the representative's name and address. No more than two representatives may receive copies of notices and communications.

The IRS will accept a **non-IRS power of attorney**, other than Form 2848. To be valid, the practitioner must sign a *Declaration of Representative*, and the taxpayer must provide the following information:

- Name and mailing address
- Social Security number and/or employer identification number
- Employee plan number, if applicable
- The name and mailing address of the representative
- The types of tax involved
- The federal tax form number
- The specific year(s) or period(s) involved
- For estate tax matters, the decedent's date of death
- A clear expression of intention concerning the scope of authority granted to a representative
- Signature and date

TIP: A married couple, in connection with a joint return, must each submit separate Forms 2848 even if authorizing the same representative(s).

The power of attorney remains in effect until a taxpayer revokes or the appointee withdraws. If a taxpayer wants to revoke a previously executed power of attorney and does not want to name a new representative, the taxpayer must send to the IRS a copy of the previously executed power of attorney with the word "REVOKE" written across the top of the first page with a current signature and date below this annotation. If a representative wants to withdraw from representation, he must write "WITHDRAW" across the top of the first page of the power of attorney with a current signature and date below the annotation and provide a copy to the IRS.

A newly filed power of attorney concerning the same matter will revoke any previously filed power of attorney. If you do not want to revoke any existing power(s) of attorney, check the box on line 6 (Retention/revocation of prior power(s) of attorney) and attach a copy of the power(s) of attorney. Filing Form 2848 will not revoke any Form 8821 that is in effect.

FORM 8821 TAX INFORMATION AUTHORIZATION

A power of attorney is not necessary to authorize the IRS to provide specific confidential tax return information to anyone designated with a Tax Information Authorization (TIA). There are two methods to grant the authorization: *Form 8821* or *Oral Tax Information Authorization* (verbal equivalent of Form 8821). However, the TIA is strictly a disclosure authorization.

> A taxpayer may <u>not</u> use Form 8821 to designate an individual as a representative. **The authorization remains in effect until a taxpayer revokes or the appointee withdraws.** A new TIA supersedes an existing TIA unless otherwise specified on Form 8821.

TIP: Form 8821 does not revoke existing authority under a power of attorney, as Form 2848 and Form 8821 do <u>not</u> affect each other in any way.

THIRD-PARTY DESIGNEE

A taxpayer can authorize the IRS to discuss his tax return with a preparer, a friend, family member, or any other person through a "checkbox authorization" indicating the *Third-party designee* directly on the tax return and providing the information required. In doing so, the taxpayer authorizes the following:

- The IRS to call the designee to answer any questions that arise during the processing of the return
- The designee to:
  1. Give information that is missing from the return to the IRS
  2. Call the IRS about the processing of the return or the status of a refund or payments
  3. Receive copies of notices or transcripts related to the return, upon request
  4. Respond to certain IRS notices about math errors, offsets, and return preparation

> The third-party designee authority **only lasts one year** from the due date of the return. The authorization automatically ends no later than the due date (not counting extensions) for filing the tax return for the following year. The CAF does <u>not</u> record information about third-party designees.

Checkbox authority applies to Form 1040-X, Amended U.S. Individual Income Tax Return, if filed within the one-year period following the original due date of the related Form 1040 (with no extensions).

CENTRAL AUTHORIZATION FILE

The IRS has a centralized computer database system called the *centralized authorization file* (CAF) system. It contains information on the authority of taxpayer representatives and those with *Tax Information Authorization (TIA)* using Form 8821. The TIA allows a third party to receive or inspect written and/or oral tax account information, subject to limitations. Individuals may represent themselves before the IRS or grant another the legal authority to represent them with a power of attorney. Entry of *Form 2848, Power of Attorney and Declaration of Representative* on the CAF system enables IRS personnel who do not have a copy of the power of attorney to verify the authority of a representative by accessing the CAF. It also enables automatic mailing of notices and other IRS communications to the representative.

An authorization on Form 2848 or Form 8821 can be recorded to the Centralized Authentication File (CAF) listing the current year/period and any tax years or periods that have already ended as of the signature date of the power of attorney. These forms may also list future tax years or periods. However, the IRS will <u>not</u> record on the CAF system future tax years or periods listed that exceed **3 years** from December 31 of the year that the IRS receives the power of attorney or tax information authorization.

WHEN IS A POWER OF ATTORNEY NOT REQUIRED?

A power of attorney is not always required when dealing with the IRS. The following situations do not require a power of attorney:

- Providing information to the IRS
- Authorizing the disclosure of tax return information through Form 8821
- Allowing the IRS to discuss return information with a third-party designee
- Allowing a tax matters partner or person (TMP) to perform acts for the partnership
- Allowing the IRS to discuss return information with a fiduciary
- The IRS may discuss tax return information with a third-party designee after receiving non-written (oral) consent. Under this temporary regulation, the IRS may disclose information to any person accompanying a taxpayer at a meeting, interview, or participating with them in a telephone conversation with the IRS.

EXAMINATIONS AND APPEALS

STATUTE OF LIMITATIONS

The collection process is controlled by statute. There are a few dates that you need to know.

In most cases, the IRS has **3 years** from the due date of the return <u>or</u> the date actually filed (whichever is later) to assess any additional taxes. This is called the *Assessment Statute Expiration Date (ASED).*

A fiduciary representing a dissolving corporation may request a prompt assessment of tax under 26 U.S. Code §6501(d). This will limit the time the Internal Revenue Service has to assess additional tax or to begin court action to collect the tax from the date the fiduciary files the request to 18 months.

When a dissolving corporation requests a prompt assessment, the IRS must assess any tax due or begin a proceeding in court within 18 months for corporations after the return was filed. Exceptions to the rule include:

- False returns
- Willful attempts to evade tax
- Extension by agreement
- Tax resulting from changes in certain income tax or estate tax credits
- Termination of private foundation status
- Failure to notify Secretary of certain foreign transfers
- Gift tax on certain gifts not shown on return
- Listed transactions

If the IRS believes a taxpayer owes additional tax (known as a *deficiency*) the IRS will propose changes to the tax return and notify the taxpayer of the right to appeal (the 30-day letter). The taxpayer can then protest the deficiency and negotiate with the IRS. The tax is not assessed at this stage.

If the taxpayer does not respond to the 30-day letter or is unable to reach an agreement with an Appeals Officer, the IRS will send a statutory notice of deficiency, also known as the 90-day letter.

The amount of the deficiency is what the IRS will assess (i.e., record as the taxpayer's liability) at the end of the 90-day period if the taxpayer does not file a petition in *US Tax Court*.

The taxpayer has an opportunity to dispute the deficiency in US Tax Court prior to the expiration of the 90-day period, so effectively, the US Tax Court hears cases before tax is assessed and paid.

> The IRS generally has **10 years** from the date of assessment to collect a timely assessed tax liability. This is called the *Collection Statute Expiration Date (CSED).*

A number of conditions can suspend or extend the general statute of limitations for collection. The most common conditions which influence the collection statute of limitations are:

- **Suspension** stops the running of the statute for a period of time. This action results in an extension beyond the general CSED. A period of suspension includes:
  1. Any period of at least 6 months the taxpayer is continuously outside the United States.
  2. The period of any extension of time for payment of estate tax.
  3. The period the IRS cannot assess (plus 60 days) or collect (plus 6 months) during chapter 11 bankruptcy.
  4. The period while an offer in compromise is pending, during the 30 days following rejection of an offer, and during an appeal of the termination or rejection.
  5. The period while a proposed installment agreement is pending, 30 days following termination or rejection of the agreement, and during an appeal of the termination or rejection.
  6. The period a request for innocent spouse relief is pending. Collection activity against the non-requesting spouse is not prohibited.
  7. The period while a Collection Due Process (CDP) hearing is pending.
  8. The period, upon a court action brought against the taxpayer prior to the CSED expiration, until the tax liability or judgment against the taxpayer is satisfied or becomes unenforceable.
- **Extension** does not suspend or otherwise affect the general 10 year period. It simply adds additional time to the end of the period if both the taxpayer and IRS consent by written agreement. The IRS must notify the taxpayer of the right to refuse to extend the period of limitations, or to limit such extension to particular issues or to a particular period of time, on each occasion when the taxpayer is requested to provide such consent.

TIP: Prior to expiration, a taxpayer can consent to an extension of the 10 year period by signing Form 872. A taxpayer has the right to refuse to sign any request to extend the collection statute, but refusal could cause the IRS to issue a statutory notice of deficiency or take other appropriate action to assess tax.

> There is **no statute of limitations for fraud.**

AMENDED RETURNS

In general, the filing of an amended return by a taxpayer does not extend the statute of limitations on assessment. It is the timely received date of the amended return not the postmark date that determines if the additional tax on an amended return can be assessed per the account posted ASED. If an amended income tax return is received within **60 days** from when the ASED would otherwise expire, a period of **60 days from the received date** is allowed for the assessment of the additional amount of income tax on that return. The 60-day period does not apply to employment taxes, excise taxes, gift or estate taxes.

IRS Notice 2020-23 provides for an **additional 30 days** to be added to the normal 60-day assessment period for timely filed amended income tax returns received on or after April 6, 2020 and before July 15, 2020, with an ASED before July 15, 2020. This does not apply to any amended income tax received after the ASED posted on the taxpayer's account.

> **EXAMPLE:** If you have an amended income tax return with a June 15, 2020, ASED that has a received date within 60 days prior to June 15, 2020, a period of 60 days plus another 30 days from the received date is allowed for the assessment of the additional amount of tax on that return. If the ASED on the amended income tax return expires on or after July 15, 2020, the additional 30 days is not provided. The normal 60-day period will apply.

IRS AUTHORITY TO INVESTIGATE

The Commissioner of the IRS, designated officers, and employees have the authority to examine any books, papers, records, or memoranda bearing upon the matters required to be included in the returns, to summon persons liable for the tax and take testimony, and to administer oaths.

TAXPAYER RIGHTS

Among other rights, a taxpayer has the right to do the following:

- Disagree with his tax bill
- Meet with an IRS manager if there is a disagreement with the IRS employee who handles his tax case
- Appeal most IRS collection actions
- Transfer his case to a different IRS office if a valid reason exists (e.g., the taxpayer moves)
- Be represented by someone when dealing with IRS matters
- Receive a receipt for any payment made

SUBSTANTIATION OF ALLEGED FACTS

The Internal Revenue Service may require a recognized representative to submit all evidence, except that of a supplementary or incidental character, over a declaration (signed under penalty of perjury) that the recognized representative prepared such submission and that the facts contained therein are true. In any case in which a recognized representative is unable or unwilling to declare his/her own knowledge that the facts are true and correct, the Internal Revenue Service may require the taxpayer to make such a declaration under penalty of perjury.

TAXPAYER ADVOCATE SERVICE

The Taxpayer Advocate Service (TAS) is an independent organization within the IRS whose goal is to help taxpayers resolve problems. If a taxpayer has an ongoing issue with the IRS that has not been resolved through normal processes, or if a taxpayer has suffered or is about to suffer a significant hardship because of the administration of the tax laws, he should contact the TAS for assistance.

CONTACT OF THIRD PARTY BY IRS

The IRS must give reasonable notice in advance that, in examining or collecting a tax liability, it may contact third parties such as neighbors, banks, employers, or employees. The IRS must also give notice of specific contacts by providing the affected taxpayer with a record of persons contacted on both a periodic basis and upon request. This provision does not apply:

- To any pending criminal investigation,

- When providing notice would jeopardize collection of any tax liability,
- Where providing notice may result in reprisal against any person, or
- When the taxpayer authorized the contact.

TIP: If a summons was served on a third-party witness, the taxpayer and any other person entitled to notice can bring a proceeding to quash (invalidate) the summons. In that proceeding, the taxpayer (or other noticee) can challenge the validity of the summons or assert privileges against production.

EXAMINATION OF RETURNS

The IRS examines (audits) returns for a variety of reasons, and examinations occur in one of several ways. An *IRS Examination Officer* may conduct correspondence examinations. Do not confuse *examination officers* with *revenue officers*, who are highly skilled employees of the IRS Collection Division. A field examination is one conducted by an *Internal Revenue Agent,* usually at the taxpayer's place of business. Generally, these audits are the most comprehensive.

- A computer program assigns a numeric score to returns after they have been processed. If a return is selected because of a high score, the potential is high that an examination of that return will result in a change to that taxpayer's income tax liability.
- A return may also be selected for examination because of information from third-party documentation, such as Forms 1099 and W-2, that does not match the return.
- A return may be selected to address both the questionable treatment of an item and to study the behavior of similar taxpayers (a market segment) in handling a tax issue.
- In addition, a return may be selected because of information received from other sources on potential noncompliance with the tax laws or inaccurate filing. This information can come from a number of sources, including newspapers, public records, and individuals.

The IRS may close the case without change, or the taxpayer may receive a refund. The IRS can conduct an examination of a taxpayer's return through the mail (correspondence audit) or in person.

REPEAT EXAMINATIONS

The IRS tries to avoid repeat examinations of the same items, but sometimes this happens. A request to discontinue an examination may be made if a tax return was examined for the same items in either of the 2 previous years and no change was proposed to tax liability.

EXAMINATIONS BY MAIL

Sometimes a taxpayer receives a 1099 or other tax forms in the mail after filing his return. Usually, the sophisticated IRS computer system catches these errors. If the information the taxpayer reported to the IRS does not match what his employers, banks, and other payers reported, the IRS sends *Form CP 2000* to inform the recipient of changes the IRS is proposing to the tax return. The IRS sends a CP 2000 to provide detailed information about those differences, the changes proposed, and what to do if the taxpayer agrees or disagrees with the proposal. The CP 2000 **reflects any corrections the IRS made** to the original return and considers those changes in a **recalculation of the tax due**. It is possible that these changes result in a decrease in tax due, but usually, an increase is the result.

An individual may receive the following documents along with the CP 2000:

- Notice 609, Privacy Act Notice
- Publication 5, Your Appeal Rights and How to Prepare a Protest if You Don't Agree
- Publication 1, Your Rights as a Taxpayer
- Publication 594, The IRS Collection Process

The CP 2000 is only a proposal that offers the taxpayer an opportunity to disagree, partially agree, or agree with the proposed changes. The IRS has not charged any additional tax at this point. It is important to respond to the CP 2000 by the due date shown on the notice. If not, the IRS assumes the proposed changes are correct and will continue processing the proposal ultimately to an assessment. If the taxpayer is unable to respond by the due date on the notice because more time is necessary to research records, the taxpayer can call the IRS to request an extension. Generally, the IRS will allow an extension 30 days beyond the response date shown on the notice. It is important to remember that additional interest and any applicable penalties will accrue on the account during the period of the extension if the tax increase is correct.

The IRS conducts some examinations entirely by mail. If the IRS conducts the examination by mail, the taxpayer will receive a letter from the IRS asking for additional information about certain items shown on his return, such as income, expenses, and itemized deductions. If the IRS conducts the examination by mail, the taxpayer may:

- Respond directly. In the case of a jointly filed return, either spouse may respond or both spouses may send a joint response.
- Have someone represent him in correspondence with the IRS. This person must be an attorney, accountant, enrolled agent, an enrolled actuary, or the person who prepared the return and signed it as the preparer. If a taxpayer wishes to have representation, he must furnish the IRS with written authorization on Form 2848, Power of Attorney and Declaration of Representative.

EXAMINATIONS IN PERSON

Internal Revenue Agents conduct field examinations, which officially begin when the IRS notifies a taxpayer that his return is selected for review. The IRS will tell the taxpayer what information to have available for the examination. Field examinations can take place in the taxpayer's home, place of business, an IRS office, or the office of the taxpayer's attorney, accountant, or enrolled agent. The examiner will try to schedule a time and place convenient for the taxpayer (or representative) that is reasonable under the circumstances considering both the convenience of the taxpayer and the requirements of sound and efficient tax administration. During an opening conference, the revenue agent explains the audit plan and the reason the taxpayer has been selected for examination. During a field examination, a taxpayer may:

- Act on his own behalf. In the case of a jointly filed return, either spouse or both may attend the interview. Each of them may leave to consult with his or her representative.
- Have someone accompany him to support his position or as a witness to the proceedings.
- Accompany someone who will represent the taxpayer. This person must be an attorney, accountant, enrolled agent, enrolled actuary, or the person who prepared the return and signed it as the preparer.
- Have his representative act for him and not be present at the audit personally. When a taxpayer chooses to have someone represent him in his absence, he must furnish written authorization to the IRS. He must make this authorization on Form 2848.

The IRS generally conducts a field examination **where the books and records are located**. The IRS will consider a written request to transfer an audit to another location, including an IRS office, on a case-by-case basis. Treasury Regulation 301.7605-1(e) indicates the IRS will take into account the **location of the taxpayer's current residence or principal place of business**, and other factors that indicate that conducting the examination at a particular location could pose an undue **inconvenience** to the taxpayer. The IRS also considers the most efficient location for the examination, and the IRS resources available at the location to which the taxpayer has requested a transfer.

RESULTS OF THE EXAMINATION

A field examination typically concludes with a closing conference. If the IRS accepts the return as filed, the taxpayer will receive a letter stating that the examiner proposed no changes to his return. The taxpayer should keep this letter with the other tax records for that year. If the IRS does not accept the return as filed, the IRS will explain any proposed changes. After the examination, if any changes to the tax are proposed, the taxpayer may either agree with those changes and pay any additional tax owed, or disagree with the changes and appeal.

FAST TRACK MEDIATION

Most cases that are not docketed in any court qualify for fast-track mediation. Mediation can take place at a conference the taxpayer requests with a supervisor, or later. The process involves an *Appeals Officer* with training in mediation. The IRS offers fast track mediation to help taxpayers resolve disputes related to:

- Examinations (audits)
- Offers in compromise
- Trust fund recovery penalties
- Other collection actions

30-DAY LETTER

A few weeks after a closing conference with the examiner, a taxpayer will receive a package containing the following:

- A notice of the right to appeal the proposed changes within 30 days (known as a **30-day letter**)
- A copy of the examination report explaining the examiner's proposed changes
- An agreement or waiver form
- A copy of Publication 5, Your Appeal Rights and How to Prepare a Protest If You Don't Agree

A taxpayer has **30 days** from the date of the 30-day letter to tell the IRS if he will accept or appeal the proposed changes. The letter explains what steps will be taken, depending on the course of action.

AUDIT RECONSIDERATOIN

An audit reconsideration request can be made any time after an examination assessment has been made on the taxpayer's account and the tax remains <u>unpaid</u>.

An Audit Reconsideration is a process used by the Internal Revenue Service to help taxpayers that disagree with the results of an IRS audit of a tax return, or a return created for the taxpayer by the IRS because the taxpayer did not file a tax return. The IRS will entertain an audit reconsideration request if the taxpayer:

- Did not appear for an audit
- Moved and did not receive correspondence from the IRS
- Has additional information to present that was not provided during the original audit
- Disagrees with the assessment from the audit

If the taxpayer disagrees with the results of the reconsideration he may request an Appeals Conference, pay the amount due in full and file a formal claim, or do nothing and the IRS will send a bill for the amount due.

APPEALS CONFERENCE

Upon receipt of the *30-day letter,* the taxpayer may elect to appeal at a conference with the IRS. The parties can settle most differences within this system without expensive and time-consuming court trials. A taxpayer's reason for disagreeing must come within the scope of the tax laws. For example, a taxpayer cannot appeal a case based only on moral, religious, political, constitutional, conscientious, or similar grounds. The Appeals Office is the only level of appeal within the IRS. In most instances, a taxpayer is eligible to take the case to court if unable to come to an agreement at the appeals conference, or if he does not want to appeal his case to the IRS Office of Appeals. When requesting an appeals conference, the taxpayer may also need to file a formal written protest or a small case request.

- **Written protest** – Taxpayers need to file a written protest in the following cases:

    1. All employee plan and exempt organization cases without regard to the amount at issue.

    2. All partnership and S corporation cases without regard to the dollar amount at issue.

    3. All other cases, unless the taxpayer qualifies for the small case request procedure or other special appeal procedures such as requesting appeals consideration of liens, levies, seizures, or installment agreements.

- **Small case request** – If the total amount for any tax period is **$25,000 or less**, the taxpayer may make a small case request instead of filing a formal written protest. This is different from the *small tax case procedure* for tax court cases of $50,000 or less. Include a proposed increase or decrease in tax (including penalties) or refund claim when considering the size of the case. If making an offer in compromise, include total unpaid tax, penalty, and interest. For a small case request, the taxpayer must send a letter:

    1. Requesting appeals consideration,

    2. Indicating the changes the taxpayer does not agree with, and

    3. Indicating the reasons why the taxpayer does not agree.

90-DAY LETTER

If the IRS does not receive a response to the 30-day letter, or if the taxpayer and an Appeals Officer cannot reach an agreement, the IRS will send a **90-day letter**, also known as a *notice of deficiency*. The taxpayer has **90 days** (150 days if addressed outside the United States) from the date of the notice to file a petition with the Tax Court. The taxpayer may <u>not</u> file a claim with the Tax Court **prior to the notice date**.

TAXPAYER PENALTIES AND INTEREST

If the taxpayer does not file a return and pay the tax by the due date, he may have to pay a penalty. Substantially understated tax, understated reportable transactions, erroneous claims for refund or credit, frivolous tax submissions, or failure to supply a Social Security number or individual taxpayer identification number may also result in the IRS assessing a penalty. The IRS may assess a civil fraud penalty if the taxpayer provides fraudulent information on a return.

- **Filing late *(failure-to-file)*** – If the taxpayer does not file a return by the due date (including extensions) the IRS may assess a failure-to-file penalty. The penalty is usually **5% for each month** or part of a month that a return is late, but **not more than 25%.** The penalty is based on the tax not paid by the due date (<u>without</u> regard to extensions).

    1. **Fraud** – If the failure to file is due to fraud, the penalty is 15% for each month or part of a month that the return is late, up to a maximum of 75%.

    2. **Return more than 60 days late** – If any return required to be filed in 2021 (generally 2020 tax returns filed in 2021) is filed more than 60 days after the due date or extended due date, the minimum penalty is the <u>smaller</u> of **$435** or **100% of the unpaid tax**.

- **Paying tax late *(failure-to-pay)*** – A taxpayer who does not pay all taxes by the due date is subject to the failure-to-pay penalty of **one-half of 1% (.50%)** of the unpaid taxes for each month, or part of a month, the tax is not paid. This penalty does not apply during the automatic six-month extension of time to file if the taxpayer paid at least 90% of the actual tax liability on or before the due date of the return and paid the balance when he filed the return.

1. The monthly rate of the failure-to-pay penalty is half the usual rate (.25% instead of .50%) if an installment agreement is in effect for that month. The taxpayer must file the return by the due date (including extensions) to qualify for this reduced penalty.
2. If the IRS issues a notice of intent to levy, the rate will increase to 1% at the start of the first month beginning at least 10 days after the day the IRS issues the notice. If the IRS issues a notice and demand for immediate payment, the rate will increase to 1% at the start of the first month beginning after the day that the IRS issues the notice and demand.
3. This penalty cannot be more than 25% of the unpaid tax.

- **Combined penalties** – If both the *failure-to-file* penalty and the *failure-to-pay* penalty apply in any month, the **5%** (or 15%) failure-to-file penalty is reduced by the failure-to-pay penalty. However, if the return is filed more than 60 days after the due date or extended due date, the minimum penalty is the smaller of **$435** or **100% of the unpaid tax** for any return required to be filed in 2021 (generally 2020 tax returns filed in 2021).
- **Accuracy-related penalty** – A penalty of 20% of unpaid tax may be due if the tax is underpaid due to:
  1. Negligence or disregard of the rules or regulations, or
  2. Substantial understatement of income tax. The understatement is substantial if it is more than the largest of **10%** (5% if the taxpayer claims section 199A deduction) of the correct tax or **$5,000**.
- **Frivolous tax submission** – A penalty of **$5,000** may be due if frivolous tax returns or other frivolous submissions are made. A frivolous tax return is one that does not include enough information to figure the correct tax or that contains information clearly showing that the tax reported is substantially incorrect.
- **Fraud** – If there is any underpayment of tax on a return due to fraud, the IRS will add a penalty of 75% of the underpayment due to fraud to the tax owed.
- **Failure to supply Social Security number** – If a taxpayer omits the SSN where required on a return, statement, or other documents, the taxpayer will be subject to a penalty of **$50 for each failure**.

Taxpayers have the right to challenge the assertion or assessment of a penalty, and generally may do so at any stage in the penalty process. Taxpayers may request the following:

- A review of the penalty prior to assessment (e.g., deficiency procedures),
- A penalty abatement after it is assessed, and either before or after it is paid (post-assessment review), or
- An abatement and refund after payment (claim for refund).

Arbitration is not an option prior to assessment. The permanent arbitration procedure may be used to resolve issues while a case is in Appeals, after settlement discussions are unsuccessful and, generally, when all other issues are resolved except specific factual issues for which arbitration is being requested.

TRUST FUND RECOVERY PENALTY

To encourage prompt payment of withheld income and employment taxes, including social security taxes, railroad retirement taxes, or collected excise taxes, Congress passed a law that provides for the Trust Fund Recovery Penalty. These taxes are called trust fund taxes because the taxpayer actually holds the employee's money in trust until making a federal tax deposit in that amount.

If trust fund taxes willfully aren't collected, not truthfully accounted for and paid, or are evaded or defeated in any way, the IRS may charge a trust fund recovery penalty. This penalty is equal to the **full amount of the unpaid trust fund tax**, plus **interest**.

The trust fund recovery penalty may apply to a person or persons responsible for collecting, accounting for and paying the trust fund taxes and who acted willfully in not doing so. If IRS can't immediately collect the taxes from the employer or business, the **IRS will decide who the responsible person or persons are and who acted willfully.**

"Willfully" means voluntarily, consciously, and intentionally. A responsible person acts "willfully" if this person knows that the required actions are not taking place for any reason. Paying other business expenses instead of trust fund taxes, including the payment of net payroll, is considered willful behavior.

The amount of the penalty is equal to the unpaid balance of the trust fund tax. The penalty is computed based on:

- The unpaid income taxes withheld, plus
- The employee's portion of the withheld FICA taxes.

For collected taxes, the penalty is based on the unpaid amount of collected excise taxes.

The IRS will send a letter to the responsible person notifying them of the proposed penalty. The taxpayer has **60 days** (75 days if this letter is addressed outside the United States) from the date of this letter to appeal the IRS proposal.

FIRST TIME PENALTY ABATEMENT

The IRS may provide administrative relief from a **penalty** that would otherwise be applicable under its *First Time Abatement (FTA)* policy. The FTA request may be made over the phone by calling the number on the notice, or in writing. An enrolled practitioner must have a power of attorney (Form 2848) on file to request abatement over the phone on a taxpayer's behalf.

A taxpayer may qualify for administrative relief from the failure-to-file, failure-to-pay, and failure-to-deposit penalties if all the following are true:

- The taxpayer was not previously required to file a return or does not have any penalties for the 3 prior tax years.
- The taxpayer has filed, or filed a valid extension for, all required returns currently due.
- The taxpayer has paid, or arranged to pay, any **tax** currently due.

TIP: The failure-to-pay penalty will continue to accrue, until the tax is paid in full. It may be to the taxpayer's advantage to wait until they fully pay the tax due prior to requesting penalty relief under the first time penalty abatement policy.

REASONABLE CAUSE

Under certain situations, a taxpayer may appeal penalties assessed against him by the IRS for non-compliance with the tax laws. These involve the use of the reasonable cause criteria. Reasonable cause involves situations that are beyond one's control after exercising normal care and prudence. Most of the time, they involve death, serious illness, unavoidable absences, the absence of needed records, and reliance on written advice from the IRS or tax professional. Similar to interest abatement, a taxpayer may use *Form 843* to claim a refund or request an abatement of certain taxes, penalties, and additions to tax.

- **Death** – This is the death (usually sudden) of a spouse, children, parents, grandparents, or siblings. This may include the tax preparer (or a member of the immediate family) or any individual on whom the taxpayer relies on for data needed to prepare the return.
- **Serious illness** – Major and (usually) unexpected illness of the individuals listed directly above. This rarely applies to sources of return information.

- **Unavoidable absences** – This is related to absences of the taxpayer (or spouse), is very rarely related to the taxpayer's preparer and is never related to sources of information. Situations include items such as incarceration, natural disasters, military deployment, and emergency hospitalization.

- **Inability to obtain needed records** – The provider of information crucial to the preparation of the return did not provide it by the date required by law, and the taxpayer has sufficient records to support unsuccessful attempts to secure the information in order to file in a timely manner. The taxpayer must also have attempted to obtain the records from any alternative sources without success; for example, if the taxpayer did not receive a W-2, he could prepare a substitute W-2 from the year-end pay stub.

- **Reliance on advice** – If the actions were taken as a direct result of, and in compliance with, written instruction from the IRS (or the oral or written advice of a tax professional) leads to the late filing and/or late payment of taxes, there are grounds for relief from the resulting penalties.

HOW TO STOP INTEREST FROM ACCRUING

If the taxpayer owes additional tax at the end of the examination, he can stop further accrual of interest by sending money to the IRS to cover all or part of the amount still owed. Interest on part or all of any amount still owed will stop accruing on the date the IRS receives this money.

SUSPENSION OF INTEREST AND PENALTIES

Generally, the IRS has three years from the date the return was filed (or the date the return was due, if later) to assess any additional tax. However, if the return was filed timely (including extensions), interest and certain penalties will be suspended if the IRS does not mail a notice stating liability and the basis for that liability, within a 36-month period beginning on the later of:

- The date on which the tax return was filed

- The due date (without extensions) of the tax return

If the IRS mails a notice after the 36-month period, interest and certain penalties applicable to the suspension period will be suspended. The suspension period begins the day after the close of the 36-month period and ends 21 days after the IRS mails a notice to the taxpayer stating liability and the basis for that liability. In addition, the suspension period applies separately to each notice received stating liability and the basis for that liability. The suspension does <u>not</u> apply to the following:

- Failure-to-pay penalty

- Fraudulent tax return

- Penalty, interest, addition to tax, or additional amount with respect to any tax liability shown on the return or with respect to any gross misstatement

- Penalty, interest, addition to tax, or additional amount with respect to any reportable transaction that is not adequately disclosed or any listed transaction

- Criminal penalty

SEEKING RELIEF FROM IMPROPERLY ASSESSED INTEREST

A taxpayer may seek relief if the IRS assesses interest for periods during which interest should have been suspended because the IRS did not mail a notice in a timely manner. If the taxpayer believes that the IRS assessed interest with respect to a period during which interest should have been suspended, submit *Form 843*, writing *"Section 6404(g) Notification"* at the top of the form, with the IRS Service Center where the return was filed. The IRS will review the Form 843 and notify the taxpayer whether or not interest will be abated. If the IRS does not abate interest, the taxpayer may pay the disputed interest assessment and file a claim for refund. If that claim is denied or not acted upon within six months from the date filed, the taxpayer may file a suit for a refund in U.S. District Court or in the U.S. Court of Federal Claims.

ABATEMENT OF INTEREST

The IRS does <u>not</u> remove or reduce interest for reasonable cause or as first-time relief. If any of tax and/or penalties are reduced, the IRS automatically reduces the related interest. Interest is charged by law and will continue until the tax account is fully paid.

The IRS may only reduce the amount of interest when due to an unreasonable error or delay by an IRS officer or employee in performing a ministerial or managerial act.

- **Ministerial act** – This is a procedural or mechanical act, not involving the exercise of judgment or discretion, during the processing of a case after all prerequisites (for example, conferences and review by supervisors) have taken place. A decision concerning the proper application of federal tax law (or other federal or state law) is not a ministerial act.

- **Managerial act** – This is an administrative act during the processing of a case that involves the loss of records or the exercise of judgment or discretion concerning the management of personnel. A decision concerning the proper application of the law is not a managerial act.

Only the amount of interest on income, estate, gift, generation-skipping, and certain excise taxes may be reduced. The amount of interest will <u>not</u> be reduced if the taxpayer or anyone related to the taxpayer contributed significantly to the error or delay. The interest is reduced only if the error or delay happened after the IRS contacted the taxpayer in writing about the deficiency or payment on which the interest is based. An audit notification letter is such a contact.

Criminal Considerations	
Title and Section	**Definition**
Title 26 USC § 7201 Attempt to evade or defeat tax	Any person who willfully attempts to evade or defeat any tax imposed by this title or the payment thereof shall, in addition to other penalties provided by law, be guilty of a felony and, upon conviction thereof: • Shall be imprisoned not more than five years • Or fined not more than $250,000 for individuals ($500,000 for corporations) • Or both, together with the costs of prosecution
Title 26 USC § 7202 Willful failure to collect or pay over tax	Any person required under this title to collect, account for, and pay over any tax imposed by this title who willfully fails to collect or truthfully account for and pay over such tax shall, in addition to penalties provided by the law, be guilty of a felony and: • Shall be imprisoned not more than five years • Or fined not more than $250,000 for individuals ($500,000 for corporations) • Or both, together with the costs of prosecution
Title 26 USC § 7203 Willful failure to file return, supply information, or pay tax	Any person required under this title to pay any estimated tax or tax, or required by this title or by regulations made under authority thereof to make a return, keep any records, or supply any information, who willfully fails to pay such estimated tax or tax, make such return, keep such records, or supply such information, at the time or times required by law or regulations, shall, in addition to other penalties provided by law, be guilty of a misdemeanor and, upon conviction thereof: • Shall be imprisoned not more than one year • Or fined not more than $100,000 for individuals ($200,000 for corporations) • Or both, together with cost of prosecution
Title 26 USC § 7206(1) Fraud and false statements	Any Person who … (1) Declaration under penalties of perjury – Willfully makes and subscribes any return, statement, or other document, which contains or is verified by a written declaration that is made under the penalties of perjury, and which he does not believe to be true and correct as to every material matter; shall be guilty of a felony and, upon conviction thereof; • Shall be imprisoned not more than three years • Or fined not more than $250,000 for individuals ($500,000 for corporations) • Or both, together with cost of prosecution
Title 26 USC § 7206(2) Fraud and false statements	Any person who …(2) Aid or assistance – Willfully aids or assists in, or procures, counsels, or advises the preparation or presentation under, or in connection with any matter arising under, the Internal Revenue laws, of a return, affidavit, claim, or other document, which is fraudulent or is false as to any material matter, whether or not such falsity or fraud is with the knowledge or consent of the person authorized or required to present such return, affidavit, claim, or document; shall be guilty of a felony and, upon conviction thereof: • Shall be imprisoned not more than three years • Or fined not more than $250,000 for individuals ($500,000 for corporations) • Or both, together with cost of prosecution

Criminal Considerations	
Title and Section	**Definition**
Title 26 USC § 7212(A) Attempts to interfere with administration of Internal Revenue laws	Whoever corruptly or by force endeavors to intimidate or impede any officer or employee of the United States acting in an official capacity under this title, or in any other way corruptly or by force obstructs or impedes, or endeavors to obstruct or impede, the due administration of this title, upon conviction: • Shall be imprisoned not more than three years • Or fined not more than $250,000 for individuals ($500,000 for corporations) • Or both
Title 18 USC § 371 Conspiracy to commit offense or to defraud the United States	If two or more persons conspire either to commit any offense against the United States, or to defraud the United States, or any agency thereof in any manner or for any purpose, and one or more of such persons do any act to effect the object of the conspiracy, each: • Shall be imprisoned not more than five years • Or fined not more than $250,000 for individuals ($500,000 for corporations) • Or both

COLLECTION PROCESS

An *Internal Revenue Officer* is a highly skilled employee of the IRS Collection Division whose role is to collect delinquent unpaid taxes and to secure tax returns that are overdue from taxpayers. A revenue officer generally conducts face-to-face interviews with taxpayers (and/or their representatives) at the taxpayer's place of business or residence. The Revenue Officer can consider alternative means of resolving tax debt issues when the taxpayer cannot pay the debt in full such as:

• Setting up payment agreements that allow the taxpayer to pay the bill over time
• When appropriate, granting relief from penalties imposed when the tax bill is overdue
• Suspending collection of accounts due to financial hardship

INJURED SPOUSE RELIEF

Sometimes a liability belongs only to one spouse. A taxpayer is an *injured spouse* if he files a joint return and all or part of his **share of the refund** was, or will be, applied against the **separate** past-due federal tax, state tax, child support, or federal non-tax debt (such as a student loan) of his spouse with whom he filed the **joint return**. An injured spouse may be entitled to recoup their share of the refund.

The injured spouse files *Form 8379* with a jointly filed tax return when the joint overpayment was—or is expected to be—applied to a past-due obligation of the other spouse. By filing Form 8379, the injured spouse may be able to get back his share of the joint refund. The taxpayer may file form 8379 with a joint return, with an amended return, or by itself at a later time.

EXAMPLE: Tom and Lucy expect a refund of $5,000 when they jointly file their tax return. Tom has $60,000 in past-due taxes that he accumulated prior to getting married. To prevent the entire refund from being applied against his past-due obligation, they can file Form 8379, to protect Lucy's share of the refund.

RELIEF FROM JOINT AND SEVERAL LIABILITY

Relief from joint and several liabilities, such as *innocent spouse relief*, is different from *injured spouse relief*. In some cases, a spouse can get relief from joint and several liabilities.

> Married taxpayers are jointly and severally liable for the tax and any additions to tax, interest, or penalties that arise because of the joint return, even if they later divorce. The term "joint and several liability" means that **each taxpayer is legally responsible for the entire liability.** One spouse may be held responsible for all the tax due, even if the other spouse earned all the income or claimed improper deductions or credits.

There are three types of relief available to married persons who filed joint returns:

- **Innocent spouse relief** – A taxpayer may be **relieved of responsibility** for paying tax, interest, and penalties because a spouse or former spouse failed to report income, reported income improperly, or claimed improper deductions or credits. A taxpayer will use *Form 8857* to request relief, provided he meets all of the following conditions to qualify:
  1. The spouses must have filed a joint return with an understatement of tax directly related to the spouse's erroneous items.
  2. The taxpayer seeking relief can establish that at the time he signed the joint return, he did not know and had no reason to know, that there was an understatement of tax.
  3. Taking into account all the facts and circumstances, it would be unfair to hold taxpayer liable for the understatement of tax.

- **Separation of liability relief** – For those who are no longer married, widowed, or legally separated and have not been members of the same household for a 12-month period. The understated tax (plus interest and penalties) on the joint return is allocated between spouses (or former spouse). The tax allocated is generally the amount the taxpayer is responsible to pay. This type of relief is available only for unpaid liabilities resulting from the understated tax. Refunds are not allowed.

- **Equitable relief** – For a properly stated but underpaid tax. If a taxpayer does not qualify for other forms of relief, the taxpayer may still be relieved of responsibility for tax, interest, and penalties.

NOTICE OF TAX DUE AND DEMAND FOR PAYMENT

If the taxpayer has not paid all that he owes, the IRS will send a bill called a *Notice of Tax Due and Demand for Payment*. The bill includes the taxes plus interest and penalties. A taxpayer may use a credit card, electronic funds transfer, check, money order, or cash to pay any taxes owed.

CURRENTLY NOT COLLECTIBLE

A taxpayer who needs more time to pay can request the IRS temporarily delay collection and report their account as *currently not collectible (CNC)*. Being currently not collectible doesn't mean the debt goes away. It means the IRS has determined the taxpayer can't afford to pay the debt at this time. If the IRS does delay collecting from a taxpayer, the debt will increase because of penalties and interest until the full amount is paid.

The IRS may temporarily suspend certain collection actions, such as issuing a levy, until the taxpayer's financial condition improves. However, the IRS may still file a Notice of Federal Tax Lien. Prior to approving a request to delay collection, the IRS may ask the taxpayer to complete a Collection Information Statement. The IRS will continue to review a taxpayer's ability to pay.

IRS COLLECTION INFORMATION STATEMENT

Form 433 is the IRS *collection information statement*, which is a statement of a taxpayer's financial condition. It includes an overview of income, expenses, assets, and liabilities. The IRS uses the information to determine how a taxpayer can satisfy an outstanding tax liability. Form 433 is a requirement to prove economic hardship. A taxpayer must file a collection information statement with an Offer in Compromise (OIC) request related to *doubt as to collectability* or to *promote effective tax administration*.

- **Form 433-A (OIC)** – Collection Information Statement for Wage Earners and Self-Employed Individuals
- **Form 433-B (OIC)** – Collection Information Statement for Businesses
- **Form 433-F** – Collection Information Statement

INSTALLMENTS

A taxpayer may request a monthly installment plan if they are unable to pay the full amount of tax owed. Before applying for any payment agreement, a taxpayer must file all required tax returns. Installment agreements generally provide up to **72 months** to pay the tax. In certain circumstances, the payment period could be longer or the amount agreed to could be less than the amount of tax owed. An installment plan is not valid unless accepted by the IRS. However, if a taxpayer **owes $10,000 or less** and meets certain other criteria, **the IRS must accept the request**. Those requirements are:

- During the past five tax years, the taxpayer (and spouse if filing jointly) has timely filed all income tax returns and paid any tax due, and has not entered into an installment agreement for payment of income tax.
- The taxpayer agrees to pay the full amount owed within three years and to comply with the tax laws while the agreement is in effect.
- The taxpayer is financially unable to pay the liability in full when due.

An *installment agreement* generally requires equal monthly payments, and the taxpayer must fully pay all of the tax owed within the time left in the 10-year period during which the IRS can collect the tax. If a taxpayer cannot pay in full by the end of the collection period, but can pay some of the tax owed, they may qualify for a partial payment installment agreement. To request an installment agreement a taxpayer can attach *Form 9465 Installment Agreement Request* to the front of their tax return, or—in cases where the return is already filed—mail it directly to the IRS.

If the IRS approves a request, they send a notice detailing the terms of the agreement and request a user fee to establish the plan. The user fee is reduced if the taxpayer is able to apply online.

> If the balance due is **$50,000 or less**, the taxpayer can apply for an installment agreement online instead of filing Form 9465. To do that, go to IRS.gov/opa.

2020 Long-term Agreement User Fees (paying in more than 120 days)			
Long-term Payment Plan Installment Agreement	Apply online	Apply by phone, mail, or in-person	Low income: Apply online, by phone, mail, or in-person
Automatic Withdrawal / Direct Debit	$31	$107	$31 fee waived
Non-Direct Debit	$149	$225	$43*
*$43 setup fee may be reimbursed if certain conditions are met			

A taxpayer whose adjusted gross income is at or below 250% of the applicable federal poverty level (low-income taxpayer) that enters into long-term payment plans may qualify to pay the low income reduced fee. The IRS will waive or may reimburse the user fee for *low-income taxpayers* only. The IRS will waive the user fee if the low-income taxpayer agrees to make electronic debit payments by entering into a direct debit installment agreement. The IRS will reimburse the user fee that was paid for the installment agreement upon completion for low-income taxpayers who are unable to make electronic debit payments through a direct debit installment agreement.

A taxpayer that can pay the full amount owed within **120 days** should not request an installment agreement on Form 9465. Instead, they can call or apply online to establish a request to pay in full. A taxpayer who can pay within the 120-day period can avoid paying the fee to set up the agreement.

Once approved, a taxpayer may submit a request to modify or terminate the installment agreement. This request will not suspend the statute of limitations on collection. While the IRS considers a request to modify or terminate the installment agreement, the taxpayer **must comply with the existing agreement.**

A taxpayer with outstanding tax liability (including penalties and interest) of $50,000 or less may file Form 9465. This is known as a *streamlined installment agreement* because the IRS **does not require a financial statement** (Form 433-F, Collection Information Statement) or substantial disclosure of financial information. A liability greater than $50,000 can be considered if the taxpayer pays down the liability to $50,000 or less prior to the agreement being granted. Generally, a taxpayer must pay off the balance due on a streamlined installment agreement within a 72-month period.

If the total amount the taxpayer owes is greater than $25,000 but not more than $50,000, the taxpayer must agree to a Direct Debit Installment Agreement (DDIA) or make payments by payroll deduction to request an installment agreement without completing a financial statement (Form 433-F, Collection Information Statement).

> The taxpayer will be charged interest and late payment penalties on any tax not paid by its due date, even if a request to pay in installments is granted. Interest and any applicable penalties will be charged until the balance is paid in full. To limit interest and penalty charges, the taxpayer should file the return on time and pay as much of the tax as possible with the return.

The IRS generally may not levy against property:

- While a request for an installment agreement is being considered,
- While an installment agreement is in effect,
- For 30 days after a request for an agreement has been rejected,
- For 30 days after termination of an installment agreement (due to taxpayer default), or
- While the IRS Office of Appeals is evaluating an appeal of the rejection or termination.

However, the IRS may file a Notice of Federal Tax Lien to secure the government's interest against other creditors. Termination of an installment agreement may cause the filing of a Notice of Federal Tax Lien and/or an IRS levy action.

OFFER IN COMPROMISE

The IRS may accept an Offer in Compromise (OIC) to settle unpaid tax accounts for less than the full amount of the balance due. The OIC program is an option for those taxpayers who are unable to pay their tax accounts in a lump sum or through an installment agreement. Taxpayers request an Offer in Compromise on *Form 656 Offer in Compromise* or on *Form 656-L Offer in Compromise (Doubt as to Liability)*.

OIC requests made in 2020 <u>must</u> include a **$205 application fee** and initial payment unless you are an individual and meet the low-income certification guidelines.

The IRS may legally compromise a tax liability for any of the following reasons:

- **Doubt as to liability** – There is doubt as to whether or not the assessed tax is correct.
- **Doubt as to collectability** – There is doubt that the taxpayer could ever pay the full tax debt. In these cases, the total amount owed must be greater than the sum of the taxpayer's assets and future income.
- **Promote effective tax administration** – There is no doubt that the assessed tax is correct and no doubt that the amount owed could be collected, but the taxpayer has an economic hardship or other special circumstances that may allow the IRS to accept less than the total balance due.

The taxpayer must select a payment option and include the payment with the offer. The amount of the initial payment and subsequent payments will depend on the total amount of the offer and which of the following payment options the taxpayer selects:

- **Lump Sum Cash** – This option requires 20% of the total offer amount to be paid with the offer and the remaining balance paid in 5 or fewer payments within 5 or fewer months of the date the offer is accepted.
- **Periodic Payment** – This option requires the first payment to be paid with the offer and the remaining balance paid in monthly payments within 6 to 24 months, in accordance with the proposed offer terms.

Under the periodic payment method, **monthly payments must continue while the IRS is evaluating the offer.** Failure to make these monthly payments may result in the return of the offer without appeal rights.

All payments sent during consideration of the offer will be applied to the taxpayer's tax debt. The payments cannot be returned unless the taxpayer pays more than the required payment and designate it as a deposit.

EXCEPTION: An individual that meets the Low-Income Certification guidelines is not required to pay the application fee, send the initial payment, or make the required monthly payments while the offer is being considered.

An offer does not stop the accrual of interest and penalties. The taxpayer will be charged interest and penalties on any tax not paid by its due date, even if the offer is accepted. Interest and any applicable penalties will be charged until the balance is paid in full.

If the offer is accepted, the taxpayer <u>must</u> continue to **timely file** all required tax returns <u>and</u> **timely pay** all estimated tax payments and federal tax payments that become due in the future. If the taxpayer fails to timely file and timely pay any tax obligations that become due within the five years after the offer is accepted (including any extensions) the offer may be defaulted. If the offer is defaulted, the taxpayer will be liable for the original tax debt, less payments made, and all accrued interest and penalties.

TIP: The IRS will return any newly filed Offer in Compromise application if you have not filed all required tax returns. Any application fee included with the OIC will also be returned. Any initial payment required with the returned application will be applied to reduce your balance due. This policy does not apply to current year tax returns if there is a valid extension on file.

LIEN

- A *lien* gives the IRS a legal claim to a taxpayer's property as security for payment of a tax debt. The federal tax lien arises when:

  1. The IRS assesses the liability,

  2. The IRS sends a client a *Notice and Demand for Payment*, and

  3. The taxpayer neglects or refuses to pay the debt within **10 days** after notification. The IRS then may file a *Notice of Federal Tax Lien* in the public records. The Notice of Federal Tax Lien tells a taxpayer's creditors that the IRS has a claim against all the taxpayer's property, including property acquired after the IRS filed the lien. The lien attaches to all property (such as homes and cars) and to all rights to property (such as the accounts receivable of a business).

- Appealing the filing of a Notice of Federal Tax Lien:

  1. The IRS is required by law to give written notice of the taxpayer's right to a *Collection Due Process (CDP) hearing* not more than five business days after the first filing of a Notice of Federal Tax Lien for each tax liability.

  2. At the conclusion of the CDP hearing, the IRS Office of Appeals will issue a determination. The taxpayer will have 30 days after the date of the determination to seek review of the determination in the U.S. Tax Court.

- **Releasing a lien** – A **lien releases automatically 10 years after a tax is assessed** if the IRS has not filed it again or issued a Certificate of Release of Federal Tax Lien. The IRS will issue a Certificate of Release of the Federal tax lien within **30 days** <u>after</u>:

  1. The date the IRS determines the entire tax liability listed in the notice of Federal tax lien (including accrued interest and penalties and other additions) is **fully satisfied** or becomes legally unenforceable, or

  2. The date the IRS accepts the taxpayer's **posted bond guaranteeing payment** of the debt.

- **Discharge of specific property** – The IRS has discretion to issue a certificate of discharge of any part of the property subject to a Federal tax lien if the fair market value of the property remaining subject to the lien is **at least double** the unsatisfied liability secured by the lien (**including any liens that have priority** over the Federal tax lien).

> **EXAMPLE:** The Federal tax liability secured by a lien is $1,000. The fair market value of all property which after the discharge will continue to be subject to the Federal tax lien is $10,000. There is a prior mortgage on the property of $5,000, including interest, and the property is subject to a prior lien of $100 for real estate taxes. Accordingly, the taxpayer's equity in the property over and above the amount of the mortgage and real estate taxes is $4,900, or nearly five times the amount required to pay the assessed tax on which the Federal tax lien is based. Nevertheless, a discharge is not permissible. In the illustration, the sum of the amount of the Federal tax liability ($1,000) and of the amount of the prior mortgage and the lien for real estate taxes ($5,000 + $100 = $5,100) is $6,100. Double this sum is $12,200, but the fair market value of the remaining property is only $10,000. Hence, a discharge of the property is not permissible because the Code requires that the fair market value of the remaining property be at least double the sum of two amounts, one amount being the outstanding Federal tax liability and the other amount being all prior liens upon such property. In order that the discharge may be issued, it would be necessary that the remaining property be worth not less than $12,200.

LEVIES

- A *levy* is a legal seizure of a taxpayer's property to satisfy a tax debt. Levies are different from liens. A lien is a claim used as security for the tax debt, while a levy actually takes the property to satisfy the tax debt. The levy will be continuous until the tax debt is paid in full, other arrangements are made to satisfy the debt, or in most instances, the time-period (usually 10 years) for collecting the tax expires. If a taxpayer does not pay taxes (or arrange a settlement):

1. The IRS can seize and sell property (such as a taxpayer's car, boat, or home), or

2. The IRS can levy property that is the taxpayer's but is held by someone else (such as wages, retirement accounts, dividends, bank accounts, rental income, accounts receivables, the cash value of life insurance, or commissions).

- The IRS usually issues a levy only when the following three conditions have occurred:

1. The IRS assessed the tax and sent the taxpayer a Notice and Demand for Payment.

2. The taxpayer neglected or refused to pay the tax.

3. The IRS sent the taxpayer a "Final Notice of Intent to Levy and Notice of Your Right to a Hearing" (levy notice) at least 30 days before the levy.

- The IRS may sell the seized property. The following conditions apply:

1. The IRS must give a notice of pending sale and wait at least 10 days.

2. If the proceeds of the sale are less than the total of the tax bill and the expenses of levy and sale, the taxpayer will still have to pay the unpaid tax.

3. If the proceeds of the sale are more than the total of the tax bill and the expenses of the levy and sale, the taxpayer may ask for a refund.

4. If the IRS sells real estate, the taxpayer has the right to buy it back within 180 days of the sale for the amount paid plus 20% annual interest.

- The following property cannot be levied:

1. School books and certain clothing

2. Fuel, provisions, furniture, and personal effects for a household (cannot exceed $9,690 in 2020)

3. Books and tools used in the taxpayer's trade, business, or profession (cannot exceed $4,850 in 2020)

4. Unemployment benefits and certain public assistance payments

5. Certain annuity and pension benefits

6. Certain service-connected disability payments and workers' compensation

7. Salary, wages, or income included in a judgment for court-ordered child support payments

8. A minimum weekly exemption for wages, salary, and other income

- **Appealing a levy** – A taxpayer may request a CDP hearing with the Office of Appeals by sending a request for a CDP hearing to the address shown on the notice. The taxpayer must file the request within 30 days of the date on the notice. At the conclusion of the CDP hearing, the IRS Office of Appeals will issue a determination. The taxpayer will have 30 days after the date of the determination to seek review of the determination in the U.S. Tax Court.

- **Filing a wrongful levy claim** –A taxpayer may be entitled to the return of the wrongfully levied property if they were not liable for the tax. For example, a taxpayer may file an administrative wrongful levy claim for the return of wrongly levied property if the taxpayer is a non-liable spouse and the IRS levies a state income tax refund or a bank account belonging to the taxpayer or spouse.

- **Releasing a levy** – In general, the IRS must release a levy if a taxpayer pays the tax along with penalties and interest. In addition, the IRS must release the levy if:

1. The IRS did not follow proper procedures,

2. An automatic stay during bankruptcy is in effect,

3. The levy is on property that the IRS is not allowed to levy,

4. The levy occurred after accepting (or while the IRS considers) an OIC or installment request, or

5. The levy occurred while the IRS Office of Appeals considers certain appeals or requests for innocent spouse relief or during review by the Tax Court (unless court permits).

COLLECTION APPEAL RIGHTS

A taxpayer may appeal many IRS collection actions to the IRS Office of Appeals (Appeals). Appeals is separate from and independent of the IRS Collection office that initiated the collection action. Appeals ensures and protects its independence by adhering to a strict policy of prohibiting certain ex parte communications with the IRS Collection office or other IRS offices, such as discussions regarding the strengths or weaknesses of the taxpayer's case. The two main procedures are *Collection Due Process (CDP)* and *Collection Appeals Program (CAP)*.

Collection Due Process (CDP) is available after the taxpayer receives one of the following notices:

- Notice of Federal Tax Lien Filing
- Notice of Intent to Levy
- Notice of Jeopardy Levy and Right of Appeal
- Notice of Levy on Your State Tax Refund
- Post Levy Collection Due Process (CDP) Notice

By law, taxpayers have the right to a CDP hearing upon receipt of a notice and a timely postmarked request for a hearing to the address indicated on the notice. Taxpayers are limited to one hearing under section 6320 (Notice and opportunity for hearing upon filing of notice of lien) and 6330 (Notice and opportunity for hearing before levy) for each tax assessment within a tax period.

> A taxpayer can contest the CDP determination in the United States Tax Court.

- **Lien Notice** – The IRS is required to notify a taxpayer the first time a Notice of Federal Tax Lien is filed for each tax and period. The IRS must notify the taxpayer within **5 business days** after the lien filing. This notice may be mailed, given to the taxpayer, or left at his home or office. The taxpayer has **30 days**, after that 5-day period, to request a hearing with Appeals. The lien notice will indicate the date this 30-day period expires.
- **Levy Notice** – For each tax and period, the IRS is required to notify the taxpayer the first time it collects or intends to collect a tax liability by taking the taxpayer's property or rights to property. The IRS does this by issuing a pre-levy or post-levy notice. The notice is mailed, given to the taxpayer, or left at his home or office. During the **30-day** period from the date of the notice, the taxpayer may request a hearing with Appeals. There are four exceptions to issuing this notice before levy:
  1. When the collection of the tax is in jeopardy.
  2. When the IRS levies a state tax refund.
  3. When the criteria for a Disqualified Employment Tax Levy is met
  4. When the IRS serves a federal contractor levy.

The taxpayer may request a hearing after the levy action in these instances.

A taxpayer may request an equivalent hearing if he did not file a timely request for a CDP hearing. To receive an equivalent hearing, the request must be postmarked on or before the end of the **one-year period** after the date of the levy notice or on or before the end of the **one-year period plus 5 business** days after the filing date of the Notice of Federal Tax Lien.

The taxpayer must identify alternatives to, or reasons for disagreeing with, the lien filing or the levy action. Alternatives or reasons for disagreeing may include:

- Collection alternatives such as installment agreement or offer in compromise.
- Subordination or discharge of lien.

- Withdrawal of Notice of Federal Tax Lien.
- Appropriate spousal defenses.
- The existence or amount of the tax, but only if the taxpayer did not receive a notice of deficiency or did not otherwise have an opportunity to dispute the tax liability.
- Collection of the tax liability is causing or will cause economic or other hardship.

The taxpayer cannot raise an issue that was raised and considered at a prior administrative or judicial hearing, if the taxpayer, or his representative, participated meaningfully in the prior hearing or proceeding. Also, the taxpayer may not challenge the existence or amount of an assessment made based on court-ordered restitution.

A taxpayer is entitled to only **one hearing relating to a lien** notice and **one hearing relating to a levy notice**, for each taxable period. In general, the IRS will deny a hearing request that only raises issues identified by the IRS as frivolous or that are made solely to delay or impede collection.

> To preserve the right to go to court, the taxpayer must request a CDP hearing no later than the **30th day** after the date shown on the notice.

COLLECTION APPEALS PROGRAM (CAP)

Collection Appeals Program (CAP) is available for the following actions:

- Before or after the IRS files a Notice of Federal Tax Lien
- Before or after the IRS levies or seizes property
- Termination, or proposed termination, of an installment agreement
- Rejection of an installment agreement
- Modification, or proposed modification, of an installment agreement

> The CAP procedure is available under more circumstances than Collection Due Process (CDP). Unlike CDP, the taxpayer may not **challenge the existence or amount of the tax liability**. A taxpayer also cannot **proceed to court if he does not agree** with Appeals' decision in a CAP case.

Collection actions taxpayers may appeal under CAP are:

- **Notice of Federal Tax Lien** – A taxpayer may appeal the proposed filing of a *Notice of Federal Tax Lien (NFTL)* or the actual filing of an NFTL at the first and each subsequent filing of the NFTL. A taxpayer may also appeal denied requests to withdraw an NFTL, and denied discharges, subordinations, and non-attachments of a lien. Third parties may file a CAP appeal regarding the filing of a notice of lien against alter ego or nominee property. There are no CDP rights available for persons determined to be nominees or alter egos. Persons assessed as transferees under Internal Revenue Code (IRC) Section 6901, however, are entitled to CDP rights.
- **Notice of Levy** – A taxpayer may appeal before or after the IRS places a levy on his wages, bank account or other property. Once the levy proceeds have been sent to the IRS, the taxpayer may also appeal the denial by the IRS of the request to return levied property. Please note that a request to return levy proceeds must be made within **9 months** from the date of such levy.
- **Seizure of Property** – A taxpayer may appeal before or after the IRS makes a seizure but before the property is sold.
- **Rejection, Modification or Termination of Installment Agreement** – A taxpayer may appeal when the IRS rejects a request for an installment agreement. The taxpayer may also appeal when the IRS proposes to terminate or terminates the installment agreement. In addition, the taxpayer may also appeal when the IRS proposes to modify or modifies the installment agreement.

- **Wrongful Levy** – If the taxpayer is not liable for the tax and the IRS has levied or seized his property, the taxpayer may appeal the denial by the IRS of the request to release the levy or seizure. Please note that a request to the IRS to return wrongfully levied property must be in writing, filed within **2 years** of the levy or seizure, and must satisfy certain specific requirements.

LESSON 4

Tax Law

THE COURT SYSTEM

If a taxpayer and the IRS still disagree after the appeals conference, the taxpayer may be entitled to take his case to the *U.S. Tax Court*, the *U.S. Court of Federal Claims*, or the *U.S. District Court*. These courts are independent of the IRS.

A taxpayer that elects to bypass the IRS appeals system may be able to take a case to one of the courts listed above. However, a case petitioned to the U.S. Tax Court will normally be considered for settlement by an Appeals Officer before the Tax Court hears the case.

If a taxpayer unreasonably misuses the IRS appeals system, or if the intent of the taxpayer in filing the case is primarily to cause a delay or the taxpayer's position is frivolous or groundless, the Tax Court may impose a penalty of up to $25,000.

U.S. TAX COURT

The U.S. Tax Court has federal jurisdiction and only hears cases related to tax. A taxpayer cannot take a case to the Tax Court <u>before</u> the IRS sends a notice of deficiency (90-Day Letter). The taxpayer has **90 days** from the mailing date of the notice (150 days if the mailing address is outside the United States) to file a petition with the U.S. Tax Court. Taxpayers represented by counsel must file all documents electronically. Generally, the **Tax Court hears cases before any tax has been assessed and paid**. Most cases are settled by mutual agreement without a trial.

A taxpayer can take his case to the U.S. Tax Court if he disagrees with the IRS over any of the following:

- Income tax
- Estate tax
- Gift tax
- Certain excise taxes of private foundations, public charities, qualified pension and other retirement plans, or real estate investment trusts

If the amount of the case is $50,000 or less for any one tax year or period, the taxpayer can request that the Tax Court handle the case under the *small tax case procedure*. If the Tax Court approves, the taxpayer can present his case to the Tax Court for a decision that is final (**cannot appeal**).

U.S. DISTRICT COURTS AND U.S. COURT OF FEDERAL CLAIMS

Generally, the *District Court* and the *Court of Federal Claims* hear tax cases only <u>after</u> the taxpayer **paid the tax and filed a claim for a credit or refund**. The taxpayer can file a claim with the IRS for a credit or refund if he believes the tax paid is incorrect or excessive. If the IRS disallows the claim, the taxpayer should receive a notice of claim disallowance. If the IRS does not act on the claim within six months from the date filed, the taxpayer can then file suit for a refund. In general, the taxpayer must file suit for a credit or refund no later than two years after the IRS informs him that it has rejected his claim. The taxpayer may file a suit for a credit or refund in *U.S. District Court* or in the *U.S. Court of Federal Claims*. However, he cannot appeal to the *U.S. Court of Federal Claims* if the claim is for credit or refund of a penalty that relates to promoting an abusive tax shelter or to aiding and abetting the understatement of tax liability on someone else's return.

TIP: *U.S. District Court* is the <u>only</u> choice if the taxpayer receives the right to a **trial by jury**.

APPELLATE COURTS

A taxpayer may appeal trial court decisions to a court of appeals, dependent upon what court handled the trial. A taxpayer may appeal a case heard in *U.S. Tax Court* or *U.S. District Court* to the *U.S. Court of Appeals* in the circuit where the taxpayer resides at the time of appeal. A taxpayer who brought his case to the *U.S. Court of Federal Claims* can appeal to the *Court of Appeals for the Federal Circuit.* In all cases, the non-prevailing party in the appeal may request that the *U.S. Supreme Court* hear the case. However, it is doubtful a tax case will go before the *U.S. Supreme Court* unless it is one of great significance.

BURDEN OF PROOF

The responsibility to prove entries, deductions, and statements made on tax returns is known as the *burden of proof*. The burden of proof is a legal term that refers to a party's duty to prove a disputed assertion. **The burden of proof is generally on the taxpayer**. This means that the taxpayer must bring to court evidence, such as documents and testimony of witnesses, to prove that the determination of the IRS is not correct and that the taxpayer's position is correct.

There are some limited circumstances where the burden of proof is on the IRS. For the burden of proof to shift to the IRS on a factual issue, the taxpayer must introduce credible evidence in court with respect to that issue. The taxpayer must also comply with substantiation and record-keeping requirements set forth in the tax laws. In addition, the taxpayer must cooperate with reasonable requests from the IRS for witnesses, information, documents, meetings, and interviews. In most cases, the burden of proof does not shift to the IRS and the petitioner must show that the IRS's determinations are wrong.

> The **IRS has the burden of initially producing evidence** (*burden of production*) in court proceedings with respect to the liability of any individual taxpayer for any penalty, addition to tax, or additional amount imposed by the tax laws. In the case of an individual, the IRS has the burden of proof in court proceedings based on any IRS reconstruction of income solely using statistical information on unrelated taxpayers.

In Tax Court the taxpayer generally bears the burden of proof, except for increases in any previously asserted deficiency and affirmative defenses pleaded in the answer to the petition. While the burden of proof may shift if the taxpayer can prove their case with credible evidence, this only applies if the taxpayer has fully cooperated with all reasonable requests for documents. As a practical matter, credible evidence and full cooperation usually do not result in a dispute, so actual instances of the shift in the burden of proof are rare.

The IRS generally has the burden of proof for any factual issue if the taxpayer has met the following requirements:

- Introduced credible evidence relating to the issue
- Complied with all substantiation requirements of the Internal Revenue Code
- Maintained all records required by the Internal Revenue Code
- Cooperated with all reasonable requests by the IRS for information regarding the preparation and related tax treatment of any item reported on the tax return
- Had a net worth of $7 million or less and not more than 500 employees at the time the tax liability is contested in any court if the tax return is for a corporation, partnership, or trust

AUTHORITATIVE HIERARCHY

TAX LAW

Tax laws are not always clear and may not provide a definitive answer or guidance to all issues. The code is further interpreted administratively by *Treasury Regulations*, *Revenue Rulings*, and *Revenue Procedures*. Many consider these interpretations and decisions to be tax law.

The IRS must follow their rulings; however, a taxpayer may contest them in tax court. If laws are in dispute or need clarification, the tax court may hear the case to clarify the intent of the code. Both *judicial* (court) and *administrative* interpretations of the code may be cited as *precedent* for future arguments in similar cases.

Internal Revenue Code

Federal tax law begins with the *Internal Revenue Code (IRC)*, enacted by Congress in Title 26 of the U.S. Code (26 USC.) The Internal Revenue Code is the basis for all tax law. Changes to tax law are proposed in the form of a "tax bill" and voted on in the U.S. Congress and Senate. If the legislature approves the tax bill and the president signs it into law, the code is amended to include the new law. Sections of the code are often referenced when citing tax laws. Sections are often referenced by "Sec." or the "§" symbol prior to the section number such as Sec. 1031 or §6695.

Treasury Regulations

In its role in administering the tax laws enacted by the U.S. Congress, the IRS must take the specifics of these laws and translate them into detailed regulations, rules, and procedures. *Treasury regulations (26 CFR)*—commonly referred to as federal tax regulations—pick up where the Internal Revenue Code leaves off by providing the official interpretation of the IRC by the U.S. Department of the Treasury. A regulation is issued to provide guidance for new legislation or to address issues that arise with respect to existing Internal Revenue Code sections. Regulations interpret and give directions on complying with the law. Regulations are published in the *Federal Register*. Generally, regulations are first published in **proposed** form. After considering public input, a **final regulation** or a **temporary regulation** is published as a *Treasury Decision (TD)*, again, in the Federal Register.

Revenue Rulings

A revenue ruling is an official interpretation by the IRS of the Internal Revenue Code, related statutes, tax treaties, and regulations. Rulings indicate how the law applies to a specific set of facts. The IRS publishes rulings in the Internal Revenue Bulletin as guidance to taxpayers, IRS personnel, and tax professionals. For example, a ruling may hold that taxpayers can deduct certain automobile expenses.

Revenue Procedures

A revenue procedure is an official statement of a procedure that affects the rights or duties of taxpayers or other members of the public under the Internal Revenue Code, related statutes, tax treaties, and regulations and that should be a matter of public knowledge. The IRS also publishes revenue procedures in the Internal Revenue Bulletin. While a revenue ruling generally states an IRS position, a revenue procedure provides return filing or other instructions concerning an IRS position. For example, a revenue procedure might specify how those entitled to deduct certain automobile expenses should compute them by applying a certain mileage rate in lieu of calculating actual operating expenses.

Case Law

Case law is born out of the decisions of the courts interpreting the law. Once a court arrives at a decision, a justice (or several justices) will write an opinion. This **judicial decision** may be cited as precedent, and any court lower in the pecking order must follow the decision as law. Lawyers and taxpayers often use these decisions to argue a position. The IRS, which is an agency within the U.S. Department of the Treasury, may disagree with a tax court determination when a ruling is against their position. IRS policy is to announce their **acquiescence** (acceptance) to follow a court ruling in future matters of an equivalent issue. The intention of the IRS to follow (or not) a court decision is published in the ***Internal Revenue Bulletin (IRB)*** and listed as ***acq.*** or ***nonacq.*** in the court citation. A decision of the U.S. Supreme court carries the same authority as the Internal Revenue Code.

LEGAL REFERENCE

Only rules of law may be cited as precedent for the purposes of defending a tax position or action. However, many other resources offer guidance as to how the IRS may treat a certain position.

IRS Notices

A notice is a public pronouncement that may contain guidance involving substantive interpretations of the Internal Revenue Code or other provisions of the law. For example, notices are used to relate what regulations will say in situations where the regulations may not be published in the immediate future.

Private Letter Rulings

The IRS Office of Chief Counsel may issue a ***private letter ruling (PLR)*** to a taxpayer, which is a written statement that interprets and applies tax laws to the taxpayer's **specific** set of facts. The IRS issues a PLR to establish with certainty the federal tax consequences of a particular transaction before the transaction is consummated or before the taxpayer files a return. A PLR issues in response to a written request submitted by a taxpayer and binds the IRS if the taxpayer fully and accurately described the proposed transaction in the request and carries out the transaction as described.

> Other taxpayers or IRS personnel may <u>not</u> rely on a PLR as precedent. PLRs are generally made public after all information has been removed that could identify the taxpayer to whom it was issued.

Technical Advice Memorandum

A technical advice memorandum, or TAM, is guidance furnished by the Office of Chief Counsel upon the **request of an IRS director or an area director** for appeals, in response to technical or procedural questions that develop during a proceeding. A request for a TAM generally stems from an examination of a taxpayer's return, a consideration of a taxpayer's claim for a refund or credit, or any other matter involving a specific taxpayer under the jurisdiction of the territory manager or the area director for appeals. A TAM issues only on closed transactions and provides the interpretation of proper application of tax laws, tax treaties, regulations, revenue rulings, or other precedents. The advice rendered represents a final determination of the position of the IRS but only with respect to the **specific issue** in the **specific case** in which the advice is issued. A TAM is generally made public after all information has been removed that could identify the taxpayer whose circumstances triggered a specific memorandum.

IRS Form Instructions and Publications

IRS Forms' instructions and IRS publications offer instructions in plain English to assist taxpayers with the preparation of returns. These informational documents do not supersede the rule of law.

Treasury Department Circular 230

Circular 230 contains the rules indicated in *31 CFR, Subtitle A, Part 10*. Circular 230 contains regulations governing the practice of attorneys, certified public accountants, enrolled agents, enrolled actuaries, enrolled retirement plan agents, and appraisers before the Internal Revenue Service. In order to practice before the IRS, a tax practitioner must understand the rules contained within Circular 230, many of which were covered earlier within this Area.

Internal Revenue Bulletin

The *Internal Revenue Bulletin (IRB)* is the authoritative instrument for announcing official rulings and procedures of the IRS and for publishing Treasury Decisions, Executive Orders, Tax Conventions, legislation, court decisions, and other items of general interest.

Internal Revenue Manual

The *Internal Revenue Manual (IRM)* is the single official source for IRS policies, directives, guidelines, procedures, and delegations of authority in the IRS.